THE GOTHIC REVIVAL
1745–1845

THE GOTHIC REVIVAL 1745–1845

JAMES MACAULAY

1975

BLACKIE

GLASGOW & LONDON

Published by

Blackie and Son Limited
Bishopbriggs, Glasgow G64 2NZ
5 Fitzhardinge Street, London W1H 0DL

© James Macaulay 1975
First published 1975

ISBN 0 216 89892 7

Printed in Great Britain by
Thomson Litho Ltd., East Kilbride, Scotland

Acknowledgements

It is pleasant to be able to acknowledge in retrospect the relatives, friends and colleagues who have assisted, in so many different ways, in the compilation of this book. I must thank especially my brother and sister-in-law, Mr and Mrs Douglas Macaulay, Miss Mary Anderson, the late Mr and Mrs Alexander Macpherson, Miss Mary C. Ramsay, and Mr and Mrs Fred M. Walker. In Perthshire Major and Mrs John Stewart of Ardvorlich gave generously of their hospitality and were unfailing sources of information. Also I am deeply grateful to Lady Hermione Cameron of Lochiel not only for many years of friendship but for constant encouragement throughout the course of this work.

It was begun, at the suggestion of Professor Frank Fielden, at the School of Architecture, the University of Newcastle-upon-Tyne where I am indebted to Emeritus Professor Jack Napper, Dr and Mrs Peter Willis, and to Miss Barbara Harbottle who read parts of the original thesis and was an invaluable source of local information. My chief debt, of course, is to Mr Bruce Allsopp who was my supervisor for more years than he might have expected. Others who have read the complete text include Miss Catherine Cruft of the National Monuments Record of Scotland and Dr Marinell Ash, who was a tireless companion on numerous field expeditions from Newcastle. Dr James Corson, Honorary Librarian of Abbotsford, has cast a critical eye on the section of the book devoted to that building. Mr Stanley Wilkinson, Head of the Scott Sutherland School of Architecture, Robert Gordon's Institute of Technology, Aberdeen, has actively supported my research and Mr Tim Robinson has taught me much about the intricacies of publishing.

To the owners of properties who gave me admittance I am duly grateful. Those who allowed their archives to be consulted included: His Grace the Duke of Argyll; His Grace the Duke of Northumberland; the Bishop of Durham; the Earl of Rosebery; Lord Barnard; Sir Donald Cameron of Lochiel; Sir Alec Douglas-Home; Mrs Home-Robertson of

ACKNOWLEDGEMENTS

Paxton; Mrs P. Maxwell-Scott of Abbotsford; Mrs D. Somervell of Fettercairn; Captain J. de B. Stansfeld. Lord Forbes kindly lent me family papers as did the late Sir Edward Collingwood and Miss J. Macintyre of Millearne. In addition other owners have permitted me to quote from family papers either still in their possession or on loan to local or national record offices. The locations of all these papers are listed at the end of the book.

Major Charles Graham, Yr of Netherby, answered many queries, while Mrs A. W. Milburn of Fowberry and Mr D. P. Graham of the Alnwick estate went to considerable trouble in helping to provide some of the illustrations. Important information was volunteered by Mr Francis Bamford, Sir John Forbes of Newe, Bt, Dr Terry Friedman, Captain P. Holderness-Roddam, Mr and Mrs R. Linzee Gordon of Cluny, Captain R. M. Macalister of Glenbarr, Major and Mrs M. Smiley of Castle Fraser, Mr H. Steuart Fothringham of Grantally and Mr D. Wedderburn. The Earl and Countess of Aboyne saved me from committing one serious error. For those that may yet be found I take full responsibility.

I have received much help from Sir John Summerson and Miss Dorothy Stroud at Sir John Soane's Museum; from Mr R. Garde of the Northumberland County Record Office; from Mr B. C. Jones of the Cumbria Record Office; and from Dr W. A. L. Seaman of the Durham County Record Office. The staffs of the National Library of Scotland, the National Monuments Record of Scotland, the Scottish Record Office and the RIBA Drawings' Collection have been consistently obliging.

I must also record my appreciation of the grants awarded during the years of my doctoral research by the Carnegie Trust for the Universities of Scotland and before that by the Charles Henry Foyle Trust. Regarding the photographic costs incurred in the production of this book, I wish to acknowledge financial assistance afforded by the Scottish Arts Council and also by the Governors of Robert Gordon's Institute of Technology, from the T. Scott Sutherland Bequest.

Finally, for their tolerance and forbearance over the past decade, I thank my family, especially George who made so many field expeditions memorable.

Photographic acknowledgements

I am grateful to the following for permission to reproduce material which appears in this book:

National Monuments Record, Plates 4, 97.

Published by permission of the British Library Board, Plate 10.

Royal Institute of British Architects, London, Plates 11, 47, 161.

Royal Commission on the Ancient Monuments, Scotland, Plates 12, 13, 41, 42, 45, 46, 48, 54, 58, 60, 61, 81–3, 87, 96, 101, 113, 115, 116, 141, 143, 177, 178, 183, 184, 187–9.

Reproduced from S. Toy, *The Castles of Great Britain*, by permission of Heinemann Educational Books Ltd, Plate 18.

The Duke of Northumberland, Plates 20, 31.

Trustees of Sir John Soane's Museum, Plates 21, 22, 26–30, 41, 45, 46, 48, 58, 60, 61

Trustees of the British Museum, Plate 23.

Cumbria Record Office, Plate 38.

The Earl of Lonsdale, Plates 39, 159, 160.

Copyright Sir John Clerk of Penicuick, Bt, Plates 52, 98.

The President and Council of the Society of Antiquaries of Newcastle-upon-Tyne and the Northumberland County Archivist, Plate 62.

The Librarian, Newcastle-upon-Tyne Central Library and the Northumberland County Archivist, Plate 64.

Mrs A. W. Milburn of Fowberry, Plates 67–9.

Country Life, Plate 72.

Crown copyright, reproduced with the permission of the Controller of Her Majesty's Stationery Office, Plate 75.

The Bishop of Durham, Plate 79.

Sir Alec Douglas-Home, Plate 83.

Published with the approval of the Keeper of the Records of Scotland, Plate 85.

Trustees of the National Library of Scotland, Plates 102, 103, 105.

The Lord Forbes, Plate 107.

Trustees of the late Lord Cochrane of Cults, Plate 113.

Perth Museum, Plates 128, 129.

The Duke of Buccleuch and Queensberry, V.R.D., Plate 141.

Trustees of the Matfen Settled Estates, Plate 166.

Laing Art Gallery and Museum, Newcastle-upon-Tyne, Plates 146, 173.

Contents

CONTENTS

CONTENTS

CONTENTS

List of Illustrations

Preface

Considering the extent of the Gothic Revival both in terms of length of time and the number of buildings executed it is a surprising fact that in a hundred years there have been only two major books devoted to the subject. In 1872 there first appeared Eastlake's monumental history to be followed fifty years later by Kenneth Clark's study of the same subject.

As both writers were concerned with the Revival as a national movement they tended to consider many of the same buildings although from different standpoints so that the idea has grown up of a steady development in the use of Gothic from Strawberry Hill to Fonthill Abbey and then on, past the mansions of Nash, to the early Victorians, the Ecclesiologists and Pugin. The present study, however, by examining two regions, Scotland and the north of England, enables them to be compared and contrasted. More importantly perhaps they can then be set beside the national movement.

The research, of which this book is the outcome, was prompted by several questions. They arose together. First, there was the question of why a Highland chief should have begun to build a Gothic castle at Inveraray in 1745. The question was the more puzzling when it was known that the Highland chief was the third Duke of Argyll who, before his succession to the dukedom, had been a noted Palladian builder in England. And when it was generally accepted that important architects of the later eighteenth century had not undertaken Gothic work, or if they had that it was not worth critical examination, what was the explanation for the creation of Robert Adam's castles, especially Mellerstain and Culzean? And why should their interiors be classical when those at Alnwick Castle in Northumberland, once it was restored by the first Duke and Duchess of Northumberland, were Gothic? Another question concerned the role of Abbotsford in architectural history. Kenneth Clark considered that it was not without influence in determining architectural style. Colleagues with whom one discussed the point thought otherwise.

Inveraray Castle, Mellerstain and Abbotsford are famous buildings. Yet there was no information which would explain convincingly the reasons for their Gothic and castellated silhouettes. Was the answer that scholars had not looked at them? Time was to show that was, indeed, a part of the answer. For instance, in Bolton's study of the achievements of Robert and James Adam the castle style was treated perfunctorily almost, indeed, as if it had been a regrettable aberration. When other writers did treat of Gothic buildings their chosen examples tended not to be in the northern half of Britain.

Ten years ago there was very little modern material which dealt with the Gothic Revival. Since then articles and books on the subject have begun to appear in increasing numbers. Even so there was not enough evidence to provide an overall picture of the significance of the Revival not only in terms of the numbers of buildings erected but to determine whether or not local events could be held up as part of a national movement either in the later eighteenth century or in the early nineteenth century. It was decided, therefore, to try to discover just how many Gothic Revival buildings there were in the chosen geographical areas. Very soon it became apparent that there were far more than had ever been suspected especially in the second half of the eighteenth century. But the very quantity began to raise problems concerning the place of Gothic architecture at that time. Was it new and exciting, something revolutionary or was it the continuation of that style which had indubitably persisted beyond the Middle Ages? And how had Horace Walpole's delicious Strawberry Hill been transformed, a hundred years later, into the pietistic Houses of Parliament when Gothic architecture put off its waywardness and became the country's official style?

Before attempting to answer these questions it was considered important to have a chapter which outlined, in general terms, the economic conditions enabling the architecture under review to be built. Also, to understand why people built as they did, a lot of emphasis has been placed on contemporary records, either published works or private documents. Although the existence of some of the latter was known, a great deal of new source material, discovered in the course of travel and of research, is here quoted for the first time.

I

The Economic Background

The Gothic Revival coincides with the later part of the Agrarian Revolution and the early Industrial Revolution and may, indeed, in some respects be said to be a manifestation or result of these two great movements. In a study of Gothic Revival architecture in the north of Britain the general background of agrarian and industrial change must be accepted as a large subject outwith the scope of an architectural study. Nevertheless, some consideration of the effects of agrarian and incipient industrial change is necessary if only because there was a differentiation between the south of Britain and the north, and Scotland especially, where agrarian change came later. Indeed, it is not possible to explain the sudden outburst of architecture in north Britain after the mid-seventeen hundreds except in terms of an economic boom which, following in the wake of a secure internal peace, brought great wealth to the landed classes in the eighteenth century and to the towns in the next. Thus areas of hitherto little architectural significance, when compared with the rich cathedral towns of the south and midlands in the Middle Ages, became studded with buildings in the Gothic or classic modes which can now be recognised as outstanding examples of their kind. Many of these are country houses which is not surprising since this was the first occasion when many of north Britain's ancient landed families acquired the wealth which is necessary for lavish architectural display. It was an opportunity which was gladly and vigorously seized, especially in Scotland where the final establishment of peace after the middle of the eighteenth century meant that for the first time it was safe for Scottish lairds and Highland chiefs to quit their tower-houses and equip their families with abodes which it was now felt their splendid ancestries warranted. The landed classes everywhere were followed in such building pursuits by the bourgeoisie either providing for a new discrimination in learning with clubs, libraries and reading-rooms or endowing the infant social services with hospitals, schools and prisons.

1

In the opening years of the eighteenth century north Britain was, in modern parlance, an underdeveloped area. An English writer could complain, somewhat jaundicedly, that, 'A field of wheat would be as great a rarity as a nightingale in any part of Scotland'.[1] Others were blunter and Defoe, writing of Westmorland, called it 'a Country eminent only for being the wildest, most barren and frightful' in England and Wales.[2] That was an honour in which the indefatigable Arthur Young was to allow the whole north of England to share[3] and the melancholy which he experienced in riding through such tracts of land[4] was in no way tempered by the knowledge that land let for a shilling an acre could, if improved, yield ten or fifteen times as much.[5] A few years later in 1776 Hutchinson recorded the same melancholy reflections. 'It is painful . . . to behold six or eight thousand acres of land . . . lying waste when the necessaries of life are so dear.'[6]

Yet changes would be introduced. The owners of estates, which in the north tended to be of princely extent, by the early nineteenth century granted long leases to their tenants sometimes extending to nineteen years although the practice was sufficiently uncommon, at least in Scotland in 1776, for Gilpin to comment on the fact that the Duke of Queensberry did grant leases.[7] These gave tenants the opportunity to effect long term improvements as did the practice of enclosure of common land. For the county of Durham alone over fifteen hundred private Inclosure Acts were passed by Parliament in the period 1756–97.[8] On the practical side of farming the most notable changes were in the introduction of new crops. The introduction varied from county to county, according to the degree of interest shown by the local landowners. It appears to be the case that compared with, say, the counties of Northumberland and Durham and parts of Scotland, and because of the difficulties created by geography and the lack of means of communication, the appearance of new types of crops tended to be later in Cumberland and Westmorland. Even there, however, turnips, to be used as winter feed, were introduced by Philip Howard of Corby Castle in 1755.[9] But progress was slow and nearly forty years later turnips were still a curiosity and people would travel for miles to see them.[10] Wheat had also been successfully grown despite a belief that grain would not ripen near the mountains 'from whence a continued moist vapour is supposed to be borne into the valley which blights the corn in its blossom'.[11]

In Scotland, 'where in the low lands, they tread very close on the heels of the English',[12] a typically progressive estate was that of the Earl of Fife. It extended along the fertile plains bordering the Moray Firth and, after the middle of the eighteenth century, a policy of improvement was begun by importing English husbandry and new breeds of black cattle, sheep and horses. Wheat, turnips and hay (all new crops) were grown in abundance with a scientific rotation of crops in enclosed fields.[13]

Another important change in north Britain was the planting of trees with the splendid results that are seen to-day. Dr Johnson in 1773 claimed to have seen not a single tree between the Scottish Border and St Andrews 'which I did not believe to have grown up far within the present century'.[14] In previous centuries, certainly, deforestation in Scotland had assumed alarming proportions but by the mid-eighteenth century tree-planting was *à la mode* for the landed classes on both sides of the Border. Around Alnwick the first Duke of Northumberland turned the countryside into one of the noblest prospects of landscape creation. The Duke of Montrose called in a follower of 'Capability' Brown to Buchanan in Stirlingshire. By the Moray Firth the Duke of Gordon transformed marshes into wooded parkland and the 'Planting' Duke of Atholl, as well as introducing the larch to Britain, had 27 million trees to his credit.[15] Such ducal activity transformed the policies around houses like Inveraray where an ecstatic traveller joyfully noted '(the woods) round the castle reciprocally borrowing from, and lending grandeur to that edifice, impressed me with such multifarious images of greatness and beauty as, I believe, will never be effaced'.[16] Another writer, obviously not so struck by ducal greatness, observed more prosaically that many of the Scottish policies 'encompassing little better than a heap of molehills and thistles, appeared like a silver fringe encircling a stiff petticoat'.[17] Whichever one's view there was no denying the fact that, aesthetics aside, trees had an economic value, especially for the charcoal used in local iron furnaces.[18]

When applied to the countryside the results of all these changes were of course quite striking. Cumulatively, they effected in time what came to be called the Agrarian Revolution. Yet as early as 1785 a correspondent to *The Gentleman's Magazine* noted of the north of England and the Scottish Lowlands that marsh land, having been drained, was producing oats or potatoes, that moors grew wheat and potatoes in fields divided by white-thorn hedges while the landscape was ornamented with clumps of pine trees and ash, beech and oaks.[19]

What were the spurs that made agricultural pursuits of such fashionable interest to the members of the landed classes? Arthur Young could eulogise thus: 'What a noble acquisition will it be to change nine hundred acres from being a barren desert, to a finely cultivated farm!'[20] More succinctly Swift found the true expression in his phrase that 'Who-ever could make two ears of corn or two blades of grass to grow upon a spot

3

of ground where only one grew before, would do more essential service to his country than the whole race of politicians put together'.[21] It was this spirit of challenge, of scientific enquiry, applied almost inevitably in that age to agriculture, which required of landowners that they should transform their ancient patrimonies. Also they were urged to such heroic exploits (which is what they were) by that atavism whereby the country seat and not the town house was held to be the chief home of any noble or landed family. True, London had its palaces but Spencer House, Bridgewater House and others, these were always few. Unlike their continental counterparts the landed classes of Britain never deserted the countryside. Finally there was the basic economic fact that the development of an urban proletariat, divorced from the countryside and its produce, together with the population explosion and, later in the eighteenth century and early in the next, the long French Wars, which blocked the supply of European grain, followed by the Corn Laws of 1815, all meant an ever increasing demand from the farmlands of Britain for agrarian produce. For those who could provide the rewards were enormous, rewards which continued until the importation of American wheat in the eighteen seventies afflicted British agriculture with a lingering malaise.

Typical of the 'Improvers' was Dr Graham of Netherby in Cumberland. On inheriting his estate in the early seventeen sixties he had a rent roll of something less than £2,000 per annum. By 1785 his son, Sir James, was expecting an income of £13,000, which had been achieved by carrying out, by then, the standard and familiar procedures for improvement of draining, manuring and planting.[22] Of course the inevitable had also happened. Rentals were increased everywhere. Frequently they doubled and sometimes quadrupled[23] and a relatively standard acreage rental was from £2 to £3.[24] It was no wonder that the first Duke of Northumberland was reputed to draw in from his landed estate an annual revenue of £150,000.[25] While it is true that there were few in north Britain (or anywhere else for that matter) who could equal Northumberland's princely revenue, nevertheless there were many others in a sliding economic scale who benefited, in however modest a manner, from the spring growth of the Agrarian Revolution, growth which was to burgeon not only in crops and cereals but in country seats; and if few edifices rivalled Alnwick Castle then it was a poor owner who could not add at least a stretch of machicolation and a brace of quatrefoils to his ancestral home.

In the Highlands of Scotland the picture was very different. Indeed, it would be no exaggeration to describe contemporary rural changes there as the negation of improvement. Of course, wherever there was agricultural advance so there was hardship in human terms. As farms became large economic units so 'the poorer sort of people remove into towns, to gain a livelihood by handicrafts and commerce...'.[26] Of the Highlands this was to prove particularly true but for very different reasons, namely the feudal position enjoyed in the country by the clan chiefs. Until the passing of the Heritable Jurisdictions Act in 1747, one of the consequences of the Forty-Five, the clan chiefs had exercised the right of 'pit and gallows' over their followers. The abolition of these powers, together with the Disarming Act of 1746, meant that the chiefs lost their immemorial rights as rulers of a patriarchal society. Thereafter, according to the distilled wisdom of Dr Johnson, 'When the power of birth and station ceases, no hope remains but from the prevalence of money'.[27] In less academic terms, the chiefs became rapacious landlords[28] as, divested of their prerogatives, they turned to the improvement of their estates, which improvement consisted for the most part of demanding more rent.[29] Such action worsened the already appalling straits of a society which lived for some of the time at subsistence level and for the other part of the time below it. In September 1776 *The Gentleman's Magazine* printed a long account entitled 'An Address to the Lairds of Scotland' in which the living conditions depicted make Crusoe's island an enviable paradise by comparison. For instance, on the island of Arran (a Hamilton possession) the inhabitants spent their time in procuring the means for paying their rent, laying in peat for the winter and in attempting to obtain a scanty pittance of food and clothing, while on Islay, where the people were worn down with poverty, 'their fare may be called rather a permission to exist'. On the Macleod stronghold of Skye the picture worsens for there 'the poor prowl along the shores, to pick up limpets and other shell-fish, the constant repast of hundreds during part of the year'. Even allowing for some journalistic exaggeration it is scarcely surprising that many died of hunger and others 'of the putrid fever'.[30] Such plights would appear to have been as bad elsewhere and not surprisingly as a labourer was paid 2s a day in summer and 1s 6d or as little as 1s 2d in winter.[31] Under these circumstances the raising of rents was to prove calamitous for the peasantry. Dr Johnson cited a case where in the space of twenty-five years the rent had been quadrupled.[32] As late as the second decade of the nineteenth century rents in the Callander area had advanced within the previous twenty years from 15s an acre to £3[33] while on the vast Breadalbane estates an increase to £3 was also considered likely though the tenants there hoped that rentals would only double from 20s and 25s an acre.[34] The rents had indeed been raised 'with too much eagerness'.[35]

With such circumstances being almost universal in the Highlands it is not to be wondered at that emigration was the order of the day. Every traveller comments upon it from Pennant briefly in 1769[36] and others with increasing detail throughout the rest of the century and into the next. It is an appalling tale and makes one of the darkest chapters in Scotland's grim history. In 1783 the catholic Bishop Macdonald reported: 'Our Highland Catholics leave us in great colonies. . . . Last year upwards of three hundred souls left Glengarry and its neighbourhood, almost all Roman Catholics, and settled in Canada, about Montreal where were already settled about eight hundred Highlanders.'[37] In 1786 one estimate put the number of emigrants at between thirty and fifty thousand[38] and the figure was to rise throughout the years ahead as sheep-runs forced the displacement of people. Sometimes as many as fifty or a hundred families would be evicted to make room for the sheep which might require only one shepherd[39] and a farm could have as many as seven thousand animals.[40] Inevitably there was trouble which, as in Ross-shire, became revolt against the flocks and their owners.[41] Not all the aristocratic families of the north were to incur the odium with which the name of Sutherland is still invested.[42] There were good landlords like Argyll and Macdonald of Staffa[43] but they were in the minority. For the rest avarice was not a sin and the rapid augmentation of their incomes was pursued unashamedly and determinedly.

Thus it must occasion no surprise to learn that an estate which in 1745 was worth five or six thousand pounds by the turn of the next century was yielding, and without any of the southern improvements, £80,000 per annum[44] while the Earl of Breadalbane had a yearly income of £40,000 and that mostly from sheep.[45] Not everyone possessed the fabulously extensive estates of Breadalbane[46] but from the island of Tiree alone the Duke of Argyll was drawing in a thousand pounds a year.[47] In the Highlands it was such wealth which paid for the rebuilding of ancestral seats on a scale previously unknown and hitherto impossible by reason of cost and the lack of peace and of communications with the remainder of Britain. After 1745 when such conditions no longer persisted then houses like Taymouth Castle (Perthshire), Inveraray Castle (Argyll), Achnacarry and Armadale Castles (both in Inverness-shire) and others could be built and very often as pioneers in architectural design and in the evolution of their particular style.

The concomitant of the Agrarian Revolution was the Industrial Revolution. Coeval in chronological sequence, in intensity and duration the latter began with the cotton industry; and in Scotland, as with tobacco before, and iron and coal later, it was the Glasgow region which witnessed the full impact of the cotton boom. In the year 1743–4 Paisley produced 353,407 yards of textiles. Forty years on and the figure was close on two million, with the silk industry itself employing ten thousand men, women and children.[48] Indeed whatever the cloth or its use then it seems to have been made in Scotland. As early as 1766 'at Killmarnoc they have set up manufactures . . . of carpeting, ruggs and broad cloath (sic), which till lately they have been obliged to furnish themselves with, out of other countries'.[49] Such a rise to economic prosperity was evident across the entire country. It continued through the eighteenth century and into the nineteenth unchecked either by foreign war or by civil strife at home after 1815. Even those regions not noted to-day for their commercial enterprises saw a tremendous increase in the movement of goods. In eight years at the opening of the nineteenth century the tonnage of the port of Edinburgh (Leith) climbed from 42,000 tons to 130,000 despite the fact that the sole manufactures were glass and paper and that there were no great industries.[50] Meanwhile Scotland's wealth was being heaped up in the west.

There in 1800 Thomas Garnett could note: 'Glasgow may, I think, without hesitation, be looked upon as the most improving place in Britain.'[51] Possibly such general satisfaction was only to be expected from one who was a native of Glasgow, and a member of that tribe which has carried its possessive loyalty around the globe. Nevertheless Garnett's pleasure, almost indeed his jubilation, and optimism, these did not arise from an idle boast. Glasgow was expanding territorially. 'I am credibly informed', writes Garnett again, 'that in this present year there are no less than five hundred buildings erecting . . . (and) most of them have been let before the foundation was laid.'[52] It was no more the city of the bishop and of the schoolmen. Instead it was one huge laboratory where new ideas were tested by machines and men for though it may have been the age of improvement the victories were hard won especially that over the River Clyde. From the late seventeenth century onwards the merchants of Glasgow had attempted to alter the course of nature, where nature was a broad river sprawling round the inches, idling over sandbanks and in most places no more than four feet deep. Only with the adoption of the ideas of James Smeaton, the celebrated engineer, was the river finally controlled by straightening its course, by dredging but chiefly by the erection of high jetties which not only deepened the channel but meant that the increased rate of flow prevented silt from being deposited in the lower reaches.[53] Glasgow made the Clyde and the Clyde made Glasgow. That marriage lasted throughout the nineteenth century. With vessels of sixteen and seventeen feet draught sailing into the very heart of the city the easy, rapid and cheap transportation of raw materials and finished products was accomplished.[54] Glasgow became the Second City. Its population rose to a quarter of a million[55] of which Irish and Highland immigrants made up a large proportion.[56] It became the greatest chemical manufactory in Britain. The largest works, producing vitriol, soda and other chemicals, were owned by a man called Tennant and, according to the foreign observer Kohl, the factory chimney (Tennant's Stalk) was four hundred and fifty feet high and 'rose over the city and its fog like the minster spire over Strasburg'. That may have been but there were other chimneys, mainly of the cotton mills. By 1834 of the 134 cotton factories in Scotland, a hundred were in Glasgow.[57] And commerce was also booming. The largest warehouse was owned by two brothers called Campbell. It employed about two hundred shopmen, which was exactly twice the number in the very largest Parisian store. It also employed a hundred and fifty women with sales in 1834 fetching in nearly £450,000.[58]

As Glasgow was to Scotland so Newcastle was to the north of England. A regional capital, its status was to be nobly enhanced by the achievements of Grainger, Dobson and others in creating a planned city centre in the eighteen twenties and thirties as the visible expression of Tyneside's wealth. Of course, there had been local industry long before then. At Seaton Sluice, in Northumberland, the landowner, Sir John Hussey Delaval, between 1761–4, provided a new entrance to improve the harbour and also formed a deep-water dock where vessels could be loaded or unloaded irrespective of the state of the tide. These improvements were necessitated by the expansion of the nearby Hartly coal trade and the establishment of a bottle factory fired by small coals. A few years later and the Delavals had a brewery, a brickworks and were exporting three hundred tons of salt.[59] In County Durham the Lambtons also had a salt-works as did the Earl of Scarborough[60] and their produce was shipped from Sunderland which, although it already manufactured lime and glass, was beginning to be associated with ship-building.[61] Over on the west coast, slate was the most famous local product being transported by coastal traffic to every part of Britain from the quarries of the Lowther dynasty—family is too mild a word.[62]

However these industries paled into comparative insignificance beside the stupendous tale of the coal trade in the north. There was nothing like it anywhere else in the country, except possibly in south Wales, and the export figures were impressive enough to be recounted with ever increasing astonishment by every writer, traveller and topographer of the late eighteenth and the nineteenth centuries. Coal and the coal-trade formed the great staple of the north whether in the east or the west.[63] By 1791 nearly two million tons of coal was annually leaving Newcastle.[64] By 1829 it had become the second port in England and old prints show huge flocks of sailing vessels, sometimes nearly a thousand, moored alongside the staithes below the castle.[65] Sunderland was not so far behind and every port was exporting on average a hundred per cent increase in all exports in the thirty years after 1791.[66]

Given the general conditions then prevailing large scale economic advances could only be made provided the traditionally wealthy classes were prepared to sink their finances into fresh outlets. It was the aristocracy which did much to create the modern world and in so doing destroyed itself. Of the first two coal-mining Lowthers it has been stated that their expenditure in the course of a century on one mine was 'upwards of half a million sterling'.[67] It was the wealth from the coal mines which enabled the Lambtons to build and re-build at Lambton Castle, which sustained Londonderry House in London and Wynyard House in the north for another Durham family as well as providing for two of the grandest examples of the Gothic Revival to survive to our own era, Ravensworth Castle in Durham and Lowther in Westmorland. Likewise in Scotland, landowners and coal-owners were one and the same with the aristocracy who allowed the black gold to be torn from their estates from Fife to Lanarkshire where at Hamilton the 'very duke of very dukes' Alexander, holder of three dukedoms, two marquisates and eight baronies was indulging himself with a £150,000 mausoleum, which has now sunk on top of the deserted, sagging coal seams.

Fortunes were made from coal and agriculture alike by the ancient aristocracy of the country for approximately a hundred years before the first chill winds set in from foreign states. In the eighteenth century the Duke of Queensberry's estate in southern Scotland drew in over a period of nine years about £70,000 of which, however, about £40,000 was returned to the country either as further investment in the estate or for public works of a charitable nature.[68] The Kennedys of Culzean paid for their Adam house by adopting the revolutionary farming techniques in Ayrshire and later running a ship-yard at Irvine. It was no wonder that in Perthshire, Strathearn could be lyrically hailed as 'bedecked by gentlemen's seats deeply imbowered and subdivided into verdant enclosures of corn fields and fertile meadows'.[69] Unfortunately, a correspondent of *The Gentleman's Magazine* found the pleasures of looking at such seats tempered by the knowledge that they did in fact belong to military men or to men lately come from the East Indies[70] though it is certain that not all of them were as rich as Captain Stewart who, on his return to Scotland, purchased the estates of Castle Stewart in Wigtownshire and St Fort in Fife.[71] If these new men were not from the East then as likely as not they came from the world of commerce as did William Russell, merchant of

Sunderland, who paid £70,000 for the Brancepeth estate in County Durham in 1796[72] or were bankers like George Harley Drummond who commissioned Gillespie Graham to build Drumtochty Castle in Kincardineshire at a cost of £30,000.[73] Everywhere the representatives of old and new families built lavishly. Sir James Campbell of Succoth had William Burn build him a Tudor mansion at Garscube on the outskirts of Glasgow while further afield Kirkman Finlay, a merchant, like Russell, and Lord Provost of Glasgow, had a castle erected at Toward Point on the Firth of Clyde. Of course not everyone was a Campbell or a Finlay but there were plenty of others, men of lesser substance who could afford a marine villa at one of the smart and rather elegant watering-places which were springing into existence at such places as Dunoon on the Clyde or Newport on the Tay. But their houses, charming though they are in whatever style, were not architecturally of first or historic importance. Throughout the hundred years from 1745–1845 it was the great aristocracy and their followers, the gentry, who set the architectural pace and it is not without significance that their century, the century of the Agrarian and the Industrial Revolutions, was also that of the Gothic Revival.

II

Aesthetic Theory

The aesthetic philosophy of the eighteenth century was born from political conditions—from the Revolution of 1688–9 which established William and Mary on the throne as the twin deities of Protestantism. Their accession was a triumph for political rationalism—despite the expediency of the English noblemen who made them King and Queen—and it marked the flowering of liberalism albeit with a Whig connotation since the Whigs ruled continuously, apart from the interregnum of Bolingbroke in Anne's time, until the succession of George III in 1760. Within that span there was established not only that the collective will of the landed aristocracy should prevail within the state but that a man (provided he was not a catholic) should have personal and religious freedom. Once such bases were accepted and elevated to political theory, becoming the *novum organum* of philosophy, then it was inevitable that the retrospective concept should project them to artifacts and environment, a common enough experience in all art but especially in architecture which is the means whereby mankind realises in volume and permanent form, philosophy, ambitions, social organisation or political and religious belief. It is only in such a context that the writings of the eighteenth century aestheticians can be understood and their importance explained since, until Pugin gave both theory and practice, architects generally followed the will of the philosophers.

Of these writers it is interesting to note that all the early ones were involved to some degree, either directly or indirectly, in Whig politics. For instance, the third Earl of Shaftesbury (1671–1713), author of *The Moralists*, and the grandson of the radical politician and earl executed by Charles II for his part in the Rye House Plot, was himself no mean politician only abandoning his parliamentary life because of chronic ill-health.[1] Burke, who introduced the term 'sublime', was a celebrated parliamentary lawyer supporting the Whig cause as did Pope before him. Similarly the third Duke of Argyll, who began to build a new Inveraray

11

Castle in 1745, was a noted Whig and Horace Walpole, of Strawberry Hill fame, was a son of the greatest Whig of them all, Sir Robert Walpole. It should then be no surprise to find that the Gothic Revival, in its prime manifestations a somewhat precious style, was the product of what to-day would be termed an 'in-group', with its members possessing similar values, taste, judgements and usually the same political beliefs and opinions. This was the Twickenham Set—an earlier and more potent Cliveden Set.

In opting for 'Sense, Order, Proportion everywhere' Shaftesbury proclaimed himself as the archetypal eighteenth century thinking man— and a British one at that since the virtues so advocated are the distillation of the age discoverable in porcelain, furniture or even in landscape and finding an echo when James Paine declared, after the middle of the century, that 'It is no wonder . . . that architecture should revive in an uncommon degree, in a nation justly celebrated for the good sense, taste and opulence of its people!'[2] True a man like Beckford in the last years of the century by his own works seemed to decry Shaftesbury's sentiments. Nevertheless, the virtues were not quite overthrown and though they may have been rocked and strained by Fonthill Abbey yet they were still the underpinning. Shaftesbury not only applied his tenets to abstract mora-lising but also to his surroundings, those surroundings depicted as views and perspectives by artists like Slezer, with panoramas of the College of Glasgow, or Kip and Knyff with plates of Lowther Castle (Westmorland) or Anderson Place in Newcastle, each set in large gardens. The elaborately contrived, petrified geometry of those Dutch inspired groves Shaftesbury scorned as 'the mockery of princely gardens' and he expanded on this by stating a preference 'for things of a natural kind; where neither Art, nor the Conceit or Caprice of Man has spoil'd their genuine Order, by breaking in upon that primitive State'.[3] Thus does Shaftesbury establish himself as one of the fundamental influences of all eighteenth century thought since it was the concept of a natural order which was to prove so attractive alike to the aestheticians and to moralists of the stature of Diderot and Rousseau. Nature was accepted neither in the wide-ranging and all inclusive twentieth century sense nor on terms presupposing a wild or primitive state but rather for qualities which were assumed to be discoverable in underlying form. It was the resultant intellectual search which so fascinated men of later generations and, indeed, if such qualities and conditions could not be presupposed then the intelligentsia would soon have abandoned its fancy for the natural world, which is what happened anyway but only after a century had passed.

Shaftesbury was followed by other writers whose lack of intellectual originality was more than compensated for by the style of their advocacy. Addision reduced Shaftesbury's dicta from the general to the particular and the practical with, 'A Man might make a pretty Landskip of his own Possessions',[4] while Alexander Pope sent up such a display of poetic pyrotechnics that his couplets remain as the summation of his day and thought, a fact later recognised by many practitioners of gardening and landscape design. His was the sarcasm that mocked

> Grove nods at grove, each alley has a brother,
> And half the platform just reflects the other.[5]

To these writers there could be no doubt that intricate formalism in gardens was overthrown. The arrogance of man's invention—distortion even—had yielded to a softer and wider understanding of nature which, like the British who 'foreign laws despise', could be found to have an order derived from its own rules and regulations.

> Nature, like liberty, is but restrained
> By the same laws which first herself ordained.[6]

Thus the epigram turned in the classic mode. Yet for men educated in the ethical rationalism of the Whigs and discovering anew, under the aegis of Lord Burlington, the intellectual disciplines and the visual strictness of Palladio's architecture, no other concept was possible. So, with the social éclat of Burlington and the Twickenham Set, the philosophical basis for eighteenth century romanticism was not just laid but well and truly mortared.

It was William Kent (1685–1748), architect, gardener and interior decorator, who was the best known exponent of the new ideas. Like Pope he, too, was a member of that coterie always in movement around Richard Boyle, third Earl of Burlington—the London *Il Magnifico*. Of Kent as landscape gardener the egregious Mr Walpole noted that 'He leaped the fence and saw all nature was a garden.'[7] If Kent was first over the fence then he did not stray very far beyond it, at least according to later notions, since his garden at Stowe was a very artificial concept making use of a variety of objects including a Temple of British Worthies, among whom, interestingly enough, Alexander Pope was numbered, while at Rousham in Oxfordshire, a few years later in 1738–41,[8] the garden was similarly eclectic with Venus' Vale and a Gothic 'eye-catcher' on the skyline. Its beauties were summarised by Horace Walpole as, 'Daphne in little, the sweetest little groves, streams, glades, porticoes, arcades, cascades and river imaginable; all the scenes are perfectly classic.'[9]

13

Such a controlled environment was very sophisticated, the mark of a high culture and an exceedingly tuned and gratified taste. In addition the emphasis on the small scale and the intimate is in direct contrast to the overall idea and the formal grandeur of a garden like Versailles or, on a lesser scale, Hampton Court. It is the rococo as opposed to the baroque. It is also that system of checks and balance, that separation of parts within an overall unity which is met with, architecturally, in Burlington's Chiswick Villa. Therefore for Walpole to use the phrase 'perfectly classic' did not betoken dichotomy of thought but was contrapuntal once the belief was accepted that nature's own rules were being applied just as in architecture it was natural laws, as re-interpreted by Palladio, which were current usage for, as Robert Morris wrote in 1728, architecture sprang from 'The Strictest Adherence to the Practice of those Unerring Rules, those perfect Standards of the Law of Reason and Nature, founded upon Beauty and Necessity.'[10] Yet what, in effect, had been achieved was the formalism of the curve for that of the straight line, of one artificiality for another. Kent was not alone in this although possibly, by his particular social connections, he may have had the greatest popular influence. Certainly, the perspective of nature had been enlarged. In practical measure it had been shown that nature could be held in a state of semi-submission; and if others later released her then theirs was the easier task. Nevertheless, once nature was accepted in the very best circles so it must conform to society's mores and not only conduct itself according to formal etiquette but must be capable of exact definition serving not only as pedigree but as a tabulator as in any other science. All this was done by Burke, the first lawyer of his day, from whose logic there emanated those terms of the beautiful and the sublime, the Scilla and the Charybdis of eighteenth century British taste.

Briefly the effect of the sublime was astonishment and that of beauty was pleasure. Not only was aesthetic vocabulary enlarged but so also were aesthetic criteria since certain fixed and immutable traits were attributed to the sublime. These included obscurity (which induced terror), power, privations (such were vacuity, darkness, solitude and silence) and vastness or greatness of dimension. Height Burke considered the most moving kind of vastness although possibly it was more so when regarded as depth. Then how much greater must be the emotion roused by infinity which had a tendency 'to fill the mind with that sort of delightful Horror' which was the most genuine effect and truest test of the sublime? Such a trait could appear in Succession and Uniformity with the former creating an illusion which continued beyond physical bounds whereas in the latter it was because there was no check to the imagination.[11]

14

Burke was at the middle of the century, that is between Shaftesbury, Addison and Pope on the one hand and Gilpin, Knight and Price on the other, and his coda therefore marks a very precise set of aesthetic judgements at the halfway stage of eighteenth century sensibility. In referring to the characteristics of his analysis it is found that those implying looseness and freedom are applicable to landscape while succession and uniformity are expressions to be associated with architecture. Thus although the *a priori* position has shifted there can still be the formal Palladian house set in the naturalistic garden in which, however, size is conceptual and not the small and the intimate. The vision has been magnified and, in time, size itself becomes the desideratum. Now, with regard to aesthetic theory earlier philosophers had been dispassionate in their observations. Quality and virtue lie in the objects perceived and by the exercise of reason and knowledge a spectator can thereby form an assessment based on intrinsic merit. By introducing the sublime and thus bringing emotion to bear on aesthetic discrimination, Burke polarised earlier attitudes. After him it is the emotional reflex of the observer which is significant and therefore to become the desired effect. The gasp of astonishment, the expression of wonder, the thrill of fear at sight or sound are all instantaneous reactions to situations. Such minutae in the range of human emotion are of such momentary duration that appreciation must consist of a rapid sequence of them if the sublime is to be maintained. As Burke defined it the sublime is yet another artificiality so that the qualities ascribed to it are neither collective nor immutable. They are individualistic and transcendental. Nevertheless, to a society as artificial and, in many respects, as limited as that of the eighteenth century, Burke's exposition of the sublime must have been a revelation compared to which Saul's conversion on the road to Damascus was but a low-powered illumination. By introducing the sublime, Burke gave the eighteenth century a handbook for meeting with nature.

That terror with which Burke distinguished the sublime was most fully and directly achieved when writers and travellers later discovered the enormity of the Lake District and the mountains of Scotland. However, such confrontations were but a vicarious thrill for as Dr Johnson noted '. . . terror without danger is only one of the sports of fancy'.[12] Indirectly such tremors as Burke depicted could be savoured and enjoyed through the medium of the immensely popular contemporary Gothic poetry, of which the origins have been traced back to Spenser and Milton. In the latter's *Il Penseroso* the following lines occur:

15

And may, at last, my weary age
Find out the peaceful hermitage,
The hairy gown, and mossy cell,
Where I may sit and rightly spell
Of every star Heaven doth shew,
And every herb that sips the dew;
Till old experience do attain
To something like prophetic strain.
These pleasures, Melancholy, give,
And I with thee will choose to live.

Imbued with the medieval, the silence of solitude and of melancholy, these lines exactly suited the facile eighteenth century literary taste for the Middle Ages. Throughout the century the flow of melancholic poetry never ceased until by the seventies and nineties almost every issue of *The Gentleman's Magazine* contained at least one gloomy and awful poem. In June, 1791, Anna Seward had a poem 'To a Coffin-Lid'. It began

Thou silent door of our eternal sleep
Sickness and pain, debility and woes
. . . Thou shuttest out for ever.

In the following month came 'Meditations Written in a Church-Yard'. This was somewhat livelier than the previous ditty since

. . . fear-created spectres stalk around,
And through the air foreboding screech owls cry.

There were monastic odes and 'The Unfortunate Maniac at Coniston Priory in Westmorland' ran to thirty stanzas.[13] That this and other such nonsense had an enormous vogue there can be no doubt which says much for eighteenth century stamina especially as thematic variation was monotonously limited. True, towards the end of the century there was more than a touch of the macabre as well as some tone-painting. In 'Rosline Abbey'

Esk, murm'ring thro' the dusky pines,
Reflects the moon's mist-mantled beam;
And fancy chills, where'er it shines,
To see pale ghosts obscurely gleam.

16

Not so the night, that, in thy halls,
Once, Rosline, danc'd in joy along;
Where owls now scream along thy walls,
Resounded mirth's inspiring song:
Where bats now rest their smutly wings,
Th' impurpled feast was wont to flow.[14]

Yet beyond that the props remained—churchyards at midnight, owls, gloom and much melancholic contemplation. Nevertheless, such poetry had a social significance for its warlike notes of the spear-encrusted Middle Ages are the psychological bolt-hole of a bored and introverted society, secure in its social stations and protected by the privilege of wealth from the hardships brought on by the wars of the time. The upper classes read of war and built warlike homes but seldom did a gentleman participate in war.

The other strain in Gothic poetry is the yearning, in that most artificial of societies, for the simple and the contemplative life. It is the Horatian ideal but in cowl and gown. Now that same wistful elegiac quality is always present in the work of certain seventeenth century landscape painters, whose influence has long been recognised as a major factor in the formation of eighteenth century British taste. Yet the appreciation of landscape was first possible only when society had lost that fear of woods, desolate roads and empty mountains which had been such a feature of medieval life. Once the earth yielded not only food and shelter to man but comfort, security and leisure then he could appreciate its beauties. Inevitably, such beauties were Roman. As writers and poets took Augustan Rome as their model so did lovers of landscape, especially if they had travelled to the Eternal City and beheld the Campagna from which Poussin and Claude Lorraine drew their inspiration. A painting like the former's *The Arcadian Shepherds*, where nobility is combined with serenity and the monumental, appealed to collectors who saw themselves as the possessors of a second Augustan age even if gout-ridden Anne and her successor, 'the wee German lairdie', did not quite match up to Augustus Caesar. Paintings by Salvator Rosa were also brought from the Continent to hang in many a great house in Britain. In time the influence of these seventeenth century artists became so pervasive that no self-respecting traveller could stir from his own doorstep without coming across some scene or other which was a reminder of either Poussin, Claude or Rosa and possibly all three together.

In Scotland Lettice described the setting of Chatelherault, the summer-palace of the Dukes of Hamilton, where trees and rocks overhung the gorge of the river, as the *belle nature* of Poussin's landscapes.[15] At Rothesay, Salvator Rosa would have sketched with rapture a cave 'particularly at the moment when a group of banditti have been celebrating their nocturnal orgies round a blazing fire, at the mouth of the chasm'.[16] Thereafter it was but a short step for some writers to see not merely a recollection of Italian landscape but a superiority. Of Derwentwater Hutchinson declared that, 'Claude in his happiest hour never struck out a finer landscape'.[17]

These artists invariably depicted landscapes set with building structures, usually temples or castellated edifices, frequently fragmentary or in a ruinous state. Perhaps not surprisingly, therefore, ruins and buildings of a quite eclectic kind became *de rigueur* for parks and gardens in Britain. Gothic became the most favoured style as Gothic remains, of one kind or another, were readily available so that a landowner might possess the genuine ruins of a medieval abbey or fortification and if not then some neighbour's fragments could easily be copied. Also Gothic was acceptable since it aroused associations in the mind of the beholder for which the poetic mood of the moment clamoured. Of course, as with any other aspect of eighteenth century gardening, ruins were a matter calling for the most detailed study and assessment. Even Arthur Young, the prime cause of whose journeyings was agrarian innovation and economy, after he had visited Fountains Abbey stated that a ruin should be set in a wilderness 'the habitation rather of bats, owls and wild beasts, than of man. . . . Ruins generally appear best at a distance.' Thus there are 'some parts that cannot be seen at all, others that are half seen; and those fully viewed broken, rugged and terrible. In such the imagination has a free space to range in, and sketches ruins in idea beyond the boldest limits of reality.'[18] Clearly, such sentiments are contrary to Palladian practice whereby a building is so positioned that all its parts are immediately visible and comprehensible to the spectator. Young's attitude, which is Burke's sublime, reflects an earlier attitude by Pope that

> He gains all points, who pleasingly confounds,
> Surprises, varies, and conceals the bounds.[19]

Yet the ultimate effect is very different since Young looks to ruins to 'impress upon the mind a kind of religious melancholy! an effect so difficult to raise by art'.[20]

Now if such were indeed the charms of ruins and bearing in mind that there was but one Fountains Abbey then a situation had arisen which that age of challenge could not fail to meet. Thus artificial ruins sprang up round many a noble and not so noble house, although such enterprises were not favoured by William Gilpin. To create an artificial ruin was an undertaking fraught with hazard since there was the necessity of 'constructing it on as regular, and uniform a plan, as if it had been a real edifice. Not only the situation, and general form of the castle, or the abbey, should be observed; but the several parts should at least be so traced out, that an eye, skilled in such edifices, may easily investigate the parts, which are lost from the parts which remain.' Then 'it is not every man who can build a house, that can execute a ruin. To give the stone its mouldering appearance—to make the widening chink run naturally through all the joints—to mutilate the ornaments—to peel the facing from the internal structure—to shew how correspondent parts have once united . . . and to scatter heaps of ruin around with negligence and ease; are great efforts of art. . . . You must put your ruin at last into the hands of nature to adorn, to perfect it. If the mosses and lychens grow unkindly on your walls—if the streaming weather-stains have produced no variety of tints— if the ivy refuses to mantle over your buttress . . . if the ash cannot be brought to hang from the cleft; or long, spiry grass to wave over the shattered battlements—your ruin will still be incomplete—you may as well write over the gate, Built in the year 1772. . . . It is time alone which meliorates the ruin.'[21]

19

III

Follies and Gothic Architecture

Despite the dire warnings of William Gilpin ruins were built along with many other folly types, some of which dated from Vanbrugh's time. One of the most famous ruins was Hagley Castle, in Worcestershire, a brainchild of the gentleman and amateur architect, Sanderson Miller in 1746. Rising over the garden, its ruined towers and shattered windows, in the well-known phrase of Horace Walpole, had 'the true rust of the Barons' Wars'. Others, too, apart from the impressionable Mr Walpole, were forcibly struck by this object of fancy even as late as 1801 when 'curiosity is on the wing to be acquainted with its history, what sieges it has sustained, and what blood has been spilt upon its walls'.[1] Such speculations, as naive as a Hollywood film handout, to the nineteenth century were wickedly frivolous when applied to gardens, like Hagley or Leasowes, consisting of superficial experiences which their creators likened to true emotional insight. And even although Dr Johnson might ask, 'Where is the pleasure of preserving such mournful memorials?'[2] humanity, being neither so sensible nor so independent of thought, revelled in the nostalgia evoked at Hagley by the Seat of Contemplation, adorned with bones and bearing an inscription contrived from thin snail shells split in two.[3] And was there not the hermitage of tree roots with a seat, covered with matting, around it, and a wooden railing and gate at the entrance[4] while beside the grotto was a moss seat, set about with tall trees and ivy and moss as 'a paradise for contemplation to indulge in'.[5] An indulgence. That was Hagley even with its Doric temple by 'Athenian' Stuart. And who should wonder then that the next century, taking its Gothic more seriously, should endeavour to dismiss Hagley and Leasowes as 'the frippery of a taste which, though constantly aspiring to something beyond mediocrity, was more prone to copy, than capable to originate'?[6] Very true and with just that touch of invective which characterises the condemnation of one generation by the next. Yet without Hagley with its castle and Leasowes and its 'ruinated priory'[7] there might never have come down to Pugin a taste for the Gothic style unless, in the first instance, it had not been so popularised that ruins appeared in every county. And not just ruins. On Loch Tayside, the Countess of Breadalbane had a hermitage in which the walls were covered with moss and the stools were upholstered with the skins of the wild cat, deer, goat and other animals.[8] Thus the visitor could view the nearby cascade in some comfort as at Blair Castle, also in Perthshire, where a similar cave existed.[9] In the south at Marston House, near Longleat, the hermitage had a small yard enclosed by horses' heads and bones.[10] Such cells, alike by fashion and material were but temporary affairs although one of the most complete must have been that at Callidon which Mrs Delany described in February, 1752. Ensconced on an island and approached by little winding walks, embellished with seats, the cell, like that at Hagley, was of tree roots. Inside, the floor was paved with pebbles, there was a matting couch and wooden stools with a manuscript and a pair of spectacles on the table while elsewhere was everything 'that you might imagine necessary for a recluse. . . . I never saw so pretty a whim so thoroughly well executed.'[11]

Of course such whims could take other forms. In northern England follies assumed the sterner air of the castle rather than of the abbey, probably because there were ecclesiastical ruins aplenty. As usual the Duke of Northumberland outdid everyone else by owning both Hulne Priory and Alnwick Abbey. In the former, 'lately purchased' in 1756,[12] 'the remains of the monastery, humbly mourning in the lowly garb of solitude, and bending down in ruins'[13] were fitted up as a gazebo (Plate 35) in the seventeen seventies while the gateway of the latter did service as a porter's lodge.[14] Further south, in County Durham, John Burdon of Hardwick Hall brought some medieval remains from Guisborough Priory to provide 'the mock ruins of a monastic house well devised', beside his lake, 'the finest sheet of water in the north of England'.[15]

Another folly was by Archdeacon Thomas Sharp of Rothbury who, in 1720, was given the living by his father, who happened to be Archbishop of York. In the topmost corner of his garden at Whitton the archdeacon built a thirty-foot high round tower which provided him with a seaview and an observatory.[16] The tower is a very smooth composition in stone and in the relationship of small round-headed windows to the overall surface is restrained and quite ungothic. Indeed, the only feature of the Middle Ages is the battlemented parapet. The exact date of building is not known but if it was built solely to relieve unemployment among local masons,[17] then it might date from the seventeen twenties as has been suggested,[18] in which case an observer would be justified in regarding the battlemented top as a survival from an earlier and traditional mode of building. If, on the other hand, the desire was not just the abatement of human suffering but also to obtain an 'eye-catcher' and a sea-view then the earliest date is probably about 1745, despite the theory that the influence of Vanbrugh's northern work might presuppose the earlier date.[19] Yet such a phenomenon should be discounted for reasons of style, geographical remoteness and the lack of other local examples in the second or third decades. By its situation and the smoothness of its architectural quality Sharp's Tower should be regarded as revivalism and not least because of the battlements atop the classical cornice. Indeed the year 1745 may be too early. After all, Kent was still alive and Hagley Castle was a year off. Nor would such a date coincide with the setting up of Codger's Fort, only eight miles to the south of Whitton. The tale is that its hilltop position on a north-facing spur and brooding over a severe dip in the road was to deter the advance of Jacobites from Scotland. That may well be true as Sir Walter Calverley Blackett, the landowner, had been Mayor of Newcastle and was the city's MP and certainly, even by mid-eighteenth century standards of Gothic, it is rough architecture, being little more than a triangular bastion of undressed masonry, pierced by long slits and having a squat, beehive-shaped block-house at either end. There are none of the usual decorative features of quatrefoils or crosslets. It is as if a section of one of those marvellously intricate and star-shaped contemporary forts had indeed been hastily set up. Yet it was commissioned from Thomas Wright of Durham as late as 1769 and was not executed until the next decade.[20] On a neighbouring crag and overlooking two manmade lakes, is Rothley Castle (Plate 1) also by the same landowner. A more elaborate and larger structure than the fort it has three equidistant towers linked by curved stretches of walling. Now this is a folly, once decorated with whalebones at the entrance and with stone figures from London's Aldersgate set atop each corner of the central tower.[21] The grouping is possessed of a cyclopean quality, yet, from a distance, the broken silhouettes and the varying masses merge and reform over the rock-face until they come close to being a medieval castle of the four-towered Northumbrian or Durham variety although the real architectural interest is the fact that the heavy castellation and the pointed niches of about 1745 are by Daniel Garrett who seems to have been the earliest Gothic practitioner in the north of England.[22] Certainly, a subtler relationship exists between the 'castle' and the site than at Codger's Fort which is arbitrarily imposed on the landscape.

22

On the coast the octagon at Seaton Sluice, near Whitley Bay, and the adjacent Starlight Castle may also have been put up in the sixties, rather than in Vanbrugh's time, when Sir John Hussey Delaval was making a new dock and entrance at Seaton Sluice.[23] As he was also the owner of Ford Castle where the medieval and Tudor house was being rendered habitable in the Gothic of the day[24] then it seems reasonable to accredit him with the octagon. Battlements apart, it is a symmetrical, though somewhat watered-down classicism in contrast with the nearby Starlight Castle on the Delaval estate, which had pointed windows and

Plate 1   Daniel Garrett. Rothley Castle, Northumberland. c. 1745.

projecting corner towers and is probably a closer relative of Ford Castle as it was. A similar type of folly is also found in Durham, at Westerton, where a circular observatory was begun by Thomas Wright (1711–86), an architect and astronomer and mathematician of international repute who was once offered the chair of mathematics at the Imperial Academy of St Petersburg. Wright's tower, being so near the end of the century, bears the typical cross-shaped slits which is a hall-mark of the period.[25]

Thus follies could be objects which, in addition to their decorative and possible associational qualities, might serve some useful but secondary purpose. But there was a third purpose—to disguise a building or object which the owner of a new-found, fashionable discrimination in visual matters might find either distasteful or vulgar and frequently both. It is such an attitude which at Swarland Old Hall accounts for the castellated screen erected across a gable.[26] As it would be glimpsed from a distance

23

the three indented arches only rise from almost the same level as the wall-head of the old house. Similarly, at Swinburne Castle a hay-loft in a field had two sides wrapped round with a castellated wall marked with Maltese crosses similar to ones at Alnwick Castle. The date of these alterations cannot be fixed although a time somewhere in the middle of the seventeen sixties or later would be appropriate. They might indeed be contemporaneous with the tower at Hartburn, also in Northumberland, erected by John Sharp, the eldest son of Archdeacon Thomas Sharp whose own tower at Whitton may be the first of these northern follies. At Hartburn walks were cut along the river-bank and a grotto formed with the front of the tower set as an 'eye-catcher' above a steep portion of the bank at a bend in the river. That was prior to 1770.[27] Later on, part of the tower was in use as a school-room[28] but to-day it is the village post office with a television aerial rising over the battlements and corner turrets. Above the ground floor, so that they might be seen, are two trefoil cusped windows below a single ogee arch with two smaller windows on the floor above. Yet despite the introduction of such Gothic features, the tower is a sham; but then it was never intended as anything else. To achieve a certain romantic effect at a certain romantic spot, that was its cause.

There is, however, a small group of structures which achieve more than this because they are planned in three dimensions and so have volume without which those spatial effects—which is what architecture in the last resort is—cannot be found. The simplest of these are the kennels at Nunwick House which bear the date 1768.[29] Two years earlier the same owners had restored part of the medieval castle of Simonburn.[30] Set on a distant hill and with turrets it was deliberately recreated as an 'eye-catcher' which was also the intention behind the formation of the kennels across the river and in front of the house. They are nothing more than a low rectangle, crowned with flat battlements and with the Y-tracery of the windows surrounded by broad flat moulding in that manner which came to be known as churchwardens' Gothic. With the dogs in their low-walled courtyards on either side and the keeper in his little house nearby the kennels at Nunwick must have been one of the most charming of follies, constructed really for no other purpose then to strike delight in the beholder.

So far nearly all the follies have been in Northumberland. Their popularity cannot be put down to a love of old forms otherwise these would be reflected elsewhere. Also the proliferation of such objects cannot be the result of a national fashion for while it is true that the Gothic style was popular and was becoming more widespread in more southern areas, there was no quick diffusion throughout the country.[31] The fact that in

24

the seventeen sixties there were so many follies in Northumberland must be related to the restoration of Alnwick Castle and the fitting up of the interior in the Gothic style by the Duke of Northumberland, the first of the new creation. The Duke was repairing the castle as early as 1752[32] and this is confirmed by *The Gentleman's Magazine* of February, 1756,[33] while it is probable that James Paine's Gothic work was begun sometime before 1758. Certainly, John Adam records a Gothic dining-room and drawing-room in the spring of 1759[34] whereas Ford Castle was not begun until 1761.[35] To Alnwick Castle then must be ascribed that impetus for the early appearance of the Gothic revival in Northumberland.

In the Palatinate of Durham, the Prince-Bishop[36] was to the county as the Percys were to Northumberland. One of the former's seats was Auckland Castle on the town edge of a deer-stocked demesne, where in 1760 Bishop Trevor, as well as constructing the gatehouse at the town entrance to the demesne, had a winter enclosure provided for the park deer.[37] An open square (Plate 2), the external arcade has low arches springing from square piers. At regular intervals crosslets are incised on the masonry which is capped with well cut battlements over a string-course. Each corner has a diagonal buttress ending above the wall-head as a crocketted finial while on three sides of the square the central arch, framed by buttresses, rises to the full height of the battlements. The fourth side has a tower, containing an upper room from which the deer could be viewed, but is treated in an otherwise similar manner to the three gateways. As one would have expected in such a setting the concept has an ecclesiastical semblance particularly as the arcades give a solemn processional air to the architectural movement. Indeed, would it be too

Plate 2   Deer House. Auckland Castle, County Durham. 1760.

far-fetched to see in this creation some subtle episcopal pun for surely the deer house is no more than a set of cloisters turned inside out? The architect, for most certainly there was one, is unknown although in 1760 or thereabouts Sir Thomas Robinson designed the main gate-house to the bishop's demesne[38] while some years before Sanderson Miller (of Hagley Castle fame) carried out some alterations at Durham Castle in the Gothic style.[39]

In the same general style is the banqueting-house at Gibside, a patrimony of the Bowes family, which was later linked by marriage to the earldom of Strathmore. In 1721 George Bowes came into possession of Gibside. Like so many of the greater sort of landowner he was a Whig, who demonstrated his beliefs by setting up in his grounds a Column of Liberty, which cost him £2,000.[40] It stood at one end of a great terrace, a mile long, terminated at the other by James Paine's superbly tactile mausoleum of 1760.[41] Overlooking these ornaments and with an avenue of trees to provide axial guidance down to the lake, was the banqueting-house built by Daniel Garrett in 1751.[42] Some steps led through the curved centre into the banqueting-room which was mirrored at the ends to give the effect of an almost limitless number of guests.[43] All that has gone and only elderberry and ivy are here now growing through and around rotting walls and fallen timbers although a smaller room still has traces of plaster-work showing a strapwork design of decidedly Jacobean flavour enclosing stylised flower patterns. Despite the ruination effected by neglect sufficient is left of the structure to see it as the product of a most skilled hand revealing a maturity of design and a competence in the handling of the Gothic motifs which is conspicuously lacking in most other Gothic follies of a similar period. For instance, the embattled side walls give a necessary balance to the central two-storeyed bay which at one time ended in a spire with three gables clustered round it.[44] These last remain with heavily crocketed outlines. There are crosslets and quatrefoils too, boldly done but never in a manner likely to detract from the overall control of the design.

Such a work as Gibside must have been the epitome of rococo Gothic never to be surpassed by Robert Adam's later works for the Duke of Northumberland around Alnwick Castle in the seventies and eighties of the century. Indeed, by that time Gothic had lost that freshness which Gibside possesses and was assuming the attenuated elegance of the later Georgian period just as Adam's own creations were becoming a trifle facile, over ornate and rather dull. But folly building did not stop at Gibside nor with Robert Adam. It was to have a long run and did not even begin in north west England until 1786. That was when the Lake

Plate 3 Spire House. Greystoke, Cumberland.

District was becoming a tourist haunt for lovers of the picturesque and when the eleventh Duke of Norfolk (1746–1815) succeeded to the Howard titles and estates.[45] On a rise above Ullswater he built and, as the designer of Arundel Castle (1791–1815),[46] may have designed, a castellated house which he called Lyulph's Tower 'from which the lines of the lake appear in a most painter-like arrangement'.[47] It was a holiday retreat where, 'His Grace usually reposes for a fortnight in the autumn, enjoying perhaps, though in a less active sense, the traditions of the Roman Saturnalia'.[48] That may have been but the Duke was renowned for his conviviality and

27

as an eccentric who so detested soap and water that his servants washed him during his drunken stupors. At his childhood home, Greystoke Castle, the Duke displayed his well-known antiquarian interests in three folly farms.[49] Spire House (Plate 3) has such a feature while Bunker's Hill was a reminder of its creator's Whiggery, the Tories having been responsible for the loss of the American colonies. Fort Putnam, the largest folly, and somewhat similar to Sebergham Castle also in Cumberland,[50] is really no more than a farmyard wall lavishly enriched with battlements, arches, round buttresses and large pointed windows. The poet Mason described such a farm when his hero, Aleander desired

> A wall embattled, and within its sward
> Let every structure needful for a farm
> Arise in castle-semblance; the huge barn
> Shall with a mock portcullis arm the gate
>   and every butress broad
> Whose proud projection seems a mass of stone
> Give space to stall the heifer and the steed.
> So shall each part, though turn'd to rural use,
> Deceive the eye with those bold feudal forms
> That Fancy loves to gaze on.[51]

Strange that a baronial cowshed should be the forebear of the Palace of Westminster. Of course, the Gothic follies were most unscholarly but then, considering the age, that was inevitable. Almost nothing, for instance, was generally known of Gothic architecture or, indeed, of its builders except that round arches were accredited to the Saxons, the pointed being reserved as a Gothic invention. Thus Carlisle Cathedral, Norman in parts, 'was built in the Saxon times with very massy pillars and round arches'[52] while the ruins of Lindisfarne Priory were similarly described as Saxon in origin.[53] It was even possible to push chronology further back as Dr Johnson did at Iona where the choir arch was 'Roman, being part of a circle; that of the additional building (nave) is pointed, and therefore Gothick or Saracenical'.[54] With such broad generalisations matters of identification, for most travellers, were allowed to rest with only an occasional and very tentative indication as to a building period usually identified, and wrongly, by the reign of a monarch.

Yet attempts to understand Gothic architecture were confounded by total ignorance of the Middle Ages. For example, in 1750 Pococke wrote of Beaulieu Abbey, 'It appears that the church was arched, and above the spring of the arch the walls are raised and Gothic windows made in them.

There is a gallery on each side, which probably was only floored at first, but now Gothic or elleiptick arches are turned over the isle . . . which makes me conjecture that the monks were in this gallery one to each window.'[55] Such misconceptions on the origin and use of a triforium indicate complete lack of knowledge on the workings of great medieval institutions, a state rendered the more confused, if that was possible, by the classical upbringing of commentators. That the language of classical architecture should be applied to Gothic buildings was inevitable and all the more so as any specific Gothic terminology was lacking, certainly prior to about the seventeen seventies. The chapter-house at Elgin had a central column 'crusted over with 16 (sic) pilasters . . . adorned with a chapter from which arise round pillars that spread along the roof';[56] and terms like Gothic-Corinthian are in no way unusual.

In the later eighteenth century travellers were ever more prone to comment on the chief Gothic remains, scattered across the countryside and in the towns, in the search for those sublime qualities now discovered in monuments erected by men of whom less was known than of the Romans. Size and magnificence were noted as well as appreciation for the intricacies and the variety of parts in Gothic decoration. Of architectural criticism there was none, in the modern sense that is, and of comment very little although attempts to convey either were hampered again by the lack of an exact etymology. When Arthur Young writes of York Minster: 'The entrance strikes the mind with that awe which is the result of the magnificent arising from vastness',[57] it could be Burke discoursing on the sublime with the qualities of landscape projected into Gothic architecture.

Of the popularity of the Gothic movement there can be no doubt. The endless flow of literature, the scholarly tomes, the horrific poetry is evidence enough as was the gradual adoption of the style for buildings. Strawberry Hill and Fonthill Abbey may have been seen by some as outlandish freaks. Yet they occupy a place in the history of the Gothic Revival which corresponds to that of the Queen's House and the recasing of St Paul's in the emergence of the classical school of British architecture. The plates in the travel books, the topographical studies and *The Gentleman's Magazine* would provide proof, if any was needed, that Gothic, the once sickly infant, by the close of the century, had become a lusty youth bawling its virtues across the landscape. Pennant in 1769 may have been in complete ignorance about Gothic architecture so that he can neither name parts nor details, but he is far from despising Gothic. Even Dr Johnson accepts Gothic for what it is worth in a rare purple passage: 'The fictions of the Gothick romances were not so remote from credibility as they are now thought. In the full prevalance of the feudal institution, when violence desolated the world, and every baron lived in a fortress, forests and castles were regularly succeeded by each other, and the adventurer might very suddenly pass from the gloom of the woods, or the ruggedness of moors, to seats of plenty, gaiety and magnificence.'[58] However, he also believes Glasgow Cathedral to be incomplete since work stopped 'before the cross isle was added, which seems essential to a Gothick Cathedral'.[59]

At the end of the century engravings in such a work as the *Letters on a Tour of Scotland* by Lettice are still very much of the earlier manner. Castles show little in the way of details save for massive machicolation and the pointed window. A scene of Bothwell Castle or of Linlithgow Palace[60] will have a tranquility and impressive strength so that it is both romantic and very associational. In ecclesiastical ruins slightly more detail is permissible. Again, however, they become pastoral scenes of great delicacy and refinement so that an 'improver' could easily convert such a ruin as Melrose or Dryburgh Abbey into a stylish habitation. The draughtsmanship is concentrated on the broad surface elements of gables, windows or buttresses which provide the readiest visual qualities without the necessity of close attention by the critic and of course as there is no emphasis on constructional elements the buildings have the flimsy quality of a theatrical back-drop. Any book, magazine or periodical of the time will have the same selection of views—lakes, mountains and ruins. *The Gentleman's Magazine* portrays them for month after month until by the seventeen nineties there is a veritable flood of plates with accompanying accounts. They are mainly of southern buildings although St Machar's Cathedral in Aberdeen is depicted in 1794[61] with Cockermouth Castle in Cumberland the following year.[62] When in 1803 a plan is given of Westminster Abbey it is without scale or measurements[63] and not for another five years are there details of bases, capitals and arch segments complete with accompanying scale[64]; only in 1811 are details given of the perforated battlements of Henry VII's Chapel at Westminster and King's College Chapel at Cambridge[65] although they had been for long and continued to be, two of the most influential sources in the anthology of the Gothic Revival.

Obviously, *The Gentleman's Magazine* was not an innovator of taste. Like any other popular journal, of then and to-day, it mirrored society and its interests so that it does not impose gothicism upon the public but rather displays a style which had come to claim much popular adherence besides attracting the attention of learned scholars. Did such taste and attention betoken then a revival of Gothic architecture or was its appearance but a survival albeit in somewhat unusual guise and purpose? Much has been written on this nice (in its original sense) academic point and more will be and, indeed, needs to be particularly with regard to those localities distant from London. Nevertheless, when Inigo Jones first began to design the Queen's House at Greenwich in 1618 Gothic architecture died. The blow did not produce instant decapitation of that style which had served Britain well in four hundred years; the Banqueting House of 1619 in Whitehall and the recasing of much of St Paul's Cathedral after 1634[66] did that. Thereafter, when Wren and Hawksmoor designed in Gothic it was in a rather dry version permeated by classicism. The breath, which gave life, had gone from the body and only the lineaments could be drawn as happened at St Mary Aldermary, one of the City churches which, according to the donor's bequest, was to be rebuilt in the Gothic idiom[67] as was the tower of St Michael, Cornhill, by request of the parishioners, after 1715 by Hawksmoor.[68] Despite the medieval plan and the fan vaulting, in plaster, of the former both examples are as much intellectual exercises as All Souls' College in Oxford (1715–40), a Gothic exterior as thin and weightless as anything put up in the later eighteenth century[69] but without the charm or the langourous grace of, say, Strawberry Hill.

As is well known a number of Gothic buildings at the universities of Oxford and Cambridge were constructed in the seventeenth century and it has been claimed that the building of St John's College library (Plate 4) in Cambridge in 1624 in a quasi-Gothic manner is a deliberate instance of

Plate 4   St John's College Library, Cambridge. 1624.

revivalism as pointed windows were preferred to the more fashionable square-headed Jacobean ones. Certainly, the cusped lights, each divided by a transom, are self-conscious although they are no more awkward looking than the amalgam of other details culled from classical or current Jacobean sources and practice. Is the statement, which dictated the shape of window, that 'some men of judgement liked the best the old fashion of church window, holding it most meet for such a building',[70] not exactly the antithesis of Wren's when he produced a plan for a Gothic steeple for Westminster Abbey in 1713? 'To deviate from the whole Form, would be to run into a disagreeable Mixture, which no Person of a good Taste could relish.'[71] While the senses are the same the attitudes bound up in each statement are at variance. One is practical; the other intellectual. One is utility; the other taste and as soon as taste enters then that is an end to honest-to-goodness building since such basic factors as plan, structure and decoration lose their polyphony becoming subordinate to taste which, on its highest level, is a calculated intellectual appraisal. On the other hand, Oxford represented that vernacular life of the nation which continued undisturbed, for the time being, by the changes in fashionable taste which prevailed in the aristocratic society around the Court. Indeed, it was not until after the Restoration in 1660 that the universities of Oxford and Cambridge turned whole-heartedly to classicism and within another two generations educated society would agree with John Macky that, 'If a man should wear the old bonnet, tunic and vest of King Henry the VIII's days now, or build a palace after the Gothic style as it was then, he would be pointed at as a madman'.[72] It was a view shared by Robert Morris whose apologia for Palladian architecture puts Gothic architecture on a par with 'the savage outrages of the Goths and Vandals'.[73]

Nevertheless one need not be surprised to find in northern Britain that the Gothic style had a life which continued for a remarkably long and healthy period after its southern demise though even there such particular instances as the noble St Mary's Church in Warwick (1694–1704) confirm Kenneth Clark's statement that Gothic architecture flowed on as a 'tiny brackish stream'.[74] In the north it was neither brackish nor tiny. The unsettled political conditions in that part of the two kingdoms lasted until the acquisition by James VI of Scotland of the English throne led to his hurried departure south to claim, like another Moses, the promised land. Castles were no longer necessary. Belsay in Northumberland shows this clearly where the owner in 1614 added a Jacobean wing with a columned entrance to his tower house.[75] In Northumberland, castles dominated the countryside and were built as late as Doddington

Plate 5   Heriot's Hospital, Edinburgh. Begun in 1628.

in 1584, and Coupland Castle after that date, when a Border Commission recommended the erection of a chain of forts to protect the frontier.[76] Coupland Castle may be as late as 1619, which is the date carved on a fireplace, and certainly the cessation of Border hostilities would not immediately end four centuries of castle building and dwelling. The Jacobean wing at Belsay is not a northern summer; it is the swallow.

The same is true in Scotland where Renaissance forms were accepted perforce after 1660 although even then the full-blooded spirit of gothicism persists at Drumlanrig Castle in Dumfriesshire (1675–89) which arose out of the hills at the behest of the first Duke of Queensberry. Drumlanrig, set on an arcaded basement and with a mask of fluted and engaged Corinthian pilasters, has been described as 'the last great gesture of the Scottish castle style'.[77] That such a structure was not alone can be borne out by the fact that Charles II's architect at Holyrood House, Sir William Bruce, when rebuilding and enlarging the ancient home of the Stewarts duplicated James V's twin towers by building another pair with battlements and other medieval trimmings at the far end of a long classical screen. Even the restored Holyrood Abbey was in a pure though rather formalistic Gothic while Heriot's Hospital (Plate 5), also in Edinburgh, and paid for from the profits of lending money to King James VI and his Queen by 'Jingling Geordie', is thoroughly Scottish in appearance and exhibits not only such castellated features as lug-turrets but on the exterior of the chapel forms which have their origins in the fourteenth century.[78] Such an enduring life is scarcely to be wondered at in Scotland where the chaste lines of the thirteenth century cathedral in Glasgow continue unchecked through two hundred years of construction and addition. Despite what has been written the crowns of King's College, Aberdeen,

33

Plate 6   Tulliallan Church, Fife. 1675

and of St Giles Cathedral in Edinburgh are not revivalism. They are the natural forms of building which continued when in 1637 the spire of the Tron Church in Glasgow was erected as a smaller version of the fifteenth century Cathedral spire.[79] As late as 1656 the Glasgow Merchants' steeple has intersecting tracery and cusped lights but banded with Renaissance openwork parapets.

That being so with major works then how much more so with the parish church in the countryside. In Britain generally there was little church building after the Reformation—that is of anything new. The old churches remained in use as the larger monastic structures and the friaries fell into disrepair or were used as handy quarries. New churches when they were needed followed medieval traditions with but few exceptions. At Drainie in Moray a belfry dated 1675 has crow-stepped gables, Gothic doorway and two light windows.[80] Of the same year the church at Tulliallan (Plate 6) in Fife has Renaissance details but with windows which only too clearly betray their Gothic ancestry.[81] Even in the next century Polworth in Berwickshire (1703) has a mixture of lancet and round-headed windows[82] while the Laigh Kirk of Paisley displays large Gothic windows

34

inspired by the nearby medieval abbey.[83] That was in 1738 when the Duke of Argyll's new castle at Inveraray was only seven years away. Is there then a link between the two? In Scotland does Gothic survival become revival? Was it the case, as one author states, that, 'There was no real interruption in the enjoyment of Gothic architecture'?[84] The answer is No because although Inveraray Castle exhibits a marvellous thirteenth century outline the motives which led to its creation were quite different from the rural and local traditions of using old forms as tangible templates or because they had been proved by use and wont to be satisfactory even although, in the later seventeenth century and the early part of the eighteenth, classicism in details and, occasionally, in plan form does appear, not as a competitor for public acclaim but as co-existence more than anything else. In any case the attitudes of mind which created Inveraray Castle and the Laigh Kirk at Paisley were worlds apart, the first sophisticated and cosmopolitan, responding to the sensory urge of fashion, and the other acting on local impulse, inbred by lack of communication, both physical and mental, with the rest of the nation and knowing nothing of the brittle whimsies of the Twickenham Set whether in poetry, prose or even bricks and plaster. Inevitably, the sets of aesthetics remained at variance one with another although it would be more accurate to state that neither would be aware, in all likelihood, of the other's existence.

It is a similar story in the north of England. There, in the later seventeenth century, ecclesiastical architecture is dominated by two outstanding characters who lived one on the west and the other on the east side of the central line of mountains. Anne, Countess of Pembroke, the last of the great family of Clifford, at the age of nearly seventy in 1649 settled on her extensive northern estates where she restored her ancestral castles of Brough, Brougham and Appleby and built or rebuilt churches at Brougham, St Wilfrid's chapel (Plate 7), nearer Brougham Castle, and Mallerstang all in Westmorland.[85] The churches have single light windows, round-headed or pointed. Other churches of the Henry VIII tradition in fenestration, as witnessed in the round-arched lights, are at Soulby (1662–3) and St Paul's at Witherslack (1669), both in Westmorland.[86] According to Professor Pevsner all this is Gothic Revival.[87] But surely not. In areas so removed geographically from the centres of change, so hedged around by physical barriers of the most daunting kind, economically backward and still medieval in the concentration of great landholdings, nothing else but the long continuance of Gothic forms should be expected. To contemplate anything else is to ignore the isolation and the poverty of the north and of the north west in particular, which

Plate 7   St Wilfrid's Chapel. Brougham, Westmorland.

endured long after this period and is exemplified in the complaint of King James VI and I in 1606 to the Archbishop of Canterbury that the principal church and the four chapels in the large parish of Arthuret in Cumberland were totally decayed. As a result the present church of Arthuret was begun three years later. A long regular building of much spaciousness it adheres strictly to medieval planning with aisles in both nave and chancel and although the side windows are late Perpendicular, the octagonal columns and the double chamfered arches of the nave arcades are Early English motifs transposed through three hundred years.[88]

In County Durham that remarkable man, John Cosin (1595–1672) rector of Brancepeth in 1626 and after the Restoration of Church, Parliament and Crown in 1660, Bishop of Durham until his death twelve years later, was the outstanding ecclesiologist.[89] Like the Countess Anne, Cosin certainly had a taste for the medieval. For the Countess the past represented pride in a long lineage; for the bishop a deliberate clinging to forms which betokened the cavalcade of the living faith of the Church. The latter reason might help to explain why Cosin adapted the late twelfth century great hall of Auckland Castle to serve as his chapel, devising for it

36

Plate 8   The courtyard, Durham Castle. 1662. The Black Staircase is in the
centre with the Great Hall on the left. The top range of windows on the right
were remodelled in 1752.

clerestory windows of fourteenth century inspiration[90] although for the
wall of his Black Staircase (Plate 8) at Durham Castle the windows with
their late Tudor character of round-headed lights, mullions and transoms
could have been commanded by the Countess Anne herself. Cosin wrote of
the staircase, 'If the outward stone case be not made to answere the Towre
at the other end of the gallery leading up to the Chappell I shall not like
the cost of a new stayre which the carpenter setts at so high rate'.[91] It is
an interesting statement which at first sight, besides signifying stylistic
good manners, might instance revivalism since, to maintain external
symmetry, Cosin's tower should match its Elizabethan predecessor. Yet
such a belief would betoken at the least a psychological gulf between the
handling of the 1662 tower[92] and its earlier neighbour which would be
evident in awkwardness of parts, proportional deviation, clumsy workmanship or poor detailing. There are none of these faults. Cosin's tower
is as idiomatic a form of building as the octagonal buttresses which he
tacked on to Bishop Antony Bec's fourteenth century great hall. It is the

classical frontispiece at the door of the hall which has a lost air as though it had strayed from its rightful setting.

Among the furnishings which the bishop commissioned for his chapel at Auckland, was a set of stalls complete with carved misericords 'to be made of the fashion of the chaires now in the Chappell at Durham Castle',[93] a reference to the early Tudor stalls removed from Auckland Castle about 1547.[94] For the cathedral Cosin ordered the colossal font cover, the symbol of the mystery and, at the same time, the supremacy of the Church triumphant after the bleak years of the Interregnum when the Church had been suppressed and the cathedral used to hold Scottish prisoners. As can still be seen from the shattered remnant of the Neville tomb in the nave, they must have caused, like any other brutal soldiery, much damage. In addition eleven years of Puritanism meant a considerable loss and destruction of church furnishings everywhere particularly those which might smack of popery.[95] Besides replacing the previous font cover, the appearance of which had caused a well-known Puritan to inveigh against 'abominable idols' in 1628,[96] the bishop ordered much carved woodwork including chancel stalls where there is a revelry of crockets, ogee arches, cusping and much else of a similar kind but all, according to one authority, to be set down as revivalism.[97] It is a debatable point as it is at Brancepeth and Sedgefield where the churches contain more of Cosin's Gothic wood carving.[98] Obviously, from surviving medieval woodwork in places like Hexham Priory (the rood screen) and St Nicholas Cathedral in Newcastle (the font cover) as well as the many parish churches, there must have been not only a great mass of woodwork lost at the Reformation and before the Restoration but also a strong tradition of woodworking which exhibits itself in much of Cosin's work when it is compared to earlier and local examples. The Durham stalls and font, as well as much else by Cosin, do not merely reveal Gothic decoration, they show it manipulated in an instinctual technical manner which became foreign to men like Kent and Walpole in the next century. On the font cover at Durham it is the stunted Corinthian columns which are mishandled whereas the Gothic is next of kin to that of the previous century.

Of course, Kent and Walpole were not interested in Gothic structure and technique. To them the Gothic style was decorative in essence, its most whimsical shapes to be availed for fresh purposes in such materials as glass, plaster, cement and gilt. There is no link between the font cover at Durham Cathedral and the banqueting-house at Gibside because in the second case the source of inspiration behind the creative force was not the locality and tradition but the dictate of London fashion. The revival came about because it stemmed from the demands and the whims of a court nobility which assuredly did not recognise a connection between itself and the lives of those who toiled on its estates or its mines to provide for the realisation of whims. Also the origins were different. They were not in the barren north—that came later—but from the gentle banks of the limpid Thames. For these reasons, and fostered by the Gothic taste and nurtured by the philosophers, the neo-Gothic of Inveraray was a court architecture and not a continuation of a folk tradition.[99]

IV

Inveraray Castle

In a report, dated 19 January 1744, William Douglas, a mason, wrote of Inveraray Castle in Argyll 'I have Narowly veiw'd the Same Inside and Outside and finde there are few parts of it Sufficient there are Large Rents in both Side walls And Gevells [gables] and run up a Great way from the foundation. In most Places it is greatly Shattered . . . to that Degree that the Air passes Sensibly throw. I am of Opinion that it cannot be Repaired for use Except at near the Expence that would build such aneother.'[1] On the basis of that report Archibald Campbell, third Duke of Argyll must have decided to demolish his ancestral tower and construct afresh the castle of Inveraray.

Archibald Campbell (1682–1761), the brother of John, second Duke of Argyll, was a younger son of the first Duke. Born at Ham House, Petersham, he was brought up to the conventional life of a member of the aristocratic classes being educated at Eton and then serving in the army under Marlborough. Afterwards, although he indulged in the building mania of his time and was a notable collector of books, his later career was chiefly devoted to politics in which he was to distinguish himself not only by the revelation of a genuine talent but also in the acquisition of many important government offices. In 1705 he was nominated Lord High Treasurer of Scotland and in the next year one of the commissioners for negotiating a treaty of union between England and Scotland being rewarded with the title of Early of Ilay when that task was successfully accomplished. By 1710 he was Lord Justice-General of Scotland and on the accession of George I was elevated to Lord Register. Indeed, so extensive was his control of Scottish affairs on behalf of the Whigs and Sir Robert Walpole that he was dubbed King of Scotland.[2]

In the south, the Earl of Ilay, as he was known, and his brother the second Duke, to whom Colin Campbell dedicated a design in the first volume of *Vitruvius Britannicus* in 1715,[3] were friends of Henry Herbert, ninth Earl of Pembroke[4] who inspired the Palladian bridge at Wilton.

Ilay was also a patron of architecture employing the services of Pembroke's architectural protégé, Roger Morris (1695–1749), clerk of works at Wilton House. Morris was the architect of Coombe Bank, a property of Ilay's in Kent. Coombe Bank, as illustrated in *Vitruvius Britannicus*,[5] was a square Palladian house of the villa type with a saloon filling the entire length of the main front on the *piano nobile*. A somewhat unusual feature of the house was the square towers projecting, and almost detached, from each corner. These towers, in a manner akin to the garden front at Wilton, rose for one further storey above the two-storeyed villa. Unusually, the staircase was in another tower set midway, and projecting from a side of the house as in the mode of Seaton Delaval. Coombe Bank was let by Ilay to his cousin, Colonel John Campbell of Mamore (later fourth Duke of Argyll) and his wife, formerly the Honourable Mary Bellenden, a friend of Henrietta Howard, Countess of Suffolk.[6]

By reputation, Lady Suffolk was the mistress of the Prince of Wales, later George II. In 1723 when the Prince made a financial settlement on her his trustees were the second Duke of Argyll and his brother, Ilay, and it was the latter who secured the land, near Twickenham in Middlesex, on which the countess erected Marble Hill from 1724 to 1729.[7] Although Lady Suffolk was advised in her architectural intentions by Lord Pembroke, the architect in charge of Marble Hill was Roger Morris, who seems to have been responsible also for Whitton Place, the villa which the Earl of Ilay caused to be built for himself on nearby land a decade later.[8] With such a close working association already existing between Ilay and Morris it is not to be wondered at that when Inveraray Castle came to be rebuilt the architect should be Roger Morris.

In October 1743 the Earl of Ilay succeeded his brother as Duke of Argyll and early in the following year he, doubtless, received the report on the condition of his ancestral home. The planning of the new castle must have been put in hand immediately for on 6 November 1744 instructions were issued to the Sheriff or Chamberlain of Inveraray for cutting down timber in Argyll although it was stated that 'if his Grace begins the building next (year), you'l have Little or no Occasion for any of the above Materials till the Year following'.[9]

The charge of the site was entrusted to William Adam 'considered as the ablest man we have in Scotland for carrying out so great a design. If Mr Adams would take charge (so wrote the Duke's agent, Archibald Campbell in July, 1746) he or his son might visit the works monthly from March till November, stay here as long as necessary and leave the proper directions till their return.'[10] Adam was also Master Mason to the Board of Ordnance, an official position which, after the Forty-Five, greatly

41

involved him with the Hanoverian forts, scattered throughout the Highlands, and especially with the new Fort George to the east of Inverness.[11] The 'Carpenter and Principal Engineer' to the Board was Morris[12] who, in Edinburgh in the summer of 1744, met Adam[13] and again three years later at Inveraray.[14] Adam had been the designer of some notable Scottish mansions such as Hopetoun House, near Edinburgh, after 1721, and in the following decade, Duff House in Banffshire, a towering ornate mass which, despite the classical detailing, swells with a neo-medieval pride much resembling certain Vanbrughian mansions. Indeed, Adam and Vanbrugh may have had a more direct association in the creation of Floors Castle, the large rectangular, battlemented block with square angle-towers erected in 1718 and traditionally ascribed to Vanbrugh with William Adam fulfilling the role of contractor at least certainly in 1723.[15]

In May 1745 Adam received a plan from Morris for digging the foundations of the castle at Inveraray.[16] In August, Morris wrote to Lord Milton, the Duke's confidential agent in Scotland,[17] explaining, 'I do not propose to put in one piece of timber till the whole Building is up, Battlement, walls finish'd and the Scaffolds taken down, and as I shall make a Moddell of the Building this Winter, Then I can give you every Particular Dimension of every Single piece of Timber in the Whole Building'.[18] Progress was slow however and was interrupted by the Jacobite rebellion[19] and only in June 1746 did a final foundation plan come to Adam. It bore a note down the left hand side. 'This Foundation to be wrought with Common rough Stone beded well and filld sound with Mortar. . . .'[20] By the end of the year consideration was being given to the walling and Adam despatched two pieces of blue Creggan stone for the Duke's inspection.[21] Then on 7 March 1747 Adam wrote to Morris. He began by stating that some masons had gone to Inveraray to work on the foundations and enclosed 'a Sketch of a Window, or Inner Door and a Chimney in the way we commonly do them in the ground storeys of good houses here, to see how you like the same'. He then continued, 'I should like wise be glad to know if the Windows will be arched on the Inside with a Gothick Arch or a Portion of a Circle. . . . It might not be Improper if you would cause make a mold for me, of what you propose should Answer for the Jambs and Arches of the Gothick Windows.'[22] However, despite the broad hint on window fashion 'in good houses' north of the Border, Morris stuck to his Gothic design and in a reply ten days later, from Green Street in London, forwarded the rather ambivalently requested drawings and measurements.[23] Nevertheless, the interchange throws an interesting sidelight on the unfamiliarity of Adam, Scotland's leading architect, with Gothic practice.

By the close of that same year William Adam's health was failing. He was already aided in architectural craft by his sons John and Robert,[24] and his correspondence with Morris reveals the assistance at Inveraray of the former.[25] In December, after some illness, William Adam dictated a letter to Morris for 'as yet I take the help of one of my sons to write for me, As I am not yet Strong Enough to undergoe a great Deal of fatigue'.[26] Come next midsummer and William Adam was dead leaving his extensive architectural practice and manifold business interests to be further continued and developed by his family of four sons.

John, the eldest, succeeded his father at Inveraray coping with the numerous troubles which hindered the progress of the great house throughout 1748 and 1749. There were labour troubles. At the quarry an unauthorised still and the attendant sale of spirits had caused drunkenness when the men should have been at work.[27] In fact, the labourers were 'so excessively bad that nothing can be made of them' but were so scarce that when any were sacked, the foreman was sometimes forced to re-employ them.[28] Problems came, too, with materials. Once stones were drawn from the Creggans quarry to the shore of Loch Fyne there was no tackle strong enough to raise them into the waiting boat.[29] That problem was overcome and in September John Adam contracted with William Cowan, a mason, to supply the blue chlorite stone at eightpence a cubic foot.[30] Later on many of the hewn stones were broken by idle townspeople, on Sundays especially, 'and by the Towns peoples Cows that often ly among the Stones, and in the Masons Shades all night, by which a good deale of damage was done'.[31] Also there must have been worries about the house itself. Morris still would not allow joisting until the roof was on and great care had to be taken to ensure that the walls remained true by binding them with temporary girders.[32]

Yet progress was being made. In October, 1751 the duke was charged £120 for 1,920 hogsheads of lime supplied in the past twelve-months.[33] Payments to the quarriers and masons William Cowan and James Gilmore of £220 and £234 respectively for a year's work were authorised by John Adam in September 1750.[34] A year later James Gilmore was due £373 and James Potter, who had succeeded Cowan 'as one of the Undertakers at the Cregans Quarry', was paid £188 8s 0d for the previous eight months leaving a balance owing to him of £19 14s $2\frac{1}{3}$d.[35] By that time the quarry was being given up[36] and, not surprisingly, therefore a letter to the duke's chamberlain in the early summer of 1752 stated, 'Some part of the Roof shall be put upon the New Castle this Season'.[37]

Work on the third Duke's house continued throughout that decade. In the autumn of 1757, however, the structure must have been nearing

43

completion for then mahogany was supplied for the windows in the central lantern tower.[38] Just over a year later John and James Adam submitted a bill for £843 19s 5d which included such materials as linseed oil, glass and white lead.[39] Yet the fabric was not to be completed until another three years had passed and even then the hall and another room were only lathed and plastered while the gallery, running the full length of the north front, had not been finished to that degree.[40] In the same year Archibald Campbell died.[41] He had been an old man when he had begun to build the great house which was as much a pious memorial to his ancestors as to himself and he had outlived both William Adam and Roger Morris, who died in 1749. To construct the shell of the house had taken eighteen years. Yet for a further decade nothing more was done and only when the fifth Duke succeeded in 1770 was the task of decoration slowly taken up with Robert Mylne becoming chief decorator of the state apartments which in their Palladian proportions and forms must have appeared very old-fashioned. Then, too, the scheme for removing the old town of Inveraray from its position between the medieval castle and the River Aray, which had been first tackled by the third Duke, who had settled for a site by the lochside, was renewed by the fifth Duke, again with Mylne as architect while both men completed works on the estate including a Gothic bridge over the Garron River in the Deer Park.[42]

As the grand project, carried through over four decades, neared fulfilment so it attracted enthusiastic encomiums from the travellers of the eighteenth century many of whom dwelt lovingly on that concomitant of social superiority, financial expenditure. 'It is said', reported Lettice, 'that the money laid out at Inveraray, since the year 1745, does now amount to the enormous sum of £250,000 and, that the present duke, . . . has expended at the rate of £3,000 per annum',[43] facts which even the sober compilers of the *Statistical Account* thought worthy of inclusion.[44] And Dr Johnson was moved to exclaim, 'What I admire here is the total defiance of expense', for, like everyone else, he was much struck by the grandeur of the house although he wished it had been a storey higher.[45] Regarding the exterior style of Inveraray (Plate 9) travellers were almost as uniform in their praise although Pennant was one of those to criticise the central lantern tower as having 'from without a most disagreeable effect'.[46] Yet for others the associations conjured up by such a castle, set by a highland loch and overshadowed by mist-ribbed hills, were enough to activate eulogies of which Lettice provided the most exact and the most romantic in that rather terse, febrile manner of eighteenth century writers when confronted by the aweful or the majestic. 'We enter (the castle) by a lofty guard-room, provided with armorial furniture, and ornaments, suitable to the stile of a highland castle. . . . There is . . . a lightness, and brilliancy, in the general fashion of the ornaments, which it was impossible not to admire, at the same time that we felt their tendency to efface the awful emotions excited, on our approach to the castle, by the stern and Gothic air of its exterior aspect, and the martial stile of its entrance. . . . The antient form of the exterior castle, and the modern

Plate 9 Roger Morris. Inveraray Castle, Argyll. Begun in 1745.

fitting up of the apartments, beyond the entrance, as they must be seen successively, cannot fail to suggest to strangers the antiquity on one hand, of the family, who inhabit it, the insecurity of barbarous times, and the necessity of strong defence; pleasingly contrasted on the other, as they penetrate, and advance into the interior, with every mark of that improved and civilised state of society and manners, which has, at length, spread itself into the remoter regions of our prosperous and happy island.'[47]

Considering this statement and others in travellers' logs of Scotland, it is an interesting fact that there is no comparable assessment of Inveraray Castle in the few modern texts which deal with the Gothic Revival. Unlike their counterparts of two hundred years ago modern writers seemingly do not visit the western highlands. Eastlake's history of the Revival (first published in 1872) yields half a page to Inveraray but comments neither on its importance nor its originality[48] while Kenneth

Clark, writing fifty years later, makes no mention of the house at all although the later Strawberry Hill is fully written up. Yet Inveraray Castle is worthier of wider notice for it was the first large Gothic Revival building in Britain, and probably in Europe, and was the progenitor of many others, all having similar characteristics, down to the next century.

Now why did Archibald Campbell replace a rambling old tower house, with corridors up-ended as stairs, by a Gothic dwelling? It is a question which it is easier for a Scotsman rather than an Englishman to answer or even to begin to understand. Strawberry Hill may be passed off as the fancy of a romantic but none of the Campbells was ever that. Nor should Inveraray be regarded as the revelation of Whig principles of liberty and freedom for in Scotland the primacy of the Campbells of Argyll came neither from the dukedom nor the Argathelia but from their ancient Gaelic patronymic of MacChailein Mor as chiefs of the clan Campbell which in the third Duke's time was the largest and most powerful of all the Scottish clans, a factor of considerable influence at Culloden where the clan chiefs for the last time could call on their clansmen to follow either for or against the Hanoverian régime. First and foremost, Archibald, third Duke of Argyll was a Campbell and Inveraray was, as it still is, a Campbell house. It was to continue the tradition that the Palladian aristocrat chose the Gothic mode. Now in Scotland such a choice was not the revolutionary break with contemporary fashion that it would have been, say, in Twickenham for in Scotland there was a continuing tradition of castle building and of castle dwelling. Craigievar Castle, rising from the hills of Mar in the north east, with corbels, turrets and false culverins creates formal and elaborate shapes so typical of early Jacobean work. Braemar Castle was given a defensive star-shaped outerwork in 1748[49] and not until 1777 did the Kennedys of Culzean ask Robert Adam to enclose their vernacular tower house with an ambitious, symmetrically castellated mansion. In Scotland the castle was the accepted and understood symbol of a landowner's suzerainty, a notion given reality by the disturbed state of the countryside and by the almost feudal powers of the highland chiefs; and that being so, the style of Inveraray was, therefore, emblematic.

Scottish factors apart, the third Duke of Argyll, when Earl of Ilay, had shown a propensity for neo-Gothic which was unusual but which bespoke an architectural awareness ahead of the time. In the grounds of Whitton he erected, during the later 1730s,[50] a neo-Gothic tower (Plate 10), triangular in plan and of brick construction. It had two rooms, one above the other, with Gothic chimney pieces and windows, and contained in one of the angle towers, a staircase of a hundred steps leading to brick

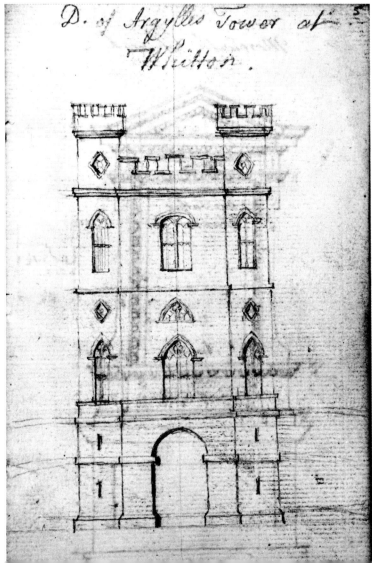

D. of Argylls Tower at Whitton.

Plates 10 and 11   The Gothic Tower at Whitton Place, Middlesex. Woollett's engraving of 1757 and as drawn by John Adam in 1748.

battlements coped with stone.[51] The tower had the appearance of being set on an earthern mound (an eighteenth century motte?) and from it a canal ran back to a colonnaded greenhouse and a wall with stoves for oranges. To the west was an Orange Walk.[52] As sketched by John Adam (Plate 11), when on a southern journey early in 1748,[53] the Whitton tower was solid and well proportioned, wearing a determined air without either the freakishness or the fragility of similar examples in the coming decades. Although the tower was probably built by Roger Morris, it seems to have been designed at a much earlier date by James Gibbs who was responsible for a very similar example at Wentworth Castle in Yorkshire.[54]

From the outset the Duke seems to have fixed on the Gothic mode for his Scottish seat for there is in the castle a large sheet entitled 'Plans, Elevations and Sections of a House for the Duke of Argyll at Inverarey (sic) designed in the Castle Stile, Defended with a Fossee and covered Way'. Inscribed 'Dugal Campbell', it was typical of the close-knit ties that bound the clan that the chief should commission such a design. The plan features five linked bastions, forming a star, set within a fosse and with a drawbridge and covered way 'to defend the House'. That is all very much in the manner of the elaborately contrived forts of the day and perhaps not unexpectedly since Campbell was designing, probably simultaneously, extensions for Fort William in Inverness-shire.[55] As to the house it would have been mostly of two flights with numerous three-storeyed towers set with battlements. It has undertones of the style of Drumlanrig and, presumably, was too old fashioned for the Palladian Duke who went to his favourite architect, Roger Morris, who created a house where the flesh is Gothic but the bones are Palladian. The facades are symmetrical and correspond alternately. They are approached by two bridges on the same axis, each resting on two huge vaults with balustrades of pierced quatrefoils. The windows are acutely pointed below hood-moulds (Plate 12) and were originally intended to be filled with the fussy tracery of the Decorated era then so much in vogue and characterised at Inveraray by the tight, flat but prim embellishments around the entrances. Such details, however, are few and the overall impression of Inveraray is of mathematical exactitude with each segment conceived according to the canons of Palladian intellectualism. By the repetition of the un-equivocal statements of each bay the well mannered reticence becomes the similitude of great strength with the marked horizontal movement of string-courses and battlements offset by the circular corner towers and the tall lantern. Nowadays the latter feature has lost much of its abrupt emphasis of height (which the disciples of Burke would have recognised as 'sublime') since the addition after the fire in 1870 of spires and a line

Plate 12   Garden front. Inveraray Castle, Argyll.

of dormers, to romanticise the skyline, obscure its bulk which must always have appeared lumpish as it squatted on the roof like a peasant on a levantine quay. Before the fire the lantern could only be viewed fully from a mid-point on any one elevation, which is a Palladian way of looking at a building, when it assumed the visual properties of a pediment with the fenestration as the tympanum. Inveraray is so logical that it is an understatement. Despite the trim, it is evocative and not romantic although the situation is. Thus it was possible to transpose the latter to the former, in the subjection of late eighteenth century picturesque theory, so that in the numerous imitations the classical qualities could be disregarded once they were borne under consciousness by the weight of associational values. Yet even the neo-classicist could have admired Inveraray for its basic shapes of the cube and the cylinder as well as the overpowering mass of punctured stone.

Of the three storeys, the basement, surrounded by a broad fosse, is below ground level. That is unusual, although at Wimbledon House for Sarah, Duchess of Marlborough, Morris employed the same technique thereby saving the old duchess the effort of climbing stairs to the *piano nobile*.[56] The same consideration may have dictated the arrangement at Inveraray although just as possible is the military plan of a ditch with bridges leading across it. Or is it nothing more than a very deep ha-ha? The house conforms to the usual three storeys of palladianism with the basement for use, then the centre for pleasure and finally with sleep or study on the top floor, all as ordained by Roger's kinsman, Robert Morris.[57] Construction, too, followed the latter's precept, copied from 'the Ancients', that the interior walls should be of a corresponding thickness to the exterior ones.[58] The plan, as originally intended (Plate 13), was also Palladian with a continuous vista on the main axis through the house thus

Plate 13 Roger Morris. Original plan of the principal floor. Inveraray Castle.

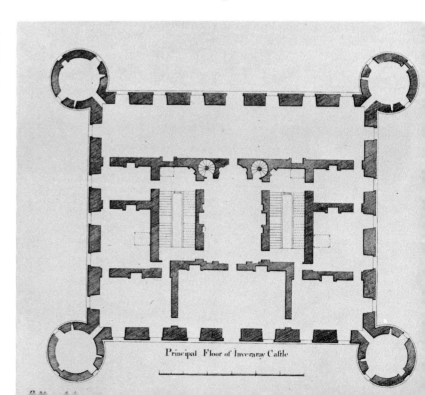

Principal Floor of Inveraray Castle

obviating a central staircase but having instead one on each side of the central entrance hall.

Yet when all is said and done the house is not Palladian in the Marble Hill sense at all for there are curious anomalies and not least in the external aspect of the circular towers and the tall lantern lighting the central hall below. The immediate comparison is with Vanbrugh's last triumphant

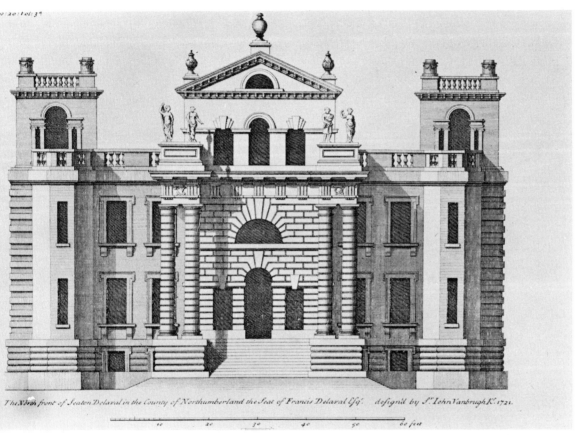

Plate 14 Sir John Vanbrugh. Entrance front. Seaton Delaval, Northumberland. 1720.

masterpiece, Seaton Delaval in Northumberland (Plate 14), long famous for its 'castle air',[59] where the corner octagonal towers contain circular rooms, as at Inveraray, and with a saloon filling the entire length of the garden front. Such an idea was contemplated by the third Duke but was later abandoned by the fifth Duke who divided the gallery into three compartments. Other Vanbrugh houses, Blenheim and Eastbury, show a comparable arrangement of staircases and lanterns with Inveraray and although not too much significance should be hazarded about such dispositions nevertheless the question must arise as to whether the comparisons are coincidental or whether they indicate a relationship between Vanbrugh, Morris and Inveraray which has so far remained unexplored.

About 1716 Vanbrugh began the designs for Eastbury in Dorset although it was not until some time after Bubb Dodington had inherited the property that building actually started. On the death of Vanbrugh in 1726 the mansion was incomplete but was carried forward by Roger Morris[60] who may well have received the commission on the strength of the friendship between Bubb Dodington and the Earl of Ilay.[61] In any case Vanbrugh and Morris would have been acquainted if, as has been suggested, the former was employed, during his last years, on military establishments for the Board of Ordnance,[62] of which Morris was 'Carpenter and Principal Engineer'.[63]

At Eastbury the final plan was, with but minor alterations, that of Inveraray.[64] More significant, however, was Vanbrugh's development of the roof top silhouette of an arcade of chimneys into a clerestory to illumine the interior staircases.[65] Although the device was discarded by Morris, it does appear, fulfilling the same function, at Inveraray. For that castle an early idea must be the roughly finished elevation among the Argyll muniments displaying a facade terminated at each end by a square two-storeyed tower topped by a recessed pavilion with a window identical to those diamond ones on the corner turrets of the Whitton tower. This drawing, a study half way between Eastbury and the completed Inveraray, owes much to Vanbrugh and his embattled manner especially in the omission of corbels, of a string-course and in the use on the towers of battlements resting on a band of semi-circular vaulting. More directly, the link between Vanbrugh and Inveraray was strengthened by the discovery, a few years ago, of a hitherto unknown Vanbrugh drawing of a plan and elevation (Plate 15) which, along with several related drawings (Plate 16), is nothing else than a small Inveraray Castle.[66] Whether this was a scheme for the second Duke cannot be stated but there can be no doubt that Morris either adapted or took over a Vanbrugh project which was already in existence. Characteristically for a Palladian, Morris omitted the caps on the towers. These Vanbrugh would have considered essential for, as he explained to Lord Carlisle in 1724, 'Towers upon Walls, are suited to them as part of the Fortifications, and are suppose'd to be lodgings or Storehouses, and as Such only require a Covering, which may however be in a degree ornamental, but shou'd not look too light and trifling'.[67]

Vanbrugh apart, consideration should, of course, be given to Longford Castle in Wiltshire where Morris was paid for a design in 1742. The late Elizabethan prodigy house is triangular in plan with an engaged round tower at each point.[68] Nevertheless, although these cannot have been

52

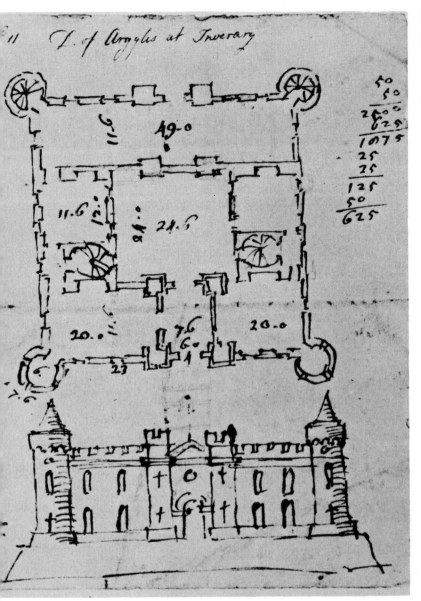
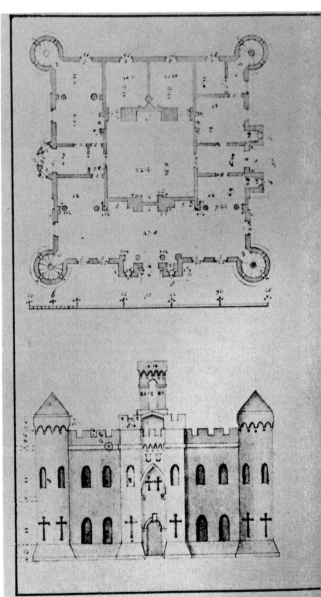

Plates 15 and 16　Sir John Vanbrugh. Design for 'D. of Argyles at Inveraray', and plan and elevation of a castle. Before 1726.

forgotten two years later, Longford, with its profusion of decoration, would have appalled Morris for what his kinsman Robert would have referred to bitingly as 'Novelty and Singleness'.[69]

Finally, having accepted the Vanbrugh relationship with the Scottish castle, it is interesting to seek for the origins of Inveraray and of Seaton Delaval and other Vanbrughian mansions, particularly with reference to the great lanterns which they possess and to find such a one in Wollaton

Plate 17   Bodiam Castle, Sussex. 1386.

Hall where even the staircase arrangements, on either side of the great hall find an echo in the eighteenth century works. Of course, it has been proved[70] that Vanbrugh did have more than a passing interest in Jacobean planning and decoration. Yet it may be that his inquiries and study of the architecture of previous ages took him back beyond the Elizabethans for it is interesting to observe that the external aspect of Inveraray is that of a thirteenth century castle. For example, in describing Inverlochy Castle, at the southern end of the Great Glen, Cruden in *The Scottish Castle* notes 'Everything about Inverlochy proclaims the thirteenth century and nothing contradicts it. The simple quadrangular layout, the high curtain walls and projecting corner towers rising from long spreading bases, the pre-eminence of one tower as the donjon, the long fish-tailed slits in the towers, the lack of openings in the curtain, the simple entrances in each of two opposite sides, and the form of a ditch are all unmistakable thirteenth century characteristics.'[71]

Where then, apart from early impressions of Chester's walls,[72] did Vanbrugh receive his inspiration from? Not from Inverlochy certainly.

54

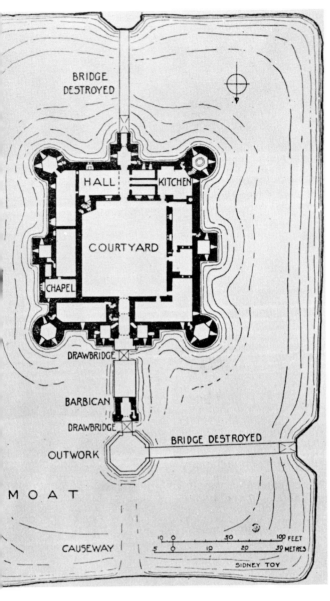

Plate 18   Plan. Bodiam Castle, Sussex.

Nor may he have seen the Welsh castles of Edward I although he must surely have known a later derivative, Bodiam Castle in Sussex (Plate 17). Like Inveraray, it has a three storey circular tower rising above ground level at each corner. Set within a moat, the body of the structure is two storeys high and internally is ranged around a central courtyard (Plate 18) as are the rooms at Inveraray. Indeed, if approximately thirty feet is deducted from the length and the breadth of Bodiam then its overall size corresponds to Inveraray Castle.[73] Thus that northern house, where there is neither a quatrefoil nor the waywardness of crockets, though conceived in the image of the fashionable court Gothic of its day, has its antecedents in the grim castles of a warrior king.

55

V

Strawberry Hill and
Alnwick Castle

The influence of Inveraray Castle, despite its honourable descent, was limited by geography. That was in marked contrast with Strawberry Hill (Plate 19), the creation of Horace Walpole, younger son of Sir Robert. Beginning his account of Strawberry Hill, Kenneth Clark observes 'Strawberry Hill has been studied at least as much as it deserves'.[1] Possibly, it has been too much studied and other seminal houses neglected for in the rose garden of the Gothic Revival Walpole's villa is a sport which, though owing something to the species of the race, is not true to form. Strawberry Hill was a whim, 'a small capricious house',[2] which Walpole had acquired in 1747 although he was not to begin gothicising it until six years later.[3] The property was in Twickenham and Walpole was, therefore, near neighbour to Lady Suffolk at Marble Hill and the Earl of Ilay at Whitton Place. Unlike them, however, Walpole eschewed the classic mode. Partly, this was the individual's desire to be different, to do as he pleased in opposition to the rules then prevailing in architecture and partly, too, the satisfaction of attracting attention for Walpole was a younger son, destined for obscurity, with no real talent for anything, except the trivial and at that he laboured and became very accomplished. Yet Walpole was interested in the Middle Ages as almost any page, from his account of Strawberry Hill, will reveal with its catalogue of *objets d'art* and paintings. He was the first serious and assiduous collector of Gothic art treasures and such connoisseurship as he exercised required some knowledge which came in part from his Committee of Taste and in part from texts on Gothic architecture.

The first serious approach to the subject had been Dugdale's *Monasticon Anglicanum* in 1655. Although followed by a few works of a similar nature it was left to the next century to begin the long and scholarly

Plate 19   Strawberry Hill, Middlesex. 1753 onwards.

tradition of inquiry. Of course, so long as any study was approached from
the Vitruvian standpoint then any attempt to understand it was doomed
to failure, as befell Batty Langley's investigation. Walpole's scholarship
came especially from the poet Gray who, it appears, was the first to attempt
to rationalise Gothic architecture by studying existing buildings without
any preconceived notions as to date or style. Gray's chief influence was
over other scholars, for example Thomas Warton, and Walpole acknowledged his own debt in 1762 in his *Anecdotes of Painting*, which contain
sensitive appreciation of Westminster Abbey, and which was followed
nine years later by Bentham's *History of Ely*.[4] Thus personal prediliction
together with considerable knowledge of the Gothic era became the straw
and the mud for Strawberry Hill which, as Walpole himself explained,
'was built to please my own taste, and in some degree to realize my own
visions'.[5] In the latter enterprise Walpole was aided by the designer
Richard Bentley (1708–82) and the gentlemen amateur architects, John
Chute of the Vyne (1701–76) and Thomas Pitt, later Lord Camelford. It
was this Committee of Taste which selected designs either from plates of
Old St Paul's or from such nearby quarries as St Albans, Canterbury and

57

Ely Cathedrals and Westminster Abbey[6] from which the theme, for the chimney-piece in the Round Drawing-Room, was 'taken from the tomb of Edward the Confessor, improved by Mr. Adam'.[7]

Yet what is the place of Strawberry Hill in architectural history? Does it have any importance or is it a toy which might have come from Mrs Chenevix's toy-shop or, in a later age, from the workshop of Carl Fabergé? Is it a phenomenon or a precursor or both? Or is it none of these things?

First, the publicity which the house has attracted both in Walpole's time and since has been immense. All too often, however, the praises have lapsed into a facile adulation equated with critical evaluation. In exercising the latter it must be remembered that Strawberry Hill was not a grand architectural concept realised and executed by an artist of genius, as one finds later with Culzean Castle and Robert Adam, but was more the outcome of the deliberations and improvisations of a man of amateur stamp whose creative zeal came in fits and starts, and was never disciplined nor harnessed to a project demanding hard work and unremitting care and zeal for years on end. In the respect that Walpole was assisted in his self-imposed task by a coterie of acquaintances, the emergence of Strawberry Hill can be compared with Sir Walter Scott's architectural activities also carried on in conjunction with advice from a circle of friends and acquaintances with the result at Abbotsford, as in the southern villa, that the achievement is more curious than beautiful. Christopher Hussey makes the remark that romantic art is imperfect,[8] a justifiable view in this context since Walpole and his friends allowed their romantic enthusiasms to get in the way of that intellectual discipline which is the hall-mark of great art.

Much has been made of the irregularity of the planning at Strawberry Hill[9] as a forerunner of later houses, like Lee Priory, but the connection should not be stressed beyond the fact that Strawberry Hill, which was no more and no less than a personal statement transformed through the continuous but albeit gradual enlargement of an idea, was succeeded later in the century by an era when symmetry in planning broke down in response to the specific ideologies of Gilpin, Knight and Price. Then, although there were rooms aplenty done in imitation of Strawberry Hill, the spirit behind their inspiration was far removed from the dilettanteism of thirty and forty years before. It became hard and professional and thereby Gothic lost the naivety of decoration and the innocence of ornament in which so much of the delight of Walpole's gim-crack edifice consists. It would, of course, be misleading to deny it any influence. The round tower, which alone rescues the grouping of the components from banality, was the first such but one which was to appear and reappear on every later Gothic and castellated concept although again for reasons

not directly attributable to Strawberry Hill. Its chief influence was not
architectural, nor in planning, nor even in the use of such substitutes as
papier maché and cement to imitate stone,[10] for others besides Walpole
were enthusiastic about such techniques, but the influence was in the
publicity accorded the house both in Walpole's time, and after his death
through the media of its owner's literary activities, and also by its close
proximity to London and therefore to the fashionable world of the
imitative. Happily, Strawberry Hill has remained much as it was. It had
begun as a sport but it matured to a bush of great size covered with a
multitude of pulchritudinous blooms whose applied brilliance and enam-
elled tints glitter like a Book of Hours. By happy chance, Walpole, the
composer of *belles lettres* and occasional scholar, concocted a fantasy and
in so doing created something of charm with the beauty of a precious work
by a goldsmith where the intricacy of workmanship and the richness of
materials amaze and rob us in the end of critical faculties. In that respect
Strawberry Hill is a triumph.

In the north of England a set of interiors having links with Strawberry Hill was at Alnwick Castle in Northumberland. Comparable to
Inveraray with all its Campbell ramifications, Alnwick, owned continuously for the past six hundred years and more by the Percys, in the
Middle Ages occupied a key position in the northern defences of the
English crown against Scotland. When in the late sixteenth century peace
came to the north the castle lost its strategic importance. In the succeeding
century the male line of the Percys failed leaving, as the last direct heir,
Elizabeth Percy who in 1682 married the sixth Duke of Somerset. Forty
years later on the death of his wife he married again. So overbearing had
he become that once, when his second wife attempted to attract his
attention by tapping him with her fan, she was rebuked 'Madam, my first
Duchess was a Percy, and she never took such a liberty'.[11] The Duke had
two grandchildren, the Lady Elizabeth (b. 1716) and Lord Beauchamp
(b. 1725).[12] As the Lady Elizabeth was not a great heiress she was not
sought after by fortune hunters. In 1740 she married Sir Hugh Smithson,
a Yorkshire baronet,[13] although the Duke of Somerset had opposed the
match doubtless because Sir Hugh's ancestor, the first baronet, had been
a haberdasher with a shop in Cheapside.[14] Four years after the marriage
the future obscurity of the Smithsons ended abruptly when the death of
Lord Beauchamp left his sister as sole heiress to the Percy name and
estates[15] which did not prevent her grandfather from doing his utmost
to have the succession diverted from her. In 1748 he died without having
achieved that and for his son, now Duke of Somerset, the ancient Percy
title of Earl of Northumberland was revived with special remainder through

the female line.[16] In 1750 the Smithsons became Earl and Countess of Northumberland and after the Earl's Lord-Lieutenancy of Ireland, first Duke and Duchess of the third creation. Inevitably, such a rise in name and fortune brought many enemies and Horace Walpole seems to have looked on it with some malice, labelling the new Earl as Earl Smithson.[17]

Lady Northumberland inherited the Percy estates only. These lay in the north of England but for half a century or more had been mismanaged. In addition the family castles of Warkworth and Alnwick were semi-ruinous[18] despite the repairs carried out on Alnwick by the sixth Duke of Somerset.[19] Shortly after succeeding to the title the Earl and Countess travelled north to inspect their inheritance and decided to renovate Alnwick as a summer residence.[20] Writing in 1868 Tate in *A History of Alnwick* declared it to have been more ruinous than Warkworth[21] and Dutens, although he was not in the service of the Earl until later, mentioned that 'Alnwick Castle . . . had entirely fallen to decay'.[22] On the other hand *The Gentleman's Magazine* of February 1756 recorded that, 'As the audits for the receipt of rent twice a year have generally been held at this castle, it has been always kept in tolerable repair',[23] which can be confirmed by Buck's prospect of 1728. In either event Warkworth had fewer historical and family associations and was smaller than Alnwick[24] where Walpole cites building as proceeding in 1752[25] when in a letter to Sir Horace Mann, he wrote of the Northumberlands, 'They are building at Northumberland House, at Sion, at Stansted, at Alnwick and Warkworth Castle! They live by the etiquette of the old peerage, have Swiss porters, the Countess has her pipers—in short, they very soon will have no estate.'[26] Such wishful thinking did not transpire. Work at Alnwick at this time was probably no more than a desire to render the building habitable for the celebrated study by Canaletto (Plate 20), which still hangs in the castle, of about this same date, besides depicting the rough nature of the foreground and the turbulence of the River Aln (the one to be smoothed and the other to be tamed by 'Capability' Brown), indicates a somewhat dilapidated castle but shows no great signs of ruination. By 1756 work was again in progress with alterations being made 'upon a most elegant plan'[27] which could suggest that a start had been made on the structural changes which ended in the restyling of the medieval castle whereby, as a contemporary verse put it

> Convenience with magnificence shall join,
> And taste adorn and judgement stretch the line;
> Proficient art on Gothic deeds lay hold,
> And modern skill improve the plans of old.[28]

60

Plate 20   Canaletto. Alnwick Castle, Northumberland. c. 1753.

When John Adam in the spring of 1759 travelled south on his way to London, he stopped the night at Alnwick 'in order to see the reparations and additions making by the Earl of Northumberland upon that Princely Pile'. He admired the new dining-room[29] and drawing room. They were, he jotted in his diary, 'extremely noble and elegant' with the walls and ceilings 'done in a very good Gothick style of stucco' although that was not his opinion of Auckland Castle in County Durham where he thought that the hall resembled the entrance to a cathedral. There is no proof but it may be that Paine was the designer of these Alnwick rooms just as he, presumably, was responsible for the octagonal neo-Gothic tower in the grounds of Belford which had also met with Adam's approval.[30]

Adam implies that extensive building operations were in progress at Alnwick and these continued into the next decade with the workmen's wages in 1763 totalling £100 a week, a sum betokening the employment

61

of large numbers of men.[31] In the next year when the stair tower was erected,[32] the greater part of the structural programme was completed, at least a bottle, found much later in the walls, contained a note to the effect that 'The Castle was built by Mathew and Thomas Mills, Master Masons. In the year 1764.'[33] As they are known to have been master masons[34] and to have been engaged at the castle the date seems likely and the more so because it was between four and five years later that the

Plates 21 and 22   Robert Adam. Section of a frieze and elevation for the banqueting-room, Alnwick Castle. 1770.

finishing touches were being put to the decoration of the state apartments. Briefly, the alterations included draining the moat and restoring the major portion of the superstructure of the keep with the exception of the armorial polygonal towers flanking the entrance from the inner bailey. Some ruinous structures, such as the chapel, were removed from the court-yards[35] and on the curtain walls three of the towers were renewed as were long stretches of wall while to the south of the barbican new coach houses and stables, with Gothic decoration,[36] appeared with a range of offices forming a link between them and the middle gateway.[37] Happily, these offices survived the fourth Duke's italianising activities in the middle eighteen fifties. The doors have thin mouldings forming two tiers of tracery and the chimney-pieces of grey stone usually have a blank arcade below the mantel with other such typical details as an ogee arch or triple shafts and the ceiling cornices bear badges and crests of the Percy family. In these modest rooms the unassuming decoration is very well done besides having a good deal of period charm.

One of the remodelled towers, in the east corner of the inner bailey, was a circular record tower for the Northumberland archives with the upper portion set aside as a banqueting room for which in 1770 Robert Adam prepared drawings. Green was the base colour of the ceiling which had, around an inner circle, a border of pink fringed ovals or vesicas with a cherub, framed in a quatrefoil, at the intersections. The frieze, for which several designs were prepared (Plate 21) as was Adam's custom, was pink with lozenges and quatrefoils alternating and, in reference to the Percy emblem, some of the latter had inset a lion couchant. The walls (Plate 22) were pale green and between the round window frames was a gilded Gothic mirror with a painted roundel above. Below was a pink dado, which approximated to that eventually chosen for the saloon and which may have been copied, albeit somewhat loosely, from the external window bays of Henry VII's chapel at Westminster Abbey. Although the banqueting room was twenty-nine feet in diameter and nearly as high none of the intricacy of the details would have been lost and the overall effect must have been spectacular.[38] Externally, the banqueting-room was ac-corded the regular Gothic architecture which pervaded the castle (Plate 23). On the walls there were crosslets and quatrefoils and the keep, where there was a marked lack of verticality, observed the conventions with a *piano nobile* delineated by large hooded lights, each one paced by a cross-shaped window above. Wherever possible regularity in the current idiom was the order of the day.

Who was the architect in charge of the renovation? In the next century Warner, referring to the transformation of the castle, had this to

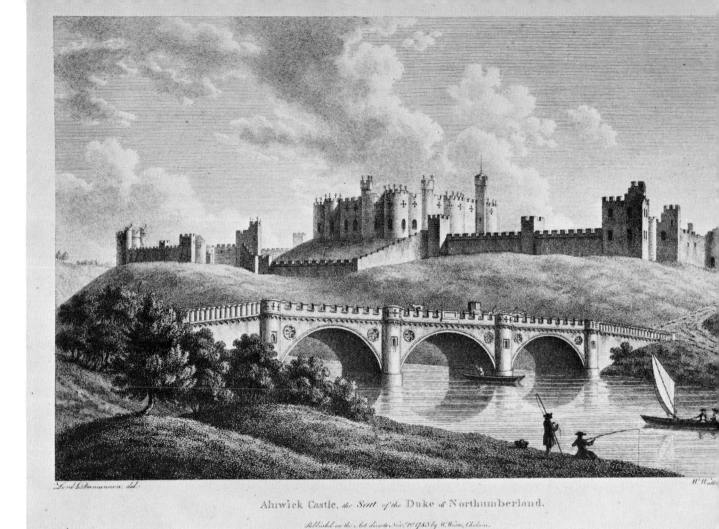

Alnwick Castle, *the Seat of the* Duke *of* Northumberland.

Published as the Act directs Nov. 1st 1783 by W. Watts, Chelsea.

Plate 23   Alnwick Castle and the Lion Bridge. 1783.

say: '. . . all within and without the mansion point out the judgement as well as taste of Messrs. Adam and Paine, who were employed to regenerate this magnificent place.'[39] None of the Adam drawings for Alnwick relates to structural changes or elevations and such telling absences would indicate that another hand was responsible for such matters. Doubtless it was Paine,[40] remembering too that the Mills brothers had previously worked under him at Belford. But why not employ Adam to carry out the entire scheme of reconstruction? It could be argued that Paine had had seventeen years of extensive architectural practice behind him by 1761 and that mainly in the north of England, whereas Robert Adam was but a newcomer to the English architectural scene and unfamiliar with the methods of building and one, moreover, whose fame was that of an innovator in interior decoration.[41] The last point is true and undeniably most of Adam's engagements at this time were the adaptation of older structures to contain his novelties even although fifteen years before he had been involved with such an important house as

64

Inveraray and also at Fort George, a government property. Surely the answer is that Robert Adam, who had only returned from Italy in 1758 and of whom society was *en fou*, was fully committed to large scale works elsewhere. In April 1759 he was at Harewood in connection with a scheme for completing the Gothic church and possibly, too, for designing interiors for the house and by the summer was absorbed in a proposal to recase internally the hall at Castle Ashby for Lord Northampton. He was being consulted about Shardeloes, Croome Court and Hatchlands where the owner was Admiral Boscawen, a Lord of the Admiralty, which may explain why the commission for the Admiralty Screen in Whitehall went to Adam in 1759. Next year a start was made at Compton Verney and the following twelve months were to be among his most productive with designs for Osterley Park, Syon and Kedleston. He was soon to be occupied with Lansdowne House and Luton Hoo as well as Moor Park and much else. With such a programme Adam was able to design the Alnwick interiors in London but was far too committed in the south to superintend the protracted operations at Alnwick where the overseer, if not at the start then certainly after 1768, would be Vincent Shepherd most of whose professional life was devoted to the service of the Earl and Duke of Northumberland. 'As a workman and an architect (for he united the powers of execution with those of design) many instances of his ability might be given' for 'in the more sublime walks of the Gothic, he stood without a rival in the county of Northumberland.'[42]

The dual relationship between Paine and Robert Adam, such as the architectural history of Alnwick hints at, was not unique. At Kedleston it is conceivable that Adam was decorator to Paine's plan (as could also be cited at Harewood) until somewhere about 1761–2 when the latter, as he himself gave out, finding himself so busy in other parts of the country that he could not give the work his attention, resigned his commission, 'whereupon it was entrusted to those able and ingenious artists Messrs. Robert and James Adam'.[43] Similarly, at Croome Court in 1761 Robert Adam was preparing drawings for the interior and the furnishings of the church which, set on a hill at a distance from the house, was by 'Capability' Brown[44] and the partnership was repeated subsequently at Hulne Priory in the park at Alnwick. Of the castle, Sir Arthur Bolton in his superb monograph on Robert and James Adam, thinks that some of the earliest Adam drawings may date from 1760.[45] That seems improbable for the Gothic rooms noted in 1759 by John Adam were still in existence towards the close of the following year.[46] Then, too, the greater part of the reconstruction was not perfected until 1764 and then the dining-room was one of the first of the new suite of apartments to be executed.[47] On this dating it would therefore appear as if the Paine-Adam partnership at Kedleston occurred prior to their combination at Alnwick and not vice-versa as Bolton was inclined to suppose.[48] Indeed Alnwick may have been one reason why Paine abandoned his interest at Kedleston.

At Alnwick it seems that the neo-Gothic style was the choice of the Duchess. Louis Dutens, once secretary to the brother of Lord Bute, the promoter of Luton Hoo, followed in the Northumberland entourage to Ireland[49] and later became historiographer-royal and rector of Elsdon from 1765 to 1812, a chaplaincy in the gift of the Duke of Northumberland.[50] In his memoirs Dutens recorded of the Duke and of the castle that it 'had entirely fallen to decay; he completely rebuilt it; and out of complaisance to the Duchess, his lady, ornamented it in the Gothic style which he himself did not like'.[51]

In the course of her numerous travels the Duchess visited many buildings and her diaries reveal some shrewd and perceptive comments on them. The Radcliffe Camera in Oxford she did not like. 'A most expensive, heavy, clumsy Pile of Building.'[52] Other entries, besides displaying her preference for lightness of ornament, express admiration for Gothic. At Warwick in 1752 she visited the church of St Mary's and the Beauchamp Chapel where, 'The Gothic Entrance . . . is extreamly [sic] handsome and the inside of it is quite charming'.[53] On another occasion she had an eye for situation rather than architecture when seeing Dunstanburgh Castle in the summer of 1760. It was, she thrilled, 'Something stupendous, magnificent in its appearance'.[54] In Scotland she admired Heriot's Hospital for the regularity of its Gothic.[55] In fact, the diaries of the Duchess prove her to have had a keen eye and considerable knowledge of painting and architecture and that she was responsive to the moods of the time, revelling in the antique and the associational. Like the Countess Anne in Westmorland, the Duchess had a lively sense of the continuity of history which was demonstrated when in 1774 she caused Malcolm's Cross, marking the spot where Malcolm III of Scotland was slain while besieging Alnwick, to be restored.[56] However, it may have been that the concept of gothicising the interior of the castle developed gradually and that from the Gothic dining-room and drawing-room came the notion of expanding the theme and utilising the fashionable talents of Robert Adam.

Preserved among the Northumberland papers is a receipt from Paine for services at Alnwick from September 1766 to 27 February 1768 'including the Last Journey to Alnwick'. With the evidence already mentioned does the last phrase not mark the termination of Paine's activities at the castle? By the same time some of Adam's schemes must

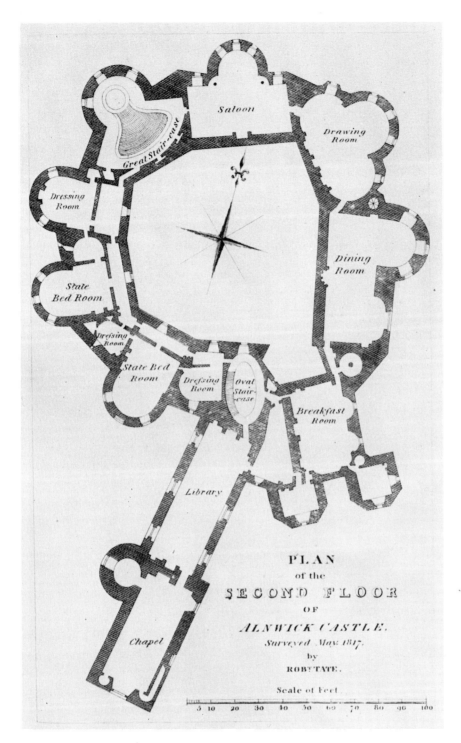

Plate 24   Plan of the principal floor. Alnwick Castle.

have been well advanced for in 1768 and 1769 furnishings, some of which at least were for the state bedrooms, were sent north from London[57] and drawings for the chief public rooms indicate that they were either finished or nearly so.[58] Also Wallis, a county historian, recorded in 1769 that the castle had been repaired 'in a very splendid and magnificent manner in the antient Saxon-gothic stile',[59] and Pennant in his tour of the same year noted, 'The apartments are large, and lately finished in the gothic style with a most incompatible elegance'.[60]

The plan of Alnwick (Plate 24) was dictated by the layout of the medieval keep, an irregular circle built around a central courtyard. The main rooms were on the first floor and except for the bedrooms in the south west were arranged *en suite*. Access to them was by two staircases, the great stair and the family stair, an oval one by the gate towers. While several smaller staircases were provided in the thickness of the walls the servicing of the residential apartments must always have been a problem. So far as the irregular outline of the keep permitted the shapes of the rooms were formalised although no two of them were identical. To what extent, if any, Adam had a hand in the planning cannot be said although it does show that skill and variety of disposition for which he was celebrated.

The entrance to the castle, then as now, was in the corner diagonally opposite the courtyard from the inner gatehouse and a small porch led into the great staircase. Paine proudly described it as 'Different, uncommon and yet elegant'.[61] One of the most admired features of the castle, it was fan-shaped with convex steps rising in diminishing width to the centre of the tower. At the landing the staircase divided into two with the steps progressing round the perimeter of the walls. Unfortunately, no illustrations of the staircase survive although there are variations on the same theme by Adam at Home House (1773–4) and at Culzean Castle in Ayrshire. At Alnwick the staircase ceiling and walls were blue and panelled in white plasterwork[62] with the cornice enriched by a hundred and twenty quarterings of the Percy family, which would be those painted 'in Oil on Paper . . . at 3 shillings each' by Joseph Edmondson in 1769 and for which he was paid £18.[63] At this period it was common for such work to be done in the studio and then pasted into position.[64]

Adjacent to the staircase on the east was the saloon. Forty-two feet long it was nineteen feet high[65] with a fan vaulted apse supported on slender many shafted columns with tiny bases and Prince of Wales capitals. Several designs are in existence[66] and each is more elaborate than the last (Plates 25 and 26) until the details become bewildering to the eye in a kaleidoscopic profusion of form and colour although the final effect may

68

not have been fussy as the plaster details were of great delicacy and of thin outline with the trim of the crockets before the apse riding the crest of the arches like sea-spume. The ceiling and walls were again blue with white tracery but with the panels for arms and trophies set in a straw-coloured background.[67] The use of the colours in large areas, their low key and the avoidance of numerous tints must have helped to promote the beauty of a room in 'the gayest and most elegant style of Gothic architecture'.[68] The chimney-piece, opposite the apse, was almost plain with a fluted surround and on each side a cluster of slim shafts carried a row of miniature fan vaults sheltering anthemion decorations.[69] Many features in the saloon were non-Gothic. Disregarding the accuracy of Adam's

Plate 25   Recess in the Saloon, Alnwick Castle.

Gothic, hardly a relevant issue for any practitioner, the room must have borne a close resemblance to many others in Adam's classical manner. Thus the apse with its plaster vault is a free translation by Adam of one of his favourite devices whereby, by means of an entablature and columns, a frontal screen bemuses perspective which lies behind in the dome of an apse where intricacy of craftsmanship is a lodestar resolving the mysteries

Plate 26   Section and plan. Saloon, Alnwick Castle.

of space. In the library at Kenwood there are such mysteries and in the
Alnwick saloon where, beyond the swelling shafts which are the biological
growth of the fluted columns of Kenwood, the recessions of the generic
planes provoke that movement which Adam instilled in so many interiors
and which found free and ready expression in the enclaves of the medieval
towers which stud the keep. Apart from the architectonic qualities, the
decorative details repay examination in the classical search. The dado,
with its series of lozenges inset with foliated designs, the reticulated surface of the walls, and the twisting plant tendrils crawling across the apse
are each and all discoverable in the formulae of such interiors as those of
Shardeloes, Harewood and other mansions; and at Alnwick the minim-
ising of the Gothic effect was carried even further in the drawing-room.

70

Apart from the chimney-piece it was a classical study and, like the saloon, had a three-windowed apse filling the tower area. On either side a lesser apse had a window bay and a door, communicating with the saloon on the one side and on the other with the dining-room. These apses, like the remainder of the room, were pink, green and white[70] and were compartmentalised by attached columns modelled in relief with arabesques and with the pedestal, as high as the dado, coated with layer upon layer of scales. The frieze had the curious device of a pair of linked dolphins alternating with a palmette. The walls were filled with round-headed panels resplendent with filigree arabesques.[71] Now at Syon the long gallery not only has a similar colour scheme as the Alnwick drawing-room but one end is terminated by a boudoir identical to the northern apses except that at Syon the panels are devoid of the infilling of the curling plasterwork. These copies at Syon and Alnwick must be near contemporaries although the former may be first since Horace Walpole mentions the gallery in 1764[72] whereas the drawing, 'Section in Alnwick Castle the Duke of Northumberland', can only date from 1766 at the earliest when the dukedom was conferred. Certainly the repetition of the colour schemes and of motifs is no coincidence. Was the Duchess then so delighted with her boudoir that it had to be recreated in her northern home or did the architect wish to elaborate upon a theme which had already pleased him? At Alnwick the drawing-room is the mid-way point in any progression through the state apartments. Also being at a tangent to the two main lines of architectural flow it therefore becomes a fulcrum. Now it was never Adam's practice to lead directly from one grand effect to another without allowing a necessary relief in the heightening of the drama by the interposition of an ante-room or of a cross-axis. As these planning tricks were not possible at Alnwick the relief instead is a visual one. After all, Adam was never a stylistic martinet.

The sole concession to the Gothic taste in the drawing-room was the chimney-piece of white statuary marble inlaid with Sienna marble.[73] On the original design (Plate 27) above a blank arcade was a band of ten quatrefoils[74] but they were replaced by a classical design incorporating a typical Adam treatment of the palmette which shows this room as a late development. The chimney-piece, in the restraint of materials and proportions, is an excellent example of its type and has survived the changes of a hundred years later. Adam's first thoughts were to have a chimney-piece of a thoroughly Gothic nature with an ogee arch, with cusping and shields, supported by pairs of columns with a pedestal and crocketted niche between each pair.[75] However that chimney-piece, too Gothic for the classical drawing-room, went to the dining-room which, of

71

all the apartments, was the most obviously Gothic since there was little of the proliferation of detail and ornaments which had appeared elsewhere, the effect depending not so much on classical motifs as on such items as cusping, crockets and pointed arches. The room was of a difficult shape being fifty-three feet long and twenty-six feet high[76] besides the complications of two unequal recesses. To impose unity a triple segmental

Plate 27   Robert Adam. Chimney-piece for the drawing-room,
Alnwick Castle. 1769.

arch was repeated across the window bays and the intervening wall space and to reduce the gaunt height a tall, elongated arcade rose above the cornice.[77] The ceiling, although it had pendants, was of a kind used in Adam's classical schemes with hexagons at the intersections of squares which enclosed designs of a classical derivation.[78] The last room in this series was the breakfast room where, although there were no projecting towers, semi-circular recesses were introduced to lend movement to an otherwise static shape and the walls were panelled with Gothic arches enclosing smaller ones.[79] It was not until 1887 that this room, the unique relic of Adam's concept, was condemned as structurally unsound and gutted.[80]

Once the grand suite of rooms within the keep was accomplished nothing more seems to have been done for some years so that in a print of 1776 the keep stands isolated although by 1784 in another print the wing, linking it to the curtain wall and containing the library and chapel, was shown. The library was the longest of the state apartments, being sixty-four feet long.[81] An early draft for it has arches and pendants akin to those in the dining room[82] but this changed considerably and became a complex diaper of small particles[83] so that, although the final effect was Gothic of a highly original kind including a battlemented cornice, much of the treatment was decidedly *cinquecento*. On the doors the rosettes, encircled by continuous bands, were comparable to those on the ceiling and over the door-cases of the red drawing-room at Syon and all with the strong refulgent character of the ornamentation in the ducal palace of Mantua.

Plate 28   Robert Adam. Carpet design. The chapel, Alnwick Castle. 1780.

Plates 29 and 30   Robert Adam. Designs for the east window and a family
tree of the Percys. The chapel, Alnwick Castle. 1777.

The last of the noble sequence of apartments was the chapel on which
building operations continued throughout the seventeen seventies only
reaching their conclusion shortly before the Duke's death in 1786 when
several of the accounts remained to be settled. The ceiling was a plaster

fan vault in green and gold[84] imitating the roof of King's College chapel in Cambridge[85]; the walls were panelled with 'the whole pedigree of the Percy's made out, shewing them to be descended from Charlemagne'.[86] Adam delineated two family trees with the first portraying a knight and his lady perched on pedestals on either side of a somewhat unkempt genealogical tree.[87] Eventually, these disparate elements were felicitously united (Plate 30) within a framework of narrow stucco arches with shields filling the spandrels,[88] an essay matched by the frontispiece to Horace Walpole's description of his villa. As so frequently occurs with Adam the carpet was patterned in the chief divisions of the ceiling. Like the carpet (Plate 28) in the circular recess or family pew[89] it was in shades of green, purple, red and gold[90] which was the overall scheme.[91] Finally, although apparently copied from the east window of York minster[92] the window in the Alnwick chapel (Plate 29) adhered only slightly to the Gothic tradition for the four lights were filled with shapes which in the tracery above shot themselves like green rockets with big floral heads into the glory of peacocks' tails.[93] Although the agreement for making the windows was signed in London in 1774,[94] some two months after the designs were prepared,[95] they were not complete until 1780 when the final account came to £373 6s 0d which included the cost of iron framing, to support the glass, and wire guards.[96] The finishing touches were put to the chapel between 1780 and 1781 when nearly fifteen hundred books of gold leaf were required.[97]

Throughout the castle the furnishings were classical but for the chapel Adam designed a lectern and chair in the Gothic mode with the chair, apart from minor details, being identical to the one for Croome Church.[98] Unlike the other furniture the Gothic pieces have a theatrical air about them although without a doubt they satisfied the rather easygoing religious standards of the day. Curiously enough, it is the furnishings which, despite their brittle elegance, have long survived the rooms for which they were intended since a hundred years after the first Duke began his renovation of Alnwick his efforts were almost fully destroyed in 1854 and subsequently by his descendant the fourth Duke who submitted the present high Renaissance interiors. Fortunately, the Duke's activities did not extend to the demesne where there is still evidence, albeit less rich and less decorative, of that style which Adam developed in the castle.

Inevitably, as a great landowner the first Duke had many responsibilities to the local community. Thus it was the Duke and not any municipality which provided the two Gothic bridges over the River Aln to the north west and to the north east of the castle. The former, the Lion Bridge, came first with the designs emanating in February 1773 from the office of Robert and James Adam at a cost to the Duke of £11 17s 6d.[99] The bridge was carried out almost exactly to the design specifications save for replacing a carved moulding by a plain band around the spandrel shields. Also although the Soane Museum drawing has a very mild looking lion atop the east parapet once cast in lead it became much more ferocious in aspect. The parapet has strong battlements except over the piers which have characteristic crosslets and the continuous corbel course is of typical Adam section frequently incorporated in his castellated houses in Scotland. On 21 August 1773 the foundation stone of the new bridge was laid with some medals deposited under it. However, in December so heavy were the rains that the rising water level covered the new piers sweeping part of them away.[100]

Once completed the bridge was an important visual element in the landscape composition for 'Capability' Brown was laying out the park during the sixties and seventies[101] with clumps and waving lines of trees crossing the landscape. In that scene the Lion Bridge is an integral part, screening as it does and mystifying the western line of the River Aln which Brown transformed from Canaletto's turbulent stream to a placid course of water stretching in gentle, easy bends to the east, its S-shape being the expression of Hogarth's line of beauty.

At the eastern extremity the park is bounded by the Denwick road where there is the second bridge. In this instance the architect may well have been Robert Mylne, a descendant of the royal master masons of Scotland and most famous as the designer of the Blackfriars Bridge in London, 1760–9. The Denwick Bridge bears the date 1773 which is when Mylne was engaged in designing a new Tyne bridge in Newcastle after the old one had been destroyed by flooding the previous year. Mylne had also worked in 1765 on Northumberland House and so must have been known to the Duke.[102] Again, the absence of any material is significant since scraps, if nothing else, have survived for almost all the Adam work; and then, too, a comparison of the bridges themselves is revealing. On the Lion Bridge Adam's three semi-circular arches establish a certain sonorous cadence with the rhythm accentuated by the relief of the armorial carvings and elaborated upon by the many corbelled vaults below the parapet plus the swelling forms of the piers. It is unfortunate that the Denwick Bridge, where the arms are weakly incised, has square section corbels in the centre and fan vaults on the terminal polygonal bays. With the linked crescents in the parapets the elements are too disparate to provide aesthetic or visual unity nor are the weaknesses redeemed by the one elliptical arch, typical of Mylne, which is a trifle too clever and grandiose for the rural setting where it is out of scale.

76

Plate 31   Robert Adam. Ecclesiastical and castellated designs for Ratcheugh Crag, Northumberland. 1784.

Apart from the bridges, the Duke dotted his estates with sundry other Gothic edifices, of which most survive, with Brown considered as the possible author of the first of them, Kielder Castle, set in the hills of Redesdale near the Scottish Border. Although surviving accounts differ in their dating and building sequences[103] both agree initially that in 1771

77

the Duke, accompanied by several of his neighbours, desiring a lodge for moor-game shooting, fixed on a site which, according to one later writer, was formerly the residence of a noted Border chieftain.[104] Building began the following year and within another three was finished although alterations may have been carried on intermittently for some years[105] which did not prevent the Duke in the late summer of 1777 from entertaining 'the herds and girls with a collation and dances distributing ribbons among the lasses'.[106]

Another rustic retreat survives unaltered at Ratcheugh Crag, to the east of the Alnwick policies, where the tea-room and gazebo, poised above an open arcade of three arches, was originally intended to be duplicated at the further end of a fanciful entrance screen of arches which was in part set up as an 'eyecatcher' along the ridge of the precipitous rockface.[107] The gazebo must have been in being by 1784 when, on the bottom left-hand corner of a fresh architectural fancy (Plate 31) is the note, referring to the plan, 'The part shaded light Already executed by the Duke of Northumberland'. Corresponding to the plan is a pastiche, highly finished in watercolour and obviously intended for the client, depicting a bevy of beflagged towers in the centre supported at each side by an elevated gazebo.[108] It is architecture of the grand gesture and would be like those many other follies which Adam was ever prone to doodle in his notebooks even as a young student but that the vast height of cliff and fortification and the limitless horizontal extent are instantly recognisable as Burke's sublime. Adam also provided an alternative idea, 'Plan and Elevation of a Monastik Building' (Plate 31), at the same time.[109] Of more solid erection, it is not so transparent as the prime scheme for there are fewer openings to allow for the escape of space and the architectural details are more convincing particularly the ruined shell-keep of which a fragment, with an attached stair-tower, was to be so constructed that it might overtop the frontal screen. However, the Duke's death in 1786 ended such novelties and only the one gazebo remains. To command the extensive view its four sides have each a trio of round-headed windows filled with the conventional intersecting glazing bars.

More interesting, however, are the follies ordered by the Duke for Alnwick park. On the highest point, Brizlee Hill, the Duke erected a tower (Plate 32) for which Adam set out designs in November 1777[110] at a cost of £21 0s 0d and in the ensuing months a total of twenty-seven working drawings were made 'at Large' plus some others.[111] Estimates of cost had already been submitted and the more detailed of the two included such items as, 'To the Shafts of the Collums' at tenpence per foot and bore the proviso that the Duke was 'to find all Scaffolding Ropes and Nails, Rows

Barrows and Tubes, Cramps and Lead, and all Moulds made and Lime and Sand Lay'd down at the Building'.[112] The mason, Matthew Mills, had also sent in an estimate which, though not so itemised, was considerably cheaper[113] and he is supposed to have been the erector which would not be surprising as he had been working on the castle. In 1779 further drawings were required and furnished, this time for doors.[114] However, the tower was now underway for the plasterer, Joseph Rose junior, was paid £56 11s 4d which included £3 4s 4d for 'Modelling, Casting and Trimming two half Capitals to be done in Stone . . . and Trimming the Leaves', which are the Prince of Wales capitals (used so much at the castle) on the fluted base columns.[115] Indeed, there are several other classical motifs incorporated into this bizarre fantasy (Plate 33), which was completed in 1783.[116] There are the familiar oval paterae on the waistband of the outer circle of

Plates 32 and 33   Robert Adam. Brizlee Tower, Alnwick Park. 1777.

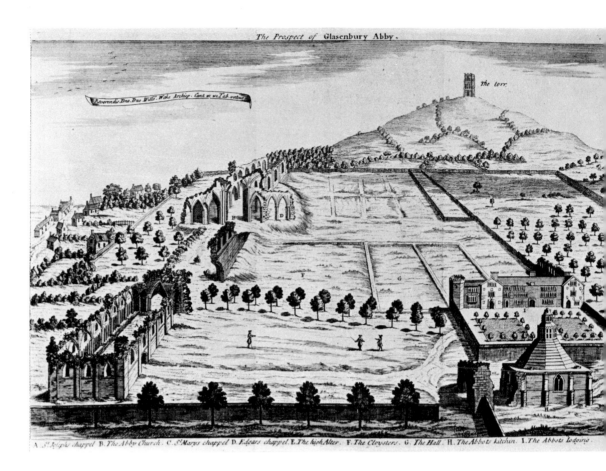

Plate 34   Glastonbury Abbey. 1776.

buttresses, the fluted string-course below the top gallery and small
medallions, either portraits of their graces or family crests, to emphasise
the apex of certain visual parts. Still, while the extravagance of the applied
surface ornament bestows an exotic air upon the tower, its situation, height
and the smallness of the openings hints at that neo-classicism which was
soon to overwhelm European architecture. Despite such sonorous claims
the tower is a confection of delight and, after all, 'The original model was,
it is said, made of pastry by a French cook. His grace was so pleased with
the ingenious design, when placed upon his table, that he ordered all the
proportions to be strictly observed in erecting this tower'.[117] Pity that
such a tale should be apocryphal.

To the east of Brizlee Hill and across the River Aln are the remains
of the Carmelite Priory of Hulne. Although acquired by Earl Hugh in
the mid seventeen fifties (Chapter III, p. 28) it was twenty years before
the ruins were renovated which was probably in response to the appearance in 1776 of the second edition of William Stukeley's *Itinerarium
Curiosum* in which the prospect of the ruins of Glastonbury Abbey (Plate

Plates 35 and 36   'Capability' Brown. The Lord's Tower and the summer-house, Hulne Priory, Alnwick Park. 1776.

34) with the tower crowning the eminence of the distant hill[118] must have prompted the construction of Brizlee Tower to complete a similar panorama in the park at Alnwick. For the priory of Hulne new Gothic arched entrances were made and Gothic tracery inserted in the gable of the former guest house 'to give a more picturesque termination to the venerable ruins'.[119] On the site of part of the west range of the cloisters[120] a summer-house was put up and linked by a bridge at first-floor level to the medieval lord's tower (Plate 35), the most substantial fragment of the pre-Reformation complex to survive with an embattled parapet and a fine, nobly proportioned oriel window both of which, by their boldness and asymmetry, may be reconstructions of previous features.[121]

The summer-house, a regular composition, has the usual features of labels, pointed lights and tracery and clearly has its origins in the Strawberry Hill fashion. The main front (Plate 36) is decorated with portraits in artificial stone of the Duke and Duchess which must have been similar to those made by George Davy in 1773 at two guineas each.[122] This building has been attributed to 'Capability' Brown by comparing the heavy, irregular castellation, then in vogue, and the niches with specimens by him at Corsham.[123] In any case, he was probably laying out the park at this time.

Inside, however, it is accepted that Adam was the designer as happened at Croome and elsewhere. Although simpler in materials and decoration than the state apartments at the castle, the rooms at Hulne convey a good idea of the Adam Gothic style which inevitably is a permutation of the classical. In the lord's tower there is a richly detailed frieze, cornice and dado and such units as doors and windows repeat one another (Plate 37) even if it means putting in a false aperture. The style has great vigour, particularly in the plasterwork of the ogee arches and the frothing crockets over the doorways and although the detail is by this date familiar, the motifs, albeit limited in range and variety, are used with skill and a play of form and part which, when set beside the aridity and the stiffness of some of Paine's classicism, say, is very refreshing. Thus beguiled it is scarcely surprising that so many of the Northumbrian gentry threw in their lot with the Gothic style. Its convoluted inventions and ingenious intricacies provided a stimulus to the jaded eye but also, by the conjuring of its historical-romantic associations, to the mind whereas Adam in the fastness of his native land was rejecting such frivolities in bringing to maturity a sterner castellated manner far removed from the gaieties of Alnwick Castle with its rich rococo interiors.

Plate 37   Details of the saloon, Hulne Priory.

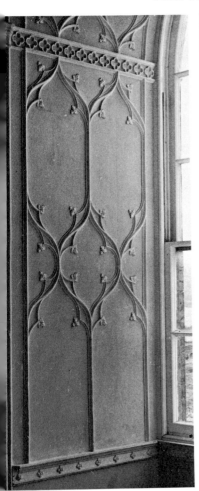

VI

Robert Adam's Northern Castles

Despite their curiosities, the interiors of Alnwick Castle must have been glitteringly beautiful. Although much of the detailing had hard gem-like colouring, the backgrounds were soft pastel tones tuned by the vibrancy of the white plasterwork. For such a large undertaking as the refurbishing of the castle, many designs must have been prepared. Though most have disappeared, those which survive testify that as much care was lavished on the Gothic as on any classical commission that came to Robert Adam. He was certainly not forced to adopt the Gothic mode against his will, as one writer would believe.[1] Indeed, if that had been so then Adam's twenty years of Gothic operations for the Percys would indicate an inventive masochism which even Robert Adam, hard and practical as he was, could scarcely have endured.

Yet apart from Alnwick, a few interiors at Mellerstain and some church designs, there is no readily identifiable Gothic work by Adam. Is it then to be said that in late middle age he consciously turned away from Gothic to create a series of castles in Scotland which in their control of deep passions are comparable to Shakespeare's later tragedies or the Beethoven quartets? Or is it that those same castles should be seen as another manifestation of the Gothic Revival? Significantly, though Adam produced many castellated schemes, it was only in Scotland, where the castle was still a meaningful symbol, that such projects were built in any number although equipped internally with all the refinements of Adamesque classicism. From the clients' point of view there may well have been good reasons for such a stylistic dichotomy. Gothic of the Alnwick and Strawberry Hill variety was a court Gothic with which many of the Scottish gentry would not be *au fait*. Also there must have been something outrageous about its defiance of hitherto accepted taste so that the Gothic interiors of the Duchess of Northumberland and Horace Walpole could be regarded as enterprises designed to shock the artistically staid.

In truth, of course, Adam's castellated architecture cannot be considered a late development. His first large schemes, for Whitehaven and Lowther Castles, date from 1766 and later. These houses, to the north west of the Pennines, were owned by the Lowthers whose ancestry was every bit as fierce and wild as that of the Percys on the east. After 1750 the head of the Lowther family was Sir James Lowther,[2] described as 'imperious and morose, tyrant of Cumberland and Westmorland'.[3] A coal-magnate and the brother-in-law of Lord Bute, one of Adam's most notable patrons, Sir James was one from whom much might be expected. In 1765 and 1766 a design for a dairy and two designs for villages were commissioned from Adam[4] whose expectations must have seemed confirmed with the request to enlarge Whitehaven Castle, on the Cumberland coast, from beneath which came the Lowthers' mineral wealth.

Adam's plans and sections are dated 1766[5] and show that he regularised a much older house by creating a castellated L-shape with a tower block at each corner and a projecting semi-oval in the middle of the longer side. Of the principal rooms, mostly along the

Plate 38   Robert Adam. Whitehaven Castle, Cumberland. 1766.

piano nobile, some were oval with semi-circular niches recessed in the walls. The structural alterations lasted for three years for then ceiling designs and friezes were worked out in London for the drawing room and dining room.[6] The ceiling of the former was elaborate being coloured light pink, green and blue with, in the corners, martial trophies incorporating shields, flags, armour and very unwarlike *putti*.[7] These designs were presumably executed although no evidence now remains so that the outcome is a rather dull building of little elegance and lacking those subtleties which one might have expected. Yet, even without such nuances, Whitehaven was a seminal concept.

In the years 1767–71 no less than four major schemes were mooted for Lowther Hall, destroyed by fire in 1720.[8] Before going to the Adam brethren, Sir James had notions of rebuilding the family seat on the model of Holkham[9] and Robert's first idea in 1767 was a classical composition with curved colonnades springing forward, like pincers, from a central rectangle.[10] In the same year James produced a Gothic scheme: as might be expected it was not very practical. Around a central courtyard of 166 feet diameter was an octagon having, at each angle, a circular turret rising for one further storey over the three storey house. Such engaged roundels were somewhat akin to late fifteenth and early sixteenth century Scottish practice, as at Holyrood, and reminiscent, too, of an Adam design of a decade before for Douglas Castle in Lanarkshire. From two sides of the octagon, hundred-foot long galleries (one was for statuary) ended in hemi-cycle blocks containing the household offices.[11] In the perspective there was also a Scottish ancestry since the house was to be approached, across a dry ditch, by a bridge with an obelisk at each corner and parapets of pierced quatrefoils all as at Inveraray.

Compared to the formula produced by James, the elder brother's undated project was simpler and was comparable to what he later achieved at Mellerstain—although the plans were of the most grandiose nature with numerous halls, libraries and galleries but all projected onto symmetrical planning arrangements[12] which have their source, ultimately, in Roman baths' planning. However, nothing materialised from these ideas and it must have been with fresh hopes, therefore, that Robert produced his 'Plan of a New Design of a Castle for Lowther in Westmorland' in 1771.[13] It was a return to his previous thought of a rectangle now enclosing a circular court, *à la* Syon, with the various apartments filling the outer faces and a gallery, 248 feet long, occupying one entire side. The plan displays to the full all Adam's skill in disposing his internal spaces in the most felicitous manner so that their very intricacies assume a rationale making their contrivance sensible and assured. Even so it is doubtful if Adam's consummate handling could have saved the enormous facade from being inordinately dull. True, the use of circular, polygonal and square towers together with protuberant bays lent some variety but that was not enough and neither were such few details as lug turrets and the precocious appearance of oriel windows.[14] Yet from a distance the great mass would have done all that Adam intended. Set above a castellated terrace, the lines of towers, over-topped by the mighty circular keep rising from the central court, would have fulfilled what Adam himself wrote of his first sight of the Emperor Diocletian's palace at Spalato as 'not only picturesque but magnificent'.[15] Indeed, such an allusion may be more than a coincidence for there can be no doubt that Adam drew upon his experiences at Spalato since not only do the rhythms of the exterior correspond to Adam's but his six storeyed tower, pushing upwards through the centre of the Lowther elevation, is an evocation, albeit in another guise, of the cathedral tower which appears in more

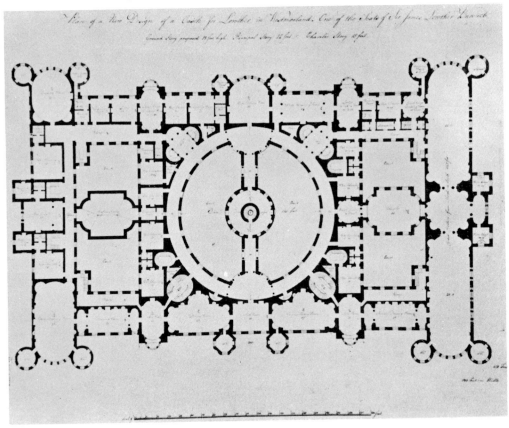

Plate 39   Robert Adam. Plan of the principal floor. Whitehaven Castle, Cumberland. 1766.

86

than one of Adam's views of the Emperor's palace.[16] In actual form, of course, the Lowther tower is like the many castellated towers which fill the Italian centuries and of which the Castel Sant' Angelo is one of the most notable.

What then was Adam's attitude to Gothic? From his earliest days he was interested in Gothic. One of his first essays in drawing was the Cross at Winchester and three years later, in 1753, in a study of his father's tomb in Edinburgh he carefully included the castle. Indeed, his notebooks are full of the *divertimenti* in the fantastical prickly Gothic of the time. When he was in Italy and studying the Baths of Caracalla and Hadrian's Villa his mentor, Clérisseau, had cause to remark on Robert's passion for things of a Gothic kind[17] which even thrust themselves forward in some of the plates of Spalato.[18] Nevertheless what was surprising was not Adam's interest in Gothic, a diversion open to gentlemen without causing alarm but, in his later years, his lack of emotional involvement with it.

The answer may be that Adam was not a romantic and that his so-called picturesque approach was due to his love of variety which can also be translated as the experimentation of the neo-classicist. Unlike Wyatt, for instance, he had little either of romantic feeling or the scholarship of Gothic. At Alnwick Adam's classicism had never been thrown overboard. More so at the start than at the finish the Adam interiors were permeated by classicism not only in the proportion but in the details. Although the chapel ceiling was copied from King's College, Cambridge, and the east window from one in York Minster,[19] Adam filigree and brilliant and complex colouring performed a service to art by abstracting the essentials which is as valid as Picasso's final reductions of portraiture from the original model. Occasionally, of course, as on the balcony of Brizlee Tower, Adam did copy a medieval detail directly. In that instance it was from the roof parapet of Trinity College, Cambridge. Yet such an example is rare because it was never Adam's intention to recreate the past. He was too much of an eclectic for that. Besides, his Gothic repertoire was limited. Unlike Wyatt, he had never worked on the restoration of great cathedrals, the vast repositories of Gothic detail, nor was he an antiquarian even where Rome was concerned. In Gothic it was almost the odd and the freakish which interested him, traits which give his Brizlee Tower an oriental quality for certainly one would swear it was blood-brother to Nash's Brighton extravaganza. There is no evidence that Robert Adam ever worked at Gothic as Wyatt later was the first to do and so become more accomplished in that school than anyone else. Adam's Gothic was a derivative of his classic thinking with many of the details culled from Batty Langley's *Gothic Architecture Improved*.

Internally Gothic interested Adam for its decorative qualities. A love of decoration was common to all the Adam brothers being a joint inheritance from their father, William Adam. With Robert, however, Gothic decoration was always disciplined so that neither in part nor in form was it ever allowed to override his guiding principles as a classicist. Of course, Gothic could also be accepted for its dramatic qualities. Although never flamboyantly overt, the dramatic tensions are the fibre of much of Adam's best compositions just as it is the plot in the Corneille tragedy which justifies the ordered elegances of the versed lines. Thus, by using forms acceptable to the eighteenth century as Gothic, Adam was able to invest a situation with a force and memorabilia which no amount of juggling with the symmetry of classicism could have brought about. In that sense Gothic was a safety valve which allowed the architect to create new formulae which, if classically garbed, would have been dismissed as monstrous aberrations. Adam's Gothic can also be regarded as the effect of an interest in planning which strained old conventions to the point where they could no longer be used. In his castles Adam's apses and hemi-cycles, having heaved against a classical planning membrane, finally burst through to free themselves.

In the shape of that architecture one writer has professed to see a deliberate attempt at creating a Roman military architecture at the expense of purely Gothic motifs, such as the pointed arch, which disappear from the Adam repertoire because Adam himself came to accept that Gothic forms should be confined to religious buildings.[20] Nevertheless, such a generalisation is an over-simplification of a most complex problem. Pointed arches with cusping appear at Brizlee in 1777 and as late as 1784 Adam was prepared to serve the Duke of Northumberland with either a castellated or an ecclesiastical folly for Ratcheugh Crag. Although lancets were introduced at Alnwick (possibly not by Adam), other castellated houses, from Whitehaven onwards, have rectangular and round-headed windows. Such combinations occur at Spalato but a nearer source must be that the Adam brothers seem to have sought inspiration in the forms of Holyroodhouse and Heriot's Hospital in Edinburgh. It is known that James Adam regarded the latter as an outstanding example of architectural composition,[21] a view Robert would doubtless have shared not only because of its regularity of form and classical planning but because in the controversy which surrounded the origins of Gothic, Adam must have been as confused as any of his contemporaries. To look to-day at Adam Gothic is to see not ecclesiastical antiquarianism but is to discover a typical eighteenth century classicist selecting whatever could be considered relevant in Gothic art for classical practice. The validity of that process may now be condemned although that does not diminish its importance since it was by such means that Adam summarised in his castles the viewpoint of educated men in the sixties and seventies who had come to terms with Gothic by accepting certain broad principles relating to its antecedents. These principles can be ascertained in *The Gentleman's Magazine* which, as an Adam primer, has been overlooked when all other sources have been gone over so sedulously that scarce a picking is left.

Before the middle of the century Gothic architecture was easily dismissed:

Where the rude plans absurdity confess,
In Gothic ornaments, and barbarous dress,
And stone and timber lie in chaos more,
Than in the quarry, or the wood before.[22]

However, as the interest and delight in such architecture became irresistible, to equate the Goths and the architecture which bore their name came to be seen as an impossibility. After all, everyone knew the Goths to be 'the most abominable of the human race' noted for 'their detestable incantations and magick, and their unbounded incest, and their cruelty in cutting off the right hand of all their captives, and, finally, their murderous oblations.'[23] How, then, could the Angel Choir at Lincoln be set against such a charge sheet? It was a disturbing dilemma for those brave enough to find virtue in the Goths. However, as 'impossibilities exist only with the vulgar',[24] a distinction came to be made between the Goths and Gothic architecture. What must have been an influential article appeared as early as 1758. 'It is well worth consideration of those who study the antiquities of this island to enquire into the origin of those buildings, generally called Gothic. It is confessed on all sides that there is an awful solemnity in these structures that makes a more lasting impression on the mind than all the studied exactness of the Grecian models. . . . The Goths rather studied strength than beauty; rather consulted how their buildings should appear bold and majestic, than rich and delicate, chose rather to animate the sentiments of posterity by a crude stateliness, than by a graceful symmetry... these rude piles are but mere disguised copies of the Grecian models.' Apparently, the Goths had used 'Greek architects as artists' and it was they 'who mellowed the grossness of the work with Grecian products'.[25]

Such an opinion, no matter how obvious its faults, however incongruous its union of facts, was one which found ready acceptance throughout the remainder of the century with the arguments turning on such niceties as 'The semicircular Grecian arch deviated by degrees into the acute angle, ... The less the deviation is from the acute angular arch, the more ancient the structure; the more the deviation the more modern.'[26] That was because it was generally held that the Grecian, meaning the Roman, arch had been transformed into the pointed Gothic arch.[27] Seriously chronicled for month upon month in *The Gentleman's Magazine* such controversies are, at first sight, of no greater consequence than the wrangles of the medieval school-men on how many angels could dance on a pinhead. Nevertheless, it would be most strange if Adam had remained unaware of the Gothic controversies and if he had then he must have been cognisant of Walpole's considered opinion that 'When men enquire who invented Gothic buildings, they might as well ask who invented bad Latin. The former was a corruption of Roman architecture, as the latter was of the Roman language. Both were debased in barbarous ages . . . but neither was restored to the original standard. Beautiful Gothic architecture was engrafted on Saxon deformity.'[28]

Probably Robert Adam's first castellated mansion to be completed in Scotland was for a family friend, Baron Mure of Caldwell, which is on the boundary of Renfrewshire and Ayrshire. Near the old castle of Caldwell, a house had been begun in 1712 by the Baron's father but with his death ten years later the project lapsed[29] and it was not until late in the Baron's career that another mansion was commenced in 1773.

It is clear that Baron Mure had known Robert Adam for some considerable time beforehand. In 1763 Adam had produced the earliest of several schemes for the Baron's uncle, 'Mr. Hutchinson Muir at Great Saxham, Suffolk',[30] and in May of the same year, in a letter discussing the establishment of a riding-house in Edinburgh, Adam several times refers to Mure of Caldwell[31] who, in 1764, was one of the subscribers to Adam's folio on Spalato.[32] The latter had intimated the type of house he required, probably early in 1770, for when Adam wrote in November of that year, after a delay occasioned by a visit to Buchanan followed by a broken shin, he promised to send on his proposals 'so soon as I hitt on what I think will answer'.[33] He was as good as his word and came up with the idea of a rusticated basement with coupled pilasters rising through two floors,[34] after which nothing more occurred until February 1772 when the Baron received a plan, from his close friend, Lord Bute,[35] with an accompanying letter. 'I have sketched out my idea of a house for you, on the principle of those in town, with a Mezzanine story, which in my opinion is worth half a house. Nesmith has not drawn it neatly but it will show my meaning.' The house was to have a basement, 'out of economy', for the domestic offices although Lord Bute would have preferred these in wings. The staircase was of Italian inspiration. Besides the mezzanine floor, there was to be a principal floor with garrets above. According to his 'rough way of calculation', Lord Bute reckoned the cost at £4,500 and he concluded, 'If you build, I present you with my labours; if not, pay me for my plan.'[36] Being a shrewd business man, the Baron probably did neither. Indeed, Adam held the Baron's judgement in such high regard that during the financial crisis provoked by the Adelphi, he arranged for Baron Mure to help evaluate the paternal estate in Kinross-shire, now belonging to John Adam, for loan purposes[37] although only once in the correspondence, and that in a postscript at the close of 1772, is there any mention of the Baron's affairs.[38]

In the next year Adam's classical scheme was superseded by a castellated design of the starkest kind without any extravagance or show whatsoever.[39] Perhaps Baron Mure was a canny Lowland laird who would have regarded lavish ornamentation not so much as costly but as unnecessary to plain living and high ideals. Certainly, the need for economy runs through the correspondence and the house, as built, reflects that for it may have been that consideration which produced plain walls topped by battlements rather than a basement and pilasters. The interior was practical and commodious for a country gentleman of the lesser sort although by the standards of other Adam houses, it was modest. The floor plans for the classical and the castellated schemes remained almost identical so that Caldwell must be an early example of that assuetude, so common in the next century, of offering a client a plan but with two sets of elevations, differing one from the other in habit.

In some senses Caldwell comes close to the old castles especially from a distance when the battlements and corner turrets, rising above the trees, match the silhouette of the old castle. On a nearer approach the gaunt walls have windows punched in them but are otherwise only lightened by flat labels and by shallow relieving arches at either end of the main front, where it is stepped backed. Despite the indeterminate design, Caldwell is the spiritual descendant of such a house as Traquair in the Borders, where Adam's next house, Mellerstain, was to be built.

The estate of Mellerstain was in the possession of George Baillie of Jerviswood. Unlike Baron Mure he seems to have been somewhat of a romantic since his portrait, painted by Ramsay in 1772 and hanging in the drawing-room, shows him in the manner and costume of Van

Plate 40   Robert Adam. South front. Mellerstain, Berwickshire. 1770.

Dyck. Such romantic historicism may have precipitated the choice of a castellated mode so breaking with past intentions to link the two wings, in existence since 1725, with a mansion very much in the repertoire of William Adam.[40] While it seems inconceivable that for nearly thirty years there was no junction between the wings, in which the owners and servants lived, such a fact must be accepted especially as parallel circumstances existed at Lowther Castle in Westmorland.

Building at Mellerstain (Plate 40) must have begun before the earliest ceiling design in 1770, when Whitehaven, of which Mellerstain is reminiscent, was being completed. Construction proceeded from the 1725 east wing in a westerly direction until, towards the close of the decade, the two wings were united by a rectangular block of the conventional three storeys accented, in the Burlingtonian manner, by a projecting centre and terminal pavilions. By its very restraints, Mellerstain is Wanstead writ large in Gothic script. At Mellerstain the elevations read well with the logic of the floor plans (Plate 41) truthfully expressed along

92

the garden front with the library filling the space between two corners and the music-room, originally the dining-room, occupying the area of the central tower. Thus through the elevations and across them there is a relationship of parts going beyond the immobility of classicism and approaching that movement of parts upon which Robert and James Adam laid so much stress.

The simple statement of the exterior is repeated in the clarity of the internal expression. There are no tricks, no devious planning but instead a series of rectangles backed by a spinal corridor along the *piano nobile*. In such a subjugation of plan to mass, of volume to control the decorative qualities of the library or the music-room are allowed to speak for themselves. There is no clamour but rather a fresh statement of the values which those inspired by the writings and the building of the ancients, had been taught to emulate. Thus the plaster panels on the library walls in their representation of classical incidents are not only decoration but like the credo, painted in the parish church, they re-vitalise faith in the classical world. Mellerstain, so often by-passed by southern writers of the Adam canon, possibly because of its distance from the metropolitan scene, appears tame when compared to the iridescence of Osterley or the efulgent luxuriance of Syon because its subtleties

Plate 41   Robert Adam. Plan of the principal floor. Mellerstain, Berwickshire. 1770.

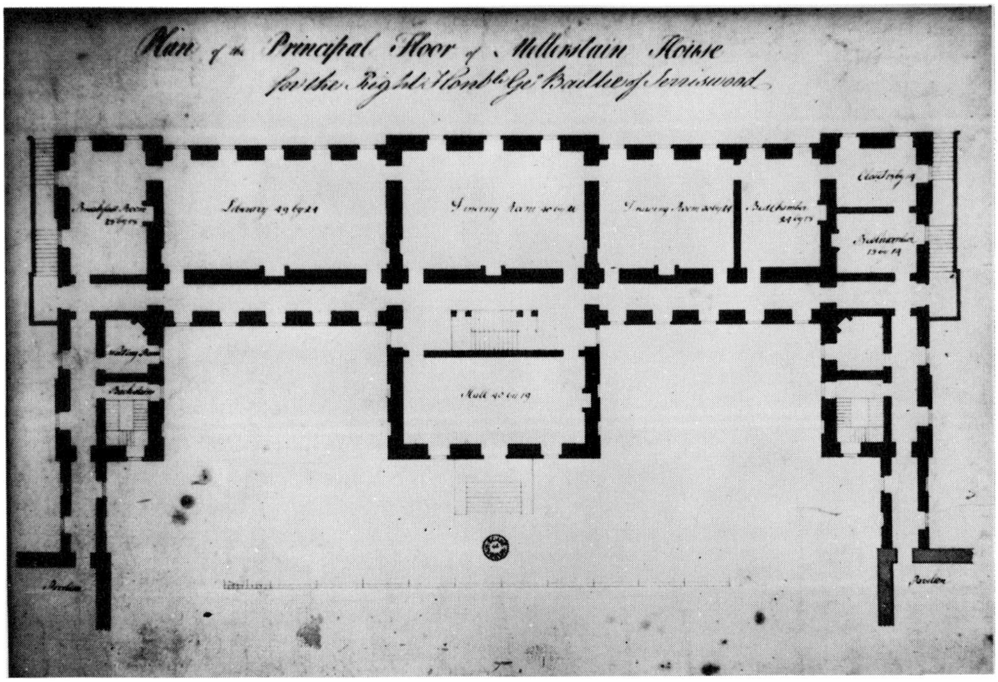

are offered up as evocations to the myrmions of ideas gleaned by Robert Adam from his seed and his travels. Yet Mellerstain is important for its interior represents Adam at the middle part of his career before he became committed to the linearisation of design and technique.

Clearly, the house was built in two sections. The ceiling designs begin with the library in 1770. Immediately to the west is the music-room of 1773 while the gallery, filling the entire top floor of that tower, is 1775.[41] Though the principal room in size, the gallery is approached by a minor stair. That, and its isolated position at the top of the house, has aroused comment.[42] Yet the gallery can only be understood in the context of Scottish tradition. In Aberdeenshire, Crathes and Craigievar Castles have galleries, filling the entire top floors, where the landowner dispensed justice and received his tenants. After the Forty-Five the former power disappeared but the tradition lingered on at Yester in 1760 and at Mellerstain, where not only was the Scottish passion for high building met with but the inclemencies of the Scottish weather, often making walking impossible, could be defeated.

At Mellerstain the drawing-room is dated 1778 as are the adjacent tower rooms[43] so that the western half was commenced only after the length from the east to the middle tower was completed. Internally, the main corridor also displays the split in the building programme for the eastern half has a tunnel vault whereas to the west the vault is groined and without the elaborate 'Perpendicular' tracery of the former.

Plate 42   Robert Adam. The breakfast-room. Mellerstain.

Plate 43   Robert Adam. Wedderburn Castle, Berwickshire. 1770–5.

Mellerstain also has one of the rare examples of Adam's Gothic in the breakfast-room, in the east tower, which has a ceiling (Plate 42) of intersecting circles containing quatrefoils while over the doorcases tiny Gothic vaulting and pencil thin shafts encase little figures. This room must be of the same date as the banqueting-room at Alnwick and like the latter would once have been richly coloured. From the evidence it might seem at first as if George Baillie, having considered Gothic interiors, changed his mind. However, that may not have been so for Arthur Young makes it clear that in the seventies Gothic was still a novelty, being used mainly out of doors for garden ornaments, although occasionally it would be introduced indoors for one or two rooms.

The singularly straightforward plan of Mellerstain has brought from writers the comment that it is untypical of Adam.[44] But then much in the Adam *oeuvre* is untypical. Yet a similar concept to the Mellerstain one had occurred at Whitehaven and occurs, too, at Wedderburn in Berwickshire (Plate 43), built from 1770 to 1775 with James Nisbet of Kelso as executant architect.[45] The plan and elevations still survive[46] and show that the design, on the sides, was altered. The front is in the Mellerstain vein, only the terminal towers are octagonal while the central tower remains locked in the main body. Inside, a single corridor again gives access to the principal rooms.

In these houses the exterior is more than usually plain for Adam, so much so that at Wedderburn it is almost sombre although the

95

medievalising features are reduced to the minimum for a Gothic effect. The elevations are unlike any others in British architecture at this time with their sources being the perimeter walls of Spalato where the terminals are three storeyed blocks, as at Mellerstain, and where octangular towers guard the entrances to the palace. Then again the arrangement of round-headed windows above a segmental relieving arch in the centre of Wedderburn is copied (Plate 44) from the east gate at Spalato.[47] On such evidence, therefore, it might be worthwhile to seek for foreign influences

Plate 44   Robert Adam. *Ruins of the Palace of Spalato*. The east gate.

at Culzean, the greatest of all the Adam castles, which as early as 1793 was hailed as 'a magnificent castle, in the Gothic style'[48] and which even Fergusson, the arch-critic of neo-Gothic, conceded to be 'one of the most successful of its class'.[49]

Culzean was a property of the Kennedys, Earls of Cassilis and later Marquesses of Ailsa, who, like many another landed family, were becoming wealthy from the agrarian changes in the county. In addition, the estates were increasing in size as a succession of rich marriages brought in further property, including some in the United States.[50] With an augmented income building could proceed for eleven years with a break of five years. Not only are the interiors striking and splendid but the interest of the building sequence has been increased by the very recent discovery of the accounts,[51] the only ones for any of Adam's Scottish castles. The accounts show that the first building programme was completed between March 1777 and 1781 under the superintendence of Hugh Cairncross, who was paid £50 yearly[52] and who was also to be in charge of the second stage between 1787 and 1792.[53] Considering the nature of the site it is not surprising that there are bills in 1777, 1778 and 1780 for excavating rock including, '270 yeards (sic) at $7\frac{1}{2}$d per yeard Cut out of the Green on South front, £8:9:2'.[54] The masons had begun

Plate 45   Culzean Castle, Ayrshire. A drawing by Robert Adam.

their operations in 1778[55] using freestone from 'Blainfeild Quarry' (sic) which in 1779 cost threepence per foot.[56]

In 1777 the Kennedys occupied a tall tower-house perched on the edge of a high sea cliff. Before Adam embarked on the building programme he made a pencil drawing of the old house.[57] With its narrow confines and crow-stepped roof set within an embattled parapet, it was but one of many such houses in Scotland. Interestingly enough the house was retained when another, more sheltered situation could have been found on the estate. However, not only did Adam change completely the character of the interior but the rugged exterior, with the removal of the steeply pitched roof, became elegant and though battlements and other medieval trappings are present, the castle is a synthesis of Adam's ideas which, drawn from a variety of sources, assume a form uniquely Adam's. Culzean should also be seen as a symbol of past ancestry, internecine strife and the domination of a hereditary warring nobility which still had a part to play as when up to date cannon were placed on a seaward battery in 1800.[58] Even so it is doubtful whether Adam, towards the close of his life, would have removed what the next century would have regarded as the most picturesque features of the vernacular castle.

Turretted wings added to it produced an oblong block containing (Plate 45) an eating room (1779) and, above it, the long drawing room (1780)[59] where the geometric ceiling of squares and lozenges has been compared to the long gallery at Syon.[60] Very unusually for Adam the entrance to the house is not in the centre of the main front but in one of the short sides. This was dictated by the planning exigencies of adding

Plate 46   Robert Adam. A design for the viaduct at Culzean Castle, Ayrshire.

to an existing core and may also have been decided by the steep fall of the ground immediately in front of the house and laid out as terraces and gardens. Adam overcame the problem admirably by adopting what now seems not only the best but, indeed, the only solution by bringing across the little glen a viaduct which, in a series of smooth bends, provides a grand approach of which every part is made interesting by the use of irregular arches and embrasures and ending in a castellated Roman triumphal arch leading into the forecourt. Adam had thought of towers along the viaduct (Plate 46) but contented himself instead with a large ruined one at the start[61] so that the ensemble of ruin, viaduct and the oblique approach to the main facade, where triple arches dominate the elevation, is a direct copy of Hadrian's Villa (Plate 47) which Adam had sketched thirty years before.[62] Less intellectually but on a more conscious and fashionable level was the inducement in *Observations on Modern Gardening*, published in 1770, that, 'In wild and romantic scenes may be introduced a ruined stone bridge, of which some arches may still be standing, and the loss of those which are fallen may be supplied by a few planks, with a rail, thrown over the vacancy. It is a picturesque object; it suits the situation; and the antiquity of the passage, the care taken to keep it still open, though the original building is decayed . . . give it an imposing air of reality.'[63] Nowhere is the dual relationship between Gothic and classical better illustrated than in the viaduct at Culzean.

Plate 47   Hadrian's Villa. A drawing by Robert Adam.

Seawards there was a range of indeterminate buildings of which the author of *The Tour to the Western Highlands in 1787* said 'had all the appearance of antiquity . . . but a nearer inspection presented us, on the opposite side with a very elegant front of castle-like features. . . .

'But I was informed his Lordship intends adding a similar front to the sea, which will be a most arduous undertaking, from the vast depth of the foundations necessary to be formed. At present it does great credit to Adam, the architect, and his Lordship's peculiar taste, and will, when complete, stand unrivalled in its way.'[64]

It was, indeed, in that same year that Adam was giving thought to the seaward aspect of Culzean. From the outset he determined on a great round tower as the central element (Plate 48) and eventually linked to the earlier landward portion by the oval staircase which, replacing the smaller one of 1780, united all the parts so that the various apartments were gathered round the centre of the house.[65] One thought by the architect was to have the sea tower's third stage recessed.[66] However, the solution decided upon was to have the second and third storeys rising continuously above the first floor but recessed within a girdling balcony and with the windows of the saloon framed by severely cut round-headed arches.[67] These marked the incorporation of another of Adam's ideas which was to have an outer casing of arches around the tower. While that would have added to the architectural force there was the practical consideration that weather conditions in Scotland do not favour the creation of shadowed recesses.

99

From his early days in Italy, Adam had been interested in circular forms and from the start of his second or London career such forms, hemicycles or domes, are frequently the climacteric in his architectural compositions. Internally, the most celebrated variable was the rotunda at Kedleston although that would have been excelled by the intended

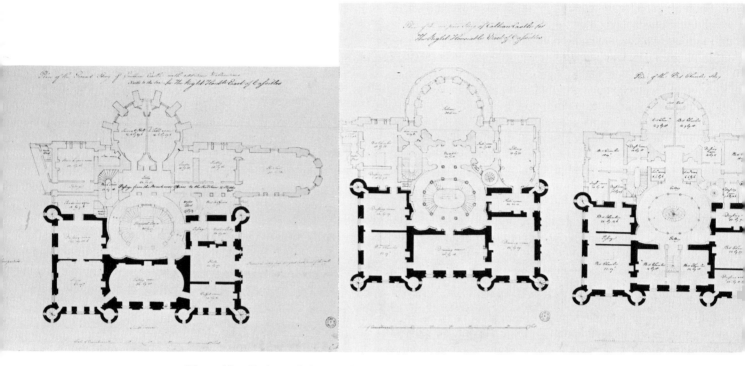

Plate 48   Robert Adam. Floor plans. Culzean Castle, Ayrshire. 1787. The lighter portions are the proposed additions to Adam's house of the previous decade.

central court at Syon. However, the form was dynamic enough to break through the structural skin and assume mastery over the entire composition as was proposed for Lowther. Culzean, however, is the first occasion when Adam brings such a feature fully forward in an elevation, allowing it an unfettered development as a feature in its own right, subordinating the mass behind it. While there had been many paper ideas and some few in stone and lime for semi-cylindrical projections, as at Whitehaven and at Oxenfoord in Midlothian (1780–5),[68] it is not until Culzean that timidity is overthrown and the form assumes an independent identity.

Two early examples which go some way towards that are David Hume's Monument in Edinburgh and the tea-house at Auchincruive in Ayrshire. The former was a memorial to be erected in the Calton Burying

Plate 49   Tomb of Caecilia Metella, Rome. c. 20 B.C. Engraving by Piranesi.

Ground in Edinburgh to David Hume, a lifelong friend of the Adam family.[69] He was probably the most distinguished and certainly the most celebrated beyond Scotland of that brilliant band of scholars who in the later eighteenth century, made Edinburgh the intellectual capital of Europe. Thus it was only fitting that Roman *gravitas* should be the theme of Adam's designs in 1777[70] which were inspired by the pre-Christian tomb of Caecilia Metella in the Eternal City (Plate 49). Adam's problem was to satisfactorily unite the upper part of the design, a ruinous cylinder, with eight arched recesses, to a base to be either square or octagonal. The concern with such basic shapes and their juxtaposed collision was a fundamental premise of the neo-classicist. It was most certainly not romantic and, although redolent with symbolism, was neither emotional nor sentimental but was a deliberate entasis of the philosophy which, inherited from Rome, was the primogenitive cause of Hume's own treatises. The memorial was not to Hume the man, whose remains lay rotting below but marked the deification of the philosopher whose place in the imperium of men's minds was assured.

The notion of a raised cylinder was given another twist at Auchincruive (Plate 50) for which the tea-house was designed in 1778.[71] At Auchincruive the violence engendered by the clash of parts is resolved by softening the lower part of the design which, though the lines are

Plate 50   Tea-house. Auchincruive, Ayrshire. 1778.

lax, is strengthened by the solid parapet and an engaged turret at each quarter. Recessed above is the domical roofed cylinder of the tea house crested with battlements and having a continuous blank arcade of twelve arches (Plate 51) with a sun motif in *basso relievo* in the head of each. The comparison with the later sea-tower at Culzean, some miles to the south, is immediate and obvious. Both structures are replicas, in one form or another, of Theodoric's mausoleum at Ravenna (Plate 52) which Robert sketched   1755.[72] A study of the monument with its arched vaults, overtopped by a saucer dome, reveals Adam's transfiguration of an Italian memory more than twenty years after first seeing it.

At Culzean the sea-tower is superbly adapted to its situation, carrying through the castle the natural drama of the site. Yet Culzean

Plate 51   Detail of the tea-house,
Auchincruive, Ayrshire.

Plate 52   Theodoric's Mausoleum, Ravenna. Drawn by Robert Adam. 1755.

has been neglected by southern historians although it might fairly be regarded not only as the finest but also the subtlest of Adam's pictorial compositions. The restrictions of the site, a narrow strip of land between the sea and a glen to the west and east and with the land falling away steeply to north and south, though formidable were turned to advantage to provide a syncretic solution where the poised blocks with their receding planes are Burkian. Much subtler is the swirl of baroque concatenation in the courtyard, between the stables to the north and the castle, in which emptiness is charged and recharged as space pulses across the terraces or is pumped along the grand viaduct and under the sea-scoured triumph of the arch. After Culzean the courtyard exacts a revolution in which the units composing a great house are centrifugally caught in a relentless theme which, losing the controlled casualness of Culzean, becomes ever more insistently passionate and sonorous until at

Plate 53   Robert Adam. Seton Castle, East Lothian. 1789.

Plate 54 Robert Adam. Dalquharran Castle, Ayrshire. 1785. The wings were added in the late nineteenth century.

Seton (Plate 53) the military beat around the walls is like a roll of drums. Though the *cour d'honneur* was not new in architecture nobody before had created a core encased in a wall, pierced perhaps by a single opening and sheltering all the castle offices. It was a plan such as could be found in great medieval castles like Alnwick where, too, the barbican is comparable with the central bow at Dalquharran (Plate 54) and Airthrey, guarded by narrowly compressed towers. At Dalquharran,[73] though the stable facade is interesting enough, the courtyard is too open whereas at Pitfour (1784),[74] it is permitted a more organic unity since small turrets on the inner side are a diminuendo of the house. Pitfour has a smaller variant at Stobs in the Borders built for Sir William Eliott of Stobs in 1792,[75] and at Seton and Airthrey. The former, with an enclosed frontal courtyard before a circular keep ringed with attached towers, comes closest

Plate 55 The ruins of old Seton Castle, 1789.

Plates 56 and 57   Robert Adam.
Airthrey Castle, Stirlingshire. 1790.

to the Alnwick plan. Even so Seton's layout might have been influenced by the old castle (Plate 55) which seems to have been polygonal with an attached tower at each angle.[76]

For Airthrey, although classical designs were produced, a castle was (Plates 56 and 57) eventually preferred possibly because its compact mass provided exactly the same accommodation (Plate 58) as the latter with its wings and terminal pavilions.[77] Airthrey was the property of Robert Haldane, of the family of Haldane of Gleneagles, who having settled at Airthrey in 1786 remained there for fourteen years before going off to become a missionary in Bengal,[78] which might explain why the outworks were never completed. Haldane was a brother-in-law of Richard Oswald of Auchincruive[79] which no doubt explains why Robert Adam was asked for designs. Haldane, however, sought to save on the cost of building, by dispensing with Adam's services as architect, and himself employing the builders, Thomas and Adam Russell. If the castle was to be of rubble with droved cornices and string-courses, their estimate was £3,500 15s 0d but

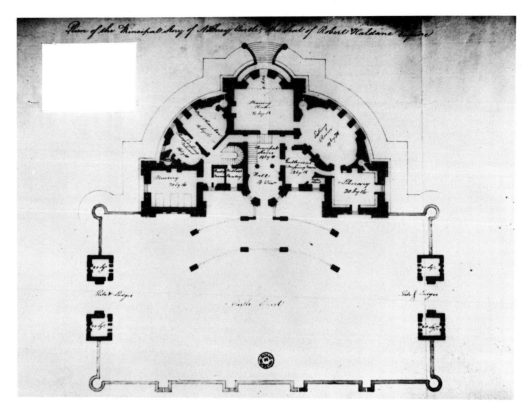

Plate 58   Robert Adam. Plan of the principal floor. Airthrey Castle,
Stirlingshire.

with another £255 to be added if it was to be of ashlar with dressed
cornices and string-courses. These estimates were substantially below
Adam's who had to content himself with sending in an account to Haldane
for £37 6s 2d for designs and expenses.[80]

The Russells had previously built Seton Castle in East Lothian.
Of all the Adam castles it is the one about which most is known for
not only does a copy of the building contract survive but so also does the
correspondence between Adam and his clerk of works, John Paterson,
who sent off to London a weekly report on progress not only at Seton
but at other Adam sites such as Edinburgh University and Charlotte
Square.[81] Such interchanges, together with the architect's annual summer
visits to his native land, ensured, despite what has been stated in the
past,[82] that there was no falling off in the quality or the execution of the
mason work or the interior finishing.

The Seton contract, between Alexander Mackenzie, an Edinburgh
lawyer, and the Russell brothers, was drawn up on 12 November 1789
and put the castle's cost at £3,400 which compares favourably with
the Russells' later estimates for Airthrey. Although the brothers were to
demolish the old castle, they were to see to it that such stone as could

be used again was retained, 'and particularly laying in one place all long Stones that will answer for lintels of doors, Windows or for Chimneys, or for steps of stairs in the offices'. Evidently, Mackenzie was a thrifty man who was not prepared to throw his money about on lavish display since the chimney-pieces in the chief rooms were 'to be of plain Statuary Marble free of spots to have little or no ornaments and not to exceed Thirty Pounds nor under Twenty Five pounds each in value'. It was further stipulated that the dining-room was to have French grey walls with darker grey on the door panels with the cornice, dado and all mouldings in white as in the drawing-room where there was to be wallpaper while the frieze, doors and skirting were to be coloured green. According to the contract, the plans were to be 'of seven leaves'[83] and these were prepared a month later in London.[84]

The site having been cleared the foundation stone was laid on 20 April 1791 and in the summer, when Adam came to Scotland, the main block was put up and roofed before the winter set in. Work restarted in spring of the following year and during the summer the final stages of construction were completed, within the time allowed for in the contract.[85] Although at Adam's death, in 1792, other castles, such as Mauldslie in Lanarkshire (Plate 60) for the Earl of Hyndford,[86] remained to be completed, Seton is supreme as Adam's last great monument in the castle style.

Yet what interpretation shall be put upon it and the other castles? Obviously, the structures themselves tell something although not as much as could be wished nor has Adam left his own views on the Gothic movement. What has remained, however, is a series of studies of fictitious castles done between 1777 and 1783.[87] In these certain traits recur again and again. Invariably, the massing is bold, sometimes asymmetrical and set on a cliff edge above water. There are viaducts, prominent shell-towers, massive round-headed arches and machicolation, all in a setting of mountains and trees. The structures are integral with the scenery but set at a distance so that the architectural details are few, consisting only of huge crosslets, corbelling and round-headed windows. Though clearly of Italian origin, nevertheless, there is frequently a Scottishness which becomes visible when turrets are corbelled out from the walls. Clearly these drawings were a form of relaxation by one who had wished to be a landscape painter,[88] whose 'numerous drawings in landscape display a luxuriance, and an effect of light and shade, which have rarely been equalled'.[89] Possibly, they were the unconscious revelation of a picturesque spirit, which must have been in tune with the contemporary theories of aesthetics. After all, the admiration of Adam for Vanbrugh is well known. Sir Joshua Reynolds also praised Vanbrugh in his thirteenth

Discourse in 1786: 'To speak, then, of Vanbrugh in the language of a painter. . . . To support his principal object, he produced his second and third groups or masses. . . . What the background is in painting, in architecture is the real ground on which the building is erected; and no architect took greater care than he that his work should not appear crude and hard; that is, it did not abruptly start out of the ground, without expectation or preparation'.[90] That exactly fulfills what Robert Adam achieved at Culzean where, in addition and for the first time, he utilised the dramatic nature of the site to enhance the drama and the monumentality of his building. Elsewhere, of course, there was no drama in the site and it was in order to prevent the structure rising 'out of the ground without expectation or preparation' that the courtyard schemes were devised for the castles. That these were rich in associations had been recognised by Sir Joshua Reynolds so that, 'whatever building brings to our remembrance ancient customs and manners, such as the castles of the Barons of ancient Chivalry, is sure to give this delight'.[91] It is a sentiment which Robert Adam would have endorsed especially as at Culzean and Seton old castles already existed. Of course the adoption of battlements and towers allowed Adam to make the most of the contrast between the profusive graces of the interiors and the sombre, powerful exteriors but it also meant that Robert could agree with James who, in 1762, had written of buildings as seen from the distance, 'We must of necessity lose all the graces and decoration so that we have nothing remaining but the beauty of a well disposed variety of high and low projections and recesses',[92] remarks corresponding to the famous line, ''Tis distance lends enchantment to the view'. Indeed, Adam's castles were intended to be looked at in a setting of woods, water and cliff. Thus, as simplicity was required then the fussiness of the usual Gothic

Plate 59   Entrance front. Seton Castle,
East Lothian.

Plate 60   Robert Adam. Mauldslie Castle, Lanarkshire. 1792.

decoration had to be omitted, which may well explain why the spire and clock intended to crown the Dalquharran stable block[93] were dispensed with possibly because, from a distance, they would have been *maigre*. It is to avoid any such danger that the roof lines are solidly proportioned with thick-cut, chunky machicolation and huge and deeply incised crosslets and with parapets which, though in the early examples are wholly battlemented, are later less so until at Seton the parapet remains unbroken as at Heriot's.

Yet as such obvious medieval trappings are dispensed with, a remarkable change overcomes the architecture. It becomes increasingly Scottish not in feeling but in detail. Thus at Pitfour, the entrance to the house is capped by a Scottish crow-stepped gable while on either side the tight little towers have the narrow vertical lines of a Scottish tower-house. The same is true at Seton where the entrance (Plate 59) broadly duplicates that of the old house.[94] At Mauldslie such atavism is even more evident for the central unit is three blocks with the outer ones having a crow-stepped gable set behind a parapet terminated at either end with the characteristic native lug-turret. While the double gable is often found worked into the larger tower-houses a more specific identification can perhaps be made with Taymouth Castle which shows a very similar pattern of features and for which, and perhaps it is of some significance, large extensions were drawn up by William Adam.[95] Even more significant at Mauldslie (Plate 60), the last of the castles, is the finish to the facade of circular towers each topped by a cap-house and candlesnuffer roof recessed within the battlements, exactly as is found at Holyroodhouse

109

Plate 61   Unexecuted design. Cluny Castle, Aberdeenshire.

or Falkland Palace. Although the castle's elevation is otherwise plain, the bold serration of the roof, albeit in keeping with Adam theories, is typical of the Scots' love for building high and then finishing with a burst of exuberant decoration, as on such notable houses as Crathes Castle or Castle Fraser, while below there might be numerous shot-holes. Perhaps it is these which are the prototypes for the indented circles in the towers at Wedderburn, Culzean and elsewhere.

Caldwell, the first of the castles in Scotland to be completed, had some few Scottish traits but though these were suppressed in the middle years, they assert themselves ever more strongly in Adam's old age until at Cluny Castle in Aberdeenshire (Plate 61) not only were all the traditional Scottish lineaments to be reproduced in the external architecture but even the characteristically Scottish Z-plan was to be duplicated in the large additions.[96] It seems then that the assertion of Seton as a Roman military station is too fanciful and, indeed, too simple an explanation for the Adam castles. Their explanation is much more complex. Adam, like all great artists, took what he wanted from the past and from his own experiences. Thus Inveraray, which must have made a deep impression on a young architect, is seen at Pitfour, where the mansion has an engaged round tower at each corner; and English medieval castle plans may have played their part just as much as Spalato or Ravenna did. Finally, Scotland of the tower-house reclaimed its heritage from the old architect in his last years. Thus Robert Adam's debt to the past was indirect but what he took his genius made its own.

110

VII

Ford Castle and Raby Castle

In Northumberland in the later eighteenth century the leading family, after the ducal house of Percy, was the Delavals of Seaton Delaval and of Ford. Their chief representative was Sir Francis Blake Delaval who, by the enormity of his debts, was obliged in 1761 to put the Ford estate up for sale. In November of the same year the family lawyer wrote to Sir John Hussey Delaval, younger brother and heir of Sir Francis, urging him to purchase the estate[1] which eventually he did.

Once in possession of his new property Sir John promptly proceeded to remodel Ford Castle.[2] A quadrangular castle of the fourteenth century (of which Chillingham is another example), the castle had been much altered in Tudor times although, like Alnwick, it had since been allowed to fall into decline. According to a statement made in 1793, presumably on the authority of Lord Delaval, the former Sir John,[3] the castle was in such a ruinous state as to be uninhabitable. Sir John, however, determined to repair the old house[4] and selected the Gothic style possibly in imitation of Alnwick where the regeneration of the medieval castle must have fired the Northumbrian gentry with enthusiasm for the Middle Ages. Certainly Ford was to be preserved 'as near its ancient form as would admit'.[5] Now, apart from a fashionable taste for Gothic, Sir John seems to have had a genuine respect for old forms. Like most of his peers he was wholly committed to architecture and in the course of a long life must have spent several fortunes on the rebuilding of his various homes. In London his town house in Hanover Square was decorated by Robert and James Adam in the early seventeen eighties and at the end of that decade work by them and other contractors was executed on Claremont House, Milbourne, and a town property in Portland Place and Conduit Street.[6] One can probably assume that all these works would be in the classical style. On the other hand, when history and tradition demanded, Sir John, like so many of the northern gentry, accepted the styles of the Middle Ages, which, so far as the eighteenth century was concerned, meant the generative term 'Gothic' and if, by later definition, further nomenclature was required then it would be, broadly speaking, Decorated. As well as the projects at Ford, which were to continue from 1761 for forty years into the next century, Sir John rebuilt at Doddington (a Lincolnshire possession) the medieval church in Gothic from 1774 to 1775 and in the next decade carried out alterations on the Jacobean hall.[7]

About Ford, tradition has it that no architect was employed during the period of rehabilitation which was supervised by Thomas Delaval, younger brother of Sir John.[8] It is likely that George Raffield, the Seaton Delaval joiner, was in charge of the daily execution of the work at the start[9] although in the seventies he was succeeded by his son John who, being introduced by Sir John to the Adams, in time not only worked on the Adelphi but became an architect himself.[10] Nevertheless a statement by Sir John in 1771 makes it clear that for some of the house at least James Nisbet, a Kelso architect,[11] had some responsibility[12] and Robert Adam's name has also been linked to it.[13] Thus when an architect was required one was employed otherwise, and this would have been in Sir John's character, the charge was entrusted to his own people.

Some of the problems encountered in bringing a medieval and Tudor house up to eighteenth century standards can be gathered from the following letter written by Thomas to his brother. 'George Raffield tells me he wrote you that it would be better to take off the arch on which my Lady's room was placed, on account of getting more room for the windows. I have been since looking at it, and told him I thought he was entirely wrong; the arch is a very fine piece of workmanship. It would not only be a great expence to pull it down and lay joists instead of it, but not the half so good for the purpose when done.' The room in question may have been Sir John's library in the north west tower and as it had no arch a hundred years later when Louisa, Marchioness of Waterford, undid her antecedent's Gothic then presumably George Raffield had his way. That would be in 1763.[14]

By that date, it is usually stated, the alterations had been completed[15] at a cost of £10,500.[16] However, from the correspondence of George and John Raffield it is evident that work continued for some time afterwards and was only coming to an end in 1771.[17] After the close of the sixties there were fewer and fewer changes to the fabric and the sur-

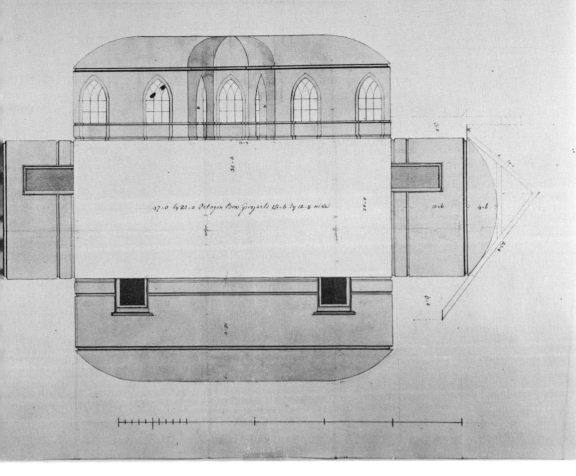

Plate 62   James Nisbet. The octagon room. Ford Castle, Northumberland.

viving papers relate increasingly to such outworks as courtyard walls
and gates although some details of the interior can be gleaned. Besides
a Gothic hall there were three Gothic looking glasses with sconces
and white frames in the drawing-room[18] where in 1771 a large fireplace
with statues was placed.[19] If it was Gothic, as seems likely, then it
would probably be similar to that designed by Adam for the dining-room
in Alnwick Castle. In the following year, when a considerable programme
of works was undertaken, the octagon room (Plate 62), in the centre of
the south front, and the adjoining one were finished while the rose
windows in the west passage were made and glazed. That was in April.[20]
Four months later one learns that the dining-room was complete and
painted blue[21] and early in the next century a letter from one Thomas
Fitzwalter to Lord Delaval, '. . . I have sent to Newcastle for the Green
for the Gallery as I could not depend on the Berwick Colour', provides
the information that the gallery was coloured green and white.[22] The
gallery would possibly be a Tudor one revamped for the eighteenth
century's taste, as Robert Adam did to the one at Syon House. Indeed,
Archdeacon Singleton, writing in 1828, infers just that. Living in the era

Plate 63   South front. Ford Castle, Northumberland. 1779.

of Rickman he doubtless felt equipped to wax righteous and castigate Ford as 'a melancholy instance of the frippery and degrading taste of George II's (sic) time. Two fine old towers are lost and overlaid with the violent gothic of Batty Langley, and Adams with his lath and plaister has attempted to form a gallery!'[23] Yet although Robert and James Adam were working at Alnwick in the sixties their executed commissions for Sir John were considerably later. Besides, Sir John was a business man who retained all his correspondence and although vast quantities will have been destroyed or lost, the available evidence on Adam relates to the southern Delaval properties.[24]

Externally, the south front of the castle was thoroughly Gothicised (Plate 63). The windows were pointed and each was surrounded by a continuous flat moulding. The basic structure of the house had not been interfered with although the pitch of the roof was screened by a parapet of colossal dimensions with large incised quatrefoils to speak of strength. Later a parapet of just such dimensions was to sprout over the roof of the Jacobean mansion at Gibside in County Durham. At Ford it seems to have been only the south elevation which was battlemented at the start since in 1787 a letter mentions raising the north passage one storey and adding battlements and is accompanied by an unsigned and undated drawing[25] showing the north front (Plate 64), three storeys high, with Gothic lights but without the final flourish of battlements.

To-day, of the neo-Gothic work at Ford, nothing remains but the courtyard walls and gates. These were erected from 1772 onwards and the greater portion of the surviving documents relates to them. At the end of 1771 Sir John was contemplating extending his building operations beyond the castle itself. Early in December George Raffield advised him that Nisbet, the architect, considered that two round towers would be most suitable for the angles of the court walls because of the

114

turnings of the drives.[26] Between Christmas and New Year matters were removed from the realm of conjecture and became factual when on 28 December the Chief Land Steward, Joseph Oxley, wrote to Sir John, '. . . the Charge is high and I think he ought not to build the porters Lodges, etc. Even at the Price he makes out in his Estemate (sic).'[27] This must be a reference to Nisbet for the very next day another letter was sent off enclosing Nisbet's estimate for building the lodges, gate and adjoining wall although the steward again complained about the price

Plate 64   James Nisbet. North elevation. Ford Castle, Northumberland. 1787.

which was 'as high as the Octagon and in Some Respects higher'. Oxley thought that his master might save a quarter on the estimate and as much as a third on what the architect, in an accompanying letter, reckoned he must have.[28] Meanwhile in London Sir John had already received the estimate and what would appear to be an earlier and cheaper one and on Christmas Eve he wrote to Nisbet from Grosvenor House to tell him

115

that he could have the contract at the cheaper rate. Then the baronet waxed furious in complaining, like his land steward, that he could not understand why he should be charged the same prices for walls and lodges as for the octagon, for which Nisbet had been responsible, nor why he should be expected to pay higher charges to the architect than his neighbours did including Blake (of Twizell).[29]

Such accusations of sharp practice set off a flurry of angry correspondence passing to and fro between the parties concerned. Nisbet must have realised that Sir John was serious in his intention to allow the work to go elsewhere and on New Year's Day he sent off a note from Kelso to justify his own actions.[30] However, neither Oxley nor his master were so easily mollified. On the contrary the language became more vituperative and the terms blunter as a first class row developed between Kelso, Ford and London. Oxley now sent off an abstract of two estimates, one was Nisbet's and the other from Ralph Lowry. To Sir John he stated that the former was shameful. Still, towards the architect he intended to be more conciliatory and despatched John Raffield, George's son, to Kelso. Jackey's mission was to discover whether Nisbet would build the porter's lodge and gateway, minus the walls, on a daily contractual basis which would be about one-third cheaper than otherwise. Oxley recognised that Nisbet was the man for the job since, although Lowry's offer was a third lower than the Kelso man's, the agent feared that Lowry, who possibly lacked the necessary ability anyway, would be unable to collect a labour force to build in lime.[31] Nisbet's abstract was for tooled ashlar at 3s 10d per yard and for 'rockwork' at 8s 4d per yard, which, one assumes, refers to the frostwork around the main entrance to the courtyard. The second estimate, not so competently drawn up and signed 'Lowry, Lowery and Lowrey', stipulated 'Touled asheler' and rockwork at the one cost, 2s 8d per yard, which made it not surprising that the agent was dubious.[32]

Next it was Nisbet's turn and in a letter in the middle of January to Sir John he went over much old ground and, stating his willingness to withdraw his men and abandon the work, implied that operations might already have been in progress although, and it is more likely, he was referring to work on hand inside the house. Yet it is clear, in this elaborate game of bluff for the best price, that he did not take his own threats seriously for at the close he dealt factually with an architectural problem. As the purpose of the south gate was to obstruct the view of some objects he contemplated a new elevation where, by building the gate in conjunction with the lodges, their former windows would be replaced by towers three feet taller than the gate.[33] On the same day as that letter

Plate 65   James Nisbet. South gate. Ford Castle, Northumberland. 1772.

went off to Sir John one arrived from Oxley. From the start it is apparent that his master's ire has cooled. Indeed, 'Sir John never said he was or had the least fear of being imposed upon by you'.[34] Nisbet refused to be placated and the next day he despatched another blast, this time to Oxley, reiterating that he did not care whether his men stayed at Ford or left.[35]

However, stay they did and at the end of February foundations were being prepared for 'the Walls before the Castle'[36] and a month later the west wall was begun[37] after which the correspondence got down to details of design for the towers and gateway. In February John Raffield was pondering the aesthetic merits of the proposed south gate and lodges about which Nisbet had put forward suggestions a month previously. Raffield thought the gate would not be bold enough for a castle. Unlike the Kelso man he did not desire height which would give it a naked and thin look especially from a side view as its forward projection was slight. To overcome such visual defects he sent to his employer an alternative, bolder and more 'Ancient-like', which was a connected pair of two storeyed lodges having a clock in the centre.[38] Meanwhile Nisbet had been having second thoughts about the round towers at the angles of the court walls. He would prefer them square and at right angles to the walls as in fortifications.[39] Of course the final decision, as in all matters, rested with Sir John so that Nisbet even had to enquire about the height

117

to which the west wall should be constructed.[40] Presumably directions were sent from the south since John Raffield was very soon writing to hint that the addition of guns to the wall would be highly ornamental and that secondhand guns could be cheaply purchased from ships 'which Would Not Be Above £20'.[41] It was possibly a more practical idea than a previous one that clay cannons should be placed on the lodges. Apart from considerations of cost, the clay, once fired, would have a deep blue colour not dissimilar to cast iron.[42] By June 1773 the lodges, walls and gate (Plate 65) were complete for then Nisbet submitted an account, which included much unspecified work, totalling £364 9s 8d. The gate was itemised at £86 6s 3½d plus two guineas for 'Canopys over the Nitches'.[43]

Until then attention throughout had been given to the west and south walls. As has been noted, the latter, partially devised to hide the view, was, in effect, a screen with terminal square towers; on the west a wall of some kind would be required because of the steep fall in the ground level and if embattled and seen from a distance would not only link the mansion and the refurbished medieval south west tower but provide a vicarious admixture of fear and pleasure for the beholder. Of the east there is no mention nor does any wall appear there in an engraving of 1779. Then Nisbet was engaged in drawing up plans for the stable and a tower,[44] the square one immediately to the east of the mansion and corresponding to those on the south screen. However, after the death of Nisbet, perhaps in 1781,[45] there is no contemporary record of further building until 1801 when Alexander Gilkie, a master builder of Coldstream, submitted an estimate for an addition to the east side of the castle.[46] From an article of the last century it has been successively repeated that Gilkie remodelled the great gateway, lodges and towers from 1791 to 1795, that Nisbet did the drawings and a William Smeaton the carvings.[47] While that may summarise in part the relationship between the three men, if the dating is correct it can only refer to the infilling of an east wall and the middle towers for Nisbet had no hand in Ford in the new century when Gilkie wrote about the small extensions on the east side of the castle.

The east towers (Plate 66) have pointed lights each protected by a hood-mould with tails. Above a double string-course, and pacing the lower lights, are large quatrefoils of raised outline which are echoed by miniature ones below the battlements. The towers were inspired by those on the keep and along the curtain wall at Alnwick where, having an original function, they are outward searching. At Ford the towers have become introspective and gaze in suppliance with sightless sockets across the green levels of the lawns to the house. Pass beneath the rigidity of the mock

Plate 66   East gate and towers. Ford Castle, Northumberland.

portcullis and the towers present nothing to the world but a surface as flat as the wall which runs away on either side.

Yet within the courtyard suspicions as to the solidity, the wholeness and the function of the towers are lulled and then quelled by the excellence of their design. There never were medieval watchtowers with such speckles of quatrefoils but at Ford one rejoices in their presence believing that without them the ensemble would be so much the poorer even if it would gain in strength. At Ford the gradual decrease in height of the proportional parts is circumscribed by string-courses which are the transcience from the vertical to the horizontal elements of the walls and their regular lines; and one suspects that Sir John may at last have used that idea which John Raffield had proposed for the south entrance of two towers connected one to the other.

By their restraint the towers graciously repress the violence, the crudity and the passions of the Middle Ages. Their evocation is contemplative whereas with the south gate a certain wildness exists which makes it, if not a peak, then at least a foothill in the history of the Gothic Revival. As it is viewed on the path to the castle, its decoration is external and in any case its decorative forms, if repeated inwardly, would only be a blur as seen from the house. Of course the weakness of the gateway is just as John Raffield prophesied. Although from the house substantial enough, it is too thin and high. But that was a budding architect's thought and not Sir John Hussey Delaval's which was two dimensional where Gothic was concerned. It is not the height of the gateway which is so striking but the forcefulness of the verticality (an unusual trait in the seventeen seventies) and the soaring sweep of the archway by which the effect of dwarfing humanity, though often sought, is here achieved as another instance of the sublime. As a frontispiece the gateway gains much from the contrast of the frostwork of the projecting

119

Plate 67   James Nisbet. North elevation. Fowberry Tower,
Northumberland. 1776.

quoins and voussoirs with the surrounding surfaces. For such a late date
it is an unlooked for treatment. Lastly, no self-respecting medievalist
considered a task complete without a peppering of quatrefoils and at Ford,
below the battlements of the gateway and the eastern towers, they are of
curious shape with each lobe scooped out towards the centre. Such a
mannerism, discoverable also at nearby Fowberry Tower (Plate 67), must
indicate the continuance of Nisbet's style, if nothing else, after the
completion of the gateway in 1773.

  Like so many of the Border homes, Fowberry was originally a
tower-house which, in the seventeenth century, was enlarged. In 1776
the estate was purchased by Sir Francis Blake of Twisel who immediately
began a programme of extending the mansion and of embellishing the
principal apartments in the Gothic taste.[48] As it finally emerged, having
been doubled in width, the house was a double-pile plan with additions
at either end of lower two-storey, one-bay wings. To the south, which
was the entrance front, there were four storeys although the rear had one
less in order to allow for the great height of the public rooms of which
two, the dining-room and the saloon, contain Gothic decorations.

Plates 68 and 69   James Nisbet. The dining-room. Fowberry Tower,
Northumberland. 1778.

The former (Plates 68 and 69) has an arcaded service screen (a relic
from the earlier house) with central quatrefoil column capped by elegant
Prince of Wales feathers. The body of the room has a heraldic cornice of
the Blake crest, granted in 1778, in trefoil panels[49] and the fireplace is of
Gothic form with slim supporting shafts. Next door in the saloon the
Gothic consists of the cornice which has the triple feathers of Wales and a
succulent quatrefoil in a repeating pattern which is a debased and mudded
version of Adam's iridescent cornice for the banqueting-room of Alnwick
Castle in 1770. The doors are also Gothic in the manner that one expects
from the later eighteenth century with wooden mouldings of slim section
delineating across the painted surface a fine reticulated web of vertical
lines which, at the mid-point of the door, plumpen into quatrefoils before
being disciplined once more into uprights drawn together at the summit
into a thin line. Framing the doorcase is a galaxy of plaster crockets
curling upwards like sea-horses to finally merge in the profulgence of the
Decorated finial. The Fowberry doors, with the ones at Hulne Priory, are

121

the finest of their type in north Britain; but wherever they appear such doors are an example of decorative charm and of an understanding and excellence of design principles making them, even if regarded as individual units, of considerable aesthetic worth.

One other Gothic feature at Fowberry is the series of miniature gilt fan vaults over the main staircase. In no way novel for this period they also occur in various guises on such Northumberland properties as Denwick Bridge and within Alnwick Castle and Hulne Priory as details on a chimney-piece and a cornice. Now although the claim has been made for the Fowberry decorations that these are products of Robert Adam there is no substantiating evidence.[50] Obviously, from their general characteristics they are of the Adam-Alnwick school and executed by an architect and craftsman familiar with the genre. Yet the application of critical criteria reveals dissimilarities of such a nature and character as to obviate anything more than kinship even although the door surrounds in the saloons at Hulne Priory and Fowberry are closely allied in form and pattern, a factor borne out by even the most cursory examination of dates. Otherwise one is not aware of one single concept being imposed ruthlessly on the fabric, as at Hulne even, but rather of disparate elements collected together. For instance, one very pointed dissimilarity at Fowberry is the dining-room chimney-piece in which the decorative parts immediately recall Adam's examples at Alnwick, particularly those of Denwick stone. On the other hand the somewhat gaunt height of the Fowberry example is so completely at variance with the Alnwick modules that it cannot be imagined as emanating from the same design office albeit that the overall general style of the Gothic trim and the quality of the craftmanship indicate that Alnwick men were employed. As to the architect, however, if it was not Adam could it have been his site architect, Vincent Shepherd? It seems unlikely bearing in mind that 'A large proportion of his professional life was almost exclusively devoted to his Grace (of Northumberland)'[51] and that he must still have been fully engaged on the alterations at Alnwick. Therefore, as the number of architects skilled in Gothic must have been few it may well be accepted that Nisbet was responsible especially as there is no evidence, at present, of his being engaged at Ford between 1773 and 1779.[52] Also as Sir John Hussey Delaval was a first cousin of Sir Francis[53] it is likely that both landowners would employ the same architect who, in fact, seems to have been working for Sir Francis as early as 1771.[54] In addition there is the stylistic comparison of the sunken quatrefoils at Ford and at Fowberry which though slight in itself might well be cited as proof. The quatrefoils bite into the rear elevation of the latter which is rendered memorable by groups of triple lights with those on the principal floor being unusually tall, like the gateway at Ford, which may be another clue leading back to Nisbet. However, the front of the house must have been finished by another hand for it has little in the way of Gothic save for some four-centred arched windows with the remainder being the usual sashes crowned on the central bay by a tight little pediment marked 1809, which was after the property had been purchased by the noted agriculturalist, Matthew Culley.[55]

The only other Gothic interiors of this period which survive in Northumberland are two rooms in Craster Tower. Lying near the coast, the tower, which predates 1415, had, as might be expected in that part of the world, a classical mansion sewn on to it in 1769.[56] At that moment, when the state apartments at Alnwick were newly finished, the Gothic sensation burst upon the Northumbrian gentry and to a society educated in the canons of architecture and recondite with the tales and legends of a heroic past, the creation of an antique style at Alnwick marked the commencement of an elaborate game of follow-my-leader which was pursued as unashamedly at Craster as elsewhere. The interiors of the original habitation were done up in Gothic with castellation being added to the wallhead and ornamenting new ranges of outworks including an entrance screen at the summit of the hill leading up from the tiny hamlet by the sea's edge. While the external work is very similar to any other of the same era, the internal resemblance to Alnwick is striking. The first-floor drawing-room has a shallow alcove on either side of the tripartite window with each part separated by slender columns which, like the cornice, are of Gothic derivation. Although the decoration is in no way uncommon, the planning does show an unmistakeable relationship with the Alnwick drawing-room which, albeit on a lesser scale, is reproduced at Craster; in the upper room the stone chimney-piece is akin to many that were at Alnwick. The designer of these rooms remains obscure and although the arrangement of two tiers of triple lights might point to the architect of Fowberry, such an hypothesis should not be pursued too vigorously since it would not have been beyond the skill of competent craftsmen to carry out the changes on their own initiative.

In the eighteenth century the Crasters of Craster were related by marriage to the Woods of Beadnell which is seven miles further up the coast. Anne, youngest daughter of John Craster of Craster, who died in 1722, married Thomas Wood of Beadnell and their son John married his first cousin, Anne Craster in 1781. Eventually, their son, another Thomas, succeeded to the Craster property, in addition to Beadnell, in the year of Queen Victoria's accession.[57] This interfamilial relationship has an architectural bearing because Beadnell Hall, like Craster Tower, was modernised. The eighteenth century front,[58] a plainer version of that at Craster, was surrounded by broad church-warden windows with intersecting wooden glazing bars and the gables, stiff with castellation, each had a pair of quatrefoil windows. But when? On the stylistic evidence the nineteenth century should be too late. Then again as any date prior to the middle seventeen sixties is to anticipate, a reasonable interpretation of evidence might be circa 1770–90 although, bearing in mind the traditional date, 1795, for the east gate and towers at Ford, then 1796, when John Wood suceeded his father, might be acceptable and although the architectural treatment would be old-fashioned, compared with Wyatt's innovations, nevertheless it was to have a long life ahead of it in many parts of the countryside.

Although the alterations at Ford, Fowberry and Craster were carried out on medieval and post-medieval structures, one new Gothic building, Twizell Castle, was begun. Yet like so many of these northern houses, its origins were in an earlier age for, writing in 1769, Wallis, an early historian of Northumbrian remains, noted that it had been 'lately repaired, with handsome additions, chiefly in the Saxon-Gothic style'.[59] These must have been the array of shot-holes and thick crosslets below the battlements exactly as at Ford.[60] Indeed Sir John Hussey Delaval in 1771 infers Nisbet's employment by the owner of Twizell, Sir Francis Blake.[61] His son, the second Sir Francis,[62] had either a penchant for Gothic or an eye to its scenic beauties for about the close of the seventeen eighties he rebuilt in a very creditable fashion the chapel of St Cuthbert at the foot of a long slope on the bank of the River Tweed where a ferry crosses into Scotland. The chapel is now ruinous but still shows three bays of lancet windows each with a tailed hood-mould and a conventional crosslet over the pointed west doorway. Though it is supposed to have been constructed from the ruins of the original chapel[63] that may not be so. Wallis certainly records that one as being in ruins in 1769[64] but writing in 1794 another local historian, Hutchinson, having verified the chapel's existence, adds 'on the side of which about five years ago, Sir Francis Blake built a small chapel'.[65] One wonders why Sir Francis did such a thing. It may have been his responsibility as a landowner or it may have been to achieve a certain scenic effect tinged with a somewhat sentimental nostalgia. At any rate the bare ruined walls are an almost unknown relic of that small band of eighteenth century Gothic churches.

Contemporary with the chapel must be the improvements which Sir Francis was making on his father's castle.[66] Hutchinson provides some valuable evidence about these for, when he was writing in 1794, they were still incomplete although 'the gallery, when finished, will be a noble apartment'.[67] However, to what extent it was completed remains unknown for in 1807, when it was five storeys high and three hundred feet long, it was dismembered by Sir Francis who used the stone to build for himself the battlemented mansion of Tilmouth Park. The core of his father's castle was left.[68] Overlooking the River Till and the celebrated Twizell Bridge and to the north turned towards Scotland and the Lowland hills, Twizell Castle has become a monumental ruin covered with ivy and thickset by elderberry interspersed with clumps of red campion growing around the base of the fallen and shattered walls. Of the eighteenth century little remains. On a side elevation there is the inevitable quatrefoil but of raised outline as at Ford. For the rest the walls are plain although they were intended to bristle with all manner of warlike devices which for all their ferocity becomes rococo abstractions. The house was an expansion of Nisbet's mansion and the sashes gave way to Gothic fenestration identical to that on Ford's towers.[69] The plan, loosely of the Inveraray type, was a rectangle with, at each corner, an attached circular tower diminishing in each stage. The impression of strength was further generated by the massive thickness of the walls, the high, shallow arched windows and internally by the stone vaulting, a precaution against fire.[70] It may be that medieval walling was incorporated in the structure for the best of the surviving towers is of rubble without the flat finish of smoothly dressed ashlar one expects. Also the sloping intakes at each stage enjoy a character not to be found anywhere else in the north at this date.

Of the medieval castle one tower is traditionally stated to have been removed to Ewart Park, an estate purchased in 1775 by Colonel Horace St Paul from his brother Robert although it was not until twelve years later that the new owner began building operations. He was at that time living at Tillmouth House, of which he had taken a lease, in order to be able to superintend the reconstruction of Ewart Park. Tillmouth is less than a mile from Twizell where, in the company of Sir Francis Blake, Colonel St Paul, watching the demolition of what must have been at least a part of the old castle, expressed regret at the action and desiring one of the corner towers, it was promptly offered to him by Sir Francis.[71] Although for long thought to be apocryphal the tale may be true for there is a tower at Ewart (Plate 70) which, while possessing many surface traits of the eighteenth century, corresponds to one that was at Twizell prior to its enlargement.[72] For the rest Ewart Park has an undeniable charm like a piece of stage scenery and indeed it is scarcely more substantial being concocted of brick and cement. As one of the acknowledged characteristics of Gothic was height the device was resorted to in this instance of

Plate 70　Ewart Park, Northumberland. 1787.　Plate 71　James Paine. The dower-house. Axwell Park, County Durham. c. 1770.

having, to the east of the tower, an upper range of false windows which, while permitting the introduction of a castellated parapet, also hid the pitch of the roof.

By comparison with Ford, Ewart possesses very little Gothic. Of course as a vogue it was irresistible to many landowners who could not be content unless, at the very least, a Gothic bay window was thrown out, as happened at Morwick Hall,[73] while other houses might have somewhat more in the way of external titillation as at Rudchester Hall where all the windows have shallow arches[74] whereas at neighbouring Eachwick Hall the square angle towers are crowned by unwarlike battlements.[75] Thus in Northumberland there is a sliding scale of Gothic descending from the princely vastness and rococo magnificence of Alnwick to the outworks of Ford and down, finally, to Roddam Hall[76] and the nearby stables, possibly the only known work, beyond Alnwick, of Vincent Shepherd.[77] At Roddam's stables the quatrefoil windows and the arrow slits are the dual emblems of romantic Gothicism as portrayed in architectural form which was utilised to add a touch of high fashion to the Northumbrian halls so distant alike in geography and architectural awareness from the London elegancies of Adam's fancies yet owning, nevertheless, lineal descent from them.

In County Durham the story is much the same although that county has the distinction, unusual for northern England, of being able to claim several completely new buildings. Naturally much of the seminal source came from the Gothic activities of the prince-bishops at their castles of Durham and Auckland thus making the programme of Gothic works very similar to that in Northumberland. At the now demolished Blackwell Hall, near Darlington, the fashionable bow windows were castellated[78] doubtless in response to the new aesthetic theories which were to be more fully exploited at Axwell Park dower-house (Plate 71). James Paine designed the mansion[79] a rather glum edifice set on a hillside. At the foot of its southern descent a serpentine lake was constructed, its north bank irregularly planted with trees and bushes while from the southern one a large meadow ran to the boundary wall. In a peaceful setting of water and trees the dower-house, at the eastern extremity of the lake,[80] is arboured by mature trees, its beauty enhanced by unpretentious proportions and overall restraint in design even to the pierced battlements lightening the solid workmanship of the body. As at Blackwell Hall, there are ground floor castellated bay windows while outbuildings are screened by walls and more castellation. The dower-house probably dates from about 1770–80 making it an approximate contemporary of Hamsterley Hall, which besides modern incorporations of seventeenth century fragments, has crenellations, ogee-headed windows and a Gothic dining-room and drawing-room.[81]

These decorous houses reveal the best eighteenth century qualities and must have been once inhabited by Jane Austen characters who would have deplored anything outrageous whether in size, form or decoration. They would be the homes of the gentry of the lesser sort unlike Castle Eden in the same county. It is the sole, large scale new work up to the turn of the century in all the north of England which, in that respect, is so different from Scotland where, as has been observed previously, the houses from the start of the Gothic Revival were not adaptations of medieval structures. In northern England, on the other hand, such conglomerate edifices as Alnwick and Raby Castles and numerous others, despite the knocks of time, were of sufficient size and durability to be brought into full use and modernised as domestic habitations.

Castle Eden is uncommon. The architect was William Newton[82] of Newcastle, of whom a contemporary wrote 'He is very able in his business'.[83] Yet Newton is an all too little known architect although his paraphrase of Adam's work in the Newcastle Assembly Rooms of 1776 would have done credit to Adam himself. After 1758 the owner of the Castle Eden lands was Rowland Burdon who instituted a series of agricultural improvements and manufacturing enterprises on the estate.[84] An undertaking of another kind was the erection of a church in 1764[85] and of the castle possibly by 1780, when the young John Soane was a visitor to Castle Eden,[86] but certainly before Rowland Burdon's death in 1786.[87] The latter structure is unusual for its period in having depressed-pointed windows; there are hood-moulds and of course battlemented wall-heads. Though now partially concealed by a coarsely detailed

127

conservatory,[88] the canted centre and the overall plainness and severity of outline of the house recall Auckland Castle although it is neither so suave nor so accomplished as parts of the latter and is completely lacking, despite its size, in the architectural excitement of medieval Gothic. That is provided in the south of the county at Raby Castle where, in the carriage hall (Plate 72), not only is there excitement but also the melodrama in which the later eighteenth century revelled but which was so seldom fulfilled when translated into solid substance.

Some sense of that impact is yielded up in the following account of a visit to the castle. 'As we passed through the outer gateway of the Castle, the vapour was dense upon the moat, and we were enveloped in night-fog, while the rolling of the carriage wheels, and the trampling of the horses' hoofs sounded dolefully over the draw-bridge; we might have fancied ourselves victims to the darkest times of Gallic despotism, condemn'd by a *lettre de cachet* to linger out our lives in the deepest dungeons of the Bastille; but lo! on the opening of a massive door, a gleam of light flash'd upon us; crack went the whips ——— we dashed forward at full trot ———, and, in a moment drew up, ——— not to a plazza, nor a vestibule ——— but before a huge blazing fire in a spacious hall.'[89]

While the carriage proceeded through another set of doors into the courtyard, and from there out of the castle, the visitor processed between a double file of columns to a shallow flight of steps leading up to the

Plate 72   John Carr. The carriage hall. Raby Castle, County Durham. 1783.

state apartments along the south front. The columns have stone bases and capitals of simple profile from which ribs support quadripartite vaulting.[90] By the sombre tones, the scagliola columns and the high, tensile vaulting, the carriage hall might be a town hall loggia or the undercroft of a university of the eighteen sixties or seventies but that the plaster vault and the spare rib sections prove otherwise. The architectural purity must surely derive from the medieval castle although it is unusual to discover an architect remaining faithful to such a source. Yet when the architect, John Carr, was altering Clifford's Tower at the castle in 1768 he utilised designs from other parts of the medieval castle[91] and two years later he ordered that corbels and parapets in the 'Small North West Tower' were to be removed pending the heightening of the wall after which they were to be replaced.[92]

The carriage hall was only a portion of the general refurbishing of the castle and its environs executed on the instructions of the second Earl of Darlington (1726–92) who succeeded to the title in 1758. He commanded the Gothic dog-kennels, folly farm[93] and lodges as well as the titivation of the castle's external fabric.[94] Internally, a variety of tastes would be employed in time with the oval dining-room being ordered in the Chinese style by the second Earl's successor for a visit of the Prince Regent[95] and later on Billings castigated the circular drawing-room 'as a wretched attempt at modern Gothic'.[96]

The construction and original planning of these apartments along the west and south fronts, completed about 1790,[97] was carried out by Daniel Garrett, James Paine and John Carr successively. At Raby Paine was responsible, before 1758, for major repairs and alterations to the structure, especially along the west side. There Garrett's state rooms were linked by the curving lines of his Hunter's Corridor with its flattened ogee arches and its coves pierced by miniature vaults rising from behind corbelled heads.[98] Although a design, in an elaborate Gothic mode reminiscent of the Alnwick interiors, was prepared for what later on became the carriage hall, it was never executed.[99] Later, when Arthur Young visited the castle in 1770, he noted that the Barons' Hall above was to be extended by thirty feet by building a circular tower, on the south front, in the same style as the rest of the building.[100] However, nothing happened until the seventeen eighties when the floor of the Barons' Hall was raised ten feet[101] to give the increased height in the carriage hall below[102] but of the proposed new tower only the ground floor, with three huge 'Strawberry-Gothic' windows,[103] was reared (Plate 73). Although the decision to build the tower and extend the Barons' Hall into it may not have been finally abandoned,[104] nevertheless it was left to the Victorians to complete the task and in so doing to replace a fire destroyed medieval feature.[105]

At Raby a sequence of formal reception rooms, frequently with apsidal ends or recesses, was contrived within the medieval walls. Indeed, so conformable to eighteenth century living were the interiors that 'when we step and find ourselves at once in modern drawing-rooms with silken

Plate 73   South front. Raby Castle, County Durham. 1792.

couches and gilt cornices, the Nevilles and their times vanish'.[106] For a later generation reared on the strong brew of Gothic such concessions to modernity were reprehensible. Still, if the interior disappointed, the exterior was rich in romantic association. 'The indescribable forms of gates, towers, walls and buttresses, that, at each adventurous step, meet the exploring eye, well reconcile our minds to give a willing belief to all the stories of warlike knights, of beauteous dames, of gallant tournaments, of noble feasts, of trophied halls and painted bowers, that fill the pages of our books of chivalry.'[107] It was a vision to which William Burn attempted to hold fast when he reshaped the Barons' Hall where once seven hundred Neville knights had assembled.

Much has disappeared at Raby and so, too, at Witton Castle which, like the former, displays an irregular profile and plan of circa 1400. By 1781 the house was in ruins;[108] sometime over the next fifteen years it was restored only to be gutted by a fire in 1796 which left the outer walls a shell.[109] Subsequently, the house was rebuilt[110] but, to judge by the internal fittings, was greatly altered in the nineteenth century. From the previous one there seems to survive much of the curtain wall where the

130

medieval character is so convincing that it must be a reconstruction and is, therefore, another early example of the desire to retain genuine medieval characteristics with a similar case history being repeated four miles to the west at Hoppyland Hall which was restored, after a fire in 1793, reputedly in imitation of Witton.[111] Certainly, its distant silhouette of two differing towers of narrow ascent with deeply cut and narrowly spaced embrasures has an authoritative air only dispelled on closer inspection by the contemporary trappings of sash windows and a maltese cross. Yet its ivy-mantled walls, bandaging the broken body, and a forlorn air have made Hoppyland such a conceit as Hagley Castle was wont to be only to-day, the world having become so sophisticated, no parties of picnickers and dilettanti come to be overawed by the crumbling remains.

Within Witton Castle are numerous bits and pieces of eighteenth century work. However, the sole complete interior is the first floor ballroom in which there hangs Reynolds' portrait of the beautiful child, Master Lambton. Judging by the thickness of the walls, the room was built within the medieval structure. The deep window embrasures have Gothic panelling with broad quatrefoils and tracery stretching across the vault; the doors are likewise treated. The apartment is three bays long with the ceiling divided by sexpartite plaster ribs which, rising from corbels, converge on the ridge-rib where the bosses of delicate leaves are clustered like rich fruits. The vault is shallow and though not an uncommon feature for both classical and Gothic settings, yet, when considered as a stylistic innovation with such parts as corbels, bosses and a ridge-rib, means a startling departure from Alnwick Castle where the ceilings were flat. Indeed so marked is the change and so unexpected the development of the Gothic mode within a span of two decades that some local derivative source should be sought especially as nothing is known of the architect. As Alnwick was the catalyst in Northumberland, so in County Durham it was the castle of the prince-bishops at Auckland where the transformation wrought by James Wyatt in 1795 would be immediately prior to the fitting up of Witton. Auckland Castle and James Wyatt, therefore, must mark a new and highly significant trend in the evolution of the Gothic mode.

131

VIII

James Wyatt

Few modern critics would wholly admire James Wyatt. Surprisingly, one of the fairest estimates of his worth was that delivered a hundred years ago by Eastlake. 'No English architect has been so overrated by his friends, or so unfairly abused by his enemies as James Wyatt.'[1] Certainly, his supporters were loud in their praises and none more so than Horace Walpole who, on the opening of the Oxford Street Pantheon in 1772, rated it as the most beautiful building in England and who was still sufficiently enthusiastic thirteen years later to claim the Gothic of Lee Priory in Kent as the 'true child of Strawberry'.[2]

After 1772 Wyatt was the most sought after architect in England, one who built up a practice which extended across the length and breadth of the country. Now while it would be foolish to assess an architect's competence or otherwise by the volume of his works, nevertheless, the confidence reposed in Wyatt by King George III, as well as by aristocratic grandees and merchant princes alike, would be surprising unless one accepts the competency of the man to realise their schemes. Beckford, for instance, foolish, intractable and unstable man that he so often was, nevertheless had an artistic percipience and sensibility which enabled him to choose the one architect in all England who could materialise the almost schizophrenic world of the artist *manqué* at Fonthill Gifford. Although he might rail about Wyatt's shortcomings to Farington,[3] he could not dispense with the man's services. Nor could many others.

So far as posterity is able to judge, Wyatt was his own worst enemy and accusations of dilatoriness, tardiness and even laziness (*vide* the famous Windham letter)[4] would doubtless be exaggerated by the inordinate size and scattered nature of his practice.[5] Even so the pettifogging mistrust and the intemperate criticism usually to be met with[6] is surprising when one considers that Wyatt's place in architectural history is between the supremacy of Adam, in the decade before the opening of the Pantheon, and the ascendancy of Soane, Nash and Smirke in the opening decades of the next century. Should one then regard the years of Wyatt's dominance as a vacuum from which important architectural innovations are absent and see the man himself as a lesser Adam content to imitate but without the ability, the originality to emulate the master? Sufficiently competent in the details to produce work indistinguishable from Adam's, he undoubtedly suffered from the standing of the Scotsman, a fact of which he himself was aware when he admitted to George III that 'there had been no regular architecture since Sir William Chambers—that when he came from Italy he found the public taste corrupted by the Adams, and he was obliged to comply with it'.[7] Inevitably, Wyatt has been beaten with the stick which he himself had cut, with one commentator mocking him for 'a lack of conscience'.[8] As a point of view not only is that unfair but it displays a lack of sympathy for an unknown and untested architect who had to make his way in the world when confronted by the zeal with which the *haut monde* had taken up Adam's niceties. These Horace Walpole dubbed as 'harlequinades' and 'gingerbread and snippets of embroidery', remarks usually regarded as waspish, if not downright malicious. Yet might it not be that Walpole's redoubtable wit had hit upon a truth which not many of Adam's admirers would care to recognise? While on occasion Adam could be as Roman and monumental (as on the front of Edinburgh's University) as Sir William Chambers, there is ample evidence in certain interiors of that fussiness which Walpole came to deride. Thus splendid though the parlour at Derby House undoubtedly was, the decorative diaper was so expansive as almost to obliterate the volumetric form of the apartment by abstracting proportions and shapes. There are other instances, too, where Adam is little better than the dancing-master of architecture.

Possibly similar complaints could be levelled against Wyatt if it were not that his Adamesque schemes have a greater restraint. The overlay is never so fulsome as to threaten the rule of form. Indeed, it was Wyatt who saved classical architecture by hacking out and pruning back much of the detail to leave a plainer but more direct and stronger classicism, as at Heveningham Hall, which in time would be further refined by his successors.

A considerable portion of Wyatt's practice was devoted to Gothic both in restoration and in new work and of his country houses a quarter were in that style. Kenneth Clark says that he loved Gothic[9] and *The Gentleman's Magazine* in its obituary notice claimed it as 'his favourite

Order'.[10] However, in his monograph on Wyatt, Antony Dale comments that 'He undoubtedly admired Gothic architecture but seems to have had a regular and classical mind, which fitted ill with the irregularities of Gothic'.[11] It is an odd remark especially when applied to Wyatt whose embryonic Gothic essays of circa 1780 at Sheffield Place, Sussex, and Sandleford Priory in Berkshire, display excursions into irregular composition at a time when other exponents of the medium, including Adam, lacked the moral courage to throw symmetry to the winds; and Wyatt's concern went beyond mobility of planning for at Lee Priory the octagon, containing the library and holding aloft the towered spire, indicated an awareness of technique marking a startling deviation from the Gothic norm. Thus before the cult of the picturesque, Wyatt was utilising Gothic as the means to compose in freer form. Gothic was a cause and not the effect of an architectural revolution which Wyatt perpetrated.

Yet Wyatt's reputation as a Gothic architect is, if anything, lower than that of the classicist[12] and words like facile and unprincipled are not uncommon. There are, of course, many reasons for this, including the contemporary antipathy aroused by the cathedral restorations and since inflamed by the comments of critics, who should know better, but especially by Pugin whose declamations, intervening between our time and Wyatt's obscure our vision of the man and his works. That has been unfortunate for Wyatt's reputation since all too often Pugin's denunciations have been accepted at face value although like the sixteenth and seventeenth century religious tractarians, Pugin was so blinded by his own virtues that his criticism becomes unbearable in its intensity and violence of language. In one sentence Wyatt is 'this monster of architectural depravity ———— this pest of cathedral architecture'.[13] Sound indeed would be the reputation to survive such an onslaught. But can one truly relate such terms to one who, when money and time were available, sensitively restored, as all critics agree, the chapel of Henry VII at Westminster Abbey? If Wyatt's efforts as a cathedral restorer only merit the title of Destroyer and the pathological enmity of Carter in *The Gentleman's Magazine*, one would wonder why patrons ever commissioned Gothic work from Wyatt. Although Carter's vituperative outpourings blocked Wyatt's election in 1796 to the Society of Antiquaries, come another year and Wyatt was elected by a huge majority.[14]

True, at the cathedrals of Salisbury and Durham especially the record of alterations seems drastic enough but was no less so than that of many another restoration either in this century or the last and in the long view of history Wyatt carried out essential work. At Durham, where his activities are most questionable, he was preceded by one Nicholson who, having built the Prebends' Bridge, in order to create work for himself, persuaded the Dean and Chapter to allow some two or three inches to be chiselled from the cathedral walls[15] and under that rude assault many fine carvings were apparently lost with the replacements, especially in the north transept spandrels, being poor substitutes.[16]

It was at Salisbury that Wyatt must have primarily realised the grand architectural effects which could be achieved by the creation of long, untold vistas. At Salisbury with its homogeneity of style, Wyatt revealed himself as the disciple of Burke by opening up the choir to the east wall, by the regular disposition of tombs in the nave arcades and even, too, in the demolition of the Hungerford and Beauchamp chantries, which, being out of period with the main fabric, would have detracted from 'succession and uniformity'. The argument that they were structurally unsound,[17] if more prosaic, was probably true. Certainly, Wyatt cannot be singled out for attempting to tidy up the muddle of the Gothic centuries. It is a task others after Wyatt have attempted and with as little and often less success.

Having completed his Wiltshire alterations the architect was invited to Durham by Bishop Shute Barrington, who was translated from Salisbury to the Palatinate by George III in 1791.[18] At Durham, Wyatt's most notorious work was the destruction of the Norman chapterhouse, the finest in England. A meeting of the chapter was convened on 20 November 1795 when 'it was ordered that the old chapter-house, being pronounced by Mr. Wyatt on his survey thereof to be in a ruinous state, be taken down by Mr. Morpeth under contract'. Morpeth put this into effect by suspending a workman over the vault and he, knocking out the keystones, the roof collapsed onto the gravestones below.[19] A pursuant attempt to have the Galilee demolished, to permit a carriage-way from the castle to arrive at the cathedral's original west door, was balked by the intervention of Carter whose denunciation so alarmed the Dean that the order was rescinded although not before the lead was off the roof.[20] While to-day one would consider the loss of the Galilee unthinkable, to Wyatt's generation there was no merit at all in a Norman product. What would be impressive about Durham was its size and bulk, the qualities which for James Wyatt made St Peter's memorable.[21] More than any other cathedral in England, Durham realised the full potential of Burke's sublime which Wyatt obviously came near to fulfilling at Salisbury and which he aimed to repeat (if Carter was correct) at Durham by throwing the choir across the Chapel of the Nine

Altars and demolishing the pierced ecstasy of the Neville Screen which, with Bishop Hatfield's throne, was to become an organ case and loft.[22] If Salisbury already possessed great height, then Wyatt intended to add to Durham's by crowning the central tower with a tall spire[23] so that the cathedral, poised aloft the straggling cliff and river, would the more fulfill Burke's dicta that the sublime was more perfect if regarded not so much as height but as depth.

Despite the public storms, which raged around his architect, Bishop Barrington, although apparently treated somewhat cavalierly,[24] did not lose faith in Wyatt who in 1795 began a series of works at Auckland Castle which are the sole remaining interiors of his mature Gothic. As has been noticed elsewhere, Barrington was not the first of the prince-bishops to evince a preference for Gothic for of his four predecessors, three contributed something in the idiom either to their palace or to Durham Castle.

At the latter in 1752 Bishop Butler had restored a great part of the north wall while on the south wall (Plate 8) a range of Gothic windows was inserted[25] obliterating the outward plasticity of Bishop du Puiset's Norman gallery. The eighteenth century windows have the glazing patterns one expects of their type and is each surmounted by an ogee hood-mould terminating in a finial flared at the summit like a grenadier's badge. These Decorated motifs were popular at that date and are also found as far north as Inveraray Castle.

When Bishop Butler died the south refacing was unfinished for the lead rainwater-head, dated 1753, bears the monogram of the succeeding bishop, Richard Trevor, who fitted up what is now the Senior Common Room where the high pointed windows have shutters resplendent with gilt carving which, embodying foliage and flowers within Gothic forms, is wholly rococo in spirit and must give some indications of the scintillations of Gibside's banqueting-hall. Other recorded work was of a minor nature and included chimney-pieces,[26] probably very much in the Strawberry manner as the designer was Sanderson Miller.[27] Although Miller did not visit Durham, Bishop Butler seems to have left the ordering of the alterations in his hands entirely only requesting, as 'our Peiple at Durham do not much understand the kind of Antique Work', that Miller should send him a 'Workman of Skill'.[28] It is an interesting sidelight, showing how dead Gothic practice was in the seventeen fifties, and is a southern echo of William Adam's request to Roger Morris in 1747. Miller, too, should probably be credited with the conduit house of 1751[29] in the College which, though modest enough, has considerable interest not least because of the corbelling below the parapet and the over-arched double lights with trefoil cusping. Nothing as authentic in its parts was to appear for the next forty years, especially as the capitals bear vertical groovings similar to those on the north porch of the cathedral. It is the first instance, in this period, of quarrying from that source and would indicate a rather free approach to his task by some 'Workman of Skill'.

Although the episcopate of Bishop Trevor lasted for almost twenty years until 1771, he contented himself at Durham with completing his predecessor's commitments whereas at Auckland Castle, to the south, he introduced several new edifices including the Deer House, described in an earlier chapter, in 1760. In the same year[30] was begun the gate-house (Plate 74) at the town entrance to the castle. For his architect, the bishop's first thoughts may have been on Richard Bentley, Walpole's ghost at Strawberry Hill, since in a volume of the latter's drawings of 1751–61, one is annotated, 'Gateway designed for Dr. Trevor, Bishop of Durham'.[31] By and large, however, weight of opinion has credited Sir Thomas Robinson of Rokeby with the design,[32] a supposition recently confirmed by the discovery of an elevation[33] subscribed, 'Sir Thos. Architect' and bearing in the opposite and bottom right hand corner the name, 'Willm. Atkinson', who was, presumably the author of the drawing and perhaps site architect. Undated, the drawing is marked, 'The Gateway at Auckland Castle Built for Lord Trevor', which implies that its origin was after the gateway's erection making it possibly a copy of the draft, mentioned in a list of Bishop Trevor's works and transcribed in the mid-nineteenth century from papers, now lost, in the Auditor's office at Durham, as 'A gateway and tower for the clock, according to a design drawn'.[34] The design is very typical of the period and could have been modelled on any one of hundreds of ceremonial gateways erected across the countryside of Britain. Its inspiration is obviously

Plate 74   Sir Thomas Robinson. Gate-house. Auckland Castle, County Durham. 1760.

Plate 75   Auckland Castle, County Durham. An engraving by S. and N. Buck. 1728.

classical and Gothic is still an applied decoration, without any integration with the structure, which, although large and bulky and unyieldingly symmetrical, lacks monumentality, a failing, however, which would not be so marked if space circulated around the building rather than the encompassing huddle of disparate buildings. Regarded as decoration the gateway is a success for the conventional machinery of Gothic is used sparingly but to effect and achieves a two dimensional modelling. One interesting feature is the spandrel infilling about which it would be hazardous and, indeed, possibly foolish to guess at a source. As an abstract it has the likeness of the head and wings of one of the cherubim with which medieval carvers and masons loved to decorate the undersides of canopies and mouldings. It is an unusual piece of design for its time and interestingly enough, was repeated around Wyatt's Durham Cathedral rose window[35] which might presuppose either that Wyatt liked the whimsy or that his builder was a local man, such as Atkinson may have been.

Prior to these subordinate works, the bishop was concerned with the fabric of his palace, at least according to a letter of 1754 from one Ralph Hodgson, who seems to have been the responsible architect, to the bishop's steward at Durham. Hodgson is sending drawings of some of the dining-room features together with one for a new drawing-room window which, he proposes, should not have 'Four Lights and as many Sashes, and therefore proposed to Bell to have the 2 small Munnions taken and the tops of the Windows closed, as the dotted line in one of them shews'.[36] The accompanying drawings have disappeared but it can be assumed that the window in question is the large four-sided bay midway on the east range but in 1754 near the southern extremity of the palace

138

as depicted in Buck's view of 1728 (Plate 75). To-day, however, the side bays are blocked up and so Ralph Hodgson had his way although the tracery in the two forward lights is of a type not found until nearer the close of the century when it would date from Wyatt's remodelling of the adjacent Great Room.

Plate 76   Auckland Castle, County Durham. John Carr's wing is on the left, James Wyatt's Great Room is in the centre and Cosin's chapel is on the extreme right.

Towards the south, simple intersecting window tracery and his episcopal arms indicate the large extension also commissioned during Bishop Trevor's time[37] for although the palace had several notable reception rooms it lacked that sufficiency of smaller apartments which the mid-century's demands for increased individual privacy required. The architectural style of the extension is simple (Plate 76) and without any decoration other than battlements and boldly modelled hood-moulds and string-course. Such features, together with the central projection of the south elevation, would betoken the typical Gothic villa of any Georgian gentleman of property if it were not for some rather curious and interesting facts.

In the early summer of 1967 there was discovered in the palace a portfolio of drawings the existence of which had hitherto been unsuspected. They included not only the Robinson elevation and a small ground plan of the gateway but numerous other drawings among which was one, initialled J.C., relating to the picture gallery, and another inscribed on the back: 'Plan of a new Drawing-room given to Bishop Trevor by Mr. Carr of York'.[38] This is for a room of sixty feet by thirty, with five windows of which the middle three protrude as a semicircular bay and it was to be built to the north of the Great Room and the chapel. However, the intention never became effective since Bishop Trevor died in 1771. He was succeeded by one of Sanderson Miller's early patrons, Bishop Egerton,[39] whom Pennant, in 1772, states furnished the southern suite of apartments.[40]

Nevertheless, the existence of the drawings must surely indicate that it was Carr who was responsible for the basis of the southern extensions. In support of such an hypothesis it is inconceivable that the prince-bishop would entrust a major extension of his country seat to a local builder. He would require an architect and although in the seventeen sixties William Newton of Newcastle was in practice someone of more than local repute would be preferred and especially someone recognised as rich in the experience of providing suitable residences for the aristocracy. In his day, Carr, the best known architect in the north of England, had just such a clientele and if his stylistic repertoire could be considered somewhat old-fashioned, that may have been no blemish in the eyes of one who was spiritual heir to Cosin. Carr's fame rests on his Yorkshire work but he did draw up a scheme for at least one Northumbrian mansion[41] and like most architects of his day he dabbled in Gothic. At the Soane Museum a bound set of drawings, copied from Batty Langley's work on Gothic architecture, has Carr's signature on the frontispiece. His proven Gothic building includes a portion of Sheffield Church, now the Cathedral,[42] as well as at least two houses[43] and the work at Raby Castle to the south of Bishop Auckland. He also worked on Workington Hall in Cumberland, a medieval and Tudor mansion which was much improved after 1782[44] and given Gothic lights.

Such postulations apart, style would also indicate Carr's authorship. The canted bay recurs again and again in his dwellings. Yet translated somewhat loosely into Gothic there is none of the exoticism of Robinson's gateway, Nisbet's wild elongation or Adam's assured manipulation but rather ponderous uncertainty and a top-heaviness increased by the lack of a third storey which the proportions would normally lead one to expect. The south elevation has the gauche air of the amateur on stage. The same lack of effect is also found at Castle Ripley in Yorkshire, a house attributed to Carr,[45] where the battlements are well developed with the pitched caps of embrasures and merlons linked by a continuous roll moulding. Within this study such a feature is only discoverable at Auckland Castle in the eighteenth century and it must, inevitably, be linked to Carr's name, which must likewise unravel what, for any architectural historian, is the most puzzling feature of the palace, namely the eighteenth century ceilings, especially the dining-room one. These ceilings, heavily symbolic and deeply modelled, cannot possibly belong to the seventeen sixties, and there is no evidence for an earlier dating, unless it is accepted that Carr was the designer when they are seen as

140

typical of his true inclination as a disciple of that school which had dominated the English architectural scene for forty years before.

The final embellishments to the castle were provided by Bishop Barrington using the offices of James Wyatt in 1795. Four years before the same architect had reconstructed the entrance to the courtyard of Durham Castle[46] by reshaping and refacing with freestone much of the existing Norman and medieval masonry, thereby creating a more ordered gateway (Plate 77) and one, which, completely symmetrical, can be compared with the gateway at Auckland Castle. Both are based on the familiar three part

Plate 77 James Wyatt. Gateway. Durham Castle. 1791.

system of a high central portion enclosing the entrance arch and supported on either side by a subsidiary wing. Yet Wyatt's work immediately reveals the advance made in the thirty years since Robinson's time. True the familiar delineations of crosslet and quatrefoil are there but then they were considered as necessary to Gothic as anthemion and palmette to the classical system. What distinguishes Wyatt's authorship is the introduction of verticality. Above the gateway the compact lodging is corsetted by unyielding turrets which, ending in tough looking battlements, have a more convincing air than any work yet seen. Certainly the misapplied label over a wooden rose window, a motif hitherto not seen, is a minor oddity above the trio of narrow windows for they, with deeply splayed reveals and acutely pointed hood-moulds are the nearest thing

141

yet, with the singular exception of the conduit house of 1751, to Gothic lights. With Wyatt in 1791 the Gothic begins to be flexed until at Auckland Castle four years later it is seen for the first time neither as pattern making nor as a decorative matrix but as architectural organisation.

At some date prior to the arrival in the north of both Bishop Barrington and James Wyatt, the former's predecessor in office, Bishop Egerton, by removing the enclosing courtyard walls at Auckland Castle, opened up vistas to the surrounding parkland.[47] However, although house and park were joined by sweeping lawns into one aesthetic and scenic creation, the approach from the town must have been very dull indeed and quite lacking in those dramatic shocks which the later eighteenth century expected from its ancient mansions. It was to create drama and possibly to partially conceal the house, soon to become *de rigueur* in aesthetic concepts but in this instance possibly to gain privacy, that Wyatt constructed the open screen of shallow arches, their lassitude stiffened by an array of buttresses. Unfortunately, Wyatt has overplayed his hand for the buttresses, instead of holding back the thrust of roof and wall as in a cloister, stand stiffly like members deprived of office. To emphasise the approach to the episcopal seat there are three huge arches joined to the bipartisan screen by uncomfortably large octangular buttresses ending over the serrated parapets as corbelled turrets. Such details apart, and although the use is misapplied so that once again there is no solidity but only space behind space, the arches cause a flicker of remembrance of some cathedral crossing to pass through the beholder but when that has gone the final impression is of sheer size, of a scale in the use of Gothic hitherto unknown. Here, at Auckland Castle is the seed of such huge florescences as Fonthill Abbey as well as Eastnor, Lowther and many another lordly excitation.

The date for the screen[48] remains unsubstantiated and so too did Wyatt's interior renovations until his drawings came to light. There are twenty-eight of these working drawings and while they relate chiefly to the staircase others refer to the reception rooms and to the chapel. For the staircase twenty survive of which thirteen are part of a numbered sequence, numbers 56 to 71 inclusive, most of which is lost. Another ten drawings relate to the anteroom, drawing-room and chapel. Out of the total fourteen bear Wyatt's name in the bottom lefthand corner, the year 1795 and in every instance, save one, the month, October. Of the remaining signed drawings none bear any indication as to year or month although as they refer to window designs they are obviously part of the same set. It is this last group which presents difficulties of interpretation for three are signed Atkinson Junr and three are signed William Atkinson, the same who signed the elevation of the town gateway. William's drawings are client's copies of window designs where each head is filled with blue and white glass as thematic variations on a fourth drawing, unsigned, which is based on an original window pattern of Cosin's time. It may be that the bishop was to select from one of these specimens although in the event, none of these designs was used, or, at any rate, so it would now seem. Atkinson Junr's drawings are in a similar vein, being a staircase window (once again of the Cosin period to judge by the cusping and blue colouring) and a more up to date version of a quartet of narrow lights with thin glazing bars. His last drawing was a suggestion for treating the window bays in the Great Room or drawing-room.

Clearly then, there were two Atkinsons, father and son, with the latter being that William Atkinson who became, supposedly through the persuasion of the bishop, a pupil of Wyatt's[49] and in time a well-known architect whose role in the Gothic Revival was of more than passing significance. Equally clearly, if he did begin life as a carpenter[50] then he was not without some architectural background since his father was probably clerk of works and site architect also. However, a third Atkinson—John—was a carpenter putting up the Gothic staircase and all the other woodwork, except the anteroom and drawing-room doors, which were sent up from London.[51]

Bishop Barrington desired to modernise the northern portion of the castle which had been left untouched by Bishop Trevor. Thus a new pastry room was provided along with many other improvements in the service quarters to which a secondary staircase gave access instead of, as formerly, through the Great Room[52] now dedicated solely to ceremonial usage. Certainly, Wyatt's skill in conjuring up such practical domestic arrangements bears out the contention by Porden, a former pupil, that his erstwhile master had 'great address in inventing and much resource in contriving alterations'.[53]

The main castle entrance, between the Great Room and the chapel, was now through a Wyatt porch[54] and from thence into the Gentlemen's Hall or Vestibule where the plaster ceiling has a band of recessed quatre-foils along the sides and down the centre. The double return staircase was not only Wyatt's favourite type but was well suited to the ceremonial functions when the Bishop as Palatine Earl held court. Mahogany was used for the slim quatrefoil balusters[55] and on the half stage the window is that drawn out by the young William Atkinson, a single sharply headed lancet of four lights with wooden intersecting tracery. From the top landing double doors lead to the anteroom and the Great Room, both of which are enfilade.

The appearance of the original Great Room is not known. That a total reconstruction took place is, however, clear from Wyatt's written instructions ordering that 'The Beams for the Great Room roof must be of Riga timber, the Principals and Spars of Memmel Timber. The whole quantity of Timber about 700 feet and there must be 20 Ton of the best Westmorland Slate',[56] which allowed the former lead roof to be melted down for gutters and other fittings.[57] In addition, although the area was seventy-six feet long by thirty-three wide, sixteen feet was partitioned off by a brick wall to form the anteroom.[58] As its cross axis is longer than the principal one (also a favourite Adam device) this creates an effective pause in the architectural progression to the episcopal presence. In any case, it is doubtful, considering the original proportions of the Great Room, if Wyatt could have handled them effectively. At any rate, the anteroom is Wyatt's first surprise. So far his Gothic has been mildly conventional and indeed almost cursory with no hint of the new techniques which from this time on made Gothic not merely a decorative trifle or a knot of fancy ribbons but an architectural concept rivalling the Roman school.

In plan the room is an irregular octagon with a square central area marked off by pairs of columns from the canted ends which contain exedrae with crocketted canopies above although these are almost flush with the wall. Narrow shafts emphasise the window gaining for it an importance equal to the tall pointed door-cases over which there are flat labels with the intervening spandrels filled with matt foliage which, though of no specific character, half a century later would unfold so luxuriantly before the radiance of Pugin's genius. The ceiling is a sexpartite vault (of plaster) with a ridge rib so that the entire room corresponds exactly to the extant sections and vault plan.[59]

Within the Great Room (Plate 78) the architectural motifs are similar and although the visual weakness of the non-structural vault is immediately apparent the proportions are saved from bleakness by the plasterwork canopies at either end with that on the south wall parclosing the bishop's chair. Inevitably, this reception room must be compared with the Alnwick interiors when it is realised that whereas Adam was not intent on faithfully reproducing medieval details, Wyatt was and in so doing became the first great architect to take Gothic seriously. He had studied and worked on cathedrals so that the interior of the Great Room is geometrically expressed by three bays with sexpartite vaulting and small bud-like bosses where ribs, rising from wall shafts, meet the ridge-line while to conceal the conflict between the maladroit length and the sum of the bays, at the north end double columns are used, a device

144

repeated at Witton Castle in the ballroom and even as late as the second decade of the next century at Duns Castle in Berwickshire by James Gillespie Graham. Clearly however, there is in 1795 an awareness of Gothic parts although little of the structural system since hood-moulds are used internally over the windows and doors. Also the appreciation of Gothic is limited to the obvious. As yet taste is unformed, because uninformed, and lacking those subtleties of appreciation which could only be revealed by studied knowledge and the tutor of understanding. Thus while Wyatt evolved a design from medieval parts, the old windows which were similar to those in the chapel,[60] that is post-1660, were replaced with Gothic sashes with the lower ones 'to slide upwards to be made of the old Oak if found'. He also instructed that the windows 'in the Bow Room in the Basement story of the new south building, must be enlarged one square nearer the floor'[61] which was done, as can be seen to-day. Lastly, Wyatt ordered anew the altar and reredos in Cosin's chapel (Plate 79). The framework of the reredos was of white wedding cake stucco[62] enclosing a painting of the Resurrection said to have been by Sir Joshua Reynolds.[63]

It is apparent that unlike Adam's petit point decoration or Carr's gauche south front at Auckland Castle, Wyatt's handiwork betokens the full genesis of early nineteenth century Gothic art. As his classical architecture was refined and drained of the Adamesque leaving the

Plates 78 and 79   James Wyatt. The Great Room and a design for the east end. The chapel. Auckland Castle, County Durham. 1795.

severities of neo-classicism so in his Gothic the attention given to the component parts enabled Wyatt to assemble them in a semblance of Gothic art so that the freshness of their forms eradicated the need for the pattern making of Robert Adam. During the first half of the nineties Wyatt had produced no original Gothic work, except for Queen Charlotte's ruins at Frogmore.[64] Then he was engaged on cathedral restorations after which he embarked on his final series of country houses which include, besides Fonthill Abbey, Norris Castle (1799) on the Isle of Wight and Ashridge (1808 onwards) for the Earl of Bridgewater. In these mature works Wyatt's expressionism burst forth in compositional form which was his greatest and most original contribution to the development of nineteenth century architecture. Nevertheless, the rooms at Auckland Castle which he decorated proclaim the new purpose of Gothic which has become a membrane. At Fonthill there were two separate membranes, inside and out but with no interrelation. To integrate the two was Pugin's achievement when he discovered the essential Gothic in structural composition.

While working on the drawings for Auckland Castle, Wyatt would also be preparing schemes for William Beckford at Fonthill where in 1795 a tower was begun on the highest part of the estate.[65] It was never completed probably because in the next year Wyatt was commissioned to erect a ruined convent of which only the chapel, parlour and dormitory had supposedly survived the ravages of the ages.[66] During the following winter the folly was enlarged to monstrous proportions with the architect creating designs for a central octagon and other buildings[67] although the tower was not, in fact, immediately commenced as the diarist Farington discovered after a morning call in August on Wyatt.[68] However, within four years he was noting that Fonthill had grown so vastly and so prodigiously that it had already cost its owner nigh on quarter of a million pounds and that as much again would be required to complete it.[69] Already it was the wonder of the epoch although even when Beckford made it his residence after 1807 it was incomplete only assuming the form known to posterity once the Great Hall, all attempts to warm it proving ineffectual, was transformed in purpose from the refectory to the state entrance[70] for which the soaring dimensions seem to have equipped it from the outset. Fonthill Abbey was the cynosure of the age but was hardly fit and scarcely less equipped for the necessities of human living. Much of it was only timber and cement and in its own day the faults were so apparent that not even the judiciously selected views which appeared in Rutter's *Delineations* could hide the flimsiness of many of the parts nor the poor detailing. As composition it was weak, chaotic

Plate 80   St Michael's Gallery. Fonthill Abbey.

and ill-organised. And yet—what would one not have given to have seen Fonthill in its heyday when its owner, seated before gold plate, was surrounded by a host of servants while light from purple and gold glass, streaming across a wilderness of paintings and the swathes of scarlet curtains, lit the crimson carpetting woven with the Hamilton cinquefoil from which house Beckford claimed descent. Coloured illustrations of St Michael's Gallery (Plate 80) still tantalise the eye and mind while the approach from the Western Hall to the octagon must have been stunning. Externally, the effects provided by the central tower, embowered by a myriad of lesser ones springing from the ranges of buildings, generated

147

an architectural melodrama seldom sustained before or since. Gone are those stand-bys, the crosslet and quatrefoil for now there were armorial bearings, capitals, foliage and the whole gamut of Gothic decoration to publicly proclaim the advance in Gothic syntax.

Yet while Fonthill was progenitor of other huge edifices such as Eastnor and Lowther, its valid architectural significance lay not in its vast scale, exciting though that was with all its possibilities of an un-realised potential. After all foreign architects, such as Ledoux, far out-stripped anything attempted in Britain. It was on the west front of the north wing with its two storeys and its range of dormers with the occasional oriel or bow which carried a secret import of what became most valid in Gothic whether in its domestic or Tudor habit and which revealed a knowledge of form and part far beyond anything ever encompassed by Adam, talented though he was. And lastly, the picturesque massing and asymmetrical grouping was also a prophecy. In 1795 the theory of the picturesque had just been advanced so that the cult had not reached full vigour. But in Fonthill there was a mansion which already met the requirements of the movement which was soon to control architecture as surely and rigorously as Palladio's canons had done eighty years before, while at the same time the rigidity of the unorthodox plan, its very regularity was a convincing evocation of the ethos of Burke's sublime.

Until Wyatt's activities Gothic was scarcely respectable but once taken up by the King's architect it became eminently so and Gothic became engrained on the consciousness of gentlemen. Indeed, it is after Wyatt's reign that the great surge of popularity occurred. In the years 1760–90 there had been, after the first flush of enthusiasm, a decline in the number of Gothic houses so that Eastlake can list less than a dozen in England.[71] Such a falling off was understandable. Walpole's Strawberry Hill, introverted play-acting, was designed to shock. Alnwick, in a style of interior decoration which only the very rich could afford, was as outré as if concocted by one of the late Helena Rubenstein's string of interior decorators. The style had to percolate through society and although Fonthill was both outré and the creation of a very wealthy man, its makeshift quality and its sudden growth suited it to the mood of the day, given impetus by the literary movement and the concept of the picturesque. Fonthill was heady stuff and though the more sober Gothic of which Auckland Castle was the microcosm was to win the day, it was at Fonthill that the potential of Gothic was first fully realised.

IX

The Scottish Contemporaries of Robert Adam

Until his death in 1792 Robert Adam was the most distinguished exponent of the revived Gothic in Scotland. Yet others also had a share in the movement. They included a younger and an older brother of Robert's as well as such architects of significance as John Baxter Junior, James Playfair and Robert Mylne, each of whom built at least one country house in regular Gothic. Almost inevitably, these houses owed something either to the Adam *ménage* or to the Inveraray canon or, indeed, to both as was the case with Douglas Castle.

Set in the fertile vales of south Lanarkshire, Douglas Castle was the seat of the first Duke of Douglas, head of that family descended from the Good Sir James, companion at arms of Robert Bruce. During the Forty-Five, the castle was considerably damaged by the Highlanders on their return from England[1] and in 1760[2] it was destroyed by fire, having been set alight, according to tradition, by the Duchess who wanted to live in Edinburgh.

Designs for a new castle were produced by John and James Adam.[3] Although the Duke had gone to the leading architectural practitioners in Scotland, and since 1748 John Adam had been supervising the erection of Inveraray Castle, the decision to build in the Gothic taste at Douglas must have been the Duke's. Yet, considering the general climate of architectural opinion in Britain at that time, such a decision must have seemed somewhat peculiar. True, the Duke was such a noted eccentric that doubts were entertained about his sanity.[4] Still, he probably had good cause for choosing as he did. As previously explained, castles in Scotland were very much the norm, playing an active role in the social and economic life of the country, while their ancient towers represented in public and

149

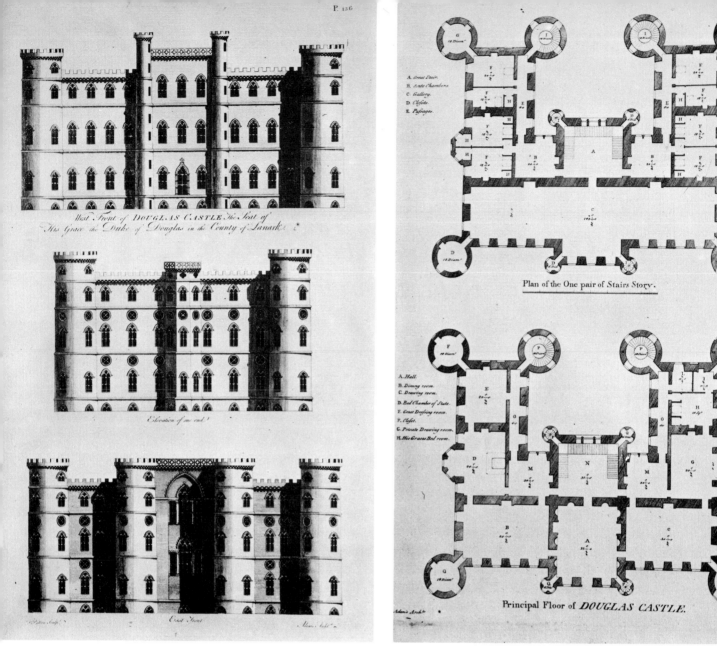

Plates 81 and 82   John and James Adam. Douglas Castle, Lanarkshire. 1757

physical form that lineage of descent of which none was more glorious than the house of Douglas. Also the Duke's acquaintanceship with the Duke of Argyll[5] may well have dictated not only the choice of architect but the size of the castle which, so legend says, was to be ten feet longer on each side than Inveraray.

Freely based on the Inveraray concept, the plan of Douglas (Plate 82) was that of a half-H.[6] As at the former, the entrance led into a hall from which the dining-room and drawing-room opened to left and right respectively. Unlike Inveraray, which was sworn to Palladianism with the

150

axial view bisecting the internal space from the entrance to the gallery intended for the garden side, the hall at Douglas was to give onto the principal staircase leading up to a gallery running the full length of the entrance front. Like the two sides it rose for three storeys above the basement with circular angle towers reaching above the wall-head (Plate 81). For the exterior most of the detailing was copied from the Argyll mansion but was so multiplied that the design, on paper at least, lost the clarity of the prototype and became obfuscate.

Although Inveraray must be regarded as the undoubted parent of Douglas Castle, it was not the vocabulary of Morris alone which was used in Lanarkshire since the attached polygonal towers, set midway on each side, have the same position and much the same form as on the early seventeenth century Heriot's Hospital in Edinburgh. It was admired in the eighteenth century for its 'regular Gothic'[7] and was to be a rich treasury for the Adam brethren and for many others in the next century. One

Plate 83   Douglas Castle, Lanarkshire. c. 1875. Demolished 1951.

must look elsewhere, however, for the half-H plan, which, owing very little to the tensions of neo-Gothic palladianism, is unusual enough for the period to warrant some comment. It seems as if the source would be the Palace of Holyroodhouse, that building more curious than beautiful in its union of Gothic and classic with a frontal presentation not dissimilar to Douglas where the arms were to end with circular corner towers. Indeed, the appearance of the ancient home of the Stewarts (a factor which, in Scotland, undoubtedly lent prestige to the building) among the collection of plates which eventually appeared as *Vitruvius Scoticus*, is some indication of the structure's significance in Adam eyes at least and the more so as, apart from some corbelling and crenellation, there is very little of the Gothic mode about the King James V tower.

According to Pennant the foundation stone of the new castle at Douglas was laid in 1757.[8] If he was correct then the castle was being constructed, not after the loss of the old tower, as has usually been supposed, but before. That can be borne out by an undated scheme, obviously from the Adam *atelier*, linking the old U-shaped castle to a new one whose layout is an early variant on the final proposals in *Vitruvius Scoticus*.[9] However, these were doomed to incompletion when in 1761 the Duke died with the request that he should be buried beneath his bowling-green[10] and although Playfair in 1791 and Gillespie Graham in 1826 submitted plans for finishing the house,[11] work was never resumed. Until the castle's demolition two hundred years later, the sole fragment of the grand idea was the drawing-room wing (Plate 83) which, nevertheless, contained between fifty and sixty rooms.[12]

For John Adam the death of the Duke of Douglas must have been a severe disappointment until, some three years later, an even more splendid ducal client appeared. The new patron was Alexander Gordon (1743–1827), fourth Duke of Gordon and seventh Marquess and twelfth Earl of Huntly. As chief of clan Gordon and Cock of the North, his rule over Scotland's north east corner was comparable to that of the Argylls in their western stronghold. A noted improver, famous for his tree-planting and for transforming the marshes of his ancestral lands, the Bog o' Gight, into extensive parkland,[13] Duke Alexander's estate became so productive that Lord Kames, himself no mean agriculturalist, was prompted to describe him as the greatest subject in Britain not only by the size of his rent roll but for the number of persons dependant on his rule and protection.[14]

In 1764 the Duke's home, like so many surviving examples in the north east, such as nearby Castle Stuart, was a tall rank tower house (Plate 84). It had been gloriously embellished by the first marquess in 1614 with chivalric collars enclosing entwined monograms and the initials of himself and his wife[15] as can still be seen on Huntly Castle, that wonder of the north, which owed its detailing to Blois where, reputedly, the marquess was governor.

To enlarge and modernise Gordon Castle two schemes were prepared by John Adam each with a centre allied by corridors to side pavilions. At first it seems, the intention was to leave the old house very much as it was internally, even to the newel stairs, but to attempt to even up the exterior by adding two bays to the eastern half of the house even although the line of the wall would have remained irregular. Short colonnades from

Plate 84   Old Gordon Castle, Morayshire.

the house connected with wings sweeping forward to form a *cour d'honneur*.[16] The elevation, likewise dated 1764 and signed by John Adam,[17] clearly shows a lack of articulation between the parts obtusely indicating John Adam's limited concept of architecture and deficient feeling for the finer subtleties, points made the more poignant when it is remembered that 1764 marked the triumph of Robert Adam at Bowood.

John Adam's elevation was unusually long, 462 feet, and it depicts a mansion of four storeys, which were necessary if the six storeyed tower was to be suitably clothed. However, the three storey wings, like the centre devoid of architectural treatment or relief, instead of complementing the main block, accentuated the barrack-like air which was made no more acceptable by such past elements as high roofs and globes atop the colonnades.

The second idea was more grandiose and intended to impose augustan canons on the old house by regularising it, a task made easier by the addition of canted bays to back and front. From the mid-point of each side five-bay corridors stretched to the terminal pavilions, thirteen bays long which, though almost identical in plan, were for stabling and kitchens.[18] Although undated and unsigned, this second lay-out and that for the ground floor,[19] belong to the 1764 group. It may, of course, be ill-luck that there are no detailed designs or sections for the same year. On the other hand the absence of such material and the general nature of what is available must indicate first thoughts by artist and patron alike, especially as it would be about this time that the Duke went abroad.[20]

153

The next designs appear in 1766 and 1767 by one A. Roumieu, who would be the Duke's surveyor, Abraham Roumieu[21] who on 15 January 1767 drew up for the Duke a building contract signed by John Mar and John Naughtie, masons of Burghead, 'to build two Lodges, two Piers and two Gateways'. This was to be accomplished by mid-July. However, as so often happens in such affairs, the work fell sadly behind schedule and the masons were only paid in December, without the penalty clause being invoked.[22]

Roumieu's first design in 1766 was a ground floor showing the old house enlarged to eleven bays[23] but that was superseded by another reverting to the century's *de rigueur* concept of a centre, colonnades and wings.[24] That it was never built is hardly surprising since the cumbersome pediment, rising over the four storeys was, to say the least, gauche. What Roumieu's architectural training or experience was nobody knows. He may have been a draughtsman who drifted north from the Adam office or the Duke may have met and brought him to Morayshire from Edinburgh. His only known work is the detailed layouts for the new town of Fochabers,[25] with its formal street pattern, beyond the castle gates. That must have been before 1769 since, although he was still in the Duke's service in May of that year,[26] by November he had left after a quarrel with one of the Duke's agents, one William Anderson who had also tried to cause trouble for John Baxter[27] who not only designed the church in Fochabers[28] but was to become the final designer and architect of Gordon Castle.

Baxter was the son of John Baxter Senior who had been a mason in the service of William Adam at Mavisbank in the early seventeen twenties[29] and a decade later executed Haddo House, in Aberdeenshire, for a kinsman of the Dukes of Gordon.[30] The son travelled to Rome where he studied architecture at the same time as James Adam[31] although as a Protestant he had to receive papal dispensation to become a member of the Academy of St Luke.[32] By 1769, having returned from Italy, he was considered sufficiently eminent to be called upon by Edinburgh Corporation to report on the collapse of the southern portion of the city's new North Bridge,[33] the gateway from the Old Town to the New. As an architect, Baxter was familiar enough, like Nisbet of Kelso and many others, with the Adam style and techniques to be able to reproduce very creditable copies whether internally or externally as on the Merchants' Hall facade in Edinburgh in 1790.[34]

In 1767 Duke Alexander had married Jane Maxwell who is remembered as the most celebrated of the Duchesses of Gordon. She was noted for her family aggrandisement[35] and that, together with the Duke's own grandiose building intentions, may well have revived his determination to build anew the family seat. At any rate 'In 1768/9 the Duke of Gordon intending an addition to his House at Gordon Castle, engaged Mr. Baxter to go North and advise him'.[36] It was an opportunity which no ambitious young architect could afford to lose. Still, there was much more to engaging an architect than a ducal command and the prime indications of conflict occur in the first exchanges. In February 1769, in a letter to the factor at Gordon Castle, Baxter Junior explained that, because his father had been unwell for the past twelve months, Baxter Senior would be quite unable to visit the Duke. With the preamble over, the son then presented his own credentials. 'As my Father has given up Businiss to me, ever since my return from Italy I therefor beg leave to Offer my selfe to his Grace's service.' Still, he was not so overawed by the prospect of the commission of a lifetime that he forgot his business acumen since 'As the Journey cannot be performed in less than three weeks, I shall agree to go North for twenty Guineas.

'If his Grace the Duke, should approve of my coming north (I) shall be glade to know, as I am engaged to be in the shire of Air, beginning of Aprile.'[37]

When April did arrive not only does it appear that Baxter was in Ayrshire but he had also to attend to some affair in Dunbartonshire so that not until 24 April was he able to reply again to the factor. The Duke had displayed some interest in Baxter by asking for prices of work which were now hurriedly sent off. 'I send You the Prices that My Father and I always have gott, and which I have establish'd as a Rule for to make Sufficient Work is as Follows.

Viz Rubble Work at £2 per Rood

Plain Ashler at eight pence per foot.'

Other charges are listed, with Baxter indicating that he would supply the workmen, before he closes with compliments to all his friends.[38] From this and other evidence it is clear that Baxter was on terms of familiarity with the Duke's servants. The work at Haddo of Baxter Senior may have laid the basis for the son's easy relationship with men like Bell and Ross,[39] successively the Duke's factors, and, of course, it would not be beyond the bounds of possibility to suggest that the Baxters had originated in the north east.

Baxter's estimates of cost were not immediately acceptable since the factor evidently wrote back querying them and may even have indicated his own thoughts on prices. At any rate, Baxter was provoked into sending off by return, on 6 May, a wordy defence. 'I was Honoured with Yours of the third of May and is [sic] Sorry to find such an Odds in the Prices, But Perhaps there may likeways be an Odds in the Workman-ship. . . .

'As my Study has always been to keep up the Character that my Father has gain'd for his making Sufficient good work . . . I hope his Grace the Duke of Gordon will excuse my not engageing in this work below the above Prices. . . .

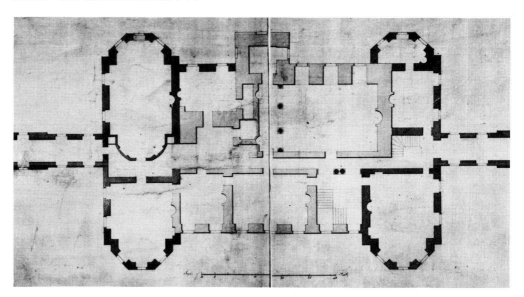

Plate 85   John Baxter. Plan of the principal floor. Gordon Castle, Morayshire. 1769.

'The three feet walls when reduced to 2 feet thick walls, would be £1 6s 8d per Rood the difference is half a crown per Rood, which I can promise would be but Trifling betwixt Sufficient and unsufficient work.

'As to the Hewenwork and furnishing Stone and workmanship for 6d per foot, Surprises Me . . . if his Grace can have his Rebbats and Ashler for the same price as others has rough Stone, I think his Grace can nott do better than employ those People Providing they do their work Sufficiently, and give every other Thing in Proportion.'[40]

The tone of the letter, especially the snide remarks about quality of workmanship, is all too common in the haggling between an architect and his potential client while the threats to leave the job to the hands of those whom Baxter considers unworthy and unsuitable rivals, is reminiscent of Nisbet's sallies against Sir John Hussey Delaval.

In June a list of the stone required for Gordon Castle was drawn up by John Mar and John Naughtie[41] who, despite their previous fault, still enjoyed the Duke's favour. That was on the 26th and it must have been about then that Baxter was at work on new plans (Plate 85). They were the third set but this time there was to be no going back and building was at last begun on 29 June.[42] About that date, John Baxter Senior died for the plans, unlike the correspondence of hitherto, lack the suffix junior. The plans are clearly derived from the schemes of five years before by John Adam for not only is there a marked continuity

Plate 86   John Baxter. Garden front. Gordon Castle, Morayshire.

of style but, in addition, a close adherence to the Adam formula of centre with protruding bays, corridors and wings which was no more subject to alteration than is usual in any large and long term undertaking except that castellation was adopted throughout, possibly to conform with the old tower which was to remain at the rear of the new house (Plate 86). The most important external change was the addition of subsidiary buildings and screens to the wings adding another hundred feet to the length, which now totalled almost 570 feet. The change was necessitated by alterations to the courts' functions which were no longer for offices exclusively since one was to be pressed into service as a residential annexe to the main block. The 'Sketch for Altering the East Pavilion G. Castle' indicated the private apartments for the family[43] as did its companion piece for the west pavilion[44] so that when the latter was eventually decided upon the stables had to be appended to it.[45] Despite such changes the plans are recognisably those by Adam. Why then did Adam not get the building of Gordon Castle into his own hands? After all, Fort

George, only thirty-seven miles along the coast, was completed in 1763.[46] Possibly, Baxter's local links were strong enough to enable him to overcome any opposition from the Adam quarter. In any event, with the approach of the seventies, the Adam family had plenty of work on hand since houses, such as Wedderburn and Mellerstain, as well as the Register House, were already under way or about to commence.

Plate 87   Gordon Castle, Morayshire in the nineteen twenties. With the exception of the original tower the central part of the house was demolished in 1961.

By the mid-seventies the number of detailed studies for the interior of Gordon indicates that construction was coming to an end on the main block and likewise on the pavilions as the roof plan for the western one is dated 1776.[47] Internally, Baxter followed Adam ideas on decoration which was freely plagiarised. The dining-room was in Robert's early Roman style and the chimney-piece had male terms with tabernacle frames on the walls. The cornice was based on one of Adam's favourite themes, the palmette surrounded by a circle[48] and the four columns, screening one end of the room, had Corinthian capitals[49] costing £16 in 1778.[50] By comparison with Adam's work in the same year at Mellerstain the dining-room at Gordon is heavy and architectonic. However, the drawing-room ceiling, designed in the previous year,[51] was in a more elegant vein, representative of Robert's halfway stage in the formation of his mature style, and if the Baxter design lacks the brilliance associated with the former, it does show how the vogue had spread helped by fashion and, doubtless, by the publication of the first volume of the Brothers' *Works* in 1773. On the design a central circle was left blank for a painting. Around it an irregular octagon in green had a blank rectangle on each of the principal sides. Beyond that white *rinceaux* were on a biscuit ground while in the corners pink and green quadrants enclosed fan ornaments, with similar motifs repeated in the window bay. Other Adam tints were the green and lavender of the dining-room ceiling[52] while the *amorini* and pairs of griffins on the staircase ceiling repeated well-known Adam traits.[53] It is small wonder, therefore, that the exterior, of white Elgin freestone,[54] should bear more than a passing resemblance to products by the Adam family. Possibly not surprisingly Hopetoun appears to have been the chief source for such things as the round-arched windows with block imposts and keystones. Even the height of the castle walls and pitched roofs recall the elder Adam's pastoral Georgic on the shores of the Forth although pitched in a lower key than the late baroque richness of its orchestration. At Gordon there was no central unifying feature so that the continuous architectural movement was without a climacteric. Indeed, what most struck observers was the castle's extraordinary length[55] making it for one 'the pride of Scotland'.[56] That apart, Gordon Castle (Plate 87) was a telling commentary on John Adam's and John Baxter's inability to handle a huge scheme in either a particularly interesting or even a significant manner.

By 1779, with the greater part of the mason work at the castle being finished, Baxter submitted an account for the ten years' work. The cost of the castle was put at £8,541 19s 9½d, with a dog kennel and bridges separately itemised, although a sum of £311 17s 11½d also fell due for work put in hand over the next two years.[57] That included finishing off the west pavilion and colonnade and smaller items such as the main staircase floor,[58] the stone for which came from Hailes quarry near Edinburgh,[59] while as late as 1782 carved chimney-pieces were being supplied for the billiard room[60] and hall.[61] Within the span of his account, Baxter had actually been paid and although the sums were not large they must have eased his outlay. His first payment had occurred on 20 October 1770 when he received £60 with sums paid at intervals to the foreman. The largest sum paid was on 25 April 1781 when £305 was accredited to the architect followed by ten guineas two months later.[62] By that time Baxter could have assumed that his commission at Gordon was coming to an end. But that was not to be for when the final reckoning was drawn up, dispute broke out between architect and employer which, although not an unknown circumstance, is, nevertheless, a very trying one.

Trouble first occurred in February 1779 when a surveyor, Alexander Ponton, went north to carry out a measurement of the work done by Baxter for the Duke.[63] Then in April 1781 Baxter's foreman, John Logie and the Duke's clerk of accounts, Robert Thomson, measured the additions since 1779[64] but without Ponton's assistance, presumably because his charge for the previous occasion was not far short of two hundred pounds.[65] Until these measurements were completed it was, of course, impossible to calculate the full cost of the building operations. Once that was established and the expenses paid in the course of building defrayed, the balance could be discovered and the interest payable thereafter settled.[66] The financial picture was made clear in a statement of October 1782, setting out the sums involved. The total cost had been fixed, after the survey, at £9,282 9s 11½d plus the architect's fee of £650, which included drawing charges. Allowing for the sums paid at different times by the Duke the balance due from him was a thousand pounds.[67] From that point the dispute grew. After some exchanges, in June of the following year the Duke brought in another architect not only to inspect the quality of the workmanship at Gordon but also to act as mediator[68] for those charges for which no rates had been laid down in the architect's original list of charges in 1769.[69] The chosen man was James Salisbury who 'was brought from England some years ago'[70] to superintend, as clerk of works, Robert Adam's Register House in Edinburgh.[71] Evidently, 'Tradesmen's Accounts have frequently been referred to him with Success But of late he has been employed by the Duke of Roxburgh and a few days ago Mr. Drummond put into his hands a Job of Consequence he means to execute at Lawers'.[72]

Three days later John Baxter despatched a letter to Charles Gordon of Braid at St John's St in the Canongate. Charles Gordon was not only a clansman of the Duke's but was a lawyer[73] who was to act as the Duke's agent with Alexander Farquharson, 'Accomptant in Edinburgh'.[74] In his note Baxter wondered why he had so far heard nothing from Gordon of Braid since Salisbury would have had time to pass an opinion on the submitted charges. After that salvo the architect then proceeded to look to his own defences. 'I must own it gave me pain to think my acct. should have been obliged to undergo the censure of aney Artist, or Workman, and if I had formerly understood by what was meant by not settling it sooner, my Charge as Architect and director of the works should have been likeways stiffened [?]; instead of the small charge of £650'.[75] It was a final flourish doubtless intended as much for his own humour as for the Duke's men.

The problem now was that Salisbury refused to give any opinion until he had visited Gordon Castle, which would cost the Duke twenty guineas.[76] Unfortunately, Salisbury was out of town a great deal and so it was with some relief that Baxter informed Gordon on July first that Salisbury, having arrived in town the previous Sunday, would remain there until the Friday when he was off to Perthshire. Baxter pleaded for the affair to be settled immediately[77] and indeed a meeting took place next day after which Gordon drafted a letter for the Duke in which the ins and outs of the entire affair were recounted. Salisbury had doubled his charge for a visit to the castle. However, that was probably more of a psychological blow than anything else since, although previously believing the prices excessive, conversation with Baxter on the quality of the workmanship and the difficulty of joining the new work to the old castle had led him to change his views so much so that he now thought the charges reasonable especially as Baxter had 'furnished Drawings and Mouldings for the Joiners, Plaisteres, Slaters, Plumbers and in short every other Artificer employed in the Work—which Artificers were all of his procuring and engaging. Insomuch that Gordon Castle had (the) best part of his time for thirteen Years; and the Charge of £50 yearly, which he made, would scarcely Indemnify the expence of his Journeys . . .'. Therefore Salisbury had begun to think that Baxter, far from over-charging, had even been undercharging and rather than have Salisbury travel north the Duke was urged to settle the account[78] which he did. The accountant drew up an agreement in September[79] and a final settlement was signed by all the parties at Gordon Castle and at Braid in October and November with the Duke authorising Baxter to be paid a final sum which, with interest,[80] came to £823.[81]

Despite such a state of affairs Gordon of Braid himself eventually yielded to the evocation of castellated architecture and supposedly engaged Robert Burn,[82] father of the more famous William Burn, to design the Hermitage at the foot of the Braid Hills on the outskirts of Edinburgh. This castellated villa, for the basement is revealed at the rear and along the sides, is a Gothic variation of Marble Hill except that, instead of the meadow-curled Thames a busybody stream rushes through a ravine at the head of which, and surrounded by thickly-wooded slopes, stands the house. Its oversailing battlements, with a lug-turret dependant at each corner, effectively block the narrow approach. Yet the classical interiors permeate this aggressive barrier with a Venetian window on either side of the entrance. The Hermitage, much admired in its time,[83] obviously derives its Gothic trim from the Adam castles but without that intellectual suppression of the emotions which in Adam created the majestic sculpture of such castles as Culzean and Seton.

Two other buildings with additions similar to the Hermitage, with which they are probably contemporaneous, are Castle Huntly in east Perthshire and Ardencaple Castle in the Lennox. Unfortunately, the architect at the former is obscured although the quality of the interiors and the introduction of oval shapes, make it tempting to imagine him to be Adam's clerk of works, John Paterson, especially as the purchaser of the estate and medieval castle in 1777 was also called Paterson.[84] Perhaps it is an early work which with its gables and rounded wings imitates nearby Pitfour (1784). Certainly, it was complete in 1792 for the compiler for the *Statistical Account*, having recorded the appearance of lug-turrets and battlements, remarked that the castle had 'assumed even a more castellated appearance outwardly than formerly'[85] when doubtless it had been a very plain old tower.

A similar transformation would also seem to have occurred at Ardencaple, the ancient seat of the Macaulays overlooking the Clyde. About 1765 Aulay, the nineteenth laird, sold the estate for debt to the fourth Duke of Argyll, who bestowed the castle on his younger son, Lord Frederick Campbell.[86] Probably finding the castle to be in need of repair, he made large additions whose circular towers with their square cut corbels and banded walls are reminiscent of Inveraray. Perhaps that is no coincidence since the architect of Ardencaple is usually stated to have been Robert Mylne[87] who was considerably impressed by the Gothic of Inveraray[88] where, from 1773, he was employed[89] by the fifth Duke who, having succeeded to the titles and estates in 1770, inaugurated the second great building period of the Argyll family. Therefore, although Mylne was at Ardencaple in 1769,[90] it is more likely that the commonly accepted date of 1786 is correct when Mylne was engaged at Roseneath, another Argyll property, on the opposite shore of the Gareloch from Ardencaple.[91]

Another house having close links with Inveraray, although on stylistic grounds only, was Melville Castle in Midlothian. The old castle was traditionally supposed to have been a hunting seat of Mary, Queen of Scots,[92] although it is also claimed that the contemporary owner was David Rizzio.[93] Whatever the past royal associations, by the middle of the seventeen eighties, the castle was the seat of another 'monarch', 'King Harry the Ninth' or Henry Dundas (1742–1811) who had come into the possession of Melville through his first wife, Elizabeth, daughter of David Rennie of Melville Castle.[94] Like the third Duke of Argyll in an earlier age, Henry Dundas, later first Viscount Melville, had an absolute control of Scotland and its affairs for thirty years and, as the government's election agent, was so successful that in the election of 1802 out of forty-five Scottish members returned to Westminster only two were Whigs.[95] As a member of the Board of Control for India and Treasurer of the Navy, it was only fitting that such a figure of consequence should have a seat 'suited to the exalted station of its owner',[96] an attitude alien to that of to-day.

The architect chosen by Dundas was James Playfair, the son of a Scottish minister.[97] Playfair practised in London[98] and Melville Castle seems to have been his first large commission so it was no doubt the patronage of the all-powerful minister which gave Playfair an extensive practice among the Scottish nobility, including the Earl of Kinnoul and the Duke of Buccleugh.[99] Possibly the first discussions about a new castle at Melville were in 1785 when, during a visit of nine and a half months to Scotland, Playfair spent eight days at Melville.[100] From an extant folder of small designs[101] it seems that the first intention was to make the existing Z-plan castle[102] more conformable to contemporary standards by additions and alterations. However, as none of the designs was worked out in any detail then the notion was probably soon abandoned perhaps on account of structural considerations for 'in 1786, Mr Dundas had the decayed old Castle taken down'[103] although not before James Playfair, in London, was employed on the designs for a new one. In March he was drawing up a site plan showing 'the manner of placing the New Castle in respect to the old'.[104] Two accompanying elevations bear some interesting details including the instruction for the string courses which 'must be cut deeper in proportion as the work is farther from the eye—so that to appearance it may all be nearly alike'.[105] In the following month he must have sent off the principal floor plan and one can assume that building operations had begun and were to incorporate a portion of the old house in one of the new wings.[106]

Like Robert Adam, Playfair apparently made at least one annual visit to Scotland to discuss the prospects for future employment with clients, such as Lord Graham, and to superintend progress at such sites as Dupplin and Kinnaird.[107] At the latter, for Sir David Carnegie, Playfair remodelled the old house into a square block with a central and square corner towers all with battlements and machicolations. A porte-cochère was before the main entrance and inside at least one room, the library, had Gothic decorations of the Alnwick variety.[108]

In the summer of 1786 Playfair left London on 3 August and did not return until the end of September and although he is not very specific in his diary, it does seem that half his time was divided between Dalkeith, where a lodge and some minor works would soon be on hand for the Duke of Buccleugh[109] and Melville[110] half a mile away. At the

163

latter progress was rapid for in October he was sending off the 'Framing of the Ceiling Floor or Garrets in the Roofs' with the injunction that 'The whole carpentry of this roof must be very accurately executed'.[111] One can imagine that the roof was on before the worst of the winter had set in since next spring interior details, such as friezes, were being prepared as well as schemes for the offices[112] although in March 1788,

Plate 88   James Playfair. Melville Castle, Midlothian. 1785.

after two further visits to Scotland, drawings, worth ten pounds, were made for the offices. Then thirty pounds was charged to Dundas after another summer's visit and on 3 December the day was spent in drawing the dairy, pantry and front stairs. These were minor items so that when Playfair next visited Midlothian in the winter and early spring of 1789 it was only for half a day or two days at a time although he did spend two more days in August 'by order of Mr. Dundas at putting up chimney piece(s)'. After that, despite the summer visit in 1791 and a prolonged stay of six days in the autumn, one can assume that the mansion (Plate 88) was complete.[113]

It was a smaller version of Inveraray but with two storey wings attached to each side to provide rooms and some of those domestic quarters which at the latter were wholly located in the basement. The abandonment of the cube form and axial planning not only indicate the loosening of the Palladian hold but are a reflection of the desire for a more variable massing. Although Robert Adam was coincidentally dealing with the identical problem of a central mass with joined subordinate groupings, it was in a markedly more individualistic way, whereas Melville merely represents an interesting stage in the elevation of the household offices from their hidden utility in the basement to their later release and expansion as architectural adjuncts capable of their

164

own positive contribution to the architectural dynamism in such houses as Taymouth (1806 on) and Balloch (1809). Yet of such a halfway stage as Melville displays it is dangerous to be too specific in making claims of architectural advance into the architectonics of the theory of the picturesque and the cult of variety. Others, such as Adam at Culzean, dispensed with a basement so that Melville is not a unique contemporary example. As is so often the case in historical study, the only conclusion, because it alone has objectivity, is that Melville dictated a solution whose happy results were seized upon and improved by later architects.

Thus Melville has an importance which neither its architect nor its architecture really warrant. Classical inside, as was almost invariably the case everywhere else, the external allegiance of Melville to the castles of Inveraray and Douglas is obvious. When it is recalled that Inveraray was commenced forty years before and that the later eighteenth century was an era of experimental vitality, such subservience to a Palladian model, at least in the external forms, although one wonders if Playfair realised that, is curious. True Robert Adam broke away from the form to mould shapes so revolutionary that they were never fully copied by his disciples who probably never understood what their master was about. But Adam was a great architect. As for Playfair he so far imitated Inveraray, at least in the towers, as to have Gothic windows, a feature dispensed with by Robert Adam.

Although a freak product of the southern school of court Gothic, Inveraray was quite acceptable in Scotland where there was a continuing function for the castle and the fort. Yet what is so surprising is how early on Inveraray became established as the exemplar for later models. At first it was the sole example and so what else was there for the unimaginative to copy? Even so, Inveraray as the idealisation of the modern Gothic castle, was acceptable *per se*. True, at Douglas there were the undertones of Holyroodhouse and Heriot's Hospital but at Melville no such historic eclecticism exists. There the style was selected for two reasons. As always in Scotland there was the habitual looking back to the past with deference to the fierce lineage of the hereditary owner. Thus at Gordon Castle, battlements were prompted by the warlike tower and at Melville there is the same atavistic urge in the desire to retain the medieval castle and, failing that, its semblance. Still, it is doubtful if Playfair's predilections were disposed to such overt rationalisation. Instead he would have seen in the situation beauties and subjective associations, so familar in writings of the time, which would have been foreign to Morris for whom intellectual precepts and not romantic musings charged the creative impulse. Therefore, although Melville and

165

Inveraray are first cousins, it is the thinking of the architects which illustrates most clearly the changes in forty years. As Playfair wrote of another house, 'The Situation is Such as to require whatever is done to be in the Style of a Castle. Such is required by the Character of the place. That in another Situation of less beauty but having more space a Modern built house would be preferable.'[114] While an echo of Pope's dictum to 'consult the genius of the place in all' is retained, it is only too apparent that the rule of the Augustans has been overthrown. Playfair's moralising is inchoate and lacks direction although he is groping fitfully towards the cult of the picturesque which was to be pinned down, like a gorgeous butterfly, by Payne Knight and Gilpin.

X

Gilpin and the Cult of the Picturesque

By the middle of the seventeen nineties Gothic might well be seen as having an established position in the canons of orthodox taste in Great Britain. After all, the study so far of the Gothic buildings in north Britain would surely support such a view. Nevertheless, it must be qualified. Such buildings did not represent a national movement having a common origin, ideals and purpose as happened later with the Greek Revival. Instead, Gothic was confined to localities so that, in Northumberland, Alnwick and Ford are the twin suns of a Gothic system. The same is true in County Durham where Raby and Auckland Castle exercise a similar centripetal force. That such local influences were of prime importance is proved by the fact that across the Pennines, to the west, where there was no aristocratic lead, there is no Gothic to speak of. True there was Whitehaven Castle but its sober outline and classical interiors would scarcely have set alight a blaze of enthusiasm for Gothic among the local landed classes. Of course, it must be borne in mind that there were fewer estates in the west. In Northumberland, for instance, the Percys were the apex of a social pyramid; in Westmorland, there were the Lowthers with, a great distance beneath them, the gentry who were never to have the financial luck of so many of their eastern neighbours of having coal discovered beneath their lands. Then, too, the separatism imposed by the lakes and mountains was, for long, a barrier of the most intractable nature. Still, even allowing for such social, financial and geographical distinctions between the north east and the north west, it remains true that, in the north of England, Gothic was begotten by the will of a very few rich individuals who, in touch with the latest cultural ideas, created Gothic buildings and interiors in the most advanced rococo taste, which was imitated in the neighbourhood. It is the local influence which makes

167

Gothic so thick on the ground in both Durham and Northumberland. In that respect they may be unlike more southerly counties.

In Scotland, on the other hand, Gothic would appear to have been much more of a national movement in the sense that it stretches from the Borders to the Highlands. Even so, what is noticeable is the dependence of the style on the Adam school so that, after the death of Robert Adam in 1792, though the movement continues for a few more years, it has become fixed without the ability to evolve new dynamic forms and shapes. In Scotland, the dominant will was not the great landowner but the architect in whose hands landowners seem content to have entrusted and left the entire management of artistic affairs. But when in northern England there are no great patrons and when Robert Adam is dead then there comes a hiatus in the Gothic movement. It falls away and only picks up again when the national movement, which involves both theoreticians and architects, spreads from the south introducing extraneous concepts which, for a time at least, overwhelm the local scene in northern England and Scotland.

A potent force in establishing a national viewpoint was *The Gentleman's Magazine*. A glance at almost any volume in the years preceding the turn of the century would reveal any number of plates of ancient churches and castles. In addition, and in marked contrast to earlier years, the virtues of Gothic were being unashamedly advocated as 'the superior elegance, richness, grace and propriety, of the Gothic architecture over the ridiculous and contemptible plainness and simplicity of the Grecian'.[1] That obviously smacks of special pleading so that in the early nineties it is better to accept Gothic as one of several styles nudging the classical mode out of its entrenched position. Therefore, in an era of stylistic change, Gothic was only as acceptable as the Chinese, Indian or Grecian. Yet Gothic had an undoubted edge over the other exotic styles for it alone lay in abundance over the countryside and was thus readily available for examination by scholars; and with native possession there was beginning to emerge the concept of Gothic as a national style. That, of course, was very much a part of the stock-in-trade of James Wyatt just as the Scottish castle became of Robert Adam. However, as early as 1781 Gothic was being firmly recommended in *The Gentleman's Magazine* for religious buildings[2] although it was not until the very late nineties that the relationship of Gothic to national identity hardened[3] after St George's Chapel in Windsor Castle had been hailed as 'perhaps the most beautiful building in the world'.[4]

While such a eulogy is indicative of a certain enthusiasm, it is as well to bear in mind the observations of Mrs Delany whose diaries over forty years[5] show Gothic to have been invariably employed as whimsy or, at best, as decoration. Nowhere, for instance, does she reveal it to have been widespread as a stylistic fashion or in use for any large undertakings. Nor is it ever considered as architecture but rather it is employed as a means to raise associations although in that respect Mrs Delany's comments are neither so exquisite as Arthur Young's nor so easily aroused. For Mrs Delany, as for that society of which she was a part, Gothic was a light-hearted ploy and despite the extent of the operations, that does seem to have been the case at Alnwick and the other great houses in the north of England. Still, there was a respect there for the medieval which does not seem to have existed or is perhaps less apparent or widespread in the south. In addition, the classical style, having come late to the north, did not have the same hold as in the south or even the midlands. In any event, many of the northern English aristocracy still inhabited ancestral halls and castles as, until the later eighteenth or the early nineteenth century, there was no money to replace them while in the rare instances where there was wealth then the family had remained for generations in the south as the Percys had done. Lastly, it should be remembered that not only did hereditary atavism ensure the retention of such castles as Ford, Alnwick and Raby but they were sufficiently commodious to be capable of modernisation while their exteriors were in accord with the new and fribblish taste, all of which was in marked contrast to Scotland.

North of the Border, as has been seen, every Gothic building meant either the demolition of an existing residence or its suppression within a new and enlarged structure. That was for two reasons. First, the vernacular castles were not the sprawling dwellings of Northumberland and Durham but tight tower-houses, whose incommodious nature was ill-matched to the conceptions of grandeur and station which new wealth was engendering. Being difficult to expand, it was, no doubt, just as cheap to demolish and build anew as to modernise these old castles although that did happen at Culzean and Oxenfoord. However, one would probably be correct in assuming that the majority of them were very decayed if the accounts of Inveraray and Melville are anything to go by. Then, too, their harsh, angular silhouettes, frequently lacking in ornament or external decoration did not appeal to the eighteenth century notion of Gothic. By and large, Alnwick and Raby with their great size, irregular outlines, spiky silhouettes and multitudinous towers and battlements were much more the castle concept although even their outlines had to be improved upon by being liberally daubed with gun-loops and crosslets.

In Scotland, there is, of course, very little internal Gothic decoration. Castles were built to display ancestry and landed power and, as such, were in the Scottish tradition whereas the interior should have all the comforts and graces of classical refinement. There is, too, the influence of Robert Adam in this respect. He seems to have preferred the division between Gothic and classical. At Alnwick, however, the interior decoration was a decision obviously imposed by the owners, and carried over into the entire estate, while in County Durham the lead was given by the predilections of certain of the Prince-Bishops. Also Henry, second Earl of Darlington, seems to have had a mind of his own in the matter. Judging by the extent and variety of his Gothic activities at Raby, both

Plate 89   Design for an alcove.
Paul Decker. 1759.

inside and outside, his was a personal commitment to Gothic. Like the Duchess Elizabeth at Alnwick, he seems to have had a romantic turn of mind which found an outlet in transforming the house and estate into something worthy of a northern prince. In addition there may well have been an element of rivalry between the Earl and the Prince-Bishops whose seat at Bishop Auckland was only eight miles to the north.

Yet despite the large scale works at Alnwick and Ford and the later ones at Raby and at Auckland Castle (until 1795 that is) it is apparent that there was very little development of Gothic as a style of interior decoration and even less when considered as architecture whether in secular architecture or in the uncommon instances of religious architecture. There are, it is true, changes but looked at broadly one can maintain that the thirty years preceding 1795 show little advance either in technique or knowledge. True the forms employed become increasingly sophisticated and complex. Yet basically they remain as variations on the early material so that by the middle of the nineties Gothic was played out. It had exhausted itself and if the Gothic movement was to continue then it had to be recharged. That, of course, is what happened.

Obviously, there were the activities of James Wyatt but whereas Auckland Castle must have caused a stir that was only local while Fonthill Abbey did not become a national curiosity until the next century. What was, therefore, of crucial importance in the life history of the Gothic movement was the appearance of a large number of pattern books in the late eighties and in the nineties so that after about 1795 architects had much more information than had hitherto been available. Previously, there had been Batty Langley's *Gothic Architecture Improved* first published in 1742. Although criticised even in its own time[6] and, when looking at the plates, easily treated as a joke, nevertheless of the few books of plates devoted to Gothic it remained the most useful for architects and if many of the actual designs in *Gothic Architecture Improved* do not seem to have been built, the slim volume was as essential an architectural source to the architect of two hundred years ago as is the *Architectural*

Plates 90 and 91   Designs for farm buildings. Thomas Lightoler. 1762.

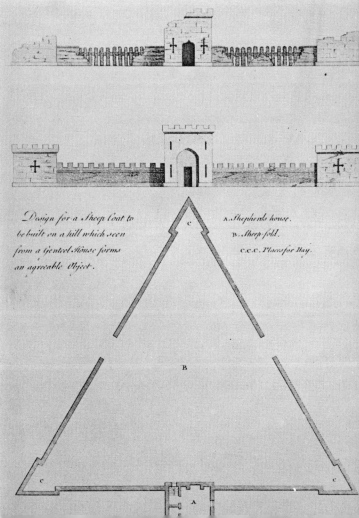

Review to to-day's practitioners. There was also Paul Decker's *Gothic Architecture Decorated* (1759) from which plate VI, a design for an alcove (Plate 89), would seem to have been the inspiration for the decorative treatment of the ceremonial gateway at Auckland Castle in 1760 while from Lightoler's *The Gentleman and Farmer's Architect* plates 24 and 25 (Plates 90 and 91), probably provided many of the elements for the courtyard at Ford Castle especially as it was 'in a great Measure intended to Obstruct Objects not wanted to be Seen'.[7] In addition, the design of the front of

Plate 92   Designs for Gothic houses. W. and J. Halfpenny. 1752.

Mauldslie Castle, despite its overt Scottishness, seems to have been an amalgamation of two elevations published as plate 11 in *Chinese and Gothic Architecture Properly Ornamented* by W. and J. Halfpenny in 1752 (Plate 92). However, Langley's book was the richest vein. In the saloon at Fowberry, the cornice is derived from a Batty Langley pattern[8] and Robert Adam's attempt at Alnwick to squeeze Gothic into a classical system, as well as many of his Gothic details, also comes from Langley. For instance, plates II and III (Plate 93) can be compared with the Adam banqueting-house cornice while the capitals of Brizlee Tower can be traced back to plate XII. In addition, 'Capability' Brown perhaps used the same pattern book[9] in his arrangement of the triple lights on the ground floor of Hulne Priory (Plate 94) while further south, in County Durham, James Paine also relied on Langley not only for the fenestration of Axwell Park dower house but also at Raby Castle. Langley's influence, too, may be seen at Inveraray Castle in some of the details, such as the entrance mouldings, while plate LXI shows quatrefoil windows placed over the main lights exactly as is found in the *Vitruvius Scoticus* design for Douglas Castle.

172

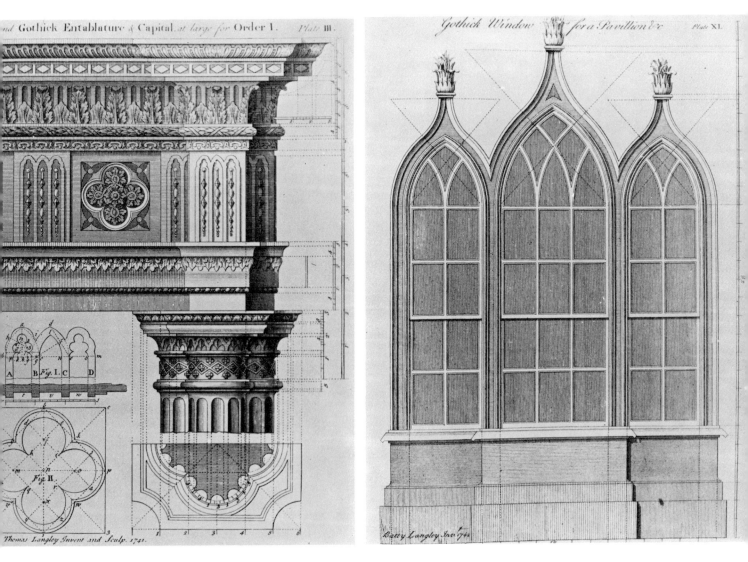

Gothick Entablature & Capital at large for Order I. Plate III.

Gothick Window for a Pavilion &c Plate XL.

Thomas Langley Invent and Sculp. 1741.

Batty Langley Inv. 1741.

Plates 93 and 94   Gothic entablature and capital and a Gothic window for
a pavilion. Batty and Thomas Langley.

In view of such a dependence on Langley, it is hardly surprising
that a complaint should be levelled in 1781 (almost forty years after the
appearance of Gothic at Inveraray) that 'this style of building is so much
neglected by us, that few of our present artists can now make a design
truly Gothick'.[10] It was an omission which over the next few years
would be rectified with the publication of Gough's *Sepulchral Monuments
of Great Britain* in 1786 with illustrations by John Carter who also
produced, in the same year, his own *Specimens of Ancient Sculpture and
Painting* to be followed in another nine years by the summation of his
antiquarian researches, *The Ancient Architecture of England*. Unlike the

173

earlier works by Langley and Decker, the new volumes, and others by Grose and Hearne, were not of that variety of books which, as Carter wrote, 'seem to answer no other purpose than merely to give satisfaction to the admiration of scenic effect, or to the collectors for county histories'.[11] The new volumes were historical studies designed to set out the origins and growth of Gothic remains but which in so doing established new standards for the neo-Gothic architect and patron alike by displaying in design and in carved decoration a range of material never before available.

However, the most important figure in the movement towards greater archaeological exactitude was neither an antiquarian nor a scholar but the publisher, John Britton.[12] With the instinct of a Northcliffe or a Beaverbrook, he realised that 'the greater number of readers require variety, picturesque effect, and general views'.[13] These needs were satisfied in the numerous and beautiful plates of the *Architectural Antiquities of Great Britain* which, appearing in five volumes from 1807 onwards, was also designed 'To elucidate some of the many doubtful and obscure circumstances relating to the origin, styles, dates and other peculiarities of the interesting ancient English edificies'.[14] That task was finally concluded in an important essay in the closing volume which, rather interestingly, was dedicated to John Nash.

It was the union of the appeal to both the scholars and the educated public which guaranteed the success of Britton's numerous publishing enterprises. Other publishers produced less costly works which demonstrated the growing popularity and strength of the Gothic Revival by their numbers. Some made important individual contributions to the movement. There was Neale's *Collegiate and Parochial Churches*, which, with plates by Le Kueux, appeared in 1824. It listed various churches, without any attempt at chronology or the assessment of individual importance and lacked plans, sections, scales and detailing. Yet it is apparent that the plates had a considerable influence on contemporary architects who put into effect many of the scenes depicted. By and large the architecture shown was Early English but without a great deal in the way of detail since the size of the plates and the selected views permitted only broad effects. What was illustrated could, therefore, be easily copied and cheaply at that.

If nothing else the sheer quantity of material produced in the early nineteenth century on Gothic, whether it was of the *Views of Seats* variety or *Sepulchral Remains*, played a part in bringing to the public notice a fresh awareness of what Gothic was all about and a greater discernment in what was required in such a building. Thus, by someone like Gillespie Graham, there would be an unfaltering distinction between baronial or castellated Gothic and ecclesiastical. Such edifices would represent the middle phase between Strawberry Hill and the entire eighteenth century movement on the one hand and the efforts of Pugin, on the other, to revive a constructional Gothic. They were, too, the products of a society which was not only more sophisticated in its taste than hitherto but was fast becoming aware of an exclusive and recondite Gothic vocabulary. That enabled Gothic, for the first time, to be analysed not as classical architecture in one comprehensible unit, but rather as individual parts with the name of each heavily evocative of 'that solemn dignity which irresistibly fills the mind with religious awe, to the excitement of which, ancient Cathedral and Monastic Churches contribute in a degree so far beyond all other ecclesiastical structures, that the art of man has ever yet produced'.[15] Similar laudatory outbursts could likewise be provoked by the chivalric notion of the Middle Ages so that in 1800 a visitor to Oatlands, the Gothic mansion then being built by the Duke of York, could report, 'How were my ears gratified to hear the workmen talk of the East tower, its hanging turret and buttress; the Saxon entrance . . . the galleries, etc., etc.! and to crown the whole I heard the Duke enquire, "When will they begin my Bower window?"'[16] Such a rhapsodising of the Gothic elements was, of course, a part of the fashionable rage for the picturesque, in which, it was generally accepted Gothic was the ideal architectural style.

The term 'the picturesque' was introduced into critical aesthetics by William Gilpin (1724–1804), a curate and schoolmaster who spent the summer vacations on sketching tours throughout Britain, the fruits of which were published at intervals after 1782.[17] Gilpin accepted many of Burke's indicatives of taste. 'In a ruin', he explained, 'The reigning ideas are solitude, neglect and desolation.' Obviously, such qualities are not so desirable around a house where the surroundings should have elegance and grandeur 'because harmony and propriety require it'.[18] Once again there is a common factor with Burke in the requirement of the large scale conjoined with wildness and regularity not in juxtaposition but as part of a total environment acceptable to the eye of the beholder. Nevertheless, if Gilpin had only restated Burke's dicta he would never be studied to-day. His importance is that by adding certain new elements to Burke's prescription he gave new force and vigour to the concept of the aesthetic.

Although Gilpin published three essays on picturesque travel and picturesque beauty in 1792 it is in the published tours that the more practical examples and conclusions are found. Thus in the 1772 tour of

175

Cumberland and Westmorland, published in 1786, Gilpin had begun to move away from Burke's philosophy. However, not until 1776, after a similar journey to Scotland, did Gilpin's aesthetical theorising, as it appears from his own writings, coalesce into a definite code of thought. In Scotland Gilpin encountered tracts of land 'intirely (sic) in a state of nature'.[19] Gilpin's immediate but conditional surrender to such a state meant that henceforth formal art could not be countenanced since art only serves to sophisticate and therefore despoil nature.[20] Agriculture must also be precluded since agriculturalists 'have miserably scratched, and injured the face of the globe. Wherever man appears . . . deformity follows his steps.'[21] Inevitably, therefore, 'all the formalities of hedge-row trees, and square divisions of property, are disgusting in a high degree'.[22] Despite such rhetorical vehemence Gilpin does allow that cultivation has its uses, not in any practical sense but because those same hedge-rows and fields can, at a 'remote' distance, form a rich aspect further embellished by a variety of architectural forms of which the finest are ruins.[23] With such a syndrome, then, it is apparent that Gilpin's view of nature was somewhat limited.

If physical formalism is out, Gilpin was still sufficiently of his time, like Burke before him, to know that there must be, nevertheless, an underlying form, a set of disciplines which existed in all things, a concept which protagonists of Gothic architecture would also accept. Thus Gilpin stated conclusively that 'the rules of picturesque beauty . . . are drawn from nature'.[24] Such an attitude is, of course, wholly subjective and indeed in his analytical discourses, and again like Burke, Gilpin makes use not only of subjective ideas but of subjection in his terminology. Certainly, in the seventeen seventies and eighties one expects to find much use of solitude and desolation but these are bedfellows with negligence, roughness and wildness (an especial favourite) and, occasionally, ferocity—traits which characterise the simplicity as well as the grandeur of nature. In Burke the subjective was passive; with Gilpin it becomes wildly active since it has been infused with the dynamic energy of passion arising from the play of the imagination when confronted with and allied to mountains, lakes and rivers.

Arising from such a fusion, Gilpin's most important additive to eighteenth century theory was the cult of the picturesque. The word occurs repeatedly in the *Tour of Scotland* especially where he claims 'that the picturesque eye has a kind of fastidiousness about it, that it is seldom pleased with any artificial attempts to please. It must find its own beauties; and often fixes . . . on some accidental, rough object, which the common eye would pass unnoticed.'[25] That being the case, then the quality of the picturesque lies not in the object perceived but in the eye of the beholder. Its applications would seem to be limitless. That was not to be. Romantic and picturesque were not synonymous so that Gilpin while not accepting Edinburgh Castle as picturesque[26] doubtless would have admitted its romantic attributes. Also certain objects were more picturesque than others. Nature, when it is simple and grand, is picturesque and, of course, so are ruins. Of the latter, while castles are very acceptable they are outclassed by abbeys although abroad 'Where popery prevails, the abbey is still intire (sic) and inhabited and of course less adapted to landscape'.[27] Animals certainly could be picturesque. Regarding people, however, Gilpin had grave doubts. People only qualified as 'picturesque appendages'[28] and those best suited to scenes of grandeur were 'clad in long, folding draperies' such as soldiers, gypsies or banditti.[29] Unfortunately, it must be admitted that in the British mountains banditti in long, folding draperies are scarce.

But if the above was all that made up the picturesque its appeal would have become common property much sooner than it did. Yet the picturesque was not for the 'common eye' but for the discerning and the knowledgeable. One had to be trained to look at a view in a particular way otherwise the picturesque response would be lacking. Even nature, after all had its imperfections although the cognoscenti could acquire a vocabulary which, while it acknowledged these defects, could attempt remedies. Therefore it cannot cause surprise to discover that another of Gilpin's favourite terms was 'improve'. Naked mountains were not attractive needing 'the drapery of a little wood'[30] to break their regularity. Even in Scotland only 'The grand outlines are all laid in; a little finishing is all we want'.[31] Thus in the foreground necessary parts were a winding road or river (reminiscent of Hogarth's line of beauty), cascades, ragged rocks and 'broken knolls'.[32] Animals could also be included and, indeed, it would have been difficult to exclude them. The Scottish specimens disappointed Gilpin. The cattle were black and white 'which make together the most inharmonious of all mixtures'. Also their horns were too wide and their countenances usually sour. The sheep were better. They were quite ordinary sheep 'but in their tattered rough attire, exceedingly picturesque'.[33] Such features presented much variety of material and form. Variety had been explicitly condemned by Burke.[34] Gilpin not only accepts but proclaims variety as one of the sources of the picturesque.[35] The other is simplicity. Now although it is never bluntly stated it is clear that the chief source of the picturesque movement lies in variety. Simplicity often springs from regularity and continuity of form, characteristics which 'will always displease' unless offset by the charms

177

of contrast.[36] By themselves simplicity promotes the sublime and variety the beautiful; together they bring forth the picturesque.[37]

That was the doctrine which was to have such revolutionary effects not only in the appreciation of landscape, so that it is still spoken of as picturesque, but when applied to architecture it permitted the softening of the symmetrical plan and elevations, hitherto all pervasive in architecture. After Gilpin, architecture was to be regarded as a series of different and surprising effects rather than one harmonious and overriding whole as with, say, Marble Hill. After all, 'Variety and intricacies are beauties and excellences in every other of the arts which address the imagination: and why not in architecture?'[38] So questioned Sir Joshua Reynolds, the President of the Royal Academy.

Gilpin's ideas—they could scarcely be termed a system of philosophy—exerted a profound influence not only on the taste of Britain but also of Europe.[39] In addition, his many books and their carefully composed illustrations not only reiterated his ideas but presented them in a manner which could win a popular acceptance beside the more academic theorists. Yet in modern works dealing with the role of aesthetics and the rise of a viewpoint, Gilpin's name is almost uniformly omitted in favour of his contemporaries, Payne Knight, Uvedale Price and Humphry Repton. Although each of these three men added something of significance to the cult of the picturesque yet it all has a common ground in Gilpin. Indeed, Price admitted the influence of Gilpin's early writings, 'From whose very ingenious and extensive observations . . . I have received great pleasure and instruction',[40] and none of the later accretions to the theory and philosophy destroyed Gilpin's vision of the picturesque which was neatly categorised by Price. 'The two opposite qualities of roughness, and of sudden variation, joined to that of irregularity, are the most efficient causes of the picturesque'.[41]

The cult was given a philosophical basis by Payne Knight with the publication in 1794 of *The Landscape, a Didactic Poem*. It was an attack on the 'Capability' Brown school of landscape.

> Hence, hence! thou haggard fiend, however call'd,
> Thin, meagre genius of the bare and bald;
> Thy spade and mattock here at length lay down
> And follow to the tomb thy favourite Brown.[42]

It was contended that Brown's followers had produced '. . . one dull, vapid, smooth, unvaried scene',[43] which Knight considered to be artificial and therefore a contortion of nature. Knight's friend and neighbour Uvedale

Price, immediately replied with *Sketches and Hints on Landscape Gardening* in which, rejecting didacticism, he favoured practicality and utility.[44]

From these and other treatises certain notable ideas, including the removal of the picturesque from landscape to architecture, emerged of which possibly the most important was Price's contribution in recognising and isolating the concept of association. 'All external objects', he wrote, 'Affect us in two different ways; by the impression they make on the senses, and by the reflections they suggest to the mind'.[45] To rouse such impressions and reflections Gothic architecture was the ideal medium. Price admitted that ruins were picturesque,[46] a common enough notion, but considered that the same quality could be fixed in abodes by creating an irregular structure which when viewed from many points would have variety and intricacy but where the angled windows would frame suitable views for the occupant.[47] In addition the domestic offices, instead of being hidden away in a basement or obscured 'behind a close plantation of Scotch firs', should be allowed to act as a connection between the house and the surrounding scenery which, if brought by means of planting to the house, would further reduce its regularity.[48] As to architectural style Price and Repton were equally agreed on the supremacy of Gothic, especially of castles which were 'The most picturesque *habitable* buildings',[49] when it came to the picturesque which demanded so much in the way of variety, irregularity and intricacy. These excellences, as Knight would have termed them, all appeared in his own irregular and castellated home, Downton Castle, built from 1774–8. Yet for its time, it was too advanced for, as Knight admitted in 1805, few had thought to copy his example[50] although within a very few more years that would no longer be the case.

Indeed, the opening decades of the new century were to witness not only a remarkable burst of activity for the entire Gothic movement but also its spread into the more distant parts of England, such as Cumberland and Westmorland, and the remoter areas of Scotland. This diffusion was hastened and aided by the increase in travel in northern Britain in the later eighteenth and early nineteenth centuries. As early as 1789 *The Gentleman's Magazine* reported that 'Travelling through the Northern parts of our island, besides being conducive to health, has become a fashionable amusement during the summer and harvest months'.[51] This was despite Arthur Young's dire warning of nearly twenty years before: 'I must in general advise all who travel on any business but absolute necessity to avoid any journey, further north than Newcastle'.[52] This was because of the poor state of the roads and, of course, until they were improved travellers had no choice but to accept Young's advice. However, improvements gradually came about. A stagecoach called The Fly began to run from London over Stanemore to Glasgow in 1774 and the Mail along the Kendal and Shap road in 1786.[53] These improvements in communication necessitated better roads. Such a state of affairs already existed in Scotland where the aftermath of the Jacobite rebellions had yielded the legacy of Wade's roads. Then for a good number of years after 1803, £20,000 was spent annually on new roads and bridges[54] which rendered the Highlands accessible to southern visitors who, even before the end of the eighteenth century, had been travelling to Scotland in considerable numbers either for shooting, hunting or the contemplation of the picturesque. In time such visits necessitated northern homes. Nevertheless, the total number of visitors was small. Garnett in his 1810 *Tour of Scotland* remarked, 'Were the roads in the highlands supported by a toll, I should suppose that half-a-crown, or five shillings a horse would be necessary to pay the interest of the money laid out in forming them, so few are the travellers'.[55] During his first three weeks in the Highlands, Garnett claimed never to have met a single other traveller[56] although Sir Walter Scott was writing in the same year: 'The number of English travellers have of late years made the Highland tours tolerable which they were not in my former visits to the mountains—so that we have no tale of hardship or even of privation'.[57] The same tale was written of the Lake District so that when in 1817 Louis Simond wrote contentedly 'England seems to be the country-house of London'[58] he was at Windermere. Nearby 'Land, half-rock is bought up at any price merely on account of the beauty of the spot'[59] and he cited as an example that two acres near Grasmere fetched £1,500[60] which was a very great increase on the few shillings an acre such land would have fetched in Arthur Young's time.

Thus in response to the picturesque and with ease of access, Gothic mansions and churches would begin to appear in large numbers in north west England and in the Highlands and along the west coast of Scotland. And though the Adam influence would flicker fitfully into the nineteenth century, the effects of the scholars' researches, changing the plan, composition and details of Gothic edifices, enabled architects to produce the variety and elaboration which the picturesque required.

XI

Paterson and the Adam Inheritance

So far the history of the Gothic Revival in north Britain has shown markedly different characteristics between England and Scotland. True, the figure of Robert Adam, and perhaps that of James Wyatt,[1] bestrides the Border which, nevertheless, fulfills its historic role of separating different cultures. Thus Alnwick with its Gothic interiors bears little affinity to the conglomerate of Adam's Scottish castles with their interest in dimensional grouping and subsidiary massing. As has already been shown, such stylistic variations of approach to the Gothic movement in England and Scotland should not be related to a division between an early and a late Adam Gothic style but rather to cultural and social differences which, stemming from separate national backgrounds of history, economic wealth and social organisation, express themselves in contradistinction north and south of the Border. Thus it is the court Gothic of Alnwick which is the pace-setter for the north of England whereas in Scotland continuing forces stem from the courtyard theme of Culzean and the symbolic importance of the castle in land tenure and *ipso facto* political dominance. Nevertheless, there comes a moment right at the end of the eighteenth century and the opening of the next when, for the first time, the divisions across the Border cease with Robert Adam's former clerk of works, John Paterson of Edinburgh. This is a unique moment for never again is there to be such harmony when the Border is of no account either in terms of commissions accomplished or of subliminal historic influences. Certainly, such a national figure as Robert Smirke would work in England and in Scotland but without influencing local architectural characteristics and it is the local men, Dobson in Newcastle and Gillespie Graham in Edinburgh, who dominate their native localities but do not cross the Border. Although affected by national trends, their works, nevertheless, bear such an individual stamp

181

that it is correct to write historically of a northern English school and a Scottish school. Indeed, the latter term was well understood by the middle of the century when the removal of William Burn from Edinburgh to the south led to its spread beyond the confines of Scotland, although, by that date, the Scottishness was being diluted in other historic styles.

Unfortunately, little is known about Paterson's career once he was practising on his own account after the death of Robert Adam in 1792. His correspondence as Adam's clerk of works survives but after that there is nothing and he remains a shadowy, enigmatic figure, whose name occurs all too infrequently on a few documents or as a footnote on a scholar's page. Yet in his time Paterson must have been well known to judge by an extensive practice and many important commissions.

Paterson's earliest individual work seems to be the stables at Castle Fraser in Aberdeenshire in 1794[2] with a plan derived from old Seton Castle and the detail of the towers from Mauldslie. Next came Monzie Castle in Perthshire (Plate 95) which was begun about 1795 for General Campbell.[3] It is a more mature and powerful composition still looking back to the

Plate 95   John Paterson. Monzie Castle, Perthshire. 1795.

architecture of Robert Adam but suppressing enough Adam traits to allow its own character to emerge. That character is neo-classical not only in the boldness of the individual parts, in the clash of hemicycle and towers against the main core, but in the stark monumentality which, eschewing decorations, relies on scale and proportion for effect. By its very plainness, the avoidance of architectural tricks, Monzie could be dismissed so easily as second rate when in fact it is the product of one who, to quote a contemporary, 'Has judiciously introduced this style of house into those parts of Scotland, which are upon a grand and a wild scale'.[4]

At Monzie several pronounced architectural details appear and although their genesis is in the Adam canon, nevertheless, their maturity becomes markedly characteristic of Paterson. There is the double string-course, a feature found on many of the Adam castles, notably at Seton and Pitfour, but without consideration of purpose except as a visual binding element. At Monzie, however, the string-courses firmly, gently and very quietly mark off the exposed basement from the *piano nobile* which is further emphasised by unusually tall windows crowned by labels. These perform no function nor are they integral to the design. Their purpose is merely to reiterate the existence of a state floor. In these respects of basement, double string-course and hood-moulds, Monzie comes close to Wedderburn, which, of all the Adam castles, has the most militaristic air. At Monzie, too, the impression of power is further stated not only by solid compactness but by the splayed bases of the corner towers while defensive interest is considered by placing each embrasure over the aligned windows of the towers. Indeed, despite their many windowed exteriors, bedizened with crosslets and shot-holes, Adam's castles are essentially studies in introversion whereas at Monzie the aspect is outward and though there are numerous windows they create, not tranquility but the angled watchfulness of many eyes.

At Eglinton Castle in Ayrshire, however, the martial mood was softened as befitted a more southern and fertile setting. Eglinton (now only a ruined fragment) was built for Hugh, twelfth Earl of Eglinton (1740–1819). In the seventeen sixties his family was living in 'a disagreeable mansion' and although a site had been laid out for a new house[5] it was not until thirty years later that Eglinton was rebuilt.[6] 'It was originally intended to preserve the old circular tower, which stood in the centre of the building; to this the staircase was sacrificed; and though it was afterwards found necessary to remove the tower, the general plan remains unaltered'.[7] Another tower was built[8] to provide, through an accident of history, a clumsy silhouette which was foreign to the general run of Paterson's output. Like Monzie, the castle (Plate 96) was of quadrilateral form but with the attached corner towers rising well above the wall-head so that there was not the clenched forcefulness of Monzie. The form was no longer static and it was given movement by low wings each pulling out from the centre. The parapets were solid but interrupted, as at Monzie, above the windows of the towers and the hemicycle where the state

Plate 96   John Paterson. The entrance front. Eglinton Castle, Ayrshire. Begun in 1797. Demolished.

apartments were marked off above and below by double string-courses. Adam had always reserved the use of a hemicycle for the rear elevations preferring to leave his entrance front flat and emphasising length as opposed to height. However, at both Eglinton and at Monzie the central bow not only included the entrance but rose high above like a soaring watch-tower. Yet at Barmoor in England, where many of the usual Paterson elements are displayed, there is a notable advance in the treatment of the centre.

Barmoor, as is so often the case in Northumberland, was originally a pele-tower which was hidden beneath the new house by Paterson in 1801.[9] His plans were never completely fulfilled which is a pity since, if they had been, Northumberland would have possessed one of the finest expressions of the neo-classical mood in the country. At Barmoor a central block, with, on either side, a subsidiary wing ending in an attached round tower, provided the basic plan. While that was similar to Eglinton it differed at Barmoor where the stables and other offices were enclosed within the same building complex to the rear. Although, as at Paterson's two Scottish houses, the hemicycle remains locked within the main structure, at Barmoor it is given its own dynamic by being recessed above

184

the entrance and flanked by buttress-like turrets which, pushing outwards, provide a sense of baroque movement to the otherwise frozen composition.

To judge from Barmoor and other later houses, there were in all these mansions classical interiors and noble staircases. Also Paterson's planning, as might have been expected from a disciple of Adam, was handled dexterously and lightly with each house containing at least one oval reception room. Within Barmoor, as well as in the apartments created at Chillingham Castle, also in Northumberland, for the Earl of Tankerville,[10] there were suites of oval rooms all decorated in a very restrained classical style, owing less to Adam than to the neo-classical movement in general.

Ovoid shapes and modified Adam decorations and colourings were also to be found at Fetteresso Castle now only a ruinous shell. Lying near the Kincardineshire coast, it was originally a home of the Earl Marischals of Scotland, by one of whom it was enlarged in 1671[11] to constitute two wings set at right angles. Despite some repairs carried out in 1783–5,[12] just after the sale of the estate to Admiral Robert Duff,[13] the building had substantially retained its late seventeenth century form until it was enlarged in 1808.[14] A fat tower, placed between the two wings, permitted a grand entrance through an elliptical hall to a fine butterfly staircase. The south wing was refaced and its great hall divided into a dining-room and drawing-room while the north wing was broadened by slapping a corridor against the old entrance facade on the west. Although there is no direct evidence that Paterson was responsible for these changes, the knowledge that he did design the parish church in 1810[15] and that much of the planning and interior decoration resembled his products elsewhere make it a fair assumption that Fetteresso Castle is from the same hand. However, unlike Robert Adam in his late years, Paterson was unsympathetic to the old vernacular work and hid the original elevations to fabricate a composition which, albeit on a weaker note, repeats the Monzie theme. Cast in the same austere mould is Fasque (1809).[16] It has polygonal angle towers and a two storey wing on either side, after the fashion of Melville, but otherwise it is devoid of decoration which would relieve its stark bluntness. Although there is no documentary evidence to link its creation with Paterson, yet its appearance in the same county as Fetteresso, the coincidence of dates, and the internal sequence of a hall and butterfly staircase leading to an oval top-lit saloon, all bespeak Paterson.

In 1811 Paterson was commissioned to produce a portfolio of designs for additions to Pitfirrane Castle in Fife.[17] What is so striking about them is not that they are in Paterson's heavy castellated manner, which so obviously eschews the mannersims of the conventional pointed neo-Gothic, but that there are no concessions whatsoever to the scale, irregularity or picturesque qualities of the vernacular tower-house. It is almost as if Paterson had neither read nor heard of the writers on the picturesque. Such an inflexible approach when confronted with the vernacular, whether in England at Barmoor or in Scotland, is in striking

Plate 97   John Paterson. The barbican. Brancepeth Castle, County Durham.

contrast to his late master's attitude when dealing with such projects as Seton and Cluny. One is left wondering, therefore, just how much respect Paterson had for the medieval castle of the Nevilles at Brancepeth in County Durham. Probably, it was very little especially bearing in mind the enthusiastic commentary which Rowland Burdon the younger, of Castle Eden sent off from Brancepeth early in February, 1819, to his friend John Soane. 'I am here in the midst of masons, etc. collected to build a huge addition to this antient Baronial Castle. My friend Mr Russell has set out very boldly, and as his powers are great he will not be easily stop'd. It is to bear the name of its founder, "the Russell Tower", and he seems to be executing it well according to the pattern of other parts of the Castle. He has got his Architect from Scotland, a Mr Patterson (sic) of whom I had not before heard, but who has been employed by some people of note in Scotland, and seems an intelligent man. Besides the Tower in question he makes extensive alterations and additions to the habitable part of the Castle so as to render it one of the largest and probably most magnificent dwellings in the

186

Island. If you visit C. Eden, as I hope you will next summer, You must allow me to bring you over to Brancepeth.'[18]

In its time Paterson's renovation of Brancepeth (Plate 97) was much admired.[19] And why not? Had not the works, starting perhaps in 1818,[20] cost their owner £120,000[21] when the purchase price of the estate, some twenty years before by his father, had been a little over half that sum.[22]

Plate 98   The castle at Volterra. Drawn by Robert Adam while on his Italian tour.

Yet a plentiful supply of money and an historic site could not provide an architectural masterpiece for, despite its burly aggressiveness, Brancepeth was emasculated by Paterson. He allowed himself to be controlled by the plan and the irregular forms but could not resist the temptation to create the architecture anew in his own style. Thus the exteriors do not read in volumetric terms but only as two dimensional design exercises bearing no relationship in terms of historical function to whatever happens behind them. Only in the barbican, perhaps copied (Plate 98) from a design by Adam,[23] is there truth because there Paterson is himself. Honest nineteenth century work, the flanking towers have their own challenging vigour and strength. But of what avail are these when there is nothing beyond the portals to defend for the courtyard ranges

187

are dull and uninspired partly because of the regularity but also because quite obviously Paterson was neither an antiquarian nor even a James Wyatt? The Adam Gothic tradition did not depend on the eclectic reproduction of medieval details for effect so that when these were required then quite clearly Paterson could not succeed. Thus the ashlar is too smooth, the buttresses too protuberant, the windows an unhappy synthesis of Norman and Decorated and the embrasures at the wall-heads too cramped as though the architect was loathe to interrupt the skyline. Altogether too cool, without the spatial excitement of the court-yard at Culzean, and without the detail, the oddities, the surprises and, indeed, the waywardness of medieval work, Paterson's attempt at re-constructing a baronial home falls flat for, although comprising genuine bits and pieces, it fails to make a valid historical statement.

It was unfortunate that Paterson should have been building at Brancepeth in the second decade of the nineteenth century when archaeo-logical exactitude was being called for, since his schemata had gelatined in the Adam mould of thirty years before. It is not perhaps to be wondered at, therefore, that Monzie should have been the finest of Paterson's works. Lacking what might be expected in the way of Gothic detailing, lancets, crosslets and such like, it is, nevertheless, a notable composition and with its successors demonstrates Paterson's importance. After all, it is he who, almost single-handed, carried the Gothic Revival forward into the nineteenth century, so that he becomes the link between Robert Adam and the second generation of his followers, men like Richard Crichton, the Elliots and even James Gillespie Graham who would hold the field until almost the middle of the century as a leader of the Gothic movement.

More directly Paterson's preference for massive, unadorned and regular castellated forms may perhaps be seen in at least three houses, beginning with Caprington Castle in Ayrshire. Its history remains obscure and what little is known comes from one source.[24] Seemingly, the design for remodelling an older house dates from 1797 although it remained in abeyance until 1820 by which date it was possible to include extensive Gothic decorations internally. Yet the exterior speaks clearly of the era of classical symmetry and proportion in a defiantly massive four-square block buttressed at the corners and with a canted tower in the centre of the main front.

The same uncompromising form also occurs at Harvieston Castle in Clackmannanshire in 1804[25] and helps to produce a block plan less grandiose but basically similar to Eglinton. Another of the same genre is Smyllum Park near Lanark (c. 1814)[26] where, to an earlier house, there has been added an imposing front which displays a return to square towers clasping the corners although these may have been inspired by Loudon Castle in Ayrshire (1804). At Smyllum the drum of the central tower is fully developed and brought well forward from the facade and supported on either side by lesser towers snuggling between it and the flat facade. The entrance is at the base of the tower but is rendered even more

Plate 99   Richard Crichton. Rossie Castle, Angus. 1800. Demolished.

insignificant by the guard of a pencil-slim tower on either side of the jambs. The loss of importance of the doorway and the ruthless juxtaposition of the hard shapes at Smyllum all reflect the neo-classical outlook. Yet there has been little development from Monzie, except that the central tower has been released, and there is nothing more to be said of those anonymous castles, Caprington, Harvieston and Smyllum.

A second line of descent from Adam, and in the end more fruitful, can be traced in those architects who remained more overtly loyal to the Adam Gothic concept. There was Richard Crichton who began his independent architectural career at the turn of the nineteenth century but died in 1817 at the early age of forty-six.[27] In those few years he was to produce half a dozen works of such signal achievement that he must be ranked as one of the seminal figures of his period. Although he was essentially a classical architect, Adam castellation was employed at Rossie Castle and at Abercairny Abbey after 1804[28] to such effect that had their author lived he must have rivalled Gillespie Graham for pre-eminence.

At Rossie Castle in Angus (1800)[29] Crichton scarcely went beyond the bounds set by Adam yet where he did it was to add something of significance. Unlike Adam, Crichton's castellated style (Plate 99) was serene and, instead of being closed in upon itself, set a gay front to the world. Though there were battlements and even a crow-stepped gable, but of the smallest, daintiest kind, the architecture was classically composed as were the interiors. Significantly, however, apart from the usual public rooms, Crichton had to provide for the new century's tastes in a museum and a conservatory[30] which was the excuse for the long colonnades rippling outwards whose glass fronts made for a harmony of solid and void. Indeed, the refulgent sophistication of Rossie Castle makes Paterson's labours in the same vein look crude by comparison.

Beside Crichton other architects were second rate although they were competent enough. Such a one was Alexander Laing who rebuilt Darnaway Castle for the Earl of Moray over a period of ten years after 1802.[31] Yet the story began quite six years before and is interesting because Darnaway is singularly well documented whereas for almost every other one of its contemporaries only second hand descriptions remain which is a marked contrast with the relatively plentiful supply of records in the previous century. The Darnaway records are also important because it is clear that for once Gothic was selected, indeed necessary, not because of hazy theoretical notions about the picturesque, but because whatever was done at Darnaway had to be linked to Randolph's Hall with its superb fourteenth century timber roof. Concern had been expressed about its safety in 1794[32] and some repairs were made.[33] However, two years later the remainder of the building was in such poor condition that a replacement at either the north or the south end of the Hall was being considered.[34] Laing charged twelve guineas for the drawings in February, 1797.[35] Later in the same year he was preparing Gothic elevations[36] 'which would have such an appearance as Darnaway Castle should have'.[37] However, an objection was raised by Lord Moray[38] and in February, 1798, another Gothic elevation and plan was drawn at a cost of three guineas.[39] Nothing further seems to have been done for three years when yet one more set of plans and elevations was prepared.[40] On this occasion there was neither objection nor delay and by the spring of the following year the working drawings had been produced,[41] the foundations had been dug[42] and the foundation stone laid with due ceremony which included four pints of whisky at 3s 6d.[43] Thereafter, the building proceeded rapidly although the documentary evidence diminishes. Yet in July 1805 a Gothic window was drawn at large for the great hall as well as sketches for porters' lodges.[44] By 1809 the works had cost well over £14,000,[45] which was seven times the modest expenditure calculated for the addition in 1796,[46] and construction was to continue for another three years.[47]

According to one nineteenth century writer, Darnaway has 'an imposing and princely appearance'[48] and for once that is true although other qualities are observable in the modesty and reticence of the even facades which remain unbroken save for the ends of the main front which step forward one pace as does the central tower. Within these facades, so carefully composed with regard to an inherited proportional system, there is no passion, no defiance but instead an aloof calm. Certainly, the entrance is enriched by a surround of Gothic lights and the skyline by a castellated trim complete with the regular quota of lug-turrets. Still, if it was necessary for sound historical reasons to accept Gothic that was no reason why the eighteenth century should be overthrown. One can understand why the classical-Gothic concept was accepted for, was it not civilised and elegant, fulfilling that moderation which is the hall-mark of so much that has been best in the British way of life? Undoubtedly, an architect like Laing, and others like him were not great. Yet it was given to them to sum up the virtues of an age; and perhaps they saw no need, or had no desire, to go beyond that. Others did for the old ways could not continue for ever and, prompted by the picturesque, men wanted to change to more exciting, less cerebral architectural forms at the same time as British architecture, because of the Napoleonic Wars and the subsequent sealing off of Europe, became introspective.

Thus architects like the Elliots and Gillespie Graham were to develop their Adam inheritance so that by its finish in 1812 Darnaway could have been looked upon as old fashioned. Yet it has its own place in the Gothic Revival for the summer of the eighteenth century fructifies at Darnaway; it is the last notable expression of the Adam school. Its debt to Adam and particularly to Mellerstain, but without its panache, is open and unashamed. That debt was also paraded at the erstwhile Newton Hall in East Lothian (1796).[49] Within the same nexus is Cluny Castle in Inverness-shire, 'presently building' in 1805[50] and even as late as 1828 Thomas Hamilton, an otherwise gifted architect, was relying on the same formula at Cumston House in Kirkcudbrightshire.[51] More directly the Adam influence was quoted at Cloncaird in Ayrshire where a masking facade of 1814[52] has a round tower which is cousin germane to the sea-tower at Culzean. A similar device, if much cruder in execution, had been contrived ostensibly twenty years before at Barnton near Edinburgh.[53]

The third strain which becomes apparent in the regular castellated architecture of the nineteenth century was a return to the Inveraray theme after its spectacular re-appearance at Taymouth Castle (1804–10). The most primitive example is Hatton Castle in Aberdeenshire in 1814.[54] In its basic outline, Hatton yields nothing to the graces and ornamentation of the age as happened at another love-child of Inveraray, Kincaid Castle. Lying at the foot of the Campsie Hills to the north of Glasgow, Kincaid was by the Glasgow architect David Hamilton.[55] Throughout his life he was to work in a variety of styles although like everyone else in Scotland his architectural philosophy was dominated by Robert Adam. For once that can be proved by the numerous drawings Hamilton made of Adam details and such houses as Syon, Luton Hoo and Mauldslie Castle while at Barnton he may have taken over an unexecuted Adam commission.[56] As a neo-classicist Hamilton was prepared to look back and accept Inveraray as a model. Yet the limitations of the neo-classical outlook and the constrictions imposed by too close a following of Adam are shown in the fact that in 1812 Kincaid[57] shows no advance whatsoever on Airth Castle, at the eastern extremity of Stirlingshire, of six years before where Hamilton added a battlemented screen to a medieval castle[58] and used the Inveraray concept, but somewhat freely, by incorporating the lantern in the central tower of the facade. Yet both these edifices, by one who, on occasions, almost reached genius, demonstrate as nothing else does the exhausted state of Gothic architecture, as descended from Robert Adam and Inveraray, and that the saving grace was to accept the picturesque as Hamilton did at Toward Castle in 1821.[59]

Clearly Scottish architects held out obstinately for as long as they could against the new movement and all that it implied and none more so than the Elliot brothers. Theirs is an interesting case for Archibald Elliot (1761–1823) was an architect of very considerable ability but he remained a prisoner of the classical world unable to shake off its shackles so that the Governor's House on Edinburgh's Calton Hill of 1815[60] is only grudgingly irregular although it was he who was to produce one of the very grandest examples of neo-Gothic architecture in Britain at Taymouth Castle.

Archibald Elliot's first independant essay in the castellated manner was the enlargement of Loudon Castle in Ayrshire, the ancient home of the Campbells of Loudon. When the fifth Earl of Loudon died he was succeeded in his titles and estates by his daughter who married Francis,

Earl of Moira and later first Marquess of Hastings (1754–1826). He had been commander-in-chief of Scotland in 1803 and in the following year married the Countess who was given away by the Prince of Wales.[61] In the same year the rebuilding of Loudon was begun[62] perhaps on the initiative of Lord Moira who, besides being a great builder, was noted not only for his charm[63] but also for his personal extravagance. It was he who commissioned William Wilkins to build the Gothic Donington Hall, 1798–1800,[64] where the hospitality was of the most princely nature and included leaving a blank cheque by the bedside of each guest. Meanwhile the Earl, perhaps mindful of the future, 'laboured earnestly to ameliorate the state of insolvent debtors'.[65]

Loudon was one of the most palatial residences in Britain although very unfortunately, because it was gutted by fire in 1941, very little is known of its internal appearance. There were ninety apartments and some of these must have been quite spectacular to judge by the entrance hall which rose through three floors, ringed by galleries supported by eight scagliola columns.[66] In 1811 work on the castle stopped, not because Lord Moira's building mania was satisfied, for it is recorded that a banqueting-hall was intended,[67] but because the Earl, having reputedly disbursed £100,000 on the castle, was in such financial straits that he could not afford to live there[68] and had to seek a foreign post in order to recoup his distraught finances.[69]

Despite the fire in World War II and the subsequent lapse of time, much of the exterior of Loudon is still intact. From the hand of a Scottish architect it falls inevitably within the Adam tradition[70] by resembling Mellerstain but without its easy calm horizontality since at Loudon there are two middle towers which close in on the entrance. Although a similar effect is found at Seton, nevertheless, the forcefulness and the brutal disruption of the traditional classical horizontality and the introduction of false machicolation over the entrance make it clear that Atkinson's Scone Palace was the model. The concentration of dramatic effect on the entrance is heatedly sustained by the approach. Indeed, to sweep up the curved ramp and enter the spectacular hall must have been sheer drama only excelled at Raby. Also the varied fenestration, the boldly corbelled balcony (perhaps modelled on the seventeenth century Moray House in Edinburgh) over the front door and the broken silhouette all show an interest in dramatic effect not through composition but in the variety and contrast of shapes placed in disharmony to one another although each is locked within the discipline of regular composition. It was such qualities which were brought to fever pitch at Taymouth Castle in Perthshire.

Taymouth was yet another Campbell home and that fact and the success of Loudon explains in part why after several false starts with other architects Archibald and James Elliot were taken into the employment of John, fourth Earl of Breadalbane (1762–1834). Within the ramifications of clan Campbell, the Breadalbanes were the senior cadet branch after the ducal house of Argyll. There had been times in the past when the Breadalbanes had attempted to wrest the leadership of the clan for themselves. Although that bid was no longer possible the extensive Breadalbane estates and his wife's fortune of £3,000 a year[71] enabled the fourth Earl to rebuild his ancestral home on a scale which would eclipse Inveraray. As the traveller Louis Simond pointedly observed later, 'Lord Breadalbane is building a castle much on the plan of the Duke of Argyll's at Inverary (sic), but larger, and in a better style'.[72]

The Elliots had already been toying with the same theorem at Stobo Castle in Peeblesshire where in 1805[73] they erected a lesser and somewhat bleak version from which offices were continued outwards as a concession to the picturesque. However, Stobo is but the pale dawn to the glorious noontime of Taymouth. Although enlarged by William Adam with square pavilions, linked by quadrants to a central block,[74] Taymouth, with its dormers and crow-stepped gables, was essentially a vernacular dwelling and as such was much criticised in the later eighteenth century. Gilpin was the first to recognise the deficiencies of the mansion in its Highland setting and noted that 'Nothing could show a more thorough inattention to every idea of beauty and taste, than the whole contrivance of the place'.[75] As these sentiments were shared by every other topographical writer just when the craze for the picturesque was coming to its zenith, then it is not to be wondered at that rebuilding was begun.

The Earl's first choice as architect was Robert Mylne. It was an obvious one for Mylne had been employed continuously by the head of the clan from 1772 to 1784.[76] In the autumn of 1789 Mylne visited Taymouth[77] and in November 'sent by the Post several Drawings of your Chateau'.[78] Although these were followed up in the spring and early summer of the next year with an estimate and a design for additions[79] nothing seems to have occurred. Then in 1801 a builder, John Gregor, contracted 'to build and erect a house in the Stile of a Castle at Taymouth'[80] at a cost of £9,035 13s 0d[81] with John Paterson of Edinburgh as the architect.[82] Although 'Many workmen were employed in building a large mansion something like that of Inverary (sic), close to the old house'[83] Lord Breadalbane became dissatisfied and in the middle of December, 1804, he sent off a letter to Gregor announcing, 'As I find it adviseable on many accounts to alter the situation of the House at

Plate 100 Taymouth Castle, Perthshire. The central portion was built by Archibald and James Elliot between 1806 and 1810 to which William Atkinson added the long straggling wing after 1818. James Gillespie Graham began to remodel the large block on the left in 1838.

Taymouth, I have determined to remove the New Building now erecting, to the Mount at Venus's Temple'. In addition it was made plain that Paterson was no longer to be the architect.[84] For once, one can have a certain sympathy with Lord Breadalbane since Paterson, who was engaged on the castles of Barmoor in Northumberland and Eglinton in Ayrshire,[85] may not have been free to devote much of his time to Taymouth. Whatever the reasons for the noble displeasure there ensued between all the parties the familiar and acrimonious legal tussle over costs. Lord Breadalbane, like many very rich men, had an almost paranoic fear of being cheated. He checked meticulously every bill that passed through his hands and commonly refused to settle builder's accounts until years after the completion of the work.[86]

With his next architects, the Elliots, Lord Breadalbane could never have cause to complain about lack of supervision at the site since James Elliot more or less became resident architect until his death in 1810.[87] It is his correspondence which fills in the details of the following years of greatest activity at Taymouth. When Gregor had been dismissed, the Earl had set down his own observations on the next Taymouth which was not only to be larger but would have '. . . A sunk storey all round of about twelve feet depth'.[88] That was omitted and the structure was lifted to ground level with the basement girdled by an arcade or cloister as it was first named in 1807.[89]

195

Almost a hundred feet long on either side, and now occupying the site of the ancestral castle, Taymouth (Plate 100) was an undertaking on a gigantic scale. A new building contract was signed in 1806;[90] by October 1807 James Elliot could report that the roof was on the huge central tower[91] and by the close of that year he was writing joyfully, 'The great Center (sic) Tower is finished. The building has a nobel (sic) effect approach it from what direction you please the appearance is truly grand. The Tower adds more dignity to the Building then (sic) I had any idea of before it was Built.'[92] When it is recalled that to arrive at the same stage at Inveraray took twelve years then the speed and the technical mastery of the operations at Taymouth is astounding. Still, although the carcase was complete, a delay of two years occurred while the Earl considered the decorations in London. At one time he had Sir John Soane produce some studies for classical interiors[93] and characteristically did not pay him until 1818.[94] Finally, in 1809 the London plasterer and sculptor, Francis Bernasconi was entrusted with the commission and although his bill would total over £6,000,[95] which would have provided many another nobleman with a dignified residence, there can be no doubt that Lord Breadalbane chose well.

In fitting up the interior of the castle no expense was spared. Thus once working drawings were prepared by Archibald Elliot and Bernasconi for parts of the staircase, the Earl ordered that one of the intended canopies should be fitted up in Bernasconi's showroom as well as having a model made '. . . Shewing the whole Size and Shape of the Drawing Room, and the Design of the Ceiling and Cornice, and how to finish the Bases'. That cost £5 16s 3d. Other models were commanded and somebody was sent down to Windsor to sketch the ceiling of St George's Chapel for the Baronial Hall at Taymouth.[96] Like Sir John Hussey Delaval at Ford, no decision concerning his home could be made by anyone other than Lord Breadalbane. Such supervision had its drawbacks. Once James Elliot received instructions for alterations which could not physically be incorporated in the fabric.[97] On the other hand, other suggestions were very sensible as when instructions were despatched from London for the Baronial Hall. 'At the End of the Room His Lordship has suggested to have the Large Arched Window made something higher. The three Windows on the side of the Room are to have square Heads. . . . The Dado to be done away and whole of the Mouldings to be made as light as the character of the thing will admit. . . .'[98]

It was intended that the Baronial Hall, in the north west corner of the house, should be the principal reception room in which the family portraits would be hung.[99] The walls were left bare while the ceiling was filled with complex tracery. Despite the eighteenth century ancestry of the house, there is little in the Baronial Hall which belongs to that century save for the ogival door-heads bursting with crockets. Discount these and the spectator could be in the Divinity School at Oxford. Of course, the vaulting is plaster. Even so, it is a superb achievement, given the respectability of credence by the breadth of the Decorated window in which the glow of the Breadalbane arms proves the right to such antique forms as ribs, bosses and lantern pendants.

Yet there is a duality which is everywhere apparent at Taymouth and which makes the house so fascinating for though the forms are always Gothic yet frequently they are handled in a manner which is wholly neo-classicism romanticised. Thus at Taymouth the entrance is set low, like a clasp, in the belt of the cloister, leading into a low dark hall in which the fan vaulting is depressed so that it loses all significance by being so crushed and deformed. How great, therefore, is the contrast with the six-storeyed tower at the foot of which lies the staircase its black lines fixed in the forever amber light. This is one of the memorable moments in neo-Gothic art (Plate 101) as the tower climbs higher and higher until finally, bursting through the roof, it explodes in a shell of light which throws the fan-vaulting dizzily skywards so that the wall-shafts pull down like hawsers under strain. For sixty years the sublime had been sought. Wyatt created Fonthill whose octagonal tower was the inspiration for a host of other grandiose towers. Fonthill collapsed; Taymouth

Plate 101   The staircase. Taymouth Castle, Perthshire. The plasterwork was executed by Francis Bernasconi.

remains, the supreme example in the neo-Gothic world of the suspension of belief. It may always have been the greater for without the purple, gold and scarlet of the former, its quality was dependant on detail and composition.

Much in the manner of Robert Adam at Culzean, a short flight of steps divides into a double stair leading to the state rooms above which the upper floors are connected by screened galleries opening on to the tower in arches, deeply cut and with the ingoes filled with shafts. Between the arches, buttresses of delicate profile rise upwards, like masts, towards the rich Perpendicular panelling which fills the last stage before the tower rises above the surrounding roof.

Bernasconi also executed the staircase at Ashridge for James Wyatt[100] but, although the scale is identical, at Taymouth the composition is subtler not only in its totality, so that nothing intrudes on the verticality, but there is also a unity of parts with canopied niches set within arcuated frames richly embellished with cusping and mouchettes. Gradually, as the chronology of Gothic rises from Decorated to Perpendicular, to fan vaulting so the conviction grows that the only worthy comparison is with the mighty cathedral towers of the Middle Ages and, indeed, it is Canterbury which is the progenitor.

The tower is not so successful when viewed as part of the external elevations in which the eighteenth century controls of Inveraray have collapsed not only before the variety of the fenestration but also in the unequivocal ruthlessness of the architecture. Inevitably, therefore, Taymouth is a turning point in the Gothic Revival which, in Scotland at least, had turned full circle in just over half a century. Taymouth was the last majestic expression of regular Gothic. Henceforth, with the increasing knowledge of medieval Gothic and supported by the picturesque, Gothic architecture would rush headlong after irregularity. Still, the Inveraray chord was not quite silent and in time some architects would return to it but never with the conviction of the Elliots for Taymouth was a delicate balancing act between Gothic and neo-classicism and that was too difficult and unnerving a trick to be repeated.

XII

Abbotsford and Its Precursors

In the eighteenth century the Scots were enthusiastic in their acceptance of Gothic architecture. However, in the middle of the seventeen nineties, when the concepts which defined the picturesque became available, the Scots did not adopt them. Instead they were content to repeat and, where possible, to refine the forms derived from Inveraray and the massive genius of Robert Adam. Such conservatism is not new in Scottish architectural history. Indeed, what else can explain the retention of the castle form in the later seventeenth century or the remarkable longevity of the Greek revival in the nineteenth century? Therefore it should be no surprise to learn that the first manifestation of irregular Gothic, Tullichewan Castle, designed circa 1808 by Robert Lugar, an Englishman,[1] provoked no native response since, until the completion of Taymouth, it was still possible to invent variations on an older theme. Thereafter, if Gothic architecture was to have any future, the principles which lay behind the cult of the picturesque would have to be utilised.

Tullichewan Castle (Plate 102), lying not very far from the southern end of Loch Lomond, showed a marked similarity to Downton Castle, which Payne Knight had built after 1774. There was the same determined irregularity of the towers, no two of which were alike in height or shape (Plate 103). Also there was a round tower which was not only the fulcrum for all the subsidiary parts but which, as at Downton, stood at the edge of a great terrace to prevent the visual slide of the entire composition down the slope.

Tullichewan was demolished twenty years ago. However, in 1809 Lugar had also built the nearby Balloch Castle[2] which, being extant, gives a very clear indication internally and externally of advanced architectural thinking, within the early years of the century, on the relationship between architecture and the picturesque. Even later, when scholarship was the criterion, Balloch (Plate 104) could still be 'allowed to be a very good specimen of the Castle-gothic'.[3] After Tullichewan

199

Plate 102　Robert Lugar. Tullichewan Castle, Dunbartonshire. 1808.
Demolished.

diversity of outline and of shape should be expected. Nevertheless, the skill
in the dispositions of the towers to fit each situation, indicates a building of
the greatest importance in the history of the Gothic Revival in north
Britain. True there is none of the epoch shattering grandeur of Taymouth,

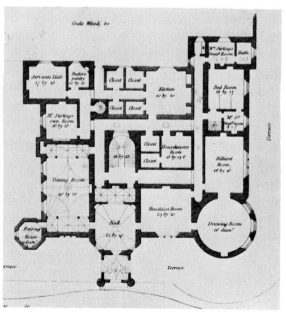

Plate 103　Plan of the
principal floor. Tullichewan
Castle, Dunbartonshire.

200

Plate 104   Robert Lugar. Balloch Castle, Dunbartonshire. 1809.

none of the controlled restraints of Robert Adam. Instead there is an attempt to provide, in a rational manner, a modest residence incorporating the very latest aesthetic theories.

Humphry Repton had accepted that 'No work of art can be great, but as it deceives'.[4] It was a consideration first proposed by Burke[5] although the extent of its influence on the architecture of the eighteenth century remains obscure. Probably, what gave it real meaning was its reappearance in several of Repton's most popular written works at the start of the nineteenth century after which the dictum became one of the mainstays of architectural philosophy, especially with regard to the Gothic Revival, helping to account for the spate of castle building and the rash of abbeys. In the later eighteenth century justification for the use of Gothic had varied from the belief that it marked the revival of a precursor or a post-Roman architectural style to the association with literature. There was, too, the desire for novelty or simply to strike a posture. However, by the start of the new century when it became necessary to reinforce the belief in Gothic it was on the basis of its inherent virtue. Therefore, although the cult of the picturesque was only indirectly concerned with Gothic, nevertheless it was that which was generally recognised as the best medium for the new movement so that, while Gothic may have lost some of its earlier charm, it became invested, through solemn philosophical concepts, with commonsense practical

201

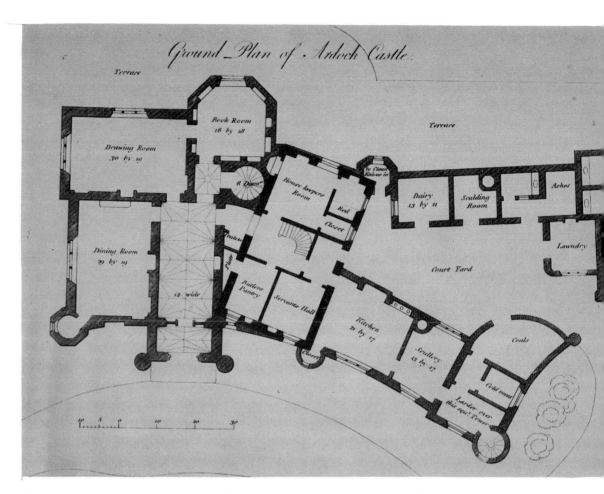

Plate 105 Plan of the principal floor. Balloch (Ardoch) Castle, Dunbartonshire.

qualities which fitted it to the new aesthetic movement. Thus it becomes clear that Balloch, for instance, owes more almost to the philosophers of the picturesque than it does to its architect. Indeed, the basic concept of the house is governed by the fact, as stated by Repton, that 'The eye of taste and experience hates compulsion, and turns with disgust from such puerile means of attracting its notice'.[6] To that Price had already propounded the positive corollary that 'The two opposite qualities of roughness and of sudden variation, joined to that of irregularity, are the most efficient causes of the picturesque'.[7] It was Repton, the practising landscape designer, who translated that into a practical terminology so that the 'great principal on which the picturesque effect of all Gothic edifices must depend' is 'irregularity of outline; first, at the top towers and pinnacles, or chimneys; secondly in the outline of the faces, or elevations, by projections and recesses; thirdly, in the outline of the apertures, by breaking the horizontal lines with windows of different

202

forms and heights; and lastly, in the outline of the base, by the building being placed on ground of different levels.'[8] With the exception of the last, Balloch has all these points. Indeed, one of its most striking features is the use of tall Tudoresque chimneys on the low entrance front. This is the first appearance in Scotland of what would become recognised as one of the standard means of adding variety. Also, to overcome the owner's insistence on retaining his old house, which Lugar considered 'A distorted feature on the face of the country',[9] the concept of 'projections and recesses' was uniquely and dramatically highlighted by pursuing a concave ground plan on the entrance front (Plate 105) which is effectively linked to the encircling trees by a diminishing line of battlemented offices, exactly as had been suggested by Uvedale Price while Payne Knight is represented by the details which, as at Tullichewan, come from Downton, particularly on the polygonal tower which dominates the south front. Though the entrance elevation is scholarly and refined, elsewhere there is coarseness and barbarity while the variety of culled details creates the impression of a building constructed at different periods of time so that the visual effect is altogether different from anything yet seen and strongly contradicts Archibald Elliot's sentiment that the exterior should be 'light and airy and partaking less of that heavy ancient Grandeur which is to be observed in Castelated (sic) Buildings...'.[10] Internally, the current philosophy is exactly followed so that, although, according to Lugar 'A mansion in the castellated style ... affords many opportunities of obtaining a number of rooms which are essential to modern habits',[11] the Gothic vaulting in the hall harks back to Repton's advice: '... it is unnecessary to retain the Gothic character within the mansion, at least farther than the hall, as it would subject such buildings to much inconvenience.'[12]

The first mansion by a Scottish architect which had asymmetry of a kind was Raehills in Dumfries-shire, built in 1786 by Alexander Stevens.[13] Although the underlying concept was classical the battlemented edifice was L-shaped. Why that should have been so is a mystery and Raehills should properly be considered an unconscious freak product so that not until Craigend Castle in Stirlingshire was completed in 1812[14] can it be accepted that asymmetry had begun in Scotland. Although Craigend was only twelve miles from Balloch of equal importance in its design must have been the publication of Lugar's *Plans and Views of Buildings Erected in England and Scotland in the Castellated and other Styles* in 1811. Not only was it the first volume of Gothic designs by an important architect but its plates of Tullichewan and Balloch ushered in a new style. Yet, as so often with the pioneers of Gothic, the designer of Craigend, at least in the initial stages, was an amateur, James Smith of Jordanhill, a relative of the owner.[15]

In that age, when land ownership was concomitant with improvement, advantage was taken at Craigend of the topography to compose a winding approach round a loch and below cyclopean crags while on the

Plate 106 Alexander Ramsay. Craigend Castle, Stirlingshire. 1812. Partly demolished.

highest part of the estate an octangular Gothic viewing-tower was erected. For the house the first proposal was the usual one of an addition 'but after the erection had gone some length, it was found more suitable to pull down the old house entirely . . .'.[16] Thereafter, the design was entrusted to a professional architect, Alexander Ramsay of Edinburgh, who preserved 'as much as possible of the internal arrangement as designed by Mr Smith'.[17] Like so many mansions of the early nineteenth century, Craigend is now a ruin. Yet prints (Plate 106) show a basic affinity with Balloch not only in the asymmetrical plan but also in the irregular grouping of diminishing horizontal planes around one dominant vertical while the incorporation of the domestic offices at the rear and a porte-cochère at the front provide pictorial connections with the trees which gently rise to the slopes above. To a greater or lesser extent all these features are to be found in the other early nineteenth century castles.

The starkest of these is Castle Forbes in Aberdeenshire, built of intractable granite roughly dressed into huge unwieldy blocks. There had been an old castle, the ancestral seat of the chiefs of the clan Forbes, but as prosperity came late to Aberdeenshire it was only in the nineteenth century that the chiefs and lairds began to think of moving out of their tower-houses into more commodious quarters, moves which were later to be given some urgency when Deeside fell prey to royalty. In plan old Castle Forbes, or Putachie as it was called before higher rent-rolls inflated family pride,[18] was a chunky, thick-set square broken in the centre by a small court to provide some light and air.[19] Lord Forbes' first thoughts, understandably, were to choose a southern architect and in 1807 John Paterson drew up plans for a neat Gothic residence followed four years later by a classical scheme[20] presented in a series of drawings in which the delicacy and beauty of line would reproach his modern successors.

When Lord Forbes did eventually decide to build, his choice was an unknown local architect, Archibald Simpson. That he had received his training in Lugar's office[21] may have been of significance although a few years later an embittered correspondent confided to John Paterson that all the subsequent troubles at the castle need never have happened if Lord Forbes, when in Aberdeen, had not been 'over-persuaded' to employ an inexperienced person.[22] Castle Forbes was Simpson's first commission in independent practice so that he would be anxious to do well by an influential patron. It was all the more unfortunate, therefore, that almost from the outset events went disastrously wrong to be succeeded by the usual litigous proceedings.

Estimates were called for in the springs of 1814 and 1815.[23] For finishing the castle it was specified that the doors were to be similar to those in 'Captain Cumming's house'.[24] Alexander Wallace was the mason and his estimate of 20 May 1814 stipulated that he agreed 'to have that part Containing the Dining and Drawing Room ready for the Roof by the first of September and the Tower finished by the end of September in a hurry on Conditions (sic) of the Building being commenced in the beginning of June'.[25]

In the past it has been accepted that construction began in the middle of June 1815 without any ceremony,[26] presumably because the owner was in Ireland. Yet Wallace's estimate of May 1814 with its phrase 'in a hurry' and a close reading of other evidence[27] seems to indicate June 1814 as the starting date. Fifteen months later the bombshell burst. Rumours having reached Lord Forbes that the building was not substantial enough, Archibald Elliot was called in to inspect it.[28] That must have been a severe blow to the architect although more than his pride was hurt since he was suffering from an ear infection.[29] As his troubles over Castle Forbes worsened so did his ailment until by the close of October it prevented him from visiting the site[30] some twenty-five miles to the west of Aberdeen. Still the affliction must have been a blessing, a painful one it is true, for he admitted that a visit would cause him distress 'after what has taken place'.[31] Simpson's reluctance to go to the site was understandable especially as an older architect, and in future his bitter rival, John Smith, had been called in, on behalf of Lord Forbes, to measure up the work already completed.[32] Simpson thought '. . . from the tenor of his Lord(ship's) letter to me that the roofing should have been stopped as well as every other part of the work except the dining-room windows as he says to me that no more work of any description be done except what is merely necessary for the protection during the winter of what has been built'.[33]

What had gone wrong? As is usually the case there was no single reason but rather a conspiracy of faults, including errors of construction. The most serious was the loss of the old castle[34] which was to have been retained as the principal feature.[35] From the outset Simpson was against that since it had neither 'architectural beauty nor even antiquity to recommend it'. As Lord Forbes refused to be persuaded and as 'Further remonstrances would have been intrusive particularly in so young an artist. His Lordship's ideas were accordingly adopted.'[36] Unfortunately,

Plate 107   Plan of the principal floor. Castle Forbes, Aberdeenshire.

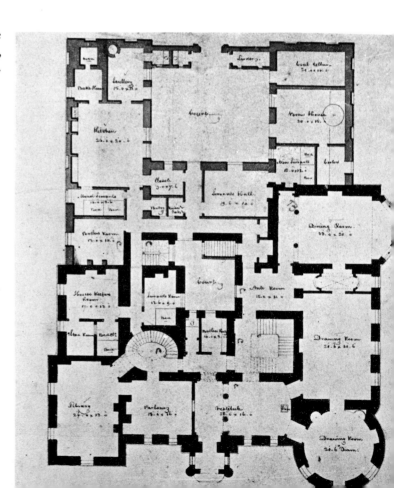

Plate 108   Castle Forbes, Aberdeenshire. Begun in 1814 by Archibald Simpson
but completed by John Smith.

in excavating for the foundations of the new work the old castle was left
unsupported so that cracks appeared and the entire castle had to be
demolished.[37] No wonder that rumours had been reaching Lord Forbes
in Ireland! Mindful of his professional status Simpson unashamedly laid
the blame on the tradesmen, particularly Wallace the mason who was
'highly blameable in hurrying on and commencing the operations before
he had his final orders so to do—and which was in a great measure the
primary cause of all the mischief that has happened'. Others were also
inculpated[38] and even Lord Forbes did not escape[39] although the truth of
the matter seems to have been Simpson's own 'want of experience in a
work rather extensive and complex'[40] as the arbiters, Paterson and James
Gillespie, later Graham,[41] would doubtless have recognised. In the meantime Simpson was pressing for payment and Lord Forbes ordered £50
to be advanced, 'in case he should require a little money'.[42]

Doubtless to the chagrin of Simpson, Castle Forbes was finished
by John Smith[43] and to him must be due the noble interior of the

drawing-room with its deep Grecian frieze. That is in the east wing where the fabric, however, is Simpson's including the four storey circular tower linked to Smith's portion, a three storey frontispiece with a higher three storey rectangular tower with the consequent changes in levels necessitating that extraordinary and expensive feature of the interior a principal staircase at either end of the building (Plate 107). In general both architects, and especially the younger one, borrowed heavily from the details of Tullichewan published in 1811 although neither man probably felt competent enough to imitate its Gothic interiors. Externally, the grouping of the various parts at Castle Forbes (Plate 108) has a bold ruthlessness accentuated by the harsh nature of the granite for as Paterson had written of one of his projects for the site, 'The Building is without any external ornament, and Suitable to the Simplicity of the Materials in the Country'.[44] Smith seems to have discovered inspiration for the rectangular south west tower in the medieval castle of Towie Barclay, near Turriff, of which the remains are remarkably similar in scale and proportion to his tower at Castle Forbes.

Elsewhere castles were created in a softer mould as with Castle Toward erected in 1821 for the wealthy merchant and Lord Provost of Glasgow, Kirkman Finlay.[45] Although in the previous century Gothic mansions were placed in level, sheltered positions, a practice imitated by their successors of the regular kind in the early nineteenth century, from the outset irregularly disposed castles were set on hilltops for, according to Lugar, 'In a well-wooded country, abounding with grand and romantic scenery, a house in the castle style is particularly suitable. . . .'[46] Thus the house and the view were considered as integral parts of a total landscape value whereas in the previous century there was a sense of detachment in contemplating, from beneath the swags and urns of the Palladian mansion, the folly set on the distant hill.

Castle Toward was by David Hamilton 'and there was none of that talented architect's plans which he himself considered more satisfactory'.[47] Certainly, it is a much more original structure than his earlier essays in regular Gothic and although, as in so much of his work, Hamilton shows himself familiar with the most advanced southern work, nevertheless Castle Toward displayed, for it was added to later, features which in the practical relationship of the working out of the theories of the picturesque were of prime importance. The design of the castle is complex, its multiplicity of towers set like the points of a diadem against the purple hills of Argyll. A porte-cochère, leading directly into the hall, was prominently marked above by a large pointed window filled with ranked tracery. There had been nothing of its size since the lantern windows at Inveraray but in future architects would enthusiastically endorse the combination of window and porte-cochère. In the new manner of Craigend, which Hamilton was bound to have known, these elements are set at one end of the structure as at Boturich Castle, a neighbour of Balloch, where additions of 1834[48] to an old keep included a circular entrance tower at one corner.

Plate 109   Robert Smirke. The gallery. Kinfauns Castle,
Perthshire. 1820–24.

At Strathallan Castle, Perthshire, in 1818[49] there was a return to earlier practice with the entrance placed in the middle of an imposing symmetrical front. Such rectitude should, of course, be expected from the architect, Sir Robert Smirke,[50] by training and even more by inclination a classicist so that, like others of that race, he would never be able to abandon himself wholly to the thrills and pleasures of Gothic freedom. Therefore his designs in that idiom, larger than anything since Fonthill, are awkward and often angular in the wrong places. Nor should his Gothic mansions, of which there are four in Scotland, be admitted without question to the irregular class since they are contrived, with an eye to symmetrical balance, of regularly composed elements set around the perimeter with no feeling of substance behind the fabric. The two

209

dimensional effect is exaggerated at Kinfauns, 1820–4,[51] where the straggling outline of pink stone is mounted on a grandiose terrace high above the bosky Tay. Of course in the early nineteenth century every country house of any pretensions had a terrace which, according to Repton, enriched the foreground and gave importance[52] and as Kinfauns is castellated therefore the terrace is provided with corner bastions to nurture the medieval complexion. Although Smirke's knowledge of classical details was immense, his Gothic repertoire was limited so that Kinfauns lacks the specialised interest of Balloch. Its lineage is from Fonthill and the entrance porch, with its dog-tooth ribbing, unique in the north at the time, and the vestibule reproduce in miniature, as it were, the extravaganza of Wyatt's state entrance at Fonthill Abbey.

Kinfauns (Plate 109) and its kind, of which there were many in the opening decades of the century, have been denigrated continuously by critics who have seen architectural merit decline in inverse proportion to the increase in size and Eastlake's comment on Eastnor Castle, that it 'might have made a tolerable fort before the invention of gunpowder, but as a residence it was a picturesque mistake',[53] is one of the kindest. Yet to expect architects to abandon their classical training for composition of the most irregular kind, was asking too much. In addition, the skill in designing for the picturesque was demanding so that where there was no expertise there was bound to be disappointment although it may be questioned whether Kinfauns, which despite its faults retains clarity and logic in the design, is not to be preferred to the later vagaries of the Scots-Baronial addicts. In comparison with Craigend, which had a tough quality, Kinfauns is too relaxed a composition and could almost fit into that second class of buildings the monastic, which intermittently filled the second and third decades of the century. The most apt description of them comes from Loudon. In the cathedral style, as he named it, 'The general masses . . . are large, of considerable length, and seldom interrupted by breaks or large projections. The roof is in general partly seen. . . . The windows of the principal apartments are similar, in general design, to those of churches. When pointed at top . . . a buttress is placed between each.'[54]

The first monastic house to be built in Scotland was Scone Palace and just as Lugar's castles were responsible for much that followed in castellated architecture so Scone, by an Englishman again, set a smart pace for the reluctant Scots. Scone is on the site of an important medieval religious foundation, which had held the Stone of Destiny on which the Kings of Scots were crowned. At the Reformation Scone, almost alone of the abbeys, was destroyed by the mob. In 1600 it was granted by

King James VI to a collateral branch of the Murrays of Atholl from one of whom was descended the celebrated Lord Chief Justice, Lord Mansfield, the creator of Kenwood. By special remainder the Earl's title passed to his nephew and it was his son, the third Lord Mansfield (1770–1840) who called in William Atkinson, the pupil of James Wyatt, and a youthful designer at Auckland Castle, to rebuild Scone.[55]

The second Earl, shortly before his death in 1796, was 'fitting up several of the apartments in a handsome style'.[56] However, within two years of succeeding his son embarked on a more thorough policy of modernisation which may have included a new dining-room and drawing-room.[57] In addition, the exterior was to have been regularised although that was probably not done since further sets of plans were prepared in 1802 by George Saunders of Oxford St.[58] He had worked for the second Earl at Kenwood;[59] his proposals for Scone included the rather drastic measure of dividing into apsidal-ended apartments the great gallery with its timber ceiling 'with painted scenes of Huntings in compartments miserably executed' or so Farington thought in 1801.[60] It was proposed, too, to enclose the courtyards using crow-stepped gables and pedimented window heads. Such a remarkable decision to imitate the original Jacobean works was perhaps prompted more by respect for the old family seat rather than by the attraction of novelty for the English architect.

Eventually, rather than refurbish, Lord Mansfield decided to be very grand and rebuild his house from plans supplied by Atkinson in April 1803.[61] 'Under the influence of Wyatt he had developed his latent love for the antique, and his study of antient forms of architecture on the Continent led him to contemplate their adaptation to modern requirements at home. He became the fashionable architect of the time amongst the upper classes and executed a greater number of important works than any of his professional contemporaries.'[62]

Scone Palace (Plate 110) was completed between 1803 and 1812.[63] Although it was proposed to retain parts of the existing fabric, because of a misunderstanding they were torn down which so incensed the Earl that he sacked all the workmen on the spot, suspending building operations for a year.[64] Some of the walling was preserved in the new structure so that Atkinson's plan, like the earlier proposals, follows much of the old monastic layout with the long gallery, for instance, on the site of its predecessor. As Atkinson made slight alterations to his own ideas a third storey heightened the south front and on the west, instead of square-headed windows on the top floor, pointed lights with a shield over each supplied a richer surface texture.[65]

211

Plate 110   William Atkinson. The south front. Scone Palace, Perthshire.
1803–12.

Although much earlier than Kinfauns, Scone is superior both in
design and execution. Thus the natural properties of the sloping site were
utilised in the Reptonian way to promote different ground levels and,
although the components of the elevations are regular, they are dramatised
by such innovations as the close set towers at the entrance, authentically
overtopped by false machicolation, and a variety of fenestration patterns.
There are square-headed lights and in the larger ones there may be
Y-tracery, quatrefoils or cusping with Perpendicular tracery while in the
heads and around the borders the glass was coloured for 'It is merely the
general effect of the gloom that pleases; as in a chapel we are soothed with
that solemn light'.[66]

Internally, Scone was the first house in Scotland in which every
room had some medieval accoutrements although, unlike in later

Plate 111   The long gallery. Scone Palace, Perthshire.

examples, these were ranged in quantity from one space to another so that after the simplicity of the dining-room comes the ante-room which, exactly as at Auckland Castle, acts as a respite before entering the drawing-room. Not only is the ante-room arranged about the cross-axis but its decorations are rich enough to hold the spectator, particularly the deep niches with oversailing canopies from which rise tiers of crocketted pinnacles. The windows have trefoil cusping, there are mouldings and label stops around the doors while the ceiling is a filigree net of ribs and splendid bosses. After the ornate drawing-room the library is subdued

Plate 112   William Atkinson. Rossie Priory, Perthshire. Built in 1810 it has since been much reduced in size.

until the decoration slowly rises again through the octagon into the crescendo of the long gallery (Plate 111) where the ceremony of architecture processes through a series of bays in the vaults of which are held the spatial volumes of the room.

For the early nineteenth century Gothic of Scotland, Scone was a rich treasure-house to be ransacked by architects, established men like the Elliots or a raw beginner like James Gillespie Graham. At Scone the underpinning was certainly Georgian classicism but the notion of a wholly Gothic mansion was a turning-point so that gradually the mixing of classical and Gothic styles would end. The introduction, too, of a specialised knowledge gave not only new features, such as galleries, but an extended range of details. Without the freakishness, Gothic was beheld as a rational style adaptable to the requirements of the age, able to give, not just a *frisson* of novelty, but associational values which were more fully stressed at Rossie Priory in Perthshire (Plate 112) in 1810[67] where low, domestically scaled conventual buildings were clustered around spire-capped towers while to the east a frontal gable, behind which was a pitched roof, marked the limits of a double range of lights. These were run into one another at Crawford Priory in Fife (Plate 113) in 1813[68] where in the Gillespie Graham portion, the wall was abolished to let huge windows fly from the ground to the wall-head. They were thick with stone Perpendicular tracery and if some of the panels were blind, to accommodate the split in floors inside, it was no matter for here was the full flavour of the monastic order even to the gabled entrance, which in its mixture of Gothic and Norman reflected various time-heralded epochs and was a transept in the rhythm of the chambered bays. Yet the difficulties of matching medieval liturgical requirements to the somewhat looser living habits of the Regency were too much and, not surprisingly, less rigorous forms were accepted for the monastic style at Ross Priory and Cambusnethan Priory.

Also less eclectic was Abercairny Abbey, after Taymouth the biggest house in Perthshire and the last one in which smoking was prohibited in all the public rooms. As is so often the case in the largest Scottish houses, every architect of note had a hand in it. The ubiquitous John Paterson noted in 1796 that Colonel Moray 'did not intend to Carry on the additions to the old house'. To do so, Paterson observed, 'would assuredly bring an Auld house about his head'.[69] Despite the prognostication, Paterson in the next year had to be content with supplying an extension which included one of his standard oval drawing-rooms.[70] Some years later Archibald Elliot sent up from London 'a Set of Sketches for your proposed Castle of Abercairny'[71] which were followed six months later by another set from an English architect at a cost of £42.[72] However, the choice finally settled on Richard Crichton.

Although there are accounts from Martinmas, 1803,[73] work seems to have seriously begun in April 1804[74] with the architect at the end of the next month sending off working drawings for the foundations, ground floor and south elevation.[75] As building at Abercairny proceeded for almost three-quarters of a century its history is extremely complex. It is sufficient, therefore, to say that by Crichton's death in 1817 the main parts of the mansion had been decided upon and constructed even

Plate 113   Crawford Priory, Fife. The first architect, in 1810, was David Hamilton. He was succeeded by James Gillespie Graham who used an ecclesiastical Gothic for his recasing of the eighteenth century house.

although progress had been slow not to say erratic for there were frequent changes of design so that neither in 1804 was a final decision made about the exterior nor two years later when Crichton was preparing drawings 'in the Monastic Style'. Such a house, he reckoned, would cost £11,000 or £1,000 less than a castellated one.[76] There were also the usual disputes about costs resulting in charges being bandied about that implicated Crichton. Matters became so serious that after Colonel Moray had dismissed all Crichton's workers and stopped the building in 1807 the architect asked for arbiters to be appointed to measure the work completed.[77] Shortly afterwards building operations were resumed[78] and the structure must have been habitable since the accounts include £105 4s 11d 'for removing castle'[79] and early in 1809 an estimate for plasterwork was itemised.[80] However, with the death of Colonel Moray in the following year work again ceased and was not resumed until four years later.

Although it is usually stated that it was after Crichton's death in 1817 that the firm of R. and R. Dickson took over at Abercairny, a memorandum from one Robert Peddie in March 1814 implies an intermediate stage. 'As it is now impossible to conform to the mode proposed by Mr Crichton for finishing that part of the House proposed to be finished. . . .'[81] The inference, clearly, is a change of control. Also, although the Abercairny papers are fairly complete there are no references

215

to Crichton after the airing of the dispute between himself and Colonel Moray in 1808 after which he was probably not reinstated by a dissatisfied client who took the management of affairs into his own hands to obtain ' the first House in N. Britain'.[82]

Hitherto, because of the acceptance of 1817 as the termination of Crichton's supervision, the assumption has always been made that certain

Plate 114   Abercairny Abbey, Perthshire. Richard Crichton's house of 1804 was enriched with Tudor decorations by R. and R. Dickson after 1820. The cloisters were not constructed. Demolished.

interiors at Abercairny were Crichton's but it would now appear that some Gothic decoration was inserted in 1814 but with the greater part coming from the Dicksons who, taking over the carcase of the house in 1820, had a free hand in finishing it. Such an hypothesis would not only account for the stylistic unity of the interiors but also the curious use of 'mode' in the 1814 memorandum implying that Crichton's ideas were old fashioned as, indeed, they would be if drawn up before 1808. By 1814 Scone had extended the Gothic vocabulary giving it a richness previously unknown and not surprisingly the gallery at Abercairny closely matched that at Scone. These galleries were part of that spoil of ideas which came to architects from Fonthill but although at Scone the concept is dictated by the Elizabethan examples, at Abercairny the prime use was to be a resplendent corridor giving access from the entrance at the east to the main staircase at the west and the public rooms along the south front. The gallery at Abercairny was put into some kind of order in 1814 with the arrival of a Gothic chimney-piece[83] and coloured heraldic glass from Birmingham[84] although it would seem to have been many years later before the gallery assumed its final appearance.[85]

Indeed, the progress of the house was punctuated by a never ending series of false starts so that after a hiatus of five years[86] drawings were prepared in 1820[87] showing not only proposed additions but also a conversion to something more thoroughly Gothic with a large porch at the east and a window bay at the west plus a conservatory and stables. While the arrangement of the rooms would remain unaltered Crichton's fenestration would be transformed into a richer and more fulsome style with stone tracery, cusping and other enrichments. It seems that the decoration of the south rooms was executed between 1820 and 1824 with the drawing-room bay windows made according to a design 'already fixed upon. The architraves of the doors and windows to be similar to those in the other public rooms, the window shutters of the patern (sic) shown by the sketch attached to this.'[88] That was done and the ceiling ribs gilded against a white background in accordance, no doubt, with an estimate promised for the autumn of 1823.[89] The library was completed probably in the following year[90] after which, although there are numerous ideas for cloisters (Plate 114), the main change was the removal of the entrance from the south front, where it had been since 1822,[91] to the east where the parlour became the entrance hall with a roof-high chimney-piece which in a bumper of trimmings had a gallery and flying-buttresses. First considered in 1826,[92] designs for the new entrance were prepared in 1827[93] after which two years passed before the finishing touches were made.[94] The old doorway was filled in with a large window [95] and another library was established.

All the interiors were in the most sumptuous style with rich plaster-work ceilings. These might be pure fantasy as in the east corridor, or of a more historical nature as in the dining-room, with its beam and panel construction, and in the libraries where fan-vaulting defied gravity. As splendid in their way as those at Taymouth the interiors were matched externally by oriels, pierced parapets and richly cut finials. Those on the towers were added after 1829[96] and others atop the buttresses in the following year.[97] Yet the facade suffered from the defects caused by the successive changes of plan. The removal of the entrance from the south to the east front meant that the broad sweep of the terrace staircase was flung against puny windows instead of a high hall while the advance of the twin towers protected nothing. Across the south facade there was an indeterminate air as though a portion had been lopped off so that, though the details were part of the picturesque, the principles of composition were ignored. Abercairny lacked the power and cliff-soaring size of Taymouth; it precluded the pre-emptive simplicity of Scone; and it is as a hybrid of many influences and styles that it finds its place in history.

That rich mixture of Perpendicular and Tudor motifs which characterised Abercairny (demolished in 1960) also appeared in the same county at Millearne Abbey. Although it would seem that Millearne (Plate 115) was from the same office as Abercairny there is no mention in any of the relevant papers of an architect. Does that and the strangely organic plan indicate perhaps that the controlling hand was that of the owner? He was John George Home Drummond, a grandson of the celebrated Lord Kames and younger brother of Henry Home Drummond of Blair Drummond. In 1812 Henry married Christian Moray, the daughter of Colonel Charles Moray of Abercairny, who died in 1810, and sister of the next two successive owners. Thus John George Home Drummond was related to the Dicksons' employers at Abercairny and must have had an intimate awareness of its building programme.

In 1820 John George Home Drummond purchased the estate of Millearne from William Keir, Younger of Huntingtower[98] and although 'the house and offices are large and very commodious and lately fitted up',[99] a builder's receipt, from David Macgibbon and Son, dating from March 1826, contains the significant phrase for 'the Buildings presently Carrying on at Millearn (sic)'.[100] Monthly builder's receipts exist for the greater part of 1826 and are attended by plumber's accounts until 1831. Indeed, apart from the architecture and decoration, the most fascinating aspect of Millearne is the collection of tradesmen's bills. For no other building in the first half of the nineteenth century is there a comparable series. For the first time one finds an element of business organisation appearing and whereas before building contraction has been either the architect, or his deputy, the clerk of works, or the estate hiring individual

Plate 115   The south front. Millearne Abbey, Perthshire. The creation, over more than two decades, of the owner, John George Home Drummond, assisted by R. and R. Dickson. Demolished.

local or itinerant craftsmen, at Millearne there were firms of plumbers and painters with offices in Crieff or Perth while for such items as glass and tiles the suppliers were in Edinburgh and, more rarely, in London and other towns in England. In other words, the age of mass production has arrived so that the specialities which the Gothic Revival was demanding, heraldic tiles, glass and ironwork, could be provided by specialist firms catering for a national market.

The most intriguing and, at the same time, the most revealing of the accounts are those for the glass. The plain glass was sent in locally, as might be expected, with the stained glass coming from a variety of sources. From William Cooper, near Leith Walk in Edinburgh, came a quantity which included such small items as '2 Fleur de lis red with Yellow ground @ 5/- (each)'.[101] In 1834 the same manufacturer invoiced for yellow and purple tracery along with a small Gothic cross and a small coronet, the last costing three shillings.[102] From another Edinburgh firm, Hunt and Co., came more stained glass accompanied by a letter of apology. 'The delay of your Stained Glass was oweing (sic) to accidents which are very liable in the Kiln. There is two (sic) of the diamond pieces wanting. I have four over the number which will be sent for spare ones. You will find 2 pieces with the Pelicans Head one of them being rather dark'. In that consignment were '3 Red waved pieces and 3 Yellow at 1/- (each)'[103] which would compose into the Drummond arms. Further glass came from the famous maker, Thomas Willement in 1841 and included 'Two figures of an Earl and a Bishop in Stained Glass' at six guineas.[104]

The intimate connection between the Gothic Revival and heraldry, with all the associations of a proven descent from some obscure worthy, is well known and has frequently been criticised. Sir John Summerson in castigating the neo-Gothic movement complains of 'The bourgeois adulation of ancestry'.[105] Yet there was nothing bourgeois about a patron who united in himself the names of Home and Drummond, two of the most ancient families in Scotland. That interest in genealogy, made so manifest at Millearne in a glowing galaxy of glass, was an integral part of the Scottish aristocratic character and starts up even amidst the classical splendours of many of the eighteenth century mansions. It was inevitable that with the progress of antiquarian scholarship more evidence should be produced of family pedigrees and that these should be set upon Gothic buildings the majority of which were the creation of the heads, or representatives of aristocratic families. Indeed, there were so few mansions for the *nouveaux riches*, whether in England or in Scotland, that merchants like William Russell at Brancepeth or Kirkman Finlay at Castle Toward were the exceptions.

The revived art of stained glass was a by-product of the Gothic Revival as was the manufacture of encaustic tiles which were demanded as a result of the increasing awareness of their use in the Middle Ages. In February 1834 two crates of paving tiles were sent off to Millearne preceded by a letter explaining that some of the same patterns had been sent 'the other day to Trentham for the Duke of Sutherland to see, who was so much pleased with them, that he beg'd he might be allow'd to retain them, which of course was granted. . .'.[106] The thought of the first Duke of Sutherland begging for anything is staggering! Finally, when Millearne was nearing completion the Worcester Royal Porcelain Works produced two sheets of tile designs for the front hall. It was the company's boast that 'Nearly all our patterns are copied from Antient specimens' from, amongst other places, the chapter house at Salisbury and Malvern and Westminster Abbeys. Yet there was a practical side to the business for such glazed tiles were not only easily cleaned but also impervious to dampness.[107] At the same time the Gothic movement would not have been what it was without some spuriousness and there came for the gallery '2 Massive, and Extra Large Size, London made Gothic Fenders, . . . enriched with Rosettes, and Shields, Battlement Tops, Supported on Octagon Turrets . . .'.[108] It was against such objects that Pugin would rail; but then he lacked the saving grace, a sense of humour.

Millearne was notable (the house was demolished in 1969) for the high quality of the detailing in the carved woodwork, the stained glass

Plate 116 The dining-room chimney-piece. Millearne Abbey, Perthshire.

and the stone carving, especially around the Perpendicular cloister and the traceried gable of the library. Inside there was the same finesse in the stone chimney-pieces, especially in the dining-room (Plate 116) and drawing-room, where they were inordinately tall and obviously from the same school as the one in the entrance hall at Abercairny. The dining-room was fashioned like the nave of a church with a high vaulted ceiling with painted blazons and with the stone chimney-piece set, like a tomb canopy, in a deep recess. At the other end of the house, beyond the cloister, was the library which was another high room but divided by a gallery and illumined by stained glass which, set within clear glass, had a very modern look.

From the accounts it is apparent that the building and fitting up of Millearne proceeded equably throughout the two decades after 1825.[109] These accounts are the only major series in this study in which there is never a hint of quarrelsomeness let alone litigation. Home Drummond seems to have been a kindly man, one to whom a glass merchant could send a copy of his treatise on glass-cutting 'Knowing that you are Curious on these Subjects'.[110] Nevertheless, the question remains: who was the architect? On stylistic grounds, historians have always linked Millearne to the Dicksons' Abercairny but without any hard and fast evidence. Among the Abercairny papers, however, in an estimate of 30 April 1830, Robert Dickson, who seems to have been the architect in the firm, mentions having been 'at Millearne last week' and in such a way that a matter of business is implied.[111] Yet there were curiosities and anomalies at Millearne which would make it wrong to ascribe that house entirely to Dickson. Thus while it is not unusual for the accounts to go direct to the owner, it is unusual never to find in them any reference to an architect. Also the room volumes were unlike anything else of the period while the rambling gait of the plan, had a makeshift, additive quality and although Millearne, with its tower, gables and lower groups of buildings spreading outwards, conformed to the ideals of the picturesque, there was a wilfulness about the composition which bespoke the self-indulgence of the wealthy amateur. There was the proud retailing of the structure's growth in the sequence of date stones and the wealth of details in bosses, tracery, chimneys, and parapets, especially over the library where helpless little lions clung to the sloping stonework. Such items not only demonstrated the scholarly, cultivated tastes of the owner but a care and an attention which no architect, however well intentioned could have bestowed. The assumption must be that Dickson 'ghosted' the building and that Home Drummond decided on the embellishments just as it was he who drew out, albeit painstakingly, a cornice and ceiling details for the library and adjacent staircase.[112]

A problem of authorship also concerns Inchrye Abbey in Fife which has been demolished without record. The few known facts are easily set down. Inchrye was built in 1827 by George Ramsay of Inchrye at a cost of £12,000 and was singular in that it was mostly single storey except at the entrance which had a tower, the roof of which lit the hall. The public rooms were large and splendid, particularly the dining-room which was over forty feet long.[113] As the decoration of the hall was imitation stone,[114] the interior, in part at least, was probably Gothic. At one time or another most of the architects of the period have been credited with Inchrye. However, the rich Perpendicular-Tudor motifs, especially the ogival capped buttresses, suggest the hand of Robert Dickson. Besides, just as Atkinson's Scone gallery was copied at Abercairny so at Inchrye the high towers on a side elevation were a crib from Rossie Priory.

Inchrye was the last of its type. At best there could only be a handful of such monastic houses if only because of the impossibility of compromising between the spiritual and the secular needs of widely separated societies. Only at Rossie and Crawford Priories were there full blown attempts at reproducing physical representations of the Middle Ages and although exciting and dramatic architecture was produced the fantasies were incapable of a prolonged development; and increasingly the monastic style was forced to rely on the importation of details from Tudor domestic architecture so that there grew up, beside the castellated and monastic styles, a third category which Loudon plainly described as 'A mixed style'.[115] It was the pragmatic approach and had been justified in a long passage by Payne Knight. 'A house may be adorned with towers and battlements, or pinnacles and flying buttresses; but it should still maintain the character of a house of the age and country in which it was erected; and not pretend to be a fortress or monastery of a remote period or distant country; for such false pretensions never escape detection'.[116] Such was the view, which, in his castellated architecture, guided Archibald Elliot finding its best expression in Lindertis in Angus (Plate 117) which, built in 1813,[117] has now been demolished. It met fully the criteria of Knight for, although there were turrets and crosslets, defence was obviously not the purpose and if there were lancets and tracery masses would not be said within the walls although the architect had fully subscribed to the picturesque even with a main block which was oppressively symmetrical. However, at Newbyth in East Lothian[118] four years later[119] the favoured block plan is pulled about by polygonal buttresses and bay windows while the entrance is deeply scored by triple recessions on both floors. An almost identical silhouette was followed in the former County Buildings at Paisley.[120]

In his later Scottish works Atkinson also departed from his overtly picturesque concepts and at Biel House in Berwickshire, 1814,[121] produced a neutral style while four years later at Tulliallan Castle in Fife[122] there was constructed an extraordinarily regressive edifice, a wholly

Plate 117   Archibald Elliot. Lindertis, Angus. 1813. Demolished.

symmetrical block which could well have been Elliot's work. Undoubtedly, however, Atkinson's most difficult commission was Abbotsford for Sir Walter Scott.

It is a surprising fact that whereas so much ink has been expended on biographies of Sir Walter and scholarly critiques of his writings, there is no account of his house. Abbotsford ranks with Strawberry Hill and Fonthill Abbey for all three were the homes of literary men who, being intensely interested in architecture and the latest theories (after all Scott was an enthusiastic admirer of Price's theories),[123] took such a close interest in the creation of their homes that the owners' creative personalities overshadowed those of the executant architects. There was, however, one essential difference between Walpole and Beckford on the one hand and Scott on the other for whereas they were amateur literati and inheritors of considerable riches, Scott became a professional writer who happened to make a great deal of money. It was that income, and in due course the expectation of income, which enabled Scott to purchase land and to build Abbotsford. In May, 1811 he stated his intentions to Lady Abercorn: 'I am about a grand and interesting scheme at present—no less than the purchase of a small property delightfully situated on the side of the Tweed, my native river. . . . I intend to build a beautiful little cottage upon the spot.'[124] Scott purchased a hundred and ten acres with entry at Whitsunday, 1812.[125] Afterwards the estate grew until by the latter part of 1816 it had reached six hundred acres[126] which was doubled within less than eighteen months.[127] Scott with his wife was 'not a little proud of being greeted as laird and lady of Abbotsford'[128] although Lord Macaulay, the famous historian, and a bitter critic of Scott, accused him of 'profuse and ostentatious expense' and of giving himself up to 'extravagant waste or rapacious speculation'.[129]

Although there are drawings and accounts at Abbotsford which relate to its growth, it is not only from these items but also from the ramifications of Scott's enormous correspondence that the full details can be gleaned. Scott drew about himself a body of like-minded friends who shared his strongly developed antiquarian architectural tastes. At the close of 1816 he first met Edward Blore the antiquarian and architect and George Bullock,[130] who had a furniture warehouse in London besides being the owner of the Mona marble works in Anglesey. He became a close friend of Scott's and was one of those most intimately involved in the creation of the first portion of Abbotsford. There were also James Skene of Rubislaw, the Aberdeenshire laird and amateur artist, and Daniel Terry the actor who, according to Scott, had originally trained as an architect in James Wyatt's office[131] so that it may have been he who was instrumental in bringing Atkinson and Scott together although the latter had a high opinion of the architect commending his work at nearby Bowhill for the Duke of Buccheuch.[132] Among this latter-day Committee of Taste, ideas for the advancement of Scott's house were bandied around. Every detail was discussed either at meetings or, more usually, in letters so that while much factual information and insight can be gained into the making of Abbotsford, it is, at times, very difficult to discover the source of the motivation behind the many changes. Like Walpole, Scott had his own ideas for the fulfilment of his dream fantasies so that for the architect he was the very worst kind of client.[133]

Scott's first architect was Stark of Glasgow who drew up a design in 1811[134] for an ornamental 'cottage'. Scott thought very highly both of

Plate 118   William Atkinson. Abbotsford, Roxburghshire. The central part was built in 1816 and was extended after 1822. The wing on the left of courtyard was built after Sir Walter Scott's death.

Stark and his plan[135] but it was not put into effect as Scott was then keeping 'the lee-side of prudence in my proceedings'.[136] In 1816 a plan, from an idea by Skene,[137] was drawn up. Blore drew out the two main elevations for a suite of rooms consisting of a boudoir, a dining-room and, adjacent to it, a study for Sir Walter with, to the south, a conservatory,[138] indicative of that early nineteenth century change in taste which not only considered nature as beautiful and worthy of close observation and study but that it should be brought indoors for greater rapport. Meanwhile, Terry had obtained another set of plans from Atkinson which Scott thought offered better accommodation although he preferred Blore's elevations 'as being less Gothic and more in the old fashioned Scotch stile (sic) which delighted in notch'd Gable ends and all manners of bartizans'.[139] Blore does not seem to have been engaged in any capacity other than a friendly one for Scott was obviously prepared to pay more attention to Atkinson, which was correct, since the latter's reputation as a Gothic architect was secure. From the outset Scott was determined to have a Gothic house for in reporting his first meeting with Blore and Bullock he mentioned having a stained glass window in the dining-room[140] and the possibility of historic monuments being ransacked either for ideas, as Horace Walpole had done, or for parts, which Walpole had not done, was under consideration. Already Scott had pedimented dormer heads from the old Tolbooth in Edinburgh besides other pieces from the old

225

College and Parliament House. Indeed, so many ancient properties were being demolished in the capital that carved stones were 'to be had for the asking' and there was even talk of the west end of St Giles being torn down which filled Scott with anticipatory glee.[141]

Although it has always been stated that Abbotsford was built to Blore's plan, the perusal of Scott's own letters makes it evident that Blore's initial draft was modified and the house executed to Atkinson's plan (Plate 118). In writing to Terry in March 1817, Scott refers to Atkinson's plans but doubts whether three windows in the conservatory 'will be sufficient to keep the plants in a healthy state'[142] while on several later occasions he expresses his gratitude to Atkinson without any reference to Blore. Even so Atkinson was one of a trio, which included Bullock, responsible until his death in 1818,[143] for the interiors and their decoration, and Terry through whom most of the correspondence flowed. Yet even while Scott was awaiting the working drawings for the ground floor plan, he was dreaming of having an armoury and though at first it may have been intended as two niches in a wall,[144] it soon became the area between the original farm-house and the extension[145] and in time would be richly ornamented with plaster ribs with bosses copied from the nearby Melrose Abbey. In the early days Bullock had made some of the casts but later on Scott counted himself fortunate in having found a plasterer who could understand Gothic plans.[146] Next door the ceiling of the dining-room was similarly elaborated. Scott was especially pleased with it. 'Mr. Atkinson', he penned, 'Has kept tryste charmingly'[147] and indeed the bosses including kail, the Scottish curly cabbage, and the thistle, have a homely look. Although by midsummer 1818, the building operations were mostly done with, Scott was complaining '. . . at present we are in a very savage state having neither grates for fire nor glass for our windows',[148] but early in the next year he could be more cheerful to Mrs Scott of Harden, 'We are just begun to get the workmen clear of the house and I think it will be one while before I am tempted to engage with them again although I have half of my house to build when I have leisure—that is—time and money'.[149]

In fact within a very few years Scott was embarking on the second stage of his programme. Early in 1822 the farm-house came down;[150] its replacement was to be not just much larger but so much more magnificent than the 1817–19 portion that Scott felt constrained to apologise lamely to his elder son. 'One is led on by degrees in these matters', and he pleaded, 'If you should be the early master of it do not be angry at me for having built too large a house'.[151] In that same month of November Scott had collected together, Jamaican cedar-wood, Chinese wall-paper and woodwork from Dunfermline Abbey to panel the entrance gallery.[152] With such acquisitions and Scott's fertile mind hatching ever more ideas it is not surprising that Atkinson was in despair over his whims.[153] By April of the succeeding year differences had occurred over the plans but as Scott generously admitted that Atkinson '...may be right only I like my own ways better',[154] there was no dispute and rapid progress was made with Scott settling a part of his account with the builders, John and Thomas Smith of Darnick, near Melrose, some nineteen months later.[155]

From that day to this Abbotsford has remained one of the most famous houses in the land and one of the most visited. In 1844 the foreign traveller Kohl, journeying by coach, was very disappointed at not having seen it. ' "You may make yourself easy about that, sir!" began one of our inside passengers, after he had taken off his right leg for greater convenience—and placed it behind him in a corner of the coach—"There are prettier seats in Scotland, than this Abbotsford; and if you have seen Taymouth Castle, Dunkeld and Dalkeith, you may travel past this comfortably enough".'[156] But what of its architectural significance? And what was Scott's attitude in the governance of its creation? Basically, he had set himself against 'a regular shape of a house' preferring 'a variety of snugg (sic) accommodation'[157] but neither did he want a castle or a priory[158] although he was not averse to following the fashionable rage of utilising medieval features to nineteenth century needs. The design of the abbot's stall in the cloister at Melrose Abbey became the gallery fire-place[159] with the courtyard porch derived from the approach to Linlithgow Palace. The consistent idea was that the house should be the 'old English hall such as a squire of yore dwelt in'[160] although when the second stage came to be built the Tudor aspect, never in truth very prominent, had been substituted by Scots-Jacobean characteristics more in keeping with the equivocal notion of a Scottish manor-house[161] which Scott recognised as being, '. . . a picturesque, appropriate, and entirely new line of archi-tecture'.[162] It was as novel as his introduction of gas lighting, the use of polychromatic stonework, the abolition of the distinction between state and private apartments and the ending of the exile of the garden beyond the house.

Abbotsford is the unsung prototype of Scots-Baronial architecture, which was to sweep across the country after the middle of the century. Yet in that nationalistic upsurge Abbotsford had no role just as it failed to influence contemporary and near contemporary architecture, with the exception of the necroscopic Scott Monument,[163] whereas the reflections from Strawberry Hill and Fonthill Abbey were infinite and varied. Why, then, should Abbotsford stand alone? Surely, not the fact that it was, in Sir

Walter's own phrase, '. . . a good deal out of the common run'?[164] In its own day, the villa of the future Earl of Orford was more than singular, while Fonthill was an eccentricity. No, the answer must be a lack of architectural publicity. Alone of the mansions of the men of literature, it had no slim volume of elegant plates to become a source book for others so that, although an interest in Scottish architecture would gradually emerge, it was to be another quarter of a century before the vision and the memory of Abbotsford would again be evoked in stone.

XIII

James Gillespie Graham

In 1803 the poet James Hogg was on a tour of the Highlands. 'Having breakfasted early we . . . left Fort William . . . we reached Achnacarry, where we spent the middle of the day, viewing the new castle of Lochiel, the building of which was then going briskly on, conducted by Mr. John Gillespie, architect; a respectable young man, possessed of much professional knowledge, who kept us company during our stay.'[1]

Hogg can be forgiven for being mistaken about the architect's christian name, which was James, since Gillespie was then unknown professionally to all but a handful of west highland landowners. James Gillespie (1776–1855) came from Dunblane in Perthshire,[2] which county would not only see his emergence as an architect of importance but much of it would remain his architectural peculiar, secured no doubt by his marriage to a Perthshire heiress, Margaret Graham of Orchill in 1815.[3] Afterwards the architect became James Gillespie Graham, the name by which he is usually known to posterity. Gillespie Graham was the first in Scotland to commence his career as a Gothic architect and not as one who turned to it as a secondary means of artistic expression and he became the leading practitioner in the second and third decades of the new century gradually being displaced by William Burn. Although Gillespie Graham had an impressive number of Gothic country houses and churches to his credit there has never been any critical appraisal of his output.

Where and what Gillespie Graham's early training was remains a mystery. Certainly, by 1800, while in his middle twenties, he was in charge of the second Lord Macdonald's building operations on Skye,[4] overseeing workmen the majority of whom were from Dunblane with the remainder from Edinburgh.[5] The workmen were engaged in February 1800 but although work on Skye was to begin on 4 March[6] there were delays. The vessel, bringing the workmen's tools, was a fortnight late in arriving[7] and there was a shortage of lime.[8] The works were for the estate

229

with some of a public benefit. Mostly of a minor nature they were diverse and included, amongst an extensive list, piers at Kylerea and Portree, a prison at the latter, several manses, smithies and lime-kilns as well as work at the Macdonald family seat, Armadale House.[9] That was in 1800 and 1801 so that, not surprisingly, in the spring of the next year the architect was 'of opinion that there are more buildings ordered than I am able to carry into effect this season'.[10] In 1803, therefore, the list of works to be erected was short although it did include further additions at Armadale House of a barn, byre and a stable.[11] In that same year Gillespie Graham's activities as 'Architect Superintendant of the buildings erecting by Lord Macdonald'[12] were taking him to another of Lord Macdonald's properties, North Uist,[13] where a factor's house had to be built.[14]

Study of the Macdonald archives for the first time has now revealed that Gillespie Graham was employed on the Macdonald estates, with one break of four years, for nearly a quarter of a century. From the outset in 1800 the architect must have been aware of the opportunities which awaited him if he gave that satisfaction 'which a young man setting out in the world and eager to acquire approbation should ever have in his eye'.[15] Therefore, the tasks between 1800 and 1803 would be well executed and, in a wide geographical area devoid of architectural expertise, the services of a skilled architect were bound to be in demand. In January 1803 Colonel Macdonald of Kinlochmoidart was charged £5 by Gillespie Graham for a plan for offices[16] which included a boat charge of £2 'in atempting (sic) to go to the spot',[17] which says much of the difficulties of communication in the Highlands. Hogg, for instance, remarked that Achnacarry had no public road near it and could not be reached by a carriage.[18]

Achnacarry, at the southern end of the Great Glen, is supposed to have been begun in 1802[19] by Donald, twenty-second Chief of clan Cameron, to whom the estates, after their forfeiture following the failure of the rebellion of 1745, were restored in 1784.[20] The old wooden house of Lochiel having been burnt by the redcoats, a new mansion was constructed nearby. Family tradition relates that while the house was being erected, Lochiel lived in the adjacent village and with regular visits to the site by the architect there would be little, if any, need for correspondence. However, the affairs of the Macdonald estates still demanded Gillespie Graham's attention so that on 24 March 1803 a southern correspondent reported that all letters for the architect were to be forwarded 'to Lochiel whither he went from Lanric (sic) Castle' in Perthshire 'on Monday'.[21] On the 28th of the same month Gillespie Graham wrote from Fort William where he expected to stay a fortnight[22]

Plate 119   James Gillespie Graham.
Achnacarry, Inverness-shire. 1802.

although on 18 April he was still in the town.[23] On 18 June he was at
Achnacarry, having arrived there from North Uist,[24] and in September,
probably to wind up the building season, he spent a fortnight at
Achnacarry en route for Skye.[25]

When Hogg saw Achnacarry in June 1803 he was able to record that
'The castle is on an extensive scale and promiseth to be a stately
structure'.[26] In the general architectural climate of its time, the house is
very much in the manner of the Adam–Paterson school. Internally it
would have been more so if the exigencies of planning had not forced the
abandonment of an oval saloon at the rear[27] in favour of a bow-ended
room. Also the departure of the chief and the subsequent lapse of over
thirty years before the house was completed[28] meant that the present
scale and platt staircase by William Burn[29] is a substitute for a more
elegant one which would have risen in a continuous curve beneath the
cupola.[30] Externally, there is a trim of battlements and corner-turrets
(Plate 119) but there is also an unyielding symmetry and to relate that to
planning meant numerous blank windows, especially on the bedroom
floor. The windows there, despite their short height, were mistakenly
given the importance of hood-moulds. Despite such architectural

231

gaucherie the house shows signs of that sophistication in manipulating the visual effects of Gothic which was to mark off Gillespie Graham from his contemporaries. Thus, although the entrance front shows two floors, the ground level slopes to the rear revealing three floors, where the central three bays curve out in a delicately formed hemicycle. These traits, the change in ground level and the hemicycle, were to become idiomatic in Gillespie Graham's early architecture and where other proof of his identity is lacking they are reasonably sure evidence of his hand.

Within the history of the Gothic Revival, Achnacarry is of considerable importance for not only did it first stretch Gillespie Graham's powers but it marked his metamorphosis from building to architecture. Achnacarry was the first Gothic house to appear in the west highlands since Inveraray and, although by its situation and architecture it might be taken as indicative of the picturesque that is probably too precocious an assumption.

The early promise which Gillespie Graham showed at Achnacarry burgeoned in the gentler air of Perthshire at Kincardine Castle. Formerly an ancient property of the dukes of Montrose,[31] it had been disposed of by the early part of the nineteenth century. The present castle was built in 1806[32] and its attribution to Gillespie Graham can be argued on two points. First, it was erected in the middle of that brief period when there is no record of Gillespie Graham being employed by Lord Macdonald although the latter's papers are remarkably complete. Secondly, Kincardine Castle is closely related to Achnacarry but with the concepts governing the style and form of the latter more fully developed. Thus the main elevation of five bays is not only bolder with open-crowned polygonal buttresses but was enriched by a Gothic porch[33] and a bay window at either end bay while above a pierced Perpendicular parapet is carried round the sides to the hemicycle at the rear. The connection with Achnacarry is obvious although Kincardine is not only surer in its massing but displays confidence in the assembly and display of such details as pointed lights, quatrefoils and corbelling. These are all very much of the eighteenth century in their handling. Nevertheless, while Achnacarry was the architectural chrysalis, Kincardine wears the joyous sumptuary of the butterfly.

In the same county is Lanrick Castle which, again on stylistic grounds, can be ascribed to Gillespie Graham. It has already been shown from the Macdonald papers that Gillespie Graham was at Lanrick in March 1803[34] and in March 1815 the architect mentioned a meeting of Lord Macdonald and his estate commissioners at the castle.[35] One of the commissioners, and the one with whom Gillespie Graham had to treat most frequently in connection with Lord Macdonald's building operations in Skye and North Uist, was Sir John Macgregor Murray, the owner of Lanrick Castle. It was an old towered house which a traveller in 1810 claimed had just been rebuilt.[36] Large symmetrical and castellated additions on each side of the four-storeyed block diminished in height until finally each ended in a single-storeyed bow. After that it was only one

Plate 120   James Gillespie Graham. Culdees Castle, Perthshire. 1810.

more step, at Culdees Castle (Plate 120), also in Perthshire, in 1810,[37] to raise the transposed hemicycle so that it became a circular tower riding above the square angle towers which beset the remaining corners of the rectangular block. A turretted porch projected boldly from a central tower in which a large Perpendicular window illuminated the staircase and hall, which were now contained in one space.[38] The same formula as at Culdees but on a smaller scale and therefore less striking was employed circa 1815 at Edmonstone Castle in Lanarkshire where the drum tower of Culdees shrinks to an octangular one scarcely more important than the three square ones. At Torrisdale in Kintyre it disappears from the exterior so that the round-ended room which the Culdees tower contained, although still present, is locked within the main fabric. Torrisdale, for General Keith Macalister, who had large estates in Skye, was identical to Edmonstone although the former was enlarged at the beginning of this century in accordance, it is said, with Gillespie Graham's original intentions.

All these houses, when set beside Scone Palace or Taymouth Castle, are modest, unassuming edifices. They cling in the main to the traditions of the Adam–Paterson school and although they show only some slight advance towards acceptance of the picturesque it would seem that Gillespie Graham had more than a passing familiarity with Lugar's houses in central Scotland. Indeed, where else could the notion of the round tower at Culdees have come from but Tullichewan? On the other hand the fenestration was copied from Scone Palace. With such a capacious dependence on colleagues' works it is surprising that the architecture is sensitive and inventive although inside there is no Gothic since with few exceptions, such as the staircase at Torrisdale, all the interiors are classical. Yet because these quiet, compact mansions are so unscholarly they possess the faint elusive charm of the Regency. Even so the sheer excitement of romanticism was not to be resisted and like most of his contemporaries Gillespie Graham embarked on ecclesiastical architecture both for houses and for churches.

The standard Gillespie Graham castle was adopted near Balloch on Loch Lomond for Ross Priory. It is Culdees in clerical habit so that instead of towers crocketted buttresses shoot upwards while the bulging end of the main elevation shows that within lies another of the bow-ended rooms.[39] Ross Priory was an old house. The property had come by marriage to Hector Macdonald Buchanan with whom Gillespie Graham had dealt over the plan for the offices at Kinlochmoidart. In September 1810 Walter Scott wrote to Lady Abercorn, 'I hear the Priory is greatly enlarged',[40] although it does not seem to have been finished for some five or six more years.[41] By comparison with the huge 'abbeys' then being erected in Scotland, Ross Priory was quite plain and much more grandiose was Crawford Priory in Fife. Although the place of the latter in the general history of the monastic movement has been noted, its importance in the career of Gillespie Graham must be touched upon.

As usual the site was not a new one, for there was already an eighteenth century mansion, Crawford Lodge,[42] whose transformation was fixed upon by the imagination of Lady Mary Crawford Lindsay and completed in 1813.[43] 'The predominant feature in Lady Mary's character was a religious reverence for feudal times and the memory of her ancestors—a reverence which she indulged in the erection of Crawford Priory',[44] in which both castle and priory were uniquely combined.

The former was designed by David Hamilton of Glasgow in domestic Gothic which replaced towers by buttresses. Early in the spring of 1810 Lady Mary had been impatiently expecting estimates from 'Messrs. Cleland and Hamilton' for 'the New Building at Craŭfurd (sic) Lodge'. In particular she was wondering if, 'I could With propriety and Without injuring my fortune go through With the Gothick (sic) Hall according to Mr. Hamilton's Superb Ideas'.[45] Two months later when the work was underway it was stopped because Cleland was not supplying drawings to the workmen. Nor did the architect, David Hamilton, escape the charge of dilatoriness so that the owner heartily wished, 'I Never had employed a Glasgow Tradesmen (sic) to plague My friends and My self'.[46] As Lady Mary's exasperation increased she decided to complete only the exterior of her castle, the servants' rooms and the great hall on which she had set her heart 'so that the Tenants May Dine in it Some Day of the Year 1811'.[47] Before then, however, 'Mr. Hamilton having declined all further trouble', Gillespie Graham had appeared. An instant success with Lady Mary he suggested that the exterior of the old house should become an abbey,[48] which by the close of the year 1811 had become the priory for 'Mr. Gillespie Wisely observes the Situation is so truly Monastic that his Part of the Building ought to Carry the Name'.[49] When the house was finished in 1813, though, pride of place in Lady Mary's eyes went to 'Earl John's Hall'[50] with its fan-vaulting and the coats-of-arms around the figure of an apostle in the west window,[51] 'the finest in any Private Building in the Kingdom'.[52]

In the Gillespie Graham portion the earlier house was left intact.[53] With his habitual flair for outclassing whatever he chose to imitate, Gillespie Graham recased Crawford Lodge, in the manner of Atkinson's Rossie Priory, with Perpendicular windows, Norman doorway and an openwork parapet similar to that at his own Ross Priory. Lady Mary, who had got the best of both medieval worlds, was so pleased with her votive offering to the past that she set up a large tablet in the ante-room commemorating her architects' achievements. In its strange duality Crawford Priory gathers into itself all the calm virtues of the age of equipoise before the dark conscience of the nineteenth century entered architecture. Yet, before confining ecclesiastical motifs to churches, Gillespie Graham did allow himself one more large monastic house,[54] Cambusnethan Priory.[55] Not surprisingly, perhaps, it is a decidely secular brand of monasticism, its towers neatly split by a pitched roof while on the rear a Culdees-type tower is opened up with numerous mullioned and transomed windows with crocketted finials set on the wallhead. Apart from a declining fashion for such fantasies, the impracticality of constructing a priory to the medieval letter must have been realised. Still, the lessons learnt from the attempt were not wasted since the biggest of Gillespie Graham's churches have a largeness of scale, although in part that must have been derived from his restorations of such genuine medieval buildings as Dunblane Cathedral[56] and the Church of the Holy Rude at Stirling in 1818.[57] Ten years later Gillespie Graham was at work on St John's, Perth,[58] and in 1835 he drew up proposals for the west end of Glasgow's cathedral.[59] It is indicative of the position he held that Gillespie Graham was commissioned to carry out these restorations; it is also indicative that they influenced but little his own ecclesiastical compositions.

Much of the middle period of Gillespie Graham's career was occupied with church building and particularly successful were the two chapels which he designed for the Roman Catholic church in 1813 and 1814 in Edinburgh and Glasgow. He had already built a church in Falkirk, on the site of the medieval Old Kirk[60] but there his Gothic was no more than a very loose assemblage of simple parts. The commissions which followed were a stroke of good fortune.[61] To be situated prominently in Scotland's major cities, the Gothic chapels were the most ambitious yet attempted in the country and were a lasting and original contribution to the Gothic Revival. Both were in the favoured Perpendicular, which appeared so frequently in Britton's *Architectural Antiquities* and in which King's College Chapel was apostrophised: 'At the period of its foundation, the ecclesiastical architecture of Great Britain had attained its highest degree of perfection'.[62] To enable his contemporaries to attain a similar perfection Britton thoughtfully provided details of groining[63] which could easily be copied in plasterwork especially as Britton treated it solely as a paper design and not as construction.

St Mary's Chapel (now the Catholic cathedral) in Edinburgh was built in 1813[64] as a rectangle a hundred feet long and just over fifty wide. There were four bays, each with a mullioned and transomed window and buttresses and pinnacles rising over the battlemented parapet. For lack of funds much of the intended ornament had to be omitted.[65] Even so, St Mary's, set in the classical splendours of Regency Edinburgh, was an advertisement for Church and architect worthy of Madison Avenue at its best. Indeed, one observer commented that the chapel 'was so much admired that it has led to the general adoption, throughout the country, of the Gothic style in the architecture of churches'.[66] No wonder that Gillespie Graham, at the start of 1814, could report 'a considerable increase of business'.[67] Later in that year he was in Glasgow[68] doubtless in connection with the erection there of the more lavish Catholic chapel.

St Andrew's Cathedral, as it is now, was the first neo-Gothic church in north Britain to have a nave and aisles closely imitating medieval precedent and fully revealed externally (Plate 121) so that the nave rides high above the crouching aisles—indeed, unduly high in order to accommodate side galleries originally. Despite the impenetrable grime, which chokes the architecture, the facade is still impressive. How much

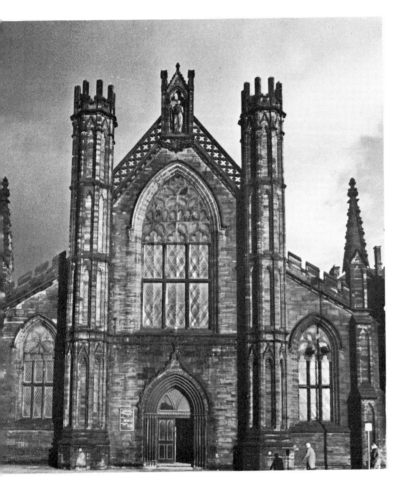

Plate 121   James Gillespie Graham. St Andrew's (Roman Catholic) Cathedral, Glasgow. 1814.

more it must have been when St Andrew's was unique, its creamy sandstone newly cut. The west window has rich tracery—solid and heavy it struggles for life, its segments pushing out in all directions like splitting amoebae; strong polygonal buttresses mark off the nave end and angled ones the aisles. Inside there is one of Gillespie Graham's favourite devices, a triple pierced screen masking the nave in which continuous shafts rise to become ribs which are collected in the bosses. Across the simple arcades the aisles have quadripartite vaults also of plaster. Although Gothic construction was beyond the powers and, let it be said, the interest of the architect, there is at St Andrew's a determination to take Gothic and force it into a new role. That purposefulness is summed up at the west door where, above the attendant shafts, there is boldly cut 'Jacobus Gillespie, Architectus. A.D. 1814'.[69] One cannot imagine Robert Adam doing such a thing; with James Gillespie it was not only pride but the assertion of self, a declaration of the right of an individual to control architecture and not be subservient to its canons. That was a fundamental change in the approach to architecture.

Usually Gillespie Graham's churches were for the Church of Scotland and for these a galleried hall was to be preferred. Of course, there were exceptions as, for example in 1826, when after a fire had destroyed the medieval building, Inverkeithing Church[70] was reconstructed on an aisles and nave plan. Externally, the structure was of the plainest with, on the side elevations, broad lights with depressed heads. Similar examples were used on the small rural church of Auchtertool in Fife which in 1833 was 'thoroughly repaired and much improved'[71] where the low lines and the almost complete absence of trimmings, save for two battlemented porches, contrast with Tain Church which bristles with crenellations.[72]

In keeping with a growing fashion towers began to appear. In 1811 at Monimail in Fife one was added to the neat, rather domestic looking eighteenth century church[73] but, coarsely proportioned and generally clumsy, especially at the summit, it lacked the soaring quality that might have been expected. In designing his first tower Gillespie Graham was clearly feeling his way. Perhaps his first Gothic church and tower was Moneydie in Perthshire, circa 1815, an exceedingly simple structure showing an interest in form, which not even St Andrew's had done, and which can be tied therefore to Gillespie Graham's first commission, Gask Chapel, also in Perthshire, of 1800.[74] At Moneydie at the liturgical west end a crenellated apse serves as an entrance porch while at the east there is the tower. Squat and stubby, it matches the other tough elementary shapes so that one wonders how the architect might have developed if there had been no surrender to the public's Gothic taste.

Until 1815 all Gillespie Graham's Gothic work was experimental followed by the mature style in which for scenic effect his designs could not be bettered. Thus, Liberton Church in Edinburgh in 1815 was well received by one observer[75] and justly so since full advantage had been taken of the townscape value of a tower. Clackmannan Church is the same date[76] and, typically, the design was repeated in the following year in the far north at Keith in Banffshire[77] where a wooded bluff gives it a commanding dignity. A smaller version was at Rafford, in Morayshire, in 1826.[78] In the same year was Muthill in Perthshire,[79] a return to the Perpendicular royal chapel style. It is doubtful if Muthill would ever be considered an architectural gem but it is a solid dependable building, well sited and with Gothic forms partly related to internal planning requirements. These had previously been more fully expressed at Dunbar Church in East Lothian in 1819[80] where the entrance tower is embraced, the end bays raised on the sides and the centre one is pitched and slightly advanced like a wall transept. There is, of course, total dependence on regularity and only at Alloa would there come a release into something dynamic.

Alloa was one of the last group of Gillespie Graham churches, those with spires. It has been criticised as too spiky[81] which is fair enough until it is remembered what other architects were doing and then the whole complex is above reproach. Although the Dunbar elevations were repeated at Alloa, the distinctive division between aisles and nave, with a resulting change of scale, make up a diverting silhouette while the two hundred foot spire and tower, asymmetrically placed, makes a truly medieval assemblage. The finest steeple is at Montrose, 1832–4,[82] where the detail is more sophisticated and the design more considered. In effect these spires, based on the medieval one at Louth in Lincolnshire,[83] are more scenic embellishments than architecture whereas at the Tolbooth Church on the Castlehill in Edinburgh[84] not only were scholarship and emotive power synthesised but the exterior, with all its rich detailing, is the membrane for the interior. In this unique work some of the detailing was, apparently, by A. W. Pugin, 'who was frequently employed by Graham'.[85]

In Gillespie Graham's later country houses, although one might expect mature designs, they seldom materialise. Certainly the scale increases and often the amount of detail but with little evidence that the architect composed in three dimensional terms. Gilpin had written: 'Painting, like poetry, is intended to excite pleasure: . . . yet he (the painter) should seize only those (images) which are easy and intelligible'.[86] That was at one and the same time the strength and the weakness of Gillespie Graham whose visual scene building incorporates, all too often, older and well-tried Gillespie Graham ideas. When new ones do occur they come from other architects but taken and used with such a flourish that the source is forgotten or overlooked in the visual excitement Gillespie Graham generated. That came, too, from a freer acceptance, than hitherto, of the principles of picturesque composition so that while there was little originality in the deepest sense there did appear a succession of comfortable, well-mannered houses in which nothing was ever taken to excess. It was no wonder that the adaptable Gillespie Graham had such a prolonged success.

The first of the mature Gothic castles was Armadale in Skye to which small additions were first made. In 1813 it was harled and in the spring of the next year a 'House and Rustic Seat' cost £4 0s 6d.[87] In the

Plate 122   James Gillespie Graham. Armadale Castle, Isle of Skye. Only a portion of the intended mansion was erected between 1814 and 1822. Now ruinous.

meantime Lord Macdonald decided 'to make certain repairs and alterations on the House of Armadale . . . and also to erect new Buildings there'. Edinburgh builders were engaged by Gillespie Graham and they agreed to have the work completed by 1 July 1815. Work had already begun at Armadale where the east wing 'already nearly finished' was to come down and the west wing 'so far as built excepting the Cellars and to take down entirely the present House of Armadale'. The total cost would have been £7,898 9s 1d.[88] A month later, in the middle of April, 1814, the works ... re 'going on by Contract'[89] and although difficulties were raised about the manner in which the contract had been placed,[90] the servants' rooms and kitchen were begun.[91] In the following spring progress was rapid[92] so that '8 Gothic Capitals and Cases' had been ordered from London

240

at a cost of £27 7s 6d[93] and payments for new furniture were made in various years[94] until in 1819 the castle was ready for its owner and £184 7s 9½d was disbursed on 'Fitting up and furnishing' the castle for his reception.[95]

Lord Macdonald had intended to have a much larger castle and

Plate 123   James Gillespie Graham. Duns Castle, Berwickshire. 1818.

published designs (Plate 122) show Gillespie Graham resorting to every trick in the picturesque rule-book for at one end of the main front was a cluster of high and variously shaped towers and at the other a solitary example to which was attached a spreading range of lesser buildings.[96] It was all in the manner of Craigend or Castle Toward. However, Lord Macdonald had to be content with a lesser edifice and a frontage of three towers, two of which belonged to the old house,[97] much of which was kept but with a suite of state rooms, hall and staircase added to it. Still those were enough for Sir John Macgregor Murray of Lanrick to express serious unease about the estate so that he would not be surprised 'if the unentailed part should be brought to the Hammer'.[98] He must have considered his foreboding justified when it was calculated that Gillespie

Graham alone had been responsible for works on the estate to the tune of nearly £29,000,[99] an enormous sum for any west highland estate to bear. Not surprisingly, therefore, Armadale after 1819 was complete except for castellated stables, presumably from Gillespie Graham, which were erected between 1821 and 1822.[100]

At Armadale Gillespie Graham had taken the towers of the old house to give an incipient drama to the composition by projection and recession in the facade as well as the contrast between high and low. The same rule was pursued at Duns Castle (Plate 123) in Berwickshire, the first of the architect's mansions which could be described as a masterpiece for not only did it obey the precepts of the picturesque but to these were added a noble scale and a mastery of detail both inside and out. These, combined with the undoubted antiquity of the building, make it an epitome of Regency Gothic, a worthy rival of the more famous mansions south of the Border. That was recognised at the time for 'the character of the new part was so planned as to harmonize in an admirable manner with the style of the old building. In preserving this, Mr Gillespie, the architect, has succeeded almost beyond precedent.'[101]

The idea of providing castellated additions at Duns was not new. In 1794 John Baxter, who had designed a Gothic gateway three years before,[102] drew up a symmetrical castellated block[103] allowing for a picture gallery, billiard room and library on the principal floor.[104] Richard Crichton's name appears on elevations and a plan in 1817,[105] the year of his death, when he was succeeded by Gillespie Graham one of whose drawings is dated 3 July 1818.[106] Duns is the sole instance where working drawings and details by Gillespie Graham appear[107] and that fact, coupled with the absence of correspondence, would seem to indicate that it was the owner, William Hay, an amateur artist, who supervised the building. That may also account for the extraordinary richness and quality not only of the total ensemble but also of the details whether in stone, plaster or wood. For these the architect had the benefit of Rickman's famous treatise of 1817 and the elder Pugin's *Specimens of Gothic Architecture* in 1821. Nevertheless, the minute attention to the details points to the close supervision of William Hay who copied, it is said, the design of an Italian ceiling for his library while his sketch of the east elevation was probably to show the architect what was wanted.[108]

Whereas at Gordon and Oxenfoord Castles attempts were made to hide an old tower, at Duns, although embellished, it remained free to become the fulcrum of the entire composition. At Armadale the towers' balance suggested a stately regularity; at Duns the parts flowing out from the tower diminished in vigour until finally the stables merged into the surrounding countryside. Set on a terrace the house rises from the park like the feudal pile it pretends to be. Although from the distance the parts are bold and simple, the facade (Plate 124) is intricately worked with windows, of many shapes and sizes, inset like devices, with broad hood-moulds standing out like coifs and gargoyles leaning out from between corbels. Some of the gargoyles, although they are supposed to represent local characters, are not very flattering for one is a devil and another is drinking from a cask held between his knees. The naturalistic carving, which makes Duns unique in its time, is also well represented internally where there are the usual features—the staircase with a huge window and vault to light and enclose it and public rooms and corridors with Gothic plaster vaults. These had first appeared at Armadale but at Duns they are complemented by superb carving in wood and stone in which the subjects not only include the oak and hop but thistles while from the stone canopies of the hall niches gnomes peep forth into a startled world from secure thickets of Decorated foliage.

The freedom which is everywhere at Duns must have come from the owner for with his next commission Gillespie Graham returned to his own basic recipe of a turretted rectangle with a circular tower at one corner so that, more than any other creation, Dunninald, in Angus, is the indictment against Gillespie Graham that his early promise was not fulfilled. Dunninald states nothing new. Yet what it does declare is done with such easy naturalness that it can be accepted without dispute as the most accomplished of the architect's achievements.

As early as 1797 James Playfair had prepared designs for Dunninald House[109] and eight years later Richard Crichton produced a scheme which attempted to clothe the old tower in castellation of the regular

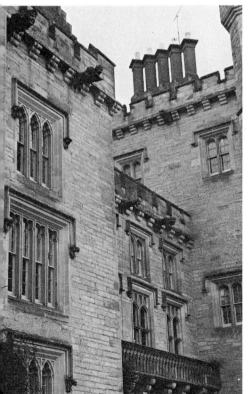

Plate 124   A detail of the south front. Duns Castle, Berwickshire.

Plate 125   James Gillespie Graham. Dunninald, Angus. 1819.

kind[110] very similar to his own nearby Rossie Castle. However, not until 1819 was anything done[111] by which date not only was the picturesque well established in Scotland but the publication of Lugar's *Plans and Views of Buildings . . .* provided a handy source book. Not surprisingly therefore, in view of Gillespie Graham's plagiarism elsewhere, it was the plates of Lugar's Tullichewan which provided not only the general silhouette of Dunninald but also the plan, and especially the eastern termination of the entrance front with a large round tower in which, for once, there is a circular room and not merely a bow protruding from the main block. Yet Dunninald can also be seen as the logical outcome of what had been begun at Achnacarry twenty years before.

At Dunninald (Plate 125) the stonework is plain and strong relying for effect neither on medieval bombast nor on the incredible insignia of war but on the antiphony rising from the sweet movement of the towers, rising and falling, advancing and retiring. Here is none of the heady intoxication of Duns, none of the pretentiousness of Armadale but an

244

unruffled reasonableness singing of the perpetual summer of the Regency. Internally, there is no extravagant Gothic decoration as Gillespie Graham had wished but which was omitted in great part, presumably for reasons of cost. The entrance hall and staircase did have Gothic plasterwork, very similar to that at Armadale, while in the dining-room a painted *trompe l'oeil* ceiling was the cheapest instant Gothic.

Plate 126   Detail of the south elevation. Drumtochty Castle, Kincardineshire.

In the same style as Dunninald was Kilmaron in Fife before the design was coarsened by the addition of bay windows. Described as 'newly constructed' in a publication of 1830,[112] Kilmaron, which cost £12,000[113] lacks the freedom of expression of Dunninald. It is much closer to Culdees since the round tower remains partially locked within the *corps de logis*. In the plan Gillespie Graham departed from his habitual practice of a central entrance on the main front and used a side elevation giving access to a broad corridor with the principal rooms to the south and the staircase opening out of the north wall.

A similar plan occurs at Drumtochty Castle in Kincardineshire which has always been accredited to Gillespie Graham on the strength of the entry in the *New Statistical Account*.[114] However the story seems to be more complex since the account books of John Smith of Aberdeen indicate a large building programme in 1815 and 1816 totalling £10,385.[115] Among the items listed are '608 feet Embrasure caps' with many others of a similar general nature including Gothic windows and arches. Some items can be specifically related to the present building. The '8 Bulls (sic) eyes' belong to the unusual octangular superstructure on the round tower (Plate 126). In addition, a comparison with Castle Forbes shows similar porches and lug-turrets at both places. Apart from the round tower, the important towers are copies of Guy's and Caesar's Towers at Warwick Castle. The curious four-lobed form of the latter was illustrated in 1814 by Britton[116] and the former much later by Pugin in the second volume of *Examples of Gothic Architecture*. Then, too, there are sections of Drumtochty where the Perpendicular stone tracery post-dates the bulk of the building. Those perhaps are the works hinted at in 1813 when Lady Mary Crawford Lindsay wrote from Crawford Priory, 'Harley Drummond & Meg Munrow (sic) have in the North a Beautiful Castle but small . . . they have got a Number of our Workmen and Mr. Gillespie has prevailed on their finishing off their House in the Outside Like this Priory'.[117] Perhaps Smith was the architect of the earlier parts of Drumtochty, which he repeated at Castle Forbes, and remained at the former as executant architect for Gillespie Graham who certainly designed the great hall by the entrance. Also it may be significant, in view of Gillespie Graham's activities elsewhere, that the lantern tower at Drumtochty is a miniature version of Taymouth's where he was engaged after 1838.

Earlier he had been inspired to reproduce the Inveraray theme, which had the attraction of a bold simplicity of outline, which was always his *forte*. The Inveraray concept was the first consideration at Dunninald[118] and it presented itself anew as a ready made solution to the problem of roofing the central courtyard when Lee Castle in Lanarkshire (Plate 127) was being renovated some time after 1822.[119] It was possibly an identical problem which led to its repetition at Wishaw House in the same county a year later[120] although in both cases the notion of a centralised plan and a dominant central feature was perhaps reinvigorated by the appearance in 1823 of Rutter's volume on Fonthill Abbey. That could help to explain why the eighteenth century concept of an isolated block was weakened at Lee and Wishaw by lines of straggling offices. Inveraray was bedded in the cold intellectualism of Palladianism whereas

Lee and Wishaw were cosseted in the swansdown of indulgent romanticism. Eventually, that movement demanded an historical accuracy in detailing which Gillespie Graham seems to have been loathe to provide so that he might well have repeated the outburst of John Nash: 'I hate this Gothic style: one window cost more trouble in designing than two houses ought to do'.[121] Yet at the moment when Gillespie Graham could no longer resist the demand for faithful historical reproductions he was to find a draughtsman who readily provided superb drawings.

Plate 127   James Gillespie Graham. Lee Castle, Lanarkshire. 1822.

Early in March 1828 Gillespie Graham first mentioned the possibility of a new castle at Murthly in Perthshire and an estimate was obtained with his assurance that it would not be exceeded.[122] In the middle of September timber to the cost of £2,275 15s 3d was delivered to the site[123] although work was not due to commence until the close of the following winter.[124] A year later two iron beams, each thirty-two feet long and weighing two and a half tons apiece, were despatched from Leith.[125] Gillespie Graham visited Murthly infrequently[126] and mostly 'I hear regularly from Murthly and find matters are going on smoothly about the Building'. That was in August 1829 while the client, Sir John

Plate 128   James Gillespie Graham. Murthly Castle, Perthshire from a photograph of c. 1875. Begun in 1829 and never completed the castle was blown up a hundred and twenty years later.

Stewart of Grantully, was abroad.[127] His health was poorly being a constant source of cause of anxiety to Gillespie Graham who was a family friend.[128]

Work at Murthly came to a sudden halt early in the new year in 1832.[129] One explanation may have been that the Baronet, as Gillespie Graham called him, was preoccupied with his forthcoming marriage[130] although more pressing were the objections from his heir, Captain William Stewart, who did not want the entailed estate encumbered with the building costs, which had been met by extensive borrowing.[131] As Sir John wrote regretfully in the autumn, 'The new House is shut up and the wood put in it and not a single workman left'.[132] Sir John died six years later[133] and the shell remained[134] as a blown folly until its demolition nearly a century and a half later.

Internally, the decorations were to have been by Pugin. In August 1829 Gillespie Graham was setting out for London[135] and in May 1830 he had 'to settle for Models in London'.[136] Pugin's name then occurs in January.[137] At that time he was short of money for in April Gillespie Graham noted: 'I have another pressing letter from Pugin and think it will be right to send him a Bill on London for £50'.[138] In the cash book for the house Pugin's name first appears on 10 October 1829, when he was paid £163 12s 0d for oak carvings, and other entries occur until the end of 1831.[139] The work referred to must surely be that which Pugin noted as the interior of a 'large mansion' for which, at the Scottish architect's

248

order, he prepared 'the great hall, Chapel, entrance hall, staircase, ante-room, library, drawing-room' all of which were of the 'James I' period except for the Louis XIV drawing-room.[140]

The exterior was Jacobean (Plate 128). As a member of the family had written, 'It combines the ideas of solidity, grandeur and elegance which ought to be the qualities of a Manor House in a fine romantic country'.[141] In an introduction to his client's plans Gillespie Graham cited Knole, Audley End and half a dozen other mansions of the same period as his sources.[142] Still, the underpinning to Murthly with its lantern tower was surely a self-conscious desire to emulate Taymouth, in the same county, and it was ironical therefore that Gillespie Graham should have been called in to finish that great house.

When Taymouth had been erected it would still have been possible to relate it to the interpretation of Burke's sublime that 'Whatever leads to raise in man his own opinion, produces a sort of swelling and triumph, that is extremely grateful to the human mind'.[143] However, with the less cerebral Repton, subjectivity came to the fore. 'A palace must not be a solitary object; it requires to be supported and surrounded by subordinate buildings, which, like the attendants on Royalty, form part of its state.'[144] At Taymouth there were still the classical wings of William Adam but on which, a writer declared in 1818, '. . . in that situation, the eye does not much love to rest'.[145] So too must have thought Lord Breadalbane for in the early twenties William Atkinson replaced the east wing with a lengthy decreet of offices compiled from unrelated Gothic units culled from the Scone Palace stock. Whether or not his plans for the west wing were fulfilled is uncertain,[146] since Gillespie Graham later wrote of its 'Tea Cadie (sic) appearance'.[147]

In 1834 Lord Breadalbane died. Although vast sums had been expended on Taymouth it was always grudgingly and he never accepted that 'Castles and palaces, particularly of the correctest style of archi-tecture, are not to be had for nothing'.[148] However, between his heir, the next peer, and Gillespie Graham there was something of that relation-ship which Disraeli described in his novel *The Young Duke* whose architect, Sir Carte Blanche, assured him that 'He would be the Lord of the most sumptuous and accurate castle, of the most gorgeous and tasteful palace in Europe'.[149]

Early in May 1838 Gillespie Graham wrote to Lord Breadalbane: 'I shall have the pleasure of forwarding by the Mail Coach to-morrow, Elevations of the West wing, which in my opinion proportion well with the high part of (the) Castle'[150] and in July further elevations with plans were despatched to Lady Breadalbane with a postscript: 'In such

249

magnificent Buildings as Taymouth Castle, a Domestic Chapel generally forms one of its appendages and which will be produced by the proposed large room'.[151] Although the chapel did not materialise the idea was not entirely abandoned since, according to the architect, 'The external appearance of this part of the Building is intended to convey the Idea of the Domestic Chapel'[152] and to that effect a huge Perpendicular window, filling the south wall, was under construction by sixteen masons early in the succeeding year.[153] Inside (Plate 129) the roof was made heavy with dark timber and £350 was spent[154] in filling its compartments with the genealogical glories of the family. From the Banner Hall, as it came to be known, a curved wooden screen gave access to the west wing heightened by one storey to contain bedrooms[155] with below a gallery and the library. Like the other apartments, the latter was rich and intricate in its carved wood-work, its dark timber ceiling set off by a blue background. These interiors are more splendid and vivid than anything that survives from the Middle Ages and quite outshine all previous ones by Gillespie Graham.

A contemporary claimed of Gillespie Graham that he had 'the merit of introducing the Gothic style into this country, in a greater degree of purity and perfection than had previously been exhibited'.[156] As a point of view that was certainly true of the Catholic chapels in 1813 and 1814 but it cannot be held to be true of such later works as Lee and Wishaw which only pay lip-service to the picturesque. Lee, for instance, had plain sashes and though at Wishaw (demolished in 1963) there were round headed lights it seems to have had as plain a classical interior as Lee where the sole Gothic was the somewhat old-fashioned decoration of the central saloon with its ritual fan vaults. Yet the fact remains that the only interiors which could justly be compared with those at Taymouth are those in the Palace of Westminster which raises the question of whether or not the former are also by A. W. Pugin. It seems likely since at Ardmaddy, designed in 1838,[157] and at Brodick Castle there is nothing comparable. The former is a prickly Gothic; the latter a towered Scots-baronial addition to an old house[158] and that Brodick is such an excellent piece of work is due no doubt to the appearance of Billings' *Baronial and Ecclesiastical Antiquities of Scotland* in 1845. For Taymouth, however, the suspicion remains that the collaboration between the architect and Pugin, about which so very little is known, may have produced a set of interiors as good as those at the latter's Scarisbrick Hall. After all, in 1838 and 1839 Pugin did prepare drawings for Gillespie Graham[159] who

Plate 129   The Banner Hall. Taymouth Castle, Perthshire. Usually credited to James Gillespie Graham it was probably designed by A. W. Pugin in 1838. The photograph was taken nearly forty years later.

commented that for the west wing at Taymouth all the details 'are taken from an old castle in Normandy'.[160] It is perhaps a significant remark especially as Pugin's father had published a volume on Normandy some time before. Whatever their authorship the Taymouth rooms were sufficiently impressive for the Austrian traveller, Kohl, to comment on them at length before concluding, 'I believe that in Great Britain may be seen, to better advantage than anywhere else, the antique models and furniture of the age of chivalry, blended with modern taste'.[161] Such a tribute Gillespie Graham would have considered he had justly deserved!

XIV

Scottish Churches

It must seem strange in a work devoted to the Gothic Revival that, save for some few passing remarks, there has been no sustained reference to churches. Yet at the end of the nineteenth century Fergusson justly pointed out: 'We must not overlook the fact that the Gothic Revival in this country is mainly an ecclesiastical movement and the real hold it has upon the people arises from their religion not from their artistic feelings'.[1] Nevertheless, although it was the motifs and occasionally the forms of the ecclesiastical architecture of the Middle Ages which, since the earliest days of the Revival, had provided such ready sources for innovations in domestic architecture, there was no corresponding ecclesiastical architecture. Therefore, in the second decade of the nineteenth century, it could be written of Gothic architecture: 'It is worthy of consideration . . . whether great advantages might not be derived from its revival, in the construction of our churches and other public buildings'.[2] Yet, so long as architects remained emotionally bound to classicism and later to the precepts of the picturesque, there was not much interest in the three dimensional aspects of medieval architecture. Certain individual forms were adapted for contemporary work but, by and large, Gothic was valuable to the eighteenth century for the fancy dress of its parts. In the second decade of the next century when there came an interest in volumes and not only planes, then there would be Gothic churches. Of course there were exceptions but prior to the opening of the nineteenth century they were few, prompted by wealthy landowners with an acquired taste for the heady Gothic spirit.

The first revived Gothic church in Scotland seems to have been at Kenmore at the eastern end of Loch Tay. Commissioned by the third Earl of Breadalbane in 1759 for six guineas[3] and erected in the following year[4] it was the product of an English architect, William Baker.[5] That fact would, doubtless, help to explain its tower and cruciform shape although these features were of importance in the setting for, set on a

Plate 130   Saltoun Church, East Lothian. 1805.

Plate 131   James Elliot. Glenorchy Church, Perthshire. 1810.

knoll, the church is opposite the Gothic entrance screen to Taymouth Castle so that the church tower effectively blocks the vista along the village street. Although remodelled in part in the nineteenth century there lingers from the previous one the use of harling, the raised dressings around the voids and the appearance of quatrefoils in the middle stage of the tower.

In 1766 John Carmichael on his Peebleshire estate built the harled T-plan Kirkurd Church with pointed arch-heads.[6] A similar plan is at Saltoun in East Lothian (Plate 130) in 1805[7] where the onset of the new century is shown by the battlements, the hood-moulds and stone mullions. Even so it is the lightness of the eighteenth century which pervades the composition especially in the changes of scale so that the tower is overwhelmed by the elegant flèche above it.

A considerable number of designs were for centrally planned churches and these were generally octagons. The best known was probably that by James Adam in Edinburgh's York Place in 1792[8] which was provided with clerestory lighting. To the same year there belongs Johnstone Church in Renfrewshire, with a pair of lights on each side and in front an octagonal tower.[9] Nearby at Lochwinnoch, again in 1792,[10] another

254

Plate 132   John Paterson. Fetteresso Church, Kincardineshire. 1810.

version but tougher and sturdier, is very much in the rural tradition. More interesting is James Elliot's Glenorchy Church for Lord Breadalbane which was supposedly completed in 1811[11] although 'a draught of the contract' had been made out in the autumn of 1809 with completion promised for late in 1810.[12] At each angle there is a buttress topped by a pyramidal pinnacle (Plate 131) and the same detail is repeated on the square tower. Likewise harled is the smaller variant, Kilmorich, also in Argyll, of five years later.[13] Its tower is banded at the summit by pierced quatrefoils. The largest of these octagonal churches and the most sophisticated is St Paul's in Perth. Costing £7,000 in 1807[14] and by John Paterson of Edinburgh[15] it has the elegance suited to a prominent building in a county town although the tower with its lug-turrets and spire lacks grace. Paterson was also responsible for the unusual church of Fetteresso (Plate 132) in Kincardineshire in 1810.[16] Hiding a rectangle there is a curved screen passage leading to the terminal towers in which there are the gallery staircases. The central tower is the porch with a turreted and battlemented corona. The windows are the usual Y-lights.

All these churches were designed to be what would be later decried as 'preaching-boxes'. The sermon being the central element of the service a centrally planned church was the ideal solution or, failing that, a rectangle with the pulpit in the centre of the south wall, for ease of lighting, and either one gallery before or several around it. With no call then for medieval planning the nave and aisles of Craig Church in Angus can only be due to the whim of Mrs Hercules Ross who paid for the building in 1799[17] and whose husband in the next year would commence Rossie Castle. As his architect was Richard Crichton then the latter may well have been responsible for Craig Church. Of three bays it has an embattled west tower with its buttressing treated as crude pilasters and with triple shafts on either side of the entrance (Plate 133). Inside there are nave arcades and plaster vaults with slim mouldings. Although the reverse has been claimed[18] it is clear that the church is a somewhat clumsy attempt to rival the astonishing virtuosity of Farnell Church in the same county.

Farnell, one of the two Scottish churches in this study about which something is known of the design process, is by James Playfair. In his diary he first mentioned 'Farnwell' in April 1788 after which there is no mention of it until the close of the year when he began to concentrate his time and energy on the design. On 16 December he recorded cryptically 'Plan and Elevation Working Drawing of Farnwell Church'

Plate 133   Craig Church, Angus. 1799.

Plate 134   James Playfair. Farnell Church, Angus. 1789.

at which he continued on the next day for 'long hours'. However, the designs were altered after a meeting with the heritor, Sir David Carnegie of Kinnaird Castle which Playfair was converting to Gothic. Two days later they met again after which the architect continued 'farther the working drawings'. That was the pattern until the close of the year and even on New Year's Day, 1789, he was 'Attending Sir D. Carnegie, Lothians Hotel' and was then at work until ten o'clock that night. On 7 January, Playfair was making an estimate of the masonry for the church and a steeple but when another week had passed not only is there no further mention of the steeple but he had made out drawings 'to Inch Scale and at Large for Windows and Masonry' having in the meantime visited Westminster Abbey and its cloisters for ideas. Finally, in the middle of January, he waited on Sir David 'with book' and then sent the estimates.[19]

Although previously attributed to the early nineteenth century[20] it must be evident that the church Playfair designed was that described as 'now building' in 1789.[21] In the characteristic manner of the period the more important side elevation has four bays which at the ends become doorways although one is false. Between them there are large windows with intersecting tracery which are blown up in scale to make the extrava-

257

Plate 135 The interior. Farnell Church, Angus.

gant east window. The canopied niche for the bell (in place of the usual bell-cote), the curved gables, and the use of buttresses and pinnacles are unique for the period (Plate 134). Inside (Plate 135) there is the same elaboration in the vaulted bays with ribs springing from angel corbels holding shields. No other church of the early Gothic Revival in Scotland is of such interest and the maturity of design and the purity of detail, rank it as one of the most important structures of its kind in Britain.

Another complex Gothic church was the Barony in Glasgow of 1794[22] with a castellated facade and a battlemented tower with a saddle-back roof. Much of the detail would seem to have been inspired by the locality, especially by the Cathedral. However, both the Barony and Farnell in their external longitudinal alignment were uncommon departures from the concept of the lateral rectangle. The pattern occurs at its simplest at Portmoak in Kinross-shire in 1832.[23] The south front has the standard four bay formula with the central ones being high pointed lights, filled with basketwork tracery, whereas the end bays are composed of sash windows set one above the other. Of the same pattern but even starker, for there are no mouldings at the openings, is Kinnettles in 1812.[24] Also in Angus is Maryton (Plate 136), dated 1791 and renovated in 1818,[25] which has demi-lights above doorways set in the customary place as at Fossoway in Kinross-shire[26] where a central mullion creates two lesser lights. At Banchory-Devenick in Kincardineshire

258

(1822)[27] there are four such windows in which the white mullions and glazing bars make a sparkling foil to the harling. Four years later and some few miles to the south Glenbervie,[28] with ashlar walls and diagonal buttresses, has the windows deeply recessed. The fenestration pattern was common and occurs at Longforgan in Perthshire as early as 1795,[29] in 1811 at Auchindoir,[30] 1812 at Kennethmont[31] and as late as 1834 at Corgarff[32] all in Aberdeenshire.

That county has an interesting group of churches which, with certain features in common, may be from the same hands. Thus the demolished Crathie Church, known to be by William and Andrew Clerk in 1804,[33] imitated the south front of Skene Church of three years before[34] where on the south elevation the central portion is projected like a gabled transept with a Gothic bell-cote perched above. The same arrangement occurs on the entrance front of Echt of the same year.[35] The doorway has an *oeil de boeuf* window above and a clock set between the rising curves of the gablet on which sits the cupola topped bell-cote (Plate 137). The same general arrangement but of double width, including the bell-cote, is at Fyvie in 1808.[36] It is the most thoroughly Gothic of the churches lacking, as it does, both classical elements and harling. On the other hand the churches of Kildrummy in 1805[37] and Bourtie of the next year,[38] both of which have an almost square plan, are so unostentatious that they become almost vernacular.

Outside that group, but with many of its superficial characteristics, is the 1812 Crimond Church.[39] Harled and with the usual granite

Plate 136   Maryton Church, Angus. 1819.

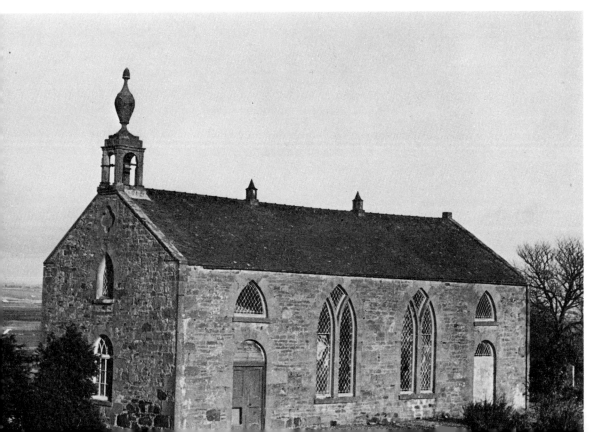

dressings it has the distinction of a tower below a spired octagon. The same theme but with stumpier proportions had been devised at Currie in Midlothian about 1785.[40] Considering the ornamental effects to be gained from spires it is surprising that there were so few, at least in the early days of Gothic churches. Perhaps that was because Gilpin condemned the spire as 'neither . . . in itself an ornament; nor has it any effect'.[41] Thirty years later there was little of either at Newburn in Fife in 1815[42] where the tower has corbels and battlements below a recessed spire. More successful by reason of its greater height is Comrie in Perthshire (Plate 138) by Stewart of Perth in 1805.[43] There, the tall tower, where battlements grip the spire's base, is perfectly proportioned to the long rectangular church in which broad windows stretch almost from floor to ceiling to light the galleries. Sited on the river and recently restored, Comrie's gleaming walls and sparkling fenestration epitomise all that is most thoughtful and charming in the Gothic Revival before, towards the close of the Regency, it became concerned with correctness. Yet the rapid proliferation of Gothic churches from then onwards can also be explained by other potent factors coming into operation.

Towards the end of the eighteenth century one compiler of the *Statistical Account* had noted: 'With us of the church of Scotland, many of our country kirks are such dark, damp, and dirty hovels, as chill and repress every sentiment of devotion'.[44] That sentiment could be answered in another quotation of only a few years earlier. 'However strongly marked

Plate 137   Echt Church,
Aberdeenshire. 1804.

Plate 138 Comrie Church, Perthshire. 1805.

were the days of our ancestors with superstition or incredulity . . . they were yet more remarkable for liberality and beneficence, for acts of charity, and for incentives to piety'.[45] As such emotion grew so it would bestow on Gothic architecture an aura of sanctity which in the long run meant that Gothic was bound to win the Battle of the Styles. Then, too, the advance of Gothic was aided by the interests of the antiquarians so that, once specialised interest became public concern, there began the campaigns to restore the monuments of the Middle Ages. It has already been seen that Gillespie Graham was employed on numerous medieval churches; he was followed by William Burn at St Giles after 1829 and Dornoch Cathedral in 1835 for the first Duchess of Sutherland. Yet what particularly accounted for the spread of Gothic were the new publications. Many have already been mentioned. In Scotland Hall's essay, in which he attempted to analyse the origins of Gothic architecture, contained useful ideas as to why Gothic should be adopted for churches. Of course, the idea was not new. As early as 1781 *The Gentleman's Magazine* had suggested a distinction between secular and religious Gothic with the latter being reserved for churches.[46] Hall expanded on such a simple premise by not only citing that 'A distant view is most favourable to the Gothic style'[47] but giving such practical reasons for preferring it as the large number of people a Gothic building will hold and the plentiful amount of light it admits.[48] While Hall's book stated

261

philosophical views on the origins of Gothic at great and tedious length, the mass of hitherto undigested Gothic memorabilia was neatly and summarily categorised by the Quaker doctor, Thomas Rickman who not only made sense of the confusion of styles in his explanatory volume but by clear and simple diagrams provided a wealth of parts which would be useful in composition, accompanied by advice as to what should or should not be copied. What the last should be was demonstrated in the *Views of the most interesting Collegiate and Parochial Churches in Great Britain* published by Neale in 1824. The preface to the first volume makes it clear that in a popular manner, that is without the architectural details of other more scholarly works, 'the characteristic beauties' of churches would be presented. The approach is best summarised in the second volume at the close of the account of Shrewsbury Abbey. 'Although barbarously defaced, and curtailed of its fair proportions, the interior of the Church has still much of that solemn dignity which inevitably fills the mind with religious awe to the excitement of which, ancient Cathedral and Monastic Churches, contribute in a degree so far beyond all other ecclesiastical structures, that the art of man has ever yet produced.' That may be a bold claim but it is evident that the *Views* had a considerable effect on architects who realised in stone and lime many of the chosen scenes. And if the influence was greater south of the Border, so far as Scotland was concerned the volumes were not without significance. Unlike Rickman, Neale made no attempt to classify his buildings either in terms of chronology or architectural importance nor did the pages have the plans, sections and details of Britton's productions beside which Neale's volumes are inferior in every respect.

When Britton in the final volume of his immensely influential *Architectural Antiquities of Great Britain* wrote his essay on Gothic architecture the number of authors he quoted is indicative of the hold which the subject had not only on architects but on the public at large. Indeed, Britton reckoned the two most important influences in raising the standards of Gothic architecture since Walpole's time to have been the number of texts and the demand for new churches.[49] In Scotland some indication of what the building programme meant can be discovered in the fact that under the direction of the energetic Dr Chalmers the Church Extension Committee from 1834 to 1841 provided two hundred new churches.[50] Previously, forty-two new churches, the so-called parliamentary kirks, for the Highlands and Islands were authorised by an act in 1824.[51] In addition, the Episcopalians and Roman Catholics, having been relieved of their religious disabilities by acts in 1792 and 1793 respectively,[52] were actively building, from the second decade of the nineteenth century onwards, for their congregations. Of these new churches a very large number were Gothic. From Hay's study of Scottish post-Reformation churches it can be found that in the years 1714–1800 eighty-four churches were erected of which six were Gothic. In the succeeding four decades there were ninety-four Gothic churches as opposed to forty others. Indeed, it can truly be claimed that in Scotland the majority of church members worship in buildings belonging to the nineteenth century. A further analysis of Hay's figures reveals that while approximately two dozen churches appeared in the burghs well over a hundred were built in the rural areas. In the former there was the need to house faiths once suppressed by edict; there was also the necessity of catering for populations in new residential areas. Thus in Edinburgh the eight new churches included the fashionable St George's in Charlotte Square but in Gothic there were, besides the Catholic St Mary's, the Episcopal chapels of St John's and St Paul's.

Within the period of this study the working classes in the towns were not a matter for religious concern. What was of concern was the condition of the rural parish church. Many of these had survived from the later Middle Ages continuing to be used throughout the centuries after the Reformation although by the start of the nineteenth century a large number were in a state of serious decay. Of Kemnay in Aberdeenshire it was reported, as a typical example, 'Owing to the thickness of the walls, and the smallness of all the windows save two, it is not well lighted. It cannot be sufficiently ventilated, for the floor is from three to four feet below the level of the burying ground . . .'.[53] More important, however, was the fact that such edifices could not house the growing populations of the parishes. In 1822 the old church of Banchory-Devenick in Kincardineshire was torn down to make way for a more sizeable one.[54] The church at Auchindoir in Aberdeenshire, built in 1811, was too small thirty years later[55] as was that at Laurencekirk in Kincardineshire which had already been extended in 1819 only fifteen years after its erection.[56] When it is discovered that such a church as Craig seated eight hundred members[57] and that other churches can be found, such as Comrie with places for over a thousand worshippers,[58] and Fetteresso, fitted to accommodate fourteen hundred sitters,[59] then the inadequacy of the existing buildings becomes apparent. For the most part they were un-roofed while a new and more commodious structure arose either nearby or, as at Fetteresso, at a more central or convenient place in the parish.

The provision of new ecclesiastical buildings in the countryside was the responsibility of the local landowners, and heritors' Gothic has always been criticised, even in its own time. In the *New Statistical Account*

Plate 139   Portsoy (Roman Catholic) Church, Banffshire. 1829.

Saltoun church was praised, for 'In its general appearance, our village sanctuary more nearly resembles the sacred structures which so frequently adorn the hamlets of England, than those less tasteful erections with which the parsimony of heritors has too often disfigured, and not embellished the parishes of Scotland'.[60] Although Saltoun was unusually rich in its decorations, it can in general be said that early nineteenth century Scottish churches were more spacious and more substantial than most of their predecessors.

It has already been seen that, with but a few exceptions, early Gothic churches were simple rectangles with, on the south side the familiar array of windows filled either with basketwork tracery or Y-tracery formed from a single wooden mullion. Although such traits would gradually disappear they persisted with the non-conformists among whom the Methodists were prominent. They were urban congregations and being few in numbers did not require high galleried edifices but met in halls which could either be above business premises, for instance at Perth in 1816,[61] or else squeezed into a narrow site between existing buildings so that only for the facade is an elaborate treatment required. In Dundee the Ward Chapel, 1833,[62] has a chunky three part facade rich with Decorated motifs. Very severe is the crenellated ashlar front of the Episcopal church in Paisley.[63] Of the same year, 1828, is the Catholic church in Fochabers, Morayshire,[64] which likewise displays a putative nave and aisles arrangement on the facade although inside there is a galleried hall as in any of the Established churches. The finest of these facades is St Mary's Catholic church in Inverness which being of 1837[65] can boast finely carved details. Although set back from the street the facade is linked to it by short curving screens which are tied to the street by buttresses. Yet in the countryside the old ways continued. At Portsoy in Banffshire the Catholic church (1829)[66] has a harled two storey front with pilaster-like buttresses and sash windows with pointed heads (Plate 139). The presbytery is attached to the church. A similar grouping occurs with Banff's Episcopal church, of 1833 by Archibald Simpson,[67] but there the dwelling is given sharp gablets.

Plate 140   The nave vault. St John's (Episcopal) Church, Edinburgh.

Although Rickman had a stated preference for Decorated 'as the perfection of the English mode'[68] it did not find such favour in Scotland where the Perpendicular came into vogue. It seems to have been introduced into church design by Gillespie Graham with his Catholic chapels of 1813 and 1814 in Edinburgh and Glasgow. The influence of these buildings, already referred to, was prodigious. In Aberdeen there is St Andrew's Episcopal chapel (now the cathedral) of 1816 which was Simpson's first ecclesiastical commission.[69] Of imported Craigleith sandstone it is a copy of St Andrew's in Glasgow. A very late imitation, in 1836, is the Catholic cathedral in Dundee[70] with the Catholic St Margaret's in Ayr of nine years before[71] being a somewhat naive version but with stone crowns on the buttresses.

VIEW OF THE EAST END, WITH THE GENERAL DESIGN OF THE NEW EPISCOPAL CHAPEL FOR THE RIGHT REVEREND BISHOP SANDFORD, TO BE ERECTED AT THE WEST END OF PRINCES STREET AND TO BE CALLED ST JOHNS CHAPEL.

Plate 141   William Burn's design for St John's (Episcopal) Church, Edinburgh. The lantern was blown down in 1818 and was never replaced.

In Edinburgh the Episcopal church also took up Perpendicular at St Paul's by Archibald Elliot in 1816[72] and St John's by William Burn in the same year.[73] Both were modelled on Tudor royal chapels and both have an aisles and nave plan. St John's, almost alone in its day, had no gallery so that the daring experiment of a plaster fan vault in the nave would lose none of its effect (Plate 140). Both churches were very expensive. St Paul's cost £12,000[74] and St John's £15,000[75] with the difference in price being accounted for by its west tower. When first built (Plate 141) this had a crowned octangular lantern[76] in imitation of the celebrated Boston 'Stump' which had appeared in the fourth volume of Britton's *Architectural Antiquities* in 1814. Before the church opened, however, the lantern was destroyed. Walter Scott wrote from Edinburgh on 17 January 1818: 'The storm was tremendous here, and the Devil has plainly proved himself to be the prince of the power of the air, for he has blown the beautiful Gothic pinnacles off the tower of Bishop Sandford's Episcopal chapel, which have fallen on the roof and much damaged the building'.[77] The lantern was not replaced. Even so, St John's, standing on a commanding site at the west end of Princes St, is a powerful and

266

evocative essay in the Perpendicular. Along with the earlier examples it set the seal on that particular style although in 1817 Rickman faulted it because the eye was 'fatigued by the constant repetition of small parts'.[78] Still, he did acknowledge that 'Of small churches there are many excellent models for imitation, so that in this style, with some care and examination, scarcely any thing need be executed but from absolute authority'.[79] Even without that authority, when financial means were limited, the Perpendicular, with its flat surfaces and lack of integral decoration and especially its use of straight or nearly straight horizontals and verticals, found ready favour.

Thus in Aberdeenshire there is a group of churches which, though following Rickman in their early stages at least, are but one remove from the Regency churches of earlier years. In 1819 Forgue[80] has Perpendicular windows alternating with circular ones set high to light the gallery. It is a unique arrangement. Of the same year but with smaller dimensions there is Simpson's first church outside Aberdeen. Designed for his uncle by marriage,[81] Kintore[82] is a granite rectangle of three bays and tall windows with thin wooden Perpendicular tracery in the heads. A stumpy bell-cote over the entrance is matched by pinnacles topping the awkwardly placed and ill-proportioned buttresses at the angles on the corners. These, save for those on Gillespie Graham's chapels of 1813 and 1814 or the precocious ones at Glenorchy in 1811, were rare features.

Resembling Kintore in plan but more refined in its detailing is Drumoak of 1835. 'The best specimen in this part of the country of what a parochial church ought to be', it cost £1,002 14s 2d.[83] It has Early English lancets along the sides. Within this same group comes Fintray of 1821 by John Smith[84] which can be linked stylistically with the handsome church at Keig[85] of red granite. Solid and monumental as only granite can be, the church has four bays of Perpendicular windows above a high base and at each corner an angle buttress with a superimposed pinnacle. The bell-cote Smith repeated at Inverurie in 1842.[86] It is a sparkling building not only in the silvery sheen of the granite but with lively detailing on the entrance front with two pairs of well worked buttresses and windows between with the central one having a finely chiselled hood-mould.

All these churches have wooden tracery. In 1820, however, at Shotts in Lanarkshire Gillespie Graham's church, its design modified by another architect[87] had stone mullions, transoms and hoods below the crow-stepped gables so beloved of its first designer. Many of these features are found too at Dunino in Fife in 1826.[88] Set in a sheltered place and more compact in scale it is the best of these rectangular kirks of the early Perpendicular period and with its compact form and logical expressionism it does much to dispel the poor reputation of heritors' Gothic. That same 'proof of the great improvement which has lately taken place in the style of ecclesiastical architecture'[89] is also to be found at Dalgety, 1830, in the same county.[90] Although seating twice the number of Dunino, it has only three bays and, without the elegant contrasts between solids and voids of the latter, is distinguished by its great height rendered more noticeable with a corbelled bell-cote with a spirelet above gabled sides. Quite the largest of this class of hall-church, in which galleries surround the pulpit, is Simpson's East Church of St Nicholas in Aberdeen which in 1834 replaced the medieval choir 'so ruinous, that it was judged necessary to pull it down'.[91] As usual economy was a prime consideration[92] but despite that Simpson's church is excellent of its kind, especially in his handling of the expansive interior with galleries filling three walls.[93]

It is, of course, obvious that few concessions were made to the double-tiered nature of Scottish churches. The addition of extra gallery windows at Forgue was a solitary concession. Only at Saline in Fife in 1810 did William Stark[94] produce a two-storeyed architectural expression. Saline is deceptive for, harled and with small windows set deep in the wall, it is totally devoid of archaeological interest although there are buttresses. But these, strong and plain, emphasise further the play of volumes. At Saline, where old forms were rethought a timeless quality was produced demonstrating that Stark's early death deprived architecture of an original mind.

In certain plan forms some attempts were made to come to terms with the nature of the church service and the use of galleries. Although central plans had been used, more common was the T-plan. Thus the addition of an aisle in 1834 converted Old Scone, notable for a Gothic Palladian window, from a lateral rectangle to a T-plan.[95] More usual, however, were the buildings specifically designed to that plan. In the past in Scotland such plans had not been uncommon since they lent themselves to a central pulpit, galleries and a laird's pew or loft facing the former. In the early nineteenth century such usage had fallen out of favour not merely because of the vogue for rectangular shapes but probably because architects did not feel capable of modelling Gothic. Thus not until the picturesque, with its claims for variable massing, was well established and there was a sufficiency of texts and patterns did T-plans re-appear. Typical is Andrew Heiton's St Martin's in Perthshire of 1842.[96] With simple Perpendicular windows and corbelled bell-cote it is part of that sequence of churches to which Dunino and Dalgety also belong although on the south front the central bay is treated like a transept. Similar but much spikier and with angle buttresses and window tracery, is David

Mackenzie's Inchture church in the same county of 1834.[97] However, the Episcopal church at Muthill, again in Perthshire, of a year later[98] is very much plainer, its austere forms rendered forbidding by tall and very thin lancets. Still, when money was available a very attractive product could be had as with the small kirk of Cranston in Midlothian, 1824, in the grounds of Oxenfoord Castle.[99] Cranston has a tower which enables the church to hold its own against the encroaching woodland. Nearby is Cockpen, a broad and expansive study by R. and R. Dickson[100] with a tower crowned by tall open parapets. Identical but on an even grander scale is Kilconqhar in Fife[101] where again re-entrant angles have curved bays although at Colessie, 1839, in the same county[102] the bays are corbelled. A similar arrangement was contrived at St Martin's.

By comparison with the grandeur of the Dicksons' products, David Bryce's two T-plan churches in Ayrshire, at Coylton in 1836[103] and at Monkton a year later[104] are disappointingly thin and unconvincing and not to be compared with Burn's work. Undoubtedly, the latter's cruciform addition to the Norman nave of Dunfermline Abbey[105] is meagre in parts but on the whole the ambitious exercise with clerestory and aisles does succeed and if the lettering in the parapet of the central tower is not exactly pleasing it does have a unique distinction. Dunfermline has survived unchanged internally. This is fortunate for all too frequently fittings, often of real beauty and excellence of workmanship and material, were swept away in the later Victorian era.

Kinnoul in Perthshire, 1826,[106] is of the same genre as Dunfermline even to the stepped plan. The later Stenton in East Lothian[107] is simpler but not unattractive with fine stonework and the tower, rising above the arms of the church, makes an elegant and fresh composition. Of course in the last years of this study changes did take place which altered the whole character of church architecture. The simple vigour of the high hall-kirks with their low-pitched roofs gave way to the products of the ecclesiologist. Yet although W. H. Playfair's Minto Church[108] in the Borders has been described as dull its sturdy tower and broad comfortable form fits well into the landscape. Of a similar nature is Dollar Church by the Englishman, William Tite and although the church itself, for such a late date as 1841,[109] is disappointing, there is a handsome tower. Finally, in this section on T-plan churches, there is Rickman's St David's (Ramshorn), Glasgow, which replaced a medieval church.

St David's is the only church of its period in Scotland for the design of which anything is known in detail. When Rickman arrived in the city in the middle of February 1824 he met 'Mr. Cleland', perhaps the same James Cleland who had built Crawford Priory. Together they went 'to

269

the Cathedral and the Ramshorn Church which is to be rebuilt and he wishes me to make a Design and is to speak to the Provost and Magistrates tomorrow about it'.[110] Some weeks later the architect received a letter from Cleland 'with the plans for the Ramshorn Church with a request for Working Drawings with some alterations'.[111] Most of the elevations were ready by early April[112] after which there came a delay so that not until the middle of the next month were the details ready.[113] At last on 8 June, Rickman could jot down that 'We have tonight by close Application finished and sent off the Drawings to Glasgow. There are 41 and I think the set is so complete that they can hardly go wrong unless they err wilfully in execution.'[114] The magistrates immediately ordered estimates to be prepared[115] and although some minor work remained to be done by Rickman, his part was more or less over.

Occupying a commanding site at the end of a long narrow approach, St David's church (Plate 142) shows all the skill and ingenuity one would expect from the architect. Not only is there a considerable range of detail, hitherto unexplored by other architects, but the composition, bold and striking, though it is, strikes a new note in church design, a note best summarised by the soaring lines of the tower with its open parapet and airy pinnacles.

Although towers had been used to some extent in the eighteenth century afterwards so far as Gothic was concerned they tended to be perfunctory and the first of the new mode was in 1809 at Bolton in East Lothian.[116] Of three stages it is a mixture of rounded and pointed voids

Plate 142   Thomas Rickman. St David's (The Ramshorn) Church, Glasgow. 1824.

with angle buttresses and a battlemented summit complete with crocketted corner pinnacles. More accurate in its fenestration is Kirkmahoe in Dumfriesshire[117] executed in the brilliant red stone of the district. Of sturdy proportions it has pairs of cusped lights on each face. However, more characteristic of the general architectural trends was Collace in Perthshire in 1813[118] which was 'much and deservedly admired'.[119] To judge by the maturity of the Perpendicular it could be by Gillespie Graham. The body of the church is a noble four bays decisively marked off by sensible buttresses which finish just below the wall-head. The windows are so large as to almost fill each bay and are rich with bar tracery and bold stone cut tracery. The tower is embraced and held by crow-steps.

It is typical of the changed status of Gothic that whereas for the early churches their designers are mostly unknown after the second decade of the nineteenth century the names of all the leading architects are to be found associated with them. Around Aberdeen, for instance, John Smith created a characteristic range of towered edifices beginning in the city with St Clement's by the harbour.[120] Although the fenestration is of the simplest kind the various components of the tall tower are well integrated especially at the summit with its tall balustrade and many pinnacles. That was in 1829. In the following year came the richer South Church in Belmont Street.[121] Beyond the city and also in 1829 is Nigg Church,[122] a typical essay whose well handled tower was a shipping landmark. Further inland, Fordoun, of the same year, and costing £3,000,[123] was more ornate with buttresses along the sides and decorated work on the tower the top of which repeated that at St Clement's. Eight years later Inverbervie's church[124] reflects a greater desire for simulation of the Middle Ages although the formula was basically much the same as before.

Further south in Stirlingshire a pair of village churches at Fintry, 1823[125] and Killearn, 1826[126] belong really to the late Georgian tradition for they are harled and each has a squat little tower with flimsy battlements and oversailing finials. Only at Killearn does the basketwork tracery survive. Both churches must be from the hand of some local mason whereas nearby Kippen, 1825[127] is the work of a professional man since it shows such advanced features as a buttress at every corner and stone window tracery.

The finest examples of towers combined with hall-churches were from David Hamilton, the learned and ingenious Glasgow architect. His Old Erskine church, near the Clyde, 1814[128] is of neat and compact proportions and although devoid of carving and enrichment that only permits the serenity of the composition to impress itself on the intelligent observer. The church itself is short, of three bays and the windows have moulded splays and tailed hood-moulds. There are simple buttresses with diagonal ones on the corners and angle ones for the tower which die away just before the summit where alone there is weakness since the pinnacles are too slight for the muscular body below. Such indeed is the simplicity of the lines that the boldness, almost the coarseness of Larbert in 1818[129] is something of a shock. There is too much at Larbert, it is too overpowering and the five bays cry out for a lessening of the architectural tension by the introduction of a chancel to reduce the power of total mass. Similar and more grandiose, so that it sits brooding on its hill like an incomplete cathedral, is Campsie Church at Lennoxtown, also in Stirlingshire.[130] Its tower is pierced by numerous windows of varying degrees of acuteness in the pointed tops so that not only is there that variety which the picturesque demanded but also a growing awareness of medieval forms. Of almost equal dimensions is Hamilton's Bothwell church in Lanarkshire of 1833.[131] Much changed internally, outside it retains its original semblance. Although towers invariably rose from the centre of the liturgical west front, at Bothwell the tower soars up from the intersection of the fragment of the medieval kirk and Hamilton's

Plate 143   William Stirling II.
Airth Church, Stirlingshire.
1818.

Plate 144   George Angus. Kinross Church. 1832.

buttressed rectangle with the junction softened by raising the bays to
transept status beneath their own gables. There is then created that
medieval complexity of plan which Hamilton's earlier churches had
demanded.

Refined and sensitive though Bothwell is, it is surpassed by Airth in
Stirlingshire. Its architect, William Stirling II,[132] like so many others,
including Gillespie Graham at his church in Keith, took as his model
Bishop Skirlaw's chapel which Britton reproduced in the fourth volume
of *Architectural Antiquities*. Airth (Plate 143) is the finest church of the
early nineteenth century in Scotland for it has all the qualities of
Hamilton's Erskine church but sophisticated by an overlay of subtle
decoration. Even the Stirlings' own Lecropt Church in Perthshire of six
years later (1824),[133] larger and more ebullient and with fine carving,
cannot match Airth for visual delight and goodly composition.

Although the hall-church gradually displaced the lateral rectangle
there were a few other plans including the aisled and arcaded Kincardine-
in-Menteith by Richard Crichton in 1814. For its day this country kirk
is uncommonly decorative but then the chief heritor, George Home
Drummond, was willing, indeed insisted on paying the extra cost involved.[134] George Angus provided an interesting trio of churches at
Kinross (Plate 144),[135] Tulliallan[136] and Kettle in Fife [137] all between 1832
and 1834. They follow the T-plan with a tower but the long leg is

273

arranged like a German medieval hall church with lofty aisle windows and a pair of gables as the frontispiece.

Although all these churches were provided with towers only a handful of spires appeared. When the picturesque mood was strong Hall praised spires as 'a very principal ornament' of the Gothic style.[138] Still, a spire was costly and what was worse difficult of execution although it was easy to add a miniature spire to a bell-cote as at St Mary's, Dumfries, 1838,[139] and elementary spires did appear at Daviot, Inverness-shire in 1826,[140] and at Denny in Stirlingshire in 1838[141] as well as at Liff in Angus[142] where rudimentary flying buttresses make a unique appearance. There was, of course, nothing to match Gillespie Graham's noble series of spires at Alloa, Montrose and, with Pugin's help, on the Tolbooth church in Edinburgh. In Aberdeen Simpson built the sole brick example for the hastily formed Free churches after the Disruption in 1843. Within three weeks of that event estimates were accepted for three churches to be erected on one site. Coursed rubble was used as the cheapest material with brick for the tower and spire which was a copy from St Elizabeth's church at Marburg in Prussia.[143] Only slightly less impressive than Simpson's triumph is Burn's spire for the West church in Dalkeith in 1840.[144]

Being so late in date Burn's church really belongs to the ecclesiologists. The steep roof impinges on the low walls, the tower is set to one side and, most importantly, the style is that of the thirteenth century. Although the ecclesiological movement is more relevant to English architectural studies, in the Episcopal churches in Scotland it was a movement of some importance. Thus the Alloa Episcopal chapel[145] is only slightly less accomplished than Burn's West church in Dalkeith where the Episcopal chapel in 1843[146] with its long low lines and chancel is typical of the new approach to ecclesiastical architecture. Other examples would include Kirkcaldy, an 1844 T-plan,[147] and the one in Dunblane by John Henderson of the same year.[148] Inside it has a sweeping chancel arch with nook shafts and an exposed timber roof and strong contrasts of light and darkness from the small windows and deep patches of colour. In their general plan these churches were part of the advances being made in English church architecture and they mark the close of that long tradition of church building which, for so long, had differentiated Scotland from its southern neighbour where the history was neither of such variety nor interest.

XV

Churches in
Northern England

Although a superficial survey might seem to indicate little difference between the Gothic Revival churches of Scotland and northern England, that would not be true. Certainly, distinctions in the ecclesiastical architecture of the two areas might individually be slight yet taken together they add up to a wide differentiation.

To an architectural observer the most obvious difference is that while in Scotland a variety of church plans was accepted that was not the case south of the Border where, although the demands of the liturgy were nothing like so ritualistic as after the late eighteen thirties, nevertheless they did necessitate a plan that went far beyond the gathering of the people and a preacher as in Scotland. Even so the lack of experiment in planning in, say, the laxer days of the late eighteenth century is surprising. Equally so is the limitation of style. When style became important in Scotland from Early English to Tudor all were used. In northern England, however, it was Early English that held the field almost without dispute so that rare indeed are the instances of Decorated or Perpendicular. Thirdly, there were far fewer buildings than in Scotland. Even accounting for the disparity in total area and the number and spread of population it is significant that in the years 1803–14 only fourteen Gothic Revival churches appear in the four northern counties of England compared to almost fifty in Scotland. Indeed so slack was Gothic church building in the north of England, and probably over the whole of England, that it can be justly claimed that the Gothic Revival as an ecclesiastical movement in England did not get under way until after the passing of the Church Building Act in 1818 and the appearance of the first churches in the next decade. Of course throughout the north there was a large existing stock of churches which could be utilised. Indeed,

275

these, constantly changed and enlarged, present the most difficult problems of analysis since rather than build a new structure the English preferred to amend and adapt a hallowed one with the result that many instances are recorded of eighteenth and early nineteenth century alterations, some of which were Gothic, but which in turn have been obliterated or done away with. These churches present complex and detailed problems and, requiring special study, have been omitted and new structures only have been taken into consideration.

When new churches were required it was, so far as can be discovered, for much the same reasons as in Scotland. Old churches had to be replaced as at Annfield Plain, a mining community in County Durham, in 1842[1] or as at Cleator in Cumberland in the previous year.[2] Less frequently it seems than in Scotland (for there is no English equivalent for those invaluable source-books, the *Statistical Accounts*) did an increasing population demand an enlarged church. At Hurworth-on-Tees the old building was so small 'that latterly the greater part of the parishioners were excluded from want of accommodation'.[3] Then, too, the expansion of old communities meant new places of worship, as at Gateshead Fell in 1824[4] while at Seaham Harbour a church was provided in 1840[5] for the township created for the export of Lord Londonderry's coal.

The first completely new Gothic church in northern England seems to have been erected at Castle Eden by Rowland Burdon in 1764.[6] 'This Sacred Fabric, which consuming Time had now reduced to ruinous Decay, was, with the addition of a Steeple, rebuilt from its old foundations.'[7] Later, aisles were added by Burdon's son[8] so that, for its day, the church, probably by William Newton of Newcastle, the architect of Castle Eden, is unusually well proportioned and developed in plan. There was, however, little decoration save for some quatrefoils on the tower. Much of that is probably original but the upper stage was an addition finished with battlements and a recessed spire. The fenestration has the characteristic raised dressings and at the east end there is another of those rare hybrids, a Gothic Palladian window. Inside there was a proprietor's gallery and below forms covered in scarlet cloth.[9]

A gallery was also inserted in 1789 at Tweedmouth[10] which had been enlarged nine years before.[11] Although since changed there are still some lights with Y-tracery and the Georgian battlemented tower. However, at Kyloe, further south, there is almost nothing of the rebuilding in 1792[12] and even less at Lowick, slightly to the west, of two years later.[13] According to an inscription the architect was Henry Penny Selby Morton[14] who was probably responsible for Kyloe which is similar in every way. These two churches with nave and central west tower are large. In that they are exceptional. Not so the tiny Hebborn chapel north of Morpeth of 1793[15] which with nave, chancel, south entrance, bell-cote and spirelet has a strong vernacular quality. On the other hand Long Horsley, also in Northumberland, of ten years before[16] could not be more thoroughly Gothic for it has all the external trimmings, including a castellated double bell-cote, while inside, amongst other Gothic decorations, a superb trefoil arch, spanning the width of the chancel, is enriched on the soffit with panels. More restrained is the mausoleum at Wetheral, in Cumberland, built in 1791 for the Howards of Corby Castle.[17] Attached to the parish church it has pilaster-like buttresses and the slimmest of lights with cast-iron mullions and tracery. Inside it has Gothic plaster work. Associated with this is the Catholic chapel at Croxdale Hall in County Durham of 1807.[18] Three bays long it has windows on the south wall which are indicated on the opposite one by blind indentations. The bays are marked off by columns with minute capitals above which there are ribs, sexpartite vaulting and flat plaster bosses. A short chancel has canted sides with canopied niches and there is a gallery on the west wall. There are other decorations, probably derived from Wyatt's alterations at Auckland Castle, which make the chapel the most elaborate ecclesiastical interior of the Gothic Revival in the north of England.

Apart from Croxdale chapel there is nothing of any real interest in the early years of the nineteenth century. There were additions and alterations to existing edifices as at Crosby Ravensworth in Westmorland where in the course of some reconstruction the summit of the tower became a copy of that at Magdalen College, Oxford, which a local proprietor 'had admired when on a visit to his nephews'.[19] Such changes apart, and they were common to any age, no school of churches emerges as in the Regency churches of Aberdeenshire for instance. Indeed, the entire Regency period in northern England is only saved from total eclipse by the quartet of churches built along the north Tyne valley as the result of an act in 1811 which, dividing the very extensive parish of Simonburn, permitted the erection of new rectories.[20] New churches were built at Wark, Greystead, Thorneyburn and Humshaugh and all were consecrated in August 1818.[21] Of these Humshaugh, perhaps because it is so unostentatious, is the pleasantest. Like the others it consists of a three bay nave (here with Y-lights) and a slight sanctuary which at Wark was dismissed by Archdeacon Singleton as 'a sort of excrescence'.[22] At the west end there is a bell-cote and below that a porch although the other three churches have an embattled west tower which at Greystead has diagonal buttresses and angle ones at Wark. But Wark, despite the monolithic tower, is very simple being without decoration save for a blind bell-cote on the east end as occurs at Thorneyburn. Although it has been claimed that Humshaugh is by John Dobson[23] the stylistic evidence both externally and internally would associate it with the other three churches known to be by H. H. Seward, once a pupil of Soane's and the clerk of works at Greenwich Hospital[24] whose commissioners were the patrons. In their severe proportions and spacious, cool interiors these churches form a unique and attractive group. However, from the descriptions of Archdeacon Singleton[25] their charms were far from being relished by the early incumbents who had to be former naval chaplains[26] and of Greystead Singleton wrote that 'the smartness of the place is gone, as the rector ... is in confinement as a lunatic at Newcastle. . .'.[27]

A church with something of the character of the later Regency period is Slaley, 1832, in Northumberland.[28] A high building with short single lancets it has a nave and chancel each of two bays. In the usual manner the latter was lower and narrower than the former and both are terminated by diagonal buttresses with double offsets. A cross over the east and a double bell-cote at the west end completes the architectural ensemble. Simpler is the church at Knaresdale in Northumberland, built in 1833,[29] which can be matched by that at Whittonstall, in the same county, of three years before.[30] Set on commanding situations their simplicity is becoming since their square forms match the bold prospects around them. Whittonstall has a west tower which scarcely rises above the ridge of the church roof and so formal and tight are its lines that it assumes a military air. These are one kind of Northumbrian church. In Cumberland much the same timeless quality is found at the church of Little Strickland[31] which with its three sets of Y-lights, corbelled bell-cote, quoins and harling speaks of an unpretentious rural simplicity. That, of course, could be deliberately sought and can be just as charming and effective as in the presbyterian church at Branton in Northumberland of 1781[32] which has a six bay facade on the south with the usual high Y-lights with white painted wooden tracery and in the end bays a doorway. That the style was persistent is proved by Embleton, also in Northumberland, with its elegantly arched framing of a pair of tall lights flanked by openings with one, now masked by a porch, being the entrance. Despite its late date, 1833,[33] the building has all the qualities of harmony of proportion and fitness of purpose of its predecessor at Branton. Of course by that date many changes had overtaken ecclesiastical architecture of which none was more important than that of style and in northern England that came to be Early English.

In Scotland where the high galleried kirks demanded a lot of light the Decorated or, better still, the Perpendicular provided the large areas

278

of glass required. In northern England, on the other hand, churches followed the old ways and tending to be long and low had no need of complex fenestration being served admirably by simple lancets. Very typical is Usworth in County Durham, 1831, by John Green,[34] which is a plain rectangle with a rhythm of buttress and lancet. In the same year and almost identical is the same architect's Catholic church at Stella also in County Durham.[35] Again in the same year and in the same county is Sadberge[36] where each bay has twin lights under linked hood-moulds. Broad, flat buttresses rise unbroken to the wall-head where they are connected by chunky corbels in the manner of the Norman bays at Durham Cathedral. Perhaps the architect of Sadberge was George Jackson of Durham since many of the Sadberge features are repeated at his Wingate church in 1841,[37] now much decayed, and in a more sophisticated way at Pelton in the next year[38] where, instead of a bell-cote, as at Sadberge, there is a small octagonal belfry and spirelet. Jackson was also responsible for the parish church at Annfield Plain, which like all his other churches is in County Durham. Annfield, being fairly late in date, 1840,[39] has a long and low chancel containing a three light window flanked by clasp buttresses and finials while each nave bay has a pair of lights.

Of simpler form because of its earlier date, 1822, is the cruciform Heworth, also in County Durham,[40] which was an old foundation rebuilt 'In consequence of a grant from the Society for promoting the Enlargement of Churches'[41] to plans supposedly prepared by John Stokoe.[42] Devoid of buttresses it has a dumpy west tower which is remarkably unforthcoming when compared with that at Lamesly of the previous year.[43] Unusually this edifice, of eighteenth century origin but gradually transformed to Gothic, has aisles of nave height carrying galleries which alone seated six hundred and fifty worshippers.[44] However, it is the tower which is the memorable feature for not only does it show an interesting fenestration but in one corner an octagonal turret rising over the parapet. Together with the stepped buttresses this tower is twenty years ahead of its time.

As might be expected there are numerous churches from the north's most famous architect, John Dobson. In 1837 he enlarged St Edmund's chapel in Gateshead which became Holy Trinity church.[45] From the thirteenth century chapel Dobson imitated the group of seven stepped lancets and improved upon the originals by increasing their slender length in a way that was true to the Middle Ages. The same theme was repeated on St Joseph's Catholic church in Birtley, also in County Durham, in 1843.[46] Unfortunately, much of the effect of the group of five lancets is spoilt since three are blind. Above is perched a corbelled bell-cote, its rude strength taken up in the massive angle buttresses with weatherings and generous offsets.

Until the age of the ecclesiologists arrived it would be true to say that Early English reigned almost supreme for Gothic church architecture in the north of England. There were good reasons. Thomas Rickman had particularly admired the products of that style from the Middle Ages. 'The general appearance of Early English building is magnificent, and rich rather from the number of parts than from its details.'[47] He then proceeded to extol its merits which included, 'perhaps, a greater variety in the Early English fronts, than in those of any other style'[48] and, 'In those buildings where very long windows are used, there is a grandeur arising from the height of the divisions'.[49] More important, however, so far as the north of England was concerned was the fact that 'in smaller buildings there is much simplicity of appearance and there is a remarkable evenness in the value of the workmanship'.[50]

Rickman's volume, besides setting forth such tenets, illustrated in considerable detail many of the architectural parts comprising a style. Perhaps of more use, though, was Neale's *Views of the most interesting Collegiate and Parochial Churches in Great Britain* which, published in 1824, came only seven years after Rickman's treatise. Neale's volumes rendered an important service to the architectural profession since as the title suggested they provided the models on which a practitioner might base his own compositions. It is, however, significant that, by and large, it is Early English which Neale depicted and since the rather small plates prevented much in the way of detail from being shown only broad effects could be aimed at. Therefore the style could be copied easily and without great expense, being without the intricacies of Decorated or Perpendicular. Neale's plates must have been of considerable importance especially for the architects in the north of England where the bulk of the surviving medieval churches were Early English.

Such was the fame of Rickman's volume that inevitably he became a national architect and not surprisingly was given commissions in the north. In Carlisle he provided Christ Church and Holy Trinity in the years 1828–30.[51] Both were eighty feet long by sixty in breadth so that for their day were large edifices. In general layout they also seem to have been similar since both were provided with galleries on cast-iron supports and a shallow chancel. Christ Church was Early English and with a steeple, now demolished, of which criticism[52] seems justified for it was indeed coarse. The church of Holy Trinity still survives although it, too, is minus its spire although that does not detract from the building which cost the large sum of £6,000 and is unusual in that it is Decorated.

By later standards the entire work could be criticised but it does have merit and not least from the careful composition of the parts. The high windows of the sides have stone tracery, with a lot of cusping, below acute arches. The buttresses, which although perhaps not of great enough width, have clear profiles while the chancel is generously treated with double polygonal buttresses which are repeated on the west tower. Internally, the most striking effect is the seven light east window. It adds immeasurably to the richness of the conception and the excellence of the overall proportions revealing Rickman's thorough handling of Gothic parts. Nowhere, perhaps, is this better demonstrated than in the deep west gallery where the screen of supporting columns creates a spatial interest.

Although for its time, and for long afterwards, Holy Trinity is unique there were many other churches which, though they fail to demonstrate any profound versatility, do show an increasing competence and confidence in the handling of Gothic particularly in the towers which after the late eighteen twenties became synonymous with Gothic. As early as 1806 Loudon had pleaded for their use. 'A case can hardly occur where both the tower (or spire) and body may not be erected. When this is not the case, churches will dwindle into mere barns, as is the case with a number of the country churches in Scotland and Wales.'[53] In Westmorland, George Webster of Kendal, a much under-rated architect, provided a series of towered churches in the local limestone which has withstood the passage of time without deterioration. Webster's largest church, perhaps inspired in part, by Rickman's work in Carlisle, is St George's (Plate 145) in Kendal in 1839.[54] At such a date the introduction of aisles is no surprise although it is not so late that galleries could be omitted. The

Plate 145   George Webster. St George's Church, Kendal. 1839.

Early English west front is unusually fine with a triple window and vesica and is distinguished by flanking polygonal towers resting on square bases. Giving access to the galleries they are flat-topped and so were probably intended to have spires.

Also in Kendal is the same architect's St Thomas's of 1837[55] which was required because of the expansion of the town.[56] Like so many of Webster's churches it is unusually long, six bays, and with a short chancel containing the *leitmotif* of the Gothic of any period in the north of England, triple lights with the centre raised above its neighbours. The same device re-appears on the embraced west tower with its stages striated by string-courses. With its broad lines and generous detailing St Thomas's is obviously an urban church whereas Milnthorpe, also of 1837,[57] could be nothing other than a country parish church. Like St Thomas's it follows the national trend with an embattled west tower complete with corner finials and buttresses. Inside, the west gallery is supported on cast-iron columns with spandrels of iron tracery as a rare example of structural honesty. Of the same general pattern is Holme church, 1839,[58] but shorter and almost identical with Casterton, built eight years before,[59] where the tower has bevelled corners and splays.

These churches, confined to one locality and by the one architect, have the regional flavour that one finds in the examples by Smith and Simpson in Aberdeenshire, a comparison which can be taken further since in both areas bold simple forms were all that could be expected given the intractable nature of the local stone. Across the Pennines to the east with softer stone and with a number of architects, churches, though conforming to the current trends, were not so standardised. Thus Winlaton in County Durham, 1827, by Ignatius Bonomi of Durham[60] is a rather surprising discovery at the top of some steep roads leading up into the hills south of Blaydon. A hall church (in the medieval sense) with aisles it has a flat ceiling supported by cast-iron braces and octangular columns without a base. The chancel, one bay deep, has roof lights above the altar supplementing a five light east window. Although the exterior is very plain it has a novelty in the round-headed late Tudor windows with mullions and transoms.

At Winlaton all the parts read as though they belong to one another. That is not so at Seaham Harbour where the church of St John the Evangelist has a very loose plan made all the more apparent by the large surround of open space. Begun in 1835 and completed five years later,[61] Seaham is a text-book pattern of what a church should be, as is Salvin's Holy Trinity in South Shields[62] except that it has aisles and a dwarf clerestory. Despite such an innovation it is a depressing building and

282

Plate 146   John Dobson. St Thomas the Martyr's Church, Newcastle-upon-Tyne. 1828.

more full-blooded is Jackson's Southwick church of 1842[63] which, though belonging to the age of the ecclesiologist, in fact seems to imitate in its outlines the 1837 church at Earsdon in Northumberland by John Green, and his son Benjamin, of Newcastle.[64] Together they designed a number of churches including Washington in County Durham in 1833[65] with a five bay nave, bell-cote and south porch while, four years later, Sugley near Newcastle,[66] though shorter, has a chancel.

John Green, who was much employed by the Duke of Northumberland, 'was a plain, practical, shrewd man of business':[67] his son had been a pupil of the elder Pugin.[68] Together their talents are probably best represented in Holy Trinity church in North Shields which, when new in 1836,[69] was probably much admired for its Geometric tracery and its galleries on cast-iron. To-day, it is gloomy—blackened and stained and only possessed of the stump of its spire. More successful is Earsdon. It, too, has a high body to allow for a gallery but the tower is complete and uncommonly has a stepped group of lights in the top stage. Even so it is all very dry and mechanical so that it is no wonder that the rubric of the ecclesiologists was so eagerly seized upon. Before then, however, there is one church which remains outstanding—John Dobson's St Thomas the Martyr's in Newcastle (Plate 146), reared to serve the new residential districts springing up to the north of the town. Opened in 1828[70] the church, by any standards, is a superb creative monument to the zeal of the Gothic Revival.

St Thomas's is probably derived in outline from St Luke's, Chelsea, finished in 1824, from which may, too, have come the idea of the ribbed vault although the style that Dobson selected was Early English, one that he would be used to from his restorations at Hexham Priory[71] and St Nicholas, now the cathedral, in Newcastle.[72] The hallmark of St Thomas's is its lightness despite the fact that there is only a tower and nave. Dobson pleaded in vain for a chancel and had to make do with a narrow sanctuary while the addition of galleries in 1837[73] has robbed his tall windows of any internal effect. Outside the coupled lancets and delicate shafts are serenely composed along the bays which are delineated by buttresses rising above the solid parapet. It is, however, the tower which really distinguishes the church for it possesses an open belfry which creates a transparency which is repeated by the open parapets and the delicately attenuated finials on the corners of the nave but doubled in number at the short east end. The unknowing would criticise the church but, to those who have eyes to see and minds trained to understand, St Thomas's remains as one of Dobson's most brilliant and original achievements.

As in Scotland there were some churches which proclaimed their spiritual function by spires although none could rival the flamboyant shapes from Gillespie Graham's calculating hand. As has already been indicated one reason for the paucity of spires was cost even although Loudon declared that 'Spires may be erected at much less expense than they commonly amount to' if they retained simplicity.[74] He considered also that 'Landed proprietors ought to encourage the introduction of spires into country villages as one of the noblest ornaments of rural scenery' in which for the passing traveller 'they convey pleasing information and useful moral instruction'.[75] While there was little of the last during the Regency once it was past 'moral instruction' became a delightful necessity and spires sprouted. In 1828 one appeared at Levens in Westmorland[76] where the church is romantically approached by a climbing path bordered by ivy and periwinkle with access made difficult by rocks and spreading tree-roots. The church itself is of the usual kind with a low short chancel and a nave entered by a south porch. The spire rests on the roof with its base dividing the gallery inside.

More ambitious was Dobson's trial effort in 1826 at Greenhead in the far west of Northumberland.[77] The high silhouette of the tower contains a fine flèche so that the vision becomes that of Stratford-on-

Plate 147 J. and B. Green.
Holy Trinity Church,
Stockton-on-Tees. 1832.

Avon rather than the wild north where spires were never a common feature. Still, they could be irresistible and doubtless an additional expense of £200 in 1824 for the spire at Gateshead Fell[78] was considered worthy of such a commanding site. The church is a nave and chancel and seems to be from the design of one John Ions who, acting as builder, contracted to build the church and tower for £2,345 with an extra £197 for the buttresses.[79]

The most spectacular examples of pre-Pugin spires were those provided by the Greens at Stockton-on-Tees and at Tynemouth. The former is the largest church so far encountered in the north of England. Although there is more than a suspicion of a determined attempt to outdo Dobson's St Thomas's, John Green was praised for a design reflecting 'the greatest credit upon his judgement and taste'.[80] Work began in 1832 and was completed two years later.[81] The nave is of four bays with galleries which the Greens, as opposed to Dobson, seem to have liked. There is a south transept with the usual Green Geometric tracery and at the west a

285

thick tower (Plate 147) which, becoming an octagon, and with four flying buttresses, supported a spire which reached a height of two hundred feet. It must have been a noble achievement, while down below fluttered a panoply of parapets, tracery, finials and crosses.

Plate 148   The chancel. St Mary the Virgin's (Roman Catholic) Church, Hexham, Northumberland. 1828.

Less ambitious but with a similar attempt to design in more expansive volumes is Holy Saviour's at Tynemouth, 1841,[82] which has also lost its spire. Once again it was a ducal Northumberland church and one of the very few churches throughout this period to employ Perpendicular. The cruciform building was equipped 'for the erection of a gallery when one may be required'.[83] The seating was painted in imitation of dark oak 'and parts of them are shaded in a manner to represent carved-work, and the pulpit, reading-desk, and altar-table all correspond. The east window contains some neatly-stained glass, including representations of the heads of the 4 (sic) Evangelists, surmounted by their names on scrolls. The building is well lighted, warmed and ventilated and has a chaste appearance inside as well as out.'[84]

No wonder that Pugin raged, castigating a wordly architecture which stressed environmental factors at the expense of holiness. Still both the account and the building are important as marking that transitional stage before Pugin and after the period when Early English could be used in a straightforward manner which was bound to give satisfaction no matter

286

how it might be used. Now a new seriousness of purpose was becoming apparent. Not only is there a mention in the earlier part of the account of the style, but there is an interest in the well developed plan with the various sub-divisions correctly named although as yet there is neither an altar nor a lectern. Clearly a new sense was coming into church architecture and furnishings. Clearly, too, the day of the ecclesiologist was not far off.

Nevertheless, it must be observed that 'the societies of Oxford and Cambridge, who introduced the custom of clerical gentlemen devoting a portion of their time to the study of ecclesiastical architecture'[85] were not everywhere victorious especially in the country districts where, as ever, the old ways died hard. For instance, in Cumberland, Rosley, constructed in 1840,[86] has Y-lights with wooden divisions. Kirklinton in the same county in 1845[87] has a tower, which with its corbelled summit, speaks nothing of Christian virtues. These are local buildings and there were many of them such as the tiny Buttermere church, again in Cumberland, which in 1841[88] boasted only a bell-cote, nave and chancel and, making no concessions to the theories of university men, fulfilled in the most work-a-day manner possible the needs of the local community. On a larger scale Houghton of 1840[89] with Y-tracery in the bell-tower and single lancets elsewhere is a duplicate of St John's, Upperby, in Carlisle of the same year.[90] Both demonstrate the continuing local influence of Rickman as does St Michael's of the next year[91] which,

Plate 149   George Webster. Holy Trinity and St George's (Roman Catholic) Church, Kendal, Westmorland. 1837.

in the tower especially, comes very close to Rickman's Holy Trinity at the other end of the town.

Almost without exception every church so far mentioned has been for the established church. There is, however, an important group of Catholic churches, important because they have a demonstrable carefree style which has no counterpart in contemporary theory. St Cuthbert's in North Shields (1821)[92] demonstrates this well for on its tower there is an exuberant mixture of random elements some of which belong to the previous century. Inside the entire east end, filled with Decorated plasterwork, has a chancel with canted sides and in front a tripartite arch from which the central columns have been omitted. At Hexham, 1828–30,[93] the west front is a confection of elements sprinkled across the facade like cake decorations while inside the east end (Plate 148) is divided into three divisions by triple shafts and enclosed by moulded arches which on the ends are blind but which in the centre opens to become the chancel. More conscious is Holy Trinity and St George's at Kendal, probably by Webster, in 1837.[94] It has the same spirited Decorated plasterwork (Plate 149) but with Early English window lancets and statues held in niches. While these and the narrowing lines of the receding chancel convey something of the innocence of Bentley's designs for Strawberry Hill, the exterior could not be more formal (Plate 150). There is a triple array of well hooded lancets and in the gable St George emerging from his niche to slay the coiled dragon, which makes it the sole example of external sculpture to appear in any of these northern churches.

Plate 150   George Webster. Holy Trinity and St George's (Roman Catholic) Church, Kendal, Westmorland. 1837.

Elsewhere many Catholic churches, especially the early ones, are much more reticent. At Darlington[95] and at Durham Ignatius Bonomi's churches of 1827[96] are in back streets while the one at Berwick of 1829[97] is hidden from the street by a stone screen. At Alnwick where the Catholic church is by John Green, built in 1836,[98] the facade is squeezed between two buildings, much as happened with the non-conformist churches in

Plate 151   The congregational chapel. Lowther St, Carlisle. 1843.

Scotland. The most original of these street facades is the Congregational chapel in Carlisle (Plate 151) 'from a design by Mr Nichol of Edinburgh'.[99] A three bay Jacobean frontispiece it has strapwork over the windows and a curved gable above the projecting centre which is quoined. It was a concept which would have startled any of the ecclesiologists.

The term ecclesiology sprang into existence from the attempt to introduce a richer liturgy and rubric into the Church of England. That meant, in consequence, a re-establishment of those forms of church planning practised before the introduction of classicism. The new ideas

Plate 152   J. and B. Green.
Holy Trinity Church, Cambo,
Northumberland. 1842.

were promoted by the Oxford Tractarians and more particularly by the
Cambridge Camden Society founded in 1833 and 1839 respectively.
Although their ideas would transform the substance of the Church of
England it would be wrong to see their success as anything but gradual
in the north although even there in the early years of the forties there
would be harbingers of the new style.

Thus Cambo in Northumberland (Plate 152) from J. and B. Green in
1842[100] shows not only what architects were beginning to learn from the
new movement but also what clerics and their congregations were
beginning to expect. Cambo, lying on the Wallington estate, is close to the
Scottish Border. Like many another Northumbrian church in a similar
situation it has a pronounced low horizontality which probably comes less
from historical considerations, relating to climate and geography, than
from liturgical mysticism. The nave is four bays and the chancel is a canted
apse. The lights, while they are Early English, are broad. Nevertheless
it is the horizontality which dictates the architectural line helped by
string-courses and mouldings.

Further south in County Durham, Blaydon church of 1845,[101] whose
architect is unknown, would at first glance also seem to indicate little
change from the Commissioners' churches of the past two decades. Yet
there are numerous small details which, taken together, speak of a whole
new attitude. For example, although the tower still stands foursquare to

290

the west front of the nave, it is entered from the south. Inside, the nave opens into a north aisle screened by an arcade of cylindrical columns. Apart from such refinements as the double chamfered arches of the arcade, there is a greater significance in the appearance of an irregular plan. Outside again early nineteenth century tradition may seem to be present in the Early English lancets of the nave. But instead of being grouped

Plate 153 Sir Edward Blackett. Holy Trinity Church, Matfen, Northumberland. 1842.

together they each have their own identity with wide splays and the irregular bonding of the jamb stones into the wall, a practice advocated and indeed illustrated by Pugin only the year before.[102] Also new is the very steep pitch of the roof and again the absence of parapets except on the tower which has become extremely rich and complex not only with an increase in the amount of detail but also in refinement so that round the entrance there are carefully articulated nook-shafts. It is by the careful placing of such details that the monotony of earlier churches is avoided.

In 1841 Pugin had written 'Every tower built during the pure style of architecture either was, or was intended to be, surmounted by a spire, which is the natural covering for a tower'.[103] Thus Pugin had given a sound practical reason for the use of spires which went far beyond Loudon's vague precept of 'moral instruction'; and one of the handsomest is Salvin's for the church of St John the Evangelist at Keswick in Cumberland in 1838.[104] Although later additions have created a handsome and, indeed, beautifully proportioned church, when first built without aisles and only a very short chancel it must have been completely dwarfed by the tower with its recessed spire. Much more to scale is the small church at Scremerston in Northumberland of 1842.[105] Although the new movement is witnessed in the low lines and the south porch, Pugin, many of whose ideas corresponded to those of the Protestant reformers, would have condemned the general lack of detailing and, in time, the positioning of the tower and broach spire in the centre of the west front. Exactly the same criticisms could be levelled at Matfen church, also in Northumberland (Plate 153), for which the foundation stone was laid in 1842 by the local landowner, Sir Edward Blackett.[106] Two years later, when certifying the materials used in the construction, Sir Edward described himself as 'Architect and Superintendant of the erection of the new Chapel at Matfen'.[107] Ten years before, when the nearby Hall was being rebuilt, Sir Edward had dismissed his architect, Rickman, taking the management of the project into his own hands with some professional help[108] as he seems to have done for the church.[109] Still that he remained the designer seems to be proved by

Plate 154   A. W. Pugin. St Mary's (Roman Catholic) Church, Warwick Bridge, Cumberland. 1840.

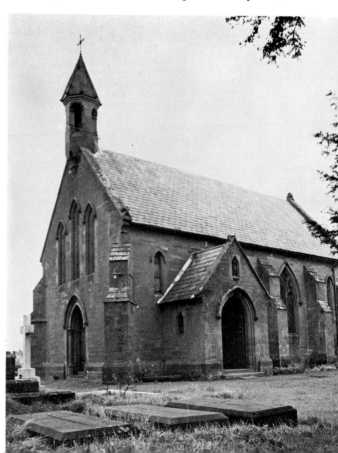

drawings, of an amateurish stamp, for the east elevation and spire.[110]

The exterior of the church is regular with lights, buttresses and a lower chancel with the overall bleakness compensated for by the great scale and display of the tower to which the spire was added in 1853.[111] Still, it was done without warmth and one can understand why Pugin moved away from the austere formalism of Early English to the warmer tones of Decorated. As Pugin wrote: 'The mechanical part of Gothic architecture is pretty well understood, but it is the principles which influence ancient composition, and the soul which appears in all the former works, which is so lamentably deficient.'[112] It was to the restoration of these qualities that Pugin set himself as in the key work of St Mary's at Warwick Bridge in Cumberland (Plate 154) which was begun two years before Matfen.[113] Of soft red stone it looks not unlike many another church with a corbelled bell-cote and triple lights below. Along the nave mere slits, alternating with Y-lights, hint at the change that inside breaks in an explosion of colour which is caught and held or flickers tremulously in bursts of light pouring themselves on red and blue ingoes or breaking up among the gilded roof timbers of the nave. Stencilled emblems of the Virgin Mary are thickly strewn on the walls of the chancel which has a screen, raised altar, sedilia and opposite a canopied recess holding the body of the church's founder. For Pugin correct church architecture was impossible 'Unless the ancient arrangement be restored, and the true principles carried out'.[114]

Much the same innovatory arrangements can be seen at the Catholic church of St Mary's in Stockton-on-Tees[115] which, with St Wilfrid's, Hulme, was the first design to practice asymmetry for the west tower is flush with the main facade at the north corner. On the south there is a porch and in the chancel an apse in which, high up, a band of low windows is a continuous bracelet of jewelled glass above the altar. Although Pugin in his *Apology* illustrated St Mary's, Stockton-on-Tees, with a spire it never materialised while at St Mary's, Newcastle, now the Catholic cathedral, the spire only appeared after a delay of fifteen years after work began in 1844.[116]

The style used throughout St Mary's, Newcastle (Plate 155), was Decorated which was most strikingly developed in the east and west elevations with their large and imaginative windows each beneath its own gable with statuary for the centre one. Still, it must be admitted that the exterior suffers overall from the use of flat ashlar so that there is not sufficient contrast between the surfaces of the glass and the stone. There is something of the same disappointment inside where, instead of a glorious stone vault, there is timber. However, the aisles and the nave have superb control in the tension provided between the solids and the voids so that movement is disciplined to progress towards the east and the altars separated one from the other by stone screens.

St Mary's, Newcastle, was an important church and as such is long and complex although it is not organic since the volumes of the areas do not interact with one another. This failing is demonstrated by the tower which, although of unrivalled magnificence, has very little to do with the building beside which it stands. Indeed, from any distance it extinguishes the church entirely. Like all Pugin's churches, St Mary's (Plate 156) can be understood best as an act of faith. 'The modulated light, the gleaming tapers, the tombs of the faithful, the various altars, the venerable images of the just—all conspire to fill the mind with veneration, and to impress it with the sublimity of Christian worship.'[117] On a November afternoon when the candlelight loiters wanly on gleaming tiles and cut stone then St Mary's does live as Pugin wished.

Plates 155 and 156   A. W. Pugin. St Mary's (Roman Catholic) Cathedral, Newcastle-upon-Tyne. 1844. The spire was added twenty years later by Hansom.

XVI

Castles and Mansions
in the North of England, 1805–45

In 1805 a correspondent to *The Gentleman's Magazine* reported: 'I am about to transform my Italian Villa, built upon the Burlington plan, into an Abbey; that is, as far as the look of the thing will allow; the open loggia to be changed into a grated gate-way (for storing corn); porticoes into cloisters (for conservatories and green-houses); the vestibule into a great-hall (for shew not use); the picture-gallery into a dormitory (for dancing) . . .'.[1] Others, however, took their Gothic more seriously so that it was with more than a touch of self-satisfaction that John Britton composed his reflections. 'The beginning of the present century was distinguished by the number, extent and costliness of the different modern Gothic mansions which were either then commenced or were in progress of execution.'[2] Such thoughts were pleasing if not indeed gratifying, to one of Britton's inclinations and he could, therefore, permit himself some slight indulgence by listing the modern Gothic mansions starting, not unreasonably, with Fonthill Abbey and including Windsor Castle, Eaton Hall, Ashridge and the castles of Ravensworth and Lowther. The last two were in the north of England which came to possess, therefore, two of the largest and most splendid houses of the entire Revival easily taking their place alongside Taymouth in Scotland.

Ravensworth Castle was the property of Sir Thomas Liddell, a descendant of Thomas Liddell, a merchant, who died in 1577. 'In the cellar under the house he had vinegar, soap and honey . . . in the shop itself mattras cords . . . combs, glue, honey, prunes, pepper, ginger, cummin, almonds, gum, brimstone, emery . . . .'[3] It was, however, coal which, in later times, had provided the family fortune and which enabled Ravensworth Castle to be built.

Originally of four towers connected by curtain walls by the end of the eighteenth century it contained a two-storeyed house.[4] In 1807 designs were drawn up for a Gothic mansion with classical interiors[5] and in the next year the greater part of the old castle was demolished[6] with the exception of two towers which, retained in the stable court, are almost all that survives to-day. The architect chosen for Ravensworth was John Nash[7] perhaps because Sir Thomas Liddell was a friend of the royal family and indeed it was for him that the title of Baron Ravensworth was revived by King George IV in 1821.[8] Although Nash certainly supplied the plans the work was not only superintended by one John Liddell[9] but a close and active interest in the design and growth of the house over many years was taken by Lord Ravensworth's eldest son, Thomas Henry Liddell, later second Baron and first Earl.[10] Indeed, Ravensworth Castle was praised as one of the 'most distinguished mansions' by Britton who credited it to Thomas Henry Liddell.[11] It is just possible that such an attribution was intended as a deliberate slight on Nash and his Gothic houses for 'There is very little to praise, or even approve in any of these works'.[12]

Whatever the truth of the matter, Liddell does seem to have had some design ability. It was he, for instance, who supplied designs for the classical 'memorial room' at Wynyard Park.[13] His contribution, though, to his own house, which when it came to be built was Gothic, can only be guessed at. There is, for example, on one plan 'shewing the Shutters of the Salon Window' the note that 'the piers and wooden sash frames are copied from Mr. Liddells's drawings but whether the Casements open outwards or inwards those drawings do not set forth'.[14] Much later it was recorded that the conservatory was built from a plan furnished by a gentleman of the family[15] and later still it was claimed that the whole of the north front was Liddell's.[16] On the evidence it would seem that he had some share in the designing of Ravensworth doubtless to the relief of Nash whose antipathy to the labours in which the Gothic style involved him is well known.

Liddell may have inherited his artistic gifts from his mother who painted numerous Italian scenes in the style of Poussin[17] whose paintings formed the bulk of the Ravensworth collection.[18] It may therefore not be without significance that, seen from a distance, Ravensworth, with its bold array of towers loosely linked, and set above verdant scenery, conforms exactly to that vision of the picturesque which had been transmitted from the campagna to Regency England.

Work was to continue at the castle for many years with the details becoming progressively more Gothic. By 1815 the 'Elevation to a larger

Scale of the Great Window at the end of the Hall' had been drawn up[19] and six years later there is a mention of '8 (sic) Sketches of Rosettes for Saloon'[20] after which in 1823 came the plan and elevation of the conservatory.[21] Among the details shown is a series of human masks gritting with their teeth the pipe which drained the parapet gutter. Whether they were executed it is impossible to say since surviving photographs of the conservatory show no such features. By 1834 there still remained to be built the greater part of the north front including the main entrance above which would be the museum and picture-gallery over a hundred feet long and lit by domes[22] which were connected to one another by ribs rising from responds. With an organ at one end the gallery was a work, which, though less well articulated, could be compared with Atkinson's one at Scone.

The chief rooms were Gothic sometimes with ceilings which hung so low on the curve that they seemed to defy the laws of gravity; there were bosses of indeterminate vegetable origin especially on those flat ceilings where sponge-like growths hung from the rib intersections. Below there were oak wainscots, which would become one of the most popular and long lasting of the early nineteenth century innovations and which seem to have been introduced at Fonthill where oak was used as a decorative and fashionable wood. At Ravensworth such decorations did little to enliven the main apartments which, enfilade along the south front, and all eighteen feet high, seem always to have been gaunt and lacking subtlety not only in ornamentation but also in plan. Behind them lay the one truly grand feature, the great hall (Plate 157). Entered from the middle of

Plate 157   The Great Hall. Ravensworth Castle. The photograph was taken early in this century.

the north side, it was filled at the west end by a double staircase rising to a statue of St George and the dragon and then to a passage along the south side. This was directly above the arcaded aisle which gave access to the state rooms. The architectural details in the hall were few yet the simplicity of the tall windows, set high in the walls, and an open timber roof, all as at Fonthill, did create something of the atmosphere of the medieval baron's hall.

Plate 158 John Nash. Ravensworth Castle, County Durham. Begun in 1808 but since demolished. The photograph was taken early in this century.

Externally, the castle (Plate 158) was more varied and complex in its massing than anything else of comparable date either in northern England or in Scotland although the surrender to the picturesque may have been due, in part, to the slow maturing over many decades. Broadly speaking the style was Edwardian but with 'a selection from the castle architecture of various periods, skilfully brought into contact'[23] although for very practical reasons the fenestration was either Perpendicular or late Tudor. In its general form Ravensworth imitated Payne Knight's Downton Castle on which Nash may have worked in 1808[24] and there was at Ravensworth a similar arrangement of three towers along the south front but avoiding any dominant element. Although Downton's famous octagonal tower with its deep corbelling did not appear on the main facade at Ravensworth it did occur terminating the west elevation. There not only did it turn the composition to the north entrance but it was the pin between the encroaching trees and the castle.

Less variable than Ravensworth and more static was Lowther Castle in Westmorland. Although the attempts of Robert and James Adam had come to naught, Sir James Lowther does not seem to have relinquished the idea of re-establishing a family home for in 1772 Gilpin noted that 'materials are now collecting for a grand structure'.[25] It was not built and shortly before his death Sir James commissioned another group of designs apparently from 'Mr. Webster' whose name appears on an accompanying letter of circa 1798.[26] Of the related designs the first was for a plain neo-classical mansion exhibiting some Adam motifs. Then came a castle within which the attempt to contrive, in a formal manner, the main rooms and the staircase around a central octagon was not a success. A matching scheme was 'a Gothic House, in the Style of an Abbey or Convent'. Although the planning was better it was not wholly satisfactory since clusters of classically shaped rooms were disposed around a baronial hall. That was integrating a very free architectural style with an inflexible plan. As so often in the past nothing came of these ideas before the death of Sir James Lowther in 1802. He was succeeded as Viscount Lowther by a cousin who in 1807 was created Earl of Lonsdale; and he became the builder of Lowther Castle.

The statement in the early thirties of the last century that Lowther Castle was begun in 1802[27] has been overlooked by modern historians who have succinctly stated that the castle was begun, as his first commission, in 1806 by Robert Smirke and completed five years later.[28] Yet, from some recently discovered correspondence, it is clear that Smirke inherited a job already underway. Attached to a letter of April 1814 he sent an account of the sums paid for the castle after May 1802[29] which fact he confirmed in another letter two months later.[30] Who the previous architect was remains unknown. However, Farington entered in his diary for 25 April 1806: 'Lord Lowther has again thanked Sir George (Beaumont) for recommending to Him Robert Smirke; at the same time the said Robert in His Plan for the House to be built at Lowther has adopted principally the idea of Dance,—which His Lordship is pleased with'.[31] From an entry of four days previously it seems that Smirke was asked 'to go to Lowther <u>alone</u>...'.[32] The use of the word 'alone' is curious, especially as it was underlined, so that the question arises as to whether or not it is an oblique reference to Dance. Apparently, Smirke had gone to Lowther to 'commence the building of the offices'.[33] It was an unusual start but may be correct since a contemporary recorded that the house was begun in 1808 and partly occupied by the family in the following summer[34] whereupon Lord Lonsdale reduced the building programme to enable Smirke to proceed with the erection of the Covent Garden Theatre.[35] Afterwards work must have continued steadily throughout the years for in May 1814, when Smirke totalled up the expenditure since 1802, it came to £73,591 19s 10¾d.[36] By any standards it was a large sum but then

Lord Lonsdale's income was 'supposed to be from 80 to £100,000 a year'.[37]

Among the craftsmen for whom Smirke itemised work were Bernasconi, the sculptor and plasterer, whose account came to over £6,000 and 'Dixon of London' for painting. Among the local men employed the name of Webster is prominent 'for Masons Work done by Contract', for supplying chimney-pieces, which cost £1,293 4s 4d, and as one of the three clerks of works.[38] It may be, therefore, that George Webster, who was responsible for many of the churches mentioned in the previous chapter, received his initial experience at Lowther.

Between December 1805 and November 1813 Smirke's travelling expenses listed thirteen journeys to Lowther[39] and still the work was incomplete. In 1811 Smirke 'said it would take many years, 8 or 10 perhaps, before Lowther Castle is completely finished'[40] but later he reported to Lord Lonsdale that very little remained to be done. 'There are no Painters at Lowther at this time, and the Plaisterers (sic) where they have finished the Cieling (sic) of the Cloister will not proceed with anything until they receive further directions'.[41] That was in 1814. Twelve years later Mrs Arbuthnot, staying at the castle, admired the principal rooms but recorded that the drawing-room and billiard-room remain unfinished. 'I used to think Ashridge beautiful', she continued, 'but it is not to be named with this house' in which she particularly admired the staircase[42] which dominated the castle both externally and internally (Plate 159). Nevertheless, filling the centre of the house as it did it ruined the planning since, with the entrance on the north, it had to be circumvented if the state appartments on the south were to be reached.[43]

The centre of the south front was filled with the saloon (Plate 160) which, sixty feet by thirty, was fitted up with oak and light grey damask

Plates 159 and 160   The staircase and the saloon. Lowther Castle.

beneath fan vaulting. In the dining-room, to the west, oak was again used with hangings of scarlet and gold while in the drawing-room, to the east of the saloon, there was white and gold embroidered satin. The family apartments and the library were along the north front (Plate 161) which, over four hundred feet long, was dragooned by eight towers set before the lantern tower (Plate 162). On the south the dichotomy of Gothic was revealed by a litany of forms so that:

> Lowther, in thy majestic pile are seen
> Cathedral pomp and grace in apt accord
> With thy baronial castle's sterner mien.[44]

Thus was Wordsworth moved to cry. Not so, however, John Britton. 'It is generally agreed that he (Smirke) has not been successful in imparting the true architectural character of either the castle or the monastery to any of his works' and he specifically named Lowther and the castellated Eastnor as failing 'to satisfy the searching and discriminating architectural critic'.[45] Yet there must be very few to-day who are not affected by the torn majesty of Lowther, its tracery plucked from its windows and robbed of its floors and roofs. One day the stonework will crack and fall but until then it will continue to dominate the surrounding park, once the most extensive in England.[46] From the park the castellated elevation is seen to have an intricacy derived from composition whereas on the south front it came from the fulsome detailing of the tracery enriching the spaces held within the outstretched wings or cloisters. Was the unequivocal distinction between castellated and ecclesiastical Gothic a unique and practical demonstration of Gilpin's profession that simplicity and variety taken together comprise the picturesque?

Plate 161   Robert Smirke. Plan of the principal floor. Lowther Castle, Westmorland.

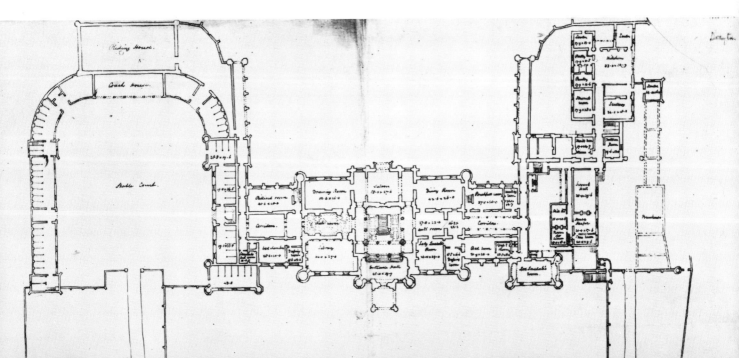

Plate 162   Robert Smirke. Lowther Castle, Westmorland. Gutted after the
Second World War.

Although there were no new developments in either Gothic practice
or scholarship at Lowther it does have an importance in the Revival. It is
evidence, in particular, of the influence of James Wyatt's Fonthill and
Ashridge. From the latter there may have come the idea for the staircase
at Lowther while the state entrance of Fonthill provided the gabled south
front. The most striking bequest, though, was the magnification of scale. It
was that which made Lowther a part of the new century whereas Fonthill
belonged in essence to the previous one. Thus Lowther, despite the symmetry of its elevations, belonged, like Ravensworth, to the picturesque so
that on west and east alike they acted as starters for the new century.

The fresh power with which Gothic had been invested was seen as
nowhere else in the court-houses at Carlisle (Plate 163), the first major

Plate 163   The Assize Courts,
Carlisle. Completed after 1811
by Robert Smirke.

Plate 164   Augill Castle, Westmorland. 1841.

piece of urban Gothic in the north. Although it has been shown that the original works were not by Smirke,[47] he did anticipate in the spring of 1810 that, through the influence of Lord Lonsdale, 'He should be the Architect to be employed in designing and carrying on buildings at Carlisle of a public nature'.[48] A year later not only had he been given the designs but the courts were underway once again.[49] Of a bright red stone they stand, twin drum towers with deep window embrasures, linked by an arched screen and with subsidiary works grouped about them. These, although fine in themselves and with rich columned openings, are dwarfed by the immense bulk of the towers which start up like shell-keeps as authoritarian statements of the feudal power of the Middle Ages.

That such a brutal encounter with the past was not everywhere acceptable is proved by Higham School at Setmurthy in Cumberland of circa 1800.[50] A symmetrical eleven bay facade with end gables, pointed lights and crosslets it has an artlessness which is repeated at Augill Castle in Westmorland forty years later (Plate 164). It was an amateur production by the proprietor who modelled some parts on Abbotsford.[51] Something of the same unreality is found at Gibside where a parapet a full storey high was added to the restored front of the Elizabethan house in 1805 by Alexander Gilkie.[52]

At Featherstone Castle in Northumberland large additions, again very Georgian in character but using much of the old castle as the model, consisted of three towers, a castellated entrance screen and garden wall all executed before 1812[53] but with further changes taking place, according to correspondence of 1818–20, after a fire.[54] Letters from his steward, William Hutton, to the Hon. Thomas Wallace relate in part to the entrance screen but mostly to the south front and the rebuilding of the drawing-room and some smaller rooms. The most significant change was the introduction of a bow window although as the roof would appear above 'if you do not like it, the Ramparts in front may be rais'd at no great expence'[55] which was done while in front there was erected a Gothic verandah. Although in general the architecture is very much of an earlier age the introduction of Tudor lights and cusping speak of a determination to take Gothic seriously as Dobson did at Newcastle in 1825 with the former Lying-In Hospital[56] 'or asylum for poor married pregnant women' where 'Each patient is required to provide a child's dress'.[57] Dobson gave the designs free.[58]

The hospital (now the BBC) has a three bay front with a Perpendicular entrance, an oriel above and to counteract that a canopied niche on either side. The building was probably a useful advertisement just when Gothic for secular buildings was beginning to appear in towns. In Carlisle Rickman produced the News Room and Library[59] for which, because of the narrowness of the site, Gothic was preferred to Greek.[60] Situated on a corner and with a tower at each important node, it is a light and airy building in which the free handling of the subject material produces an extremely original product.

Rickman owed his influence in the north to Bishop Percy of Carlisle who, when he was raised to the see in 1827, found Rose Castle, the episcopal seat, to be in a dilapidated state. 'The floors were rotten, the roofs gave little or no protection against the weather, and the exterior presented a strange mixture of styles, according to the periods at which the several parts were erected or restored.'[61] It was Rickman's task, two years later,[62] to sort out the muddle of the centuries. In fairness, while he did produce what was tantamount to a new building, it was one with coherence even if the chapel was Decorated and the new dining-room and drawing-room were vaguely Tudor with long bays. To order the past in such a way was probably preferable to trying to lay hold of some distant century by the heels and much the same was done, and is attributed to Rickman, at Scaleby Castle, a few miles east of Carlisle, in 1835.[63] Although the alterations on the south front loosely belong to the Middle Ages the predominant ideas of comfort and sensible management are indicated by the spacious Tudor casements each with its mullion and drip-mould. It was much the same considerations which dictated the form of the nearby Brunstock, an entirely new form of building which is best described not so much as a diminutive mansion surrounded by its own policies but rather as a Tudor villa.

Although the date of Brunstock is usually put at 1827–8,[64] it must surely come after Rose Castle after which, having received the episcopal blessing, Rickman extended his activities to other parts of the north. It would seem, therefore, that the date 1833 which a contemporary writer gave to Brunstock is the likelier.[65] The main portion of the house is two storeys with an exposed roof and deep overhanging eaves and the first appearance of barge-boards. The chimneys are octagonal and grouped for effect in clusters and the windows have the same Tudor quality, especially the oriel. A long extension contains the library and is Perpendicular. It is indeed the refusal to be historically precise which makes Brunstock so important for the future development of Gothic for it is neither a castle nor an abbey. Instead it is an upper middle-class home primarily designed with comfort and convenience in mind so that neither show nor make-believe has a use.

Some indication of the same trend also appeared at Whelprigg House, near Barbon in Westmorland, an old house rebuilt in 1815[66] but given its present shape in 1834.[67] Unlike Brunstock with its easy, informal lines, Whelprigg is stiffer with each facade consciously composed with gables at the corners and, in the centre of each, stepped mullioned windows. There are oriels but they are awkward and without the composure of Rickman's. Something of the same overall angularity also occurs at Hames Hall, supposedly by Smirke[68] and at his Edmond Castle erected for T. H. Graham near Carlisle.

Smirke's drawings are still in Edmond Castle and prove that the main block was erected after 1824[69] and that it was doubled in size twenty years later when a library, conservatory, chapel and study were added.[70] The earlier portion is a rather dry Tudor with regularly composed fronts each with bay windows or a porch. A touch of whimsy is provided by curling gablets and the outline is softened by the later extension to the rear where it is almost a detached wing. Much larger and with a certain state is the front which Salvin added to Greystoke Castle in Cumberland[71] with tall windows, of the Hardwick type, filling the facade. Of course, as time passed it was almost inevitable that Jacobean should be revived so that at Netherby, near Longtown, the mansion was titivated by William Burn with Jacobean dressings especially on the old pele-tower by the entrance which was given strapwork.[72]

One entire Jacobean mansion was, however, constructed in northern England at Underlay Hall in Westmorland (Plate 165) which was designed

Plate 165   George Webster. Underlay Hall, Westmorland. 1825.

and built by George Webster of Kendal in 1825.[73] It is a very remarkable building and not least for such a precocious date. One would like
to know why the decision to employ Jacobean was taken and whether
the rich Jacobean interiors with their plaster ceilings and carved woodwork
belong to the early nineteenth century or to the enlargement of the hall
after 1872.[74] Even so the first portion of the house is impressive enough
with seven bays and with the centre and the ends projecting. The centre
is a double-tiered columned porch, probably imitating that at Hatfield,
and across it is carried the pierced parapet which at the corners meets slim
towers with lead cupolas. The other main front is round the corner
and not at the rear, as it would have been in earlier mansions, and
was similar but with a single-storey porch crowned with strapwork and
beyond that the offices had finials with curly gables set between them.
Underlay is unique in northern England and although the Jacobean
would, in time, enjoy a prolonged vogue, for most northern patrons the
Tudor era was as far forward in history as they were prepared to be led
by the architectural pundits.

After the exuberant outburst of medievalising at Ravensworth and
Lowther the Gothic movement in the north of England subsided until the
later twenties and thirties when, in a rush of building activity, Tudor
came to hold the field against castellated Gothic. That was in response
to the awakening appeal of the 'old English style' or 'Queen Elizabeth's
Gothic' to national sentiment. Repton, whose profound impact on nine-

teenth century architecture has never been fully admitted, had lamented the 'mutilation of the old halls and manor houses, where the large bay-windows, the lofty open chimneys and picturesque gables of Queen Elizabeth's time, give place to the modern sashes and flat roofs. . .'.[75] His sympathy for the style also took a practical bent since he recognised that its asymmetry rendered it both more adaptable and potentially more convenient than any other.[76] Kerr, looking back from after the middle of the century, made a similar judgement. 'Convenience . . . lies at the root of the medieval or irregular type' of plan[77] since it not only gave privacy and comfort in the diversity of the rooms but met the requirements of views[78] with bay-windows which he rated as 'one of the most useful and pliant of all contrivances'.[79] It was, of course, unfortunate that many Tudor houses included Renaissance details but since it was accepted that 'The outlines of the Elizabethan mansions are decidedly Gothic'[80] all that was required was 'a severe correction of the style of their ornaments'.[81]

The kind of house that Repton had in mind was Matfen Hall, a grandiose Tudor mansion, of a southern stamp, in Northumberland. The facts concerning it are generally stated as follows. Rickman, having been engaged by Sir Edward Blackett, began work in 1828. Shortly afterwards they quarrelled, one reason being Sir Edward's preference for Elizabethan rather than the architect's Gothic. Rickman was dismissed and Sir Edward completed the house himself.[82] While that is indeed what happened the story is not just so clear cut.

Sir Edward Blackett and Rickman met through the agency of Bishop Percy of Carlisle early in May 1832.[83] Rickman was invited to Northumberland[84] and at first all went well although the architect noted that his employer 'seems quite determined on Elizabethan'.[85] Although Sir Edward approved of Rickman's plan, on the day that the latter left Matfen,[86] Sir Edward wrote to his wife that 'several alterations in the plan have struck me since Rickman left'.[87] It was the first sign of future upsets. The note which Rickman received asked for 'more accommodation for Lady Blackett and a larger Hall and a museum'[88] and, after much difficulty, plans and drawings were produced and despatched from Birmingham.[89]

The plans[90] varied in details and scale but both provided Tudor elevations with bays with the main rooms, such as drawing-room, library and dining-room, along the south front although, in the second plan, these rooms were increased in number. Each elevation was regular on plan and elevation with the entrance, in the centre of the north side, set in a projecting tower. That led to a vestibule and across a passage to a hall filling the middle of the house. In the first plan the hall, surrounded by passages, was square with the staircase opening from one side. The second plan (Plate 166), though, showed a much grander hall still entered from the north but with an arcade of columns along the south confirming the thought that Ravensworth was in Sir Edward's mind.

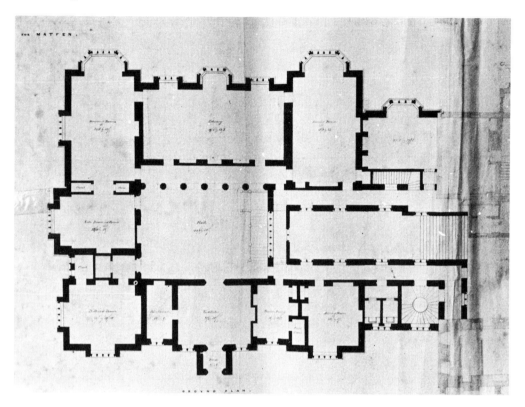

Plate 166   Thomas Rickman. Plan of the principal floor. Matfen Hall, Northumberland.

In the late summer Sir Edward proposed numerous and complex changes involving construction, planning and the raising of the south front to three storeys.[91] Having duly overcome these obstacles, Rickman began work on the interior and 'settled the staircase'[92] the position of which in the hall had never been decided upon. Thus when the architect next went to Matfen and met 'Sir Edward and Lady Blackett at dinner, they were very kind and friendly but he talks of various alterations'[93] which all next day Rickman struggled to resolve.[94] In December Sir Edward proposed changes in the projection of the oriels to his architect[95] who, by now, was weary of a client 'so very capricious that he says things quite contrary to what he has said before'.[96] It was at this time that Rickman produced his 'plan for joining the two houses'[97] which, although a compilation of the earlier plans, was more compact and not so wasteful of space.[98] The hall was shortened and, although it still had its arcade, two of the three surrounding passages disappeared so that it was no longer an island but the heart of the house approximating closely to the great halls of the Middle Ages. Along the south there was still the sequence of three public rooms from the first plan but the drawing-room and the dining-room were turned at right angles to the library and all three had curved bays.

Some seven months previously Rickman had set down his thoughts on the hall before sending off two sets of plans. 'The Set A proceeds on the supposition that a building of earlier date had existed the Hall of which being found in sufficiently good condition has been retained and a house of later character built round it. . .'.[99] It was a subtle and ingenious suggestion on Rickman's part since the appeal to the past anthology of Gothic allowed Rickman to introduce it into the house. Still, the staircase remained unsettled and other changes altered the position of the coat-of-arms on the porch.[100] Although no details of events for the next ten months are available there is no reason to suppose that the pattern changed. In February 1835 they came to a climax when Rickman was dismissed.[101] Later on, Sir Edward gave as the reason the architect's bad health 'rendering him unable to attend to business'.[102] Certainly, Rickman's health had given way, yet, all things considered, the surprising thing is that the break had not come sooner than it did. Afterwards Sir Edward, who falsely claimed that he 'chiefly planned and superintended my building myself'[103] took charge of its finishing although it was well advanced since in March 1834 Rickman had sent off the roof drawings[104] and the famous chimney-piece, which Chantrey had cut for Buckingham Palace, arrived in the autumn of 1835.[105] As ever, the outstanding problem was the staircase and Sir Edward turned for help to Lewis Cottingham, a London architect specialising in Gothic, who sent up drawings in 1836 although there is every reason to suspect that it was Sir Edward who altered the proposed cast-iron to wood.[106]

The staircase starts on the west wall and, passing the window with its fourteen divisions and glorious with saints, kings and prelates, rises along the north to meet the east corridor screened from the hall by an arcade of columns which continues round the south wall. Immediately below is the south aisle which, giving access to the main rooms, has an arcade of Early English columns with thin archivolts rising from the figured representations which include a knight, duke, king and bishop. High above is the hammer-beam roof its timbers flecked by shots of light from the west window. Superb though Ravensworth's hall must have been, much more recondite is Matfen with its mysterious lights glancing on the rose coloured stone. An unknown masterpiece, the hall at Matfen is the most splendid single interior of the entire Revival in the north of England.

Externally, the facades of Matfen (Plate 167) are rather plain and consist of ashlar stone with crisply cut mullions and transoms for the numerous windows. However, the design does suffer from the abrupt

Plate 167   Thomas Rickman. Matfen Hall, Northumberland. 1832.

change on the side elevations from two storeys to three with a disturbing change in scale as a result. Although the south front is symmetrical later additions of a somewhat different character do prevent monotony in the undecorated planes.

The second great Tudor house in Northumberland, and much richer in its massing and decoration, is Lilburn Tower which is altogether more skilful in its parts. The architect was John Dobson who had already tried his hand at Tudor with Angerton Hall in 1823.[107] A somewhat stiff and unyielding house (Plate 168) with an L-plan it has the entrance near the re-entrant angle. The main fronts, turned towards the garden, are battlemented except where sharp gables break through and the fenestration is regular with mullions and flat hood-moulds. An interesting house it dispenses with the more lavish detailing of true Elizabethan architecture. Indeed, where that style was too costly then Dobson recommended the 'Manor House style' not only as a good substitute but because in some cases it might be more in harmony with the landscape.[108]

Plate 168   John Dobson. Angerton Hall, Northumberland. 1823.

Dobson, like others of his time, valued Tudor architecture and there still exists a volume of his topographical drawings which include half a dozen sketches, done over a period of years after 1831, of Haddon Hall.[109] At Gainsborough he drew towers with large Decorated windows and details of cusping and hood-moulds; he also recorded the gateways of St John's College, Cambridge, and the Bishop's Gate at Norwich, both in 1837, as well as the Tudor portions of Hampton Court Palace six years before. From such study he learnt that 'much of the picturesque effect came from chance' since convenience had been the prime objective so that for domestic use 'Much might be said of the advantages of Tudor architecture'.[110]

These advantages were demonstrated at Lilburn Tower,[111] an estate which Henry Collingwood inherited in 1827. He tore down the old house and, having commissioned designs from Dobson, laid the foundation stone of the new mansion on 3 January 1829 when the architect 'exhibited several highly-finished drawings of the intended structure'. Afterwards the owner and his friends retired for a meal while 'The workmen and neighbouring people were plentifully regaled with bread and cheese, and strong ale'.[112] During the first few years of construction detailed accounts were kept[113] and up to the middle of June 1832 the house had cost £11,500. Within that period Dobson was paid £300 and a similar sum during the next three years after which the accounts cease although work continued until 1840 when, after a delay of three years, the project was completed.

Being so late in date the picturesque grouping (Plate 169) is disposed with such skill that it can be accepted as the sole solution to the client's requirements. The same praise also attaches to the detail which, although extremely scholarly, is made fully complementary to the architectural scheme. The main fronts are symmetrical but whereas on the south the centre, flanked by tall octagonal buttresses, projects on the west

Plate 169   John Dobson. The entrance front. Lilburn Hall,
Northumberland. 1829.

it is recessed and scarcely observed because of the large porte-cochère. It has been shifted from its original position but it formerly led into the saloon and grand staircase which have been closed off by lowering the roof to the height of the ground floor rooms.

Although the Tudor style would eventually win the nation's allegiance the castellated style was still vigorous especially in the hands of Dobson. Late in life he recollected that when, as a young man, he had devoted time to sketching castles his friends considered his time wasted since he was not likely to be much employed on castle building. However, just after he had spent three months at Conway, Caernarvon and Beaumaris Castles he won the competition for the Northumberland county prisons and court-house to be built at Morpeth.[114] The ground plan was octagonal with a 'chapel, house of correction, wards for debtors and felons' with Caernarvon as the model.[115] Only the gateway (Plate 170) of Dobson's building remains to-day. Over seventy feet high the entrance

Plate 170 John Dobson. The gatehouse. The county prison. Morpeth, Northumberland. 1822.

is guarded by towers with bevelled corners which although a thirteenth century trait may perhaps have a local origin in the Percy stronghold at Warkworth. Battlements set on machicolation and carried all the way round the wall-head (Plate 171) add up to an impressive testimonial to Dobson's skill which equals that of Smirke in the Carlisle towers.

Clearly such a style had to be considerably modified to allow castles as dwellings to be created and of these perhaps the first by Dobson is

Plate 171   Detail of the gatehouse. The county prison. Morpeth, Northumberland.

Plate 172   John Dobson. Beaufront Castle, Northumberland. 1837.

Benwell Tower now within the Newcastle city boundaries. Built on the site of the old Benwell Tower in 1831,[116] the higher portion, much of which is windowless, has the appearance of an old pele-tower although for other areas there are well proportioned windows arranged according to a classical prescription. Much more bellicose is Brinkburn Priory or at least that portion which Dobson tacked onto the Georgian Gothic house of

Plate 173   The saloon. Beaufront Castle, Northumberland. A watercolour painting by John Dobson with the figures drawn by J. Carmichael.

1810.[117] Facing the ruins of the medieval priory church, Dobson's work has strong shaping. The entrance, like the Angerton one, is a porch with an upper room, a favourite arrangement of Dobson's and one that he had sketched repeatedly. Above the battlements a broad tower is overtopped by a corner stair turret; all the windows are of late Tudor origin with one large oriel held on a corbelled shoulder-arch.

Brinkburn was the precursor to Dobson's later works at Holme Eden Hall in Cumberland[118] and Beaufront Castle in Northumberland both of which were begun in 1837.[119] The former has a two-storey frontage into which is cleverly slotted an entrance tower with polygonal buttresses only slightly larger than the ranks of chimney-stalks which have become an important feature of the skyline. Holme Eden is refulgent with ease and good living. In contrast Beaufront, although more sumptuous in its detailing, is of a sterner cast doubtless because of its setting on a high bluff above the River Tyne. The western approach is dominated by a high tower (Plate 172) which, though rather similar to the one at Holme Eden, is, however, the Brinkburn essay set loose from the lock of the walls and then increased in height and grandeur. All these towers had a common origin in such college towers as St John's, Cambridge, which Dobson had sketched, and others which Pugin had engraved for the second volume of the *Examples*. Thirty years before at Lowther the entrance tower was the climax to a carefully graduated frontage along which were ranged the family apartments. Since then, in response to more informal living and the desire for greater privacy, family rooms gradually disappeared from public view. At Beaufront there was the western entrance, on the south side a block containing the public rooms and, stepped back from these, there was the family wing with a garden entrance in the re-entrant angle. Inside most of the main interiors were of a mild Jacobean flavour being placed off the saloon (Plate 173) which, with an aisle along one side, again shows a response to Ravensworth.

Good of their kind though these castles were they were quite outclassed by the seat which the Lambtons reared from their coal fortunes in County Durham. Of no other building is there so much conflicting evidence making any interpretation an immediate matter of dispute. However, the main facts seem to be as follows. Old Harraton Hall, an Elizabethan house,[120] was largely demolished prior to 1787[121] and a new one started in the following year.[122] This was a two-storeyed classical house. When General Lambton died in 1794 there was a gap and once work was restarted two years later it was to the designs of Joseph Bonomi, the Italian follower of the Adams, for W. H. Lambton[123] who refers to it in a letter at the close of the year.[124] An account for the years 1797–1801 gives the sum disbursed as £22,000 much of which was probably spent on foundations for the terrace.[125] Once again, however, after the death of the owner there was an interruption and not until George Lambton, later the first Baron Durham, came of age was building resumed in 1822. When completed after eight years, to the designs of Joseph's son, Ignatius,[126] the mansion, according to one account, had been given battlements.[127] After subsidence later on, much of the house was rebuilt or reconstructed by Dobson and, after his death in 1865, by his son-in-law, Sydney Smirke;[128] and in this century a great deal of that work has been demolished. Remaining from Bonomi's time may be the mighty entrance hall, at least externally, with its fugue of round-headed windows leading into the clock-tower, the pivot of the entire composition. The richest decoration is along the south front and what survives is a conventional block of four bays and three storeys. To the east (Plate 175) there stands an octagonal tower with a splayed base clearly copied from Guy's Tower at Warwick Castle but with a window of thirteenth century outline in one face which bears a striking resemblance to the solar window at Aydon Castle. Between the tower and the west block are the private apartments with the windows of the upper two floors (Plate 174) linked by one frame with the intervening floor level masked by carved panels bearing coats-of-arms. To allow the retention of Lord Durham's balcony on the ground floor detached flying buttresses were designed and since, according to Bonomi, 'The upper part seemed to require a more chapel-like termination to correspond with the tower . . . I have added the pinnacles'.[129]

Plate 174   The private apartments. Lambton Castle, County Durham.

Plate 175   The south front. Lambton Castle, County Durham.

Lambton Castle, perhaps the first great house to have gas lighting,[130] was the last expression of castellated Gothic in the north of England. Belonging in spirit to such earlier castles as Ravensworth and Lowther it was already old-fashioned when completed. That Lambton would never procreate was ensured by the competition in 1835 for the Houses of Parliament for henceforth Tudor was the mode. Thus the Greens designed the Master Mariners' Asylum at Tynemouth in 1837[131] with an E-plan and a forest of gablets and seven years later Dobson produced a similar essay for the town hall at North Shields.[132] These buildings with their utilitarian functionalism are a part of the new age of railways, workhouses, municipal baths, and town halls. No more could it be said that, 'Hitherto, Gothic architecture has made very little progress in towns and cities'[133] for Gothic had gone public and was no longer the preserve of the gentry and the aristocracy.

317

XVII

William Burn and the Country House

In the north of England the Tudor style established itself, despite earlier sporadic appearances, as a coherent style circa 1830 although as a specialised product of the Gothic Revival it had a vigorous rival in the stylistically unified castellated architecture of John Dobson. The historical development of the Revival was, however, very different in Scotland. There, not only was Tudor architecture well established before the close of the second decade of the nineteenth century but in the capable hands of William Burn of Edinburgh it became, starting in the twenties, the generally accepted style for a country house despite Britton's comment in 1840 that most new Gothic mansions in Scotland were castellated.[1] Of course, castle building continued but it faltered and with a loss of confidence that continuity of development, which had been such a marked feature of the later eighteenth and early nineteenth centuries, was irretrievably broken.

As so often occurs in the history of the Gothic Revival in Scotland the introduction of a new style was effected by an Englishman, William Wilkins. When the fourth Earl of Rosebery succeeded to his titles in 1814 he chose Wilkins as the architect for a new house on his West Lothian estate[2] where the house and gardens were 'much neglected'.[3] As with the creation of so many other country houses there was a long gestation before the old castle of Barnbougle by the shore of the Firth of Forth was replaced. Robert Adam had prepared a series of careful designs for a spectacular triangular castle which, set by the water's edge, would have conjured up an image of the imperial palace of Spalato.[4] Nevertheless, nothing was done until, according to family tradition, a wave from the Forth, crashing into the dining-room at Barnbougle, knocked over Lord Rosebery who thereupon selected an inland site for a new seat.

Plate 176   William Wilkins. Dalmeny House, West Lothian. 1815.

Wilkins' first design was Grecian[5] but rather fortunately, considering the climate, instead of a long pillared front the sunnier Tudor was preferred with the design based on those examples in East Anglia, particularly East Barsham Manor in Norfolk,[6] with which Wilkins would have been familiar from boyhood. As the site at Dalmeny sloped to the south there was a good excuse for a terrace, that prerequisite for any residence of importance. The elevation above is a formal arrangement of seven bays and two storeys with the centre raised a further storey and formed into a tower supported by buttresses. These were repeated on the end bays which are topdressed with false gables. The windows are large with the characteristic Elizabethan grid of mullions and transoms and above each one is a flat hood-mould. There are battlements but for show and not in imitation of defence. Clearly neither an abbey nor a castle Dalmeny (Plate 176), with its easy horizontality and delicate projections belying the formal patterning, was a new kind of house in Scotland. In its plan, too, it was just as original. In the main the public rooms overlooked the east and, not to disturb the privacy of the occupants, the entrance lay on the south. It led into a vestibule and from there to a staircase hall from which a cloister, with ribbed vaults and with stained glass windows, gave access to the public apartments. These, decorated in a restrained classical idiom, also broke with precedent being 'calculated more for comfort, and convenience than show'.[7] The domestic functions were further broken down by having a private family wing overlooking a secluded garden and with suites of servants' offices set out to the north.

319

Plate 177   William Burn. Design for Dunmore Park, Stirlingshire. 1820.

Perhaps because Wilkins can so easily be dismissed as an architect of the second rank, Dalmeny's revolutionary principles in design and in planning have been overlooked by historians even although Fergusson, the most punctilious critic of the early Gothic Revival, grudgingly conceded Wilkins' domestic work 'a fair amount of success'.[8] That 'appearance of novelty to his designs',[9] which Fergusson also observed, occurred too in Wilkins' second Scottish mansion, Dunmore Park in Stirlingshire (Plate 177), for the fifth Earl of Dunmore, which was commenced in 1820.[10] Although Wilkins had produced Tregothnan in Cornwall by then[11] Dunmore shows little of the former's irregular composition and, instead, it closely imitated Dalmeny even to the courtyard plan (Plate 178) and the

Plate 178   William Burn's plan of the principal floor. Dunmore Park, Stirlingshire.

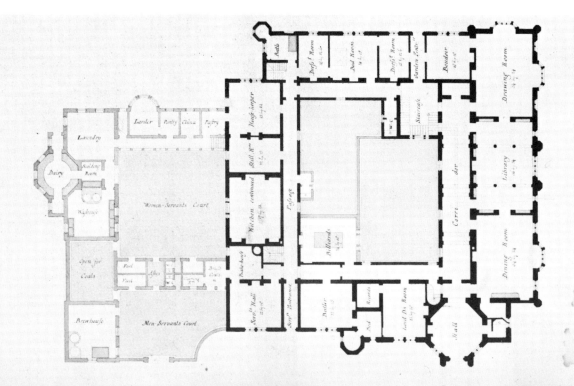

placing of the entrance and public and private apartments on different fronts.[12] Still, the formula which had been so successful at Dalmeny was less so at Dunmore, perhaps because of the bold porte-cochère. With a room above, it became too powerful for not only did it overwhelm the entrance front but from any distance it became an appendage to the south elevation upsetting the formal balance. The visual confusion was worsened by the assorted fenestration and the jumbled chimneys on the skyline which indicated, even since Dalmeny, a greater desire for variety and contrast.

These last elements were provided to the full by William Burn (1789–1870), the most prolific of country house practitioners. It was the Elizabethan and, later, the Jacobean modes which were to prove Burn's *forte* and although he has left no record as to the reasons for his choice they seem clear enough. Primarily, there was the gradual acceptance of Tudor architecture as the national style. That, of course, did not apply in Scotland. Nevertheless, when in 1829 Sir John Forbes of Craigievar was considering building a new house a friend recommended 'the Manor style. It admits of being added to—it is neat and light and airy within and it affords a good opportunity . . . for your paying respect to your Ancestors by erecting (?) what may seem to have been of their day. You are not a proud man nor vain of your familie's (sic) antiquity . . . and in this feeling I would put up a house with an elevation that I would think more than twice about, were I a new man.'[13] There was also the consideration that 'notwithstanding all the facilities which we possess in inexpensive decoration' Tudor architecture, while avoiding pretentiousness, gave that comfort and convenience which were coming to be regarded as the hallmarks of the gentlemanly way of life.[14]

Yet perhaps all these notions only fell to Burn in time so that his initial acceptance of the Tudor style was because of its novelty. Burn was shrewd and would have realised the advantages of picking up the style which he could have seen at Dalmeny while working in 1818[15] on the neighbouring Dundas estate where his rather conventional and staid castellated block (Plate 179) was rendered old fashioned by Wilkins'

Plate 179   William Burn. Dundas Castle, West Lothian. 1818.

achievement. As nearly always seems to happen in Scotland there was a medieval tower at Dundas although when it was left to show off its stocky vernacular silhouette against Burn's extensions then a new movement was about to begin.

The castle which Burn devised eschewed many of the more usual symbols in favour of an eclectic range of window types including an oriel and a Jacobean bay. Despite these assertions of individuality it is to Lowther that Dundas bows in homage for like Lowther it has contrasting castellated and ecclesiastical elevations. The entrance was on the south with the main rooms along the east reached by a corridor or cloister at the start of which rose the staircase.[16] Although there had been corridor galleries at Scone and Abercairny, the Dundas example, together with the courtyard plan, must have come from Dalmeny.

So far as Burn is concerned the corridor is one of his most easily recognised characteristics. For instance, it was repeated in 1821 at Carstairs House in Lanarkshire[17] where, eighty feet long and with a staircase at one end, it ran parallel to and separated the main elevations. The mansion, which replaced a much older house,[18] is Tudor with a rather severe entrance facade in which the elements from the south facade of Dalmeny were re-assembled but bringing the false gables into the sides of the tower. Like the entrance the south front (Plate 180) at first glance appears wholly regular although it is not so and is, indeed, unusual in not having a dominant central feature. Still it is made distinctive with scrolled gables and heavily carved Tudor buttresses and window heads all of which made it 'this truly splendid residence of a British merchant'.[19]

A house of a very different stamp, although stylistically similar, is Ratho Park in Midlothian, 1824,[20] which can be said to mark the emergence of the distinctive architecture of Burn. Although Dundas could be praised for its combination of excellent planning and domestic comfort[21] that was not the case at Carstairs where the offices lay beyond the corridor so that it became a longitudinal thoroughfare for owners and servants alike although for the former there was a less public route through the intercommunicating public rooms. At Ratho Park the lines of communication for the servants were shortened by placing the domestic offices and the residential accommodation on either side of the corridor. The servants entered the corridor by the side of the staircase which was contained in its own recess breaking into the courtyard to the north, an idea which had come to Burn perhaps from a perusal of Britton's plan of Longleat in the second volume of his *Architectural Antiquities*. At Dundas the family apartments had been placed beside the entrance[22] as they were at Lowther, but at Ratho Park there was a gain in privacy

322

Plate 180   William Burn. The south front. Carstairs House, Lanarkshire.

by having them in a self-contained suite to the west of the corridor. In addition, as the public rooms were to the south, the corridor became a vacuum so that neither sight nor sound of the servants at work to the north need ever disturb the tranquil lives of the owners. In that respect so successful was Burn's planning that the young wife of the fourth Duke of Montrose when at Buchanan Castle (one of Burn's most famous corridor mansions) of her fourteen servants only saw the butler and complained bitterly of her isolation.

It was, of course, Burn's prime claim to fame that he first devised 'that scientific mode of arrangement'[23] which, though basically unchanged, would be further categorised at such later mansions as Falkland and Whitehill with a multitude of servants' offices spilling over from the basement into wings. What made such an expansion all the more remarkable was that the number of public rooms contracted. Apart from the occasional appearance of a business room, there were only three or four public rooms. How different from the Adam period with its hosts of drawing-rooms and its summer and winter apartments!

The new approach to planning was revealed externally at Ratho (Plate 181) where to prevent draughts, the doorway was offset from the middle of a short elevation which, with a mullioned bay and a two storey Tudor porch, was copied from East Barsham Manor.[24] Furthermore, to

323

mark the break with the residential accommodation there was a sharp reduction in the scale of the adjacent offices which were terminated by a low two storey tower.

Plate 181   William Burn. Ratho Park, Midlothian. 1824.

A somewhat similar pattern had already been put into effect by Burn at Blairquhan Castle in Ayrshire (Plate 182). Designed in 1820[25] for Sir James Hunter Blair the castle was a return to the courtyard plan of Dundas but dispensing with peripteral routes by enclosing the centre with a lantern tower after the manner of those at Lowther and Taymouth. Beneath the

Plate 182   William Burn. Blairquhan, Ayrshire. 1820.

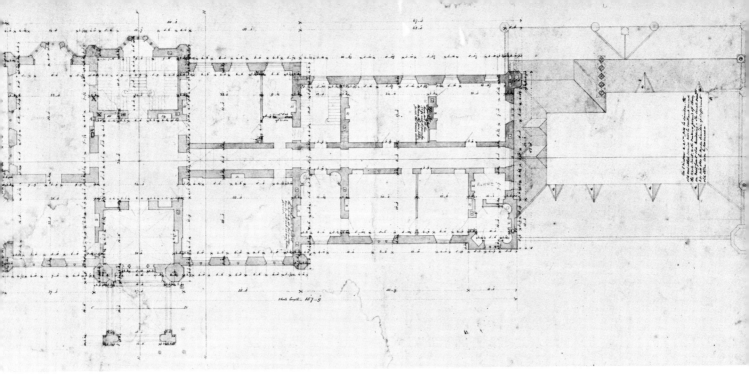

Plate 183   William Burn's plan for the principal floor. Blairquhan, Ayrshire.

tower was a galleried saloon (Plate 183), sixty feet high, and beyond it a staircase, all forming an assemblage almost identical to Gillespie Graham's at Lee Castle in 1822 so that perhaps not unjustly, Burn complained: 'Of Mr. Gillespie, there is nothing he would hesitate about and therefore his conduct surprises no one'.[26] With the hall, saloon and staircase in axis at Blairquhan (Plate 184) there was a complete separation of the drawing-

Plate 184   The saloon. Blairquhan, Ayrshire.

room and billiard-room from the dining-room and library beyond which lay the family suite with bathroom, nursery and secondary stair.

Burn's last Tudor house within this study, and in some respects his finest, was the riparian Garscube House built in 1827[27] in a sylvan setting near Glasgow. Although there was a saloon the presence of an older house prevented that rigorous separation of functions which had occurred at Blairquhan. As the entrance hall and its adjacent business room were on the north the family apartments and the servants' quarters were set east and west respectively of the saloon with the public rooms intervening on the south. Garscube was demolished in the nineteen-fifties but surviving photographs show that the interior was lavishly Gothic. The boudoir, for example, had fan vaulting and the drawing-room, which led into the

Plate 185   William Burn. Fettercairn House, Kincardineshire. 1826.

conservatory, had a beam and panel ceiling on which were armorial insignia. The exterior was equally ornate in the Dalmeny or East Anglian manner with an entrance tower linked to terminal ones by two storey ranges with curved Tudor window heads. It was a front which, in general, was copied from Eton College.[28]

The designs for Garscube were made in 1826.[29] Earlier that year Burn had been at work enlarging Fettercairn in Kincardineshire,[30] a Restoration mansion of three storeys (Plate 185). The ground floor became a basement with a *piano nobile* above. To counter the horizontal movement every window had its own curled gable, copied probably from Montacute, with majestic bays for the dining-room and drawing-room. Between them was the entrance with an oriel above and, showing Burn's love of strong end uprights, helmetted polygonal buttresses. It was a strong grouping and one that was derived perhaps from the entrance at Burghley House. To the rear, however, few changes disturbed the rubble walls and crow-steps of the vernacular architecture where the added gablets became, in effect, Scottish dormers.

Plate 186   William Burn. Auchmacoy, Aberdeenshire. 1831.

Garscube had been a very grand mansion. Fettercairn, though, with its indolent sprawl really belonged, despite its ornate gables, to the manor class of house which in previous centuries would have been erected by the middling sort of landowner. The style was not new. Scott had considered it for Abbotsford and there are late examples at Tayfield in Fife of circa 1835[31] which copied Burn's St Fort of six years earlier,[32] and Glendelvine, now Raffel House, of 1839[33] which imitated another Burn house, Snaigow. The first of the manor class, however, was Smirke's Cultoquhey in Perthshire which, although it was designed in 1818,[34] was delayed until at least four years later for reasons of cost.[35] Eventually, the owner's wish for a residence 'as plain as possible'[36] was fulfilled to the letter for there are undecorated walls and gables and only a few minute corbels on the tower near the entrance. A tower, with the same medieval stockiness, also dominated the entrance to The Grove in Dumfries-shire by Rickman[37] who designed the nearby Terraughtie, again in 1825,[38] with an E-plan and Jacobean porch. Much less austere was Blore's series of stepped facades at Corehouse in Lanarkshire in 1824.[39] It was akin to the warm comfortable fashion of the Cotswolds, and was repeated at Kirklands in Berwickshire, circa 1835,[40] with a half H-plan and a porch in a re-entrant angle. Just as lively was Lugar's Hensol in Kirkcudbright-shire, before 1828,[41] with mullioned windows, ogee capped corner towers and another one for the entrance. A comfortably scaled house it closely followed Lugar's own precepts. 'The site having been determined on, the next important point is to arrange the distribution of the living rooms that they may not be overlooked in approaching the door; and that the indispensable privacy of a country residence be not invaded; and then

327

carefully to adjust the subordinate offices . . . so that each may obtain the contiguity and facility of access which its utility requires.'[42] These were Burn's sentiments exactly.

Several manorial houses were built by Burn beginning with the now demolished Snaigow in Perthshire,[43] Strathendry in Fife, both in 1824,[44] and the larger and more interesting Auchmacoy in Aberdeenshire seven years later.[45] In the main an Elizabethan house (Plate 186) it was, like Fettercairn, to be an important architectural contribution to the northern architectural scene not just because of its shafted chimneys and numerous gables, although these in themselves were novelties in the north, but because it introduced such Scottish elements as dormers, *tourelles* and harling which, by throwing the granite dressings into relief, imparted vivacity to the entire composition. In the same year, 1833, Kirkmichael House in Dumfries-shire[46] revealed much the same indulgent attitude to the past with corbelling and Scots-Jacobean dormers.

Although Burn established his canon in the early seventeenth century he did make some sorties into the Middle Ages and castellated architecture. After 1817 he was engaged on Saltoun Hall in East Lothian[47] where the core was a medieval castle with classical additions, perhaps by John Adam.[48] Burn encased it all in a grandiloquent medieval garb, perhaps with Taymouth in mind, but more probably Lowther. After all, not only had Burn worked in Smirke's office[49] but later on he praised him unstintingly. 'There is not so worthy and kind hearted a man in existence.'[50] And it may have been from Smirke and Lowther that there came to Burn that easy-going approach to the authenticity of style which marks out Burn's early architecture at both Dundas and at Saltoun. At Saltoun the former courtyard was enclosed with a Gothic version of the dome of St Paul's cathedral even to a circular gallery although below there were medieval screens allowing for east–west communications at

Plate 187   William Burn. Milton Lockhart, Lanarkshire. 1829. Demolished.

first floor level. To the east the library was approached from a north facing cloister, an idea culled perhaps from Britton's plan of Audley End.[51]

Large additions were also made by Burn to Dalhousie Castle, in Midlothian[52] and its thirteenth century drum tower re-appeared at Inverness Castle[53] and to the north at Beaufort Castle in 1839.[54] Yet clearly these medieval structures had no interest for Burn who would have agreed with Pugin. 'What can be more absurd than houses built in what is termed the castellated style? . . . What absurdities, what anomalies, what utter contradictions do not the builders of modern castles perpetrate! . . . On one side of the house machicolated parapets, embrasures, bastions, and all the show of strong defence, and round the corner of the building a conservatory leading to the principal rooms. . . .'[55] Probably such practical considerations first influenced Burn's approach to Scottish architecture. At Dundas, for instance, although the old castle was retained, Burn's architecture had ignored it; at Saltoun it was obliterated; at Riccarton[56] the tower house was split from top to bottom with Tudor lights which the higher they rose the smaller they became, exactly as at Layer Marney Tower. However, as Burn worked on an ever increasing number of Scots tower houses there gradually came to the fore a respect for traditional Scottish features. Some of these had been used by Robert Adam, a practice which had died out with him so that it was left to Burn to establish a lasting appreciation through his personal influence. Thus while Hoddam Castle in Dumfries-shire seems to have made little impact on his additions in 1826,[57] at Pitcaple Castle in Aberdeenshire four years later[58] they were made subservient to the Z-plan tower and given crow-steps and attenuated *tourelles* and turrets. Much sturdier was the sober house wrapped round two sides of Kilconquhar Castle in Fife[59] and although the corbelled turrets were still too slim that was remedied at Castle Menzies[60] where Burn learnt

Plate 188   A design by Burn for the entrance front of Milton Lockhart.

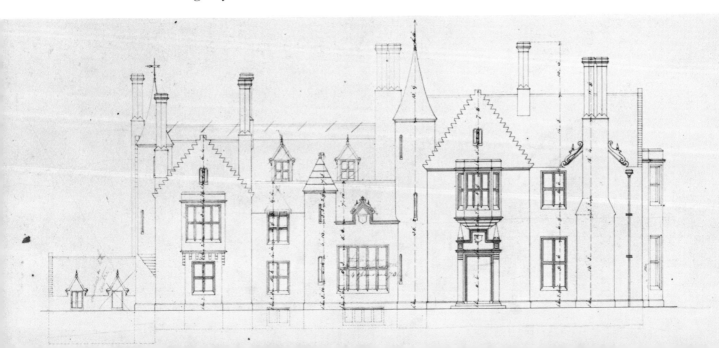

something of the balance between solid and void as well as the careful detailing of Renaissance dormers with finely carved pediments. At first, of course, Burn's Gothic decorations were much the same as anybody else's and only gradually did he develop a repertoire of rich Jacobean ornament beginning with Niddrie Marischal, near Edinburgh, in 1823.[61] There Burn provided a saloon with a Jacobean staircase, taken, in all probability, from a plate of Crewe Hall in Cheshire,[62] but with a ceiling, with ribs, monograms and heraldic devices, which was a replica of those of 1661 already in the house. Thus there gradually emerged in Burn's work the inheritance of the late Scottish castles and Scots-Jacobean enrichments in stone and plaster. These strands, when put together, produced what came to be called Scots-Baronial.

Burn's finest example of Scots-Baronial was Milton Lockhart[63] on a site in the Clyde valley selected by Sir Walter Scott and with a library which was a duplicate of that at Abbotsford.[64] Now a ruin, photographs show that Milton Lockhart (Plate 187) had an advanced two storey entrance with an oriel and crow-stepped gable. To the left, in the re-entrant angle, was a round tower, then lesser elements and finally another stepped gable with a corbelled bay-window. A lively composition it was further diversified by high chimney stacks and scrolled dormer-heads. As one observer wrote: 'The details are taken from ancient Scottish buildings, and it is generally considered one of the best works of that distinguished architect.'[65] Indeed, as an original composition, Milton Lockhart (Plate 188) can be ranked with Garscube and the later Falkland as Burn's best work making the loss of the first two more acutely felt. Fortunately, Auchterarder House, Perthshire, of 1832,[66] does remain although it is primarily Scots-Jacobean with a columned porte-cochère supporting a pedimented armorial tablet while behind, characteristic Scottish gables die away into a round tower set with a classical parapet on corbels exactly as on many an early seventeenth century castle. One of the largest of these Scots-Jacobean houses is Tyninghame in East Lothian[67] although, in point of interest it is surpassed by Falkland House in Fife. Built for Onesophorous Tyndall Bruce it became, after 1887, the property of the Marquess of Bute.

Falkland must be acknowledged as one of the finest mansions of the early nineteenth century not only because of its richness, both internally and externally, but also because of its planning. It is alleged to have cost £30,000[68] although the original estimate in the summer of 1839 was £17,833 8s 0d.[69] The contract was signed at the end of that summer but because of the richness of the parts the carcase was not complete until three years later.[70] The clerk of works was William

Spottiswoode and from his letters to the client some indications can be gained of the progress of the work particularly in the two years after 1842.[71] In July of that year the drawings for the staircase ceiling arrived from the architect[72] though it was not until the autumn that the preparations for the stair itself were under way. That was on 8 November and although the gas fitters had left on the previous day there were still glaziers and masons at work with the latter engaged in carving and in erecting the chimneys.[73] By late spring in 1843 the masons' tasks were more or less complete.[74] In June the chimney-piece for the entrance hall had been selected but, as the quarries were not working because of the rain, the carvers were kept busy cutting balusters for garden seats.[75] When the chimney-piece was finished the cost was £77 11s 0d;[76] it is the last recorded item before the architect submitted his account. By then Burn had settled in London, where 'My folks are all delighted with their change of residence', leaving David Bryce to complete the job at Falkland[77] for which £1,000 was charged. That included the designs, working drawings and specifications as well as supervision while for travelling expenses, for the five years after November 1838, the architects charged £40 1s 6d.[78]

A great deal of thought had gone into the lavish decoration of Falkland House. Thus in October 1841 Burn had written to his client: 'The Ceilings as Shewn by the drawings are much richer than I originally Contemplated, but I was taken with the style and character, and regarding them as particularly suitable to your house.'[79] In the drawing-room, library and dining-room the painted decorations were to be imitation

Plate 189   The entrance elevation as designed by Burn for Falkland House, Fife. 1839.

oak with the walls of the last painted to represent damask.[80] However, within a month of the estimate being agreed upon there was a dispute between Burn and the decorator over the dining-room ceiling[81] so that the latter was provoked into a wordy explanation. 'It is now considered better taste to varnish the wainscoting allowing the natural colour of the wood to appear and in order that the ceiling may now be in keeping it certainly ought to be painted in imitation of the wainscot. . . . .'[82]

The exterior of Falkland (Plate 189) was comprised of past forms but brought together in an original manner. On the important elevations there were two storeys separated by a string-course. The south front was composed of four bays of mullioned and transomed windows and at either end a canted bay was overtopped by a crow-stepped gable with square Jacobean turrets. The entrance, on the north, was asymmetrical with a square tower and before it a broad single storey hallway and porch leading into the usual corridor from one side of which rose the staircase. Very similar in its general outlines was Burn's next house, Whitehill in East Lothian in 1840[83] where the Scottish elements were either removed or else overwhelmed by the exuberance of the pronounced English Jacobean motifs which included, besides much fretwork and strapwork, an oriel copied from the seventeenth century Bramshill. Burn's most explicit statement of English Jacobean was Madras College in St Andrews in 1831[84] although he had already begun to move towards that with Dupplin Castle in Perthshire of three years before[85] which Lord Cockburn described as 'one of the few modern Scotch houses not absurdly large. . . . It seems to me to be Burn's best.'[86] In the year following Dupplin, St Fort, in the same county,[87] repeated many of its parts, particularly the large square tower with a double cupola roof copied from Audley End.

Despite these English overtones, Burn's achievement was the genesis of the 'Scotch style'[88] which Kerr described as having 'spread over Scotland and the North of England from the head-quarters of Edinburgh'.[89] That was not quite true for in Scotland much of the north east remained closed to Burn. There, country-house practice was divided between those bitter rivals John Smith and Archibald Simpson both classical men at heart but prepared to work in the new style which had first manifested itself in the north at Fettercairn where the site architect may have been John Smith. Certainly he was already well known to Burn[90] when they came to collaborate over Fintray House some nine miles to the north west of Aberdeen.

Fintray was an estate belonging to Sir John Forbes of Craigievar who early in January 1827 received from Smith a design for the ground floor of a new house at Fintray which was estimated to cost £5,000

Plate 190 A model of Castle Newe, Aberdeenshire, built in 1831 by Archibald Simpson but since demolished.

with an additional £1,500 for additions to the existing house.[91] Five months later, though, Sir John wrote to William Burn, whom he seems to have heard of through Lord Blantyre and Robert Wallace of Kelly, near Greenock. Sir John bluntly stated his requirements. 'Something of the old Manor House will suit place (sic) and also enable me to build a part at present and add thereto when I wish it.' He wanted the usual three public rooms and as 'I do not wish any Sunk Storey' the offices were to be to the rear.[92] Burn's charges were 5% for the whole job or $2\frac{1}{2}$% without superintending it with a reduction in his travelling costs since he expected to be working both at Aberdeen and at Fettercairn.[93]

After that first exchange there was a hiatus. Burn was working on a plan in which he altered Lady Forbes' arrangements for the bedroom and ground floor, especially the hall which had overlooked 'the dressed ground, and private road to the garden'. Changes were made, too, in the servants' quarters to bring part of them more directly under the control of the butler.[94] After that the specification could be made out and, with the plans, it cost £84.[95]

Sir John accepted Burn's plan but wanting 'the assistance of a professional person close at hand' suggested Smith[96] to which Burn readily agreed 'having lately found him most liberal and conciliatory in his conduct towards myself'.[97] However, when in December Smith estimated the cost of the additions and alterations at £4,500 he included the remark that 'A new Mansion House of Granite Stone in the Grecian Style would only be £6,000'.[98] It may be that Smith, in the true professional way, was hoping to supplant Burn which it seems he did since in 1830 a contract was drawn up with Sir John for a new house to 'conform to a Plan,

Plate 191   John Smith. Slains Castle, Aberdeenshire. Enlarged in 1836 and
gutted in the twentieth century.

Elevations and Measurement designed, drawn and Subscribed by John
Smith, Architect in Aberdeen'.[99]

In April 1829 specifications had been issued for demolishing much
of old Fintray House, part of which at least was classical.[100] Nearly two
months later a contract provided for the manufacture at Fintray of
between sixty to a hundred thousand bricks[101] which was later increased to
a hundred and twenty thousand[102] although the exterior was in the
polished grey granite which Sir John had initially considered[103] with
dressings of Morayshire freestone.[104] By the autumn of 1829 the foundations were dug[105] although it was not until another two years had passed
that the principal rooms were being finished.[106]

While the documentary evidence points to Smith as the architect of
Fintray House, it did, as might be expected, owe a great deal to Burn.

Plate 192   John Smith. Forglen, Banffshire. 1839.

Plate 193   John Smith. Cluny Castle, Aberdeenshire. 1836.

Thus, as at Auchmacoy, it had an asymmetrical entrance elevation but with a symmetrical one for the public rooms. There was stone corbelling at the entrance and curved gables and gablets for the second storey windows. As a 'Jacobethan' mansion, to use a modern term, Fintray was rivalled by Castle Newe in Strathdon, an old house of 1604 enlarged by Archibald Simpson for another member of the Forbes clan, Sir Charles Forbes once a merchant in Bombay.[107] When a contemporary praised Castle Newe (like Fintray now demolished) for 'The portico, the vestibule, and the corridor, which are lighted with stained glass'[108] there is more than a hint of Burn's planning. Externally, Simpson's Jacobean mansion was very plain (Plate 190) with the chief facade being symmetrical and ending in round towers covered with cupolas. Simpson also made Jacobean additions to Craig Castle, also in Aberdeenshire, circa 1832,[109] although elsewhere he made full use, like other architects in that 'era of "Omnium Gatherum"',[110] of both Tudor and, later on, of Scottish architecture. His collegiate Tudor at Marischal College in Aberdeen in 1837[111] was his public reply to Smith's Perpendicular Gothic at King's College in Old Aberdeen of twelve years before.[112] In 1838 Simpson used Jacobean for the Gordon Schools at Huntly, built for the Duchess of Gordon[113] and between 1836 and 1841 he was adding extensions to such houses as Lessendrum,[114] Meldrum[115] and Pittodrie[116] which, though ostensibly Jacobean, had Scottish elements although with a noticeable lack of artistic commitment.

335

Much more positive were Smith's houses of which three, Easter Skene of 1832,[117] and Menie[118] and Candacraig[119] both dating from circa 1835 show a strong kinship with Auchmacoy. Nor could Smith break away from that source even when ambitiously transforming Slains Castle (Plate 191) into Scots-Tudor for Lord Erroll after 1836.[120] However, Banchory House of 1839,[121] on the south bank of the River Dee, although basically

Plate 194   David Hamilton. Dunlop House, Ayrshire. 1833.

Tudor, did show an awareness of Scottish architecture which with Smith finally came into its own at Learney House, Aberdeenshire, in 1837[122] with crow-steps and dormers. On the other hand Forglen House (Plate 192) of 1839 onwards,[123] thick with mullions and gables, can best be described as English Jacobean. It was perhaps a calculated contrast to Cluny Castle,[124] a monstrous swelling of a small Z-plan castle which was buried beneath towers eight storeys high. It is a curiously archaic building indigestible in its parts. Twenty years out of date it is like a Regency buck, grown cankerous and old, flaunting the colours of the picturesque.

Within this study Cluny (Plate 193) was the last testament of the castle style. Other architects either preferred to copy William Burn or attempted to emulate him. In 1833 David Hamilton produced his Scots-Jacobean prodigy, Dunlop House in Ayrshire[125] which was laced round with strap-work (Plate 194). Five years before W. H. Playfair had reproduced the gate-house of Falkland Palace as the centre of Belmont

Castle in Perthshire.[126] A very early example of revivalism in Scottish architecture it was followed by others, as sensitive and beautifully and accurately detailed, from the same architect. At Prestongrange[127] his Scots-Jacobean extension was as exquisitely mannered as it was five years later, in 1835, at Craigcrook Castle[128] for Lord Jeffrey while for a second judge, Lord Cockburn, he built a pele-tower at Bonaly in 1837.[129] Finally, as if in recompense for such austerity, in 1838 he began to re-case Floors Castle in Roxburghshire[130] in the most florid Elizabethan dress which he also adopted for Donaldson's Hospital in Edinburgh in 1842.[131] Rising from their parklands and with grouped clusters of towers they were indeed the true offspring of Burghley. Yet such painstaking reproductions, while undoubtedly successful in terms of visual exuberance both at Floors and at Donaldson's, were disturbing portents. In the long run, though, the future of architecture could not lie in the meticulous setting out of past forms. That had never been Burn's way. He had striven consciously to make the past subservient to his present requirements. His reputation has always been as a planner so 'that the most convenient houses in the kingdom have for many years back come from the hands of certain Scotch architects. The name of Mr. Burn particularly has long been distinguished in connexion with this circumstance'.[132] But it was Burn, too, who, by dissolving old forms had produced a new formula, Scots-Baronial. By such means 'more abstract and grammatical than imitative',[133] not only would the Gothic Revival be prolonged but there would emerge, in time, the modern movement of the first half of the twentieth century.

Epilogue

When considering the Gothic Revival in northern England and in Scotland obvious differences come to the fore. In the eighteenth century there is, in general, the conservative attitude of the northern English landowners who preferred, whenever possible, to retain their ancestral castles by adapting them to new modes. In Scotland such a policy does not seem to have been either so possible or as desirable. Certainly many Scots wanted to be rid of their cramped tower-houses although the castle, as a symbol of social status and of land ownership, was of more consequence north of the Border where the Gothic villa, such as at Axwell, is unknown. Similarly there is no Scottish equivalent of the Gothic suite of rooms at Alnwick Castle or of the carriage-hall at Raby Castle. In Scotland, almost without exception, the interiors of Gothic houses were classical whereas in northern England Gothic was a fashionable novelty which could be readily identified with old forms.

A more serious attitude to the concerns of life may help to explain why it was in Scotland rather than in England that Robert Adam's castles were built. Archaeological and scholarly, they are infused with a deep personal philosophy which places castles, such as Culzean and Seton, in the first rank of European architecture. One would like to know more, too, about the guiding philosophy of the neo-classical John Paterson. His works and those of others before him bely the notion that the Gothic architecture of the middle and later eighteenth century was entirely frivolous and unscholarly. The very prevalence of such notions has prevented, until very recently, the proper study and assessment of Inveraray Castle which is not only the first major building of the Gothic Revival but one of the most important monuments of the second half of the eighteenth century.

Such an oversight is, of course, a part of the general neglect of the regions in assessing the history of architecture. It is an attitude which has been bolstered, so far as the Gothic Revival has been concerned, by the assumption that, with the exception of the wayward James Wyatt, no major architect of the later eighteenth century was involved seriously with Gothic architecture so that Gothic buildings must have been the

338

handiwork of local practitioners. However, once it is realised that such figures as Paine, Carr and various members of the Adam family did take Gothic architecture seriously then a radical reassessment of the place of the Revival in the architectural history of the later eighteenth century becomes necessary.

With only a slight degree of modification the same is true for the opening decades of the nineteenth century. Until then the predominant influences both in northern England and in Scotland were those which had been imported initially from southern Britain. Throughout the remainder of the eighteenth century the Scots in particular were resistant to further change and remained content with the dual sources of Inveraray and Robert Adam. But when change did come it was both sudden and extensive for within the span of a dozen years after 1803 the Englishmen, Atkinson, Lugar and Wilkins, had introduced and established monastic, irregular castellated and Tudor architecture. Although the Scots were slow to adopt irregular composition, there were surprises nevertheless. Lugar's Tullichewan and Balloch Castle date from 1808 and 1809 respectively. Craigend Castle was begun in 1812 and Castle Forbes, Aberdeenshire, in 1814. After the early eighteen-twenties the tide of southern influence began to ebb with the rise to prominence in Scotland and in northern England respectively of William Burn and John Dobson. In part, of course, the success of both these architects was based on their practical approach to the problems of their day. In particular the solutions adopted by Burn in planning a country house, which combined privacy for the owner with ease of management, appealed both to the aristocrat and to the man of newer substance.

The practical element was always evident in the design of places of worship. Nevertheless, Presbyterian Scotland is remarkable for the variety of church plans in the later eighteenth century. There was also the appearance in the second decade of the next century of the large Catholic and Episcopalian chapels both in Edinburgh and in Glasgow. By comparison English church architecture was much more narrowly conceived until the advent of Pugin.

Overall it is tempting to view the Gothic Revival, both the secular and the ecclesiastical buildings, as a movement which is capable of being divided into neat categories or into a tidy scheme of descent of from one or two sources. In fact there are many sources and while the influence of some, such as the social and philosophical ones, may be obscure nevertheless they remain potent. Sometimes, of course, the movement seems to regress, particularly in Scotland, with the continued use in the nineteenth century of the Inveraray formula. Yet the extent of change in the forward movement of the Revival can be gauged from the fact that a century after the commencement of Inveraray Castle in 1745 the Houses of Parliament, the most important public building of the nineteenth century, was encapsulated in Gothic architecture.

Until within the past decade the general neglect of the Revival by scholars has led to many losses including the castles of Ravensworth and Lowther in northern England and Abercairny, Inchrye and Millearne as well as Tullichewan and Gordon Castle in Scotland. That such losses went unchecked is not inexplicable when it is realised that Taymouth Castle remained unknown to all but a handful of scholars even although it is one of the largest and most dramatic architectural compositions in the British isles. Therefore it becomes clear that further regional studies may well reveal other buildings of national importance which require to be placed within the history of the Gothic Revival.

References

ABBREVIATIONS

A.A.	*Archaeologia Aeliana.*
APSD	*Architectural Publication Society's Dictionary.*
A.R.	*Architectural Review.*
CRO	Cumbria Record Office.
C.L.	*Country Life.*
D.N.B.	*Dictionary of National Biography.*
G.M.	*The Gentleman's Magazine.*
H. of N.	*History of Northumberland.*
NLS	National Library of Scotland.
NMRS	National Monuments Record of Scotland.
NRAS	National Register of Archives (Scotland).
NRO	Northumberland Record Office.
N.S.A.	*New Statistical Account.*
RCAHMS	Royal Commission on the Ancient and Historical Monuments of Scotland.
RHP	Register House Plan.
RIBA	Royal Institute of British Architects.
RIBAJ	*Royal Institute of British Architects' Journal.*
S.A.	*Statistical Account.*
S.M.	Soane Museum.
SRO	Scottish Record Office.
Trans. C. & W.A. & A.S.	*Transactions of the Cumberland and Westmorland Antiquarian and Archaeological Society.*
V.B.	*Vitruvius Britannicus.*
V.C.H.D.	*Victoria County History : Durham.*
V.S.	*Vitruvius Scoticus.*

I

1. E. Burt, *Letters from a Gentleman* (1818), Letter XIII, Vol. I, p. 245.

2. D. Defoe, *A Tour* (1927), Vol. II, p. 679. See also G. P. Jones, 'The Poverty of Cumberland and Westmorland'. *Trans. C. & W. A. & A. S.,* N. S., Vol. LV (1955), p. 199.

3. A. Young, *A Six Months' Tour* (1771), Vol. IV, p. 338. 'The journey lies through the counties of Northumberland, Cumberland and Westmorland, and through the uncultivated parts of Yorkshire, which are amongst the most barren in the kingdom.'

4. Ibid, Vol. III, p. 92.

5. Ibid, Vol. IV, p. 378.

6. W. Hutchinson. *An Excursion to the Lakes in Westmorland and Cumberland* (1776), p. 341.

7. W. Gilpin, *Observations on . . . the Highlands of Scotland* (1808), Vol. II, p. 94.

8. *V.C.H.D.*, Vol. II, p. 357.

9. Pringle, *A General View of the Agriculture of the County of Westmorland*. Quoted by T. H. Bainbridge in a very comprehensive survey 'Eighteenth Century Agriculture in Cumbria'. *Trans. C. & W.A. & A.S.*, N. S., Vol. XLII (1942), p. 56.

10. Ibid, p. 60.

11. Hutchinson, op. cit., p. 37.

12. 'Pleasing Improvements in the North; Particularly at Netherby'. *G.M.*, Vol. LV, pt. II (Nov. 1785), p. 844.

13. J. Hall, *Travels in Scotland* (1807), Vol. II, pp. 337–8.

14. S. Johnson, *A Journey to the Western Isles of Scotland, 1773* (1951), p. 9.

15. J. Handley, *The Agricultural Revolution in Scotland* (1963), p. 64.

16. J. Lettice, *Letters on a Tour . . . of Scotland, 1792* (1794), p. 240.

17. H. Skrine, *Three Successive Tours in the North of England and a great Part of Scotland* (1795), p. 94.

18. J. Hodgson, *A Topographical and Historical Description of the County of Westmoreland* (1823), p. 13.

19. *G.M.*, op. cit., pp. 843–5.

20. Young, op. cit., Vol. II, p. 416.

21. J. Swift, *Gulliver's Travels* (1941), pp. 119–20.

22. *G.M.*, op. cit., p. 844.

23. G. Tate, *History of the Borough, Castle and Barony of Alnwick* (1869–9), Vol. I, p. 361.

24. *V.C.H.D.*, Vol. II, p. 361.

25. L. Simond, *Journal of a Tour and Residence in Great Britain, During the Years 1810 and 1811, by a French Traveller* (1817), Vol. II, p. 73.

26. 'Observations on Improvements lately made in Cumberland'. *G.M.*, Vol. LX (June 1790), pp. 505–6.

27. Johnson, op. cit., p. 85.

28. Ibid, p. 81.

29. Ibid, p. 85. 'The chiefs divested of their prerogatives, necessarily turned their thoughts to the improvement of their revenues, and expect more rent, as they have less homage.'

30. 'An Address to the Lairds of Scotland'. *G.M.*, Vol. XLVI (Sept. 1776), pp. 397–8. This account is largely drawn from Pennant's *Voyage to the Hebrides*. It also quotes Dr Johnson, op. cit.

31. Simond, op. cit., Vol. I, p. 404.

32. Johnson, op. cit., p. 33.

33. Simond, op. cit., Vol. I, p. 420.

34. Ibid, Vol. I, p. 408.

35. Johnson, op. cit., p. 86.

36. T. Pennant, *A Tour in Scotland, 1769* (1790), p. 229.

37. Quoted by P. F. Anson, *The Catholic Church in Modern Scotland, 1560–1937* (1937), p. 120.

38. J. Knox, *A Tour through the Highlands of Scotland and the Hebride Isles . . . in 1786* (1787), p. xc. See also Garnett, op. cit., Vol. I, p. 184.

39. Knox, op. cit., p. lxxxix.

40. Simond, op. cit., Vol. I, p. 395.

41. Lettice, op. cit., p. 341.

42. The most recent account of the Highland Clearances is by J. Prebble (1963).

43. For Argyll see Lettice, op. cit., p. 243. For Macdonald of Staffa see Sir Walter Scott's letter to Joanna Baillie of July 19, 1810 quoted by H. J. Grierson, *Letters of Sir Walter Scott* (1932–7), Vol. II, p. 361.

44. Simond, op. cit., Vol. I, p. 412.

45. Ibid, Vol. I, p. 395.

46. Ibid. 'The Earl of Breadalbane's estate extends twenty-five miles west of Tyndrum, and farther east. . . .' On p. 408 Pennant is quoted as saying 'That Lord Breadalbane could travel a hundred miles on his own estate in a straight line'.

REFERENCES

47. Knox, op. cit., p. 72.
48. 'Progress of the Linen and Cotton Manufactory at Paisley'. *G.M.*, Vol. LVII (May 1787), p. 372 and (June 1787), p. 465.
49. 'Account of a Journey into Scotland'. *G.M.*, Vol. XXVI (May 1766), p. 209.
50. Simond, op. cit., Vol. I, p. 353.
51. T. Garnett, *Tour in Scotland, 1800* (1810), Vol. II, p. 185.
52. Ibid.
53. J. Kohl, *Scotland, Glasgow, the Clyde ... to the Lakes* (1844), pp. 17–18.
54. Ibid.
55. Ibid., p. 26.
56. Hall, op. cit., Vol. II, p. 567. 'The half of the people of Glasgow, at least of the lower classes, appear to be Highlanders.'
57. Kohl, op. cit., pp. 19–20, 26.
58. Ibid, pp. 21, 23.
59. *H. of N.*, Vol. IX, pp. 128, 133.
60. R. Surtees, *History and Antiquities of the County Palatine of Durham* (1816–40), Vol. II, p. 385.
61. Ibid, Vol. I, pp. 261–2.
62. Hodgson, op. cit., p. 19; Hutchinson, op. cit., p. 80.
63. 'Observations on Improvements lately made in Cumberland'. *G.M.*, Vol. LX (June 1790), p. 505; Hodgson, *Northumberland* (The Beauties of England and Wales) (1813), p. 16; Hutchinson, op. cit., p. 211.
64. 'Present State of Newcastle'. *G.M.*, Vol. LXI, Pt. I (April 1791), p. 325.
65. E. Mackenzie and M. Ross, *A View of the County Palatine of Durham* (1834), Vol. I, pp. ciii, cv.
66. W. Parson and W. White, *Gazetteer of Durham and Northumberland* (1827), Vol. I, p. cxxvii.
67. J. Nicolson and R. Burn, *History and Antiquities of the Counties of Westmorland and Cumberland* (1777), Vol. II, p. 44.
68. Gilpin, ibid.
69. J. McNayr, *A Guide from Glasgow to the Highlands of Scotland* (1797), p. 75. See also the Anonymous, *A Tour in the Highlands of Scotland, 1818* (1819), where similar sentiments are expressed.
70. 'Pleasing Improvements in the North; Particularly at Netherby.' *G.M.*, Vol. LV, Pt. II (Nov. 1785), p. 844.
71. A. H. Millar, *Fife: Pictorial and Historical* (1895), Vol. II, p. 282.
72. *The Journal* (Feb. 1850). Obituary of William Russell, grandson of the merchant.
73. *N.S.A.*, Vol. XI, pp. 88–9. 'The estate was purchased about thirty years ago by George Harley Drummond, Esq. of the well-known banking-house in Charing Cross. ....'

II

1. *D.N.B.*
2. J. Paine, *Plans, Elevations and Sections of Noblemen's and Gentlemen's Seats* (1767), Vol. I, p. i.
3. N. Pevsner, 'Genesis of the Picturesque', *A.R.* (Nov. 1944), Vol. 96, p. 140; E. W. Manwaring, *Italian Landscape in Eighteenth Century England* (1965), p. 122. See, however, W. A. Brogden, 'Stephen Switzer: La Grand Manier'. *Furor Hortensis* ed. by P. Willis (1974), pp. 21–30, for an interesting re-assessment of recent attitudes to the landscape garden in the early 1700s and in particular the concept that there was an anti-French, anti-Baroque element in English design of the early eighteenth century.
4. Pevsner, op. cit., p. 142; Manwaring, op. cit., p. 125.
5. A. Pope, *To Richard Boyle, Earl of Burlington, 1731* (London, 1970), lines

117–18; Manwaring, op. cit., p. 127.

6. A. Pope, *An Essay on Criticism* (1711) lines 90–1.

7. Manwaring, op. cit., p. 130.

8. H. Colvin, *A Biographical Dictionary of English Architects, 1660–1840* (1954), p. 345.

9. Quoted by S. Sitwell, *British Architects and Craftsmen* (1960), p. 211.

10. R. Morris, *An Essay in Defence of Ancient Architecture* (1728), p. xviii.

11. C. Hussey, *The Picturesque* (1927), pp. 58–9.

12. S. Johnson, *A Journey to the Western Isles of Scotland, 1773* (1951), p. 18; Manwaring, op. cit., p. 191.

13. M. Langley: 'The Unfortunate Maniac at Coniston Priory, in Westmoreland'. *G.M.*, Vol. LXIX, Pt. I (Jan. 1799), p. 62.

14. 'A Journey to the Highlands of Scotland'. *G.M.*, Vol. XLVIII (Feb. 1778), p. 83.

15. J. Lettice, *Letters on a Tour . . . of Scotland, 1792* (1794), p. 50.

16. Ibid, p. 154.

17. W. Hutchinson, *An Excursion to the Lakes in Westmoreland and Cumberland* (1776), pp. 156–7; Manwaring, op. cit., p. 192.

18. A. Young, *A Six Months' Tour* (1771), Vol. I, p. 301. See also Manwaring, op. cit., p. 180.

19. A. Pope, *To Richard Boyle, Earl of Burlington* (1731), lines 55–6.

20. Young, op. cit., Vol. I, p. 301.

21. W. Gilpin, *Observations on . . . Cumberland and Westmoreland* (1808), Vol. I, pp. 72–4. See also C. P. Barbier, *William Gilpin. His Drawings, Teaching, and Theory of the Picturesque* (1963), pp. 117–21.

III

1. 'Inscriptions at Hagley', *G.M.*, Vol. LXXI, Pt. II (July 1801), p. 593.

2. S. Johnson, *A Journey to the Western Isles of Scotland, 1773* (1971), p. 5.

3. R. Pococke, 'Travels Through England During 1750, 1751 and Later Years'. *Camden Society* (1888–9), Vol. II, p. 233.

4. Ibid, Vol. I, p. 224.

5. A. Young, *A Six Months' Tour* (1771), Vol. III, p. 294.

6. 'Tour to the Lakes of Cumberland and Westmorland'. *G.M.*, Vol. LXXVI, Pt. I (March 1806), p. 226.

7. 'Priory at the Leasowes.' *G.M.*, Vol. LXV (1795), p. 457.

8. J. McNayr, *A Guide from Glasgow to the Highlands of Scotland* (1797), p. 122.

9. Ibid, p. 149.

10. R. Pococke, op. cit., Vol. II, p. 40.

11. Lady Llanover (ed), *Autobiography and Correspondence of Mary Granville, Mrs Delany* (1861–2), Vol. II, p. 492.

12. 'Alnwick Described'. *G.M.*, Vol. XXVI (Feb. 1756), p. 74.

13. W. Hutchinson, *A View of Northumberland* (1778), Vol. II, p. 249.

14. W. Parson and W. White, *Gazetteer of Durham and Northumberland* (1827), Vol. I, p. 385.

15. W. Hutchinson, *History and Antiquities of the County Palatine of Durham*, Vol. III (1794), p. 65; N. Pevsner, *County Durham* (1953), pp. 37, 156.

16. *H. of N.*, Vol. XV, p. 317.

17. Ibid.

18. N. Pevsner, *Northumberland* (1957), p. 323. 'Archdeacon Thomas Sharp in 1720 . . . built a folly tower. . . .'

19. Ibid.

20. J. Hodgson, *History of Northumberland* (1820–40), Part II, Vol. I, p. 306; N. Pevsner, op. cit., p. 284. 'Cadger's (sic) Fort built in 1745 as a (somewhat romantic) defence against the Stuart menace from Scotland. . . .' There are

several designs at Wallington which are by Thomas Wright. They include a Gothic entrance screen as well as the designs for 'Codjah's Fort'. They are dated 1769. See also E. Harris, 'Architect of Rococo Landscapes. Thomas Wright—III'. *C.L.*, Vol. CL (9 Sept. 1971), pp. 614–15.

21. J. Wallis, *Antiquities of Northumberland* (1769), Vol. II, p. 525 ('Sir Walter Calverley Blacket, Bart. . . . built the Tower.'); Hodgson, op. cit., Part II, Vol. I, p. 305 footnote; J. Hodgson, *Northumberland* (Beauties of England & Wales) (1813), p. 181; W. Hutchinson, *View of Northumberland* (1778), Vol. I, p. 223; Pevsner, op. cit., p. 284. 'The two towers called Rothley Castle built as an eye-catcher at about the time when the lake was made. Barbara Jones gives 1776 as the date. . . .'

22. Garrett had been employed by Sir Walter Blackett on the remodelling of his seat, Wallington, which was completed by 1743. P. Leach, 'In the Gothick Vein. The Architecture of Daniel Garrett. Pt. III'. *C.L.*, Vol. CLVI (26 Sept. 1974), pp. 834–7; J. Cornforth, 'Wallington, Northumberland'. *C.L.*, Vol. CXLVII (April 1970), p. 857.

23. *H. of N.*, Vol. IX, p. 128; Pevsner, op. cit., p. 189 and on p. 289 'the Octagon, perhaps the Harbour Master's house and perhaps an after-dinner idea of Vanbrugh's.'

24. *H. of N.*, Vol. XI, p. 416.

25. *D.N.B.*; 'Mr Wright's Description of his Villa at Byer's Green.' *G.M.*, Vol. LXIII, Pt. I (March 1793), p. 216, states that Wright was 'thinking of erecting a Gothic tower' and the editor adds in a footnote that although the tower was begun, Wright did not live to complete it; E. Mackenzie and M. Ross, *A View of the County Palatine of Durham* (1834), Vol. II, p. 302; N. Pevsner, *County Durham*, p. 238 ('A circular, medieval-looking tower in the village, built c. 1780–90. . . .'); F. Rutherford, 'Pevsner on the Palatinate', *Trans. Architectural and Archaeological Society of Durham and Northumberland*, Vol. XI, Parts I and II (1958); E. Harris, 'The Wizard of Durham'. *C.L.*, Vol. CL (26 Aug. 1971), pp. 493–4.

26. N. Pevsner, *Northumberland*, p. 295.

27. J. Hodgson, *History of Northumberland* (1820–40), Part II, Vol. I, pp. 301 and 297, where a footnote explains the relationship between John and Thomas Sharp; Pevsner, op. cit., p. 165; Wallis, op. cit., Vol. II, p. 526.

28. J. Hodgson, *Northumberland* (1813), p. 180.

29. *H. of N.*, Vol. XV, p. 199; Pevsner, op. cit., p. 271.

30. *H. of N.*, Vol. XV, pp. 193–4; Hodgson, op. cit., p. 137 but is quoting Wallis, op. cit., Vol. II, p. 55; Hutchinson, op. cit., Vol. I, p. 215; Pevsner, op. cit., p. 292.

31. Although some follies were built in Scotland they were few in number and do not have the close architectural relationship of follies in Northumberland and County Durham. The earliest Gothic folly in Scotland was perhaps the Whim, a castellated 'eye-catcher' set on the hill above Blair Castle, Perthshire, in 1756 for which there is a drawing in the house. Gothic decorations embellished estate buildings at Inveraray and as far apart as Midmar Castle in Aberdeenshire and Cardross in Stirlingshire stables were screened with mock fortifications either at the end of the eighteenth century or early in the next.

32. Quoted from a remark by Horace Walpole by A. Bolton, *The Architecture of Robert and James Adam* (1922), Vol. I, p. 253. See also Pevsner, op. cit., p. 69.

33. 'Alnwick Described'. *G.M.*, Vol. XXVI (Feb. 1756), p. 73.

34. J. Fleming, *Robert Adam and His Circle* (1962), p. 263; A. C. S. Dixon, 'The Restoration of Alnwick Castle, 1750–86', pp. 11 and 12, unpublished B.Arch. dissertation, School of Architecture, University of Newcastle-upon-Tyne, 1960.

35. *H. of N.*, Vol. XI, p. 416.

36. Although shorn of many of their secular powers the bishops of Durham, throughout the eighteenth century and in the early nineteenth century, continued to exercise their secular jurisdiction over the Palatinate. After the passing of the 1832 Reform Act and on the death of Bishop van Mildert, Lord Melbourne separated the Palatinate from the see of Durham vesting the former in the Crown in 1836. See *V.C.H.D.*, Vol. II, p. 173.

37. J. Raine, *Account of the Episcopal Castle or Palace of Auckland* (1852), pp. 126–7. The cost is given as £379. See also Pennant, *A Tour in Scotland . . . 1772* (1790), Vol. II, p. 343.

38. N. Pevsner, *County Durham*, p. 52, gives the date 1760; F. Rutherford, op. cit., p. 79, says Sir Thomas Robinson may have been the designer and also quotes H. Colvin, *Biographical Dictionary of English Architects, 1660–1840* (1954), p. 511. It is noted, ibid, p. 73, that a drawing, 'Gateway designed for Dr Trevor Bishop of Durham', was executed by Richard Bentley. However, an elevation recently discovered at Auckland Castle bears the inscription in the bottom left hand corner, 'Sir Thos. Robison (sic) Architect'.

39. Pevsner, op. cit., p. 120.

40. J. Boyle, *The County of Durham* (1892), p. 596; Pevsner, op. cit., p. 153.

41. Paine, *Plans, Elevations and Sections of Noblemen's and Gentlemen's Seats* (1767), Vol. I, pls LXVII–LXIX; C. Hussey, 'Gibside, County Durham'. *C.L.*, Vol. CXI (Feb. 1952), p. 356.

42. *C.L.*, ibid, p. 357.

43. Boyle, op. cit., p. 596.

44. Ibid.

45. *D.N.B.*

46. I. Nairn and N. Pevsner, *Sussex* (1965), p. 91; N. Taylor, 'A Duke's Library'. *A.R.*, Vol. CLXII (Oct. 1967), p. 287.

47. W. Green, *Guide of the Lakes* (1819), Vol. I, p. 329; N. Pevsner, *Cumberland and Westmorland* (1967), p. 160, gives 1780 as the date for Lyulph's Tower but without indicating the source of the information; H. Skrine, *Three Successive Tours in the North of England and a great Part of Scotland* (1795), p. 30, states, ' . . . the Duke of Norfolk has erected a Gothic building, to which he has given the name of Lyulph's Tower . . .'.

48. 'Tour to the Lakes of Cumberland and Westmorland'. *G.M.*, Vol. LXXVI, Pt. I (March 1806), p. 223.

49. Pevsner, op. cit., pp. 133–4.

50. W. Whellan, *History and Topography of the Counties of Cumberland and Westmoreland* (1860), p. 250; Pevsner, op. cit., p. 188.

51. W. Mason, *English Garden*, 4th Book, 1781, quoted by C. Hussey, *The Picturesque* (1927), p. 145.

52. T. Pennant, *A Tour in Scotland, 1769* (1790), p. 272.

53. Ibid, p. 50.

54. Johnson, op. cit., p. 135.

55. Pococke, op. cit., Vol. I, p. 83.

56. Pennant, op. cit., p. 302.

57. Young, op. cit., Vol. I, p. 180.

58. Johnson, op. cit., p. 69.

59. Ibid, p. 145; see also 'Strictures on Dr Johnson, Mr Pennant and Mr Walpole' *G.M.*, Vol. XLV (May 1775), p. 227.

60. J. Lettice, *Letters on a Tour . . . of Scotland, 1792* (1794).

61. *G.M.*, Vol. LXIV, Pt II (Aug. 1794), p. 697.

62. Ibid, Vol. LXVII (Jan. 1797), p. 9.

63. Ibid, Vol. LXXII (May 1803), p. 458.

64. Ibid, Vol. LXXVIII (Nov. 1808), p. 977.

REFERENCES

65. Ibid, Vol. LXXXI (Nov. 1811).
66. J. Summerson, *Inigo Jones* (1966), pp. 44, 48, 99.
67. M. S. Briggs, *Goths and Vandals* (1952), p. 94.
68. H. Colvin, 'Fifty New Churches'. *A.R.* (1950), Vol. 107, p. 193.
69. M. S. Briggs, op. cit., p. 119; J. Summerson, *Architecture in Britain, 1530–1830* (1963), p. 186.
70. N. Pevsner, *The Englishness of English Art* (1956), p. 56; N. Pevsner, *Cambridgeshire* (1954), p. 148.
71. Briggs, op. cit., p. 103.
72. B. S. Allen, *Tides in English Taste* (1958), Vol. I, p. 54.
73. R. Morris, *An Essay in Defence of Ancient Architecture* (1728), p. 11.
74. K. Clark, *The Gothic Revival* (1964), p. 1.
75. Inscription over entrance.
76. *H. of N.*, Vol. XI, p. 227; N. Pevsner, *Northumberland*, pp. 138 and 133, where of Coupland Castle he writes, 'The date on the big fireplace of the first-floor Hall—1619—seems almost unbelievably late'.
77. Summerson, op. cit., p. 332.
78. Ibid, pp. 332, 334.
79. Ibid, p. 333; G. Hay, *The Architecture of Scottish Post-Reformation Churches, 1560–1843* (1957), p. 171.
80. Ibid, p. 56.
81. Ibid, p. 61.
82. Ibid.
83. Ibid, pp. 75, 111.
84. Allen, op. cit., Vol. II, p. 68.
85. *D.N.B.*; N. Pevsner, *Cumberland and Westmorland*, pp. 28–9, 234–5, 275.
86. Ibid, pp. 30, 292, 298.
87. Ibid, p. 28. See also introduction by J. Mordaunt Crook, p. [30] to Eastlake, *History of the Gothic Revival* (1970).
88. C. G. Bulman, 'The Parish and Church of St. Michael, Arthuret'. *Trans. C. & W.A. & A.S.*, N.S., Vol. LXVI (1966), pp. 179–89.
89. *D.N.B.*; 'Correspondence of John Cosin'. *Surtees Society*; Vol. LV (1870), Vol. II, Appendix XIV, pp. 356–82.
90. N. Pevsner, *County Durham* (1953), p. 54; Eastlake, op. cit., p. 11.
91. 'Durham Castle'. *C.L.*, Vol. XXIII (25 Jan. 1908), p. 134; *V.C.H.D.* Vol. III, p. 76.
92. The date is on a lead rainwater-head.
93. Correspondence of John Cosin, op. cit., Vol. II, Appendix XIV, p. 382. 'Six chaires of wenscoate gross worke for to be placed on the insides of the skreene within Auckland Chappell, on the right and left hand, in the middle Ile, and to be made of the fashion of the chaires now in the Chappell at Durham Castle, adjoyning to the skreene on the right hand going in, where my Lord uses to sit at prayers. The seates must be to turne up, with a little seate when turned up, and carving underneathe it.' Extract from a contract for joinery work between Cosin's steward, Edward Arden and Marke Todd and James Hull, joiners, 29 May 1665.
94. *Guide to Durham Castle* (n.d.), p. 25.
95. Correspondence of John Cosin, op. cit., Intro., p. xvii.
96. Ibid (Vol. LII, 1868), Vol. I, p. 168.
97. Pevsner, op. cit., p. 32.
98. Ibid, pp. 61–2, 207–8; Eastlake, op. cit., p. 12, in discussing Cosin's Gothic woodwork at Brancepeth Church, 'The whole of the woodwork, though naturally deficient in purity of detail, is thoroughly Gothic in motive'.
99. The term 'court Gothic' is used in this work not to indicate an architecture sponsored by the monarch but rather by people like the third Duke of Argyll and the Duke of Northumberland who, holding Crown appointments were at the centre of the political and artistic life of the country. In an age when the Crown was not an innovator of architecture, it was left to the fashionable aristocracy to set in train new ideas in architecture.

1. Argyll MSS at Inveraray Castle. For a complete account of the building of Inveraray Castle see I. G. Lindsay and M. Cosh, *Inveraray and the Dukes of Argyll* (1973), Chs I and II.

2. *D.N.B.*

3. *V.B.*, Vol. I, p. 4. 'And as it's my greatest Honour to receive my Blood from his August House, I thought I could nowhere so properly consecrate the first Essay of my Inventions.' Also pls 19, 20.

4. J. Lees-Milne, *Earls of Creation* (1962), p. 61.

5. H. Colvin, *Biographical Dictionary of English Architects 1660–1840* (1954), p. 396; *V.B.*, Vol. IV, pls 75–77. They are inscribed, 'R. Morris Arch.'

6. Lees-Milne, op. cit., p. 81; M. Cosh, 'Two Dukes and their Houses'. *C.L.*, Vol. CLII (13 July 1972), p. 80, implies that Coombe Bank was owned by Colonel Campbell.

7. M. P. G. Draper and W. A. Eden, *Marble Hill House and Its Owners* (1970), pp. 12–14, 36; Colvin, ibid, gives 1728–9 as the date.

8. Ibid; Lees-Milne, op. cit., pp. 81, 94. Whitton Place was built from 1736–9. M. Cosh, 'Lord Ilay's Eccentric Building Schemes. Two Dukes and their Houses—II'. *C.L.*, Vol. CLII (20 July 1972), pp. 144–5.

9. Roger Morris to the Shireff (sic) or Chamberlain of Inverara (sic), London, 6 Nov., 1744. Argyll MSS., Morris Letter Book.

10. Quoted by J. Fleming, *Robert Adam and His Circle* (1962), pp. 64–5.

11. Ibid.

12. Colvin, op. cit., p. 395.

13. Letter from William Adam to Andrew Fletcher of Saltoun (Lord Milton), 23 Aug. 1744 stating that he and Morris dined together. NLS, Fletcher of Saltoun MSS, Box 41.

14. Letter from William Adam to Fletcher of Saltoun, 15 Sept. 1747, from Inveraray. 'His Grace and Mr Morris are exceedingly well pleased with the works at this place.' NLS, Fletcher of Saltoun MSS, Box 73.
Morris also supplied Gothic designs for Roseneath Castle, an Argyll property on the River Clyde. In August 1745, William Adam sent off a statement about Roseneath. In November three years later John Adam, on the Duke of Argyll's instructions, sent to Fletcher of Saltoun 'the plans and Elevations of Mr Morriss's last designs for Roseneath'. NLS, Fletcher of Saltoun MSS, Boxes 403, 53.

15. J. Dunbar, *Historic Architecture of Scotland* (1966), p. 110; Fleming, op. cit., pp. 34–6, 330.

16. R. Morris to W. Adam, 3 May 1745. Argyll MSS, Morris Letter Book.

17. *D.N.B.*

18. R. Morris to Lord Milton, London, 1 Aug. 1745. Argyll MSS, Morris Letter Book.

19. *S.A.*, Vol. V, p. 296; J. Lettice, *Letters on a Tour . . . of Scotland* (1794), p. 242.

20. R. Morris to W. Adam, London, 19 June, 1746. Argyll MSS, Morris Letter Book.

21. 'A Memorial Relating to the Work at the Castle of Inverara (sic) by William Adam. Edinburgh. 6 Dec. 1746.' Adam sent off two pieces of dressed Creggan stone so that the Duke might see its quality. Argyll MSS, Morris Letter Book.

22. William Adam to Roger Morris, Edinburgh, 7 March 1747. Argyll MSS, Morris Letter Book.

23. The letter is addressed to Mr Adam from Green Street in London, 17 March 1746. Argyll MSS., Morris Letter Book. See also J. Fleming, op. cit., pp. 65–6.

24. Ibid, p. 66.

REFERENCES

25. W. Adam to R. Morris 5 Feb. 1747. Argyll MSS, Morris Letter Book.

26. W. Adam to R. Morris 22 Dec. 1747. Argyll MSS, Morris Letter Book.

27. Ibid; 'Memorial Concerning the Duke of Argyll's Works at Inveraray, March, 1748.' Argyll MSS, File I. For an account of the building and labour problems at Inveraray see M. Cosh, 'Building Problems at Inveraray'. *Bulletin of the Scottish Georgian Society.* Vol. II (1973), pp. 58–67.

28. Memorial of 14 Sept. 1749. Argyll MSS, File I.

29. Memorial of March 1748. Argyll MSS, File I.

30. 'Agreement with Cowan the Mason, 12 Sept. 1748.' Argyll MSS, File I.

31. Memorial of 14 Sept. 1749. Argyll MSS, File I.

32. Ibid.

33. Account certified by John Adam, 14 Oct. 1751. Argyll MSS, File I.

34. Accounts certified by John Adam, 1 Sept. 1750. Argyll MSS, File I.

35. The accounts bear the signature of John Adam. Argyll MSS, File I.

36. Ibid.

37. Letter of 12 July 1752 from Robert Campbell to the Chamberlain. Argyll MSS, File I.

38. Account, dated Sept. 1757. Argyll MSS.

39. Account Dec. 1757—Oct. 1758 from John & James Adam. Argyll MSS.

40. Memorial of 29 June 1761. Argyll MSS, File I.

41. Details of the third Duke's will were published in 'A Copy of the Last Will of the late Duke of Argyll'. *G.M.*, Vol. XXXI (May 1761), pp. 206–7. The Duke left all his real estate in England to 'Mrs Elizabeth Anne Williams, otherwise Shireburn, of Whitton Dean in the county of Middlesex and of Marlborough St. in London. . . . I also give one year's wages to each of my servants in London and Daniel Craft, my gardiner (sic) at Whitton, and my housekeeper there, excepting my cook, whose wages are too high.'

42. C. Gotch, 'Inveraray Castle, Argyllshire', *C.L.*, Vol. CXIII (25 June 1953), p. 2,062.

43. Lettice, op. cit., p. 242.

44. *S.A.*, ibid.

45. Boswell, *Journal of a Tour to the Hebrides* (1951), p. 400.

46. T. Pennant, *A Tour in Scotland, 1769* (1790), p. 239; H. Skrine, *Three Successive Tours in the North of England and a great Part of Scotland* (1795), pp. 47–8; W. Gilpin, *Observations on . . . the Highlands of Scotland* (1808), Vol. I, p. 185.

47. Lettice, op. cit., p. 247.

48. C. L. Eastlake, *A History of the Gothic Revival* (1970), p. 58.

49. S. Cruden, *The Scottish Castle* (1963), pp. 237–8.

50. The Whitton tower appears in a print of 1757 by William Woollett. There is a copy in the Duke of Argyll's collection at Inveraray Castle. Eastlake, op. cit., p. [47] gives the date of the Whitton tower as 1725 without any supporting evidence.

51. Catalogue of the sale of the Whitton Estate on 30 May 1765, plan and p. 7. Argyll MSS, File A.

52. Ibid, plan.

53. It was done in 1748 in a sketchbook, p. 5. RIBA Drawings' Collection, L12/2. See also J. Fleming, op. cit., p. 83.

54. Cosh, op. cit., pp. 143–44; Lindsay and Cosh, op. cit., pp. 10, 30. Dr Terry Friedman indicated the stylistic connection between the Gothic towers at Whitton and at Wentworth Castle. See also N. Pevsner, *Yorkshire, the West Riding* (1967), p. 548.

55. Campbell's designs for Fort William for the Board of Ordnance are dated 1744.

56. Lees-Milne, op. cit., p. 93. Horace Walpole wrote of the Duchess of Marlborough and Wimbledon House that 'She had directed my Lord Pembroke not to make her go up any steps; "I won't go up steps", and so he dug a saucer to put it in, and levelled the first floor with the ground'.

57. Robert Morris, *An Essay in Defence of Ancient Architecture* (1728), p. 71. For country seats the storeys should be arranged with 'the Ground or Basement for Conveniency or Use, the State for Pleasure and Delight, and the Attick for Sleep and Retirement, or Study'.

58. Ibid, p. 74. 'The Ancients had always a peculiar regard to discharge the exterior Walls from the Weight of the other necessary parts belonging, that they always made their inner or partition Walls when any considerable distance from each other of a Magnitude equal, if not larger than those of the exterior Part.'

59. It is of some interest in this connection that the first Duke of Argyll died at his property, Chirton House, near North Shields in Northumberland. In 1703 the house was sold and passed out of the Argyll family. See *Procs. of the Soc. of Antiquaries* (Newcastle), 3rd Series, Vol. I (1903–4), p. 41.

60. L. Whistler, *The Imagination of Vanbrugh and His Fellow Artists* (1954), pp. 156–7, 174.

61. Fleming, op. cit., pp. 255, 367.

62. Whistler, op. cit., pp. 212–16; Colvin, op. cit., p. 637.

63. Ibid, p. 395.

64. Whistler, op. cit., pl. 73.

65. Ibid, pl. 72.

66. H. Colvin and M. Craig, 'Architectural Drawings in the Library of Elton Hall'. *Roxburghe Club* (1964), pl. XXXVIb, Drawing No. 79. See also pl. XXXV and pp. xxvii–xxviii.

67. Whistler, op. cit., p. 196.

68. Colvin, op. cit., p. 396; N. Pevsner, *Wiltshire* (1963), p. 272.

69. Morris, op. cit., p. 21.

70. N. Pevsner, 'Good King James's Gothic'. *A.R.*, Vol. 107 (1950), pp. 117–18.

71. Cruden, op. cit., p. 61.

72. Whistler, ibid.

73. S. Toy, *The Castles of Great Britain* (1966), pp. 213–14.

V

1. K. Clark, *Gothic Revival* (1964), p. 34.

2. H. Walpole, *A Description of The Villa of Mr Horace Walpole*. (1969), p. iv.

3. Ibid, pp. 1–2.

4. Clark, op. cit., pp. 22–31, 59.

5. Walpole, op. cit., p. iv.

6. J. Summerson, *Architecture in Britain, 1530–1830* (1963), pp. 240–1; Clark, op. cit., pp. 46–7.

7. Walpole, op. cit., pp. 52, 53; S.M., Vol. XXII, Drawing 227. 'Chimney Piece for the Honble Horace Walpole 1766.'

8. C. Hussey, *The Picturesque* (1927), p. 5.

9. Summerson, ibid.

10. Clark, op. cit., p. 52. Referring to the use of substitute materials at Strawberry Hill he states that 'Walpole killed craftsmanship'.

11. G. Brenan, *History of the House of Percy* (1902), Vol. II, p. 418.

12. Ibid, Vol. II, p. 421.

13. Ibid, Vol. II, p. 436.

14. Ibid, Vol. II, p. 428.

15. Ibid, Vol. II, p. 437.

16. Ibid, Vol. II, p. 442.

17. Ibid, Vol. II, p. 443.

18. Sykes, *Tracts* (1829).

19. A. C. S. Dixon, 'The Restoration of Alnwick Castle, 1750–86', p. 7. Unpublished B.Arch. dissertation, School of Architecture, University of Newcastle-upon-Tyne. 1960.

20. 'Alnwick Described.' *G.M.*, Vol. XXVI (Feb. 1756), p. 73; A. Bolton, *The Architecture of Robert and James Adam* (1922), Vol. I, p. 41.

21. G. Tate, *History of Alnwick* (1868–9), Vol. I, p. 357.

22. Quoted by Bolton, op. cit., Vol. I, p. 253; W. Hutchinson, *View of Northumberland* (1778), Vol. II, p. 205. 'The castle was become quite a ruin.'

23. *G.M.*, ibid.

24. Tate, ibid.

25. N. Pevsner, *Northumberland* (1957), p. 69.

26. Bolton, ibid.

27. *G.M.*, ibid.

28. Quoted by Sykes, op. cit., as being 'occasioned by the Earl and Countess's visit to Alnwick, in 1750, and his Lordship's design of repairing the Castle there'.

29. An unsigned and undated drawing at Alnwick Castle may be this room. Northumberland MSS.

30. J. Fleming, *Robert Adam and His Circle* (1962), pp. 263, 369, credits Paine with the authorship of these Alnwick rooms. For Benwell Tower, the Northumberland property of Robert Shafto, Paine designed, on stylistic evidence at least, the intricate Gothic facade for the 'Temple for the Mount in the Garden'. The drawing was pasted into Shafto's memoranda book with its sketches, probably by the owner, for numerous estate buildings such as the castellated hen-house and the seat, for the 'Fan Grove', thatched and lined inside with moss and paved with bones. Shafto's book also contains plans for additions to Benwell Tower, 'according to Mr.

Payne' (sic). Whether the changes were made or the estate buildings erected, it is impossible to say, NRO, MBE III/1. After Shafto's death the estate was sold by his daughter in 1781 and by 1811 the tower was in ruins. NRO, MBE/V/3,6a.

31. Sykes, op. cit.

32. Dixon, op. cit., p. 32.

33. W. Ryle Elliot, 'The Work of Robert Adam in Northumberland', *A.A.*, Vol. XXX, 4th Series (1952), p. 110.

34. Ibid; Dixon, op. cit., p. 33.

35. Ryle Elliot, ibid, says, 'The buildings within the inner and outer baileys were removed in 1755' but gives no evidence for this dating.

36. In 1773 part of a bill, now at Alnwick Castle, U.I. 46, submitted to the Duke from Robert and James Adam included the following: 'June 26th To a design for the Stable with a Groind Ceiling, a quarter done in Lines—£5 5s 0d.
'June 29. To another design for the Stable with a flat Ceiling a quarter done in Lines only.—£2 2s 0d.
'To a Cornice for the Stables at full size.—£0 5s 0d'.
As there is no further record or mention of such designs it is likely that they were never carried out.
See too Dixon, op. cit., p. 28.

37. Tate, op. cit., Vol. I, p. 374.

38. S.M., Vol. XI, no. 30. 'Ceiling of Circular Room at Alnwick. Janry 1770.' (A section of Vol. XXXIX, no. 39.)
Vol. XXVII, no. 39. 'Impost for the Circular Room at Alnwick.'
Vol. XXXIX, no. 10. 'Part of the Section of the Circular Room at Alnwick. Duke of Northumberland' and no. 13, 'Ceiling of Alnwick Castle for the Duke of Northumberland.' Vol. XI, no. 29. 'Ceiling of Alnwick Castle for the Duke of Northumberland.'
In addition there are at Alnwick

351

Castle coloured drawings of the ceiling, the frieze and one section.

39. R. Warner, *A Tour Through the Northern Counties of England* (1802), Vol. II, p. 19.

40. A. Rowan: 'Gothick Restoration at Raby Castle'. *Architectural History. Journal of the Society of Architectural Historians of Great Britain*, Vol. XV (1972), p. 29. Memorandum by James Paine, 'Observations upon the intended alterations and additions at Raby Castle', 13 April, 1771 in which he refers to Alnwick Castle where 'the forms of all those rooms arose chiefly from the plan of the old castle.'

41. Bolton: op. cit., Vol. I, pp. 232, 236.

42. 'Obituary; with Anecdotes of remarkable Persons.' *G.M.*, Vol. LXXXII, Pt. I (June 1812), p. 601; H. Colvin, *A Biographical Dictionary of English Architects, 1660–1840* (1954), p. 540.

43. Bolton, op. cit., Vol. I, p. 232.

44. D. Stroud, *Capability Brown* (1950), pp. 47–9.

45. Bolton, op. cit., Vol. I, p. 41.

46. Ibid.

47. Hutchinson, op. cit., Vol. II, p. 206; Jones, *Views of the Seats . . . of Noblemen and Gentlemen* (1829) Vol. II.

48. Bolton, op. cit., Vol. I, p. 43. 'The mention of James Paine is singular, because if correct, it would appear that Robert Adam was working with him earlier than their meeting at Kedleston.'

49. Ibid, Vol. I, p. 253.

50. *Procs of Soc. of Antiquaries* (Newcastle), Vol. VIII (1899), p. 77.

51. Bolton, ibid.

52. J. Greig (ed.), *The Diaries of a Duchess* (1926), p. 3. 18 Sept. 1752.

53. Ibid, p. 8.

54. Ibid, p. 13. 23 July 1760.

55. Ibid, p. 22. 8 Aug. 1760.

56. M. A. Richardson, *Local Historian's Table Book* (1841–6), Vol. II, p. 231; Pevsner, op. cit., p. 72.

57. Accounts from Walle and Reilly for 1768 and 1769. Northumberland MSS. U.I. 27 (2).

58. The earliest dated drawings in the Soane Museum which relate to Alnwick are marked 1769. They are chimney-piece designs for the saloon, drawing-room and library. Vol. XXII, nos 50–54.

59. J. Wallis, *Antiquities of Northumberland* (1769), Vol. II, p. 381.

60. T. Pennant, *A Tour in Scotland, 1769* (1790), p. 42; A. Young, *A Six Months' Tour* (1771), Vol. II, p. 29. Of Alnwick Castle he writes '. . . most of it new built by the present Duke, and not yet finished'.

61. Rowan, op. cit. Paine memorandum.

62. Dixon, op. cit., p. 35.

63. Northumberland MSS.

64. Bolton, op. cit., Vol. I, p. 286.

65. Hutchinson, op. cit., Vol. II, p. 205.

66. S.M., Vol. XXVII, no. 37 and Vol. XXXIX, no. 14, 'Section of one of the apartments in Alnwick Castle', are precursors for the final design in Vol. XXXIX, no. 16, 'Chimney side of the Saloon at Alnwick Castle. The Duke of Northumberland.'

67. Dixon, ibid.

68. Hutchinson, ibid.

69. S.M., Vol. XXII, no. 50. 'Design of a Chimney Piece for the Salon at Alnwick Castle. 1769.'

70. Dixon, op. cit., pp. 38–9.

71. S.M., Vol. XXXIX, no. 15. 'Section in Alnwick Castle the Duke of Northumberland.'

72. Bolton, op. cit., Vol. I, p. 269.

73. S.M., Vol. XXII, no. 52. 'Chimney Piece for the drawing room at Alnwick Castle. 1769.'

74. Ibid, Vol. XXII, no. 53. 'Design of a Chimney Piece for the Drawing Room at Alnwick Castle. 1769.'

75. Ibid, Vol. XXII, no. 51. 'Drawing Room Chimney Piece for Alnwick Castle, 1769.'

76. Hutchinson, op. cit., Vol. II, p. 206.

77. Plan and section of window wall. Northumberland MSS.
78. Ibid, Vol. XI, no. 29.
79. Dixon, op. cit., p. 41.
80. Ibid.
81. Hutchinson, ibid.
82. S.M., Vol. XXIV, no. 212. 'Library at Alnwick.'
83. Ibid, Vol. XXXIX, no. 12. 'Side of a Room and Chimney in Alnwick Castle for the Duke of Northumberland.'
84. Dixon, op. cit., p. 43.
85. Hutchinson, ibid; T. Rose, *Westmorland, Cumberland, Durham & Northumberland*. (1832), Vol. I, p. 7.
86. J. Greig (ed.): *The Farington Diary* (1923), Vol. I, p. 320. Entry for 15 Sept. 1801.
87. S.M., Vol. XXVII, no. 38.
88. Ibid, Vol. XXXIX, no. 19. 'Design for finishing the Pannells in the Chapel at Alnwick containing the Pedigrees of the Family proposed to be partly done in Stucco and partly in Painting. R. Adam Archt. 1777.'
89. Ibid, Vol. XVII, no. 201. 'Carpet for the Circular Recess or Pew in the Chapel at Alnwick Castle. N.B. The whole of the original was finished 5th Decr., 1780.' (The drawing shows only one segment in colour.)
90. Ibid, Vol. XVII, no. 202. 'Design of a Carpet for the Chapel at Alnwick Castle, in two different ways. One full half of the Original finished. Adelphi. 5th Decr. 1780.'
91. Dixon, op. cit., p. 47, suggests on evidence from Wadel's description of 1785 that a cheaper floor covering was used for the chapel although in the family's recess there was a very fine carpet.
92. Hutchinson, ibid; Rose: ibid.
93. S.M., Vol. XXXIX, no. 18. 'Castle of Alnwick Chaple. Duke of Northumberland.'
94. 'March 9 1774. Mr. James Pearsons Agreemt. for Chapel Windows.' At Alnwick Castle.
95. 'His Grace the Duke of Northumberland To Robert and James Adam For Designs For Alnwick.' It includes, '1773 Dec. 22d. To Two Different Designs for Painting the Chaple Window £10:10:0.' Northumberland MSS.
96. 'To James Pearson Dr. Jan. 7 and March 1780.' Northumberland MSS. U.I. 46.
97. 'His Grace the Duke of Northumberland for Materials made use of and Mens time employed in repairing, Painting, Gilding and Ornamenting the Chaple at Alnwick Castle from February 1780 to March 1781.' Northumberland MSS.
98. Ibid, Vol. L, no. 21.
99. Ibid, Vol. LI, no. 35. 'Design of a Bridge proposed to be Built at Alnwick. One of the Seats of His Grace the Duke of Northumberland.' A smaller elevation is at Alnwick Castle as well as the account, 'His Grace the Duke of Northumberland To Robert and James Adam For Designs for Alnwick'. Northumberland MSS., U.I. 46.
100. Richardson, op. cit., Vol. II, p. 222; Pevsner, ibid.
101. Stroud, op. cit., pp. 140–1.
102. Colvin, op. cit., pp. 399–403; Dixon, op. cit., p. 56; Pevsner, ibid, gives Adam the credit for the Denwick Bridge but adduces no evidence.
103. *H. of N.*, Vol. XV, p. 266; J. Fleming, 'Adam Gothic', *Connoisseur*, Vol. CXLII (Oct. 1958), p. 78; Pevsner, op. cit., p. 199.
104. J. Hodgson, *Northumberland* (1813), p. 139.
105. Fleming, ibid, quotes an old account, 'In 1780 the east part of the castle was built, and soon after it the west part to an equal height. The stable block to the north was built some years later.'
106. Ibid, and gives the date as 1779.

107. S.M., Vol. XXXIX, no. 22. 'Gateway for Alnwick Castle the Seat of His Grace the Duke of Northumberland'; see also Pevsner, op. cit., p. 72.

108. S.M., Vol. XXXIX, no. 20. 'Elevation of a Building proposed to be erected upon the top of a Rock near Alnwick Castle, One of the seats of His Grace the Duke of Northumberland. Adelphi, 21st Nov. 1783.'
The Alnwick Castle drawing is 'Elevation of a Building proposed to be erected on the top of a Ridge of Rocks near Alnwick Castle. The part shaded light already executed by the Duke of Northumberland. Robt. Adam Archt. Invt. Deluit. 1784.' Northumberland MSS.

109. S.M., Vol. XXXIX, no. 21. 'Another Elevation of a Building proposed to be built on the top of a Rock near Alnwick by his Grace the Duke of Northumberland.'
The Alnwick Castle version is 'Plan and Elevation of a Monastik Building for His Grace the Duke of Northumberland and proposed to stand on a Ridge of Rocks near Alnwick Castle. Designed and Drawn by Robt. Adam Archt. 1784.' Northumberland MSS.

110. S.M., Vol. XIX, no. 156, 'Design of a Tower for Briesley'; no. 157, 'Diagonal Front of the Tower for Briesley'; no. 158, 'Section of the Tower for Briesley. 18th Nov. 1777.' At Alnwick Castle there are two copies of each of these drawings. See also Pevsner, ibid.

111. 'To Robert and James Adam'. It details work from August, 1777 to July, 1778. Northumberland MSS.

112. 'An Estimation of the Mason work, for the Tower at Briesley Hill . . . by Robt. Shepherd, Ed. Bruce and John Sinclair.' Northumberland MSS.

113. 'Prices of Different Sorts of work for a tower Intended to be Built at Briesley . . . by Matthew Mills.' Northumberland MSS. See too A. Dixon, op. cit., p. 67.

114. 'To Robert and James Adam. May 28, 1779 to April 16, 1785.' Northumberland MSS.

115. 'His Grace the Duke of Northumberland To Jos. and Jos. Rose. May 29th, 1777.' Northumberland MSS., U.I. 46. Another plasterer who may have done work at Alnwick was William Staniforth who on several occasions in the years 1774, 1777 and 1787 wrote to Sir John Hussey Delaval from Alnwick Castle. NRO., Delaval (Waterford) MSS., 2 DE 5/8/4, 9, 10, 15.

116. Richardson, op. cit., Vol. II, p. 281.

117. Fleming, op. cit., p. 76, is quoting from E. Mackenzie: *View of Northumberland* (1825); Parson and White, *Gazetteer of Durham and Northumberland* (1827), Vol. I, p. 386.

118. W. Stukeley, *Itinerarium Curiosum* (1776).

119. W. Davison, *A Descriptive and Historical View of Alnwick* (1822), p. 284.

120. Pevsner, op. cit., pp. 196–7.

121. Hutchinson, op. cit., Vol. II, p. 249, 'the tower a square building with exploratory turrets at each corner, is in good repair'. However, Brown did build stables at Burghley House with round-headed windows and at Tong Castle, 1765, a gazebo has an affinity with the Hulne Priory oriel. See Stroud, op. cit., pp. 41, 209; Colvin, op. cit., pp. 101–2.

122. 'To George Davy for Artificial Stone. Oct. 5, 1773.' Northumberland MSS., U.I. 28 (2).

123. Stroud, op. cit., p. 209.

REFERENCES

VI

1. K. Clark, *The Gothic Revival* (1964), p. 68.
2. *Burke's Peerage, Baronetage and Knightage* (1970), p. 1,651.
3. A. Bolton, *The Architecture of Robert and James Adam* (1922), Vol. II, Index of Clients' Names, p. 78.
4. These designs are dated and signed 'Robt. Adam, Architect', CRO., Lonsdale MSS., Scarlet portfolio, 8 and 9.
   N. Pevsner, *Cumberland and Westmorland* (1967), p. 274; Bolton, op. cit., Vol. I, p. 65, wrongly describes the Lowther village layout as Whitehaven.
5. The drawings, each 14 by 20 inches, include five plans, a roof section and a section through the house. All but one are signed and dated, 'Robt. Adam 1766'. In addition, there is an unsigned and undated sheet of window details. Entitled 'Part of the Plan of the Window at Large', it belongs demonstrably to the same group as the dated designs. CRO., Lonsdale MSS., Blue portfolio. In the Soane Museum, drawings also relate to Whitehaven. In Vol. XXXIII, nos 59 and 60 are elevations of the west and north fronts. No. 61 indicates the enlargement and regularisation of the old house by Adam and this can be compared with the 'Plan of the Ground Storey' in the Lonsdale series which is subscribed, 'N.B. These parts shaded dark shews what is new and those of a lighter colour is what remains of the old building'.
   Bolton, ibid, makes no distinction between the castles of Lowther and Whitehaven.
   J. Swarbrick, *Robert Adam and His Brothers* (1916), p. 218 merely says of the family's operations for Sir James Lowther, 'It is by no means improbable that they carried out work at Penrith Castle and Whitehaven Castle'.
   Pevsner, op. cit., p. 205.
6. S.M., Vol. XI, no. 261. 'Ceiling for the Dining room for Sir James Lowther's House at Whitehaven. 1769.' The design was a rectangle with a central circle and partially coloured blue semi-circles on the short sides. The remaining area was of lozenges of pale pink and green with the latter containing large paterae.
   Vol. LIII, no. 30 is uncoloured friezes of a classical design and typical of that era in Adam's London career which marked the emergence of the famous Adam style.
7. S.M., Vol. XI, no. 262.
8. J. Hodgson, *A Topographical and Historical Description of the County of Westmoreland* (1823), p. 124; T. Rose, *Westmorland and Cumberland* (1823), Vol. I, p. 38; Pevsner, op. cit., p. 272.
9. Of the numerous drawings for this proposal one is dated 1764. CRO., Lonsdale MSS.
10. The drawings are signed and dated. CRO., Lonsdale MSS., Maroon portfolio, 17–19.
11. It is signed. Lonsdale MSS., Maroon portfolio, 21.
12. Lonsdale MSS., Maroon portfolio, 32, 33.
13. Lonsdale MSS., Maroon portfolio, 29.
14. Ibid, 30.
15. R. Adam, *Ruins of the Palace of Spalatro* (1764), p. 2.
16. Ibid, pl. IV et passim.
17. J. Fleming, *Robert Adam and his Circle* (1962), p. 310. Clérisseau remarked to James Adam that Robert was 'very ignorant of architecture when he came to me, except the Gothic: but I put him off that and gave him some taste for the antique'. See also J. Fleming, 'An Italian Sketchbook by Robert Adam, Clérisseau and Others', *Connoisseur* Vol. CXLVI (Nov. 1960), p. 191.
18. Adam, op. cit., pls XVII, XX, XXVIII.

19. W. Hutchinson, *View of Northumberland* (1778), Vol. II, p. 206.

20. J. Fleming, 'A "Retrospective View" by John Clerk of Eldin, with some Comments on Adam's Castle Style' *Concerning Architecture*, ed. by Sir J. Summerson, p.76. Also J. Fleming, 'Robert Adam's Castle Style'. *C.L.*, Vol. CXLIII (23 May 1968) pp. 1, 356–9. For a comprehensive analysis of Adam's castle style see A. Rowan, 'The Adam Castle Style'. *Journal of the Royal Society of Arts*, Vol. CXXII (Sept. 1974), pp. 679–94.

21. This is clear from an incomplete essay on architectural theory by James Adam quoted by J. Fleming, *Robert Adam and his Circle* (1962), p. 316.

22. 'To the Rev. Mr. Lionel Seaman.' *G.M.*, Vol. XVI (Feb. 1746), p. 100.

23. 'Celtic Animadversions on Gothic Reflexions.' Ibid, Vol. LX (July 1790), p. 604.

24. A. Young, *A Six Months' Tour* (1771), Vol. II, p. 396.

25. 'Observations on Gothic Buildings.' *G.M.*, Vol. XXVIII (Nov. 1758), pp. 517–9.

26. 'Remarks on Gothic Buildings'. *G.M.*, Vol. LII (Oct. 1782), pp. 480–2.

27. Ibid.

28. H. Walpole, 'Anecdotes of Painting', Vol. I, p. 181. Quoted in *G.M.*, Vol. LIII (May 1783), pp. 375–6.

29. A. H. Millar, *Castles and Mansions of Renfrewshire and Buteshire* (1889).

30. Bolton, op. cit., Vol. I, p. 49. This drawing is S.M., Vol. XXI, no. 228.

31. Bolton, ibid, Vol. I, pp. 60–1.

32. Adam, op. cit.

33. Bolton, op. cit., Vol. I, p. 116. Also quoted in full in 'Selections from the Family Papers Preserved at Caldwell'. *Maitland Club*, Part II, Vol. II, pp. 78–9.

34. S.M., Vol. XLII, nos 7 and 8.

35. *D.N.B.*

36. Caldwell Papers, op. cit., p. 195, Lord Bute to Baron Mure, London, 25 Feb. 1772; Bolton, op. cit., Vol. I, p. 69.

37. Caldwell Papers, op. cit., p. 208, Robert Adam to Baron Mure on 1 Dec. 1772; Bolton, op. cit., Vol. I, p. 118.

38. Caldwell Papers, op. cit., p. 210, letter of Robert Adam to Baron Mure of 28 Dec. 1772; Bolton, ibid.

39. S.M., Vol. XXXVII, nos 70, 71, 72.

40. The foundation stone is dated 11 Sep. 1725. The central block was to have been very much in William Adam's late manner and would have been similar to Pollok House in Glasgow.

41. S.M., Vol. XII, nos 59, 60, 61. There is a client's copy of the last drawing at Mellerstain. It is inscribed, 'Adelphi, 5th Aug., 1775'. See also Bolton, op. cit., Vol. II, p. 258.

42. M. Girouard, 'Mellerstain, Berwickshire'. *C.L.*, Vol. CXXIV (4 Sept. 1958), p. 479.

43. S.M., Vol. XII, nos 62, 63, 64; Bolton, ibid.

44. Ibid; *C.L.*, ibid (28 Aug. 1958), p. 417.

45. The Home-Robertson MSS. include payments to James Nisbet for superintending the building at Wedderburn, 1770–5. By 1775 the cost of the house was £8,276 with an additional £3,724 being estimated for finishing the inside and for furnishings. A. Rowan, 'Wedderburn Castle, Berwickshire'. *The Country Seat* ed. by H. Colvin and J. Harris (1970), pp. 174–7; J. Dunbar, *Historic Architecture of Scotland*, p. 125; A. Rowan, 'Paxton House, Berwickshire' *C.L.*, Vol. CXLII (24 Aug. 1967), p. 424; A. Rowan, 'Wedderburn Castle, Berwickshire'. *C.L.*, Vol. CLVI (8 Aug. 1974), pp. 354–7.

46. S.M., Vol. XXXVII, nos 78–80. *The Country Seat*, ibid.

47. Adam, op. cit., pl. X.

48. 'Earl of Cassilis'. *G.M.*, Vol. LXIII, Pt. I (Jan. 1793), p. 34.

49. J. Fergusson, *History of Modern Archi-*

tecture (1902), Vol. II, p. 97.

50. *G.M.,* ibid.

51. SRO., Ailsa MSS., GD 25, Section 9, Boxes 9 and 10.

52. Discharged account by Hugh Cairncross for the years 1777–81. SRO, GD 25/9/9. In another document, dated 17 Nov. 1779, he is described as the 'Undertaker of the new building at Cullean'. SRO, GD 25/9/9.

53. 'Account book of Hugh Cairncross, clerk of the works for Lord Cassilis, 1787–92.' SRO., GD 25/9/10.

54. William Key charged £29 6s 7d on 29 July 1777, £48 11s 8d eleven months later and a further £1 4s 11d on 12 Feb. 1780. For removing old walls his charge was £3 14s 10d. SRO, GD 25/9/9.

55. The masons in an account of 14 March 1778 were John McGlover and Andrew Morton. SRO, GD /9/9.

56. Account of 20 [ ] 1779 from John McCrorie. SRO, GD 25/9/9.

57. S.M., Vol. XXI, no. 6.

58. Bolton, op. cit., Vol. II, p. 263.

59. The eating-room is dated 1779 in S.M., Vol. XIV, no. 90, The drawing-room ceiling is dated 11 April 1780 in S.M., Vol. XIV, no. 61.

60. A. T. Bolton: 'Culzean Castle, Ayr.' *C.L.,* Vol. XXXVIII (11 Sept. 1915), p. 360.

61. S.M., Vol. XXXVII, nos 11 and 10.

62. RIBA, Drawings' Collection, L 12/5.

63. T. Whately: *Observations on Modern Gardening* (1770), p. 75. See also R. Macaulay, *Pleasure of Ruins* (1966), p. 26; E. W. Manwaring, *Italian Landscape in Eighteenth Century England* (1965), pp. 146–7.

64. Quoted by Bolton: op. cit., Vol. II, p. 274.

65. S.M., Vol. XXXVII, nos 3–8. Nos 4 and 5 are dated '4th May, 1787'. The two tiers of staircase capitals seem to have been carved by William Cleland from Edinburgh who spent a hundred and twenty days carving capitals and was paid £35 14s 0d in August 1789. In the previous month P. M. Van Gelder was paid £14 19s 7d for 'a Statuary Marble Mantle and Jamb Chimney Piece with wood dressing carved'. It is probably the one in the round drawing-room. The majority of chimney-pieces were carved by the mason Peter Henderson with William Cairncross, perhaps a brother of the clerk of works, carving wooden ones for the bedrooms. From Hugh Cairncross's account book it seems that the enlargement of Culzean after 1787 cost £7,353 1s 1½d with repairs to Cassilis House and Kirkmichael Church being additional. SRO, GD 25/9/10/I, II, IVA, VIII.

66. S.M., Vol. XXXVII, no. 9.

67. Ibid, no. 1.

68. Oxenfoord Castle in Midlothian was an old house remodelled by Robert Adam in the early eighties for Sir John Dalrymple. In 1841 it was redone and enlarged by William Burn. See W. Angus, *Seats of the Nobility and Gentry* (1787); H. H. Dalrymple, *An Account of Oxenfoord Castle* (1901), pp. 50–51; T. Hannan, *Famous Scottish Houses* (1928), p. 141; A. Rowan, 'Oxenfoord Castle, Midlothian.' *C.L.,* Vol. CLVI (15 Aug. 1974), pp. 430–33. S.M., Vol. XXX, nos 126–9 are dated Adelphi, 29 July 1780 and show the existence of a tower-house which doubtless accounts for the unusual height of the central portion. In March 1782 designs were made for the library and drawing-room ceilings and are in S.M., Vol. XIV, nos 80, 81.

69. Fleming, op. cit., pp. 5, 101–102 et passim.

70. S.M., Vol. XIX, nos 76, 78, 84 and are dated Feb. 1777. Bolton, op. cit., Vol. I, p. 13.

71. S.M., Vol. XIX, no. 161, 'Tower for Richard Oswald Esqr at Auchincrue

19 June 1778'. Nos 160, 159, 162 are a section and plans.
A. Oswald: 'Auchincruive, Ayrshire', *C.L.*, Vol. LXXII, (17 Dec. 1932), p. 695, gives the date of the tower as 1780. Also A. Rowan, 'Robert Adam's Last Castles'. *C.L.*, Vol. CLVI (22 Aug. 1974), p. 495.

72. The drawing is no. 129 in a volume of drawings in the Clerk of Penicuik collection. See J. Fleming, 'An Italian Sketchbook by Robert Adam, Clérisseau and Others', *Connoisseur*, Vol. CXLVI (Nov. 1960), p. 193.

73. S.M., Vol. XXXI, no. 43. 'Plan of the Principal Story of Dalquharran Castle the Seat of Thomas Kennedy of Dunure. Adelphi, 6th April, 1785.'
See also nos 39–44. The stable designs were altered in 1789, Vol. XXXI, no. 49, when designs for chimney-pieces were produced in Vol. XXIII, no. 184. Rowan, ibid, p. 496.

74. Dunbar, op. cit., p. 126; Rowan, ibid, pp. 496–97.

75. S.M., Vol. XXX, no. 85. 'The East Front of Stobs Castle the Seat of Sir William Eliott Bart. Albemarle Street 28th Jan., 1792.' See also nos 86, 89–91. The old castle of Stobs had been destroyed by fire at some date prior to 1770. The Adam castle was completed in 1793 and three years later Sir William Eliott wrote, suggesting extensive alterations, to the architect William (sic) Elliot. Dowager Lady Eliott of Stobs and Sir Arthur Eliott of Stobs, *The Elliots. The Story of a Border Clan* (1974), pp. 103, 105. See below ch. XI, refs. 70, 87. Also Rowan, ibid, p. 497.

76. F. Grose, *Antiquities of Scotland* (1789), Vol. I, pl. opp. p. 64.

77. S.M., Vol. XLVIII, nos 75–87. None of the drawings is dated or signed.

78. A. Haldane, *Memoirs of the Lives of Robert Haldane of Airthrey and of his brother James Alexander Haldane* (1852), p. 39.

79. Ibid, p. 98.

80. J. Fleming, 'Seton Castle's Debt to Ancient Rome', *C.L.*, Vol. CXLIII (30 May 1968), p. 1,444.

81. Ibid.

82. Bolton, op. cit., Vol. II, p. 197.

83. 'Copy Contract for Building Seton Castle between Alexander Mackenzie Esqr and Adam and Thomas Russel, Signed by them 12 Novr., 1789.' SRO, Clerk of Penicuik MSS., GD 18/4965.

84. S.M., Vol. XXXIII, nos 90–6. They are dated December 1789 from Albemarle Street.

85. Fleming, ibid.

86. Bolton, op. cit., Vol. II, p. 200n.
S.M., Vol. XXIX, no. 8 a main elevation is signed by Robert Adam and dated 1791, nos 10 and 11 plans of the principal floor from Edinburgh on 12 April 1792, no. 12 'Bed chamber St., Albemarle St., 11th Augt., 1792', no. 13 'Joisting for principal storey. Edinburgh, 28th June, 1792', no. 14 drainage plan, no. 15 the elevation of the offices from Albemarle St. on 22 Aug. 1795, no. 16 a plan of the same date and address.
After Robert Adam's death in March, 1792 continuity was maintained at Mauldslie first by James and latterly by William Adam after the death of James in 1794.

87. Bolton, 'The Classical and Romantic Compositions of Robert Adam', *A.R.*, Vol. 57 (Jan. 1925), p. 28 *et al.* *RIBAJ.*, Vol. XL, 3rd Series (10 Dec. 1932) frontispiece; P. Oppé, 'Robert Adam's Picturesque Compositions', *Burlington Magazine*, Vol. LXXX (March 1942), pp. 56–59; A. A. Tait, *Robert Adam in Scotland. The Picturesque Drawings* (1972).

88. J. Fleming, *Robert Adam and his Circle* (1963), p. 81.

89. 'Biographical Account of the late Robert Adam, Esq. Architect.' *Scots*

Magazine, Vol. LXV (May 1803), p. 8.

90. Quoted by C. Hussey, *The Picturesque* (1927), p. 193.

91. Quoted by N. Pevsner, *Outline of European Architecture* (1961), pp. 266–7.

92. Fleming, op. cit., p. 315.

93. S.M., Vol. XXXI, nos 49 and 51, inscribed 'Albemarle St., 2nd Jan., 1789'.

94. Grose, ibid.

95. *V.S.*, pl. 51.

96. S.M., Vol. XXXIV, nos 79–85. The drawings are dated 1793, that is the year succeeding Robert Adam's death, and are probably by James Adam. It is clear that they are based on earlier studies, S.M., Vol. I, nos 112, 113. On 1 September 1790, Adam, while in Edinburgh, drew up a 'Particular description of Building and finishing an addition to Clunie Castle, Aberdeenshire', and estimated the cost to be £2,724 8s 8½d. SRO, Clerk of Penicuik MSS., GD 18/4965.

Bolton, *The Architecture of Robert and James Adam* (1922), Vol. II, Index of Adam Drawings, p. 7, erroneously refers to the Perthshire Clunie Castle.

VII

Unless otherwise stated correspondence relating to Ford Castle is in the Northumberland County Record Office, Delaval (Waterford) MSS.

1. Letter from M. Coulthurst to Sir John Hussey Delaval, 20 Nov. 1761. Quoted in *Procs of Soc. of Antiquaries* (Newcastle), 4th Series, Vol. IX (1934–41), p. 264.

2. W. Ryle Elliot, 'The Work of Robert Adam in Northumberland', *A.A.*, 4th Series, Vol. XXX (1952), p. 109, says, 'About 1760 there were designs for the interior of Ford Castle'. However, *Procs of Soc. of Antiquaries* (Newcastle), Vol. V (1893), p. 62, gives 1761 as the commencing date and this is repeated in *H. of N.*, Vol. XI, p. 416.

3. A. Bolton, *The Architecture of Robert and James Adam* (1922), Vol. II, Index of Clients, p. 68. Sir John was created a Baronet in 1761 and in 1783 was raised to the peerage as Baron Delaval of Redford, Co. Wicklow and in the peerage of the United Kingdom, Baron Seaton Delaval, Co. Northumberland.

Bolton mistakenly gives the date of Lord Delaval's death as 1783. In fact he died in 1801 when the honours became extinct.

4. *H. of N.*, ibid.

5. Ibid.

6. NRO, Delaval (Waterford) MSS. They include letters and accounts for alterations and decorations to Sir John's house in Hanover Square, London, by Robert and James Adam and other contractors, including the agreement with Robert and James Adam (1781) and one letter and accounts from Robert Adam (1780–2). 2 DE 23/2/1–24.

Also an account book for alterations by Robert, James and William Adam and other contractors for alterations at Claremont House, Milbourne Place and a town property in Portland Place and Conduit Street, 1789–90. 2 DE 23/3.

The letter referred to above must be that quoted verbatim in *Procs of Soc. of Antiquaries* (Newcastle), 4th Series, Vol. IX (1934–41), p. 266 and dated 19 Aug. 1780.

See also Bolton, op. cit., Vol. II, Topographical Index, pp. 7, 36, 39, 53, 68.

7. Delaval (Waterford) MSS. Corres-

pondence of William Portisland, agent at Doddington, for rebuilding the church (2 DE 20/6/1–30) and of William Lumby, architect, for alterations to the Hall, 1786–8 (2 DE 21/2/1–68). H. Colvin, *Biographical Dictionary of English Architects, 1660–1840* (1954), p. 371, records work on the Hall by Lumby in 1761–2.
See also F. Askham, *The Gay Delavals* (1955), p. 133; N. Pevsner and J. Harris, *Lincolnshire* (1964), p. 516.

8. *Procs of Soc. of Antiquaries* (Newcastle), Vol. V (1893), p. 62.

9. Ibid, p. 63; *H. of N.*, ibid.

10. *Procs of Soc. of Antiquaries* (Newcastle), ibid; Colvin, op. cit., p. 483.

11. Although the surname is spelt Nasbet, Nesbit and Nisbit the form Nisbet has been uniformly adopted in accordance with the architect's own spelling. The christian name occurs in a letter from Joseph Oxley, the chief land steward, to Sir John on 28 March 1772 (2 DE 4/10/55) and in Nisbet's account of 4 June 1773 (2 DE 18/1/13) as well as in other Nisbet documents.

12. Letter of Sir John Hussey Delaval to Nisbet on 24 Dec. 1771 (2 DE 18/1/9). See also the letters of James Nisbet of 18 January and 25 March 1771 to Sir John Hussey Delaval in which the former details his activities at Ford Castle. NRO, Society of Antiquaries, Newcastle-upon-Tyne, MSS, M17/29.

13. *H. of N.*, Vol. XI, p. 417; N. Pevsner, *Northumberland* (1957), p. 155.

14. *Procs of Soc. of Antiquaries* (Newcastle), ibid.

15. Ibid, p. 62; Hodgson, *Northumberland* (1813), p. 220, 'It was rebuilt by the late Lord Delaval in 1761'; W. Hutchinson, *View of Northumberland* (1778), Vol. II, p. 335, 'The work was begun in the year 1761, and completed in two or three years'; J. Wallis, *Antiquities of Northumberland* (1769),

Vol. II, p. 479, says the castle had been 'lately repaired after a handsome manner'. In addition a painting of c. 1765, besides showing the completed house, also depicts the medieval south east tower, which was demolised at some date prior to 1779 as it does not appear in a print of that year.

16. *H. of N.*, Vol. XI, p. 416.

17. Delaval (Waterford) MSS, correspondence of George Raffield. 2 DE/18. Correspondence of John Raffield, Joicey MSS, NRO, 429/8/3–5.

18. Inventory of household furniture, Feb. 1786, Joicey MSS, NRO, 429/4.

19. Letter of John Raffield, 8 Dec. 1771. 2 DE 18/4/3.

20. Letter of John Raffield, 15 April 1772. 2 DE 18/4/12.

21. Letter of Joseph Oxley to Sir John Hussey Delaval, 15 Aug. 1772. 2 DE 4/10/69.

22. Letter from Thomas Fitzwalter to Lord Delaval, 11 May 1806. 2 DE 4/51/39. According to John Raffield, in a letter to Sir John Hussey Delaval of 28 April 1769, the gallery was in the east tower. Joicey MSS, NRO, 429/8/1. In the 1786 inventory no mention is made of a gallery. It may be that it was in fact the Gothic hall next to the dining-room.

23. *H. of N.*, Vol. XI, p. 417.

24. Pevsner, ibid, says that the house was gothicised about 1761–5 and that from a letter it is known that Robert Adam had a hand in this. The letter cannot now be traced but may have been that, already mentioned, of 19 Aug. 1780.

25. Both among the Delaval (Waterford) MSS. 2 DE 18/1/28.

26. Letter of John Raffield, 8 Dec. 1771. 2 DE 18/4/3.

27. Letter of Joseph Oxley to Sir John Hussey Delaval from Ford Castle, 28 Dec. 1771. 2 DE 4/10/46.

28. Ibid to ibid, Ford Castle, 29 Dec. 1771. 2 DE 4/10/47.

REFERENCES

29. Letter of Sir John Hussey Delaval to Nisbet from Grosvenor House, 24 Dec. 1771. 2 DE 18/1/9. Francis Blake of Twizell (1708–80) was created a baronet in 1774. See *D.N.B.*

30. Letter from Nisbet to Joseph Oxley from Kelso, 1 Jan. 1772. 2 DE 18/1/9.

31. Letter to Sir John Hussey Delaval from Joseph Oxley, 3 Jan. 1772. 2 DE 18/1/9.

32. 2 DE 18/1/9, 8.

33. Letter of Nisbet to Sir John Hussey Delaval, 18 Jan. 1772. 2 DE 18/1/11.

34. Letter of Joseph Oxley to Nisbet from Ford Castle, 18 Jan. 1772. 2 DE 4/10/50.

35. Letter of Nisbet to Oxley, 1 Jan. 1772. 2 DE 18/1/9. Two and a half weeks later the former despatched a letter, couched in similar terms, to Sir John. 2 DE 18/1/11.

36. Letter of John Raffield, 24 Feb. 1772. 2 DE 18/4/8.

37. Joseph Oxley to Sir John Hussey Delaval, 28 March 1772. 2 DE 4/10/55.

38. Letter of John Raffield, 14 Feb. 1772. 2 DE 18/4/7.

39. Letter of John Raffield, 21 March 1772. 2 DE 18/4/10.

40. Nisbet to Sir John Hussey Delaval, 22 April 1772. 2 DE 18/1/12.

41. Letter of John Raffield, 9 May 1772. 2 DE 18/4/13.

42. Letter of Oxley to Sir John Hussey Delaval from Ford Castle, 29 Dec. 1771. 2 DE 4/10/48.

43. Account of Nisbet to Sir John Hussey Delaval, 4 June 1773. 2 DE 18/1/13. Also Hutchinson, ibid, in 1776 'the area is enclosed by a wall embrazured and garnished with Turrets'.

44. Letter of Nisbet to Sir John Hussey Delaval, 30 Jan. 1779. 2 DE 18/1/15.

45. In a letter to Lord Delaval dated 23 April 1793, James Nisbet's widow stated 'My Husband died about twelve years ago'. 2 DE/18/35.

46. Letter from Alexander Gilkie from Coldstream, 16 Oct. 1801, 2 DE 18/1/30.

47. *Procs of Soc. of Antiquaries* (Newcastle), Vol. V, p. 63; *H. of N.,* ibid; Pevsner, ibid; Colvin, op. cit., p. 237; C. Hussey, 'Ford Castle, Northumberland'; *C.L.,* Vol. LXXXIX (11 Jan. 1941), p. 34, says that the screen wall and gateway were built in about 1790 by Nisbet.

48. *H. of N.,* Vol. XIV, pp. 218, 224; Pevsner, op. cit., p. 157.

49. *H. of N.,* op. cit., p. 220.

50. Ryle Elliot, op. cit., pp. 114–17. On very dubious grounds he awards Adam the credit for the Fowberry decorations.

51. 'Obituary; with Anecdotes of Remarkable Persons', *G.M.,* Vol. LXXXII, Pt. I (June 1812), p. 601; Colvin, op. cit., p. 540.

52. In 1773 Nisbet with John Laidlaw and John Purves was preparing plans for Kelso Church. See RCAHMS, *Roxburghshire* (1956), Vol. I, p. 246.

53. *H. of N.,* Vol. IX, pp. 172–3, and Vol. XI, p. 402.

54. Letter of Sir John Hussey Delaval dated 24 Dec. 1771. 2 DE 18/1/9. In the Joicey MSS, an earlier letter, 19 April 1771, of John Raffield to Sir John states, '. . . for Mr. Nisbet and Mr. Blake is far from being friendly at present'. NRO, 429/8/3.

55. *H. of N.,* ibid, pp. 219, 224. The date of purchase was 1807.

56. Ibid, Vol. II, p. 168; Pevsner, op. cit., p. 135.

57. *Burke's Landed Gentry;* Vol. I (1965), p. 170.

58. Pevsner, op. cit., p. 82.

59. Wallis, op. cit., Vol. II, p. 452.

60. Among the papers of Colonel Horace St Paul of Ewart Park is a drawing, 'South View of Twysil (sic) Castle towards the River Till, as it was, before the New Castle was built'. On the bottom right hand corner is inscribed:

'Taken by Thomas Younger in 1786, 1787 or 1788'. NRO, Butler (Ewart) MSS, ZBU. B5/6/33.

61. Letter of Sir John Hussey Delaval to Nisbet, 24 Dec. 1771. 2 DE 18/1/9.

62. Sir Francis Blake (1738?–1818), second baronet, succeeded his father in the baronetcy in 1780. See *D.N.B.*

63. Pevsner, op. cit., p. 298 where it is stated that there is a cross on the east gable.

64. Wallis, op. cit., Vol. II, p. 458.

65. W. Hutchinson, *History and Antiquities of the County Palatine of Durham* (1794), Vol. III, p. 413.

66. A drawing, 'Twysell (sic) Castle as it was before the Alterations. South Front . . .' and dated 'Tilmouth, 3rd July, 1787' is among the papers of Colonel St Paul. NRO, ZBU. B5/6/32.

67. Hutchinson, op. cit., Vol. III, p. 414.

68. Blake (Twisel) MSS, NRO, 508/23. Pevsner, op. cit., p. 299, states that George Wyatt was working on Twizell Castle in 1812. Colvin, op. cit., p. 722, gives the information that George Wyatt, a pupil of James Wyatt from 1798 to 1800, altered Tarzell House in Northumberland for P. J. Selby, c. 1811.

69. Elevation 'The North View of Twisel (sic) Castle'. NRO, ZBU. B5/6/34.

70. Hutchinson, ibid.

71. *H. of N.*, Vol. XIV, pp. 185–7; Pevsner, op. cit., p. 150. The house was further enlarged to the west c. 1814 and in 1867.
Among the Butler (Ewart) MSS there are many plans and drawings relating to the Ewart estate. Some are dated either 1788 or 1789. The more grandiose ideas for the mansion were never realised and now, almost forgotten, it is one of the most charming of ruins. One proposal was for a castle with square angle towers and an oval one, containing the staircase, rising above the centre. The drawings (ZBU. B5/7/ 9–11) not only owe a debt to Inveraray Castle, of which there is a plate in the same volume, but also to Mellerstain. More specifically the notion of an oval shape rising through the centre of the house to appear above the roofline became typical of John Paterson. Although the drawings, of an elevation and several floors, are unsigned they belong to the project which Robert Adam drew up for Colonel St Paul in 1779. See Bolton, op. cit., Vol. II, Index of Adam Drawings, p. 57.
Other drawings are derived from one of Hampton Court in Herefordshire and show a gradual diminution in concept until finally the most modest version is given the porch from the Adam elevation. NRO, ZBU. B5/6/19, 18.

72. The tower at Ewart can be compared with the drawing, 'South View Twysil (sic) Castle . . .' NRO, ZBU. B5/ 6/33.

73. Pevsner, op. cit., p. 217.

74. Ibid, p. 284.

75. Ibid, p. 142. The Gothic work at Eachwick was most likely done by Ralph Spearman (1749–1823) a local antiquary commonly supposed to have been the original of Jonathan Oldback in Walter Scott's novel *The Antiquary*. Spearman probably inherited the estate on his mother's death in 1792. See *H. of N.*, Vol. XIII, p. 92.

76. Hodgson, op. cit., p. 214; Pevsner, op. cit., p. 282; *H. of N.*, Vol. XIV, p. 278, which credits the house, of a date before 1767, to Lancelot Coxon, an otherwise unknown architect, but who may have designed Killingworth Hall, also in Northumberland, for a member of the same family.

77. The stables are a smaller and less elaborate version of a scheme prepared in 1796 and inscribed on the back 'Mount Athelston by Shepherd'. Mount Athelston is on the Roddam

estate but the plan and elevations seem to have been adapted for a site nearer the Hall. The drawing is at Roddam Hall.

78. N. Pevsner, *County Durham* (1953), p. 56.

79. J. Paine, *Plans, Elevations and Sections of Noblemen and Gentlemen's Seats* (1767), Vol. I, Pls LVI–LX; Pevsner, op. cit., p. 43.

80. Ibid.

81. Ibid, p. 155; R. Surtees, *History and Antiquities of the County Palatine of Durham* (1816–40), Vol. II, p. 290, 'a handsome mansion-house, built by the Swinburns, and much improved by its present owner', which was after 1806. The property was inherited by Henry Swinburne in 1763. Four years later he married a lady with a large West Indian fortune and proceeded to adorn Hamsterley where he 'laid out the estate with a painter's eye'. That would be before 1774 when he and his wife went abroad. See C. Hussey, Hamsterley Hall, Durham'. *C.L.,* Vol. LXXXVI (21 Oct. 1939), pp. 418–22.

82. *Local Biography,* Vol. II, p. 120; *Procs of Soc. of Antiquaries* (Newcastle), 3rd Series, Vol. VI (1913–14), pp. 28–9; Colvin, op. cit., pp. 413–14. In Newcastle the other notable building by William Newton (1730–98) is St Anne's Church, 1768. In the county of Northumberland he was the architect of Howick Hall.

83. Letter of John Oxley to Sir John Hussey Delaval, dated 9 July 1772. NRO, Delaval (Waterford) MSS, 2 DE 2/10/63.

84. E. Mackenzie and M. Ross, *A View of the County Palatine of Durham* (1834), Vol. I, p. 403; Surtees, op. cit., Vol. I, p. 44.

85. M. A. Richardson, *Local Historian's Table Book* (1841–6), Vol. II, p. 126.

86. A. T. Bolton, *Portrait of Sir John Soane* (1927), pp. 17, 39. Soane visited Castle Eden on 6 Oct. 1780.

87. Hutchinson, op. cit., Vol. III, p. 1, 'Mr. Burdon has lately rebuilt Castle Eden house on an elegant and extensive plan'; Mackenzie and Ross, ibid; Surtees, ibid; Pevsner, op. cit., pp. 64–5.

88. W. Fordyce, *History of Durham* (1857), Vol. II, p. 365, mentions that the gallery and staircase had been 'recently fitted up, and that the conservatory was 'erected about two years ago'.

89. Ibid, Vol. II, p. 110, in a footnote where the date of the visit is erroneously given as 1775.

90. Wilhelmina, Duchess of Cleveland, *Handbook for Raby Castle* (1870), p. 84, says that in the carriage hall the pillars are probably original 'but Lord Darlington probably added or at least repaired, the bases and capitals, and the first Duke, after his return from abroad, conceived the unhappy idea of coating them with scagliola, in imitation of porphyry'. In fact, the columns are eighteenth century although it does seem that the original ones were used as models. The chimney-pieces were made to Carr's design, 'Chimney Piece for the Hall', dated 1783. The drawing is still at Raby. See A. Rowan, 'Raby Castle, Co. Durham', *C.L.,* Vol. CXLVII (8 Jan. 1970), pp. 66–69; A. Rowan, 'Gothick Restoration at Raby Castle', *Architectural History. Journal of the Society of Architectural Historians of Great Britain,* Vol. XV (1972), pp. 23–50 and P. Leach, 'In the Gothick Vein. The Architecture of Daniel Garrett. Pt. III'. *C.L.,* Vol. CLVI (26 Sept. 1974), pp. 834–37.

91. The sheet of instructions and sketches, initialled 'J.C.' and dated 1768, is in the Raby Castle muniments.

92. The instructions, inscribed 'J.C. Archt., 1770', are at Raby Castle.

93. Hutchinson, op. cit., Vol. III, p. 268.

94. In his instructions in 1770 Carr was

363

writing of the 'intended long South front' where he proposed a remodelling and the addition of a further storey. The latter was never done and the introduction of a Gothic facade was only partially completed. See *C.L., ibid.*

95. Wilhelmina, Duchess of Cleveland, op. cit., pp. 49, 117.

96. Fordyce, op. cit., Vol. II, p. 111. The remark quoted would seem to have been directed against the 'Gothic drawing-room at Raby Castle', the design for which was exhibited at the Royal Academy by R. Hughes in 1820. See A. Rowan, 'Raby Castle, Co. Durham', *C.L.*, Vol. CXLVII (22 Jan 1970), p. 187.

97. 'Raby Castle'. *G.M.*, Vol. LXII (Oct. 1792), p. 893, says that 'several parts of the South aspect' are new. A plate shows the partially reconstructed south front.

98. There is an incomplete design at Raby for the Hunter's Corridor. It is unsigned and undated and has been attributed to Daniel Garrett. Several Paine drawings are initialled and one, 'Sides of the Square Court', is signed. See A. Rowan, 'Raby Castle, Co. Durham', *C.L.*, Vol. CXLVII (1 Jan. 1970), p. 20 for a full account of Paine's work at Raby. Also A. Rowan, 'Gothick Restoration at Raby Castle', *Architectural History. Journal of the Society of Architectural Historians of Great Britain,* Vol. XV (1972), pp. 23–50 and P. Leach, 'In the Gothick Vein. The Architecture of Daniel Garrett. Pt. III'. *C.L.*, Vol. CLVI (26 Sept. 1974), pp. 834–37.

99. The drawing, showing the four sides of the room, is undated and unsigned. It is for a hall ninety feet long and must date from before Carr's proposed tower of 1770. From the style of the Gothic decoration an acceptable date would be c. 1768 when Carr first began to work at Raby.

100. A. Young, *A Six Months' Tour* (1771), Vol. II, p. 428.

101. J. Boyle, *County of Durham* (1892), p. 717.

102. The drawing, 'Chimney Piece for the Hall', is dated 1783. A flooring plan for the carriage hall bears the same watermark as the signed Carr drawing, 'The South Elevation of Henderson's House and Barn'. These drawings are at Raby Castle.

103. Wilhelmina, Duchess of Cleveland, op. cit., p. 73.

104. H. Skrine, *Three Successive Tours in Northern England and a great part of Scotland* (1795), p. 81. 'Lord Darlington is making great additions to the house, which do not exactly correspond to its structure; and intends enlarging the great hall which is at the top of the house to the length of 150 feet.'

105. Wilhelmina, Duchess of Cleveland, ibid.

106. Fordyce, ibid.

107. 'The Pursuits of Architectural Innovation. No. IX'. *G.M.;* Vol. LXIX, Pt. I (April 1799), p. 295.

108. *Procs of Soc. of Antiquaries* (Newcastle), Vol. VI, pl.

109. Richardson, op. cit., Vol. II, p. 386, gives the date of the fire as 27 Dec. 1796, and that the castle had not been long rebuilt; Mackenzie and Ross, op. cit., Vol. II, p. 277, refer to Witton Castle as 'a large oblong building . . . and was nearly rebuilt during the last century; but on Dec. 27th, 1796, it was discovered to be on fire, and the flames raged with such violence, that all attempts to stop their progress were ineffectual. All the elegance of the internal structure was destroyed, and the outer walls only left standing.'

110. Pevsner, op. cit., p. 245, gives the date of the present eighteenth century remains as c. 1790–5.

111. Pevsner, ibid., p. 169.

REFERENCES

VIII

1. C. L. Eastlake, *A History of the Gothic Revival* (1970), p. 93.
2. J. Summerson, *Architecture in Britain, 1530–1830* (1963), p. 242. 'Short Memoirs of the Life of James Wyatt, Esq.', *G.M.*, Vol. LXXXIII (Sept. 1813), p. 296, recorded of the Oxford St Pantheon that 'Never, perhaps, was so high a reputation in the Arts obtained by a first effort'.
3. J. Greig (ed.): *The Farington Diary* (1923), Vol. II, p. 217. Entry for 29 March 1804.
4. C. R. Turnor, *James Wyatt* (1950), p. 12; A. Dale, *James Wyatt* (1956), p. 198.
5. H. Colvin, *A Biographical Dictionary of English Architects, 1660–1840* (1954), pp. 725–31, lists eighty-seven country houses either built or altered by Wyatt as well as fourteen churches or cathedrals. There were, of course, the many public commissions which Wyatt also received especially at Oxford.
6. J. Lees-Milne, *The Age of Adam* (1947), pp. 151–52.
7. Greig, op. cit., Vol. II, p. 180. Entry for 8 Jan. 1804.
8. Turnor, op. cit., p. 11. For a similar criticism see also Summerson, op. cit., p. 280, where Wyatt is referred to as a 'stylistic weather-cock'.
9. K. Clark, *The Gothic Revival* (1964), p. 69.
10. *G.M.*, ibid.
11. Dale, op. cit., p. 114.
12. Lees-Milne, op. cit., p. 152. Wyatt's 'indolence and growing intemperance so accentuated his artistic shortcomings that he finally allowed himself to be enmeshed in a facile Gothicism, and he became bored with the execution of serious undertakings'. C. Hussey, *English Country Houses* (1958), Vol. III, p. 13, refers to Wyatt's 'facile but unprincipled applications of ecclesiastical gothic'. For more in the same vein see Eastlake, op. cit., p. 95; Turnor, op. cit., pp. 33–4.
13. M. S. Briggs, *Goths and Vandals* (1952), p. 157.
14. 'Ballot at the Society of Antiquaries'. *G.M.*, Vol. LXVII, Pt. II (Nov. 1797), pp. 930–1: 'Mr. Wyatt's Election'. Ibid, p. 1, 089. Wyatt was elected by 143 votes to 20. See also Dale, op. cit., pp. 117–18; Colvin, op. cit., p. 724.
15. J. Boyle, *The County of Durham* (1892), p. 207.
16. Ibid, p. 208.
17. 'Ancient and Present State of the Cathedral at Salisbury', *G.M.*, Vol. LIX (Oct. 1789), p. 874; 'Defence of Mr. Wyatt's Alterations in Salisbury Cathedral' (Dec. 1789), pp. 1,064–6.
18. Dale, op. cit., p. 111.
19. Boyle, ibid.
20. Ibid, p. 210.
21. Greig, op. cit., Vol. I, p. 218. Entry for 7 Nov. 1797. See also Dale, op. cit., pp. 4–5.
22. Boyle, ibid.
23. Ibid.
24. Dale, op. cit., p. 199.
25. W. Parson and W. White, *Gazetteer of Durham and Northumberland* (1827), Vol. I, p. 189; *V.C.H.D.*, Vol. III, pp. 78, 79.
26. W. Hutchinson, *History and Antiquities of the County Palatine of Durham* (1787), Vol. II, p. 288.
27. N. Pevsner, *County Durham* (1953), p. 120; L. Dickins and M. Stanton, *An Eighteenth Century Correspondence* (1910), p. 279.
28. Ibid, p. 280.
29. Pevsner, op. cit., p. 117.
30. Ibid, p. 52.
31. Colvin, op. cit., p. 73.
32. J. Raine, *An Account of the Episcopal Castle or Palace of Auckland* (1852), p. 127; T. Pennant, *A Tour in Scotland . . .*

1772 (1790), Vol. II, p. 341; Pevsner, op. cit., p. 52; J. Cornforth, 'Auckland Castle, Co. Durham', *C.L.*, Vol. CLI (3 Feb. 1972), p. 270.

33. There is also a very simple plan which accompanies this elevation. Bishop of Durham's MSS.

34. Raine, op. cit., p. 107n.

35. Boyle, op. cit., p. 208, gives the date as 1795.

36. Raine, op. cit., p. 108n.

37. Pevsner, op. cit., p. 53, gives the date of the extension as 1775–80, that is during the episcopate of Bishop Egerton.

38. Bishop of Durham's MSS.

39. Dickins and Stanton, ibid. 'In 1754 Miller was helping his friend John Egerton, Rector of Ross . . . , in the work of repairing the chancel of the parish church and it is probable that his assistance was also claimed for the re-modelling of the rectory at Ross which was accomplished about this date'.

40. Hutchinson, op. cit., Vol. III, p. 354; 'Memoirs of Dr. John Egerton, late Bishop of Durham', *G.M.*, Vol. LXVII (Sep. 1797), p. 735.

41. Colvin, op. cit., p. 123.

42. S. D. Kitson, 'Carr of York', *RIBAJ*, 3rd Series, Vol. XVII (Jan. 1910), p. 257.

43. Colvin, op. cit., p. 124; M. E. Ingram, 'John Carr's Contribution to the Gothic Revival', *Trans. East Riding Georgian Society*, Vol. II, Part III (1949), pp. 43–52.

44. S. Jefferson, *History and Antiquities of Allerdale* (1842), p. 250; N. Pevsner, *Cumberland and Westmorland* (1967), p. 210.

45. Colvin, op. cit., p. 125; C. Hussey, 'Ripley Castle, Yorkshire', *C.L.*, Vol. LXXII (13 Aug. 1932), p. 183.

46. E. Mackenzie and M. Ross, *A View of of the County Palatine of Durham* (1834), Vol. II, p. 406, gives the date 1791; Boyle, op. cit., p. 184; N. Pevsner, *County Durham*, p. 118.

47. *G.M.*, ibid.

48. T. Rose, *Westmorland, Cumberland . . .* (1832), Vol. I, p. 57; N. Pevsner, op. cit., p. 52.

49. *APSD*. It should be noted that Dale, op. cit., p. 3, mentions Wyatt as having been a pupil of a W. Atkinson about whom nothing would seem to be known. It would appear that the Bishop Auckland Atkinsons were local men.

50. *APSD*.

51. 'Some of the Repairs made at Auckland Castle by Bishop Barrington, 1791–1826', p. 4, a memorandum copied in 1894 from one originally belonging to Bishop Barrington's secretary, Mr Emm. Bishop of Durham's MSS.

52. Ibid, pp. 4–5.

53. Dale, op. cit., p. 80, quoting from Farington's diary of 26 Dec. 1804. For a short account of Wyatt's alterations at Auckland Castle see J. Cornforth, 'Auckland Castle, Co. Durham', *C.L.*, Vol. CLI (10 Feb. 1972), pp. 336–7.

54. Emm Memorandum, p. 4. There is also a drawing at Auckland Castle, 'Elevation of the Porch', which, although unsigned and undated, is part of the Wyatt sequence. Bishop of Durham's MSS.

55. Drawings, nos. 56, 60, 61, 62, 64, 65, 66, 67, 68, 69, 70, 71 at Auckland Castle. Bishop of Durham's MSS.

56. Bishop of Durham's MSS.

57. Emm Memorandum, p. 3.

58. Ibid.

59. The drawings include a plan of the ceiling vault, 'Wyatt's Plan of Anti-Room' (inscribed in a later hand) and a door and a window section inscribed 'Details of anti-room mouldings, etc.' Bishop of Durham's MSS.

60. Emm Memorandum, ibid.

61. Wyatt Instructions. Bishop of Durham's MSS.

62. The drawing is inscribed in a later hand 'Wyatt's Design for the Chapel Altar Piece'. Bishop of Durham's MSS.

63. Raine, op. cit., p. 89.

64. Dale, op. cit., p. 143.
65. J. Rutter, *Delineations of Fonthill and its Abbey* (1823), p. 108.
66. Ibid, p. 109.
67. Ibid.
68. Greig, op. cit., Vol. I, p. 213. Entry for 6 Aug. 1797.
69. Ibid, Vol. I, p. 308.
70. Rutter, op. cit., p. 111.
71. Eastlake, op. cit., pp. 57–61.

IX

1. *D.N.B.*
2. 'Review of New Publications'. *G.M.*, Vol. LXVI, Pt. I (March 1796), p. 221, 'The old castle at Douglas was burnt by accident about 33 years ago'. See *S.A.*, Vol. VIII, p. 85. The date of the fire is given as 1760 in *N.S.A.*, Vol. VI, p. 488.
3. *V.S.*, pls 135–6 are inscribed 'Adam's Archts'. Robert Adam was abroad from 1754–8 and on his return was occupied in London. The youngest brother, William, seems never to have been a designer.
4. *D.N.B.*
5. Ibid. T. Smollett, *Humphry Clinker* (1960), p. 269, 'the late duke resolved, as head of the first family of Scotland, to have the largest house in the kingdom . . .'.
6. *V.S.*, ibid, shows elevations and plans. There is a small collection of material in the possession of Sir Alec Douglas-Home illustrating earlier stages in the design.
7. J. Greig (ed.), *The Diaries of a Duchess* (1926), p. 22.
8. T. Pennant, *A Tour in Scotland . . . 1772* (1790), Part 1, p. 133.
9. The plan is in Sir Alec Douglas-Home's collection. It shows that a tower was to be built onto the two angles of the old castle. The surviving tower at Douglas indicates that one may have been constructed before the fire, which destroyed the old castle, after which the single tower was allowed to stand.
10. *D.N.B.*
11. These are in Sir Alec Douglas-Home's collection at the Hirsel.
12. *G.M.*, ibid.
13. J. Fitler and J. C. Nattes, *Scotia Depicted* (1804), pl. VI.
14. *D.N.B.*
15. RHP, No. 1075. Elevation of Gordon Castle. The date, 1614, occurs intertwined in one of the monograms. The elevation, in ink, is of the same period as the plans for a new house but so far the draughtsman has not been indentified although he may have been Roumieu who was the Duke's surveyor certainly in the years 1767–9.
16. RHP, No. 1053.
17. RHP, No. 1052. 'East Front of Gordon Castle with Pavilions, etc. The Seat of His Grace the Duke of Gordon'.
18. RHP, No. 1051.
19. RHP, No. 1050.
20. J. Balfour Paul (ed.): *The Scots Peerage* (1907), Vol. IV, p. 556. 'The Duke had raised the 89th Regiment of Foot for the service of Government in 1759. . . . The regiment was disbanded at the Peace of Paris in 1763, and the Duke then travelled abroad for some time.' The *D.N.B.* says that the Gordon Highlanders were disbanded in 1765 in India but though the regiment was sent home the Duke remained behind and did the Grand Tour.
21. The *APSD* says that Roumieu was employed by the Duke of Gordon c. 1750. He was probably descended from Paul Roumieu, a clock-repairer in Edinburgh in the late seventeenth

century. See R. K. Marshall, *The Days of Duchess Anne* (1973), p. 46.

22. The building contract is in the Gordon Castle accounts in SRO, GD 44/49/16.

23. RHP, No. 1073. It is marked 'A.R.'

24. RHP, No. 1072 and signed 'A. Roumieu'.

25. J. Dunbar, *The Historic Architecture of Scotland* (1966), p. 198, gives the foundation of Fochabers as the last decade of the eighteenth century whereas P. Nuttgens, 'Regional Planning in the North-East', *Prospect* (Spring 1960), puts it at c. 1780. However, from information kindly supplied by Mr Grant of SRO, a date in the early sixties should possibly be considered especially as Abraham Roumieu is known to have left the Duke's service in 1769.

26. Letter of 6 May 1769 from John Baxter Junior to William Bell, the factor to the Duke of Gordon at Gordon Castle. SRO, GD 44/49/16.

27. Letter from Peter May, Cullen House, 16 Nov. 1769 to James Ross, factor to the Duke of Gordon at Gordon Castle. SRO, GD 44/49/22. My attention was drawn to this letter by Mr Grant of SRO.

28. Dunbar, ibid.

29. J. Fleming, *Robert Adam and His Circle* (1962), pp. 37, 38.

30. Ibid, pp. 56–7.

31. Ibid, p. 331.

32. A. and J. Simpson, 'John Baxter, Architect, and the Patronage of the Fourth Duke of Gordon', *Bulletin of the Scottish Georgian Society*, Vol. II (1973), p. 47.

33. A. Bolton, *Architecture of Robert and James Adam* (1922), Vol. II, p. 203.

34. Ibid, Vol. II, pp. 250–1.

35. *D.N.B.*

36. Memorandum for James Salisbury. SRO, GD 44/49/16.

37. Letter of 25 Feb. 1769 from John Baxter Junior. SRO, GD 44/49/16.

38. Letter of 24 April 1769 from John Baxter Junior. SRO, GD 44/49/16.

39. According to Peter May's letter of 16 Nov. 1769 James Ross was the factor by then and after that date Baxter's correspondence is to him. SRO, GD 44/49/22.

40. Letter of 6 May 1769 from John Baxter Junior to William Bell, the factor at Gordon Castle. SRO, GD 44/49/16.

41. A List of Stone for Gordon Castle, 26 June 1769. SRO, GD 44/49/16.

42. 'Accot. His Grace the Duke of Gordon to John Baxter Architect for Mason Work from June 29th, 1769 to 1779'. SRO, GD 44/49/16.

43. RHP, No. 1083.

44. RHP, No. 1085. 'Sketch of Second Story of the West Pavilion'. This and No. 1083 obviously belong to the 1769 period and are by Baxter.

45. RHP, No. 1091.

46. Dunbar, op. cit., p. 62.

47. RHP, No. 1060. It is signed 'Jn Baxter Archt 1776'.

48. RHP, No. 1059. 'Section across the Principal Stair, and Dining Room, etc.' and is signed 'John Baxter Archt 1776'.

49. RHP, Nos 1068 and 1079. Sections of the dining-room.

50. Copy of an account from John Baxter in 1778. SRO, GD 44/49/16.

51. RHP, No. 1063. 'Ceiling of the Drawing Room Gordon Castle' and is signed 'J. Baxter 1775'.

52. RHP, No. 1064. 'Dining Room Ceiling Gordon Castle' and is signed 'John Baxter Archt. 1775'.

53. RHP, No. 1065. 'Ceiling (sic) of the Principal Staircase'. Uncoloured, it is signed 'John Baxter Archt. 1776'.

54. F. H. Groome (ed.), *Ordnance Gazetteer of Scotland* (1894), Vol. III, p. 201.

55. *S.A.*, Vol. XIV, p. 265; *N.S.A.*, Vol. XIII, p. 119; H. Skrine, *Three Successive Tours in the North of England and a great Part of Scotland* (1795),

REFERENCES

pp. 125–6; J. Hall, *Travels in Scotland* (1807), Vol. II, pp. 358–9.

56. Fitler and Nattes, ibid.

57. 'Accot. His Grace the Duke of Gordon to John Baxter Architect for Mason Work from June 29th 1769 to 1779'. SRO, GD 44/49/16.

58. 'Measure of Mason Work done for His Grace the Duke of Gordon by Mr. John Baxter Architect 1779' by Alexander Ponton. SRO, GD 44/49/16/2.

59. Memorandum for James Salisbury. SRO, GD 44/49/16.

60. The billiard room chimney-piece is mentioned in the 'Report by John Logie and Robert Thomson of Mr. Baxter's Additional Work at Gordon Castle 20th April, 1781'. SRO, GD 44/49/16.

61. The inlaid marble chimney-piece for the hall cost £33 7s 0d according to the copy of an account, 'Settled with Mr. Ross, June 29th, 1782'. SRO, GD 44/49/16.

62. 'Payments to and upon account of Mr. John Baxter Architect for carrying on the buildings at Gordon Castle'. SRO, GD 44/49/16.

63. 'Alexr. Ponton enclosing account of measurements of Mr. Baxter's work at Gordon Castle to Mr. James Ross, 8th Feb. 1779'. SRO, GD 44/49/16.

64. 'Report by John Logie and Robert Thomson of Mr. Baxter's Additional Work at G. Cas., 20th April 1781'. SRO, GD 44/49/16.

65. 'Measurement of Mason Work done for His Grace the D. of Gordon by Mr. John Baxter Architect, 1779'. SRO, GD 44/49/16/2.

66. This is explained in the final settlement of the dispute in October and November 1783. SRO, GD 44/49/16/1.

67. 'State of Mr. Baxter's account with the Duke of Gordon, Oct. 1782'. SRO, GD 44/49/16.

68. The letter, dated 8 June 1783, SRO, GD 44/49/16, was sent from Glenfiddich which is perhaps the house designed by John Plaw for the Duke of Gordon of which there are designs in the Soane Museum. See H. Colvin, *A Biographical Dictionary of English Architects, 1660–1840* (1954), p. 463.

69. A copy of a letter to Baxter dated 12 June 1783 and also a letter from Baxter to Charles Gordon of Braid on 1 July 1783. SRO, GD 44/49/16.

70. A copy of a letter from Charles Gordon of 4 July 1783. SRO, GD 44/49/16.

71. Bolton, op. cit., Vol. II, Ch. XXXII.

72. Copy of a letter from Charles Gordon dated 4 July 1783. It was probably to the accountant, Alexander Farquharson. SRO, GD 44/49/16.

73. This is stated in the final settlement of the dispute signed in October and November, 1783. SRO, GD 44/49/16/1.

74. Farquharson's profession is explained in a note from Baxter to Charles Gordon. SRO, GD 44/49/16.

75. Letter from Baxter to Charles Gordon of Braid on 11 June 1783. SRO, GD 44/49/16.

76. Letter from Charles Gordon to the Duke of Gordon, 24 May 1783. SRO, GD 44/49/16.

77. Letter from John Baxter to Charles Gordon of Braid on 1 July 1783. SRO GD 44/49/16.

78. Draft letter of Charles Gordon to the Duke of Gordon, dated Edinburgh, 2 July 1783. SRO, GD 44/49/16.

79. SRO, GD 44/49/16/1.

80. Ibid.

81. Copy of a bill sent by the Duke of Gordon authorising payment to John Baxter. The bill was sent from Gordon Castle on 10 Oct. 1783. SRO, GD 44/49/16.

82. Dunbar, op. cit., p. 126, gives 1785 as the date and names Robert Burn as the architect. If this is correct then the Hermitage is at least twenty years

before any other proven work by Burn. Yet J. Stoddart, *Remarks on Local Scenery and Manners in Scotland during the years 1799 and 1800* (1801), Vol. I, p. 102, says 'The present building is new'; M. Warrender, *Walks near Edinburgh* (1895), p. 22, gives 1789, which seems likely, as the date. Charles Gordon had purchased the Braid estate in 1772. SRO, GD 244, Box 36.

83. Ibid.

84. *S.A.*, Vol. XXI, p. 82.

85. Ibid, Vol. XIX, p. 478.

86. E. R. Welles, *Ardincaple Castle and Its Lairds* (1930), p. 154.

87. *APSD*; *D.N.B.* The additions are very similar in their basic form and plan to what had been proposed for Ardencaple in 1774 by Robert Adam. See S. M., Vol. X, nos 30–31; Vol. XII, no. 152; Vol. L, no. 51.
However, the drawings in Vol. XXII, nos 72–4, and dated 1762, though ascribed to Ardencaple (see also Bolton, op. cit., Vol. II, Topographical Index, Section I, p. 2) on the evidence of chronology must be for another property of Lord Frederick Campbell's, possibly Coombe Bank. Though the prescience of the Campbells of Argyll was notorious one would not go so far as to allow them the gift of second-sight.

88. A. E. Richardson, *Robert Mylne, Architect and Engineer, 1733–1811* (1955), p. 23.

89. R. S. Mylne, *The Master Masons to the Crown of Scotland* (1893), Chap. 13, pp. 276–7; H. Colvin, op. cit., p. 402.

90. Richardson, op. cit., quoting from Mylne's diary.

91. Mylne, op. cit., p. 276.

92. W. Angus, *Seats of the Nobility and Gentry in Great Britain and Wales* (1787), pl. XXIX.

93. *N.S.A.*, Vol. I, p. 333.

94. *D.N.B.*

95. Ibid.

96. *S.A.*, Vol. X, p. 287.

97. Colvin, op. cit., p. 463.

98. Ibid.

99. Ibid.

100. James Playfair's *Journal of Architecture, 1783–92.* NLS, Adv. MSS. 33.5.25. It consists of a series of jottings concerning visits to houses, the length of the journey and the time taken as well as the time spent on drawings. The diary was obviously used as an aide-memoire in calculating expenses and fees.

101. These designs are part of the Melville MSS. RHP, 3154.

102. RHP, 6699, Drawing No. 5. It is dated 25 March 1786 and signed by James Playfair.

103. Angus, ibid.

104. RHP, 6699, Drawing No. 5.

105. Ibid, Drawing No. 2.

106. Ibid, Drawing No. 8, 'Plan of the Principal Storie, April, 1786'.

107. Playfair, ibid. Entry for July to October, 1788. Also 31 Dec. 1788, 'Attended Marquis of Graham in the morning'. Playfair carried out alterations to the old castle of Buchanan in Stirlingshire and built the stables, all in a classical style for Lord Graham, later Duke of Montrose. Throughout the eighteenth and nineteenth centuries the Dukes of Montrose commissioned various designs for rebuilding Buchanan entirely, from such architects as William and Robert Adam, Playfair and Charles Barry. Eventually, after Buchanan was destroyed by fire, William Burn erected, on a nearby site, a splendid castle (1854) which is now ruinous.

108. The date for Playfair's work at Kinnaird Castle is variously given. He did visit it in 1787 and again the next year during his two journeys to Scotland. Then, in his journal, on 24 Jan. 1789, he noted: 'Elevations of West front

(of) Kinnaird. A finished drawing with portico and Square Tower and Sundry other proposed alterations.' In the Soane Museum collection of Playfair drawings the plan of the principal storey at Kinnaird is dated 16 Dec. 1789, with a sheet of chimney-piece designs marked August 1790. The library drawings are from the following year. Kinnaird was rebuilt in 1855 by David Bryce.

Playfair also produced a scheme for Urie House, near Stonehaven, which was to have pointed windows and circular towers.

109. Colvin, ibid.
110. Playfair, ibid.
111. RHP, 6699, Drawing No. 25, 'Framing of the Ceiling Floors or Garrets in the Roofs, October, 1786'.
112. These drawings are dated April. RHP, 6699.
113. Playfair, ibid.
114. Ibid, Sept. 1788. Playfair was referring to Urie House. See footnote 108.

X

1. *G.M.*, Vol. LXIX (Oct. 1799), p. 832.
2. Ibid, Vol. LI (May 1781), p. 217.
3. 'The Pursuits of Architectural Innovation. No. VII', *G.M.*, Vol. LXIX (Feb. 1799), pp. 92–3.
4. 'Improvements made, and still wanted to be made, at Windsor', *G.M.*, Vol. LX (Aug. 1790), p. 690.
5. Lady Llanover (ed.), *Autobiography and Correspondence of Mary Granville, Mrs. Delany* (1861–2).
6. 'The Pursuits of Architectural Innovation. No. VII', *G.M.*, Vol. LXIX (Feb. 1799), p. 93.
7. Letters from James Nisbet to Sir John Hussey Delaval dated Kelso 18 Jan. 1772. NRO, Delaval (Waterford) MSS, 2DE.18/1/11.
8. B. Langley, *Gothic Architecture Improved* (1747), pl. I.
9. Ibid, pl. XL.
10. 'Print of W. Front of Old St. Paul's', *G.M.*, Vol. LI (May 1781), p. 217.
11. J. Carter, *The Ancient Architecture of England* (1845), preface.
12. J. M. Crook, 'John Britton and the Genesis of the Gothic Revival'. *Concerning Architecture* ed. by Sir J. Summerson (1968), pp. 98–119.
13. J. Britton, *Architectural Antiquities of Great Britain* (1807 on), Vol. III, introduction.
14. Ibid, Vol. I, Prefatory Testament.
15. J. P. Neale, *Views of the Most Interesting Collegiate and Parochial Churches in Great Britain* (1824), Vol. I, preface.
16. 'Architectural Alterations Making at Oatlands', *G.M.*, Vol. LXX, Pt I (May 1800), p. 426.
17. *D.N.B.* For an analysis of Gilpin's theory of the Picturesque see C. P. Barbier, *William Gilpin. His Drawings, Teaching, and Theory of the Picturesque* (1963), Ch. VIII.
18. W. Gilpin, *Observations on Several Parts of Great Britain; particularly the High-lands of Scotland* (1808), Vol. I, p. 24. See also *Observations on . . . the Mountains and Lakes of Cumberland and Westmoreland* (1808), Vol. I, p. xiii.
19. Gilpin, *Observations on . . . the Highlands of Scotland* (1808), Vol. II, p. 111.
20. Ibid, p. 112.
21. Ibid.
22. Gilpin, *Observations on . . . Cumberland and Westmoreland* (1808), Vol. I, p. 7.
23. Gilpin, *Observations on . . . the Highlands of Scotland* (1808), Vol. II, p. 117.
24. Gilpin, *Observations on . . . Cumberland and Westmoreland* (1808), Vol. I, p. xxii.
25. Gilpin, *Observations on . . . the Highlands of Scotland* (1808), Vol. I, p. 49.

26. Ibid, Vol. I, p. 63.
27. Gilpin, *Observations on . . . Cumberland and Westmoreland* (1808), Vol. I, p. 14.
28. Ibid, Vol. II, p. 45.
29. Ibid, p. 46.
30. Gilpin, *Observations on . . . the Highlands of Scotland* (1808), Vol. I, p. 50.
31. Ibid, Vol. II, p. 119.
32. Ibid, p. 118.
33. Ibid, p. 136.
34. C. Hussey, *The Picturesque* (1927), p. 59.
35. Gilpin, op. cit., Vol. II, p. 121.
36. Gilpin, *Observations on . . . Cumberland and Westmoreland* (1808), Vol. I, p. 89.
37. Gilpin, *Observations on . . . the Highlands of Scotland* (1808), Vol. II, pp. 121–2.
38. Sir Joshua Reynolds, Thirteenth Discourse, 1786. Quoted by C. Hussey, *The Picturesque*, p. 186.
39. W. Hipple, *The Beautiful, the Sublime, and the Picturesque in Eighteenth-Century British Aesthetic Theory* (1957), p. 192.
40. U. Price, *Essays on the Picturesque, as Compared with the Sublime and the Beautiful* (1810), Vol. III, p. 38; Hipple, op. cit., p. 221.
41. Price, op. cit., Vol. I, pp. 50–1.
42. R. P. Knight, *The Landscape, a Didactic Poem* (1795), Book I, ll. 297–300.
43. Ibid, Book I, l. 286.
44. J. Summerson, *British Architecture, 1530–1830* (1963), pp. 288–9.
45. Price, op. cit., Vol. II, p. 247; Hipple, op. cit., p. 206.
46. Price, op. cit., Vol. I, p. 52, and Vol. II, p. 262.
47. Ibid, Vol. II, p. 268.
48. Ibid, Vol. II, pp. 180–1; Hipple, op. cit., pp. 218–19.
49. Price, op. cit., Vol. II, p. 265.
50. Quoted by C. Hussey, *English Country Houses* (1956), Vol. II, p. 148.
51. 'The Plan of Knox's Picturesque Scenery of Scotland', *G.M.*, Vol. LIX (April 1789), p. 326.
52. A. Young, *A Six Months' Tour* (1771), Vol. IV, p. 434.
53. J. Hodgson, *A Topographical and Historical Description of the County of Westmoreland* (1823), p. 43.
54. *A Tour in the Highlands of Scotland 1818* (1819), p. 126.
55. T. Garnett, *Tour in Scotland, 1800* (1810), Vol. I, p. 109.
56. Ibid, footnote.
57. H. J. Grierson (ed.), *Letters of Sir Walter Scott* (1932–7), Vol. II, p. 363.
58. L. Simond, *Journal of a Tour and Residence in Great Britain During the Years 1810 and 1811 by a French Traveller* (1817), Vol. I, p. 440.
59. Ibid.
60. Ibid, Vol. I, p. 448.

XI

1. It is traditionally stated at Glamis Castle in Angus that the rebuilding of the wings was by James Wyatt. A. H. Millar, *Historical Castles and Mansions of Scotland* (1890), p. 238, 'Important structural alterations were made in 1811 . . . and also in 1849'.
2. Plans, dated and signed, are still at Castle Fraser. The existence of these plans would seem to indicate that Paterson was responsible for the contemporary alterations, including a domed staircase, which were carried out within the castle and which were removed in 1951 by the present owner.
3. The traditional date for Monzie Castle is 1795. J. Stoddart, *Remarks on Local Scenery and Manners in Scotland during the years 1799 and 1800* (1801), Vol. II, p. 301, records that Monzie 'a magnificent pile, in the Gothic taste, is nearly finished'.

REFERENCES

4. J. Fitler, *Scotia Depicted* (1804).

5. 'Account of a Journey from Lancashire into Scotland', *G.M.*, Vol. XXXVI (April 1766), p. 167.

6. J. M. Leighton and J. Swan, *Select Views on the River Clyde* (1830), p. 152, state that Eglinton Castle was begun in 1797 and finished three years later. F. H. Groome (ed.), *Ordnance Gazetteer of Scotland* (1894), Vol. II, p. 530, gives the date 1798.

7. Stoddart, op. cit., Vol. II, p. 313.

8. This tower was made the excuse for a circular top-lit saloon which was one of the finest of the apartments in Eglinton Castle. See A. H. Millar, *Castles and Mansions in Ayrshire* (1885).

9. *H. of N.*, Vol. XIV, p. 108. 'In 1801 a new mansion was built round the old tower by John Patterson (sic) the Edinburgh architect.'
   At Barmoor a set of plans, signed by Paterson, shows how the old house was disguised.

10. Ibid, p. 336. The date was 1803. See also N. Pevsner, *Northumberland* (1957), pp. 54, 125.

11. The date and a carved representation of the Earl Marischal's arms are visible on keystones once on the external wall but now within the inner fabric.

12. Estimates and accounts in SRO, GD 105/766, 769–71.

13. A. and H. Tayler, *The Book of the Duffs* (1914), Vol. II, p. 309.

14. Tracings of the now vanished drawings, which were apparently signed and dated are in NMRS, KCD/34/1–2; Groome, op. cit., Vol. III, p. 18, says of Fetteresso that 'it was partly rebuilt and greatly extended about 1830 by Colonel Duff'.

15. Ibid.

16. *N.S.A.*, Vol. XI, p. 119; Groome, op. cit., Vol. III, p. 11.

17. NLS, MS 6511.

18. A. T. Bolton, *The Portrait of Sir John Soane* (1927), p. 306.

19. M. A. Richardson, *Local Historian's Table Book* (1841–6), Vol. III, p. 194. 'This year (1819) Brancepeth Castle ... was restored ... under the able direction of Mr. John Patterson (sic) of Edinburgh'. See also T. Rose, *Westmorland, Cumberland, Durham and Northumberland* (1832), Vol. I, p. 28; E. Mackenzie and M. Ross, *View of the County of Durham* (1834), Vol. II, p. 323.

20. Richardson, ibid, indicates that the date 1819 marked the completion of the restoration of Brancepeth. However research among the Brancepeth Estate MSS has produced some Paterson letters of 1822 and 1823 (D/Br./F.28) describing the completion of the library, billiard-room and entrance tower as well as alterations to the chapel. *Procs of Soc. of Antiqus* (Newcastle), Vol. III (1889), p. 415, states that the castle was 'greatly altered and enlarged in 1818 by J. Patterson (sic), Edinburgh', adding that the later alterations were 'by the late Mr. Salvin'. See also N. Pevsner, *County Durham*, p. 60.

21. Ibid.

22. *The Journal*, Feb. 1850, mentions a sum of £70,000 as the purchase price paid in 1796 for the Brancepeth estate by the merchant and mine-owner, William Russell. Pevsner, op. cit., p. 59, gives the price as £75,000.

23. The drawing by Robert Adam, one of his Italian studies, is probably the castle at Volterra. It is numbered 126 and is in the possession of Sir John Clerk of Penicuik, Bt.

24. T. Hannan, *Famous Scottish Houses* (1928), pp. 53–4.

25. *N.S.A.*, Vol. VIII, p. 72; Groome, op. cit., Vol. III, p. 249.

26. *N.S.A.*, Vol. VI, p. 18, in 1834 says of Smyllum Park that it 'was built about twenty years ago'.

27. NMRS.

28. M. Girouard, 'Abercairny, Perthshire'. *C.L.*, Vol. CXXIX (9 March 1961), pp. 507–8.

29. *N.S.A.*, Vol. XI, p. 252.

30. Jones, *Views of the Seats . . . in Scotland* (1829).

31. J. Watson, *Morayshire Described* (1868), p. 65.

32. Letter from the factor to the Earl of Moray, 20 Jan. 1794. Moray MSS, Box 11/1202.

33. Factor's letter to the Earl of Moray, 13 May 1794. Moray MSS, Box 11/1206.

34. Memorandum from Alexander Laing to the Earl of Moray, 13 Sept. 1796. Moray MSS, Box 18/742.

35. Account of Alexander Laing to Lord Moray, 23 Feb. 1797. Moray MSS, Box 18/742.

36. Account of 1 Aug. 1797. Moray MSS, Box 18/742.

37. Letter of 1 Aug. 1797, from Alexander Laing in Edinburgh to Lord Moray. Moray MSS, Box 18/742.

38. Letter from Alexander Laing in Edinburgh to the Earl of Moray, 23 Feb. 1798. Moray MSS, Box 18/742.

39. Account of 23 Feb. 1798. Moray MSS, Box 18/742.

40. Account of 13 and 20 June 1801 at Darnaway Castle. Moray MSS, Box 18/701.

41. Account of 24 Mar. 1802. Moray MSS, Box 18/701.

42. Memorandum of 28 May 1802. Moray MSS, Box 18/701.

43. Account of 19 June 1802. Moray MSS, Box 18/701.

44. Account of 9 July 1805. Moray MSS, Box 18/701.

45. The abstract of the account for building the castle is still at Darnaway. The exact cost from 12 Aug. 1802, to 29 Aug. 1809 was £14,691 18s 3d. Moray MSS, Box 18/544.

46. Memorandum of 13 Sept. 1796. Moray MSS, Box 18/742.

47. Watson, ibid.

48. Ibid.

49. NMRS.

50. Two estimates, one of which is for plumber work, are dated May and July 1805. The architect of Cluny Castle remains unknown. The house is of three storeys and is battlemented with lug-turrets. SRO, GD 80/711.

51. NMRS.

52. *N.S.A.*, Vol. V, p. 500.

53. J. Small, *Castles and Mansions of the Lothians* (1883).

54. *N.S.A.*, Vol. XII, p. 994; Groome, ibid. The Inveraray concept was created economically at Hatton by tacking facades onto two connected sides of the medieval tower.

55. David Hamilton's drawings, Vol. I, p. 110. (Photostat copy in NMRS.) 'The Plan of the principal floor of Mr. Kincaid's House' is undated and unsigned.

56. Hamilton's involvement at Barnton is obscure. His drawings include one of the circular four-storey tower (Vol. I, no. 39) and a design for the gateway (Vol. II, no. 269). Yet an east coast commission in 1794, if that is the date of Barnton, is difficult to explain since Hamilton was born in Glasgow and nearly all his works are in the west.
The Adam drawings are S.M., Vol. XXIX, nos 72, 73, 74, 76–9 and bear a strong resemblance to Barnton as it was completed.
Barnton was demolished c. 1920.

57. RCAHMS, *Stirlingshire* (1963), Vol. II, p. 357.

58. Hamilton prepared two schemes for Airth. The first was to create a triangular house with Adam style interiors. However, the house, as enlarged, followed the second scheme which was less grandiose. Plans were also submitted by William Stirling of Dunblane. See Jones, op. cit.; *APSD*; *Stirlingshire*, Vol. I, p. 232.

59. Jones, op. cit.
60. *APSD.*
61. *N.S.A.*, Vol. V, pp. 840–3.
62. *APSD*; G. Richardson; *New Vitruvius Britannicus*, Vol. II (1808), p. 7, 'This magnificent edifice, to which additions are now making . . .' See pls LI–LVI.
63. J. Greig (ed.), *The Farington Diary* (1923), Vol. III, p. 290, 11 Dec. 1814; H. J. Grierson (ed.), *Letters of Sir Walter Scott* (1935), Vol. I, p. 271.
64. Farington, op. cit., Vol. VII, p. 115, 17 Oct. 1812; H. Colvin, *Biographical Dictionary of English Architects, 1660–1840* (1954), p. 674.
65. *D.N.B.*
66. Millar, op. cit.
67. Ibid.
68. Ibid.
69. Ibid.
70. On his last journey to Scotland in the summer of 1791, Robert Adam kept a diary recording the places he visited and the people he saw. He left Edinburgh for the last time on Friday, 6 Jan. 1792 and on the following day, 'Dined with Sir Gilb(ert Elliot), & Mr. Elliot Archt. at Hawick'. Whether the architect was Archibald or James Elliot is not known. Bearing in mind that Archibald Elliot, in contemporary printed material, is designated esquire, an unusual title for an architect, it makes one wonder if the usual view of his humble origin is correct. See above Ch. VI, n. 75.
71. Quoted from the *Scots Magazine* by A. H. Millar, *Historical Mansions and Castles of Scotland*, p. 148.
72. L. Simond, *Journal of a Tour and Residence in Great Britain During the Years 1810 and 1811 by a French Traveller* (1817), Vol. I, p. 404.
73. RCAHMS, *Peebleshire* (1967), Vol. II, p. 308. The plans are still in the house. There are two sets. The first is dated 1804 and signed; the second set, undated and unsigned, seems to represent a revised scheme as carried out.
74. *V.S.*, pls 50, 51.
75. W. Gilpin, *Observations on . . . the High-lands of Scotland* (1808), Vol. I, p. 158.
76. Colvin, op. cit., p. 402.
77. A. E. Richardson, *Robert Mylne, Architect and Engineer, 1733–1811* (1955), p. 134.
78. Letter from Robert Mylne to Lord Breadalbane of 23 Nov. 1789. SRO, GD 112/20/2.
79. Richardson, op. cit., pp. 137–8.
80. The Final Decreet in the submission between Lord Breadalbane and John Gregor, 1807. SRO, GD 112/20/1.
81. 'Memorandum for the Earl of Breadalbane in the submission between his Lordship and Mr. John Gregor'. SRO, GD 112/20/1.
82. Letter from John Paterson to Lord Breadalbane dated 16 Nov. 1807. SRO, GD 112/20/2. Among the Breadalbane papers there are many other records demonstrating Paterson's connection with Taymouth which seems to have begun in 1797 when he submitted an estimate for a castellated porch and other additions. SRO, GD 112/20/4.
83. D. Wordsworth, *Recollections of a Tour Made in Scotland, A.D. 1803* (1874), p. 193.
84. Copy letter from Lord Breadalbane to John Gregor of 19 Dec. 1804. SRO, GD 112/20/1.
85. On 12 Jan. 1804 Paterson wrote from Eglinton Castle to the Edinburgh lawyer John Campbell. SRO, GD 112/20/2.
86. In 1829 Paterson submitted an account to Lord Breadalbane for £658 15s 2d and not until 1812 were the accounts of Gregor's successor as builder settled. SRO, GD 112/20/1, 4.
87. It would seem that James Elliot was brought to the notice of Lord Breadalbane by Alexander Trotter of

Dreghorn. In a letter of 13 Sept. 1800 Trotter described James Elliot as 'a young man of but very mean appearance but of Considerable Abilities as a draftsman and designer. He proposes to Join in business with a Brother whom he has got in London and who has had a regular Education there and much experience under the best Masters'. SRO, GD 112/20/7. See above n. 70.

88. Copy letter from Lord Breadalbane to John Gregor of 19 Dec. 1804. SRO, GD 112/20/1.

89. Letter from James Elliot to Lord Breadalbane dated 24 Oct. 1807. SRO, GD 112/20/1.

90. The contract was signed by James Miller and Allan Johnston as the builders. It was stipulated that they should 'take down the Battlements, Cornices and the upper part of the Walls, and the Towers of the South front of the Building already erected'. SRO, GD 112/20/4.

91. Letter from James Elliot to Lord Breadalbane of 24 Oct. 1807. SRO, GD 112/20/1.

92. Letter from James Elliot to Lord Breadalbane dated 11 Dec. 1807. SRO, GD 112/20/2.

93. The drawings are in the Soane Museum. See A. Rowan, 'Taymouth Castle, Perthshire'. *C.L.*, Vol. CXXXVI (8 Oct. 1964), p. 915.

94. Miss Dorothy Stroud, assistant curator at the Soane Museum has discovered that Soane was paid £105 in 1818.

95. Account of Francis Bernasconi. SRO, GD 112/20/1.

96. Ibid.

97. Letter of James Elliot to Lord Breadalbane, Edinburgh, 14 Sept. 1809. SRO, GD 112/20/1.

98. Copy of a letter to James Elliot of 24 Aug. 1809. SRO, GD 112/20/1.

99. Millar, op. cit., p. 150.

100. G. Beard, *Georgian Craftsmen and Their Work* (1966), p. 162.

XII

1. The year c. 1808 seems a much more likely one for the building of Tullichewan than the hitherto accepted one of 1792. (See J. Dunbar, *The Historic Architecture of Scotland* (1966), p. 127.) There is really no evidence to support a late eighteenth-century attribution and, indeed, in 1792 Lugar, if the birth date of 1773 is correct (H. Colvin, *A Biographical Dictionary of English Architects, 1660–1840* (1954), p. 369) was only nineteen years old.
   R. Lugar, *Plans and Views of Buildings Executed in England and Scotland in the Castellated and Other Styles* (1811), p. 13, describes Tullichewan as, 'The Seat of John Sterling, Esq.' That is

obviously a printer's error and plate I, 'Plan of the principal Floor of Tillicheun' with its references to Mr and Mrs Stirling, proves it to have been a Stirling property so that Tullichewan is obviously, if indirectly referred to when in the entry under Lugar the *APSD* states '1808 a house in a castle style now building for J. Stirling, esq., of Cordale, near Dumbarton'. See also Colvin, op. cit., p. 370.

2. *APSD*; Jones, *Views of the Seats . . . in Scotland* (1829); Colvin, ibid. Yet the date on the clock tower at Balloch is 1803.
   Balloch, or Ardoch Castle was built for John Buchanan of Ardoch although his first thoughts had been to have an

'abbey'. See Lugar, op. cit., pp. 18, 21.

3. Jones, ibid.

4. H. Repton, *An Inquiry Into the Changes in Landscape Gardening* (1806), p. 96.

5. Ibid. See also C. Hussey, *The Picturesque* (1927), p. 57.

6. Repton, op. cit., pp. 25–6; see also Hussey, op. cit., p. 177.

7. Quoted by N. Pevsner, *Studies in Art, Architecture and Design* (1968), Vol. I, p. 129.

8. Quoted by W. J. Hipple, *The Beautiful, the Sublime, and the Picturesque in Eighteenth-Century British Aesthetic Theory* (1957), p. 234, from *Fragments,* vi in *Works,* p. 247.

9. Lugar, op. cit., p. 18.

10. Archibald Elliot to Col. Moray Stirling, 25 June 1803. SRO, GD 24/1/624.

11. Lugar, op. cit., p. 10.

12. Repton, op. cit., p. 74.

13. The accounts are in the house which was enlarged outrageously by William Burn in 1834. See also *N.S.A.*, Vol. IV, pp. 158–9: Dunbar, op. cit., p. 126.

14. *N.S.A.*, Vol. VIII, p. 82.

15. Jones, op. cit.

16. Ibid.

17. Ibid.

18. In volume II of the John Smith MSS in the NMRS, Castle Forbes is referred to by the old name of Putachie until May 1817 and after that by its modern designation.

19. A plan of the old house is in a set of drawings by John Paterson of Edinburgh and dated 1807. Lord Forbes' MSS.

20. The drawings for both schemes belong to the present Lord Forbes at Balforbes, Aberdeenshire.

21. G. M. Fraser, *Archibald Simpson, Architect, and His Times,* Ch. III. In a letter of 24 Feb. 1811 Simpson wrote 'I have been assisting Lugar of late occasionally—who is a very affable sort of man, and I generally dine with him on such days'.
This unpublished material in Aberdeen Central Reference Libary was compiled from early twentieth-century newspaper articles.

22. Letter of Sir John Hay to John Paterson of 5 Oct. 1816. SRO, GD 52/349.

23. The first estimate, for the mason work, was submitted to Archibald Simpson by Alex. Wallace on the 20 May 1814. The second, 'for finishing Putachie' by Harry Leith was sent on '7th May, 1815.' SRO, GD 52/349.

24. Ibid.

25. Estimate of Alex. Wallace.

26. It is on the recollections of a mason at the castle that the claim for June 1815 has always been advanced. See A. and H. Tayler, 'The House of Forbes' *Third Spalding Club Miscellany* (1937), p. 284.

27. In support of 1814 it should be observed that the carpenter went bankrupt in December 1814 (memorandum of William Scott of 14 Nov. 1816) and that Simpson was engaged from 1 May 1814 to 20 Sept. 1815. SRO, GD 52/349.

28. Letter of Archibald Simpson of 29 Sept. 1815. SRO, GD 52/349. Curiously, Simpson appears not to have heard of Archibald Elliot before.

29. Ibid.

30. Letter of Simpson to William Scott, 24 Oct. 1815. SRO, GD 52/349.

31. Ibid.

32. Letter from Simpson to William Scott, 21(?) Oct. 1815. SRO, GD 52/349.

33. Ibid.

34. Memo by William Scott of 14 Nov. 1816. SRO, GD 52/349.

35. Answer of Archibald Simpson to the Case of Lord Forbes, 25 Dec. 1817. SRO, GD 52/349.

36. Ibid.

37. Memo by Scott, 14 Nov. 1816. SRO,

GD 52/349.

38. Letter from Archibald Simpson to William Scott on 29 March 1816. SRO, GD 52/349.

39. Letter of 26 Oct. 1816. SRO, GD 52/349.

40. Memo by Scott of 14 Nov. 1816. SRO, GD 52/349.

41. Letter of William Scott of 26 Oct. 1816. Also on 30 Jan. 1822, James Gillespie and John Paterson asked for condescendences from both parties to the dispute. SRO, GD 52/349.

42. Letter of William Scott, 26 Oct. 1816. SRO, GD 52/349.

43. John Smith kept very detailed notes and accounts of his work at Castle Forbes where, on the evidence available, he seems to have begun in November 1815 (Vol. I) although the surviving accounts date only from May 1816. These indicate that the greater part of the house was finished by the summer of 1818. Besides the usual entries there is a cryptic note on 27 Aug. 1818, 'Cleaning Surgeon's Instruments'. The Smith MSS are in the NMRS.

44. From the introductory notes by John Paterson to his 'Sketches and Designs' of 1811. Lord Forbes' MSS.

45. J. M. Leighton and J. Swan, *Select Views on the River Clyde* (1830), p. 135; Jones. op. cit.; *N.S.A.*, Vol. VII, p. 609.

46. Lugar, ibid.

47. *N.S.A.*, Vol. VII, p. 610.

48. Ibid, Vol. VIII, p. 215; J. Irving, *History of Dunbartonshire* (1857), p. 469.

Boturich was built by John Buchanan of Ardoch who had previously enlarged nearby Balloch Castle.

49. NMRS.

Strathallan was an old house which was enlarged and regularised by Smirke. F. H. Groome (ed.), *Ordnance Gazetteer of Scotland* (1894), Vol. VI, p. 407.

50. Colvin, op. cit., p. 546.

51. Kinfauns was built for the 15th Baron Gray who had inherited the estate from his mother, formerly Miss Blair of Kinfauns. Lord Gray must have been very proud of his new house for he printed abstracts of its cost which, including the furnishings and offices, came to £41,664 2s 5d. SRO, GD 46/17/77.

Kinfauns came by descent to the Morays of Darnaway whose present representative, the Earl of Moray, has the Smirke drawings. There are a large number of these which begin in March 1820 and continue at intervals until September 1824.

Jones, op. cit.; A. H. Millar, *Historical Castles and Mansions of Scotland* (1890), pp. 108–9; Colvin, ibid.

52. Repton, op. cit., p. 120n.

53. C. Eastlake, *A History of the Gothic Revival* (1872), p. 79.

54. J. Loudon, *Treatise on Forming, Improving and Managing Country Residences* (1806), Vol. I, pp. 107–8.

55. Colvin, op. cit., p. 47.

56. H. Skrine, *Three Successive Tours in the North of England and a great Part of Scotland* (1795), p. 61.

57. T. Garnett, *Tour in Scotland, 1800* (1810), Vol. II, p. 119.

There are drawings at Scone Palace by Andrew Cock dated 1798 which may relate to the change of the time. D. Walker, 'Scone Palace, Perthshire'. *The Country Seat*, edited by H. Colvin and J. Harris (1970), pp. 210–14, gives the date for these drawings as 1789.

58. The drawings are at Scone Palace.

59. Colvin, op. cit., p. 527.

60. J. Greig (ed.), *The Farington Diary* (1923), 27 Sept. 1801, Vol. I, pp. 326–7.

61. The Atkinson drawings are at Scone Palace. The earliest are the plans of the basement and principal floors and elevations which are signed and dated

April 1803.

62. Millar, op. cit., p. 13.

63. Memorandum of Building and Repairs at Scone Palace and Estate, 1802–1959, p. 1. A Copy is in the NMRS. *N.S.A.*, Vol. X, pp. 1060–1; Jones, op. cit.; F. O. Morris, *A Series of Picturesque Views of Seats* (1866–80), Vol. I, p. 83. These all give the terminal date as 1806.

64. Memorandum of Building and Repairs at Scone Palace and Estate, ibid.

65. Atkinson's drawing of the south elevation shows it to have been intended to be two storeys. The changes on the west are indicated by comparing the 'West Elevation to Plan B' and the 'West Elevation for Scone' of April 1803.

66. J. Gilpin, *Observations on . . . the High-lands of Scotland* (1808), Vol. I, p. 7.

67. *N.S.A.*, Vol. X, p. 833, gives the date 1807; Colvin, op. cit., p. 48, quoting Neale, *Seats*, 2nd series, ii, 1825, gives the dates as 1810–15.
Jones, op. cit.; Millar, op. cit., pp. 13–28, have very full accounts of Rossie Priory and its interiors.

68. *N.S.A.*, Vol. IX, p. 568; J. M. Leighton, *History of the County of Fife* (1840), Vol. II, p. 243; A. H. Millar, *Fife: Pictorial and Historical* (1895), Vol. I, pp. 191–2.

69. Letter of John Paterson to 'Mr. Menzies Factor to Charles Moray of Abercairny Esq. by Crieff' of 25 Jan. 1796. SRO, GD 24/1/624.

70. Letter of J. Paterson of 21 Oct. 1796 and accompanying elevations and plans. SRO, GD 24/1/624.
For a short account of the development of the Abercairny see M. Girouard, 'Abercairny, Perthshire'. *C.L.*, Vol. CXXIX (9, 16 March 1961), pp. 506–9, 584–7.

71. The drawings are referred to in a letter from Archibald Elliot of 25 June 1803 and were despatched 'in a tin case along with some plans for Mr. Maclauren which I hope you will have the goodness to let him have'. SRO, GD 24/1/624.

72. A letter from C. H. Tatham, dated 19 Jan. 1804, acknowledges the receipt of £42 for designs. SRO, GD 24/1/624.

73. SRO, GD 24/1/624.

74. Memo for commencement of new house, 9 April 1804. SRO, GD 24/1/624.

75. Letter from Richard Crichton to Col. Moray of 30 May 1804. SRO, GD 24/1/624.

76. Richard Crichton to Col. Moray on 5 Feb. 1806. SRO, GD 24/1/624.

77. Letters of Crichton of 16 and 21 March and 8 April, 1808. SRO, GD 24/1/624.

78. Building account from 4 March 1809 to Dec. 1809. SRO, GD 24/1/624.

79. Building account for 1808. SRO, GD 24/1/624.

80. SRO, GD 24/1/624.

81. Memo by Robert Peddie, 28 March 1814, Perth. SRO, GD 24/1/624.

82. Letter from J. Paterson to Col. Charles Moray of 25 Jan. 1796. SRO, GD 24/1/624.

83. Account of 18 Aug. 1814. The total was £126 6s 0d. SRO, GD 24/1/624.

84. Account of Ralph Egerton of Birmingham of 29 Oct. 1814. SRO, GD 24/1/624.

85. 'Plan of Part of Ground Floor showing proposed new Staircase', 24 Dec. 1824. RHP, 1017/37.

86. Drawings were prepared for the library on 31 Aug. 1815. RHP, 1017/22.

87. These drawings were produced in May and June 1820. RHP, 1017/2, 3, 20, 21.

88. Estimate, 13 Sept. 1823, from R. and R. Dickson (SRO, GD 24/1/624), and 'Elevation of South side of Drawing room', Sept. 1822. RHP, 1017/48.

89. Estimate of 13 Sept. 1823. SRO, GD 24/1/624.

90. 'Estimate for library chimney-piece in dove marble £108' from Robert Dickson dated 14 Jan. 1824 (SRO, GD 24/1/624). However, on 25 Oct. 1822, in a letter concerning designs for the hall floor, an intended alteration to the library chimney-piece is mentioned. RHP, 1017/19.

91. 'Design of Portico', 9 Nov. 1822 by R. and R. Dickson. RHP, 1017/34.

92. There is a drawing, 'Opening Between Library and Present Entrance Hall', dated 22 April 1826. RHP, 1017/49.

93. 'Plan of New Entrance Hall', 26 Feb. 1827. RHP, 1017/17. See also Nos 5 and 45. All are inscribed R. and R. Dickson.

94. 'Abercairny Abbey. Finishing of New Entrance Hall', 3 Feb. 1829. RHP, 1017/26.

95. Letter of Robert Dickson dated 23 March 1829. RHP, 1017/19.

96. Ibid.

97. Estimate from Robert Dickson of 30 April 1830. SRO, GD 24/1/624.

98. There is a promissory note at Millearne which is dated, 'Edinburgh, 11th Nov., 1820'. Macintyre MSS, 1. According to a letter of 12 May 1820. 'The price upon the property is £16,000 Stg.' Macintyre MSS, 2.

99. Macintyre MSS, 1.

100. It is dated 4 March 1826 and is still at Millearne as are all the other accounts and receipts. Macintyre MSS, 4.

101. Account from William Cooper for glass supplied from 4 Oct. 1832 to 1 Aug. 1833. It totalled £20 19s 6d. Macintyre MSS, 23.

102. Account from William Cooper of 25 Oct. 1834. Macintyre MSS, 24.

103. The letter and account from E. Hunt for Hunt and Co., 57 Abbey Hill, Edinburgh, are not dated. The latter came to £22 15s 6d. There is another letter of 24 Jan. 1833 and an account which totalled £38 3s 6d. Macintyre MSS, 29, 28.

104. Account of Thomas Willement from 25 Green St, Grosvenor Square, for £11 10s 2d. Macintyre MSS, 33.

105. J. Summerson, Architecture in Britain, 1530–1830 (1963), p. 320.

106. Letter and account from Samuel Wright, Staffordshire Potteries, Shilton, dated 20 Feb. 1834. The total was £20 11s 0d. Macintyre MSS, 30.

107. Letter from Chamberlain and Co., Worcester Royal Porcelain Works, dated 14 Aug. 1843. Macintyre MSS, 37.

108. Account from Harris Watson, 16 Oxford St, London, dated 15 July 1836 for £23 16s 0d. Macintyre MSS, 32.

109. There is an account from James Bruce, Glazier, 100 High St, Perth, dated 23 March 1846 which totals £42 15s 0d and which includes work done on the stable and the cloister which formed the west entrance to the house. The receipt is dated 27 March 1846. Macintyre MSS, 35, 36. See A. Rowan; 'Millearne, Perthshire'. C.L., Vol. CLI (24 Feb. and 2 March 1972), pp. 452–6, 498–501.

110. Letter of William Cooper of Edinburgh to J. G. Home Drummond which accompanies the account for glass supplied between 30 Nov. 1833 and Jan. 1835. Macintyre MSS, 25.

111. Estimate from Robert Dickson of 30 April 1830. SRO, GD 24/1/624.

112. Sheet of pencilled details initialled J.G.H.D. and dated 26 June 1845. Macintyre MSS, 40. Although the library had been painted in 1833 it seems to have received its final form in 1845.

113. N.S.A., Vol. IX, p. 52; Millar, op. cit., Vol. II, p. 357; Leighton, op. cit., Vol. II, p. 150.

114. Jones, op. cit.

115. Loudon, ibid.

REFERENCES

116. Quoted by Hussey, op. cit., p. 213.
117. *N.S.A.*, Vol. XI, p. 681; Jones, op. cit.; *APSD*, Groome, op. cit., Vol. IV, p. 512.
118. *APSD*.
119. In April 1816 Robert Baird stated his intention to rebuild Newbyth 'in consequence of the Mansion House . . . having lately been destroyed by fire'. SRO, GD 236/3.
    Dunbar, op. cit., p. 127; T. Hannan, *Famous Scottish Houses* (1928), p. 129, has a full description of Newbyth but wrongly attributes it to Robert and James Adam.
120. According to the *N.S.A.*, Vol. VII, Pt I, p. 199, they were erected 1818–20 at a cost of about £28,000. When Elliot died in 1823 he was still due £527 from the Paisley Jail Commissioners.
121. *APSD*; Colvin, ibid; *N.S.A.*, Vol. II, p. 57, 'The late Mr. Nisbet, after the death of his mother Mrs. Hamilton, added greatly to the mansion-house at Beil (sic), from a plan by Atkinson; and extended the range along the face of the bank on which the building stands to about 500 feet. In a series of about 7 years nearly £40,000 were expended'. See also Hannan, op. cit., pp. 17–18; J. Small, *Castles and Mansions of the Lothians* (1883), Vol. I.
122. There was an old castle nearby, the ruins of which were visible in the early nineteenth century. See J. Stoddart, *Remarks on Local Scenery in Scotland . . . 1799 and 1800* (1801), Vol. II, p. 235; A. Campbell, *A Journey Through Parts of North Britain* (1810), Vol. II, p. 352.
    Millar, op. cit., Vol. II, p. 267, gives the information that Tulliallan was built for Viscount Keith in 1818. See also *APSD*, where the date is given as 1817–20, and Colvin, ibid.
123. *D.N.B.* See also H. J. Grierson (ed.), *Letters of Sir Walter Scott* (1932–7),

Vol. III, p. 240n.
124. Ibid, Vol. II, p. 496. Letter of 17 May 1811 to Lady Abercorn.
125. Ibid, Vol. II, p. 500.
126. Ibid, Vol. IV, p. 308. Letter of 29 Nov. 1816 to Lady Abercorn.
127. Ibid, Vol. V, p. 44. To Daniel Terry, 8 Jan. 1818.
128. Ibid, Vol. II, p. 537. Letter of 25 Aug. 1811.
129. Ibid, Vol. I, p. xxx.
130. Ibid, Vol. IV, p. 289. To Daniel Terry, 12 Nov. 1816.
131. Ibid, Vol. V, p. 272. To James Skene, 10 Dec. 1818.
132. Ibid, Vol. IV, p. 333. To D. Terry, 28 Dec. 1816.
133. Ibid.
134. Ibid, Vol. III, p. 34. To Joanna Baillie, 1811.
135. Ibid, Vol. III, p. 65. To Patrick Murray, 18 Jan. 1812.
136. Ibid, Vol. III, pp. 34, 514.
137. Ibid, Vol. IV, p. 333. To D. Terry, 28 Dec. 1816.
138. Ibid, Vol. IV, p. 289. To D. Terry, 12 Nov. 1816.
139. Ibid, Vol. IV, p. 333.
140. Ibid, Vol. IV, p. 289.
141. Ibid, Vol. IV, p. 333.
142. Ibid, Vol. IV, p. 397. To D. Terry, March, 1817. At Abbotsford there is a drawing, 'Section across Greenhouse', dated Aug. 1818 from Atkinson. Other drawings survive from 1817 to 1824.
143. Grierson, op. cit., Vol. V, p. 136. To D. Terry, 4 May 1818.
144. Ibid, Vol. IV, p. 422. To D. Terry, 28 March 1817.
145. Ibid, Vol. IV, p. 526. To D. Terry, 26 Sept. 1817.
146. Ibid, Vol. V, p. 61. To D. Terry, 8 Jan. 1818.
147. Ibid, Vol. V, p. 133. To D. Terry, 30 April 1818.
148. Ibid, Vol. V, p. 191. To D. Terry, 11 Sept. 1818.

149. Ibid, Vol. V, p. 298. To Mrs Scott of Harden, 20 Jan. 1819.
150. Ibid, Vol. VII, pp. 73, 75. Letters of Feb. 1822.
151. Ibid, Vol. VII, p. 274. To Walter Scott, Younger of Abbotsford, 1 Nov. 1822.
152. Ibid, Vol. VII, p. 278. To D. Terry, 10 Nov. 1822.
153. Ibid, Vol. VII, p. 111. To Lord Montagu, 27 March 1822.
154. Ibid, Vol. VII, p. 367. To Lord Montagu, 5 April 1823.
155. Ibid, Vol. VIII, p. 423.
156. J. G. Kohl, *Scotland, Glasgow, the Clyde . . . to the Lakes* (1844), p. 247.
157. Grierson, op. cit., Vol. IV, p. 301. To Joanna Baillie, 26 Nov. 1816.
158. Ibid, Vol. VII, p. 111; Vol. VIII, p. 246.
159. Ibid, Vol. VI, p. 298. To D. Terry, 9 Jan. 1823.
160. Ibid, Vol. V, p. 91. Also Vol. IV, p. 301.
161. Ibid, Vol. VII, p. 111.
162. Ibid, Vol. VI, p. 323.
163. The Scott Monument in Edinburgh was built from 1840–6 to the designs of G. M. Kemp and was inspired by the architecture of Melrose Abbey.
T. Bonnar, *Biographical Sketch of George Meikle Kemp* (1892); W. Forbes Gray, 'The Scott Monument and its Architect', *A.R.*, Vol. 96 (July 1944), pp. 26–7.
164. Grierson, op. cit., Vol. VIII, p. 246. To Lady Louisa Stuart, 4 April 1824.

XIII

1. J. Hogg, *A Tour in the Highlands in 1803* (1888), p. 38.
2. It has always been stated that Gillespie Graham was the son of a joiner in Dunblane. However, Miss Catherine Cruft has discovered that his father was a solicitor in the town and that James had a brother who was hanged at Aberdeen for embezzlement.
3. *APSD*; B. Crombie, *Modern Athenians* (1882), p. 142; L. G. Graeme, *Or and Sable* (1903), p. 448.
In the archives of Major John Stewart of Ardvorlich is a charter of resignation by James, Duke of Montrose, to Mrs Margaret Gillespie and her husband James in which the succession to the Orchill estate was settled.
4. The Lord Macdonald MSS are in SRO. 'A List of the tradesmen's wages, who are employed in erecting the Buildings and executing the works of the Right Honble. Alexander Lord MacDonald under J. Gillespie'. SRO, GD 221/52.
5. 'List of tradesmen engaged for the works of Lord Macdonald in the islands of Skye and North Uist, by James Gillespie, Edinb., 24th Feby., 1800'. SRO, GD 221/52.
6. Ibid.
7. 'Report by James Gillespie on the buildings in Skye, 28th Dec., 1800'. SRO, GD 221/73.
8. Ibid.
9. 'Memo from James Gillespie relative to buildings in Skye, Edinb., 18th Jany., 1802'. SRO, GD 22/73.
10. Letter from J. Gillespie to J. Campbell, 3 April 1802. SRO, GD 221/73.
11. 'Buildings to be erected in Skye, 1803'. SRO, GD 221/73.
12. 'Docquet to Accounts for Improvements on Lord Macdonald's Estate, 1803'. SRO, GD 221/73.
13. Letter of J. Gillespie, 29 May 1803. SRO, GD 221/91.
14. Ibid from Achnacarry, 18 June 1803. SRO, GD 221/91.
15. 'Report by James Gillespie on the buildings in Skye, 28th Dec., 1800'. SRO, GD 221/73.

REFERENCES

16. Account from James Gillespie to Colonel Macdonald. NLS, Robertson-Macdonald MSS, 3983, f. 198.
17. Receipt from James Gillespie to Mr Hector Macdonald Buchanan of 11 Jan. 1803. NLS, Robertson-Macdonald MSS, 3947, f. 1.
18. Hogg, op. cit., p. 42.
19. A. Mackenzie, *History of the Camerons* (1884), p. 225.
20. Ibid.
21. Letter from Mal(colm) Coldstream to John Campbell, W.S., of 24 March 1803. SRO, GD 221/91.
22. Letter of James Gillespie, 28 March 1803. SRO, GD 221/91.
23. Letter from J. Gillespie to John Campbell, 18 April 1803, SRO, GD 221/91.
24. Letter from J. Gillespie, 18 June 1803. SRO, GD 221/91.
25. Ibid.
26. Ibid, 10 Sept. 1803. SRO, GD 221/91.
27. At Achnacarry there is a small booklet of plans marked with measurements. The plan of the principal floor shows clearly that an oval saloon in conjunction with the hall and the entrances to the adjacent rooms would have been difficult to effect in an efficient and functional way.
28. Mackenzie, ibid.
29. Plans at Achnacarry of 22 Dec. 1837 from 131 George St, Edinburgh, the office of William Burn.
30. Booklet of plans at Achnacarry.
31. T. Pennant, *A Tour of Scotland and a Voyage to the Hebrides, 1772* (1790), Vol. II, p. 106, noted that Kincardine was 'an antient (sic) seat of the Montrose family'. See also J. Hall, *Travels in Scotland* (1807), Vol. I, p. 244.
32. Jones, *Views of the Seats . . . in Scotland* (1829).
33. Ibid. The porch has been removed.
34. Letter from Mal(colm) Coldstream to John Campbell, 24 March 1803. SRO,

GD 221/91.
35. Letter from J. Gillespie to John Campbell, 10 March 1815. SRO, GD 221/74.
36. A. Campbell, *A Journey Through Parts of North Britain* (1810), Vol. I, p. 102. See also the 'Description of Lanrick Castle'. *Scots Magazine*, Vol. LXXIX (June 1817), p. 403, which says that Lanrick Castle 'was built by Sir John (Macgregor Murray) himself'.
37. *APSD*; Jones, op. cit.
38. Culdees Castle was built for General Drummond. It was modified and enlarged in the Scots-baronial style in 1867 by David Bryce whose drawings are still at the castle.
39. Jones, op. cit., gives the information that the house had been built in 1693 with projecting wings and that these were removed in 1812. See also *N.S.A.*, Vol. VIII, p. 215; F. H. Groome (ed.), *Ordnance Gazetteer of Scotland* (1894), Vol. V, p. 273.
40. H. J. Grierson (ed.), *Letters of Sir Walter Scott* (1932–7), Vol. II, p. 378. Letter of 30 Sept. 1810.
41. Ibid, Vol. IV, p. 308. Writing on 29 Nov. 1816 to Lady Abercorn, Scott remarked 'I conclude that all the improvements at the priory are now complete and that you are in quiet possession'.
    APSD gives the date of the mansion as 1812.
42. J. M. Leighton, *History of the County of Fife* (1840), Vol. II, p. 243.
43. Ibid; *APSD*; A. H. Millar, *Fife : Pictorial and Historical* (1895), Vol. I, p. 191.
44. Ibid, Vol. I, p. 194.
45. Letter from Lady Mary Crawford Lindsay to Hugh Hamilton, of 12 March 1810. SRO, GD 142/2/10/2.
46. Ibid to ibid, 23 May, 1810. SRO, GD 142/2/10/2.
47. Ibid to ibid, 2 June, 1811. SRO, GD 142/2/10/2.

48. Ibid to ibid, 23 Dec., 1810. SRO, GD 142/2/10/1.

49. Ibid to ibid, 15 Dec., 1811. SRO, GD 142/2/10/1.

50. Ibid to ibid, 13 Feb., 1813. SRO, GD 142/2/10/1.

51. Leighton, ibid.

52. Letter from Lady Mary Crawford Lindsay to Hugh Hamilton, 13 Feb. 1813. SRO, GD 142/2/10/1.

53. Eighteenth-century plans at Crawford Priory show that the ground plan of Crawford Lodge corresponds to the eastern or monastic portion of the Priory.

54. On the west coast of Kintyre, across the peninsula from Torrisdale Castle, is Glenbarr House. About 1815, when it belonged to the younger brother of General Keith Macalister of Torrisdale, it received 'monastic' additions, most likely by James Gillespie Graham, and became Glenbarr Abbey.

55. A stone tablet on the south front records that an earlier house was destroyed by fire in 1816 and that Gillespie (Graham) was the architect of Cambusnethan Priory.
See J. M. Leighton and J. Swan, *Select Views on the River Clyde* (1830); *N.S.A.*, Vol. VI, p. 615.

56. NMRS.

57. Ibid.

58. *N.S.A.*, Vol. X, p. 107.

59. A. Gomme and D. Walker, *Architecture of Glasgow* (1968), p. 28.

60. The tower of the old church was retained.

61. In his introduction to the Victorian Library edition of *Contrasts*, p. 12, H. R. Hitchcock states that Gillespie Graham was a Catholic. Such a statement appears to be groundless for in 1838 in a letter to the Catholic baronet, Sir William Drummond Stewart, Gillespie Graham wrote, 'I am well acquainted with all the details of an altar from having been extensively employed by the Catholics, who have been sincere friends to me'. SRO, GD 121/21/87.

62. J. Britton, *Architectural Antiquities of Great Britain* (1807), Vol. I, p. 1.

63. Ibid, Vol. III, p. 42.

64. 'Description of the Edinburgh Catholic Chapel', *Scots Magazine*, Vol. LXXIX (Feb. 1817), p. 85; T. H. Shepherd, *Modern Athens* (1829), p. 73; *N.S.A.*, Vol. I, p. 668; I. Lindsay, *Georgian Edinburgh* (1948), p. 33.
For the events leading up to the building of St Mary's, see J. F. S. Gordon, *Scotichronicon and Monasticon* (1867), pp. 431, 436, 459; P. F. Anson, 'Catholic Church Building in Scotland, 1560–1914', *Innes Review*, Vol. V (1954), pp. 128–9.

65. *Scots Magazine*, ibid; Shepherd, ibid. P. Stanton, *Pugin* (1971), p. 200, records that St Mary's was remodelled and enriched internally by Gillespie Graham in 1840–1 and that Pugin was paid £200 by him for unspecified work.

66. *Scots Magazine*, ibid.

67. Letter from J. Gillespie to John Campbell, Glasgow, 10 Jan. 1814. SRO, GD 221/24.

68. Ibid to ibid, 2 Nov. 1814.

69. *N.S.A.*, Vol. VI, p. 194; *Glasgow and Lanarkshire Illustrated* (1904), p. 10; Gomme and Walker, op. cit., p. 171. For the events leading up to the building of St Andrew's see Gordon, op. cit., p. 265.

70. *N.S.A.*, Vol. IX, p. 245; Leighton, op. cit., Vol. II, p. 241.

71. *N.S.A.*, Vol. IX, p. 258. In 1812 Gillespie Graham had built the manse.

72. G. Hay, *Architecture of Scottish Post-Reformation Churches, 1560–1843* (1957), p. 116.

73. Leighton, op. cit., Vol. I, p. 127; Millar, op. cit., Vol. I, p. 211.

74. A tablet on the south wall of Gask

Chapel is dated 1800. Groome, op. cit., Vol. III, p. 83.

75. *N.S.A.*, Vol. I, p. 11.
76. NMRS.
77. The date is above the entrance.
78. *N.S.A.*, Vol. XIII, p. 254.
79. NMRS.
80. *N.S.A.*, Vol. II, pp. 79–80. It replaced a cruciform church.
81. Hay, op. cit., p. 177; *N.S.A.*, Vol. VIII, p. 43.
82. Ibid, Vol. XI, p. 282.
83. Britton, op. cit., Vol. IV, p. 1.
84. Crombie, op. cit., pp. 141–2.
85. Ibid, p. 141.
86. Quoted by C. Hussey, *The Picturesque* (1927), p. 124.
87. Account between J. Gillespie and Lord Macdonald for 1813, dated 18 March 1814. SRO, GD 221/48.
88. 'Contract Between the Right Hon. Alex. Wentworth, Lord Macdonald and Alex. Shearer, Builder and John Shannon, Wright, Edinburgh, 1813'. SRO, GD 221/74.
89. Letter from James Gillespie to J. Campbell, Edinburgh, 15 April 1814. SRO, GD 221/24.
90. Letter from J. Campbell to Colonel J. Macgregor Murray, 16 April 1814. SRO, GD 221/74.
91. Ibid which contains the reply of Colonel Macgregor Murray on 17 April.
92. Letter from J. Gillespie to J. Campbell, 2 March 1815. SRO, GD 221/74.
93. Account between J. Gillespie and Lord Macdonald for 1814. It was submitted on 3 March 1815. SRO, GD 221/48.
94. The payments for new furniture are recorded in the accounts which J. Gillespie sent annually to Lord Macdonald.
95. Account for the years 1819 and 1820 which was submitted on 26 July 1820. SRO, GD 221/48.
96. Jones, op. cit.
97. A water-colour showing Armadale House before it was enlarged and Gothicised by Gillespie Graham is in NMRS.
98. Sir John Macgregor Murray to J. Campbell, 21 May 1817. SRO, GD 221/73.
99. The account is dated July 1818. SRO, GD 221/49.
100. The papers relating to the building of the stables at Armadale are in the Lord Macdonald MSS. The stables were erected by McNaughton and Macpherson who in 1820 wrote from Craigend. SRO, GD 221/88.
101. Jones, op. cit.
102. The design, inscribed 'Jn. B. 1791', is at Duns Castle.
103. A booklet, 'Plan of Duns Castle, 1794', has several pages signed by John Baxter. The booklet is at Duns Castle.
104. The plan for the principal floor is in 'Plan of Duns Castle'.
105. 'Elevations of the East Front, Edinr. 9th May, 1817 Rich. Crichton Archt.' are at Duns Castle.
106. The drawing, 'No. 30. Elevation. J.G. 3rd July, 1818' is of the oriel window above the entrance porch. The drawing is at Duns Castle.
107. All these drawings are at Duns Castle.
108. The preliminary study of the east elevation is a pencil drawing quite unlike any of Gillespie Graham's hastily produced sketches. It can be compared stylistically with the drawings which are signed by William Hay. He is supposed to have designed the episcopal church in Duns.
109. H. Colvin, *A Biographical Dictionary of English Architects, 1660–1840* (1954), p. 463.
110. 'View of a House designed for David Scott, Esq.' is in the Soane Museum.
111. 'Plan of the Pleasure Grounds of Dunninald by James Gillespie, Architect, 1819' is at Dunninald House. See A. Rowan, 'Dunninald, Angus'.

C.L., Vol. CXLVI (14 Aug. 1969), pp. 384–7.

112. B. Botfield, *Journal of a Tour Through the Highlands of Scotland* (1830), p. 31.

113. Millar, op. cit., Vol. I, p. 131. See also *N.S.A.*, Vol. IX, p. 8; Leighton, op. cit., p. 36.

114. *N.S.A.*, Vol. XI, pp. 88–9; Groome, op. cit., Vol. II, p. 375.

115. John Smith's account book, Vol. I. Although the entries for Drumtochty are undated the volume opens with Castle Forbes as well as dealing with valuations from November, 1815. The volume is in the NMRS.

116. Britton, op. cit., Vol. IV, p. 181.

117. Letter from Lady Mary Crawford Lindsay to Hugh Hamilton, 4 Jan. 1813. SRO, GD 142/2/10/4. There is also a letter from Andrew Gammell, proprietor of the Drumtochty Castle estate, of 28 May 1839 in which he writes of 'rebuilding' parts of the castle and offices. SRO, GD 52/367. The letter may refer to the western portion of the castle which includes the copy of Guy's Tower at Warwick Castle.

118. The drawing is at Dunninald. There is a copy in the NMRS.

119. Leighton and Swan, op. cit., p. 25. See also *N.S.A.*, Vol. VI, p. 18; Jones, op. cit.; Groome, op. cit., Vol. IV, p. 479.

120. *APSD*; *N.S.A.*, Vol. VI, p. 616; Jones, op. cit.; Groome, op. cit., Vol. VI, p. 499.

121. M. S. Briggs, *Goths and Vandals* (1952), p. 149.

122. Letter from J. Gillespie Graham to Lady Stewart, mother of Sir John Stewart of Grantully, dated 5 March 1828. SRO, GD 121/97/XX/83.

123. Letter from David W. Dickson and Co., Leith of 11 Sept. 1828. SRO, GD 121/97/XX/98.

124. Letter of 18 Feb. 1829, from J. Gillespie Graham to John Stewart, Union Bank, Perth. He was, along with the architect, a trustee for the building of the new house at Murthly. John Stewart was a close friend of Gillespie Graham's as shown by many of the latter's remarks and frequent expressions of goodwill in his letters. SRO, GD 121/97/XX/107.

125. Advice from John and George Anderson, Leith Walk Foundry, 15 Feb. 1830. The beams cost £688 14s 10d. The receipt is dated 11 Dec 1830. SRO, GD 121/97/XX/145, 172.

126. Letter to John Stewart of Perth from J. Gillespie Graham of 18 June 1829, in which he proposes to visit Murthly. He wanted arrangements made to have some chicken soup ready for his youngest child on their arrival at the George Inn. Ibid to ibid, 26 Sept. 1829 and 4 Dec. 1830. SRO, GD 121/97/XX/116, 122, 171.

127. Ibid to ibid, 28 Aug. 1829. SRO, GD 121/97/XX/118.

128. Ibid to ibid, 22 Sept. 1829; 26 Sept. 1829 (two letters); 27 Sept. 1829; 8 May 1830; passim. SRO, GD 121/97/XX/121–4, 150.

129. Ibid to ibid, 2 and 4 Jan. 1832. SRO, GD 121/97/XXI/1, 3.

130. Ibid to ibid, 30 Dec. 1831 and 4 Jan. 1832. SRO, GD 121/97/XX/219 and XXI/3.

131. J. M. Melville to John Stewart, 2 Feb. 1832. SRO, GD 121/97/XXI/6.

132. Sir John Stewart to Captain William Stewart, 25 Sept. 1832. SRO, GD 121/XXI/22.

133. Letter from Lord Breadalbane of 25 May 1838. SRO, GD 121/97/XXI/84.

134. 'It is a singular coincidence, that the twin houses of Dunkeld and Murthly have both lost their founders, and have remained ever since unfinished.' So lamented a contributor to the *N.S.A.*, Vol. X, pp. 963–4, when referring to Dunkeld Palace which had been begun by the 4th Duke of Atholl replacing the 'plain west house' which Garnett saw in 1810 (Vol. II, p. 64). The palace,

designed by Thomas Hopper, was a Gothic fantasy even more splendid than Murthly for besides a private chapel it had a gallery, ninety-six feet long. Two floors were nearly completed and some fine Gothic windows were cut by the time of the Duke's death in 1830 when 'a mournful dispersion of the work people instantly took place'. *N.S.A.*, ibid.

135. J. Gillespie Graham to John Stewart, Perth, 28 Aug. 1829. SRO, GD 121/97/XX/118.

136. Ibid to ibid, 5 May 1830. SRO, GD 121/97/XX/149.

137. Ibid to ibid, 27 Jan. 1831. SRO, GD 121/97/XX/179.

138. Ibid to ibid, 23 April 1831. SRO, GD 121/97/XX/182.

139. Entries in 'Cash Book for New Mansion House at Murthly'. SRO, GD 121/68.

140. Stanton, op. cit., p. 195. The relationship between Gillespie Graham and Pugin after 1829 explains why, when the latter was shipwrecked at Leith in the following year, he sought out the Scottish architect in Edinburgh. Pugin produced several series of drawings in 1835, 1836 and 1837 for Gillespie Graham and they included those which the latter submitted in the competition for the Houses of Parliament in 1835.

141. Letter to Sir John Stewart from Harriet Drummond, Naples, 26 March 1830. SRO, GD 121/97/XX/148.

142. The plans are at Murthly Castle.

143. Quoted by Hussey, op. cit., p. 58.

144. H. Repton, *An Inquiry Into the Changes in Landscape Gardening* (1806), pp. 29–30.

145. *A Tour in the Highlands . . . 1818* (1819), p. 70.

146. Papers relating to the changes by Atkinson are in SRO, GD 112/20/1, 6 et passim.
A. Rowan, 'Taymouth Castle, Perthshire'. *C.L.*, Vol. CXXXVI (15 Oct. 1964), pp. 978–81 gives a full account of the developments at Taymouth after 1818.

147. Letter from J. Gillespie Graham to Sir William Drummond Stewart, 12 Nov. 1838. SRO, GD 121/97/XXI/87.

148. B. Disraeli, *The Young Duke* (1831), p. 43.

149. Ibid, pp. 43–4.

150. J. Gillespie Graham to Lord Breadalbane, 8 May 1838. SRO, GD 112/20/5.

151. J. Gillespie Graham to Lady Breadalbane, Edinburgh, 2 July 1838. SRO, GD 112/20/1.

152. Letter from J. Gillespie Graham to Sir William Drummond Stewart, 12 Nov. 1838. SRO, GD 121/97/XXI/87.

153. Letter from William Gray to J. Wyllie, Taymouth, 21 Jan. 1839. SRO, GD 112/20/1.

154. Account from Frederick Crace and Son, 14 Wigmore St, London, 1842. SRO, GD 112/20/2.

155. Letter from J. Gillespie Graham to Sir William Drummond Stewart, 12 Nov. 1838. SRO, GD 121/97/XXI/87.

156. Jones, op. cit.

157. Ardmaddy, on the coast of Argyllshire, was an old house to which additions were made in 1790. Gillespie Graham designed an extension to it which was not built until 1862 under the superintendence of David Bryce.

158. *APSD*. Gillespie Graham's portion of Brodick Castle was designed in 1844 as an enlargement of a medieval and seventeenth-century structure. It was a property of the Duke of Hamilton.

159. Stanton, op. cit., pp. 198–9.

160. Letter from J. Gillespie Graham to Sir William Drummond Stewart, 12 Nov. 1838. SRO, GD 121/97/XXI/87.

161. J. Kohl, *Scotland, Glasgow, the Clyde . . . to the Lakes* (1844), p. 41.

XIV

1. J. Fergusson, *History of Modern Architecture* (1902), Vol. II, p. 3.
2. J. Hall, *Essay on the Origin, History and Principles of Gothic Architecture* (1813), p. 145.
3. H. Colvin, *A Biographical Dictionary of English Architects, 1660–1840* (1954), p. 55.
4. *S.A.*, Vol. XVII, p. 461; *N.S.A.*, Vol. X, p. 479.
5. Colvin, ibid.
6. *N.S.A.*, Vol. III, p. 132; RCAHMS, *Peeblesshire* (1967), Vol. II, p. 199.
7. *N.S.A.*, Vol. II, p. 122. The date is above the entrance.
8. A copy of the original plan, signed and dated 1792, is in NMRS. However the *N.S.A.*, Vol. I, p. 667, says that it was built in 1794, a statement repeated by T. H. Shepherd, *Modern Athens* (1829), p. 42.
9. *N.S.A.*, Vol. VII, Pt I, pp. 226–7. The spire was added in 1823. Ibid, p. 203.
10. G. Hay, *Architecture of Scottish Post-Reformation Churches, 1560–1843* (1957), p. 96.
11. *N.S.A.*, Vol. VII, Pt II, pp. 100–1; Hay, op. cit., p. 176.
12. Letter from James Elliot to Lord Breadalbane from Edinburgh, 14 Sept. 1809. SRO, GD 112/Box 2.
13. Hay, op. cit., p. 123. The date is on the tower.
14. *N.S.A.*, Vol. X, p. 85.
15. Hay, ibid.
16. F. H. Groome (ed.), *Ordnance Gazetteer of Scotland* (1894), Vol. III, p. 18.
17. *N.S.A.*, Vol. XI, p. 258.
18. Hay, op. cit., p. 117.
19. James Playfair, *Journal of Architecture, 1783–92*. NLS, Adv. MSS 33.5.25.
20. Hay, op. cit., p. 116.
21. Colvin, op. cit., p. 463; *N.S.A.*, Vol. XI, p. 112, gives the date as 1806.
22. A. Gomme and D. Walker, *Architecture of Glasgow* (1968), p. 64n, who think the Barony Church may have been designed by Robert Adam's nephew, John Robertson, who acted for him in certain Glasgow jobs.
23. The date is on the south side of the church.
24. *N.S.A.*, Vol. XI, p. 218.
25. *N.S.A.*, Vol. XI, p. 120; Hay, op. cit., p. 246.
26. Ibid, pp. 116, 117, 260.
27. Ibid.
28. Ibid, p. 260.
29. *S.A.*, Vol. XIX, p. 481. The tower belongs to the seventeenth century but the church was rebuilt in 1795.
30. *N.S.A.*, Vol. XII, p. 413; Hay, op. cit., pp. 116, 170, 242.
31. *N.S.A.*, Vol. XII, p. 587; Hay, op. cit., pp. 116, 243.
32. *N.S.A.*, Vol. XII, p. 547; Hay, op. cit., pp. 116, 242, gives the date as 1836.
33. An inscribed stone from Crathie church is now in the manse garden. *N.S.A.*, Vol. XII, p. 652, says that the church was rebuilt in 1805 and finished in the next year.
34. *N.S.A.*, Vol. XII, p. 1,100; Hay, op. cit., pp. 117, 244.
35. *N.S.A.*, Vol. XII, p. 741; Hay, op. cit., pp. 117, 242. The date of erection is on the church.
36. *N.S.A.*, Vol. XII, p. 338; Hay, op. cit., p. 243.
37. Hay, op. cit., pp. 117, 243.
38. *N.S.A.*, Vol. XII, p. 628; Hay, op. cit., pp. 117, 242.
39. *N.S.A.*, Vol. XII, p. 713; Hay, ibid.
40. *S.A.*, Vol. V, p. 317: 'The present kirk is a neat modern edifice, built a few years ago.' Groome, op. cit., Vol. II, p. 332; Hay, op. cit., pp. 84, 264.
41. W. Gilpin, *Observations on . . . the High-lands of Scotland* (1808), Vol. I, p. 5.
42. J. M. Leighton, *History of the County of Fife* (1840), Vol. II, p. 128; Hay,

op. cit., pp. 118, 258.

43. *N.S.A.*, Vol. X, p. 591; Hay, op. cit., pp. 116, 117, 268.

44. *S.A.*, Vol. VIII, p. 352.

45. 'Lavenham Church', *G.M.*, Vol. LVII (May 1787), p. 377.

46. 'Print of W. Front of Old St. Paul's', *G.M.*, Vol. LI (April 1781), p. 217.

47. Hall, op. cit., p. 147.

48. Ibid, p. 145.

49. J. Britton, *Graphic Illustrations of Toddington* (1840), pp. 16–17.

50. Hay, op. cit., p. 109.

51. Ibid.

52. Ibid.

53. *N.S.A.*, Vol. XII, p. 819.

54. Ibid, Vol. XI, p. 185.

55. Ibid, Vol. XII, p. 413.

56. Ibid, Vol. XI, p. 145.

57. Ibid, Vol. XI, p. 258.

58. Ibid, Vol. X, p. 591.

59. Ibid, Vol. XI, p. 265.

60. Ibid, Vol. II, p. 123.

61. T. H. Marshall, *History of Perth* (1849), p. 397.

62. Hay, op. cit., p. 245.

63. Ibid, pp. 150, 271.

64. Ibid, pp. 156, 266.

65. Ibid, pp. 156, 259.

66. *N.S.A.*, Vol. XIII, p. 188; Hay, op. cit., p. 155.

67. *N.S.A.*, Vol. XIII, p. 33; G. M. Fraser, *Archibald Simpson, Architect, and His Times*, Ch. XVII.

68. T. Rickman, *An Attempt to Discriminate the Styles of Architecture in England* (1848), p. 5.

69. *APSD*; Fraser, op. cit., Ch. IV.

70. Hay, op. cit., p. 245. George Mathewson was the architect. See also P. F. Anson, 'Catholic Church Building in Scotland, 1560–1914', *Innes Review*, Vol. V (1954), p. 130.

71. Hay, op. cit., p. 248; J. E. Shaw, *Ayrshire, 1745–1950* (1953), p. 102; Anson, ibid.

72. I. Lindsay, *Georgian Edinburgh* (1948), p. 33. See also 'Description of the Episcopal Chapel now Erecting in York Place, Edinburgh'. *Scots Magazine*, Vol. LXXVIII (June 1816), p. 403; Shepherd, op. cit., p. 63.

73. Ibid, p. 72; Lindsay, ibid.

74. *N.S.A.*, Vol. I, p. 666.

75. Ibid, Vol. I, p. 667.

76. 'Architectural Description of the New Episcopal Chapel, Princes St'. *Scots Magazine*, Vol. LXXIX (Jan. 1817), p. 3.

77. H. J. Grierson (ed.), *Letters of Sir Walter Scott* (1932–7), Vol. V, p. 60.

78. Rickman, ibid.

79. Ibid, p. 231.

80. *N.S.A.*, Vol. XII, p. 604, gives the date as 1819; Hay, op. cit., p. 242, gives it as 1821.

81. Fraser, op. cit., Ch. VI.

82. *N.S.A.*, Vol. XII, p. 664; Hay, op. cit., p. 243. The date is over the entrance.

83. *N.S.A.*, Vol. XII, p. 895.

84. J. Smith, *Account Books*, Vol. VIII, in NMRS.

85. *N.S.A.*, Vol. XII, p. 955; Hay, op. cit., p. 242. Keig Church was erected in 1835.

86. *N.S.A.*, Vol. XII, p. 685.

87. Hay, op. cit., p. 263.

88. Leighton, op. cit., Vol. II, p. 83; Hay, op. cit., pp. 118, 257.

89. *N.S.A.*, Vol. IX, p. 190.

90. Ibid; Leighton, op. cit., Vol. II, p. 244; Hay, op. cit., p. 257.

91. *N.S.A.*, Vol. XII, p. 33.

92. Fraser, op. cit., Ch. XVI; APSD.

93. A. Gammie, *The Churches of Aberdeen* (1909), p. 10, records that in 1874 the East Church of St Nicholas was completely destroyed by fire but was restored in the same style.

94. Hay, op. cit., pp. 141, 258.

95. *N.S.A.*, Vol. X, p. 1,073; Hay, op. cit., p. 270.

96. The date is on the bell-cote. See Hay, op. cit., pp. 122, 270.

97. Ibid, pp. 122, 269.

98. Ibid, p. 270.

99. *N.S.A.*, Vol. I, p. 194, gives the date of Cranston Church as 1825. Hay, op. cit., pp. 122, 264.

100. Ibid.

101. *N.S.A.*, Vol. IX, p. 333; Leighton, op. cit., Vol. II, p. 121; Hay, op. cit., pp. 121, 257.

102. Ibid, pp. 122, 256.

103. *N.S.A.*, Vol. V, pp. 662–3; Hay, op. cit., p. 248.

104. *N.S.A.*, Vol. V, p. 176; Hay, op. cit., p. 249.

105. *N.S.A.*, Vol. IX, p. 872; Leighton, op. cit., Vol. II, p. 222; Hay, op. cit., pp. 129, 257.

106. *N.S.A.*, Vol. X, p. 942; Hay, op. cit., pp. 130, 270.

107. Ibid, p. 255.

108. *N.S.A.*, Vol. III, pp. 372–3; Hay, op. cit., pp. 125, 274.

109. *N.S.A.*, Vol. VIII, p. 109; Hay, op. cit., pp. 121, 253.

110. Diary of Thomas Rickman, 14 Feb. 1824 in the RIBA Drawings' Collection.

111. Ibid.

112. Ibid, 6 April 1824.

113. Ibid, 15 May 1824.

114. Ibid, 8 June 1824.

115. Ibid, 25 June 1824.

116. *N.S.A.*, Vol. II, p. 278; Hay, op. cit., p. 255.

117. *N.S.A.*, Vol. IV, p. 64; Hay, op. cit., pp. 119, 254.

118. *N.S.A.*, Vol. X, p. 216; Hay, op. cit., p. 268.

119. *N.S.A.*, Vol. X, p. 212.

120. Fraser, op. cit., Ch. XI. The plans and elevations were passed by the Town Council in August, 1827 and the church completed two years later. See Hay, op. cit., p. 241.

121. Ibid.

122. Ibid; Fraser, op. cit., Ch. XIII.

123. Smith, *Account Books*, Vol. VIII; *N.S.A.*, Vol. XI, p. 104; B. Botfield, *Journal of A Tour Through the Highlands of Scotland* (1830), p. 54; Hay, op. cit., p. 260.

124. Ibid; *N.S.A.*, Vol. XI, p. 9.

125. Ibid, Vol. VIII, p. 46; RCAHMS, *Stirlingshire* (1963), Vol. I, p. 169; Hay, op. cit., p. 275.

126. Ibid; *N.S.A.*, Vol. VIII, p. 66.

127. Ibid, Vol. VIII, p. 270; Hay, op. cit., p. 275.

128. *N.S.A.*, Vol. VII, Pt I, p. 514; Hay, op. cit., pp. 141, 271, gives the date as 1814.

129. *N.S.A.*, Vol. VIII, p. 357.

130. Ibid, Vol. VIII, p. 259, gives the date as 1829. Hay, op. cit., p. 278, gives the date as 1828.

131. *N.S.A.*, Vol. VI, p. 799; Hay, op. cit., pp. 141, 177, 262.

132. RCAHMS, op. cit., Vol. I, p. 142; Hay, op. cit., p. 275; D. Walker, 'The Stirlings of Dunblane and Falkirk'. *Bulletin of the Scottish Georgian Society*, Vol. I (1972), pp. 48–9.

133. Hay, op. cit., p. 269; Walker, ibid.

134. *N.S.A.*, Vol. X, p. 1265; 'Description of the New Parish Church of Kincardine in Monteith (sic)'. *Scots Magazine*, Vol. LXXVIII (April 1816), pp. 243–4.

135. *N.S.A.*, Vol. IX, p. 14; Hay, op. cit., p. 261.

136. *N.S.A.*, Vol. IX, p. 21; Vol. X, p. 870.

137. Ibid, Vol. IX, p. 109; Leighton, op. cit., Vol. II, p. 239; Hay, op. cit., p. 257.

138. Hall, op. cit., p. 147.

139. Hay, op. cit., p. 253.

140. Ibid, pp. 132, 259.

141. The church was built in 1813. See *N.S.A.*, Vol. VIII, p. 122; RCAHMS, op. cit., Vol. I, p. 158; Hay, op. cit., p. 275.

142. *N.S.A.*, Vol. XI, p. 586; Hay, op. cit., p. 246, gives Burn as the architect.

143. Fraser, op. cit., Ch. XXIV.

144. *N.S.A.*, Vol. I, p. 502; Hay, op. cit., p. 264.

145. *N.S.A.*, Vol. VIII, p. 43, names Angus as the architect.

146. Ibid, Vol. I, p. 502; F. Trench, *Scotland, Its Faith and Its Features* (1846), Vol. II, p. 133.

147. NMRS.

148. Ibid.

XV

1. W. Fordyce, *History of Durham* (1857), Vol. II, p. 663.

2. W. Whellan, *History and Topography of Cumberland and Westmoreland* (1860), p. 373.

3. E. Mackenzie and M. Ross, *View of the County of Durham* (1834), Vol. II, p. 98.

4. Ibid, Vol. I, pp. 107–8.

5. Fordyce, op. cit., Vol. II, p. 591.

6. Mackenzie and Ross, op. cit., Vol. I, p. 404.

7. Fordyce, op. cit., Vol. II, p. 368, quoting from an inscription in the vestry.

8. Ibid.

9. W. Hutchinson, *History and Antiquities of the County Palatine of Durham* (1794), Vol. III, p. 1.

10. J. Raine, *History and Antiquities of North Durham* (1852), pp. 245–6.

11. Ibid; N. Pevsner, *Northumberland* (1957), p. 298, gives the date as 1783.

12. Raine, op. cit., p. 190; Pevsner, op. cit., p. 202.

13. Raine, op. cit., p. 214n, says that 'The church was long in a ruinous state'; *H. of N.*, Vol. XIV, p. 89, mentions that c. 1833 the obelisks on the tower were replaced by the present saddleback roof. After the present lancet windows were introduced the walls were roughcast to hide the discrepancies caused by the insertion of the windows. The chancel was added in 1887. See also Pevsner, op. cit., p. 209; H. Colvin, *A Biographical Dictionary of English Architects, 1660–1840* (1954), p. 397.

14. The inscription is above the entrance.

15. M. A. Richardson, *Local Historian's Table Book* (1841–6), Vol. II, p. 362; J. Hodgson, *History of Northumberland* (1820–40), Pt II, Vol. II, p. 130.

16. Pevsner, op. cit., p. 208.

17. N. Pevsner, *Cumberland and Westmorland* (1967), p. 201.

18. The date is on the monument to William Thomas Salvin in the chapel. See Mackenzie and Ross, op. cit., Vol. II, p. 439.

19. C. J. Gordon, 'Crosby Ravensworth Church'. *Trans. C. & W.A. & A.S.*, New Series, Vol. VIII (1908), p. 219; Pevsner, op. cit., p. 244. Smirke was the architect.

20. *H. of N.*, Vol. XV, p. 173.

21. Richardson, op. cit., Vol. III, pp. 190–1. See also N. Pevsner, *Northumberland* (1957), pp. 311, 160, 297. On p. 197 Pevsner wrongly gives the date of Humshaugh church as 1819. Colvin, op. cit., p. 534.

22. Quoted in *H. of N.*, Vol. XV, p. 296.

23. M. J. Dobson, *A Memoir of the late John Dobson* (1885). See also *Procs of Soc. of Antiquaries* (Newcastle), 5th Series, Vol. I (1951–6), p. 346.

24. Pevsner, op. cit., pp. 160, 297, 311; Colvin, op. cit., pp. 534–5.

25. *H of N.*, Vol. XV, p. 175.

26. Ibid, Vol. XV, p. 173.

27. Ibid, Vol. XV, p. 272.

28. Richardson, op. cit., Vol. IV, p. 121; *H. of N.*, Vol. VI, p. 380; Pevsner, op. cit., p. 292.

29. Richardson, op. cit., Vol. IV, p. 176; Pevsner, op. cit., p. 202. Archdeacon Singleton on a visitation in August, 1832 stated that the church then standing was in an unsafe condition. See *Procs of Soc. of Antiquaries* (New-

castle), Vol. VII (1897), p. 128.

30. *H. of N.*, Vol. VI, p. 200; Pevsner, op. cit., p. 323, names the architect as Jonathan Marshall. The chancel was added in 1896.

31. N. Pevsner, *Cumberland and Westmorland* (1967), p. 270.

32. *H. of N.*, XIV, p. 393; N. Pevsner, *Northumberland* (1957), p. 104.

33. *H. of N.*, Vol. II, p. 9; Pevsner, op. cit., p. 148.

34. Richardson, op. cit., Vol. IV, p. 86; Fordyce, op. cit., Vol. II, p. 743; N. Pevsner, *County Durham* (1953), p. 235; Colvin, op. cit., p. 246.

35. Mackenzie and Ross, op. cit., Vol. I, p. 193; Pevsner, op. cit., p. 219; Colvin, op. cit., p. 179, credits Stella church to John Dobson.

36. Pevsner, op. cit., p. 200.

37. Richardson, op. cit., Vol. V, p. 322; Fordyce, op. cit., Vol. II, p. 386; Pevsner, op. cit., p. 243; Colvin, op. cit., p. 312.

38. Fordyce, op. cit., Vol. II, p. 620. See also Richardson, op. cit., Vol. V, pp. 314–16. Pevsner, op. cit., p. 190, mistakenly names John Green as the architect as does Colvin, op. cit., p. 246.

39. Colvin, op. cit., p. 312; Pevsner, op. cit., p. 43. See also Fordyce, op. cit., Vol. II, p. 663; Richardson, op. cit., Vol. V, p. 193.

40. Fordyce, op. cit., Vol. II, p. 749; Pevsner, op. cit., p. 167. See also J. R. Boyle, *Comprehensive Guide to the County of Durham* (1892), p. 577.

41. Mackenzie and Ross, op. cit., Vol. I, pp. 17–18.

42. Pevsner, ibid; Colvin, op. cit., p. 573.

43. Fordyce, op. cit., Vol. II, pp. 638–9; Boyle, op. cit., p. 607; Pevsner, op. cit., p. 177.

44. Mackenzie and Ross, op. cit., Vol. I, p. 147.

45. Fordyce, op. cit., Vol. II, p. 763; Richardson, op. cit., Vol. IV, p. 391;

Pevsner, op. cit., p. 150.

46. Fordyce, op. cit., Vol. II, p. 624; Colvin, op. cit., p. 179.

47. T. Rickman, *An Attempt to Discriminate the Styles of Architecture in England* (1848), p. 131.

48. Ibid, p. 124.

49. Ibid, p. 131.

50. Ibid.

51. Whellan, op. cit., pp. 143, 145; S. Jefferson, *History and Antiquities of Carlisle* (1838), pp. 271–2; *APSD*; Colvin, op. cit., p. 500; N. Pevsner, *Cumberland and Westmorland* (1967), p. 97. See also C. G. Bulman, 'Two Recently Demolished Carlisle Churches'. *Trans. C. & W.A. & A.S.*, New Series, Vol. LV (1956), pp. 311–14.

52. Ibid, p. 314.

53. J. Loudon, *Treatise on Forming, Improving and Managing Country Residences* (1806), Vol. I, p. 120.

54. T. Bulmer, *History, Topography and Directory of Westmorland* (1885), p. 460; Whellan, op. cit., p. 841; Colvin, op. cit., p. 659; Pevsner, op. cit., pp. 254, 256.

55. Whellan, ibid; Pevsner, op. cit., p. 256.

56. Bulmer, ibid.

57. Bulmer, ibid, p. 420; Whellan, op. cit., p. 831; Pevsner, op. cit., p. 277.

58. Whellan, op. cit., p. 885; Pevsner, op. cit., p. 252.

59. Whellan, op. cit., p. 891; Bulmer, op. cit., p. 667; Pevsner, op. cit., p. 238.

60. Mackenzie and Ross, op. cit., Vol. I, p. 197; Fordyce, op. cit., Vol. II, p. 674; W. Parson and W. White, *Gazetteer of Durham and Northumberland* (1828), Vol. II, p. 185; N. Pevsner, *County Durham* (1953), p. 243; Colvin, op. cit., p. 83.

61. Richardson, op. cit., Vol. IV, p. 231, Vol. V, p. 171; Fordyce, op. cit., Vol. II, p. 591; Pevsner, op. cit., p. 206; Colvin, op. cit., p. 478.

62. Richardson, op. cit., Vol. IV, p. 212; Fordyce, op. cit., Vol. II, p. 716; Pevsner, op. cit., p. 212.

63. Richardson, op. cit., Vol. V, p. 377; Fordyce, op. cit., Vol. II, p. 443; Pevsner, op. cit., p. 215; Colvin, op. cit., p. 312.

64. Richardson, op. cit., Vol. III, p. 391; *H. of N.*, Vol. IX, p. 18; N. Pevsner, *Northumberland* (1957), p. 142; Colvin, op. cit., p. 246.

65. Fordyce, op. cit., Vol. II, p. 740; N. Pevsner, *County Durham* (1953), p. 235.

66. *H. of N.*, Vol. XIII, p. 134; N. Pevsner, *Northumberland* (1957), p. 294; Colvin, op. cit., p. 246.

67. J. Hodgson, *Local Biography*, Vol. II, p. 309.

68. Ibid, Vol. II, p. 313.

69. Richardson, op. cit., Vol. IV, pp. 212–4; *H. of N.*, Vol. VIII, p. 360; Colvin, ibid; Pevsner, op. cit., p. 267.

70. W. Collard and M. Ross, *Architectural and Picturesque Views in Newcastle-upon-Tyne* (1841), pp. 55, 56; Pevsner, op. cit., pp. 56, 232; Colvin, op. cit., p. 179.

71. Dobson, op. cit., p. 37.

72. Ibid, p. 41.

73. Collard and Ross, op. cit., p. 56.

74. Loudon, op. cit., Vol. I, p. 121.

75. Ibid, Vol. I, pp. 121–2.

76. Whellan, op. cit., p. 835; Bulmer, op. cit., p. 432; N. Pevsner, *Cumberland and Westmorland* (1967), p. 268.

77. J. Hodgson, *History of Northumberland*, Pt II, Vol. III, pp. 134–5; Dobson, op. cit.; Colvin, op. cit., p. 179; N. Pevsner, *Northumberland* (1957), p. 160.

78. Parson and White, op. cit., Vol. I, p. cxlv.

79. Ibid; Mackenzie and Ross, op. cit., Vol. I, pp. 107–8; Fordyce, op. cit., Vol. II, p. 789.

80. Richardson, op. cit., Vol. IV, p. 271.

81. Ibid, Vol. IV, p. 221, Vol. V, p. 18; Fordyce, op. cit., Vol. II, pp. 163–4; Colvin, op. cit., p. 246, gives the date as 1834–5. N. Pevsner, *County Durham* (1953), p. 221, puts it as late as 1857.

82. Richardson, op. cit., Vol. V, pp. 133–4, 291; *H. of N.*, Vol. VIII, p. 360; N. Pevsner, *Northumberland* (1957), p. 300; Colvin, op. cit., p. 246, gives the date as 1839–40.

83. Richardson, op. cit., Vol. V, p. 257.

84. Ibid.

85. J. Dobson, 'Inaugural Address, April 1859'. *Procs of Northern Architectural Association* (1858–9).

86. N. Pevsner, *Cumberland and Westmorland* (1967), p. 182.

87. Ibid, p. 149.

88. Ibid, p. 82.

89. Ibid, p. 139.

90. Ibid, p. 97.

91. Ibid. The architect was J. Hodgson.

92. Parson and White, op. cit., Vol. I, p. 464; *H. of N.*, Vol. VIII, p. 376; N. Pevsner, *Northumberland* (1957), p. 267, names the architect as Robert Giles.

93. Richardson, op. cit., Vol. III, p. 373, Vol. IV, p. 62. The builder was William Oliver of Durham. Pevsner, op. cit., p. 179, states John Green to be the architect. However, it seems to be too clever and imaginative a building to be from him.

94. Whellan, op. cit., p. 841.

95. Richardson, op. cit., Vol. III, p. 353; Colvin, op. cit., p. 83.

96. Richardson, op. cit., Vol. III, p. 354; Mackenzie and Ross, op. cit., Vol. II, p. 402; R. Surtees, *History and Antiquities of the County Palatine of Durham* (1816–40), Vol. IV, p. 85; N. Pevsner, *County Durham* (1953), p. 124; Colvin, ibid.

97. Richardson, op. cit., Vol. IV, p. 26; N. Pevsner, *Northumberland* (1957), p. 90.

98. Richardson, op. cit., Vol. IV, p. 316;

G. Tate, *History of the Borough, Castle and Barony of Alnwick* (1868–9), Vol. II, p. 204; Pevsner, op. cit., p. 66; Colvin, op. cit., p. 246.

99. Whellan, op. cit., p. 123; N. Pevsner, *Cumberland and Westmorland* (1967), p. 98.

100. Richardson, op. cit., Vol. V, p. 313; N. Pevsner, *Northumberland* (1957), p. 110; Colvin, ibid.

101. Fordyce, op. cit., Vol. II, p. 685.

102. A. W. Pugin, *The True Principles of Pointed or Christian Architecture* (1841), p. 18.

103. Ibid, p. 10.

104. Whellan, op. cit., p. 343; N. Pevsner, *Cumberland and Westmorland* (1967), p. 146.

105. Raine, op. cit., p. 385; N. Pevsner, *Northumberland* (1957), p. 285.

106. Richardson, op. cit., Vol. V, pp. 394–5; Pevsner, op. cit., p. 210.

107. Certificate from Sir Edward Blackett dated 30 Oct. 1844. NRO, ZBL 265/6.

108. Matfen Hall building accounts and correspondence. NRO, ZBL 187/4

and 257.

109. Bill of Business Sir Edward Blackett to Henry Wm. Fenwick of December, 1842 for 'Attending(?) you on the subject of a new Church which you contemplated building at Matfen'. See also items dated 7 April 1843 and July 1843. NRO, ZBL 265/5.

110. NRO, ZBL 265/5.

111. Pevsner, op. cit., p. 210.

112. A. W. Pugin, *Contrasts* (1841), p. 43.

113. Whellan, op. cit., p. 196; N. Pevsner, *Cumberland and Westmorland* (1967), p. 198; P. Stanton, *Pugin* (1971), pp. 95–7.

114. Pugin, op. cit., p. 57.

115. Richardson, op. cit., Vol. V, p. 267; Mackenzie and Ross, op. cit., Vol. II, p. 30; N. Pevsner, *County Durham* (1953), p. 221; Stanton, op. cit., pp. 125, 129.

116. Parson and White, op. cit., Vol. I, p. 69; N. Pevsner, *Northumberland* (1957), p. 228; Stanton, op. cit., pp. 133, 135.

117. Pugin, op. cit., p. 5.

XVI

1. 'Pursuits of Architectural Innovation. No. XC'. *G.M.*, Vol. LXXV (Nov. 1805), p. 1,013.

2. J. Britton, *Graphic Illustrations of Toddington* (1840), p. 18.

3. C. Walton, *Romantic Ravensworth* (1950), p. 5.

4. W. Hutchinson, *History and Antiquities of the County Palatine of Durham* (1785–94), Vol. II, p. 317, plate and p. 417.

5. These designs, part of the collection of fifty-one drawings relating to Ravensworth Castle, are in the RIBA drawings' collection.

6. M. A. Richardson, *Local Historian's Table-Book* (1841–6), Vol. III, p. 78; E. Mackenzie and M. Ross, *View of the County of Durham* (1834), Vol. I, p. 150; T. Rose, *Westmorland, Cumber-*

land, Durham and Northumberland (1832), p. 21.

7. *APSD*; J. Summerson, *John Nash* (1952), p. 95; N. Pevsner, *County Durham* (1953), pp. 195–6; H. Colvin, *Biographical Dictionary of English Architects, 1660–1840* (1954), p. 408.

8. Walton, op. cit., p. 11.

9. Mackenzie and Ross, ibid.
In the Ravensworth Castle drawings in the RIBA, E4/3(48), there is a letter from Nash to John Liddell in 1824.

10. *Burke's Peerage, Baronetage and Knightage* (1970), pp. 2, 226–7.

11. Britton, op. cit., p. 26.

12. Ibid, p. 21.

13. W. Fordyce, *History of Durham* (1857), Vol. II, p. 321.

14. RIBA drawings E4/3(23).

REFERENCES

15. Mackenzie and Ross, ibid.
16. Pevsner, ibid.
17. Fordyce, op. cit., Vol. II, p. 642.
18. Ibid.
19. RIBA drawings E4/3(12).
20. The watermark is 1821. RIBA drawings E4/3(28).
21. The watermark is 1823. RIBA drawings E4/3(15).
22. Mackenzie and Ross, ibid.
23. Ibid.
24. A. Rowan, 'Downton Castle, Herefordshire'. *The Country Seat*, ed. by H. Colvin and J. Harris (1970), pp. 170–3.
25. W. Gilpin, *Observations on . . . Cumberland and Westmoreland* (1808), Vol. II, p. 149.
26. The drawings are watermarked 1794 but it is 1798 on the letter which accompanied 'A Plan showing the Situation and Aspect of the Buildings at Lowther according to a Sketch given by Mr. Webster'. CRO, Lonsdale MSS.
27. Rose, op. cit., p. 38.
28. Colvin, op. cit., p. 546; N. Pevsner, *Cumberland and Westmorland* (1967), p. 272.
29. Letter from R. Smirke to Lord Lonsdale, dated 11 April 1814. CRO, Lonsdale MSS.
30. Ibid to ibid, 2 June 1814. CRO, Lonsdale MSS.
31. J. Greig (ed.), *The Farington Diary* (1923), Vol. III, p. 205. Entry for 25 April 1806.
32. Ibid, Vol. III, p. 198. Entry for 21 April 1806.
33. Ibid.
34. J. Hodgson, *Topographical and Historical Description of the County of Westmoreland* (1823), p. 124.
35. Greig, op. cit., Vol. V, p. 112. Entry for 11 Feb. 1809.
36. Account attached to a letter from R. Smirke and dated 11 April 1814. CRO, Lonsdale MSS.
37. Greig, op. cit., Vol. V, p. 67. Entry for 19 May 1808.
38. Account attached to the letter from R. Smirke dated 11 April 1814. CRO, Lonsdale MSS.
39. Account attached to the letter from R. Smirke dated 2 June 1814. CRO, Lonsdale MSS.
40. Greig, op. cit., Vol. VI, p. 251. Entry for 19 March 1811.
41. Letter from R. Smirke dated 11 April 1814. CRO, Lonsdale MSS.
42. F. Bamford and the Duke of Wellington (eds), *The Journal of Mrs. Arbuthnot* (1950), Vol. II, p. 42.
43. A plan of Lowther Castle and some details are in the RIBA drawings' collection. J11/12, 1–8.
44. Quoted by D. Sutherland, *The Yellow Earl* (1965).
45. Britton, op. cit., p. 23.
46. Sutherland, op. cit., pp. 192–3. The park at Lowther was greatly extended by Hugh, the 'Yellow Earl', to surpass that of his neighbours, the Howards of Greystoke Castle, which had been the largest park in England.
47. Pevsner, op. cit., p. 101, refers to Colvin who states that the courts in Carlisle were begun by Telford and Chisholm, continued in 1808 by Peter Nicholson and only completed by Smirke. For a full discussion of the problem of authorship see J. Hughes, 'The Building of the Courts, Carlisle, 1807–22'. *Trans. C. & W.A. & A.S.*, N.S., Vol. LXX (1970), pp. 209–19.
48. Greig, op. cit., Vol. VI, p. 27. Entry for 21 March 1810.
49. Ibid, Vol. VI, p. 251. Entry for 19 March 1811. See S. Jefferson, *History and Antiquities of Carlisle* (1838), pp. 278–9; W. Whellan, *History and Topography of Cumberland and Westmorland* (1860), p. 128.
50. Pevsner, op. cit., p. 188.
51. Whellan, op. cit., p. 736; Pevsner, op. cit., p. 232, gives the date as 1842.

52. C. Hussey, 'Gibside, County Durham'. *C.L.*, Vol. CXI (8 Feb. 1952), p. 356; N. Pevsner, *County Durham* (1953), p. 152; F. Rutherford, 'Pevsner on the Palatinate', *Trans. Architectural and Archaeological Society of Durham and Northumberland*, Vol. XI (1958), p. 81, tentatively suggests that the re-modelling of Gibside Hall was by David Stephenson of Newcastle. However the colossal parapet which was added above the entrance front is similar to that at Ford Castle where Gilkie worked for Lord Delaval who recommended him 'to Lord Strathmore for the rebuilding of Gibside'. See Colvin, op. cit., p. 237.

53. Hodgson, ibid; N. Pevsner, *Northumberland* (1957), p. 152.

54. Letters from William Hutton to Thomas Wallace. NRO, Middleton (Belsay) MSS, ZMIs 76/46–48.

55. Letter from William Hutton, dated 30 Oct. 1818. NRO, ZMIs 76/46/19.

56. Richardson, op. cit., Vol. III, p. 313; Pevsner, op. cit., p. 247, gives the date of the Lying-In Hospital as 1826; Colvin, op. cit., p. 181.

57. W. Parson and W. White, *Gazetteer of Durham and Northumberland* (1827), Vol. I, p. 82.

58. Richardson, ibid.

59. Whellan, op. cit., p. 130; *APSD*; N. Pevsner, *Cumberland and Westmorland* (1967), p. 103.

60. Jefferson, op. cit., p. 289.

61. Whellan, op. cit., p. 164.

62. Ibid; Jefferson, op. cit., p. 381; *APSD*; J. Wilson, *Rose Castle* (1912), pp. 103–4; Pevsner, op. cit., pp. 181–2. See also C. M. L. Bouch, 'Rose Castle', *Trans. C. & W.A. & A.S.*, N.S., Vol. LVI (1957), p. 140.

63. Pevsner, op. cit., p. 185. See also Jefferson, op. cit., p. 385.

64. *APSD*; Pevsner, op. cit., p. 139.

65. Jefferson, op. cit., p. 405.

66. Whellan, op. cit., p. 890; T. Bulmer, *History, Topography and Directory of Westmorland* (1885), p. 665.

67. The date is over the doorway. See Pevsner, op. cit., p. 224.

68. Ibid, p. 109.

69. Ibid, p. 137. See also Jefferson, op. cit., p. 403.

70. Smirke's drawings, from 24 Berkeley Square, for the extensions to Edmond Castle are dated for each year from 1844–6.

71. Pevsner, op. cit., p. 133.

72. Ibid, p. 169; Rose, op. cit., p. 101.

73. Ibid, p. 37; Whellan, op. cit., p. 889.

74. F. Morris, *Picturesque Views of Seats* (1866–80), Vol. IV, p. 73; Bulmer, op. cit., p. 663; Pevsner, op. cit., p. 295.

75. Quoted by W. J. Hipple, *The Beautiful, the Sublime, and the Picturesque in Eighteenth-Century British Aesthetic Theory* (1957), p. 234.

76. Ibid, pp. 233–4.

77. R. Kerr, *The Gentleman's House* (1864), p. 81.

78. Ibid, p. 83.

79. Ibid, p. 103.

80. A. Pugin, A. W. Pugin and E. J. Willson, *Examples of Gothic Architecture* (1839), Vol. II, p. xviii.

81. Ibid.

82. N. Pevsner, *Northumberland* (1957), p. 210; Colvin, op. cit., p. 501; J. Farthing, 'The Matfen Estate'. Unpublished B.Arch. dissertation School of Architecture, University of Newcastle-upon-Tyne, 1964.

83. Rickman's Diary, 2 May 1832.

84. Ibid, 7 May 1832.

85. Ibid.

86. Ibid, 22 May 1832.

87. Letter from Sir Edward Blackett to Lady Julia Blackett, dated 25 May 1832. NRO, ZBL 253.

88. Rickman's Diary, 30 May 1832.

89. Ibid, 31 May, 1, 2, 5 June 1832.

90. Plans No. 1 and 2 for Matfen Hall are in the Matfen Estate office.

91. Letter from T. Rickman to Sir Edward

Blackett of 3 Sept. 1832. NRO, ZBL 257.

92. Rickman's Diary, 13 Oct. 1832.

93. Ibid, 19 Nov. 1832.

94. Ibid, 20 Nov. 1832.

95. Letter of 10 Dec. 1832, from T. Rickman to Sir Edward Blackett. NRO, ZBL 257.

96. Rickman's Diary, 5 Sept. 1833.

97. Ibid, 4 Sept. 1833.

98. The plan is in the Matfen Estate office.

99. Letter from T. Rickman to Sir Edward Blackett, dated 13 Feb. 1833. NRO, ZBL 257.

100. Ibid to ibid, 15 April 1833. NRO, ZBL 257.

101. Ibid to ibid, 9 Feb. 1835. NRO, ZBL 257.

102. Letter to Sir Matthew W. Ridley, Bart. Although unsigned it is clearly from Sir Edward Blackett and was probably a draft. In addition a letter from Richard Thomas Hussey of 11 Feb. 1835 goes into the question in some depth of Rickman's dismissal by Sir Edward Blackett. NRO, ZBL 257.

103. Letter to Sir Matthew W. Ridley, Bart. NRO, ZBL 257.

104. Rickman's Diary, 29 March 1832.

105. Letter from Messrs Kinson and Browne, London, 29 Sept. 1835. NRO, ZBL 257.

106. Letter to Sir Edward Blackett from L. N. Cottingham, Waterloo Bridge Rd, of 1 Oct. 1836. NRO, ZBL 260. Lewis Nockalls Cottingham (1787–1847) was a well known Gothic scholar and antiquarian. A friend of Carter, he published several works on medieval architecture. See Colvin, op. cit., pp. 153–4.

107. M. J. Dobson, *Memoir of the Late John Dobson* (1885); Pevsner, op. cit., p. 76; Colvin, op. cit., p. 177.

108. J. Dobson, 'Inaugural Address'. *Procs. Northern Architectural Association* (1858–9), p. 13.

109. Dobson's topographical drawings are in the Laing Art Gallery, Newcastle-on-Tyne.

110. J. Dobson, ibid.

111. Rose, op. cit., p. 145; M. J. Dobson, op. cit., Pevsner, op. cit., p. 205; Colvin, op. cit., p. 178. W. Hutchinson, *View of Northumberland* (1778), Vol. I, p. 237, mentions that 'The ancient Tower and Mansion of the Lilburns is in ruins'.

112. *H. of N.*, Vol. XIV, p. 438.

113. The agent's accounts for the building of Lilburn are still at Lilburn Tower. They are in two notebooks. The first is a monthly account of expenditure from 1828–32; in the second notebook the expenses are itemised.

114. J. Dobson, op. cit., p. 12.

115. Richardson, op. cit., Vol. III, p. 249.

116. Ibid, Vol. IV, p. 109; *H. of N.*, Vol. XIII, p. 214; Pevsner, op. cit., p. 88.

117. M. J. Dobson, op. cit.; Pevsner, op. cit., p. 106; Colvin, ibid. J. Wallis, *Antiquities of Northumberland* (1769), Vol. II, p. 522, describes the house as 'in decay' although later Hutchinson, op. cit., Vol. II, p. 280, refers to it without comment. The Georgian portion of the house was built in 1810. NRO, ZFE/21, p. 4. See *Procs of Soc. of Antiquaries* (Newcastle), Vol. X (1902), p. 200.

118. M. J. Dobson, op. cit.; N. Pevsner, *Cumberland and Westmorland* (1967), p. 199; Colvin, ibid.

119. M. J. Dobson: op. cit., gives the date of Beaufront Castle as 1835; *H. of N.*, Vol. IV, p. 199; N. Pevsner, *Northumberland* (1957), pp. 82–3; Colvin, ibid. Beaufront Castle replaced a Georgian mansion erected for the Errington family one of whom was a subscriber to James Paine's, *Plans, Elevations and Sections of Noblemen and Gentlemen's Houses* (1767). Since all the other Northumbrian landed proprietors listed had mansions built for them by Paine, then Beaufront should, per-

haps, be included in his works. However, in John Carr's copy of *Select Architecture* (in the Soane Museum) there is, opposite pl. V, a plan and elevation of a three-storeyed house with two-storey wings. Below is written, 'Design'd for —— Errington, Esqr'.

Hutchinson, op. cit., Vol. I, p. 174, described Georgian Beaufront as 'an extensive modern plan' and Hodgson, *Northumberland* (1813), p. 158, said that 'it exhibits a long and handsome front'. In Dobson's house there is still one complete room from this house.

120. J. R. Boyle, *Comprehensive Guide to the County of Durham* (1892), p. 438; Fordyce, op. cit., Vol. II, p. 627.

121. W. Hutchinson, *History and Antiquities of the County Palatine of Durham* (1787), Vol. II, p. 413.

122. The plan was prepared by John Dodds. See C. Hussey, 'Lambton Castle, Durham'. *C.L.*, Vol. CXXXIX (24 and 31 March, 1966), pp. 665–7, 726–9, for a full account of Lambton Castle. See also N. Pevsner, *County Durham* (1953), p. 177.

John Dodds was a builder and architect in Newcastle. See Colvin, op. cit., p. 181.

123. Sketches by J. Bonomi relating to Lambton and dated 1796 are in the Lambton MSS at Lambton. See also Richardson, op. cit., Vol. II, p. 395; Fordyce, ibid; Colvin, op. cit., p. 85.

124. S. Reid, *Life and Letters of the first Earl of Durham* (1906), Vol. I, p. 30.

125. The 'Costs of Lambton Hall New Buildings to Sept., 1801' is in the Lambton MSS.

126. The correspondence for the reconstruction of Lambton Hall is in the Lambton MSS.

127. Parson and White, op. cit., Vol. II, p. 150, recorded in 1828 that Lambton Castle had 'recently been surmounted with battlements'.

128. Fordyce, op. cit., Vol. II, p. 628; M. J. Dobson, op. cit., pp. 32–4.

129. Quoted in *C.L.*, Vol. CXXXIX, p. 728.

130. J. Gore (ed.), *Creevey's Life and Times* (1934), p. 223.

131. N. Pevsner, *Northumberland* (1957), p. 300; Colvin, op. cit., p. 247.

132. Pevsner, op. cit., p. 267, credits the Town Hall at North Shields to Dobson although there is no mention of such a commission in the list of works compiled by M. J. Dobson, the architect's daughter.

133. Pugin, op. cit., Vol. II, p. xv.

XVII

1. J. Britton, *Graphic Illustrations of Toddington* (1840), p. 27.

2. *APSD*; H. M. Colvin, *Biographical Dictionary of English Architects, 1660–1840* (1954), p. 676.

There is a water-colour view of Dalmeny, dated 1815, in the RIBA drawings' collection, CC7/11.

3. L. Simond, *Journal of a Tour and Residence in Great Britain, During the Years 1810 and 1811, by a French Traveller* (1817), Vol. I, p. 432.

4. A. Bolton, *The Architecture of Robert and James Adam* (1922), Vol. II, Index of Adam Drawings, p. 3.

There are designs by Robert Adam for the new castle of Barnbougle at Dalmeny House.

5. Wilkins' design for a Grecian mansion is at Dalmeny House along with the volume of plans for its Tudor successor. There has recently been discovered at Dalmeny a set of small elevations in coloured wash showing a series of Tudor fronts which, although simpler and lacking the tower

in the centre of the east front, are not dissimilar to the mansion that was built. Each elevation is signed 'Jeffry Wyatt Archt. 1814'. Whether they were commissioned by the 3rd Earl of Rosebery or by his heir is uncertain.

6. C. Hussey, *English Country Houses* (1958), Vol. III, Late Georgian, 1800–1840, p. 145.

7. Jones, *Views of the Seats . . . in Scotland* (1829); J. Small, *Castles and Mansions of the Lothians* (1883).

8. J. Fergusson, *History of Modern Architecture* (1902), Vol. II, p. 100.

9. Ibid.

10. *APSD* gives the date of Dunmore Park as 1826; Colvin, ibid; RCAHMS, *Stirlingshire* (1963), Vol. I, p. 230, and Vol. II, p. 341.

11. Colvin, ibid.

12. NMRS, STD/86/1, 4–6. Jones, ibid.

13. Letter from Robert Wallace of Kelly to Sir John Forbes of Craigievar of 9 July 1828. SRO, GD 250/41/3.

14. R. Kerr, *The Gentleman's House* (1864), p. 57.

15. The date 1818 is carved on the exterior of Dundas Castle. Jones, op. cit.; *N.S.A.*, Vol. II, p. 98; Small, op. cit.

16. T. Hannan, *Famous Scottish Houses* (1928), p. 94.

17. The drawings for Carstairs House in NMRS, LAD/5/3, 5, 6, are dated 30 June 1821. J. M. Leighton and J. Swan, *Select Views on the River Clyde* (1830), p. 1; Jones, op. cit.

18. Ibid.

19. Leighton and Swan, op. cit., p. 2.

20. Burn's plans, dated 1824, are in NMRS, MLD/71/2–7. The contract for building was signed on 17 Jan. 1825.

21. Jones, op. cit.

22. Hannan, op. cit., p. 94.

23. Kerr, op. cit., p. 55.

24. J. Britton, *Architectural Antiquities* (1807), Vol. II.

25. The drawings, in NMRS, AYD/38/3, 5–8, are dated 18 Sept. 1820. *N.S.A.*, Vol. V, p. 338 states that Blairquhan was finished in 1824; Jones, op. cit.; Hannan, op. cit., p. 29; M. Girouard, *The Victorian Country House* (1971), p. 22.

26. Letter from William Burn to C. R. Cockerell dated 9 July 1824. NLS, Cockerell MSS, 638, f. 63.

27. The contract for Garscube House was signed on 26 Jan. 1827. *N.S.A.*, Vol. VIII, p. 49.

28. Britton, op. cit., Vol. II.

29. The designs for Garscube House, dated 25 Oct. 1826, are in NMRS, DBD/10/4, 6, 12, 15, 17.

30. The designs for Fettercairn House, dated 8 March 1826, are still at Fettercairn House. Copies in NMRS, KCD/32/4–6.

31. *N.S.A.*, Vol. IX, p. 508; J. M. Leighton, *History of the County of Fife* (1840), Vol. II, p. 64.

32. Burn's designs for St Fort, dated 9 May 1829, are in NMRS, FID/164/1–6. *N.S.A.*, ibid; Leighton, ibid and p. 282.

33. *N.S.A.*, Vol. X, p. 676.

34. Ibid, Vol. X, p. 257; E. Maxtone Graham, *The Maxtones of Cultoquhey* (1935), p. 154.

35. Ibid.

36. Ibid, p. 155.

37. *APSD*; Colvin, op. cit., p. 501.

38. *APSD*; Colvin, ibid.

39. Leighton and Swan, op. cit., pp. 17–18; Colvin, op. cit., p. 80.

40. *N.S.A.*, Vol. III, p. 245.

41. R. Lugar, *Villa Architecture* (1828), p. 23, describes The Hensol as, 'This newly erected mansion'; *APSD*; Colvin, op. cit., p. 370; J. Dunbar, *Historic Architecture of Scotland* (1966), p. 129.

42. Lugar, op. cit., p. vii.

43. The plans for Snaigow are in NMRS, PTD/96/2–17. *N.S.A.*, Vol. X, p. 676.

44. The plans for Strathendry House are in NMRS, FID/169/1–12. *N.S.A.*, Vol. IX, p. 116; Leighton, op. cit., Vol. II, p. 189; A. H. Millar, *Fife: Pictorial and Historical* (1895), Vol. II, p. 79.

45. The plans for Auchmacoy, dated 3 Feb. 1831, are in NMRS, ABD/13/4–8, 9.

46. *N.S.A.*, Vol. IV, p. 71.

47. The plans for Saltoun Hall are in NLS, Fletcher of Saltoun MSS, Accession No. 2933 with copies in NMRS. The plan of the principal floor is signed and dated 16 Oct. 1817. Elevations are dated 2 April, 1818. Small, op. cit.; Hannan, op. cit., pp. 157–9. See also *N.S.A.*, Vol. II, p. 116.

48. The correspondence of John Adam which relates to Saltoun Hall is in NLS, Fletcher of Saltoun MSS.

49. Colvin, op. cit., p. 546.

50. Letter from William Burn to C. R. Cockerell, dated 26 Dec. 1822. NLS, Cockerell MSS, 638, f. 18.

51. Britton, op. cit., Vol. II.

52. Burn's plans for the additions to Dalhousie Castle in 1825 are in NMRS, MLD/23/1–6.

53. Inverness Castle was built in two stages in 1834 and 1843. Burn's plans are in NMRS, IND/5/1–25. *N.S.A.*, Vol. XIV, p. 16.

54. The plans for Beaufort Castle are in RIBA.

55. A. W. Pugin, *True Principles of Pointed or Christian Architecture* (1841), pp. 58–9.

56. Small, op. cit., gives the information that the alterations were completed in 1827.

57. Burn's plans for additions to Hoddam Castle are in NMRS, DFD/70/1–13.

58. Copies of Burn's plans for Pitcaple Castle are in NMRS.

59. The plans for the extensions to Kilconquhar Castle are in NMRS, FID/110/1–22.

60. Although the drawings for Castle Menzies, in NMRS, PTD/3/2–17, are dated 14 May 1836 work was delayed for four years. See A. H. Millar, *Historical Castles and Mansions of Scotland* (1890), p. 45.

61. NMRS.

62. Britton, op. cit., Vol. II.

63. Burn's plans for Milton Lockhart are in NMRS, LAD/23/5, 8, 11, 13.

64. *Glasgow and Lanarkshire Illustrated* (1904), p. 116.

65. *N.S.A.*, Vol. V, p. 582.

66. The drawings for Auchterarder House are in NMRS, PTD/30/1–15. *N.S.A.*, Vol. X, p. 289.

67. The drawings for Tyninghame House are in NMRS, ELD/103/1–12.

68. Millar, op. cit., Vol. I, p. 236.

69. The total expense for Falkland House was calculated in an abstract of estimates despatched on 22 June 1839 by Burn to O. Tyndall Bruce. SRO, GD 152/58. *N.S.A.*, Vol. IX, p. 930. The plans and elevations, dated 7 May 1839, are in NMRS, FID/101/3, 5–8.

70. The contract was signed on 7 Sept. 1839. SRO, GD 152/137.

71. Letter from William Spottiswoode to O. Tyndall Bruce of 8 Nov. 1842. SRO, GD 152/58.

72. Ibid to ibid, 11 July 1842. SRO, GD 152/58.

73. Ibid to ibid, 8 Nov. 1842. SRO, GD 152/58.

74. Ibid to ibid, 18 May 1843. SRO, GD 152/58.

75. Ibid to ibid, 5 June 1843. SRO, GD 152/58.

76. 'Statement of expence of Chimney piece for Ent (sic) Hall'. SRO, GD 152/58.

77. William Burn to O. Tyndall Bruce, 29 Oct. 1844. SRO, GD 152/58.

78. SRO, GD 152/58.

79. William Burn to O. Tyndall Bruce, 22 Oct. 1841. SRO, GD 152/58.

80. Estimate from D. R. Hay, 90 George

St, Edinburgh of April, 1843. SRO, GD 152/58.

81. D. R. Hay to O. Tyndall Bruce, 23 May 1843. SRO, GD 152/58.

82. Ibid to ibid.

83. Burn's designs, dated 2, 12 Aug. and 12 Sept. 1839, are in NMRS, MLD/80/3, 6–8. N.S.A., Vol. I, pp. 611–12; Small, op. cit. The building contract, dated 16 and 19 Nov. 1840, put the price of the new mansion at £18,217 16s 7d. The house was to be completed by the end of August, 1842. Burn's account, from his first examination of the ground in 1843 to the autumn of 1843, totalled £1,301 6s 6d. The price of Whitehill far exceeded the original estimate. NRAS 0227/8G(1).

84. Burn's plans are in NMRS, FID/149/1–27. N.S.A., Vol. IX, p. 484; Leighton, op. cit., Vol. II, p. 40.

85. The drawings for Dupplin Castle are in NMRS, PTD/53/1–45. A. H. Millar, Historical Castles and Mansions of Scotland (1890), p. 125.

86. Ibid, p. 126.

87. The drawings for St Fort are in NMRS, FID/164/1–6.

88. Kerr, op. cit., p. 359.

89. Ibid.

90. Letter from William Burn to Sir John Forbes of Craigievar, dated 27 Sept. 1828. SRO, GD 250/41/3.

91. J. Smith to Sir John Forbes, 5 Jan. 1827. SRO, GD 250/41/2.

92. Sir John Forbes to William Burn, 5 June 1827. SRO, GD 250/41/3.

93. William Burn to Sir John Forbes, 6 June 1827. SRO, GD 250/41/3.

94. Ibid to ibid, 11 April 1828. SRO, GD 250/41/3.

95. Account from William Burn dated 13 March 1829. SRO, GD 250/41/3.

96. Sir John Forbes to William Burn, 22 Sept. 1828. SRO, GD 250/41/3.

97. William Burn to Sir John Forbes, 27 Sept. 1828. SRO, GD 250/41/3.

98. J. Smith to Sir John Forbes, 29 Dec. 1828. SRO, GD 250/41/2.

99. Copy contract of 1830. SRO, GD 250/41/3.

100. The first specification for 'the South division', dated 4 April 1829, mentions a pediment. The second specification of the same date was 'for pulling down and removing the East division of the present Building'. SRO, GD 250/41/3.

101. 'Contract for making Bricks at Fintray House, 30 May, 1829'. SRO, GD 250/41/3.

102. 'Contract for making Bricks at Fintray House, 13th October, 1829'. SRO, GD 250/41/3.

103. Sir John Forbes to William Burn, 5 June 1827. SRO, GD 250/41/3.

104. Specification for mason work. SRO, GD 250/41/3.

105. The receipt for digging the foundations is dated 3 Oct. 1829. SRO, GD 250/41/3.

106. 'Estimate for doors, shutters, etc. of 3 principal rooms——29th Oct., 1831'. SRO, GD 250/41/3.

107. G. M. Fraser, Archibald Simpson, Architect, and His Times, Ch. XII.

108. N.S.A., Vol. XII, p. 546; APSD.

109. W. D. Simpson; Archibald Simpson, Architect, 1790–1847 (1947), p. 14.

110. Kerr, op. cit., p. 358.

111. N.S.A., Vol. XII, pp. 104 and 1181–3; APSD; Fraser, op. cit., Chs VII, IX, XVIII. Simpson and Smith had recommended a new building for Marischal College in 1824 but although both were asked to submit plans only Simpson did so. However, Treasury funds for a new building were not advanced until 1836.

112. APSD; Fraser, op. cit., Chs VII, IX; Smith's accounts in NMRS.

113. N.S.A., Vol. XII, p. 1038; APSD; Fraser, op. cit., Ch. XXI.

114. N.S.A., Vol. XII, p. 304; APSD.

115. Ibid.

116. Ibid.

117. *N.S.A.*, Vol. XII, p. 1097. The date is over the entrance.
118. NMRS.
119. *N.S.A.*, Vol. XII, pp. 546–7.
120. *APSD*; J. B. Pratt, *Buchan* (1870), p. 52.
121. Smith's plans are in the house.
122. Smith's accounts, Vol. VIII in NMRS.
123. *N.S.A.*, Vol. XII, p. 834. See also Smith's accounts.
124. Smith's accounts.
125. *N.S.A.*, Vol. V, pp. 294–5; *APSD*; R. Chambers, *Biographical Dictionary of Eminent Scotsmen* (1875), Vol. II, p. 205.
126. *APSD*.
127. Ibid; Small, op. cit.
128. *APSD*; Hannan, op. cit., pp. 69, 71.
129. *N.S.A.*, Vol. I, p. 120; *APSD*; Hannan, op. cit., pp. 33–5; Small, op. cit.
130. *N.S.A.*, Vol. III, p. 320; RCAHMS, *Roxburghshire* (1956), Vol. I, p. 250. Playfair's drawings are still at Floors.
131. *N.S.A.*, Vol. I, p. 726. The date and Playfair's name are carved over the entrance.
132. Kerr, op. cit., p. 476.
133. Ibid, p. 386.

Bibliography

Books

Adam, Robert. *Ruins of the Palace of Spalatro*. London, 1764.

Adam, William. *Vitruvius Scoticus*. Edinburgh, n.d.

Allen, Barbara S. *Tides in English Taste, 1619–1800*. 2 vols. New York, 1958.

Angus, William. *Seats of the Nobility and Gentry in Great Britain and Wales*. Islington, 1787.

Anson, Peter F. *The Catholic Church in Modern Scotland, 1560–1937*. London, 1937.

Askham, Francis. *The Gay Delavals*. London, 1955.

Barbier, Carl Paul. *William Gilpin. His Drawings, Teaching, and Theory of the Picturesque*. Oxford, 1963.

Bamford, Francis, and the Duke of Wellington (eds). *The Journal of Mrs. Arbuthnot*. 2 vols. London, 1950.

Beard, Geoffrey. *Georgian Craftsmen and Their Work*. London, 1966.

Bolton, Arthur T. *The Architecture of Robert and James Adam*. 2 vols. London, 1922.

Bolton, Arthur T. *Portrait of Sir John Soane*. London, 1927.

Bonnar, Thomas. *Biographical Sketch of G. Meikle Kemp*. Edinburgh, 1892.

Boswell, James. *Journal of a Tour to the Hebrides*. Oxford University Press Edition of Standard Authors. London, 1951.

Botfield, Beriah. *Journal of a Tour Through the Highlands of Scotland during the summer of 1829*. Norton Hall, 1830.

Boyle, John R. *Comprehensive Guide to the County of Durham*. London, 1892.

Brenan, Gerald. *A History of the House of Percy*. 2 vols. London, 1902.

Briggs, Martin S. *Architect in History*. Oxford, 1927.

Briggs, Martin S. *Goths and Vandals*. London, 1952.

Britton, John. *Architectural Antiquities of Great Britain*. 5 vols. London, 1807.

Britton, John. *Graphic Illustrations of Toddington*. London, 1840.

Bulmer, T. F. *History, Topography and Directory of Westmorland*. Manchester, 1885.

Burke's Peerage, Baronetage and Knightage. 105th edn, London, 1970.

Burt, Edward. *Letters from a Gentleman in the North of Scotland*. 2 vols. 5th edn, London, 1818.

Campbell, Alexander. *A Journey Through Parts of North Britain*. 2 vols. London, 1810.

Campbell, Colin. *Vitruvius Britannicus*. 3 vols. London, 1715–25.

Carter, John. *The Ancient Architecture of England*. London, 1845.

Chambers, Robert. *Biographical Dictionary of Eminent Scotsmen*. 3 vols. London, 1875.

Clark, Kenneth. *Gothic Revival*. Pelican edn, Harmondsworth, 1964.

Colgrave, Bertram. *Durham Castle*. Derby, n.d.

Collard, W., and Ross, M. *Architectural and Picturesque Views in Newcastle-upon-Tyne*.

Newcastle-upon-Tyne, 1841.

Colvin, Howard M. *A Biographical Dictionary of English Architects, 1660–1840*. London, 1954.

Colvin, Howard M., and Craig, Maurice (eds). 'Architectural Drawings in the Library of Elton Hall by Sir John Vanbrugh and Sir Edward Lovett Pearce'. *Roxburghe Club*. Oxford, 1964.

Colvin, Howard M., and Harris, John (eds). *The Country Seat. Studies in the History of the British Country House*. London, 1970.

'Correspondence of John Cosin, Bishop of Durham'. *Surtees Society*. Vols LII, LV. Newcastle-upon-Tyne. Pt. I, 1869 and Pt. II, 1872.

Crombie, Benjamin W. *Modern Athenians*. Edinburgh, 1882.

Cruden, Stewart. *The Scottish Castle*. Edinburgh and London, 1963.

Dale, Antony, *James Wyatt*. Oxford, 1956.

Dalrymple, Sir Hew Hamilton. *An Account of Oxenfoord Castle*. 1901.

Davison, William. *A Descriptive and Historical View of Alnwick*. 2nd edn, Alnwick, 1822.

Decker, Paul. *Gothic Architecture Decorated*. London, 1759. Reprinted Farnborough, 1968.

Defoe, Daniel. *A Tour Thro' the Whole Island of Great Britain*. 1724. 2 vols. London, 1927.

Denholm, James. *History of the City of Glasgow and Tour to the Principal Scotch and English Lakes*. 3rd edn, Glasgow, 1804.

Dickins, L., and Stanton, M. (eds). *An Eighteenth Century Correspondence*. London, 1910.

Dictionary of Architecture. Issued by the Architectural Publication Society. 8 vols. London, 1848–87.

Dictionary of National Biography.

Disraeli, Benjamin. *The Young Duke*. 3 vols. London, 1831.

Dobson, Margaret J. *A Memoir of the Late John Dobson*. Newcastle-upon-Tyne, 1885.

Draper, M. P. G., and Eden, W. A. *Marble Hill House and Its Owners*. London, 1970.

Dunbar, John. *Historic Architecture of Scotland*. London, 1966.

Eastlake, Charles L. *A History of the Gothic Revival*. London, 1872. Reprinted Leicester University Press, 1970, with an introduction by J. Mordaunt Crook.

Eliott of Stobs, Dowager Lady and Sir Arthur. *The Elliots. The Story of a Border Clan*. Chatham, 1974.

Fergusson, James. *A History of Modern Architecture*. 2 vols. 3rd edn, London, 1902.

Ferrey, Brian. *Recollections of A. W. Pugin*. London, 1861.

Fitler, J., and Nattes, J. C. *Scotia Depicted*. London, 1804.

Fleming, John. *Robert Adam and His Circle in Edinburgh and Rome*. London, 1963.

Fordyce, William. *The History and Antiquities of the County Palatine of Durham*. 2 vols. Newcastle-upon-Tyne, 1857.

Forsyth, Robert. *Beauties of Scotland*. 5 vols. Edinburgh, 1805–8.

Fraser, G. M. *Archibald Simpson, Architect, and His Times*. Collected articles in the Central Reference Library, Aberdeen.

Gammie, Alexander. *The Churches of Aberdeen*. Aberdeen, 1909.

Garnett, Thomas. *Observations on a Tour Through the Highlands and Part of the Western Isles of Scotland*. 2 vols. London, 1810.

Gilpin, William. *Observations on Several Parts of England, Particularly the Mountains, and Lakes of Cumberland, and Westmoreland, relative chiefly to Picturesque Beauty, Made in the Year 1772*. 1786. 2 vols. 3rd edn, London, 1808.

Gilpin, William. *Observations on Several Parts of Great Britain, Particularly the Highlands of Scotland, relative chiefly to Picturesque Beauty, Made in the Year 1776*. 1789. 2 vols. 3rd edn, London, 1808.

Girouard, Mark. *The Victorian Country House*. London, 1971.

Glasgow and Lanarkshire Illustrated. Edinburgh and Glasgow, 1904.

Gomme, Andor, and Walker, David. *Architecture of Glasgow*. London, 1968.

Gordon, J. F. S. *Scotichronicon and Monasticon*. Glasgow, 1867.

Gore, John (ed). *Creevey's Life and Times*. London, 1934.

Graeme, Louisa G. *Or and Sable*. Edinburgh, 1903.

Graham, E. Maxtone. *The Maxtones of Cultoquhey*. Edinburgh and London, 1935.

Green, William. *The Tourist's New Guide, Containing a Description of the Lakes, Mountains and Scenery in Cumberland, Westmorland and Lancashire*. 2 vols. Kendal, 1819.

Greig, James (ed). *The Diaries of a Duchess*. London, 1926.

Greig, James (ed). *The Farington Diary*. 8 vols. 4th edn, London, 1923.

Grierson, Herbert J. (ed). *Letters of Sir Walter Scott*. 12 vols. Centenary edn, London, 1932–7.

Groome, F. H. (ed). *Ordnance Gazetteer of Scotland*. New edn, 6 vols. London, Edinburgh and Glasgow, 1894.

Grose, Francis. *Antiquities of Scotland*. 2 vols. London, 1789–91.

Haldane, Alexander. *Memoirs of the Lives of Robert Haldane of Airthrey and of his Brother, James Alexander Haldane*. London, 1852.

Halfpenny, William and John. *Chinese and Gothic Architecture Properly Ornamented*. London, 1752. Reprinted New York and London, 1968.

Hall, Sir James. *Essay on the Origin, History and Principles of Gothic Architecture*. London, 1813.

Hall, James. *Travels in Scotland*. 2 vols. London, 1807.

Handley, James E. *The Agricultural Revolution in Scotland*. Glasgow, 1963.

Hannan, Thomas. *Famous Scottish Houses*. London, 1928.

Hay, George. *The Architecture of Scottish Post-Reformation Churches, 1560–1843*. Oxford, 1957.

Hipple, Walter J. *The Beautiful, the Sublime, and the Picturesque in Eighteenth-Century British Aesthetic Theory*. Illinois, 1957.

History of Northumberland. 15 vols. Newcastle-upon-Tyne, 1893–1940.

Hodgson, John. *History of Northumberland*. 3 Parts. Newcastle-upon-Tyne, 1820–40. Part 1 was subsequently written by J. H. Hinde to complete the work and was published in 1858.

Hodgson, John. *Local Biography*. A collection of newspaper cuttings and other items in the Central Library, Newcastle-upon-Tyne.

Hodgson, John. *Northumberland. Beauties of England and Wales*. London, 1813.

Hodgson, John. *A Topographical and Historical Description of the County of Westmoreland*. London, 1823.

Hogg, James. *A Tour in the Highlands in 1803*. Alex. Gardner (ed). Paisley, 1888.

BIBLIOGRAPHY

Hussey, Christopher. *English Country Houses, 1715–1840.* 3 vols. London, 1955–8.

Hussey, Christopher. *The Picturesque : Studies in a Point of View.* London and New York, 1927.

Hutchinson, William. *An Excursion to the Lakes in Westmoreland and Cumberland in the years 1773 and 1774.* London, 1776.

Hutchinson, William. *The History and Antiquities of the County Palatine of Durham.* 3 vols. Newcastle-upon-Tyne, 1785–94.

Hutchinson, William. *A View of Northumberland.* 2 vols. Newcastle-upon-Tyne, 1778.

Irving, Joseph. *History of Dunbartonshire.* Dumbarton, 1857.

Jefferson, Samuel. *History and Antiquities of Allerdale.* Carlisle, 1842.

Jefferson, Samuel. *History and Antiquities of Carlisle.* Carlisle, 1838.

Johnson, Samuel. *A Journey to the Western Isles of Scotland, 1773.* Oxford University Press Edition of Standard Authors. London, 1951.

Jones' Views of the Seats, Mansions, Castles, etc. of Noblemen and Gentlemen in England, Wales, Scotland and Ireland. 3 vols. London, 1829. Series of Scottish Seats. London, n.d.

Jones, Barbara. *Follies and Grottoes.* London, 1953.

Kerr, Robert. *The Gentleman's House.* 2nd edn, London, 1864.

Knight, Richard Payne. *The Landscape, A Didactic Poem.* 2nd edn, London, 1795. Reprinted Farnborough, 1972.

Knox, John. *A Tour Through the Highlands of Scotland and the Hebride Isles in 1786.* London, 1787.

Kohl, Johann G. *Scotland, Glasgow, the Clyde to the Lakes.* London, 1844.

Langley, Batty and Thomas. *Gothic Architecture Improved.* 2nd edn, London, 1747. Reprinted Farnborough, 1967.

Lees-Milne, James. *The Age of Adam.* London, 1947.

Lees-Milne, James. *Earls of Creation.* London, 1962.

Leighton, John M. *History of the County of Fife from the Earliest Period to the Present Time.* 3 vols. Glasgow, 1840.

Leighton, John M., and Swan, Joseph. *Select Views on the River Clyde.* Glasgow, 1830.

Lettice, John. *Letters on a Tour Through Various Parts of Scotland, 1792.* London, 1794.

Lightoler, Thomas. *The Gentleman and Farmer's Architect.* London, 1762. Reprinted Farnborough, 1968.

Lindsay, Ian. *Georgian Edinburgh.* Edinburgh, 1948.

Lindsay, Ian, and Cosh, Mary. *Inveraray and the Dukes of Argyll.* Edinburgh, 1973.

Llanover, Lady (ed). *The Autobiography and Correspondence of Mary Granville, Mrs. Delany.* 6 vols. London, 1861–2.

Loudon, John C. *A Treatise on Forming, Improving and Managing Country Residences.* 2 vols. London, 1806. Reprinted Farnborough, 1971.

Lugar, Robert. *Plans and Views of Buildings Executed in England and Scotland in the Castellated and Other Styles.* London, 1811.

Lugar, Robert. *Villa Architecture.* London, 1828.

406

BIBLIOGRAPHY

Macaulay, Rose. *Pleasure of Ruins*. 1953. Reprinted London, 1966.

Mackenzie, Alexander. *History of the Camerons*. Inverness, 1884.

Mackenzie, Eneas. *An Historical, Topographical and Descriptive View of the County of Northumberland*. Newcastle-upon-Tyne, 1825.

Mackenzie, Eneas, and Ross, M. *An Historical, Topographical and Descriptive View of the County Palatine of Durham*. Newcastle-upon-Tyne, 1834.

McNayr, James. *A Guide from Glasgow, to Some of the Most Remarkable Scenes in the Highlands of Scotland and to the Falls of Clyde*. Glasgow, 1797.

Manwaring, Elizabeth Wheeler. *Italian Landscape in Eighteenth Century England*. 2nd Impression. London, 1965.

Marshall, Rosalind K. *The Days of Duchess Anne. Life in the Household of the Duchess of Hamilton, 1656–1716*. London, 1973.

Marshall, Thomas H. *The History of Perth*. Perth, 1849.

Millar, Alexander H. *Historical and Descriptive Accounts of the Castles and Mansions of Ayrshire*. Edinburgh, 1885.

Millar, Alexander H. *Castles and Mansions of Renfrewshire and Buteshire*. Glasgow, 1889.

Millar, Alexander H. *Historical Castles and Mansions of Scotland*. Paisley and London, 1890.

Millar, Alexander H. *Fife : Pictorial and Historical*. 2 vols. Cupar (Fife), Edinburgh and Glasgow, 1895.

Morris, Francis O. *A Series of Picturesque Views of the Seats of the Noblemen and Gentlemen of Great Britain and Ireland*. 5 vols. London, 1866–80.

Morris, Robert. *An Essay in Defence of Ancient Architecture*. London, 1728.

Mylne, Robert S. *The Master Masons to the Crown of Scotland*. Edinburgh, 1893.

Nairn, Ian, and Pevsner, Nikolaus. *Sussex. Buildings of England*. Harmondsworth, 1965.

Neale, John P. *Views of the Most Interesting Collegiate and Parochial Churches*. 2 vols. London, 1824.

New Statistical Account of Scotland. 15 vols. Edinburgh, 1845.

Nicolson, Joseph, and Burn, Richard. *History and Antiquities of the Counties of Westmorland and Cumberland*. 2 vols. London, 1777.

Paine, James. *Plans, Elevations and Sections of Noblemen and Gentlemen's Seats*. 2 vols. London, 1767 and 1783.

Parson, W., and White, W. *Gazetteer of Durham and Northumberland*. 2 vols. Newcastle-upon-Tyne, 1827–8.

Paul, Sir James Balfour (ed). *Scots Peerage*. 9 vols. Edinburgh, 1904–14.

Pennant, Thomas. *A Tour in Scotland, 1769*. 5th edn, London, 1790.

Pennant, Thomas. *A Tour in Scotland and a Voyage to the Hebrides, 1772*. 2 vols. London, 1790.

Pevsner, Nikolaus. *Cambridgeshire. Buildings of England*. Harmondsworth, 1954.

Pevsner, Nikolaus. *County Durham. Buildings of England*. London, 1953.

Pevsner, Nikolaus. *Cumberland and Westmorland. Buildings of England*. Harmondsworth, 1967.

Pevsner, Nikolaus. *Englishness of English Art*. London, 1956.

Pevsner, Nikolaus. *Northumberland. Buildings of England*. Harmondsworth, 1957.

Pevsner, Nikolaus. *Outline of European Architecture.* 5th edn, Harmondsworth, 1961.

Pevsner, Nikolaus. *Studies in Art, Architecture and Design.* 2 vols. London, 1968.

Pevsner, Nikolaus. *Yorkshire: The West Riding. Buildings of England.* 2nd edn, Harmondsworth, 1967.

Pevsner, Nikolaus. *Wiltshire. Buildings of England.* Harmondsworth, 1963.

Pevsner, Nikolaus, and Harris, John. *Lincolnshire. Buildings of England.* Harmondsworth, 1964.

Pococke, Richard. 'Tours in Scotland, 1747, 1750, 1760'. *Scottish History Society.* Edinburgh, 1887.

Pococke, Richard. 'Travels Through England During 1750, 1751 and later years'. *Camden Society.* 2 vols. London, 1888–9.

Pope, Alexander. *Selected Poetry.* Signet Classic edn, New York, 1970.

Pratt, John B. *Buchan.* 3rd edn, Aberdeen, 1870.

Price, Uvedale. *Essays on the Picturesque, as Compared with the Sublime and the Beautiful.* 3 vols. London, 1810. Reprinted Farnborough, 1971.

Pugin, Augustus Welby. *Contrasts.* 2nd edn, London, 1841. Reprinted Leicester University Press, 1969, with an introduction by H. R. Hitchcock.

Pugin, Augustus Welby. *The True Principles of Pointed or Christian Architecture.* London, 1841.

Pugin, Augustus, and Pugin, Augustus Welby, and Willson, Edward J. *Examples of Gothic Architecture Selected from Various Ancient Edifices in England.* Vol. II. 1836. 2nd edn, London, 1839.

Pugin, Augustus Welby, and Walker, Thomas L. *Examples of Gothic Architecture Selected from Various Ancient Edifices in England.* Vol. III. 1836. 2nd edn, London, 1840.

Pugin, Augustus, and Willson, Edward, J. *Examples of Gothic Architecture Selected from Various Ancient Edifices in England.* Vol. I. 1836. 2nd edn, London, 1838.

Raine, James. *A Brief Historical Account of the Episcopal Castle or Palace of Auckland.* Durham, 1852.

Raine, James. *History and Antiquities of North Durham.* London, 1852.

Reid, Stuart (ed). *Life and Letters of the First Earl of Durham.* 2 vols. London, 1906.

Repton, Humphry. *An Inquiry into the Changes in Landscape Gardening.* 1806. Reprinted Farnborough, 1969.

Richardson, Albert E. *Robert Mylne, Architect and Engineer, 1733–1811.* London, 1955.

Richardson, George. *New Vitruvius Britannicus.* 2 vols. London, 1802–8. Reprinted New York, 1970.

Richardson, Moses A. *Local Historian's Table-Book.* 5 vols. London, 1841–6.

Rickman, Thomas. *An Attempt to Discriminate the Styles of Architecture in England.* 1817. 5th edn, London, 1848.

Rose, Thomas. *Westmorland, Cumberland, Durham and Northumberland.* 3 vols. London, 1832.

Royal Commission on the Ancient and Historical Monuments of Scotland. *Peeblesshire.* 2 vols. Edinburgh, 1967. *Roxburghshire,* Edinburgh, 1957. *Stirlingshire.* 2 vols. Edinburgh, 1963.

Rutter, John. *Delineations of Fonthill and its Abbey.* London, 1823.

'Selections from the Family Papers Preserved at Caldwell'. *Maitland Club.* 2 Parts. Paisley, 1883, 1885.

BIBLIOGRAPHY

Shaw, James E. *Ayrshire*, 1745–1950. Edinburgh and London, 1953.

Shepherd, Thomas H. *Modern Athens or Edinburgh in the Nineteenth Century*. London, 1829.

Simond, Louis. *Journal of a Tour and Residence in Great Britain, during the years 1810 and 1811, by a French Traveller*. 2 vols. 2nd edn, London, 1817.

Simpson, W. Douglas. *Archibald Simpson, Architect, 1790–1847*. Edinburgh, 1947. Reprinted from the *Quarterly Journal*, Royal Incorporation of Architects in Scotland.

Sitwell, Sacheverell. *British Architects and Craftsmen*. Pan edn, London, 1960.

Skrine, Henry. *Three Successive Tours in the North of England and a Great Part of Scotland*. London, 1795.

Small, John. *Castles and Mansions of the Lothians*. 2 vols. Edinburgh, 1883.

Statistical Account of Scotland. 21 vols. Edinburgh, 1791–9.

Stanton, Phoebe. *Pugin*. London, 1971.

Stillman, Damie. *Decorative Work of Robert Adam*. London, 1966.

Stoddart, Sir John. *Remarks on Local Scenery and Manners in Scotland during the years 1799 and 1800*. 2 vols. London, 1801.

Storer, James and H. S. *Views in Edinburgh*. London, 1820.

Stroud, Dorothy. *Capability Brown*. London, 1950.

Stukeley, William. *Itinerarium Curiosum*. 1724. 2nd edn, London, 1776.

Summerson, John. *Architecture in Britain, 1530–1830*. Pelican History of Art. 4th edn, Harmondsworth, 1963.

Summerson, John (ed). *Concerning Architecture. Essays on Architectural Writers and Writing Presented to Nikolaus Pevsner*. London, 1968.

Summerson, John. *Inigo Jones*. Harmondsworth, 1966.

Summerson, John. *John Nash*. London, 1952.

Surtees, Robert. *History and Antiquities of the County Palatine of Durham*. 4 vols. London, 1816–40.

Survey of Moray. Elgin, 1798.

Sutherland, Douglas. *The Yellow Earl*. London, 1965.

Swarbrick, John. *Robert Adam and His Brothers*. London, 1916.

Swift, Jonathan. *Gulliver's Travels*. 1726. Oxford, 1941.

Sykes, John. *Tracts*. Newcastle-upon-Tyne, 1829.

Tait, Alan A. *Robert Adam and Scotland. The Picturesque Drawings*. Scottish Arts Council Exhibition Catalogue. Edinburgh, 1972.

Tate, George, *History of the Borough, Castle and Barony of Alnwick*. 2 vols. Alnwick, 1868–9.

Tayler, Alistair and Henrietta. *Book of the Duffs*. Edinburgh, 1914.

Tayler, Alistair and Henrietta. 'House of Forbes'. *Third Spalding Club Miscellany*. Aberdeen, 1937.

Tipping, H. Avray. *English Homes*. 9 vols. London, 1920–37.

Tour in the Highlands of Scotland, 1818. London, 1819.

Townend, Peter (ed). *Burke's Landed Gentry*. 3 vols. 18th edn, London, 1965–

Toy, Sidney. *Castles of Great Britain*. 4th edn, London, 1966.

Trench, Francis. *Scotland, Its Faith and Its Features*. 2 vols. London, 1846.

Turnor, Christopher R. *James Wyatt*. London, 1950.

Victoria History of the Counties of England. *Durham*. 3 vols. London, 1905–28.

Wallis, John. *The Natural History and Antiquities of Northumberland.* 2 vols. London, 1769.

Walpole, Horace. *A Description of the Villa of Mr. Horace Walpole.* 1784. Reprinted Farnborough, 2nd impression, 1969.

Walton, Clarence R. *Romantic Ravensworth.* Newcastle-upon-Tyne, 1950.

Warner, Richard. *A Tour Through the Northern Counties of England and the Borders of Scotland.* Bath, 1802.

Warrender, Margaret. *Walks Near Edinburgh.* Edinburgh, 1895.

Watson, J. *Morayshire Described.* Elgin, 1868.

Welles, Edward R. *Ardincaple Castle and Its Lairds.* Glasgow, 1930.

Whately, Thomas. *Observations on Modern Gardening.* London, 1770.

Whellan, William. *History and Topography of the Counties of Cumberland and Westmorland.* Pontefract, 1860.

Whistler, Lawrence. *The Imagination of Vanbrugh and His Fellow Artists.* London, 1954.

Wilhelmina, Duchess of Cleveland. *Handbook of Raby Castle.* 1870.

Willis, Peter (ed). *Furor Hortensis. Essays on the History of the English Landscape Garden, in Memory of F. H. Clark.* Edinburgh, 1974.

Wilson, James. *Rose Castle.* Carlisle, 1912.

Wordsworth, Dorothy. *Recollections of a Tour Made in Scotland, A.D. 1803.* Edinburgh, 1874.

Young, Arthur. *A Six Months' Tour Through the North of England.* 4 vols. 2nd edn, London, 1770–1.

Articles

'Account of a Journey into Scotland'. *The Gentleman's Magazine.* Vol. XXXVI. April and May, 1766.

'An Address to the Lairds of Scotland'. *The Gentleman's Magazine.* Vol. XLVI. September, 1776.

'Alnwick Described'. *The Gentleman's Magazine.* Vol. XXVI. February, 1756.

'Ancient and Present State of the Cathedral at Salisbury'. *The Gentleman's Magazine.* Vol. LIX. October, 1789.

Anson, Peter F. 'Catholic Church Building in Scotland, 1560–1914'. *Innes Review.* Vol. V. 1954.

'Architectural Alterations Making at Oatlands'. *The Gentleman's Magazine.* Vol. LXX. Part I. May, 1800.

'Architectural Description of the New Episcopal Chapel, Princes St.' *Scots Magazine.* Vol. LXXIX. January, 1817.

Bainbridge, T. H. 'Eighteenth Century Agriculture in Cumbria'. *Transactions of the Cumberland and Westmorland Antiquarian and Archaeological Society.* New Series. Vol. XLII. 1942.

'Ballot at the Society of Antiquaries'. *The Gentleman's Magazine.* Vol. LXVII. Part II. November, 1797.

'Biographical Account of the late Robert Adam, Esq., Architect'. *Scots Magazine.* Vol. LXV. May, 1803.

BIBLIOGRAPHY

Bolton, Arthur T. 'The Classical and Romantic Compositions of Robert Adam'. *Architectural Review*. Vol. LVII. 1925.

Bolton, Arthur T. 'Culzean Castle, Ayr'. *Country Life*. Vol. XXXVIII. 11 September, 1915.

Bouch, C. M. L. 'Rose Castle'. *Transactions of the Cumberland and Westmorland Antiquarian and Archaeological Society*. New Series. Vol. LVI. 1957.

Bulman, C. G. 'The Parish and Church of St. Michael, Arthuret'. *Transactions of the Cumberland and Westmorland Antiquarian and Archaeological Society*. New Series. Vol. LXVI. 1966.

Bulman, C. G. 'Two Recently Demolished Carlisle Churches'. *Transactions of the Cumberland and Westmorland Antiquarian and Archaeological Society*. New Series. Vol. LV. 1956.

'Celtic Animadversions on Gothic Reflexions'. *The Gentleman's Magazine*. Vol. LX. July, 1790.

Colvin, Howard M. 'Fifty New Churches'. *Architectural Review*. Vol. CVII. 1950.

'A Copy of the last Will of the late Duke of Argyll'. *The Gentleman's Magazine*. Vol. XXXI. May, 1761.

Cornforth, John. 'Auckland Castle, Co. Durham'. *Country Life*. Vol. CLI. 3 and 10 February, 1972.

Cornforth, John. 'Wallington, Northumberland'. *Country Life*. Vol. CXLVII. 16 April, 1970.

Cosh, Mary. 'Building Problems at Inveraray'. *Bulletin of the Scottish Georgian Society*. Vol. II. 1973.

Cosh, Mary. 'Lord Ilay's Eccentric Building Schemes. Two Dukes and their Houses. Pt. II'. *Country Life*. Vol. CLII. 20 July, 1970.

Cosh, Mary. 'Two Dukes and their Houses'. *Country Life*. Vol. CLII. 13 July, 1970.

'Defence of Mr. Wyatt's Alterations in Salisbury Cathedral'. *The Gentleman's Magazine*. Vol. LIX. Part II. December, 1789.

'Description of the Edinburgh Catholic Chapel'. *Scots Magazine*. Vol. LXXIX. February, 1817.

'Description of the Episcopal Chapel now Erecting in York Place, Edinburgh'. *Scots Magazine*. Vol. LXXVIII. June, 1816.

'Description of Lanrick Castle'. *Scots Magazine*. Vol. LXXIX. June, 1817.

'Description of the New Parish Church of Kincardine in Monteith (sic)'. *Scots Magazine*. Vol. LXXVIII. April, 1816.

Dobson, John. 'Inaugural Address'. *Proceedings of the Northern Architectural Association*. 1859.

'Durham Castle'. *Country Life*. Vol. XXIII. 25 January, 1908.

'Earl of Cassilis'. *The Gentleman's Magazine*. Vol. LXIII. Part I. January, 1793.

Elliot, W. Ryle. 'The Work of Robert Adam in Northumberland'. *Archaeologia Aeliana*. 4th Series. Vol. XXX. 1952.

Fleming, John. 'Adam Gothic'. *Connoisseur*. Vol. CXLII. October, 1958.

Fleming, John. 'An Italian Sketchbook by Robert Adam, Clérisseau and Others'. *Connoisseur*. Vol. CXLVI. November, 1960.

Fleming, John. 'Robert Adam's Castle Style'. *Country Life*. Vol. CXLIII. 23 May, 1968.

Fleming, John. 'Seton Castle's Debt to Ancient Rome. Robert Adam's Castle Style. Part II'. *Country Life*. Vol. CXLIII. 30 May, 1968.

Girouard, Mark. 'Mellerstain, Berwickshire'. *Country Life*. Vol. CXXIV. 28 August and 4 September, 1958.

Girouard, Mark. 'Abercairny, Perthshire'. *Country Life*. Vol. CXXIX. 9 and 16 March, 1961.

Gordon, C. J. 'Crosby Ravensworth Church'. *Transactions of the Cumberland and Westmorland Antiquarian and Archaeological Society*. New Series. Vol. VIII, 1908.

Gotch, Christopher. 'Inveraray Castle, Argyllshire'. *Country Life*. Vol. CXIII. 25 June, 1953.

Gray, W. Forbes. 'The Scott Monument and Its Architect'. *Architectural Review*. Vol. XCVI. 1944.

Harris, Eileen. 'The Wizard of Durham'. *Country Life*. Vol. CL. 26 August, 1971.

Harris, Eileen. 'Architect of Rococo Landscapes. Thomas Wright—III'. *Country Life*. Vol. CL. 9 September, 1971.

Hughes, J. 'The Building of the Courts, Carlisle, 1807–22'. *Transactions of the Cumberland and Westmorland Antiquarian and Archaeological Society*. New Series. Vol. LXX. 1970.

Hussey, Christopher, 'Ripley Castle, Yorkshire'. *Country Life*. Vol. LXXII. 13 August, 1932.

Hussey, Christopher. 'Hamsterley Hall, Durham'. *Country Life*. Vol. LXXXVI. 21 October, 1939.

Hussey, Christopher. 'Ford Castle, Northumberland'. *Country Life*. Vol. LXXXIX. 11 January, 1941.

Hussey, Christopher. 'Gibside, Co. Durham'. *Country Life*. Vol. CXI. 8 February, 1952.

Hussey, Christopher. 'Lambton Castle, Durham'. *Country Life*. Vol. CXXXIX. 24 and 31 March, 1966.

'Improvements made, and still wanted to be made, at Windsor'. *The Gentleman's Magazine*. Vol. LX. August, 1790.

Ingram, M. Edward. 'John Carr's Contribution to the Gothic Revival'. *Transactions of the East Riding Georgian Society*. Vol. II. Part III. 1949.

'Inscriptions at Hagley'. *The Gentleman's Magazine*. Vol. LXXI. Part II. July, 1801.

Jones, G. P. 'The Poverty of Cumberland and Westmorland'. *Transactions of the Cumberland and Westmorland Antiquarian and Archaeological Society*. New Series. Vol. LV. 1956.

'A Journey to the Highlands of Scotland'. *The Gentleman's Magazine*. Vol. XLVIII. February, 1778.

Kitson, S. D. 'Carr of York'. *Royal Institute of British Architects' Journal*. 3rd Series. Vol. XVII. January, 1910.

Langley, Margaret. 'The Unfortunate Maniac at Coniston Priory in Westmorland'. *The Gentleman's Magazine*. Vol. LXIX. Part I. January, 1799.

BIBLIOGRAPHY

'Lavenham Church'. *The Gentleman's Magazine*. Vol. LVII. May, 1787.

Leach, Peter. 'In the Gothick Vein. The Architecture of Daniel Garrett. Part III'. *Country Life*. Vol. CLVI. 26 September, 1974.

'Memoirs of Dr. John Egerton, late Bishop of Durham'. *The Gentleman's Magazine*. Vol. LXVII. September, 1797.

'Mr. Wright's Description of his Villa at Byer's Green'. *The Gentleman's Magazine*. Vol. LXIII. Part I. March, 1793.

'Mr. Wyatt's Election'. *The Gentleman's Magazine*. Vol. LXVII. Part II. 1797.

Nuttgens, Patrick. 'Regional Planning in the North-East'. *Prospect*. Spring, 1970.

'Obituary; with Anecdotes of Remarkable Persons'. *The Gentleman's Magazine*. Vol. LXXXII. Part I. June, 1812.

'Observations on Gothic Buildings'. *The Gentleman's Magazine*. Vol. XXVIII. November, 1758.

'Observations on Improvements lately made in Cumberland'. *The Gentleman's Magazine*. Vol. LX. June, 1790.

Oppé, Paul. 'Robert Adam's Picturesque Compositions'. *Burlington Magazine*. Vol. LXXX. March, 1942.

Oswald, Arthur. 'Auchincruive, Ayrshire'. *Country Life*. Vol. LXXII. 17 December, 1932.

Pevsner, Nikolaus. 'Genesis of the Picturesque'. *Architectural Review*. Vol. XCVI. 1944.

Pevsner, Nikolaus. 'Good King James's Gothic'. *Architectural Review*. Vol. CVII. 1950.

'The Plan of Knox's Picturesque Scenery of Scotland'. *The Gentleman's Magazine*. Vol. LIX. April, 1789.

'Pleasing Improvements in the North; Particularly at Netherby'. *The Gentleman's Magazine*. Vol. LV. Part II. November, 1785.

'Present State of Newcastle'. *The Gentleman's Magazine*. Vol. LXI. Part I. April, 1791.

'Print of W. Front of Old St. Paul's'. *The Gentleman's Magazine*. Vol. LI. April, 1781.

'Priory at the Leasowes'. *The Gentleman's Magazine*. Vol. LXV. Part I. June, 1795.

Proceedings of the Society of Antiquaries, Newcastle-upon-Tyne. Vol. III. 1889; Vol. V. 1893; Vol. VII. 1897; 2nd Series. Vol. X. 1902; 3rd Series. Vol. I. 1903–04; 3rd Series. Vol. VI. 1913–14; 4th Series. Vol. IX. 1934–41; 5th Series. Vol. I. 1951–6.

'Progress of the Linen and Cotton Manufactory at Paisley'. *The Gentleman's Magazine*. Vol. LVII. May and June, 1787.

'The Pursuits of Architectural Innovation. Nos. VII, IX, XC'. *The Gentleman's Magazine*. Vol. LXIX. February and April, 1799; Vol. LXXV. November, 1805.

'Raby Castle'. *The Gentleman's Magazine*. Vol. LXII. October, 1792.

'Remarks on Gothic Buildings'. *The Gentleman's Magazine*. Vol. LII. October, 1782.

'Review of New Publications'. *The Gentleman's Magazine*. Vol. LXVI. Part I. March, 1796.

Rowan, Alistair. 'Taymouth Castle, Perthshire'. *Country Life*. Vol. CXXXVI. 8 and 15 October, 1964.

Rowan, Alistair. 'Paxton House, Berwickshire'. *Country Life*. Vol. CXLII. 24 August, 1967.

Rowan, Alistair. 'Dunninald, Angus'. *Country Life*. Vol. CXLVI. 14 August, 1969.

Rowan, Alistair. 'Raby Castle, Co. Durham'. *Country Life*. Vol. CXLVII. 1, 8 and 22 January, 1970.

Rowan, Alistair. 'Millearne, Perthshire'. *Country Life*. Vol. CLI. 24 February and 2 March, 1972.

Rowan, Alistair. 'Gothick Restoration at Raby Castle'. *Architectural History. Journal of the Society of Architectural Historians of Great Britain*. Vol. XV. 1972.

Rowan, Alistair. 'Wedderburn Castle, Berwickshire'. *Country Life*. Vol. CLVI. 8 August, 1974.

Rowan, Alistair. 'Oxenfoord Castle, Midlothian'. *Country Life*. Vol. CLVI. 15 August, 1974.

Rowan, Alistair. 'Robert Adam's Last Castles'. *Country Life*. Vol. CLVI. 22 August, 1974.

Rowan, Alistair. 'The Adam Castle Style'. *Journal of the Royal Society of Arts*. Vol. CXXII. September, 1974.

Rutherford, Frank. 'Pevsner on the Palatinate'. *Transactions of the Architectural and Archaeological Society of Durham and Northumberland*. Vol. XI. Parts I and II. 1958.

'Short Memoirs of the Life of James Wyatt, Esq.' *The Gentleman's Magazine*. Vol. LXXXIII. September, 1813.

Simpson, Ann and James. 'John Baxter, Architect, and the Patronage of the Fourth Duke of Gordon'. *Bulletin of the Scottish Georgian Society*. Vol. II. 1973.

'Strictures on Dr. Johnson, Mr. Pennant and Mr. Walpole'. *The Gentleman's Magazine*. Vol. XLV. May, 1775.

Taylor, Nicholas. 'A Duke's Library'. *Architectural Review*. Vol. CLXII. 1967.

'To the Rev. Mr. Lionel Seaman'. *The Gentleman's Magazine*. Vol. XVI. February, 1746.

'Tour to the Lakes of Cumberland and Westmorland'. *The Gentleman's Magazine*. Vol. LXXVI. Part I. March, 1806.

Walker, David. 'The Stirlings of Dunblane and Falkirk. Fragments of Five Architectural Biographies'. *Bulletin of the Scottish Georgian Society*. Vol. I. 1972.

Unpublished Dissertations

Dixon, A. C. S. 'The Domestic Architecture of the Gothic Revival in Northumberland'. B.A. dissertation, School of Architecture, University of Newcastle-upon-Tyne, 1955.

Dixon, A. C. S. 'The Restoration of Alnwick Castle, 1750–86'. B. Arch. dissertation, School of Architecture, University of Newcastle-upon-Tyne, 1960.

Farthing, J. 'The Matfen Estate'. B. Arch. dissertation, School of Architecture, University of Newcastle-upon-Tyne, 1964.

Fisher, David J. 'The Parliamentary Commission in the Highlands and Islands of Scotland'. Diploma dissertation, Scott Sutherland School of Architecture, Aberdeen, 1974.

Scott, James Y. 'An Historical Study of Woodlands Hill, Glasgow'. Diploma dissertation, Scott Sutherland School of Architecture, Aberdeen, 1973.

List of Manuscripts Quoted

Private Collections

The Duke of Argyll's MSS at Inveraray Castle

Lord Barnard's MSS at Raby Castle

Sir Donald Cameron of Lochiel's MSS at Achnacarry

The Trustees of the Late Lord Cochrane of Cults' MSS at Crawford Priory

Sir Edward Collingwood's MSS at Lilburn Tower

Sir Alec Douglas-Home's MSS at The Hirsel

The Bishop of Durham's MSS at Auckland Castle

Lord Forbes' MSS at Balforbes

Mrs Hay of Drumelzier's MSS at Duns Castle

Captain P. R. Holderness-Roddam's MSS at Roddam Hall

Mrs Home-Robertson of Paxton's MSS at Paxton House

Lord Joicey's MSS at Etal Manor

Miss J. Macintyre's MSS at Millearne

The Earl of Mansfield's MSS at Scone Palace

Mrs P. Maxwell-Scott of Abbotsford's MSS at Abbotsford

The Earl of Moray's MSS at Darnaway Castle

The Duke of Northumberland's MSS at Alnwick Castle

The Earl of Rosebery's MSS at Dalmeny House

Captain J. de B. Stansfeld's MSS at Dunninald

Mrs D. Somervell's MSS at Fettercairn

D. Steuart Fothringham, Esq. of Murthly's MSS at Murthly Castle

Major J. Stewart of Ardvorlich's MSS at Ardvorlich

Carlisle Record Office

The Earl of Lonsdale's MSS

Cumberland County Council

Edmond Castle MSS at Edmond Castle

Durham County Record Office

Brancepeth Estate MSS

Northumberland County Record Office

Benwell Manorial MSS (MBE)

Blackett (Matfen) MSS (ZBL)

Blake (Twisel) MSS (NRO. 508)

Butler (Ewart) MSS (ZBU)

Delaval (Waterford) MSS (2DE)

Fenwick (Brinkburn) MSS (ZFE)

Joicey MSS (NRO. 429)

Society of Antiquaries, Newcastle-upon-Tyne MSS (M 17)

Middleton (Belsay) MSS (ZMIs)

Scottish Record Office

Abercairny MSS (GD24)

Ailsa MSS (GD25)

Baird of Newbyth MSS (GD236)

Breadalbane MSS (GD112)

Clerk of Penicuik MSS (GD18)

Fetteresso MSS (GD105)

Forbes MSS (GD52)

Gordon Castle MSS (GD44)

Gordon of Cluny MSS (GD244)

Grantully (Murthly) MSS (GD121)

Hamilton Bruce MSS (GD152)

Hamilton of Pinmore MSS (GD142)

Lord Macdonald MSS (GD221)

Macpherson of Cluny MSS (GD80)

Melville MSS (GD51)

Seaforth MSS (GD46)

Sempill of Craigievar MSS (GD250)

National Library of Scotland

Cockerell MSS

Fletcher of Saltoun MSS

Halkett of Pitfirrane MSS

James Playfair. *Journal of Architecture*

Robertson-Macdonald MSS

National Monuments Record of Scotland, Royal Commission on the Ancient and Historical Monuments of Scotland

The Day Books of John Smith

Royal Institute of British Architects

Thomas Rickman's Diary

Appendices

A *Chronological Index of Ecclesiastical Buildings in Scotland*
B *Chronological Index of Ecclesiastical Buildings in Northern England*
C *Chronological Index of Secular Buildings in Scotland*
D *Chronological Index of Secular Buildings in Northern England*

NOTE. Where they are known the dates which appear in the following tables are those for the commencement of building.

A

Chronological Index of Ecclesiastical Buildings in Scotland

Year	Building	Architect	
1760	Kenmore, Perthsh.	William Baker	Cruciform; tower
1766	Kirkurd, Peeblessh.		T-plan
1785	Currie, Midloth.		Spire
1787	St Cuthbert's, Dundee, Angus	S. Bell	
1789	Farnell, Angus	J. Playfair	Gothic interior
1791	Montrose, Angus	D. Logan	
1792	St George (Episc.), Edinburgh	James Adam?	Octagon
	Johnstone High, Renfrewsh.		Octagon; spire later
	Calder, Lochwinnoch, Renfrewsh.		Octagon
1794	Barony, Glasgow	John Robertson?	Dem.
1795	Longforgan, Perthsh.		Tower earlier
1799	Craig, Angus		Aisles, Gothic inter.; tower
1800	Gask, Perthsh.	Gillespie Graham	
1801	Skene, Aberdeensh.		Cf. Echt
	Dingwall, Ross-shire		
1803	Strathblane, Stirlingsh.	J. Brash	
	Monzievaird and Strowan, Perthsh.		Dem.
1804	St Peter (R.C.), Aberdeen	J. Massie	
	Cluny, Aberdeensh.		
	Crathie, Aberdeensh.	W. & A. Clerk	Cf. Echt. Dem.
	Echt, Aberdeensh.		Harled; lateral rect.
	Fettercairn, Kincardinesh.		Tower

Year	Building	Architect	
	Old Scone, Perthsh.		Aisle added 1834
1805	Kildrummy, Aberdeensh.		Cf. Echt
	St John (Episc.), Pittenweem, Fife		
	Saltoun, E. Loth.		Cruciform; spire
	Comrie, Perthsh.	Stewart of Perth	Spire
1806	Bourtie, Aberdeensh.		Cf. Echt
	Ceres, Fife		Steeple only
	Fossoway, Kinross-shire		Lateral rect.
	Anti-Burgher chapel, Falkirk, Stirlingsh.		Hexagon
	Muiravonside, Stirlingsh.		Harled
1807	Kirkcaldy, Fife	A. & J. Elliot	A rebuilding
	St Paul, Perth	J. Paterson	Octagon
1808	Fyvie, Aberdeensh.		Since altered
1809	Bolton, E. Loth.		Tower
1810	Glenorchy, Argyll	J. Elliot	Octagon; tower
	Fetteresso, Kincardinesh.	J. Paterson	
	Dunning, Perthsh.		T-plan remodelled
	Saline, Perthsh.	W. Stark	Cf. Muirkirk
	Falkirk Old, Stirlingsh.	Gillespie Graham	A rebuilding
1811	Auchindoir, Aberdeensh.		
	Monimail, Fife	Gillespie Graham	Tower only
1812	Crimond, Aberdeensh.		Harled; spire
	Kennethmont, Aberdeensh.		
	Kinnettles, Angus	S. Bell (attrib.)	
	Monikie, Angus		
	Muirkirk, Ayrsh.	W. Stark	
	Old Kilpatrick, Dunbartonsh.		
	St Paul, Dundee, Angus		
	St Andrew (Episc.), Fortrose, Ross & Cromarty		
1813	Chapel of Garioch, Aberdeensh.		
	St Mary (R.C.), Edinburgh	Gillespie Graham	Since altered
	Tongland, Kirkcudbrightsh.		Tower
	Collace, Perthsh.	Gillespie Graham?	Tower
1814	Peterhead (Episc.), Aberdeensh.	R. Mitchell	
	Kemback, Fife		
	Borgue, Kircudbrightsh.		
	St Andrew (R.C.), Glasgow	Gillespie Graham	Aisles

Year	Building	Architect	
	Kincardine-in-Menteith, Perthsh.	R. Crichton	Aisles, clerestory
	Old Erskine, Renfrewsh.	D. Hamilton	
1815	Oathlaw, Angus		Tower
	Clackmannan, Clacksh.	Gillespie Graham	
	Newburn, Fife		Small spire
	Liberton, Edinburgh	Gillespie Graham	Tower
	Moneydie, Perthsh.	Gillespie Graham?	Tower
	Tain, Ross & Cromarty	Gillespie Graham	
	Kilsyth, Stirlingsh.		Tower
1816	Kilmorich, Argyll		Octagon; tower
	Dunoon High, Argyll	Gillespie Graham	Enlarged, 1834 by D. Hamilton
	St Rufus, Keith, Banffsh.	Gillespie Graham	Cf. Clackmannan
	St John (Episc.), Edinburgh	W. Burn	Tower. Gothic interior
	St Paul (Episc.), Edinburgh	A. Elliot	Gothic interior
	Methodist chapel, Perth		
	St John (Episc.), Arpafeelie, Ross & Cromarty	A. Ross?	
1817	St Andrew (Episc.), Aberdeen	A. Simpson	
	Channelkirk, Berwicksh.		
	St Mungo, Alloa, Clacksh.	Gillespie Graham	Spire
	Largo, Fife		T-plan
1818	Edzell, Angus		Tower
	Airth, Stirlingsh.	W. Stirling II	Tower
1819	Kintore, Aberdeensh.	Simpson	
	Maryton, Angus		Remodelling
	Dunbar, E. Loth.	Gillespie Graham	Tower
	Dunfermline Abbey, Fife	W. Burn	Cruciform
	St John's, Bell St, Glasgow	D. Hamilton	Dem.
	Laurencekirk, Kincardinesh.		Remodelling of 1804 building
	Larbert, Stirlingsh.	D. Hamilton	Tower
1820	Forgue, Aberdeensh.		
	Rescobie, Angus		
	Dunsyre, Lanarksh.		Tower and additions
	Shotts, Lanarksh.	Gillespie Graham & J. Brash	
	Cockpen, Midloth.	R. & R. Dickson	T-plan; tower
	Nicolson St, Edinburgh	Gillespie Graham	Gothic front
1821	Fintray, Aberdeensh.	J. Smith	
	Udny, Aberdeensh.	J. Smith	Tower

421

Year	Building	Architect	
	Glenisla, Angus		
	Kilconquhar, Fife	R. & R. Dickson	T-plan; tower
1822	Kirkmahoe, Dumfries-sh.		Tower
	Banchory-Devenick, Kincardinesh.		
1823	Fintry, Stirlingsh.		Tower; cf. Killearn
1824	Lochlee, Angus		
	St David (Ramshorn), Glasgow	Rickman	T-plan; tower
	Banchory-Ternan, Kincardinesh.		Tower
	Congregational chapel, Perth		
	Blairgowrie, Perthsh.	W. Stirling I?	
	Lecropt, Perthsh.	W. Stirling I & II	Tower
	Ettrick, Selkirksh.		T-plan; tower
1825	St Mary (R.C.), Dufftown, Banffsh.		
	St Andrews (Episc.), Fife	W. Burn	Dem.
	Cranston, Midloth.		T-plan; tower
	? Dron, Perthsh.	W. Stirling I & II	
	Kippen, Stirlingsh.	W. Stirling I & II	Tower
1826	Kilchoman, Argyll		
	Dunino, Fife		
	Inverkeithing, Fife	Gillespie Graham	Rebuilding
	Daviot, Inverness-sh.		Tower
	Glenbervie, Kincardinesh.		
	Govan, Glasgow	Smith of Jordanhill	Copy of Stratford-on-Avon. Dem.
	Elgin (Episc.), Moraysh.	W. Burn	
	Rafford, Moraysh.	Gillespie Graham	Tower
	Kinnoul, Perthsh.	W. Burn	Cruciform
	Muthill, Perthsh.	Gillespie Graham	Tower
	Killearn, Stirlingsh.		Tower
1827	Duror, Argyll	Telford	T-plan
	St Margaret (R.C.), Ayr	Gillespie Graham?	
	Berriedale, Caithness	Telford	T-plan
	Kiess, Caithness	Telford	T-plan
	Tillicoultry, Clacksh.	W. Stirling I & II	
	Abdie, Fife	W. Burn	
	Croick, Ross & Cromarty	Telford	T-plan
	Kinlochluichart, Ross & Cromarty	Telford	T-plan
	Plockton, Ross & Cromarty	Telford	T-plan
	Shieldaig, Ross & Cromarty	Telford	Dem.
	Stoneykirk, Wigtownsh.		

Year	Building	Architect	
1828	St Clement, Aberdeen	J. Smith	Tower
	Cortachy, Angus	D. Paterson	
	Iona, Argyll	Telford	
	Tobermory, Argyll	Telford	Dem.
	Ulva, Argyll	Telford	
	Stenton, E. Loth.	W. Burn	T-plan; tower
	St Mary (R.C.) Fochabers, Moraysh.		
	Blair, Perthsh.	A. Elliot	Tower
	Holy Trinity (Episc.), Paisley, Renfrewsh.		Gothic front
	Poolewe, Ross & Cromarty	Telford	
	Strathy, Sutherland	Telford	T-plan
1829	Nigg, Aberdeensh.	J. Smith	Tower
	Acharacle, Argyll	Telford	
	Ardgour, Argyll	Telford	
	Strontian, Argyll	Telford	Altered
	Mauchline, Ayrsh.		Tower
	Portsoy (R.C.), Banffsh.	Bishop Kyle	
	Tombae (R.C.), Banffsh.		
	Thurso, Caithness	Burn	
	Ardkenneth (R.C.), Inverness-sh.		
	Berneray, Inverness-sh.	Telford	
	Staffin, Inverness-sh.	Telford	T-plan.
	Trumisgarry, Inverness-sh.	Telford	T-plan. Ruin
	Fordoun, Kincardinesh.	J. Smith	Tower
	Ullapool, Ross & Cromarty	Telford	T-plan. Ruin
	Minto, Roxburghsh.	W. H. Playfair	Tower
	Campsie, Stirlingsh.	D. Hamilton	Tower
	Kinlochbervie, Sutherland	Telford	T-plan
	Stoer, Sutherland	Telford	T-plan
1830	St Nicholas South, Aberdeen	Smith	T-plan; tower
	St Patrick (R.C.), Dumbarton		
	Creich, Fife	W. Stirling I & II	
	Dalgety, Fife	W. Burn	
	Monzie, Perthsh.	W. Stirling I & II	
	Strathconan, Ross & Cromarty	Telford	
1831	Arbroath Old, Angus	J. Henderson	Steeple only remains
	Liff, Angus	W. McKenzie	Tower
	Ardnamurchan, Argyll	W. Burn	
	Bracadale, Inverness-sh.		

Year	Building	Architect	
1832	Brechin (Episc.), Angus		Dem.
	Montrose, Angus	Gillespie Graham	Steeple only
	Duirinish, Inverness-sh.		
	Kinross, Kinross-sh.	Angus	Tower
	Portmoak, Kinross-sh.		
	Fochabers (Episc.), Moraysh.	Simpson	
	Baptist chapel, Perth		
	St John the Baptist (R.C.), Perth		
	Rosskeen, Ross & Cromarty		Tower
	Balfron, Stirlingsh.		
	Dunipace, Stirlingsh.	W. Stirling I & II	
1833	Ward Chapel, Dundee, Angus	J. Brewster	Gothic front
	Eassie & Nevay, Angus		
	Banff (Episc.), Banffsh.	Simpson	
	Auchtertool, Fife	Gillespie Graham	Remodelling
	St Catherine, Newburgh, Fife	W. Burn	Dem.
	Tullialian, Fife	Angus	Cf. Kinross
	Bothwell, Lanarksh.	Hamilton	Tower
	St Peter (Episc.), Peebles, Peeblessh.	W. Burn	
1834	Corgarff, Aberdeensh.	'Mr. Daniel'	
	Kettle, Fife	Angus	Cf. Kinross
	Inchture, Perthsh.	D. Mackenzie	T-plan
	Galashiels Old, Selkirksh.		Dem.
1835	East Church of St Nicholas, Aberdeen	Simpson	
	Keig, Aberdeensh.	Smith	
	Kilmartin, Argyllsh.	J. G. Davis	Tower
	Kirkcudbright, Kirkcudbrightsh.	W. Burn	
	St James (Episc.), Muthill, Perthsh.		T-plan
1836	Drumoak, Aberdeensh.	Simpson	
	St Andrew (R.C.), Dundee, Angus	G. Mathewson	
	Coylton, Ayrsh.	Bryce	T-plan; tower
	St Marnock, Kilmarnock, Ayrsh.	J. Ingram	
	Glencairn, Dumfries-sh.		T-plan; tower
	Bonhill, Dunbartonsh.		Tower
	Minigaff, Kirkcudbrightsh.	W. Burn	Tower

Year	Building	Architect	
1837	Gaelic chapel, Ardrossan, Ayrsh.		
	Monkton, Ayrsh.	Bryce	T-plan
	St Mary (R.C.), Inverness,	Robertson of Elgin	Gothic front
	Inverbervie, Kincardinesh.	Smith	Tower
1838	St Michael (R.C.), Tomintoul, Banffsh.		
	St Mary, Dumfries	J. Henderson	
	Holy Trinity (Episc.), Edinburgh	J. Henderson	
	Newlands, Peeblessh.		
	Denny, Stirlingsh.		Spire
1839	Blairdaff, Aberdeensh.		Gutted
	St Andrew (R.C.), Braemar, Aberdeensh.		
	New Deer, Aberdeensh.		
	Wallacetown, Dundee, Angus	G. Mathewson	
	Alloa (Episc.), Clacksh.		
	Collessie, Fife	R. & R. Dickson	T-plan; tower
	Petty, Inverness-sh.		
	St Peter's (Episc.), Stornoway, Ross & Cromarty		Tower
1840	Dudhope Free, Dundee, Angus	G. Mathewson	
	Kingoldrum, Angus		
	Carnock, Fife	J. Henderson	
	Scarista, Harris, Inverness-sh.		
	Dalkeith West, Midloth.	W. Burn	Steeple
	Holy Trinity (Episc.), Melrose, Roxburghsh.	J. Henderson	
1841	Kilmun, Argyll	T. Burns	
	Portsoy (Episc.), Banffsh.	J. Ross	
	Olrig, Caithness	D. Cousin	
	Dollar, Clacksh.	W. Tite	Tower
1842	Aboyne, Aberdeensh.	Simpson	
	Inverurie, Aberdeensh.	Smith	
	Inverurie (Episc.), Aberdeensh.	Simpson	
	Menmuir, Angus	D. Smith	
	Sanquhar, Dumfries-sh.		
	St Mary (R.C.), Glasgow	Goldie & Childe	
	Tolbooth, Edinburgh	Gillespie Graham & Pugin	Spire

425

Year	Building	Architect	
	Blairgowrie (Episc.), Perthsh.		
	St Martins, Perthsh.	A. Heiton, senr	T-plan
	Edderton, Ross & Cromarty		
1843	St James (Episc.), Cruden Bay, Aberdeensh.		Octagonal tower; spire
	St Mary (Episc.), Dalkeith, Midloth.	W. Burn	
1844	Free Churches, Aberdeen	Simpson	Steeple
	Kemnay, Aberdeensh.	James Henderson	T-plan
	St Peter, Kirkcaldy, Fife	John Baird I	
	St Sylvester (R.C.), Elgin, Moraysh.		
	Urquhart, Moraysh.		Tower
	St Mary (Episc.), Dunblane, Perthsh.	J. Henderson	
1845	Boddam, Aberdeensh.		
	Rothesay (Free), Butesh.	C. Wilson	
	St John (Free), Glasgow	Rochead	Dem.
	St Peter (Free), Glasgow	C. Wilson	Dem.

426

B

Chronological Index of Ecclesiastical Buildings in Northern England

Year	Building	Architect	
1764	St James, Castle Eden, Co. D.	W. Newton?	A rebuilding; tower
1781	St Michael, Alnwick, North.	V. Shepherd	Gothic chancel. Dem.
1783	St Helen, Long Horsley, North.		Gothic interior
	St Bartholomew, Tweedmouth, North.		Tower
1789	St Cuthbert, Tilmouth, North.		Derelict
1790	St Cuthbert, Carham, North.	R. Hodgson Huntley	Nave only
1791	Mausoleum, Wetheral, Cumb.		Cast iron tracery; Gothic interior
1792	St Nicholas, Kyloe, North.		Cf. Lowick
1793	Hebborn, North.		Nave and chancel
1794	St John, Lowick, North.		Tower; chancel later
1797	Methodist chapel, Berwick, North.		Remodelled 1878
1806	St Mary, Long Newton, Co. D.		Rebuilt 1856
	St Lawrence, Crosby Ravensworth, West.	R. Smirke	Altered since
1807	Chapel, Croxdale Hall, Co. D.		Gothic interior
	St Cuthbert, Allendale, North.		Altered

Year	Building	Architect	
1810	St John, Beckermet, Cumb.		Rebuilt 1878
	St Andrew, Dacre, Cumb.		W. tower rebuilt
1811	St Mary, Harrington, Cumb.		Chancel only
1813	St Peter, Elwick, Co. D.		Tower rebuilt
1814	St Mary, Little Strickland, West.		
1818	St Luke, Greystead, North.	H. H. Seward	Cf. Wark
	St Peter, Humshaugh, North.	H. H. Seward	Cf. Wark
	Congregational chapel, N. Shields, North.		
	St John Lee, North.	Dobson	Altered since
	St Aidan, Thorneyburn, North.	H. H. Seward	Cf. Wark
	St Michael, Wark, North.	H. H. Seward	Tower, nave and chancel
1821	St Andrew, Lamesley, Co. D.		Remodelling
	St Cuthbert (R.C.), N. Shields, North.	R. Giles	Tower; Gothic interior.
1822	St Mary, Heworth, Co. D.	J. Stokoe	Cruciform; tower
	Christ Church, Carshield, North.		Dem.
	Pres. Chapel, Newcastle, North.	J. Green	
1823	St Oswald, Burneside, West.		Additions 1861, 1869
1824	Gateshead Fell, Co. D.	J. Ions	Steeple
	St Mary, Rydal, West.		Hexagonal tower
1825	St Mary, Sebergham, Cumb.		Tower
	St Peter, Allenheads, North.	W. Crawhall	
1826	Ryhope, Co. D.		
1827	John St Chapel, Bishopwearmouth, Co. D.	P. W. Wyatt	
	St Augustine (R.C.), Darlington, Co. D.	I. Bonomi	
	St Cuthbert, Durham, Co. D.	I. Bonomi	Tower; Gothic interior
	Winlaton, Co. D.	I. Bonomi	Tower; aisles
	St Bartholomew, Loweswater, Cumb.		Altered 1884
1828	Christ Church, Carlisle,	Rickman	Dem.

Year	Building	Architect	
	Cumb.		
	Holy Trinity, Carlisle, Cumb.	Rickman	Tower
	St Hilda, Westward, Cumb.		Tower
	St Mary, Belford, North.	Dobson	Restoration
	St Mary the Virgin (R.C.), Hexham, North.		Elaborate W front
	St Mary, Horton, North.		Altered 1864, 1902
	St Thomas the Martyr, Newcastle, North.	Dobson	Tower; Gothic interior
	St John the Evangelist, Levens, West.		
	St Stephen, New Hutton, West.	G. Webster	Tower and spire
1829	St Mary & St Cuthbert (R.C.), Berwick, North.		
1830	St Mary, Stapleton, Cumb.		Tower, nave, chancel
	St Philip & St James Whittonstall, North.		Tower; nave
1831	All Saints, Hurworth-on-Tees, Co. D.		Altered 1870
	St Andrew, Sadberge, Co. D.	Jackson?	
	Holy Trinity, Seaton Carew, Co. D.	T. Pickersgill	Chancel 1842 by Jackson
	St Mary & St Thomas Aquinas (R.C.), Stella, Co. D.	J. Green?	
	Holy Trinity, Usworth, Co. D.	J. Green	
1832	Hetton-le-Hole, Co. D.		
	St Mary's, Slaley, North.	Milton Carr	Nave, chancel
1833	Holy Trinity, S. Shields, Co. D.	Salvin	Tower; transepts later
	Holy Trinity, Washington, Co. D.	J. Green	Tower
	Pres. Church, Embleton, North.		
	Holy Trinity, Casterton, West.		Tower
1834	Holy Trinity, Stockton-on-Tees, Co. D.	J. & B. Green	Spire; transepts
1835	St John the Evangelist, Seaham Harbour, Co. D.	Prosser	Tower, nave, chancel, transept

429

Year	Building	Architect	
	St Mary (R.C.), Sunderland, Co. D.		
	St Cuthbert (R.C.), Wigton, Cumb.		Nave, chancel, transept
	St John, Shotley, North.		Chancel 1903
1836	St Mary (R.C.), Alnwick, North.	J. Green	Gothic front
	Holy Trinity, N. Shields, North.	J. Green	Tower
1837	Holy Trinity, Gateshead, Co. D.	Dobson	Enlargement of 13th cent aisle
	St Cuthbert (R.C.), Wigton, Cumb.	Bonomi	
	St Alban, Earsdon, North.	J. & B. Green	Tower; chancel 1889
	Holy Saviour, Sugley, North.	B. Green	
	Holy Trinity & St George (R.C.), Kendal, West.	Webster	
	St Thomas, Kendal, West.	Webster	Tower
	St Thomas, Milnthorpe, West.	Webster	Tower
1838	St John the Evangelist, Keswick, Cumb.	Salvin	Steeple
	St Mary & St Michael, Doddington, North.	Bonomi	Chancel only
	Knaresdale, North.		Nave only
	St John, Grayrigg, West.		Tower 1869
	St Thomas, Selside, West.		
1839	St Oswald (R.C.), Bellingham, North.	Bonomi	
	Holy Trinity, Dalton, West.		
	Holy Trinity, Holme, West.		Tower
	St George, Kendal, West.	Webster	
1840	St Thomas, Annfield Plain, Co. D.	Jackson	
	Holy Trinity, Wingate, Co. D.	Jackson	
	St John, Carlisle, Cumb.		Tower
	Holy Trinity, Rosley, Cumb.		Tower
	St Bartholomew, Whittingham, Co. D.	Green	Tower and alterations
	Our Lady & St Wilfrid	Pugin	

430

Year	Building	Architect	
	(St Mary) (R.C.), Warwick Bridge, Cumb.		
1841	St John, Elton, Co. D.		
	St Mary (R.C.), Stockton-on-Tees, Co. D.	Pugin	Tower at NW
	Buttermere, Cumb.		Spire 1853
	St Michael, Carlisle, Cumb.	J. Hodgson	Tower: cruciform
	St Leonard, Cleator, Cumb.		
	St Thomas of Canterbury (R.C.), Long Horsley, North.		
	St Mary (R.C.), Swinburne Castle, North.		
	Holy Saviour, Tynemouth, North.	J. & B. Green	Cruciform; steeple
1842	Holy Trinity, Pelton, Co. D.	Jackson	
	Holy Trinity, Southwick, Co. D.	Jackson	Tower
	St Cuthbert (R.C.), Ushaw College, Co. D.	Pugin	Rebuilt
	Holy Trinity, Cambo, North.	J. & B. Green	Tower later
	Holy Trinity, Matfen, North.	Sir E. Blackett?	Spire
	St Peter, Scremerston, North.	Bonomi & Cory	Broach spire
	All Saints (R.C.), Thropton, North.		
	S Stainmore, Brough, West.		
1843	St Joseph (R.C.), Birtley, Co. D.	Dobson	
	Holy Trinity, Darlington, Co. D.	Salvin	Altered 1883, 1890
	Wesleyan chapel, Sunderland, Co. D.		
1844	St Paul, Hunwick, Co. D.	W. Thompson	Rebuilt 1887
	St Cuthbert, Farne Is., North.		Restoration
	St Mary (R.C.), Newcastle, North.	Pugin	Spire added 1860
1845	St Cuthbert, Blaydon, Co. D.		Tower
	St Paul, Holme Low, Cumb.	W. Armstrong	
	Holme St Cuthbert, Cumb.	W. Armstrong	

GOTHIC REVIVAL

Year	Building	Architect	
	St James, Ireby, Cumb.		
	St Cuthbert, Kirklinton, Cumb.		Tower
	St John, Nenthead, Cumb.	Bonomi & Cory	
	St Theobald, Musgrave, West.	G. R. Appleby	Tower

C

Chronological Index of
Secular Buildings
in Scotland

Year	Building	Architect	
1745	Inveraray Cas., Argyllsh.	Roger Morris	
1756	The Whim, Blair Cas., Perthsh.		
1757	Douglas Cas., Lanarksh.	John & James Adam	Cf. Inveraray. Dem.
1769	Gordon Cas., Moraysh.	J. Baxter	Centre dem.
1770	Mellerstain, Berwicksh.	R. Adam	
	Wedderburn, Berwicksh.	R. Adam	
1773	Caldwell, Renfrewsh.	R. Adam	
1776	Observatory, Calton Hill, Edinburgh	J. Craig	
1777	Culzean Cas., Ayrsh.	R. Adam	
	Auchincruive tea-house, Ayrsh.	R. Adam	Cf. Theodoric's Tomb
1778	?Town House, Bo'ness, W. Loth.		Cf. Inveraray. Dem.
1780	Oxenfoord Cas., Midloth.	R. Adam	Adds by Burn
1784	Pitfour Cas., Perthsh.	R. Adam	Adds by Burn
1785	Dalquharran Cas., Ayrsh.	R. Adam	Derelict
	Melville Cas., Midloth.	J. Playfair	Cf. Inveraray
1786	Kinnaird Cas., Angus	J. Playfair	Recased by Bryce
	Raehills, Dumfries-sh.	A. Stevens	Asymmetrical
	Ardencaple Cas., Dunbartonsh.	R. Mylne?	Adds. Dem.
1787	Culzean Cas., Ayrsh.	R. Adam	
1789	Seton Cas., E. Loth.	R. Adam	
	Hermitage of Braid, Edinburgh	R. Burn	

Year	Building	Architect	
	Garscadden House, Glasgow	C. Ross	Gothic gates. Dem.
	Mausoleum, Duff Ho., Banffsh.		
	Dunvegan Cas., Inverness-sh.	W. Boak	Adds
1790	Castle Huntly, Perthsh.	J. Paterson?	Adds
	Airthrey Cas., Stirlingsh.	R. Adam	Altered by Bryce
1791	The Bridewell, Edinburgh	R. Adam	Dem.
1792	Stobs Cas., Roxburghsh.	R. Adam	Cf. Pitfour
1793	Mauldslie Cas., Lanarksh.	R. Adam	Dem.
1794	?Barnton Cas., Midloth.	D. Hamilton	Adds. Dem.
1795	Monzie Cas., Perthsh.	J. Paterson	
1796	Newton Hall, E. Loth.		Dem.
1797	Caprington Cas., Ayrsh.		Built c. 1820
	Eglinton Cas., Ayrsh.	J. Paterson	Dem.
1800	Rossie Cas., Angus	R. Crichton	Adam type. Dem.
1802	Gillespie's Hospital, Edinburgh	R. Burn	Dem.
	Woodlands Ho., Glasgow	D. Hamilton?	Dem.
	Achnacarry, Inverness-sh.	Gillespie Graham	Burn staircase
	Darnaway Cas., Moraysh.	A. Laing	Adam type
1803	Cortachy Cas., Angus		Adds
	Scone Palace, Perthsh.	W. Atkinson	Gothic interiors
	Airth Cas., Stirlingsh.	D. Hamilton	Add. to old cas.
1804	Harvieston Cas., Clacksh.		Cf. Inveraray. Dem.
	Abercairny Abbey, Perthsh.	R. Crichton	Eccles. Dem.
1805	Cluny Cas., Inverness-sh.		Adam type
	Dreghorn Cas., Midloth.	J. Elliot	Dem.
	Stobo Cas., Peeblessh.	A. & J. Elliot	Cf. Inveraray
1806	Kincardine Cas., Perthsh.	Gillespie Graham	Cf. Achnacarry
	Taymouth Cas., Perthsh.	A. & J. Elliot	Cf. Inveraray
1807	Nelson Monument, Edinburgh	R. Burn	
1808	Loudon Cas., Ayrsh.	A. & J. Elliot	Gutted
	Tullichewan Cas., Dunbartonsh.	R. Lugar	Asymmetrical. Dem.
	Fetteresso Cas., Kincardinesh.	J. Paterson	Dem.
	Nelson's Monument Forres, Moraysh.	C. Stewart	
	?Lanrick Cas., Perthsh.	Gillespie Graham	Adds
1809	Balloch Cas., Dunbartonsh.	R. Lugar	Asymmetrical
	Fasque Cas., Kincardinesh.	J. Paterson?	
	Dunkeld House, Perthsh.	A. Elliot	Adds

	Ochtertyre Mausoleum, Perthsh.	C. H. Tatham	
1810	Ross Priory, Dunbartonsh.	Gillespie Graham	Eccles.
	Crawford Priory, Fife	D. Hamilton; Gillespie Graham	Castell. and eccles.
	Culdees Cas., Perthsh.	Gillespie Graham	Adds by Bryce
	Rossie Priory, Perthsh.	Atkinson	Eccles. Much dem.
1811	Dowland, Midlothian		Castell. Dem.
	Dunvegan Cas., Inverness-sh.		Adds.
1812	Craigend Cas., Stirlingsh.	A. Ramsay	Asymmetrical. Dem.
	Kincaid Cas., Stirlingsh.	D. Hamilton	Cf. Inveraray
1813	Lindertis, Angus	A. Elliot	Asymmetrical. Dem.
	Broomhouse, Berwicksh.		Castell. Derelict
	Torry, Fife	J. Sands	Asymmetrical. Dem.
	?Drumtochty Cas., Kincardinesh.	Smith & Gillespie Graham	Altered since
1814	Castle Forbes, Aberdeensh.	Simpson & Smith	Asymmetrical
	Hatton Cas., Aberdeensh.		Cf. Inveraray
	Cloncaird Cas., Ayrsh.		Adds. Cf. Culzean
	Biel, E. Loth.	Atkinson	Partly dem.
	Tolbooth, Glasgow	D. Hamilton	Dem.
1815	Druminnor, Aberdeensh.	Simpson	Adds. Dem.
	Fetternear, Aberdeensh.	J. Massie	Adds. Derelict
	?Glenbarr Abbey, Argyllsh.	Gillespie Graham?	Eccles. adds.
	Torrisdale Cas., Argyllsh.	Gillespie Graham	Adds later
	The Castle, Newport, Fife		
	Armadale Cas., Inverness-sh.	Gillespie Graham	Gothic interiors
	Kirkcudbright Jail		
	Ogscastle, Lanarksh.		Single storey
	Edmonstone Cas., Lanarksh.	Gillespie Graham	Cf. Torrisdale
	Calton Jail, Edinburgh	A. Elliot	Mostly dem.
	Dalmeny House, W. Loth.	Wilkins	Tudor
1816	Duns Town Hall, Berwicksh.	Gillespie Graham	Dem.
	Abbotsford, Roxburghsh.	Atkinson	Scots-baronial
1817	Newbyth, E. Loth.	A. Elliot	Asymmetrical; Gothic interiors
	Saltoun Hall, E. Loth.	W. Burn	Cf. Inveraray
	?Bonskeid, Perthsh.		

Year	Building	Architect	
1818	Duns Cas., Berwicksh.	Gillespie Graham	Gothic interiors
	Tulliallan Cas., Fife	Atkinson	
	Strathallan Cas., Perthsh.	Smirke	Gothic interiors
	Taymouth Cas., Perthsh.	Atkinson	E wing
	Dundas Cas., W. Loth.	W. Burn	Tudor. Cf. Dalmeny
1819	Dunninald, Angus	Gillespie Graham	Cf. Tullichewan
	Cambusnethan Priory, Lanarksh.	Gillespie Graham	Eccles
	?Carberry Tower, Midloth.		
1820	Blairquhan, Ayrsh.	W. Burn	Tudor
	Corehouse, Lanarksh.	Blore	Manorial
	Kinfauns Cas., Perthsh.	Smirke	Gothic interiors
	Millearne Abbey, Perthsh.	R. & R. Dickson	Eccles. Dem.
	Jedburgh Cas., Roxburghsh.	A. Elliot	Cf. Inveraray
	Dunmore Park, Stirlingsh.	Wilkins	Tudor
	The Binns, W. Loth.		Adds.
1821	Toward Cas., Argyll	D. Hamilton	Later adds.
	Carstairs House, Lanarksh.	W. Burn	Tudor
	Millburn Tower, Midloth.		Dem.
1822	Lee Cas., Lanarksh.	Gillespie Graham	Cf. Inveraray. Dem.
	Abbotsford, Roxburghsh.	Atkinson	Adds.
1823	Wishaw House, Lanarksh.	Gillespie Graham	Cf. Inveraray. Dem.
	Niddrie Marischal, Midloth.	W. Burn	Jacobean. Dem.
	Riccarton, Midloth.	W. Burn	Tudor adds. Dem.
	Cultoquhey, Perthsh.	Smirke	Manorial
1824	Castle House, Dunoon, Argyllsh.	D. Hamilton	
	Greenlaw Prison, Berwicksh.		Dem.
	Strathendry, Fife	W. Burn	Manorial
	Duchrae, Kirkcudbrightsh.	W. Burn	Tudor
	Duke St Prison, Glasgow		Dem.
	Ratho Park, Midloth.	W. Burn	Tudor
	?Brodie Cas., Moraysh.	W. Burn	Adds (dem?)
	Westerton, Moraysh.		Castell. Dem.
	Snaigow, Perthsh.	W. Burn	Manorial. Dem.
1825	King's College, Aberdeen	Smith	Perpendicular
	Craighall-Rattray, Angus		Scots-Tudor adds.
	Drumfin (Aros) Ho., Argyllsh.	W. Burn	Jacobean. Dem.
	Terraughtie, Dumfries-sh.	Rickman	Manorial
	The Grove, Dumfries-sh.	Rickman	Manorial

Year	Building	Architect	
	Keith's Tower, Kincardinesh.		
	Dalhousie Cas., Midloth.	W. Burn	Castell. adds.
	?Dunkeld House, Perthsh.	Hopper	Perpendicular. Dem.
1826	Duntrune, Angus	W. Burn	
	Hoddam Cas., Dumfries-sh.	W. Burn	Castell. adds. Dem.
	Garscube House, Dunbartonsh.	W. Burn	Tudor. Dem.
	Fettercairn, Kincardinesh.	W. Burn	Tudor adds.
	Holmehill, Perthsh.	W. Stirling I	Tudor
	Pitcairn, Perthsh.	W. Burn	Manorial
1827	Balcaskie, Fife	W. Burn	Adds.
	Inchrye, Fife	R. & R. Dickson?	Eccles. Dem.
	The Hensol, Kirkcudbrightsh.	R. Lugar	Manorial
	Laurieston Cas., Midloth.	W. Burn	Scots-Jacobean adds.
	Duke of York Tower, Moraysh.		
1828	Raehills, Dumfries-sh.	W. Burn	Adds.
	United College, St Andrew's Univ, Fife	R. Reid	Jacobean
	Cumston Ho., Kirkcudbrightsh.	T. Hamilton	Adam type
	Belmont Cas., Perthsh.	W. H. Playfair	Scottish
	Dupplin Cas., Perthsh.	W. Burn	Jacobean. Dem.
	Erskine Ho., Renfrewsh.	Smirke	Tudor
1829	Kilmaron Cas., Fife	Gillespie Graham	Dem.
	St Fort, Fife	W. Burn	Jacobean. Dem.
	Milton Lockhart, Lanarksh.	W. Burn	Scots-baronial. Dem.
	Murthly Cas., Perthsh.	Gillespie Graham	Jacobean. Dem.
1830	Fintray Ho., Aberdeensh.	Smith	Scots-Jacobean. Dem.
	Pitcaple Cas., Aberdeensh.	W. Burn	Scots-Tudor adds.
	Cassilis Ho., Ayrsh.	W. Burn	Adds.
	Ayton Cas., Berwicksh.	W. Burn	Burnt
	Boturich Cas., Dunbartonsh.		
	Prestongrange Ho., E. Loth.	W. H. Playfair	Scottish adds
	Tyninghame Ho., E. Loth.	W. Burn	Scots-Jacobean
	Muirhouse, W. Lothian		Tud. adds. Dem.

Year	Building	Architect	
1831	Castle Newe, Aberdeensh.	Simpson	Jacobean. Dem.
	Auchmacoy, Aberdeensh.	W. Burn	Scots-Tudor
	Wallace Tower, Ayr	T. Hamilton	
	Kilconquhar Cas., Fife	W. Burn	Scots-Jacobean adds
	Madras College, St Andrews, Fife	W. Burns	Jacobean
	Muirtown Ho., Inverness		Adds.
	Grange Ho., Edinburgh	W. H. Playfair	Scottish
1832	Craig Cas., Aberdeensh.	Simpson	Scots-Jacobean adds.
	Easter Skene, Aberdeensh.	Smith	Cf. Auchmacoy
	Spottiswoode Ho., Berwicksh.	W. Burn	Scots-Jacobean. Dem.
	Dawyck Ho., Peeblessh.	W. Burn	Scots-Jacobean
	Auchterarder Ho., Perthsh.	W. Burn	Scots-Jacobean
1833	Dunlop Ho., Ayrsh.	D. Hamilton	Scots Jacobean
	Kirkmichael Ho., Dumfries-sh.	W. Burn	Scots-Jacobean
	Inverness Cas.	W. Burn	Asymmetrical castell.
	Leys Cas., Inverness-sh.	S. Beazley	Cf. Inveraray
	Lurgan Ho., Perthsh.	W. H. Playfair	Jacobean
	Teviotbank, Roxburghsh.	W. Burn	Manorial
1834	Thurso Cas., Caithness	W. Burn	Gutted
1835	Candacraig, Aberdeensh.	Smith	Scots-Jacobean
	Menie Ho., Aberdeensh.	Smith	Cf. Auchmacoy
	Masonic Rooms, Forfar, Angus	J. Brewster	Gothic
	Bourhouse, E. Loth.	D. Bryce	Tudor
	Balcarres Ho., Fife	W. Burn	Adds.
	?Tayfield, Fife		Manorial
	Craigcrook Cas., Edinburgh	W. H. Playfair	Scottish
	Kirknewton Ho., Midloth.	W. H. Playfair	Dem.
	Kirklands Ho., Roxburghsh.	Blore	Manorial
1836	Marischal Coll., Aberdeen	Simpson	Tudor
	Cluny Cas., Aberdeensh.	Smith	Castell. adds.
	Meldrum Ho., Aberdeensh.	Simpson	Scots-Jacobean. Dem.
	Slains Cas., Aberdeensh.	Smith	Scots-Tudor. Dem.
1837	Lessendrum Ho., Aberdeensh.	Simpson	Jacobean. Dem.
	Invergowrie Ho., Angus	W. Burn	Adds.
	Greenock Library, Renfrewsh.	Blore	Collegiate Gothic

Year	Building	Architect	
1838	Learney Ho., Aberdeensh.	Smith	Scots-Jacobean
	Armaddy Cas., Argyllsh.	Gillespie Graham	Built by Bryce
	Burgh Buildings, Banchory, Kincardinesh.		Tudor Gothic
	Taymouth Cas., Perthsh.	Gillespie Graham	W wing
	Floors Cas., Roxburghsh.	W. H. Playfair	Tudor adds.
1839	Forglen Ho., Banffsh.	Smith	Scots-Jacobean
	Ninewells Ho., Berwicksh.	W. Burn	Dem.
	Falkland Ho., Fife	W. Burn	Scots-Jacobean
	Beaufort Cas., Inverness-sh.	W. Burn	Cf. Dalhousie
	Banchory-Devenick Ho., Kincardinesh.	Smith	Scots-Jacobean
	Bonaly Tower, Edinburgh	W. H. Playfair	Scottish
	Forres Town Hall, Moraysh.		Scottish
	Glendelvine (Raffel) Ho., Perthsh.		Manorial
	?Leckie, Stirlingsh.		Tudor
1840	Gordon Schools, Huntly, Aberdeensh.	Simpson	Jacobean
	Garth Cas., Angus	A. Heiton	
	Hospitalfield Ho., Angus	P. Allan Fraser	Scots-baronial
	Scott Monument, Edinburgh	Kemp	
	Dunvegan Cas., Inverness-sh.	R. Brown	Adds
	Whitehill Ho., Midloth.	W. Burn	Jacobean
	Castle Menzies, Perthsh.	W. Burn	Scots-Jacobean
	Carbeth Ho., Stirlingsh.		
1841	Pittodrie Ho., Aberdeensh.	Simpson	Scots-Jacobean adds.
	Water tower, Montrose, Angus	W. Middleton	
	Trinity College, Perthsh.	J. Henderson	Tudor
1842	Knockdolian Cas., Ayrsh.		Tudor
	Gartnavel Hosp., Glasgow	C. Wilson	Tudor
	Donaldson's Hosp., Edinburgh	W. H. Playfair	
1843	Garvel, Ayrsh.	W. Burn	Adds
	Inverness Cas.	W. Burn	Castell. add.
	Woodhouselee, Midloth.	Kemp	Scots-baronial. Dem.
1844	Carradale Ho., Argyll.	W. Burn & Bryce	Scots-baronial
	Kilberry Cas., Argyllsh.	Bryce	Add.

GOTHIC REVIVAL

Year	Building	Architect	
	Brodick Cas., Butesh.	Gillespie Graham	Scottish
1845	Clatto Ho., Fife	Bryce & W. Burn	Scots-baronial
	Leny Ho., Perthsh.	Bryce & W. Burn	Scots-baronial

D

Chronological Index of Secular Buildings in Northern England

Year	Building	Architect	
1745	Rothley Cas., North.	D. Garrett	Ruinous
1751	Conduit Ho., The College, Durham Cath.		
1752	Durham Cas.	S. Miller	Alterations
	Banqueting-ho., Gibside, Co. D.	D. Garrett	Ruinous
	Raby Cas., Co. D.	D. Garrett & J. Paine	Alterations
1756	Alnwick Cas., North.	J. Paine	Gothic interiors
	White House, Appleby, West.		
1760	Deer House, Auckland Cas., Co. D.		
	Gatehouse, Auckland Cas., Co. D.	Sir Thomas Robinson	
1761	?Ford Cas., North.	J. Nisbet	
	?Starlight Cas., Seaton Sluice, North.		Mostly dem.
1764	?Castle Eden, Co. D.	W. Newton	
1766	Whitehaven Cas., Cumb.	R. Adam	Interiors lost
	Simonburn Cas., North.		Dem.
1767	?Auckland Cas., Co. D.	J. Carr	Adds
	?Hamsterley Hall, Co. D.		Alterations
1768	Raby Cas., Co. D.	J. Carr	Alterations
	Pottergate Tower, Alnwick, North.		Spire dem.
	Kennels, Nunwick Ho., North.		
1770	Axwell Park, Dower Ho., Co. D.	J. Paine	

Year	Building	Architect	
	Codger's Fort, Rothley, North.		
	?Craster Tower, North.		Gothic interiors
	Twizell Cas., North.	J. Nisbet?	Derelict
1772	Kielder Cas., North.		
1773	Denwick Bridge, Alnwick Cas., North.	R. Mylne	
	Lion Bridge, Alnwick Cas., North.	R. Adam	
1776	Hulne Priory, Alnwick Cas., North.	R. Adam & Brown	
	Fowberry Tower, North.	J. Nisbet	Adds.
1777	Brizlee Tower, Alnwick Cas., North.	R. Adam	
1782	Workington Hall, Cumb.	J. Carr	Alterations
1783	?Gazebo, Ratcheugh Crag, Alnwick Park, North.	R. Adam	
1785	?Westerton Tower, Co. D.	T. Wright	
1787	Ewart Park, North.		
	Twizell Cas., North.		Adds.
1790	?Lyulph's Tower, Cumb.		
1792	?Eachwick Hall, North.		Embattled adds.
1793	?Hoppyland Hall, Co. D.		Derelict
1795	Auckland Cas., Co. D.	J. Wyatt	Gothic interiors
1796	Witton Cas., Co. D.		Cf. Auckland Cas.
	Stables, Roddam Hall, North.	V. Shepherd	
1800	Choir School, Durham Cath.		Tudor front
	Cockermouth Cas., Cumb.		Adds.
	?Higham School, Setmurthy, Cumb.		Symmetrical facade
1801	Barmoor Cas., North.	Paterson	
1802	?Stables, Muncaster Cas., Cumb.	S. Culling?	
	Lowther Cas., West.		
1803	Hospital of God, Greatham, Co. D.	Jeffrey Wyatt	
1805	Gibside Hall, Co. D.	A. Gilkie?	Jacobean adds.
1806	Lowther Cas., West.	Smirke	
1808	Ravensworth Cas., Co. D.	Nash	
1810	Brinkburn Priory, North.		

Year	Building	Architect	
1811	Assize Courts, Carlisle, Cumb.	Smirke	
	Market House, Appleby, West.	Smirke	
1812	Blenkinsopp Hall, North.		Castell. adds.
	Featherstone Cas., North.		Castell. adds.
1817	Moot Hall, Brampton, Cumb.		
	Jesmond Towers, Newcastle, North.	Dobson	
1818	?Brancepeth Cas., Co. D.	Paterson	Baronial adds.
	Featherstone Cas., North.		Adds (after fire)
1820	Union Building, Durham Univ.		Castell.
	?Coupland Cas., North.		Add. to tower
1822	Register Office, Durham		
	Lambton Cas., Co. D.	I. Bonomi	
	County Prison, Morpeth, North.	Dobson	Dem.
1823	Stanhope Cas., Co. D.		Castell. adds.
	Angerton Hall, North.	Dobson	Manorial
	Jesmond Towers, Newcastle, North.	Dobson	Add.
1824	Edmond Cas., Cumb.	Smirke	Tudor
1825	Tudhoe House, Co. D.		
	Underlay Hall, West.	G. Webster	Jacobean
1826	Lying-in-Hospital, Newcastle, North.	Dobson	
1827	County Jail, Carlisle, Cumb.	W. Nixon & C. Hodgson	Dem.
1829	Rose Cas., Cumb.	Rickman	Tudor adds.
	Vicar's Pele, Elsdon, North.		Gothic interior
	Lilburn Tower, North.	Dobson	Tudor
1830	?The Hermitage, Chester-le-Street, Co. D.		Tudor
	News Room & Library, Carlisle, Cumb.	Rickman	Gothic
	Brinkburn Priory, North.	Dobson	Castell. adds.
	?Brougham Hall, West.	L. Cottingham	Castell. Dem.
1831	Benwell Tower, Newcastle, North.	Dobson	Castell.
1832	Matfen Hall, North.	Rickman	Tudor. Gothic hall.
1833	Brunstock, Cumb.	Rickman	Gothic
	Netherby Hall, Cumb.	Burn	Jacobean adds.

Year	Building	Architect	
	Blenkinsopp Cas., North.	Dobson	Castell. add. Dem.
	Jesmond Towers,	Burdon & Sanderson	Gothic add.
	Newcastle, North.	Sanderson	
1834	Whelprigg Ho., Barbon, West.		Manorial
1835	?Scaleby Cas., Cumb.	Rickman?	
	Savings Bank, Alnwick, North.	Wm. Smith	
	Blenkinsopp Hall, North.	Dobson	SE tower
1837	Holme Eden Hall, Warwick, Cumb.	Dobson	Tudor
	Beaufront Cas., North.	Dobson	Castell.
	Tyne Master Mariners' Asylum, Tynemouth, North.	J. & B. Green	Tudor
	Low Bridge Hall, Selside, West.		Elizabethan. Altered 1875.
1838	Bishop Cosin's Alms-Houses, Durham.		Tudor
1839	Greystoke Cas., Cumb.	Salvin	Elizabethan adds.
1841	Trinity Ho., Newcastle, North.		Tudor
	Augill Cas., Brough, West.		Castell.
1842	Raby Cas., Co. D.	Burn	Adds. Alterations
1844	Infirmary, Seaham Harbour, Co. D.		
	Edmond Cas., Cumb.	Smirke	Tud. adds.
	Town Hall, N. Shields, North.	Dobson	Tudor

Index